Making the Presidency

John Adams after Gilbert Stuart, c. 1815. National Portrait Gallery, Smithsonian Institution.

Abigail Smith Adams by Gilbert Stuart, 1800/1815. Courtesy National Gallery of Art, Washington. Gift of Mrs. Robert Homans.

Making the Presidency

John Adams and the Precedents That Forged the Republic

LINDSAY M. CHERVINSKY

OXFORD
UNIVERSITY PRESS

Oxford University Press is a department of the University of Oxford. It furthers the University's objective of excellence in research, scholarship, and education by publishing worldwide. Oxford is a registered trade mark of Oxford University Press in the UK and certain other countries.

Published in the United States of America by Oxford University Press
198 Madison Avenue, New York, NY 10016, United States of America.

Library of Congress Cataloging-in-Publication Data
Names: Chervinsky, Lindsay M., 1988– author.
Title: Making the presidency : John Adams and the precedents that forged the republic / Lindsay M. Chervinsky.
Other titles: John Adams and the precedents that forged the republic
Description: New York, NY : Oxford University Press, 2024. |
Includes bibliographical references and index.
Identifiers: LCCN 2024001996 (print) | LCCN 2024001997 (ebook) |
ISBN 9780197653845 (hardback) | ISBN 9780197653869 (epub) |
ISBN 9780197653876
Subjects: LCSH: Adams, John, 1735-1826—Influence. |
United States—Politics and government—1817–1825. |
United States—Politics and government—1789–1797. |
Washington, George, 1732–1799—Influence. |
Presidents—United States—Biography. |
Cabinet officers—United States—History—18th century.
Classification: LCC E322 .C447 2024 (print) | LCC E322 (ebook) |
DDC 973.4/4092 [B]—dc23/eng/20240227
LC record available at https://lccn.loc.gov/2024001996
LC ebook record available at https://lccn.loc.gov/2024001997

DOI: 10.1093/oso/9780197653845.001.0001

Printed by Sheridan Books, Inc., United States of America

For my parents, who taught me how to work hard and insisted with unflinching conviction that there was nothing I couldn't achieve if I set my mind to it.

Contents

A Note on Language ix

Introduction 1

1. An Address to the People of the United States 10

2. Washington Recedes 26

3. The Die Is Cast 39

4. The "Sublimest Thing" Ever Exhibited in America 54

5. A Scene of Ambition 63

6. A Dishonorable Infidelity 78

7. Expect Nothing but the Most Unqualified Injustice 87

8. Not a Sixpence! 98

9. Poured in from All Quarters 110

10. Massacre the Inhabitants 122

11. Decisive Measures 136

12. The "Majic" of His Name 149

13. The Tocsin of Insurrection 161

14. All Evidences That They Are Sincere 168

15. Solely the President's Act 180

16. Struck by a Thunderbolt 191

17. The Spirit in the City Is Very High 197

18. A Paltry Insurrection 204

19. The Air of an Abdication 211

20. An Apple of Discord to the Federalists 220

21. The Late President of the United States, Is No More! 231

22. Their Gag in My Mouth 237

23. Hocus-Pocus Maneuvers 247

24. A Change in the Administration 253

25. The Seat of Government 262

26. Death or Liberty 273

27. The Unqualified Conviction of His Unfitness for the Station 281

28. Storms of a New Character 294

29. Nothing but a Forest and Woods Along the Way 304

30. The Prey of Anarchy and Faction 321

31. The New Order of Things Begins 329

Epilogue: May None but Honest and Wise Men 335

Acknowledgments 341

Notes 345

Bibliography 407

Index 419

A Note on Language

Eighteenth-century language poses a few challenges for twenty-first-century readers. I have largely left quotes untouched but have sparingly updated the spelling within quotations to facilitate comprehension.

Political parties in the United States tend to reuse names and descriptions, which can muddy our understanding of their platforms. In the 1790s, Thomas Jefferson founded one of the first two political parties, sometimes called the Democratic-Republican Party or the Jeffersonian Republican Party. He called it the Republican Party. I prefer to use his language whenever possible, but this version of the Republican Party should not be confused with the party of Abraham Lincoln in 1860 or the Republican Party that exists today. On the other side, the more radical faction of the Federalist Party has been described as Arch Federalists, High Federalists, or Ultra Federalists. I choose to employ Arch Federalists.

The United States can be called both a representative democracy and a republic. For clarity, I have adopted the terms "democratic institutions" when referring to branches of government, elections, and core practices, and "republic" when referring to the country.

Making the Presidency

Timothy Pickering. Pickering served as secretary of state from 1795 to 1800 under Presidents George Washington and John Adams. He was from Massachusetts and a leader of the Essex Junto, a radical wing of the Federalist Party. The Miriam and Ira D. Wallach Division of Art, Prints and Photographs: Print Collection, New York Public Library.

James McHenry by Charles Balthazar Julie Févret de Saint-Mémin, 1803. McHenry served as secretary of war from 1795 to 1800 under Presidents George Washington and John Adams. He was from Maryland, an ally of Alexander Hamilton, and a member of the Federalist Party. National Portrait Gallery, Smithsonian Institution; gift of Mr. and Mrs. Paul Mellon.

Oliver Wolcott Jr. by John Trumbull, ca. 1790. Wolcott served as secretary of the treasury from 1795 to 1800. He was from Connecticut, a member of the Essex Junto, and an ally of Alexander Hamilton. Yale University Art Gallery, Gift of Nicholas Roosevelt. Photo: Christopher Gardner.

Charles Lee by Cephas Thompson, c. 1810–11. Lee served as the attorney general from 1795 to 1801. He was from Virginia, a moderate member of the Federalist Party, and loyal to both Washington and Adams. National Portrait Gallery, Smithsonian Institution; gift of Mrs. A. D. Pollock Gilmour.

Introduction

ON MARCH 21, 1797, John Adams walked two blocks from his lodgings at Francis Hotel to the President's House on the corner of Sixth and Market Streets in Philadelphia. A few minutes later, his carriage and the cart with his possessions pulled into the courtyard beside the large, brick mansion. The second President of the United States walked through the door of his new home and into a terrible mess.

Adams wandered through the rooms, inspecting the state of the house with sinking dismay. The green floral carpets under his feet were threadbare and fraying at the edges. The paint on the walls was flaking off, the mantels were darkened from smoke and soot, and the tables were scratched. Adams felt the draperies on the windows, which were faded from the sun and hanging in tatters. He opened the cabinets in the servants' hall and in the kitchen. Only a few pieces of chipped china, cracked crystal, and dented cookware remained.[1]

He walked up the staircase to the second floor, where he found an empty public drawing room. The elegant green upholstered sofas, armchairs, and stools that had once filled the reception space, had been sold.[2] Red damask upholstered chairs and sofas filled the family drawing room, but not one chair was "fit to sit in." Adams continued to the bedrooms, where the bolsters were lumpy, and the feather beds required mending.

After spending his first night in the house, Adams wrote to his wife, Abigail, describing the scene. "Don't expose this Picture," he cautioned.[3] He had taken the oath of office as the second president two weeks earlier and he knew Americans had enough on their minds. The nation was in disrepair, they didn't need to know the President's House was too.

The presidency had survived the ordeal of creation. George Washington had served successfully for eight years and painstakingly filled out the contours of the office, which gaps and vagaries in the Constitution had left

FIGURE I.1 President's House: "Residence of Washington in High Street." Watercolor by William L. Breton. Collection of the Historical Society of Pennsylvania.

for him to resolve. But no one else possessed his stature or enjoyed the same level of public trust—and no one else ever would again.

Adams was tasked with navigating the presidency without that unique prestige. He was guaranteed to fall short in comparison to Washington. The challenge of the second president, therefore, called for someone to battle the growing partisan divisions without Washington's presence to provide unity, to withstand cabinet schemes fomented by department secretaries to increase their authority at the expense of the president, and to combat European countries' efforts to exploit the United States's weaknesses for their own imperial aims. The office required a president willing to sacrifice his reputation and popularity on behalf of the nation.

Whoever came next was going to mold the office for all the chief executives to follow. John Adams was an experienced diplomat and a thoughtful constitutional thinker. He was also irascible, stubborn, quixotic, and certain that he knew best most of the time. He proved the right man for the moment.

John Adams was born on October 30, 1735, on a small farm in Braintree, Massachusetts. A fifth-generation New Englander, Adams followed the family tradition. He was raised in the Congregationalist faith, farmed, received an education at Harvard University, and then turned to the study of law.

An early supporter of the colonies' resistance movement against Great Britain, Adams burst onto the national scene in October 1770 when he defended the British officers charged with murdering civilians in the Boston Massacre. Adams's decision to accept the British as clients was deeply unpopular with his neighbors, but he was determined to show that the revolution was one based on laws and principles, not passion and mobs. This stubborn commitment to do what was right, despite the political costs, would prove to be Adams's guiding principle years later as president.

Over the next twenty-seven years, Adams devoted himself to public service. He worked tirelessly on dozens of committees in the Continental Congress, engineered the nomination of George Washington as commander-in-chief of the Continental Army, and harangued his fellow delegates to declare independence.

Starting in November 1777, Congress sent Adams to France, The Hague, and London to represent the new nation abroad and negotiate treaties with European nations. He authored a treaty with the Netherlands, which served as the model for similar agreements with several other nations, and staunchly defended American interests in the negotiations over the Treaty of Paris, which ended the Revolutionary War in 1783.

The end of the war did not bring stability to American relations with Europe, however. Across the Atlantic, European empires still coveted North American territory and were all too pleased to exploit American weakness or pick off wavering states when opportunities arose. Great Britain and France traded places again and again as the greatest threat or ally to the United States, depending on their economic and naval policies of the moment. Dutch bankers held sizable American debts while Spain lingered in western parts of North America and controlled key waterways.

Adams's years abroad convinced him that the European empires would continue to wage war against each other and seize what they wanted whenever possible. He understood that they cared little for the goals and priorities of the United States and instead saw the new nation as a pawn to be leveraged in their centuries-old squabbles. He also developed a deep commitment to neutrality, eager to avoid battles that would harm American trade, threaten the safety of the nation, and sacrifice lives and treasure.

Adams's fellow citizens recognized his sacrifices by rewarding him with the vice presidency in 1789. Faithfully representing the Washington administration, he presided over the Senate almost every day for eight years and cast twenty-nine tie-breaking votes.

From his perch in the Senate, Adams watched as many of his predictions about Europe proved prescient. In 1789, France appeared to be following in American footsteps when it started its own revolution for liberté, égalité, and fraternité. But within a couple of years, the French Revolution took a dark turn toward the Reign of Terror. Revolutionary leadership ordered the execution by guillotine of King Louis XVI and Queen Marie Antoinette, as well as tens of thousands of innocent men and women, without trial.

The revolutionary fervor quickly collided with American economic interests. In 1793, the militant French Directory declared war on Great Britain. For the next several decades, Britain and France battled for European supremacy and regularly meddled with American merchants, who conducted a brisk business carrying food and supplies from the United States to combatants.[4]

Meanwhile, enslaved laborers on sugar plantations in Saint Domingue, inspired by the rebellious rhetoric flowing from France, staged their own uprising, which became known as the Haitian Revolution. Over the next decade, European and Haitian forces vied for control of the colony and its profitable sugar industry.

Many Americans watched the violence and anarchy spread from France to the Caribbean and feared it would soon wash onto American soil, perhaps carried by the thousands of refugees fleeing the slaughter in Paris and Saint Domingue.[5] The influx of refugees fueled a rising wave of xenophobia and radicalism.

On the eve of Adams's inauguration as the second president, Americans viewed foreign policy, immigration, disease, violence, and citizenship through an increasingly partisan lens. The political divisions threatened to snap the recently forged and still fragile bonds between the states, the people, and the federal government.

On one side, the Federalists supported a stronger central government, believed a standing army was essential for national defense, and preferred close ties to Great Britain to facilitate trade. They advocated for government investment in infrastructure, trade, military preparedness, and banking to promote a cosmopolitan future. They drew their support from urban gentry, New England residents, and some plantation elites in the South. While not all Federalists had served in the Continental Army during the Revolution, nearly all officers threw their lot in with the Federalist Party.

Few Federalists hailed from extraordinary wealth. Instead, most came from less hierarchical communities that lacked the extreme social stratification of southern plantations. Yet, they nursed a burning conviction that the country should be led by the "best men," or a natural aristocracy, which, of course, meant themselves. Leading Federalists like Theodore Sedgwick, Timothy Pickering, Alexander Hamilton, George Cabot, and Rufus King were fueled by their belief in their own innate superiority and were sensitive to any slight to their status or threat to their place atop the fragile hierarchy. They also distrusted immigrants, who tended to vote against Federalists, and blamed them for instigating political violence and importing disease.

The Federalists had dominated the national government since the opening days of the First Federal Congress in April 1789, but by the time Adams assumed the presidency, deep divisions in the party were rising to the surface. The Essex Junto or the "flaming Essex Men," a secret network of like-minded Federalists, emerged on the extreme wing of the party. Originally named by John Hancock during the Revolutionary War, the cabal originated in Essex County, Massachusetts, where many of the members were born, but quickly spread to far corners of New England and laid deep roots in the president's cabinet.[6]

The moderate wing of the party coalesced around Adams, who was much more ideologically temperate than the Arch Federalists. Benjamin Stoddert, Noah Webster, Charles Lee, and Harrison Gray Otis were among Adams's strongest supporters. They favored neutrality, ardently supported the fleet of merchants which drew much of their supplies, ships, and sailors from New England before carrying American goods across the globe, and distrusted both the British and the French. For Adams, these views derived from his experience in the world and his hard-won understanding of the complex dynamics of the global community.

Although Adams was much more sensible than the Essex Junto on matters of foreign policy, he shared their fears of a growing domestic infestation of radicalism and anarchy. There was evidence everywhere he looked. In 1794, protests in western Pennsylvania over a whiskey excise tax had turned violent when rebels exchanged fire with tax officials and burned the home of a collector. The resistance collapsed when faced with federal forces, but the short-lived rebellion convinced many Americans that a widespread network was attempting to destroy the republic with the assistance and encouragement of French allies.

Federalists concluded that their rivals, the Republican Party, spearheaded that widespread network. Led by Thomas Jefferson, James Madison, James Monroe, and Aaron Burr, the party emerged in opposition to the Federalists, pieced together initially from a coalition of Antifederalists, who had opposed the ratification of the Constitution; southerners, who were generally wary of strong central government and its threat to slavery; and westerners, who distrusted eastern elites. Republicans preferred a small central government, aligned themselves with the interests of wage workers and farmers, and shared an ideological affinity with France. They resented the influence of bankers and merchants, viewed cities as dens of corruption and cronyism, and abhorred standing armies. All these qualities endeared them to immigrants from France, Ireland, and Haiti, who voted overwhelmingly for Republican candidates.

Exiled from power during the Washington administration, the Republican Party built a network that harnessed the growing political influence of westerners as well as laborers in the North, while benefiting from the constitutional advantages granted to slave states. Article I, Section II of the Constitution appointed representation in Congress based on population, calculated as the "whole Number of free Persons" plus "three fifths of all other Persons." In 1797, nearly 4.5 million people lived in the United States, roughly 750,000 of whom were enslaved.[7] Although enslaved Americans did not count as citizens, they were included in population totals and artificially inflated southern representation in Congress and the Electoral College.

In opposition, Republicans developed party unity and instilled a strict discipline among their members, which they planned to put to good use battling the Adams administration and Federalist measures in Congress. Republican newspapers flourished, connecting the disparate groups that constituted the party and trumpeting Republican messaging.

As Americans built walls between themselves, Adams offered a pessimistic view of the nation he had been elected to lead. "Alass my Poor Country!" he lamented.[8] Convinced that humans by nature were greedy and power-hungry, Adams worried that Americans were just as prone to corruption, anarchy, and violence as Europeans. Most of all, he wasn't sure Americans possessed the civic virtue necessary to survive the trials ahead.[9]

Three interconnected and bedeviling problems dominated the Adams administration. First, Washington's retirement triggered a series of unprecedented experiences. The first competitive presidential election, the first transition, and the first transfer of power loomed on the horizon. Furthermore, Washington's absence destabilized the nation domestically. Although partisan divisions had intensified during his presidency, he was the closest thing to a unifying figure the nation possessed. Before the flag acquired emotional significance, before the states had cemented ties with one another, and before citizens cherished a national identity, Washington offered a shared touchstone. The nation would need to forge an identity without him at the helm. How would the nation survive crises, partisan conflict, or wars without Washington's steadying presence? Would it endure? John Adams and his fellow Americans were not sure.

Second, Adams and his fellow citizens had to determine if the presidency as an institution, with all its trappings, privileges, and power, worked without Washington. Executive branch officials and Congress had largely deferred to Washington's decisions and respected his authority.[10] It remained to be seen if the other branches of government or Adams's direct subordinates would respect the office regardless of its occupant, or whether they might try to run roughshod over executive authority.

Third, European powers threatened war and destruction from day one of Adams's administration. The transition from Adams to Washington, the partisan divide, and squabbles over executive power undermined the nation's ability to defend itself. Recognizing this weakness, European empires were tempted to strike, disrupt American trade, and seize North American territory. Most citizens remembered the costs of war, but they also demanded respect as an independent nation. Adams had to navigate a fine line between self-defense and provocation.

President John Adams offered several critical contributions to guarantee the nation's survival at this tempestuous moment. First, Adams proved that someone else could be president. He never enjoyed Washington's vaunted reputation, but he did his best to instill the office with prestige and respectability. Washington established countless executive precedents, but until they were repeated, they were little more than historic anomalies. Adams forged the parameters of the presidency for everyone that followed.

Second, he ensured the presidency's durability by staunchly defending executive authority. Adams's cabinet secretaries conspired with other Arch Federalists to weaken the presidency, transfer authority to the executive departments, and undermine civilian leadership of the military. Defying the loudest voices in his party, Adams reasserted control over the military, foreign policy, and executive branch personnel, leaving a strengthened office for his successors.

Third, Adams secured peace and the United States' place on the world stage. War is always unpredictable, but never more so than when a fledging nation is at its weakest. In 1798, the American people clamored for revenge against French depredations on American shipping and insults to American sovereignty. While Adams initially relished the "rally round the flag" effect, he knew that war with France might prove fatal to the country. Relying on his own judgment, diplomatic expertise, and intelligence networks across the globe, Adams negotiated for peace. The resulting treaty reaffirmed American sovereignty and guarded the nation's future.

Fourth, Adams knew that diplomacy would threaten his popularity and leadership in the Federalist Party. He pursued peace anyway, putting the nation's interests above those of his party and his own career. His determination fractured the Federalist Party, cost him his reelection, and complicated his legacy. Adams's persistence is less likely to earn a monument or a place on Mount Rushmore than winning a war, but it was an extraordinary demonstration of civic virtue.

Finally, Adams's presidency was bookended by the first two peaceful transfers of power. There was no tradition of peaceful transition; it had to be crafted from scratch. Washington, Adams, and Jefferson carefully laid the foundation for the norms and precedents that serve as critical scaffolding for the democratic institutions in the American political system. These norms and customs largely held firm until January 6, 2021, when Americans were reminded of the preciousness and fragility of republics. Adams never took for granted that peaceful transfer of power lay at the heart of American republic. Over two centuries later, the peaceful transfer of power remains essential to democracy and requires the same vigilance demonstrated by President Adams.

The United States of 1797, therefore, faced enormous challenges, provoked by enemies foreign, domestic, and invisible. Upon taking office, John Adams was as prepared as a president can be to meet these challenges—and to this day, he remains one of the most qualified presidents in American history. He had served as a lawyer in the Boston Massacre trials, one of the biggest cases in the eighteenth century; a delegate to the Continental Congress; a representative at the Confederation Congress; a minister to France, the Netherlands, and Great Britain; the author of the Massachusetts Constitution; and the vice president before his election as the second President of the United States. But he had never held an executive position. Instead, Adams would rely on his *ideas* about executive power, the Constitution, politics, and the state of the world to navigate the hurdles of the presidency. He knew it would be his last public service position and would require every ounce of intelligence, political savvy, diplomatic experience, and courage he could muster.

Not all of Adams's contemporaries believed he was up to the demands of the office, however. In July 1783, Adams drove Benjamin Franklin to his wit's end when they were together in France. "I am persuaded," Franklin wrote to Robert Livingston, secretary of Foreign Affairs, that Adams "means well for his Country, is always an honest Man, often a Wise One, but sometimes and in some things, absolutely out of his Senses."[11]

Had Adams known of this letter, he probably would have been amused. He had a wicked sense of humor, especially about himself, and he knew when he was being ridiculous. The very attributes that make John Adams accessible to Americans today made him somewhat an anathema to his contemporaries.

For all his doubts about humanity and himself, Adams remained unfailingly patriotic and committed to the future of the United States. He believed the nation could grow into something extraordinary and was willing to use every tool at his disposal to protect that future.

In these convictions, Adams was buoyed by a sense of providence and an unwavering hope that future generations would appreciate his dedication to the country. Adams also received immeasurable support and courage from a marriage that ranks among history's greatest love stories. Abigail Adams could have easily been one of the billions of women lost to history books or briefly noted in their husbands' biographical descriptions. Instead, she became a highly influential political thinker of the Founding era.

Previous biographies of Adams have given short shrift to his presidential years, but his tenure in the highest office was one of his most important contributions to the nation.[12] John Adams's unique background, inimitable personality, and extraordinary marriage shaped his approach at several pivotal turning points during his administration. As he stood in the frayed and dusty living room of his new home in Philadelphia, Adams knew that the next four years would be nearly impossible, but he accepted the burden anyway. When he left the presidency in 1801, he did so satisfied that it was stronger than when he assumed office.

George Washington created the presidency, but John Adams defined it.

1

An Address to the People of the United States

ON SEPTEMBER 19, 1796, Secretary of State Timothy Pickering carefully cut the Farewell Address from his copy of the *Daily Advertiser*. He then picked up his quill and wrote a quick note to John Adams: "The President set out early this morning for Mount Vernon; and soon after, his address to the people of the United States appeared in Claypoole's news-paper. Of this public declaration . . . I supposed it would be grateful to you to receive the earliest advice. The sentiments he has expressed on the occasion may be imagined to be interesting: The news-paper is inclosed."[1]

The Boston newspapers reprinted the address in their Thursday publications and confirmed the news that George Washington was retiring.[2] After reading Pickering's note, Adams picked up the newspapers and saw the announcement plastered across the headlines. Adams left no record of his reaction. His diary fell quiet, and he didn't pen a letter until the end of October. For the previous several months, Adams had kept up a steady stream of correspondence and documented his daily farm activities in his diary. The sudden silence was no accident. Adams did not want his thoughts recorded for posterity.

In the age of monarchs, emperors, and military dictators, this moment reverberated around the globe. Few men ever willingly relinquished power—Washington had now done so twice. The president's announcement also revealed existing divisions in the executive branch: who enjoyed his trust and who was excluded.

Washington planned to retire in 1792, at the end of his first term. On February 19, he sent a note to James Madison asking, "if convenient," could he "spare half an hour from other matters." If so, "G. W. would be glad to see him at 11 oclock to day."[3]

Madison was born in 1751 to a wealthy, slave-owning, Virginia plantation family. During the Revolution, he served on the Virginia Committee of Safety and Virginia House of Delegates, helped craft the Virginia Constitution and Declaration of Rights, and won a seat in the Second Continental Congress in 1777, where he likely met General Washington as he convened with legislators to report on the status of the war. Although they hadn't known each other long, Madison quickly became one of Washington's most trusted advisors. He was instrumental in convincing Washington to attend the Constitutional Convention in Philadelphia in 1787, and they quietly strategized to secure ratification of the constitution produced by the delegates.[4] Later, Madison drafted Washington's first inaugural address and advised Washington on most issues during the first year of his term.

FIGURE 1.1 James Madison by Bradley Stevens (after Charles Willson Peale). Collection of the US House of Representatives.

At 11 A.M., Madison arrived at the President's House on the corner of 6th and Market Streets. Washington welcomed Madison into his study on the second floor, where they could speak confidentially. The study was small, only about fifteen by twenty-one feet, and stuffed with furniture. A French mahogany desk, over five feet wide, occupied one corner, with a tall swiveling leather chair. Mahogany bookshelves lined one wall, and across the room stood a dressing table and mirror. In the corner diagonal from the desk, an iron stove provided heat during the winter, and a standing globe completed the final corner. Busts, medals, and other gifts presented to the president adorned the shelves and the walls. In this room, Washington wrote his correspondence, met with his department secretaries, dressed, and received his morning shave from his enslaved manservant, Christopher Sheels. Few people were granted access to this room, the president's most private space.[5]

Washington revealed to Madison that he planned to retire the following spring. Men in his family had an unfortunate tendency to die young, and he had already survived two life-threatening illnesses in his first term. He did not want to spend his final days as president, subject to increasingly partisan attacks. When Washington entered office, his reputation was unparalleled.[6] Every day he remained as president, Washington risked sullying this unblemished reputation.

Washington acknowledged that he had "spoken with no one yet on those particular points" and desired Madison's advice on how best to make the announcement.[7] By 1792, Madison had split with the administration over several key pieces of legislation and Washington took these political differences personally. Although their relationship had cooled, Madison still understood public opinion and the mood in Congress better than anyone else.

Madison immediately balked at the president's request. Washington's retirement would "give a surprize and shock to the public mind." He insisted that "retiring at the present juncture, might have effects that ought not to be hazarded." Madison might not agree with some of the president's choices, but Washington was better than any of the alternatives.

But Washington seemed immovable, so Madison grudgingly suggested that he publish an address to the American people. A newspaper publication would be a powerful demonstration that the president represented all Americans, rather than an address to Congress, which would appear more elitist. With Washington's approval, Madison spent the next few months crafting the first draft. Most of the address focused on the president's retirement, but it also included a call for national unity: "We may be considered as the children of one country."[8]

Madison alone couldn't convince Washington to stand for another term, but the combined pressure of his cabinet over the next several months proved more effective. Washington had carefully selected the first cabinet secretaries to bring diverse experience, expertise, and geographical representation into the administration. The secretaries rarely agreed on substantive issues, but they were unanimous on the importance of Washington's second term.

Secretary of the Treasury Alexander Hamilton was born in the Caribbean to an unwed mother and orphaned by the age of fourteen. He escaped near death from disease and natural disasters, before sailing to New York City with the support of patrons, where he enrolled at King's College (now Columbia University). During the Revolution, Hamilton demonstrated his intelligence and bravery, which sometimes bordered on insanity. He captured Washington's attention and joined headquarters as the commander-in-chief's right-hand man.

After the war, Hamilton worked to secure financial reform in New York, the Confederation Congress, and the Constitutional Convention. As secretary of the treasury, Hamilton spearheaded financial legislation on the federal level that righted the country's economy and restored national credit. His relationship with Washington had endured significant bumps and bruises during the war, but in the administration, they grew closer, and Washington once again found his assistance invaluable.

Secretary of State Thomas Jefferson was everything Hamilton was not. He was born to a wealthy, slave-owning plantation family and had first risen to prominence in the Continental Congress, where he served as the primary author of the Declaration of Independence. After two disastrous terms as the governor of Virginia, in which the British invaded the state twice and met little resistance, Jefferson retired with his reputation in tatters. An official inquest cleared him of charges of dereliction of duty, but the taint stuck.

Jefferson enjoyed the second of his many political lives when the Confederation Congress appointed him minister to France. After several years abroad, he accepted the position of secretary of state. He encouraged and supported Washington's energetic use of executive authority but found himself increasingly in opposition to the administration's agenda. Jefferson especially resented Hamilton's growing influence and loathed their heated debates in cabinet meetings. When Jefferson's persuasive efforts failed to turn Washington against Hamilton, he founded a partisan newspaper to attack the administration—while continuing to serve as secretary of state.

Although they disagreed on nearly everything, Jefferson and Hamilton both insisted that Washington must serve another term. "The confidence of

FIGURE 1.2 Alexander Hamilton by William J. Weaver, ca. 1794–1806. Courtesy of the Diplomatic Reception Rooms, US Department of State.

the whole union is centered in you," Jefferson urged Washington. "Your being at the helm will be more than an answer to every argument which can be used to alarm and lead the people in any quarter into violence or secession." Jefferson knew that Washington worried about the Union's future, and he played on those fears. "North & South will hang together, if they have you to hang on," he said.[9]

Hamilton agreed. "Your declining [reelection] would be to be deplored as the greatest evil, that could befall the country at the present juncture," he wrote to Washington. In case the threat of national collapse wasn't persuasive, Hamilton warned Washington that his retirement after only one term would actually be "critically hazardous to your own reputation . . . that indeed it would have been better, as it regards your own character, that you had never consented to come forward, than now to leave the business unfinished and in danger of being undone."[10]

FIGURE 1.3 Thomas Jefferson. Cornelius Tiebout, engraver. United States, ca. 1797 and 1800. Library of Congress Prints and Photographs Division, LC-DIG-pga-12975.

In the fall of 1792, Washington reluctantly shelved Madison's draft of the Farewell Address and agreed to stand for election one more time.[11] Vice President John Adams was excluded from all these conversations.

As Washington's second term progressed, he lost the support of his remarkable first cabinet. Jefferson retired at the end of 1793, Secretary of War Henry Knox retired at the end of 1794, Hamilton retired in January 1795, and Edmund Randolph, first the attorney general and then the secretary of state, resigned in August 1795.

Washington tried to find equally meritorious replacements, but few of the leading minds were willing to serve in the cabinet. Cabinet positions were not nearly as prestigious as they would become in later decades. The pay was relatively low, and the hours were long. The demands of the job kept secretaries in Philadelphia for most of the year, away from their homes, families, and businesses. Additionally, travel was uncomfortable, dirty, and time-consuming, making it difficult for secretaries to regularly visit their families. The positions also made the secretaries vulnerable to considerable public criticism and the potential damage to their reputations was enough to give most men pause.

Washington promoted Oliver Wolcott Jr. to be secretary of the treasury. Wolcott came from a long line of Connecticut Federalists, including his father, the original Oliver Wolcott. Both Olivers served as governors of Connecticut, and their family belonged to the Standing Order, the Connecticut aristocracy. Wolcott wasn't a creative financial genius like his predecessor, but after serving as Hamilton's comptroller treasurer for several years, he was at least a competent manager.

The same cannot be said for Washington's other appointments. After months of searching for an alternative, Washington finally settled on Timothy Pickering as secretary of state. Pickering had been serving as the secretary of war after Knox's departure and was perfectly adequate for that office during peacetime. But he was wildly unsuited to the nation's top diplomatic position. Pickering was always convinced he was the smartest person in the room, despite spending time with many of the greatest minds in American history. His intensity can be partly attributed to his hardscrabble upbringing and his family's deep connection to its Puritan roots. Pickering's large family was always overworked and short on funds. As one historian said, however, perhaps it's unfair to the Puritans to blame them for Pickering's tyrannical personality.[12] After serving together in office, Adams later joked that "Pickering could never be happy in heaven, because he must there find, and acknowledge a superiour."[13]

Pickering had risen to the top position in the cabinet through sheer force of will but brought little of the experience expected of a secretary of state. He had never traveled outside the United States, had held no diplomatic positions, and spoke poor French (the language of eighteenth-century diplomacy). Perhaps most important, he viewed compromise as a moral failing and anyone who disagreed with him as an enemy to be crushed—a dangerous combination for any politician, let alone the top official charged with diplomacy.

With Pickering at the state department, Washington selected James McHenry as secretary of war. Born into a wealthy Irish family that relocated to Maryland in 1771, McHenry trained as a doctor in Philadelphia before serving as a surgeon in the Continental Army. He was charming, friendly, and brave—all the qualities necessary for a low-ranking officer. He was unfailingly loyal to his friends and worshiped Washington. But he was far from brilliant or imaginative, lacked executive management skills, and generally struggled to handle a large portfolio.

Although Washington had appointed this second cabinet, he rarely convened a cabinet meeting to request their advice. In 1796, Washington was determined to retire, and he once again returned to his most trusted advisors to draft the updated Farewell Address. Four years earlier, Madison had held that place in Washington's circle. Now, Madison and Washington weren't speaking, and Hamilton was the president's choice.

On February 17, 1796, Hamilton arrived in Philadelphia to argue the government's case in *Hylton v. United States* in front of the Supreme Court.[14] For the next several days, Hamilton holed up in his boarding house on Market Street to prepare.[15] On February 22, he was officially sworn in as a "Counsellor of the Supreme Court" and argued his case two days later.[16] Hamilton spoke with "astonishing ability, and in a most pleasing manner," and the audience provided its "profoundest attention," despite his giving a "speech [that] lasted about three hours."[17]

Afterward Hamilton called on the president. During their conversation, Washington revealed that he planned to retire. Hamilton tried to convince the president to run again, like he had at the end of the first term. Once it was clear Washington would not waver this time, Hamilton agreed to help craft an address.[18]

Washington unlocked a cubby in his large desk, pulled a piece of parchment out of the drawer, and handed it to Hamilton. Hamilton scanned the writing and realized that it was a draft of a farewell address.

Washington clarified that he had worked on it with Madison four years earlier. This news came as quite a surprise to Hamilton, who had been embroiled in a messy political battle with Madison around the same time. Casting the document aside, he suggested that they start from scratch, but Washington insisted that the final address must contain specific passages from this older draft.[19]

Washington explained why this inclusion was so essential. The substance of the paragraphs was less important than the author of those words. Madison and Jefferson were "now stronger, & foremost in the opposition to the Government." Washington knew they might be tempted to criticize the address and accuse him of seizing additional power for the executive branch. Washington wanted to remind them of three critical facts: he had wanted to retire four years earlier; they had encouraged him to stay in office; and they had known about the draft's existence since 1792 and remained silent. Washington calculated that using Madison's words would "blunt, if it does not turn aside," some of the criticism that would inevitably follow his retirement announcement.[20]

Once Hamilton returned to New York, he wrote to the president, alluding to Madison's draft: "When last in Philadelphia you mentioned to me your wish that I should *re dress* a certain paper which you had prepared." Hamilton asked for a copy of the exact language Washington wanted included in the draft, "as it is important that a thing of this kind should be done with great care."[21]

Washington wasted no time replying. A few days later, he sent Hamilton the document, as well as some notes on other items he wished to include. He gave Hamilton wide berth to rewrite the entire address but reminded him to include Madison's initial two paragraphs.

From late May to early July, Hamilton worked on a revised draft in between meeting with clients, arguing cases, and attending to his family. On July 5, he informed the president that he would soon be ready to share his draft. Washington asked him to consult with John Jay, another trusted advisor, just to get a second set of eyes—and maybe a more level head.

Washington trusted Hamilton's writing abilities, but perhaps not always his political judgment.[22] Jay, however, had shown constant and reliable shrewdness over the past several decades. Hailing from an old, distinguished family in New York, Jay was educated at King's College and joined the New York bar. He served in the Continental Congress before accepting a series of diplomatic posts, including working closely with John Adams in Paris to negotiate a treaty to end the war with Great Britain. When Washington assumed the presidency, he offered Jay his choice of secretary of state or chief justice of the Supreme Court. Jay chose the court and helped establish many of the first legal precedents in the new nation while also tackling occasional diplomatic duties for the president. He negotiated a treaty, which bore his name, resolved the lingering disputes from the Revolutionary War between Britain and the United States, reestablished the crucial trade relationship between the two nations, and preserved neutrality.

Hamilton was happy to work with Jay on Washington's address; they were close and had frequently consulted at the president's direction over the past seven years. A few days later, Hamilton walked one block from his home to the recently completed governor's mansion overlooking the Bowling Green, where Jay had lived since his election as governor of New York in 1795. Every room enjoyed sweeping views of the Hudson River and was outfitted with the latest decor imported from Paris and London. Typically, the Jay family would have welcomed guests into the parlor, but Jay ushered Hamilton into his

FIGURE 1.4 Portrait of John Jay by Gilbert Stuart, 1794. Courtesy National Gallery of Art, Washington. Gift of the Jay Family.

private office, perhaps signaling that the secret nature of their conversations required a more intimate setting.[23]

Hamilton shared copies of his draft, but he also read the address out loud for Jay. Newspapers were regularly passed around to friends and neighbors, and read aloud at both family hearths and taverns, where illiterate citizens could partake in the daily news. The men spent the next several hours finessing the language to please the ear and eye, before Hamilton returned home to prepare a clean draft.[24] After receiving Hamilton's draft, Washington made his own edits and asked Hamilton to return previous versions, wanting to retain all evidence of Madison's earlier involvement.[25]

Washington shared his plans with the department secretaries on September 15. Many months earlier, he had indicated to them that he planned to retire, but their objections carried far less weight than those of the cabinet in 1792. He did not ask for their input on the substance of the address but wanted them to have advance notice.

In these conversations, much like the rest of the administration, Washington intentionally excluded his vice president.

Washington and Adams had met for the first time in Philadelphia in September 1774, when they served as delegates at the First Continental Congress. Initially, they shared tremendous respect for one another, though the pressures of war soon complicated their exchanges. In 1776 and 1777, Adams had been particularly critical of Washington's leadership in low moments of the military campaign. These critiques eventually reached Washington, and he rarely forgave his critics. After the war, Adams resented the enormous praise heaped on Washington, while his own sacrifices for diplomatic service rarely received such attention or appreciation from the American public.

Despite these tensions, both Washington and Adams entered their respective offices with high expectations for a cordial working relationship. Ten days after his inauguration, the president wrote and requested Adams's advice. Washington said that he desired "to maintain the dignity of Office," but he also hoped to avoid "unnecessary reserve." He recognized that every decision had the potential to establish powerful precedent, including daily social interactions. For example, could the president host guests at private events? Could he attend events at his friends' homes? Should he make himself available to visitors? Should he embark on a tour of the states to offer more access to the average citizen? Washington conceded that these issues may "appear of little importance in themselves and at the beginning," but "may have great and durable consequences from their having been established at the commencement of a new general Government."[26]

Yet just a few months after requesting advice, Washington appeared to distance himself from his vice president. Adams's role in the controversy over the president's title was at least partly to blame for the cooling in their interactions. In the spring of 1789, Congress debated what to call the president. On one hand, Adams preferred a more elaborate title like "His Highness, the President of the United States of America and the Protector of their Liberties."[27] Adams had spent years surrounded by the finery and ostentatiousness of European courts, and he worried that foreign diplomats would scoff at the new United States government and its lack of gravitas. He argued that a lofty title would demand respect from both visiting foreigners and local citizens. On the other hand, Madison and many of his colleagues in the House of Representatives preferred a simple title, such as "Mr. President."

Washington did not interfere in the debate or indicate his preference, but later expressed his relief when Congress adopted Mr. President and confessed, "Happily, the matter is now done with, I hope never to be revived."[28] Disappointed at the result, Adams bore the brunt of criticism from his congressional opponents. Dubbed "His Rotundity" and "The Royal Vice" by his critics, Adams never escaped rumors that he preferred the trappings of monarchy. Washington took notice and no longer trusted Adams's political instincts. He excluded Adams from every single cabinet meeting and shared little information with him about state affairs.

With no job in the daily governing of the executive branch, Adams threw himself into his role as president of the Senate. Every day the Senate was in session, he walked from his hotel to the Senate chambers on the second floor of the new courthouse at the corner of Sixth and Chestnut Streets. The Senate debates were an exercise in patience. Adams had initially hoped that he would play a leadership role, guiding the senators through high-minded deliberations. But by the end of the first legislative session, the senators objected to Adams's lengthy lectures and tasked John Trumbull, a Revolutionary War veteran, respected painter, and friend of the vice president, with delivering a message to Adams to stay silent.[29] Adams thanked Trumbull for the private communication, but the criticism stung. He wrote back, "I have no Desire ever to open my mouth again, upon any question."[30] He rarely spoke in the Senate after this warning.

At the end of the Senate's daily sessions, Adams maintained a busy schedule. He made regular appearances at the President's House for social events, including the male-only levees, or standing mixers, on Tuesday afternoons. On Thursday evenings, he was a frequent guest at the Washingtons' state dinners. On Friday afternoons, he attended Martha Washington's "drawing rooms," where enslaved attendants passed lemonade, punch, and light refreshments among a "great Circle of Ladies and a greater of Gentlemen."[31]

In between his circuit of official events, he socialized with visiting dignitaries, other public officials, and old friends. In late January, he enjoyed meals with Martin Lincoln and Josiah Quincy III, and regaled them with tales of their fathers' exploits during the Revolution.[32]

Adams also patronized a bookstore owned by French émigré Médéric-Louis-Élie Moreau de Saint-Méry at the corner of Front and Walnut Street. After stopping at the post office one block away to mail letters to Abigail in Quincy several times per week, Adams passed free time flipping through the books, stationery, newspapers, and supplies on the shelves. The publications in French, English, German, Dutch, and Latin tested Adams's intellect, and

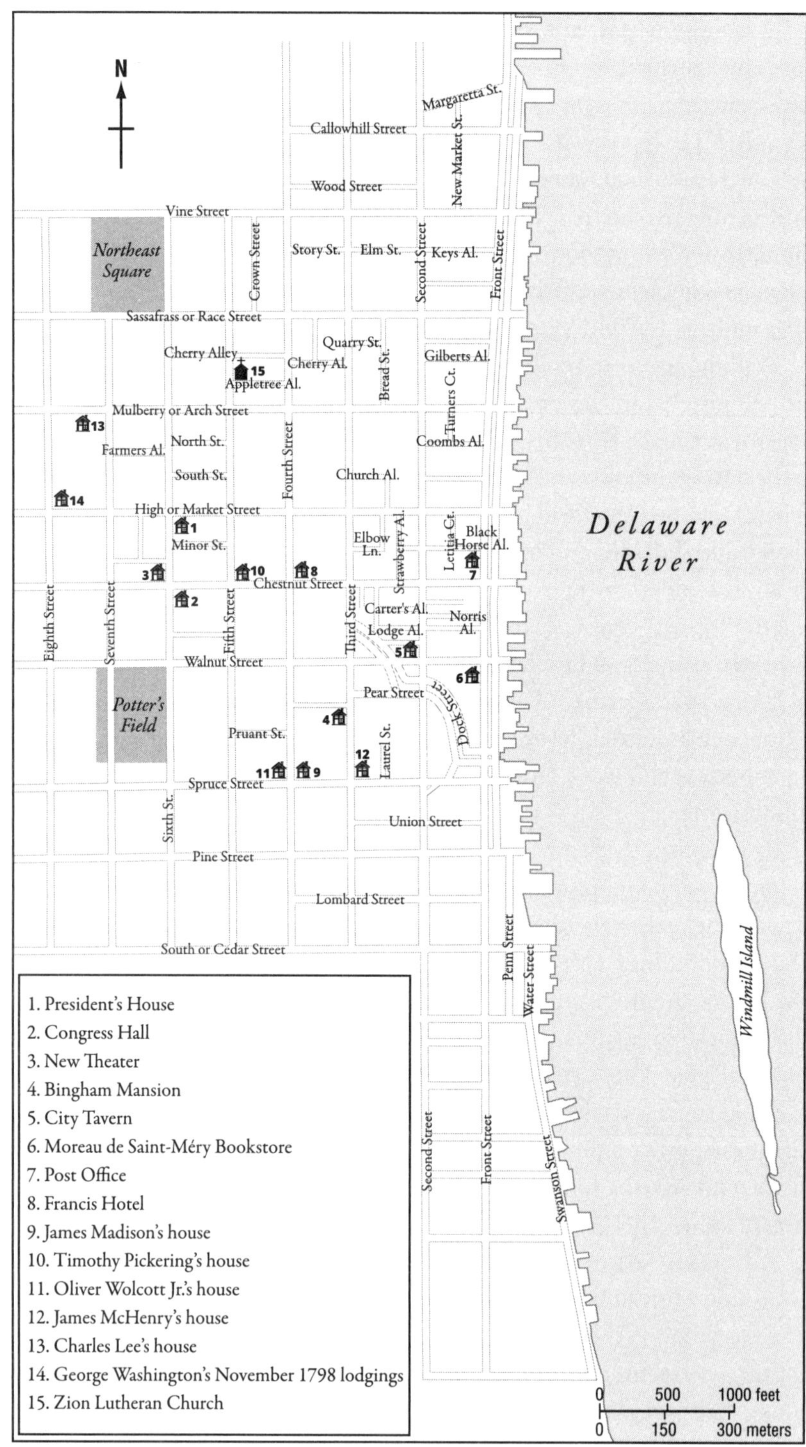

FIGURE 1.5 Map of Philadelphia

he looked forward to bantering with Moreau to maintain his French fluency. The bookshop offered the political arguments, scientific discoveries, cultural developments, and economic ideas that Adams found lacking in the Senate.[33]

In late March 1796, Washington hosted a lavish state dinner attended by Adams, Secretary of State Pickering and his wife, Rebecca, as well as all the visiting foreign ministers and their wives. After the guests finished their meal, the ladies moved to the parlor, while the men remained in the dining room for some political conversation, before joining the women upstairs. The president and vice president remained in the dining room.

Washington invited Adams to take a seat closer to the head of the table. For the next several hours, they discussed every element of the current political situation, including Great Britain, France, and the emerging political parties. Washington's candor and openness shocked Adams. The vice president acknowledged that Washington had "never [been] more frank and open upon Politicks." Adams was delighted to find Washington's "Opinions and sentiments are more exactly like mine than I ever knew before."[34] Most important, Washington indicated that his "Reign would be very short." He repeated this hint "three times at least." Adams had no trouble grasping Washington's meaning.

Although they had attended the same social events several times per week since 1789, this conversation was their first intimate exchange—a shocking admission from Adams nearly eight years into the first administration and twenty-two years into their professional relationship.[35]

On May 6, Adams left Philadelphia to spend the summer in Quincy. He did not hear from the president until his return to the city on December 2. This silence wasn't out of the ordinary, as Adams and Washington hadn't exchanged any letters during their previous summers in office. But this year was different: the president had news worth sharing.

On the afternoon of September 15, 1796, Tobias Lear hand-delivered a note to printer David Claypoole at the office of the *American Daily Advertiser* at 66 Spruce Street. The note was from President George Washington requesting Claypoole's presence the next day.

Claypoole reported to the President's House at the "appointed time" the following morning. After welcoming Claypoole into the drawing room on the second floor, Washington revealed that he planned to retire at the end of his term. "He had some thoughts and reflections on the occasion, which he deemed proper to communicate to the people of the United States, in the form of an address," and wished to publish them in the *American Daily Advertiser*. The editor immediately expressed his honor at "being singled out for that purpose" and recommended that they run the address the following Monday, September 19.[36]

Washington had selected the *Daily Advertiser* with great care. He knew Claypoole personally from their time together in the Continental Army and he trusted him to handle the assignment with discretion. The *Daily Advertiser* held many of Congress's printing contracts, including printing copies of the Constitution after the Constitutional Convention in 1787, and it had avoided the partisan reputations of the *Gazette of the United States* and the *Aurora*. As an avid consumer of news, Washington picked the newspaper that would reach the greatest number of citizens.

After they agreed to the date, Claypoole rushed back to his offices to prepare for the manuscript. The following day, Lear delivered the papers and Claypoole spent the entire night laying each word of type by hand and printing a proof copy for the president to review. Washington made just a few minor "alterations from the original, except in the punctuation, in which he was very minute."[37]

Claypoole's printing presses whirred and clanked through the night, churning out thousands of copies of the Monday edition. Before the sun rose, Claypoole's clerks began their rounds distributing newspapers to their subscribers across Philadelphia and depositing copies at the post office to be mailed around the country. Each copy contained Washington's Farewell Address.[38]

The same day Washington met with Claypoole, he convened his cabinet and shared the text of the address with the department secretaries. He did not want them to be surprised when they opened their newspapers. He did not extend the same courtesy to his vice president.

Why Washington didn't warn Adams about the Farewell Address remains a mystery. He had written to Jay months earlier on May 8, revealing his retirement plan, and had exchanged numerous letters about the address with Hamilton over the summer. His silence, therefore, wasn't a question about the trustworthiness of the mail. Washington rarely confided in Adams, and this time was no different. He simply didn't want to tell Adams or felt no obligation to do so.

Whatever his motivations, the president's decision to keep the Farewell Address a surprise was only the first in a long line of important facts he kept from Adams. As vice president, Adams kept abreast of developments at home and abroad as best as he could, but public information paled in comparison to the details Washington could have provided. Washington had never invited him to observe a cabinet meeting or sit in on important discussions. Finally, Adams remained unaware of the poor quality of the department secretaries or how Washington carefully managed their interactions. In short, he had no idea how the executive branch worked.

Washington and Adams's communication challenges would dominate the next four years and shape the coming battles over executive power. From the first days of his administration, Washington had carefully forged the beginnings of the presidency. But he failed to appreciate the enormity of the challenges facing the person holding the office after he retired. Whoever followed him was bound to fail. No one could compare in the public's estimation, and the pressure to live up to his lofty standards was impossible. By keeping critical information from his successor, Washington undermined the second president from the very beginning.

2

Washington Recedes

THE 1796 ELECTION posed a slew of new questions and challenges for the fledging nation. The country had already conducted two presidential elections, but the Electoral College had selected Washington unanimously, twice, a historic anomaly never to be repeated. For the first time, the two emerging parties had to select candidates and organize campaigns around their chosen personality. They had waged campaigns at the state level, but never on a national scale. Both sides endeavored to establish campaign etiquette, the states counted votes in earnest, and politicians struggled to protect the sanctity of elections from foreign interference which threatened to undermine the system. Finally, the American people tried to determine how to elect a president other than Washington and started to learn how to cherish the norms and customs that bolstered democratic elections as the foundation of the republic.

Under the terms of Article II of the Constitution, the president was selected by electors in the Electoral College. The Constitution granted electors to each state based on the number of representatives they had in the House plus two for their senators. For example, Delaware had three electors: one for the state's representative plus two for the senators. During presidential elections, citizens voted for electors with stated candidate affiliations rather than for candidates themselves. In the coming election, for instance, Elbridge Gerry announced that he would stand as a John Adams elector, so if voters cast a ballot for Gerry, they knew his Electoral College vote would be for Adams.

In 1788 and 1792, the process had been relatively straightforward. All electors voted for Washington for president with little thought, then selected their regional favorite for vice president. The process would not be so simple in 1796, and state legislatures began considering how to choose electors to produce their desired political outcome. Eight states authorized the legislature to select the electors, meaning that whichever party won control of the legislature would also effectively decide the state's vote for president. The other eight states held statewide elections for their electors, giving an advantage to the party with better organization at the local level.[1]

This sort of maneuvering was possible in 1796 because the terms of the Constitution called for each elector to select two candidates, and one candidate had to hail from a different state than the elector. Each party put forth two candidates and verbally agreed which candidate was intended for president and vice president. But the electors did not cast different votes for each role or fill out two separate ballots.*

Retail politics was especially effective at a time when very few Americans were eligible to vote. Most women, people of color, wage laborers, the enslaved, and immigrants were excluded. Reaching the "right voters," meaning white men of property, was easier because there were so few of them and each vote carried enormous weight.

The campaigns did not articulate party platforms, nor did they host conventions or primaries. Although most voters knew that the Federalist and Republican parties existed, many Americans had no strong party affiliations. Eighteenth-century social customs demanded that politicians abstain from campaigning for themselves or appearing too eager to win. Their supporters were tasked with cultivating favor among voters and, if politicians won, then they would graciously agree to answer the call of the people and serve.

The reality was much messier. As early as February 1796, James Madison, a leader of the fledgling Republican Party, began speculating about the candidates for the upcoming election. He confided to James Monroe, "It is now pretty certain that the president will not serve beyond his present term." He speculated that Adams would be the Federalist candidate.[2] Moore Furman, a Republican and Revolutionary War veteran, concurred. Because Adams was "so near [Washington]," he wrote, the Federalists supposed he was the "only man that can tread in Washington's steps."[3]

Federalists, led by Adams supporters in Massachusetts, agreed. In April, Colonel Elliot's Independent Cadets toasted Adams's political future: "When WASHINGTON recedes from upholding the New World, may this Atlas balance our sphere."[4] The Federalists embraced Adams because of his position

* This system remained in place until the ratification of the 12th Amendment in June 1804. The 12th amendment created separate votes for the president and vice president to avoid ties or confusion in the future.

as Washington's natural heir, but they were also keen to retain their support in New England and knew a native son would be popular.

After solidifying their presidential choice, Federalists turned their attention to the vice-presidential candidate. While there were plenty of options for the second spot on the Federalist platform, they chose Thomas Pinckney from South Carolina to provide regional balance.

Pinckney also benefited from the support of Alexander Hamilton, who remained a leading voice in the Federalist Party. Hamilton, however, had ulterior motives. He distrusted Adams's political instincts and questioned his commitment to the Federalist agenda. At the very least, Hamilton knew Adams was independent, stubborn, and difficult to control. Pinckney would make a far more malleable president. Accordingly, Hamilton devised a secret campaign to sneak Pinckney past Adams and into the presidency.[5]

The vagueness of the language of the original Constitution offered Hamilton this opportunity. He realized that if all Federalist electors cast a vote for Pinckney but threw away a handful of the Adams votes, Pinckney would win. He concocted a plan to convince all northern voters to vote unanimously for the two Federalist candidates, then covertly encouraged southern electors to throw away a handful of Adams votes.

Hamilton left little written evidence of his intrigues, but his allies were less discreet. New York Federalist Robert Troup, Hamilton's former college roommate, revealed their plans in a letter to Rufus King, the American Minister to Great Britain and a staunch Federalist. Troup pledged that all the New York electors would "vote unanimously for Adams and Pinckney," and explained that they were writing "to all our Eastern friends and endeavoring to make them accord with us in voting unanimously both for Mr. Adams and Mr. Pinckney."[6] This part of the plan was essential because if New England voters heard rumors of the scheme, they might deprive Pinckney of "some of their votes, under an idea that if they vote for him unanimously they may injure Mr. Adams."

Robert Goodloe Harper, another Revolutionary War veteran and Hamilton ally in the House of Representatives, was even more explicit. He confessed to friends and family in South Carolina that "Major Pinckney" was nominated with "the intention of bringing him forward . . . to make him President, and that he will be supported with that view."[7]

Meanwhile, Hamilton enlisted the assistance of Washington's cabinet secretaries to supplement the work of Harper and other Federalist allies in Congress. Secretary of the Treasury Oliver Wolcott Jr. was entrusted with monitoring the election in his home state of Connecticut, a bedrock of

Federalist support. Connecticut voters were eager to rally around Adams but were more suspicious of the South Carolinian Pinckney. Hamilton tasked Wolcott with writing to allies at home, urging them to support both candidates.[8]

From the beginning of the election, the Federalist Party was deeply divided. Over the following decades, party divisions proved to be a regular occurrence every four years. But in 1796, the Federalist Party was still new and relatively weak. The party had not yet developed a practice of setting aside differences and pursuing a shared agenda after the election. If Adams won, his presidency would be hobbled by internal party divisions from day one.

On the other side of the aisle, Madison set his mind to electing his oldest friend as the next president. "The republicans, knowing that Jefferson alone can be started with hope of success, mean to push him," he wrote to Monroe, another Jefferson protégé.[9] There was no set process for selecting a nominee. Instead, like-minded elites shared letters, met behind closed doors, and conducted whisper campaigns. Geographic differences hampered these efforts, as Virginia networks did not always translate to New York, Pennsylvania, or New England. Newspapers with national distribution, like Benjamin Franklin Bache's *Aurora General Advertiser*, helped bridge the distance between communities. The *Aurora*, which featured pro-Jefferson editorials and articles, was printed in Philadelphia, then carried to Baltimore, Charleston, and Boston, where newspapers would reprint these articles and extend the unofficial Republican campaign.

Although most Republicans accepted Jefferson as their candidate, Federalist opposition to his campaign sealed the deal.[10] As early as 1795, Hamilton and his Federalist allies accused Jefferson of running for president in their Fourth of July toasts. Later that year, Hamilton published a series of essays under the pen name "Camillus," in which he charged Republicans with scheming to replace leading Federalists with Jefferson and Governor of New York, George Clinton.

While Jefferson appeared to be the only choice for the Republican presidential candidate, party elites were less certain about the vice-presidential candidate as late as mid-September. Several options were mentioned, but no one stood out. In late spring 1796, Republicans in Congress met secretly and agreed that they needed to coalesce around a vice president if they had any hope of winning. Aaron Burr of New York was the compromise choice, selected to provide geographic balance to Jefferson's Virginia. Originally from New Jersey, Burr distinguished himself at Princeton University before serving in the Continental Army during the Revolution. He joined the New York bar after the war and served a term in the US Senate, before returning to the state assembly, where he acquired influence as a power broker in New York City.

Washington's shadow loomed over the entire process. If Washington had decided to stand for a third term, no one would have challenged him. Certainly not Jefferson, who had no desire to engage in that particular fight.[11] As long as Washington remained reticent about his intentions, the election was hypothetical at best.

Republicans suspected that Washington's silence was "designed to prevent a fair election, and the consequent choice of Mr. Jefferson."[12] They were right. Washington had originally planned to announce his retirement at the close of the congressional session on June 1. As Hamilton worked on a draft of the Farewell Address, he urged the president to "hold the thing undecided to the last moment."[13] By postponing the announcement until September, Hamilton successfully limited the campaign season to seven weeks before the first state cast its votes on November 4.

Finally, on November 8, as electors went to the polls, William Smith wrote, "Burr . . . is to be run on the antifederal ticket with Jefferson in some of the states; tho I believe the party are not perfectly agreed among themselves as to the Vice President—the plan of the leading men, I am told, is to vote for Jefferson and any other man, except Adams and Pinckney, and instructions have been issued to that effect."[14] Americans were trying to figure out how to choose a leader in real time with no model to follow.

The campaign may have been short, but it was vicious. Republicans launched their campaign in mid-September when Burr set out on a six-week trip across New England. He met with local leaders and cultivated support for Jefferson in Connecticut, Rhode Island, and Vermont before ending his trip in Massachusetts. He spent several days with local Republican leaders, including Benjamin Austin Jr., a senator in the Massachusetts legislature; William Eustis, who had served several terms in the Massachusetts House of Representatives; and Dr. Charles Jarvis, a perennially unsuccessful candidate for House and Senate seats. Burr hoped that the state politicians could help swing Massachusetts' electoral votes away from Adams to Jefferson and, by extension, to himself.[15]

In accordance with political norms, Burr presented his campaign as strictly on Jefferson's behalf to avoid any accusations of impropriety. But many observers suspected Burr harbored ulterior motives. John Beckley, a leading Pennsylvania politician, alerted Madison that Burr's efforts were "more directed to himself than any body else."[16] Beckley suggested that Madison might consider reaching out to his Virginia allies and throwing a few votes to George Clinton, another Republican contender, to ensure that Burr didn't edge out Jefferson in the final vote tally.

Meanwhile, in his own state, Beckley took no chances. Under his supervision, Jefferson supporters printed 1,000 copies of a pamphlet authored by "A Republican." The pamphlet warned of the dangers of monarchy, aristocracy, and British influence, and tied these threats to Adams.

In two phases, Beckley ramped up his efforts to turn out the Republican vote. First, Beckley urged his friends to fill out by hand as many ballots with the Republican candidates as possible and distribute them to local voters in their community.[17] Under Pennsylvania election law, each voter was required to write out the names of their preferred candidates by hand on the ballot. Critically, while the ballots had to be hand-written, the script did not need to be in the voter's own hand. These measures were extreme, but they were legal.

In phase two, Beckley blanketed western Pennsylvania with 30,000 pamphlets, printed with the names of all Republican candidates. These pamphlets provided a useful guide for voters who struggled to remember all the names, many of whom were strangers. Only 12,000 of the 90,000 residents in Pennsylvania were eligible to vote, meaning Beckley distributed more than two pamphlets for each voter.[18] Madison applauded Beckley's efforts in the swing state and concluded that the upcoming election "*will probably turn on* the *vote of Pennsylvania.*"[19]

While Beckley monitored the pivotal campaign in his home state, Republicans began a door-to-door campaign in New England. Tench Coxe, writing under the pseudonym "Federalist," penned a series of articles describing Adams as a friend of monarchy.[20] Republican supporters printed copies of Coxe's articles and other handbills. Experienced horsemen then crisscrossed the Massachusetts countryside with saddlebags full of these campaign materials and nailed them to gateposts, doors of houses, tavern walls, and roadside posts. Whereas Paul Revere had warned of the imminent arrival of British regulars twenty years earlier, these riders left Boston to warn of a subversive British influence in the guise of Adams's candidacy for president.[21]

Republican efforts to curry favor in Massachusetts received support from an unlikely source. Pierre Adet, the French minister to the United States, described Jefferson and Burr as "our friends" and "devoted to us." In late September, Adet traveled from Philadelphia to Boston, determined to help sway the election in Jefferson's favor.[22] It was one of the first, but not the last, instances of foreign interference in American elections.

After meeting with Republican leaders in Boston, Adet returned to Philadelphia and wrote a letter to the Washington administration accusing it of betraying the Franco-American alliance and announcing a new policy recently adopted by the French Directory. Going forward, the Directory would replicate the British navy's stance toward neutral vessels. In other words, when British ships seized American vessels, France would too. If Britain respected neutral trade, so would France.[23] On its face, this policy seemed relatively innocuous. Except that the British navy had regularly attacked neutral vessels and Americans had mostly ignored the depredations, which both Adet and Secretary of State Timothy Pickering knew well.

On October 27, Adet's clerk delivered the message to Pickering. While Adet waited for an irate response, he drafted a public address to the American people. That afternoon, Pickering replied, demanding a justification for this change in policy.[24] Rather than sending his explanation directly to the secretary or Washington, Adet published his response in Philadelphia newspapers.[25]

The address assured readers that "the neutral governments or the allies of the Republican have nothing to fear." However, if Americans allowed the English to meddle with "that neutrality, and turn it to their advantage," then they should expect France "to restore the balance of neutrality to its equilibrium." This statement targeted Republican suspicions that the Federalists sought to cozy up to the British and was designed to influence the election on behalf of Jefferson and Burr.[26]

Both sides acknowledged the impact of Adet's meddling. Madison and leading Republicans were furious: "Adet's note . . . is working all the evil." He lamented that the minister's actions provided Federalists with a powerful political talking point and appeared to offer evidence of "an electioneering maneuvre" executed by "the French Government" in cahoots with the Republicans.[27]

Beckley, Coxe, and Adet's articles framed the election in foreign policy terms. Opponents accused the Federalists of British sympathies and Republicans of pro-French bias. These affinities belied more pressing concerns about the future of the American republic. Republicans worried Federalists were working to morph the presidency into a monarchy. Federalists fretted that Republicans were importing French radicalism and violence into American society. These fears played an oversized role in the election of 1796 because the president almost single-handedly controlled foreign policy and foreign policy was the president's main responsibility.

While Federalists, Republicans, and foreign actors ginned up support through letters, publications, local meetings, and door-to-door efforts, Adams and Jefferson remained silent at their homes. Eighteenth-century political expectations suited Jefferson's preferences perfectly, as he had no interest in leaving Monticello or campaigning for public office. Republicans kept Jefferson removed from the process entirely because Madison was not sure Jefferson would even agree to have his name put forth. He confided in Monroe that he feared "that he will mar the project" through "public protest."[28] To avoid the possibility that Jefferson might say no, Madison simply avoided him so as "to present [Jefferson] no opportunity of protesting to his friend against being embarked in the contest."[29] Madison also skipped his annual summer visit to Monticello—the only summer he and Jefferson did not see each other except for the years Jefferson spent in Europe.

Adams similarly held himself to eighteenth-century political norms, but it was painful. For six weeks, he sent no letters and left no notes in his diary. Finally, on October 28, he picked up his pen and wrote to his eldest son, John Quincy Adams, the American minister at The Hague, acknowledging that the election was taking place: "If you read The Chronicle, the Aurora and all the other Papers which Attack me, you will See a manifest insincerity in every Writer and every Paragraph which relates to me. They seem to take no Pains to disguise themselves."[30]

Adams tried to ignore the slurs, but he confessed "nothing affects me so much as to see" friends set up "in opposition to me."[31] Abigail also questioned decades-old friends and refused to put sensitive details in letters, lest they be leaked to the press or opened by Republican rivals. She urged her correspondents, "Pray burn this Letter," cautioning that "Dead Men tell no tales." Her letters were "really too bad to Survive the Flames," Abigail insisted.[32]

John and Abigail did their best to muddle through the first competitive election, unsure which of their friends and acquaintances they could trust. They had no control over events unfolding across the country and even worse, they had no idea when they would receive information about the outcome of the election. Voters had been casting ballots for weeks, but the tallies would not be counted in the states until early December. Congress would not certify the results until February 8, 1797. Months of uncertainty lay before the Adamses and their fellow citizens.

In late fall, congressmen left their homes and traveled to Philadelphia for the upcoming legislative session. As they bumped along the rocky roads, voters went to the polls to cast their ballots. On November 23, 1796, several weeks into voting, Adams reluctantly departed his home in Quincy, Massachusetts, with only his valet, John Briesler, as company. Abigail remained behind to care for their home and John's mother, who was almost ninety years old and failing. A week later, Adams arrived in New York City, where he spent the day in Eastchester with his children and grandchildren, and assured Abigail that their new granddaughter was "as fat & rozy and hearty as a Country Girl can be."[33]

On the night of November 30, he enjoyed a "very happy" dinner at the governor's mansion, where he and John Jay reminisced about their shared adventures and travels.[34] The two men had been friends since they both served as delegates to the Continental Congress and worked together to secure support for the Declaration of Independence. The meal was a welcome distraction from the ongoing election.

While in New York, Adams learned of the efforts underway to "smuggle in" Pinckney to "first place." Perhaps Adams heard these rumors from Jay or maybe he received a warning from his children.[35] If Jay knew that Hamilton, his regular correspondent, was the source of these machinations, he kept it to himself.

The next day, Adams left New York for the final leg of his journey, still uncertain about the outcome of the election. The presidency was going to be a challenge for anyone after Washington, but Adams was not sure he wanted the job after learning of the internal divisions that faced the next president. He was relieved of all "envies of Mr. Jefferson, or Mr. Pinckney, or Mr. Burr, or Mr. anybody who may be chosen President or Vice-President," he confessed to Abigail.[36]

Leading figures in both parties were equally eager to receive poll results from the states. Burr lingered in New York for several weeks after the start of the session, skipping his duties in the Senate to keep tabs on the election. On November 27, he received gossip about the Pennsylvania votes and wrote, "Adams has, we think, no chance, the race will be between Jefferson and Pinkney." Three days later, he wrote to Elbridge Gerry in Massachusetts and speculated that if "the Eastern Votes should be unanimous or nearly so," then Pinkney "will be the President."[37]

On December 5, now that all the votes were cast, Madison finally wrote to Jefferson for the first time in six months.[38] Madison assumed Jefferson would accept the presidency, but urged, "You *must* reconcile yourself to the secondary as well as the primary station, if that should be your lot."[39]

Jefferson quickly reassured Madison that he would be delighted if the election kept him from the presidency: "There is nothing I so anxiously hope, as that my name may come out either second or third." Jefferson continued, "These would be indifferent to me; as the last would leave me at home the whole year and the other two-thirds of it."[40]

Jefferson knew whoever came after Washington was likely to fail. He had no desire to invite comparisons between him and Washington, or to manage the rising partisan tensions at home or the looming conflict with France abroad. He would happily wait for a more opportune moment to assume the highest office.

In fact, Jefferson went so far as to dictate instructions if the election was a tie and thrown to the House of Representatives. A tie would produce enormous "embarrassment," uncertainty, and threaten the future of the republic. Therefore, it is "both my duty & inclination," Jefferson wrote to Madison, to help avoid the questions and confusion that might arise in a tied election. "I pray you and authorize you fully to sollicit on my behalf that mr. Adams may be preferred." Jefferson shared his reasoning: Adams had "always been my senior from the commencement of our public life, and the expression of the public will being equal, this circumstance ought to give him the preference." If needed, "the addition of my wish" might tip "the scale," he concluded.[41]

It was a remarkable statement for a politician. Jefferson's letter displayed the requisite eighteenth-century humility, but it was also an honest confession of his political desires and ambitions. Although Jefferson preferred Republican leadership, he retained a lingering fondness for Adams based on their years together in Europe, and he respected Adams's decades of public service.

Madison appreciated Jefferson's willingness to accept second place, but he wasn't about to make that announcement public until absolutely necessary. He replied, "the prevailing idea is that Pinkney will have the greatest number of votes: & I think that Adams will be most likely to stand next."[42] Even without the results, Madison suspected "that this turn," meaning Pinckney's apparent lead over Adams, had "been secretly meditated from the beginning" by Hamilton and Secretary of the Treasury Oliver Wolcott Jr.[43]

Adams received the same reports and concluded his days in Philadelphia were numbered. At night, Adams confessed to Abigail that he did not worry about losing. But he dreaded having to endure the "foolish, mortifying, humiliating, uncomfortable residence [in Philadelphia] for two tedious months after I shall be known to be Shimmed." He comforted himself that he could flee the city as soon as his responsibilities as president of the Senate had expired. "The 16 of Feb will soon come and then I will take my leave forever," he wrote to Abigail. There was much to look forward to in retirement: "Frugality and independence—poverty and patriotism—love and a carrot bed." Not wanting to appear weak or mopey, he reminded his wife, "Don't show this stuff" to anyone else.[44]

Just a few days later, as a bitter cold enveloped the city and citizens ice-skated on the Delaware River, reports of the results of the last state elections trickled into Philadelphia. Adams dined at the home of Anne and William Bingham, where he enjoyed "Something like a political Conversation" with Anne, who he reported "has more ideas of the Subject than I Suspected: and a correcter Judgment." The election was certainly one of the subjects of "political Conversation" at dinner. Adams reported to his wife that the rumored results indicated "that neither Mr Pinckney nor Mr Jefferson can be President." He had "not made the Calculations" yet, but it appeared likely that he would win the election.[45]

Madison had tallied the numbers and agreed with Adams's tentative conclusion. He reported to Jefferson that Adams almost certainly obtained "the highest number. It is highly probable, tho' not absolutely certain, that Pinkney will be third only on the list." He reaffirmed his earlier plea one more time: "You must prepare yourself therefore to be summoned to the place Mr. Adams now fills."[46]

Meanwhile, Madison discreetly, but intentionally, shared Jefferson's earlier letter, written in the event of a tie, with other officials in Philadelphia. He began with Benjamin Rush, who adored both Adams and Jefferson. Madison was certain that Rush would reveal the contents of the letter to Adams, and sure enough, on January 1, John wrote to Abigail that the letter was "in the mouth of every one."[47] Adams considered the letter "as Evidence of his Determination to accept—of his Friendship for me—And of his Modesty and Moderation."

Madison also ensured that the letter reached other Federalist readers. The following week, Congressman Chauncey Goodrich sent Oliver Wolcott Sr., a Connecticut Federalist and the father of the secretary of the treasury, an account of Jefferson's letter expressing "esteem" for Adams.[48] Madison had done his job well.

Not until December 27, nearly two months after voting commenced, did Adams feel confident enough in the reported results to write with certainty to Abigail that he would be president with roughly 71 votes.[49] Jefferson received 68 votes and "will be Daddy Vice," the nickname Adams bestowed on the vice presidency.[50] Pinckney came in third. And yet, these results were still provisional, based on rumors and word of mouth reporting. Adams knew that assumptions in politics were a dangerous business, and he took nothing for granted until the results were certified in Congress.

Despite Hamilton's efforts, regional loyalties had foiled his plans. Many New Englanders had heard about his schemes and rallied around their native son. They voted unanimously for Adams and threw away their second vote on other New England-based candidates, including Chief Justice Oliver Ellsworth. These voters did not object to Pinckney, but they gave their votes to other candidates to ensure Pinckney would not win the presidency as Hamilton intended. Similarly, South Carolina electors voted unanimously for Pinckney, their native son, and Jefferson, the Republican candidate and another southerner. The results proved that regional affiliation counted for more than party identity, at least for the moment.

As Adams came to grips with the outcome of the election, he also began to grasp the extent of the machinations behind the scenes. He was embarrassed that he had been duped by Hamilton: "As great an hypocrite as any in the U.S., his intrigues in the election I despise," he wrote to Abigail. "I shall take no notice of his puppyhood," he resolved, and pledged to "maintain the same conduct towards him that I always did—that is, to keep him at a distance."[51] Perhaps more hurtful than Hamilton's duplicity were the reports that long-time friends from Massachusetts, including Stephen Higginson and George Cabot, had conspired against him.[52]

Abigail soothed her husband's feelings, "Oh I have read his heart in his wicked eyes many a time," she said of Hamilton. "The very devil is in them." She cautioned him to "Beware of that spare Cassius," a reference to the Roman senator who had instigated the assassination plot against Julius Caesar.[53]

Adams intended to follow her advice and never trusted Hamilton again. The damaged relationship between Adams and Hamilton, two of the leading figures in the Federalist Party, would define politics and the presidency for the next four years.

Adams's changed status in the Philadelphia community served as a balm to his ego. No longer the thoroughly irrelevant vice president, he was seen as a source of future power and prestige. Friends and foes alike visited to pay their respects.[54] Adams also relished the acknowledgments from his Republican rivals that he would make an honest and decent president. He overheard Representative William Branch Giles, one of Jefferson's allies from Virginia, say "The old man will make a good President, too." Even the *Aurora*, which regularly criticized the Washington administration and had published countless editorials opposing Adams, confessed that the vice president might be better than his predecessor. At least he would "not be a *puppet*," as Adams possessed "great integrity" and "would not sacrifice his country's interests at the shrine of party."[55]

Martha Washington's comments were perhaps the most pleasing of all. On January 10, Adams attended one of Washington's Tuesday afternoon levees. After the event concluded, he walked upstairs to the family parlor to call on Martha. She quietly acknowledged that it had given both her and the president "great Pleasure to find that the Votes" had gone to Adams. Washington never mentioned the election results, but for Adams, it was enough to know that the president and first lady supported the outcome.[56]

As he slowly inched toward the presidency, Adams found his feelings about his future shifting almost daily. One moment, he wished that he "could retire," but it was "too late." The next, he was preoccupied with the uncertainties on the horizon. "The Examination is to be tomorrow after which We shall soon see what turn Things are to take," he wrote to Abigail on February 7.[57] Despite the months of speculation, breathless reporting in the newspapers, rumors, and campaigning, Adams could not be sure what would happen next until he opened the ballots the next morning. If the reports were accurate and he had won, then he had to face the burdens and cares of the presidency.

Determined to meet the moment, Adams rose from his bed and stood in front of the dying fire. He practiced declaring "Thomas Jefferson to be chosen President of the United States" until he was confident that he could deliver the message "with firmness & a good grace." Just in case. Only then could he fall asleep.[58]

3

The Die Is Cast

THE NEXT MORNING, Adams rose before the sun as usual. After eating a quick breakfast and tending to his correspondence, he walked the two blocks to Congress Hall. Most days he took the stairs to the Senate chambers on the second floor, but on this morning, he crossed the threshold into the chamber of the House of Representatives. He walked down the aisle, past the rows of desks arranged in a semi-circle, and toward the raised dais at the front of the room.[1] He climbed four steps and sat in the large armchair behind the Speaker's desk, covered in green, fringed cloth. While he waited for enough congressmen to arrive to reach a quorum, he tried not to fidget.

George Washington, the cabinet secretaries, several foreign ministers, "many ladies," and leading Philadelphia families crammed into the "crowded assemblage." When the room was full, Adams gaveled the joint session into order. Following the procedures laid out in resolutions previously passed by the House and Senate, he opened the envelope from Tennessee, declaring that "it has been the practice heretofore . . . to begin with the returns from the State at one end of the United States, and to proceed to the other." Adams read the certificate before handing it to the clerk of the Senate, who read the report aloud: three votes for Thomas Jefferson and three for Aaron Burr. The clerk then handed the paper to the tellers who marked the vote tallies. Adams repeated this process for each state.

While everyone in the room had a pretty good idea Adams had won, no one could be certain until all the envelopes were opened. After announcing each state one by one, he then read aloud the vote counts for each candidate: 71 votes for John Adams, 68 votes for Thomas Jefferson, and 2 votes for George Washington from stubborn electors who refused to accept his retirement. Adams reminded the audience, new to tracking a close race in the

Electoral College, that there were 138 electoral votes. Therefore, "70 votes" makes a majority, "so that person who has 71 votes . . . is elected president." He then sat down in silence.[2]

A moment later, he stood up once more and spoke with great solemnity:

> In obedience to the Constitution and Law of the United States, and to the commands of both Houses of Congress, expressed in their Resolution pass'd in their present session, I now declare that: John Adams is elected President of the United States for four years to commence with the fourth of March next, and that Thomas Jefferson is elected Vice President of the United States.

The surrealness of the situation was not lost on Adams nor anyone else in the room. Adams had just announced his own election. "The Die is cast," he wrote to Abigail.[3]

Over the next few weeks, Adams would navigate the first transition between presidents. He had to manage the fiery partisan tensions stirred up by the election, establish a foreign policy and explain to foreign diplomats what the change would mean for their nations, and staff the executive branch. These three challenges would plague every future transition, but they were unprecedented in 1797.

The next morning, every newspaper in Philadelphia, regardless of party affiliation, printed a special edition announcing the results of the election. The postal service carried these copies across the country and local papers reprinted the news for readers from Maine to Georgia. Almost no one was fully satisfied with the results. Arch Federalists were disappointed their schemes had failed to place Thomas Pinckney in the presidency, all Federalists were convinced Jefferson would be a fox in the hen house as the next vice president, and Republicans were convinced Adams would try to recreate a monarchy as the next president.

Nonetheless, there was much to celebrate. The nation had campaigned, cast votes, and counted the returns in the first competitive election. There were no allegations of fraud, no confusion about the outcome, no widespread political violence, no civil war. The nation had survived. Adams, Jefferson, and their contemporaries recognized that the first peaceful election was an accomplishment to be proud of and a rarity in their history books.

With this widespread feeling of goodwill in the air, partisans on both sides were willing to temporarily set aside their differences and offer good wishes to the new administration. In this brief spirit of bipartisanship, Congress authorized $14,000 (in 1797 currency) for new furniture for the President's House. This enormous sum for the time revealed the shoddy state of the building and offered Adams great relief, as he was fretting about how he would afford the requisite repairs. Adams recognized this vote as the olive branch it was intended to be. Similarly, the First Presbyterian Church in Philadelphia offered a large front pew for the president-elect's special use.[4]

Many Republican newspapers made gestures of conciliation and offered encouragement to their readers. Adams was particularly pleased that a newspaper in Baltimore described him as "old fielder," which he explained to Abigail was "a tough, hardy, laborious little horse that works very hard and lives upon very little. Very useful to his master at small expense."[5]

Adams did indeed have a near-limitless capacity for hard work and put that trait to good use preparing for his inauguration. His first task was wrapping up his responsibilities to the Senate. Confident that Washington no longer needed him present to cast a tie-breaking vote, Adams requested a leave of absence for the remaining few weeks of his official term as vice president. With so much to do, he simply couldn't afford to spend his days listening to Senate debates.

On February 15, Adams delivered a farewell speech to the Senate, expressing his gratitude for the "confidence" placed in him by the voters and offered his fervent wish for the "continuation of the virtues, liberties, prosperity, and peace of our beloved country."[6] One week later, a committee made up of Senators Aaron Burr, Theodore Sedgwick, and Uriah Tracy called on Adams to deliver the Senate's reply.[7] The president-elect received them in the small drawing room attached to his sleeping chamber. The senators remained standing while offering their prepared remarks.

The address emphasized Adams's "undeviating impartiality" and commended his loyalty. Few civil servants had carried the burden of Americans' trust for longer and that "steady confidence . . . has never been betrayed or forfeited." They closed by expressing their utmost certainty that he would continue to uphold the Constitution and pledged their loyalty to support the administration.[8]

Adams did not know whether Federalists Tracy and Sedgwick had preferred him or Pinckney for president, but he assumed they would be loyal to the Federalist administration. Burr, however, had just been dealt a crushing

FIGURE 3.1 Theodore Sedgwick by Edgar Parker (after Gilbert Stuart). Collection of the US House of Representatives.

blow in the election. Yet, just one week after the defeat, he joined his colleagues and confirmed his loyalty to the administration and the nation. He established precedent for what it meant to be a citizen participant in a republic.[9] Knowing that the honeymoon period would likely be brief, Adams did not take Burr's loyal opposition for granted.

Partisan divisions, the first of the transition hurdles, threatened to rend the fragile bonds between fellow citizens and their states. Over the last two years, Republicans had become increasingly outspoken in their criticism of the Federalist administration. Washington had endured "the abuse of Party" but his unique position insulated him from unrestrained attacks. As one of the most insightful political observers in the 1790s, Abigail surveyed the scene and accurately described what she saw. Washington had enjoyed a "Combination of circumstances which no other Man can look for," including a unanimous election and an unparalleled reputation "by having commanded their Armies." Washington's stature shielded him from Republican attacks as well as those from within his own party. Now that he was gone, however,

Abigail expected that the pent-up partisan tensions would explode. She couldn't help but wonder, if Washington "was reviled and abused, his administration perplex'd and his measures impeded," then "What is the expected Lot of a Successor?"[10] She feared the second president would be "fastned up Hand and foot and Tongue to be shot at as our Quincy lads do at the poor Geese and Turkies."[11]

Adams was more preoccupied with foreign policy, the second big challenge posed by the transition. In short succession, he received visits from Philippe André Joseph de Létombe, the French consul general, and Robert Liston, the British minister to the United States. Both Létombe and Liston called to get an early sense of the president-elect's intentions for foreign policy and how the transition from Washington to Adams might affect their own countries. Adams knew exactly why they were visiting. He assured both sides that he intended to pursue friendly relations with all nations and follow "the system of impartial Neutrality bet[ween] the belligerent Powers, until it should be otherwise ordained by Congress."[12]

Adams's assurances were genuine. Neutrality had been the driving force behind his vision for American foreign policy since the nation declared independence in 1776. Adams believed wars would be damaging, unprofitable, and contrary to the country's best interests. European nations thought only of their own interests and cared little for the survival of the United States. Therefore, Adams argued, the United States should avoid war and entangling alliances with European nations whenever possible. His positions should not be confused with isolationism, however, because Adams was also a fervent supporter of intellectual, financial, and diplomatic engagement on the world stage.[13]

He was so convincing that both ministers wrote to their supervisors that the new president would benefit their nation, which was impossible, as France and Britain had long been bitter rivals. Létombe's dispatches predicted that Adams would follow the counsel of no man, least of all the anti-French forces gathered behind Hamilton. Liston's letters argued that the British should consider Adams's election "as favorable to the interests of His Majesty." This judgment was "not because I perceive in Mr. Adams any partiality of sentiment towards Great Britain," Liston explained, "but because he detests the principle and dreads the predominance of our enemy, [France], and because the firmness of his character removes all danger of his being bullied into measures which he does not approve."[14]

Privately, Adams predicted that his dreams of neutrality would come under fire from "the open Assaults of France and the Secret Plotts of England."[15]

Abigail, his closest advisor, agreed that "Our Government is in as Critical a state, as it respects our Foreign connections," than it had faced "Since its commencement."[16]

As Adams surveyed the international scene, he saw one bright spot in the morass of foreign policy. His eldest son, John Quincy Adams, had proven himself to be a promising diplomat. As news of Adams's victory reached the American ministers in Europe, John Quincy planned to return home to preempt any charges of nepotism. When Abigail asked about his plans, John Quincy assured her that he would never ask for an appointment under his father's administration. Frankly, he was offended she could even think such a thing and told her that he "had hoped that *my mother* knew me better." He was not just posturing. He was proud of his diplomatic successes and no insult cut deeper than insinuations he owed his success to his familial connections. Abigail forwarded the letter to John, who "could not withhold it," and sent it along to Washington like the proud father he was.[17]

FIGURE 3.2 John Quincy Adams, by John Singleton Copley, American (1738–1815), 1796. Bequest of Charles Frances Adams. Photograph © 2024 Museum of Fine Arts, Boston.

Washington agreed that special treatment should be avoided, but he encouraged Adams not to "withhold merited promotion" from his son just because they were related. "Mr Adams is the most valuable public character we have abroad," Washington wrote, and "he will prove himself to be the ablest, of all our diplomatic Corps." The loss of John Quincy's talents would harm national security, Washington concluded. Adams confessed that the exchange and sentiments contained in the letters was "the most beautiful Thing I ever read."[18] Convinced by Washington's praise, Adams insisted his son remain abroad.

Confident in the diplomatic corps, Adams then turned his attention to building his administration—the last and most time-consuming of his transition duties. While some appointments and open offices would have to wait until after his inauguration, he focused on selecting the attorney general and the secretaries for the war, state, and treasury departments. Appointing subordinates was a new challenge. As a lawyer, congressman, and diplomat, Adams had proven he could work alone or with colleagues on behalf of his nation, but he had never served in an executive capacity. Even so, he had copious ideas about presidential authority and had probably spent more time thinking about the role of the executive than almost anyone.[19]

Adams's ideas about power undergirded key political discussions. He had authored the Massachusetts state constitution, which remains the longest surviving written constitution, and he had published his multi-volume *A defense of the constitutions of government of the United States of America.* Both documents had served as important models for the United States Constitution and were referenced by the delegates at the Constitutional Convention.[20] At the core of Adams's political ideology, he was deeply committed to the principle of executive power.[21]

While Adams brought nearly unparalleled theoretical knowledge of executive power to the presidency, he had never exercised it, nor had he observed how to delegate responsibility within the executive branch.[22] Adams had never witnessed the cabinet deliberations or realized the importance of interpersonal relationships. Adams didn't realize that while Washington delegated a great deal of authority to the secretaries, he kept a close eye on them.

Adams sat down at his writing desk to craft a list of potential candidates for these positions. Topping the list were his closest friends and advisors, including Elbridge Gerry, Benjamin Rush, and John Jay. As an avowed Republican, Adams concluded Rush was out of the question. Adams intended to appoint Gerry to a diplomatic position, so he couldn't hold a demanding cabinet office as well. Jay had recently retired as chief justice of the Supreme

Court in favor of the governor of New York, so he was unlikely to accept a cabinet position, which he would have seen as a considerable demotion.

By the end of Washington's administration, the only men willing to serve were those who lived close to Philadelphia (like Wolcott), desperately needed the paltry salary (like Pickering), or worshiped the president (like McHenry).[23]

Adams knew that Washington had endured significant frustration trying to fill cabinet vacancies toward the end of his administration. The president had to distribute "the offices about the states in some proportion to their numbers."[24] But few men were willing to endure "the expenses of living at the seat of government," when "the sure reward of integrity . . . is such obloquy, contempt, and insult." Adams was surprised that Washington could find anyone "willing to renounce his home, forsake his property for the sake of removing to Philadelphia, where he is almost sure of disgrace and ruin."[25] Ultimately, Adams concluded "it is very difficult to find gentlemen who are willing to accept of public trusts, and at the same time capable of discharging them." If Washington had trouble filling these positions, then Adams certainly would too.

Without the benefit of firsthand experience in the cabinet, Adams assumed the structure of the presidency kept the rest of the executive branch in line. He had no reason to think he shouldn't keep the existing cabinet secretaries. There was no precedent suggesting removal. If the secretaries were loyal to Washington, then surely they would be loyal to him.

Adams also had to consider the partisan implications of his cabinet choices. Replacing Pickering, who had taken a strident anti-French tone in newspaper publications during the election, would offer a powerful symbolic gesture that Adams was committed to peace with France. However, Pickering was well-liked and well-connected in the Federalist Party. Adams didn't consider himself particularly partisan, but he also didn't want to provoke a party split before taking office.[26]

Party implications would prove a perennial challenge for Adams's successors, but he had one last, unique concern. He feared replacing the cabinet secretaries would appear as a rebuke of Washington's administration. Many Americans already felt as though the "World [had turned] Upside down" when Washington announced his retirement. Adams felt he had no choice but to trust Washington's judgment and have faith his predecessor would guide him.[27]

All these factors weighed on the president-elect as he evaluated his choices. The problem was that Adams "had never had much intercourse with any of the Secretaries of Department." He had interacted with them at Washington's levees, drawing rooms, and state dinners but never worked with them on any executive department activity. But he also had "no particular objection against any of them," so it was his "duty to look into them."[28]

A couple of days after opening the Electoral College votes in Congress, Adams began a morning of visits to the secretaries to determine if they could work together as colleagues. Swathed in layers of wool to protect against the bitter winter wind, he left his lodgings and walked three blocks to "the Treasury" at 100 Chestnut Street. After wiping the ice and dirt off his boots, he "conversed with Wolcott" while warming his hands in front of the fire.

There were no written rules governing this situation and Wolcott was not sure what the moment required of him. During this conversation, Wolcott offered his resignation. Relying on the only precedent he could find, Wolcott borrowed from British cabinet practice and offered to vacate the office, just as privy counselors did when prime ministers were replaced.[29] Adams turned down the resignation but appreciated the gesture.

After that conversation, Adams walked to the corner of Arch and Sixth Streets, where he stopped "at the office of State and conversed with Pickering."[30] Next, Adams likely went one block farther west on Arch Street to Charles Lee's residence. Finally, he finished his rounds at the offices of the war department on Fifth and Chestnut Streets. None of the other secretaries offered their resignations. Perhaps they were waiting to discuss the subject with Wolcott and discover whether his offer had been accepted, or maybe they were waiting for Adams to request it.

After concluding his conversations with the secretaries, Adams returned to his rooms, thawed out from his journey, and wrote to Gerry, "Pickering and all his Colleagues are as much attached to me as I desire I have no Jealousies from that Quarter."[31]

While the secretaries mulled over Adams's offer, Washington entered the fray. He did not speak directly to the president-elect, but he encouraged the secretaries to remain in office. He urged Pickering to think of "the near prospect of peace" and his "facility in executing it." Washington did not explain his rationale for interference, but he likely hoped the secretaries would provide institutional stability and continue his foreign policy of neutrality and peace with all nations.[32]

Behind their backs, he offered a very different assessment. In his final years in office, Washington convened few cabinet meetings, especially compared to the daily or weekly meetings he had organized with Hamilton and Jefferson.

FIGURE 3.3 High Street, from Ninth Street—Philadelphia, 1800. William Russell Birch & Son. Courtesy National Gallery of Art, Washington. Corcoran Collection (Museum Purchase, Mary E. Maxwell Fund).

He liked Pickering, Wolcott, and McHenry less than their predecessors and almost always asked for second opinions from Hamilton or Jay.

Beyond considering them poor advisors, Washington judged the secretaries incompetent at their bureaucratic responsibilities. He regularly complained to Hamilton about McHenry's unfitness for office: "I early discovered, after he entered upon the Duties of his Office, that his talents were unequal to great exertions, or deep resources."[33] Similarly, Hamilton concluded that Pickering "has nevertheless something warm and angular in his temper & will require much a vigilant moderating eye."[34] These warnings proved prescient. Pickering would indeed require a "vigilant moderating eye" in the coming years, but neither Hamilton nor Washington shared these concerns with Adams.[35]

Washington left no record explaining his silence, nor did Adams speculate as to why his predecessor kept him in the dark. Perhaps Washington felt it would be inappropriate to offer advice, as Adams might view this guidance as unwelcome meddling. Given that Washington intervened behind the scenes to encourage the secretaries to accept the positions, however, a more likely answer lies in Washington and Adams's uneasy relationship. He did not completely trust Adams's instincts. By leaving the secretaries in place, Washington could help ensure the continuation of his agenda and provide stability for Americans shaken by the transition. Their silence in the transition marked another missed opportunity for honest communication. Had Washington spoken with Adams, he would have discussed their foreign policies, noting that they were closely aligned.

When the secretaries accepted their offers a few days later, Adams was relieved. He believed that he had resolved a critical obstacle of the first transition and established his presidency on firm footing. As he prepared to take office, Adams sent the secretaries a letter requesting that they "Make reports of their Opinions in writing" of the many tensions that plagued the Franco-American relationship.[36] He intended to rely on their guidance and expected that he would need their help managing the significant challenges to come.

Adams still had one more piece of the administration to settle—the vice president. Adams had played a small role in Washington's administration, and they had represented the same party. Adams wanted to include Jefferson in the governing process but was not sure how to work with a vice president he had just defeated in the election. Jefferson had no idea what role he should play, nor did he have any idea how to craft that role for himself. Both men followed their political instincts and hoped for the best.

To start, they had engaged in a series of backchannel conversations through their friends and the press. Adams had assured Gerry, their mutual friend, that he trusted Jefferson's political values and honesty. Gerry quickly passed on these assurances to Jefferson.[37] In return, Jefferson had written to John Langdon that he had no "feelings which would revolt at taking a station secondary to Mr. Adams. I have been secondary to him in every situation in which we ever acted together in public life for twenty years past."[38] Adams was particularly gratified when Langdon, an old friend from the Continental Congress, shared the contents of this correspondence, as Jefferson expected he would.

Jefferson thought he should reach out directly to the president-elect as well. He wrote to Adams expressing his great pleasure that Hamilton's election schemes had failed. Indeed, he continued, "no one then will congratulate you with purer disinterestedness than myself." Jefferson also referred to their long history together and pledged that he still retained "for you the

FIGURE 3.4 Elbridge Gerry by Nathaniel Jocelyn (1744–1814). Harvard Art Museums/Fogg Museum, Louise E. Bettens Fund, Photo © President and Fellows of Harvard College, 1943.1816 F.

solid esteem of the moments when we were working for our independance, and sentiments of respect and affectionate attachment." In closing, Jefferson hoped that the Adams administration would enjoy the greatest success and "be able to shun for us this war by which our agriculture, commerce and credit will be destroyed. "The glory will be all your own," Jefferson said, assuring Adams that he wouldn't get in his way or overshadow him.[39]

Then, at the last moment, before mailing the note, Jefferson had second thoughts. Could the letter be misinterpreted? Would Adams know what he meant? Would the letter establish a dangerous precedent? Would it be a political embarrassment if leaked? Unsure how to proceed, Jefferson resorted to his usual practice whenever he was conflicted about what to do—he sent the letter to Madison.

Horrified, Madison pocketed the letter. Unsure how long the harmony between the president and vice president would last, Madison warned Jefferson that Adams was notoriously touchy about his reputation. He might take offense at the mention of Hamilton and the election. Furthermore, Jefferson had already expressed his congratulations and he might come to regret the effusive letter if it was made public at some point in the future.[40]

Jefferson accepted Madison's advice, as he did so often, and filed away the draft. This exchange revealed much about their relationship. Though he was Madison's senior in age, reputation, and expertise, Jefferson regularly consulted his friend on decisions big and small. When Madison advised against a policy, Jefferson often listened. Their contemporaries might have viewed Madison as the subordinate, but they both knew they were partners.

Unaware of these machinations, Abigail encouraged John to reach out to Jefferson. It was the right thing to do, she reminded him. Jefferson was not "an insincere or a corruptible Man," she said, and it was also the smart political choice. By aligning himself with Jefferson, Adams could undermine potential political attacks from both sides. He could defend against accusations of partisanship launched by Republicans, while building a broad base of support in the event the Arch Federalists turned on him.[41]

Adams knew his wife was right, and he remained hopeful that he and Jefferson could work together in harmony to lead the nation through the tumultuous transition from the first to the second administration. Adams vowed to speak with the vice president-elect as soon as he arrived in Philadelphia.

In late January, Jefferson wrote to Madison that he planned to leave Monticello in the next few weeks, traveling most of the way to Philadelphia by public stage to "escape into the city as covertly as possible." Jefferson didn't know how the president would receive him and which policies he planned to pursue. Until Jefferson had this information, he wanted his role in the administration to be as discreet as possible. He requested that Madison keep his ear to the ground. If "Governor Mifflin should show any symptoms" of planning a welcoming ceremony, Jefferson begged Madison to intercede on his behalf.[42]

On February 20, Jefferson reluctantly began his journey north, resting each night at a local tavern or public house. A few days later, Jefferson arrived in Alexandria, one of the biggest port cities at the time. A congressional messenger was waiting to intercept him and delivered the official certificate of election.

Jefferson pushed onward to Georgetown, where he was delayed by "the failure of the stages." He lost three more days at Baltimore, where bad weather stymied several attempts to cross the Chesapeake Bay. Already grumpy about the trip, Jefferson suffered a "very rough passage" north, before one last stop in Wilmington.[43]

Ten days after he left home, Jefferson entered the city early on the morning of March 2. Despite his best efforts, his arrival was celebrated by a company of artillery who discharged sixteen rounds of ammunition out of two twelve-pounder cannons. The soldiers carried a flag that proclaimed Jefferson "THE FRIEND OF THE PEOPLE."[44]

After acknowledging the troops' efforts, Jefferson made his way to Madison's home on 115 Spruce Street, where he planned to spend the night.[45] He ate a quick meal and freshened up before walking two blocks to the Francis Hotel. He asked the housekeeper for directions, made his way upstairs, and knocked on the door of the president-elect.[46]

Adams and Jefferson had last seen each other four years earlier when Jefferson retired as secretary of state. They had once considered the other a most valued friend and treasured their shared time together in Europe. Then they returned to politics in the United States and spent the next several years criticizing each other's diverging politics. Adams thought Jefferson was a naïve optimist about the violence and danger of the French Revolution, and Jefferson worried that Adams had grown too fond of the monarchies in Europe and wanted to replicate the same system at home. The election had exacerbated their differences, as their supporters slung criticism and falsehoods at the other in newspapers.

As Jefferson knocked on the door, he hoped that his letters in support of Adams's presidency had softened existing tensions. Jefferson was relieved when Adams welcomed him warmly and spoke enthusiastically about their shared administration. The visit was a short one—Jefferson was tired from his travels—but it was a good start.

The next morning, Adams found Jefferson alone in his room at Madison's house. The visit was rather remarkable. Adams was scheduled to take the oath of office and deliver his address the following day, yet he took time out of the final morning before the official beginning of his presidency to return Jefferson's call. Eighteenth-century social custom dictated that the social inferior should make the first call, then if the person of superior class wished to continue the relationship, he should return the visit. Adams's call on Jefferson was in accordance with this norm, but as president, Washington had never returned calls. Adams could have avoided the second meeting if he wished.[47]

Aside from the symbolic gesture, Adams had substantive matters to discuss. He was already planning his first diplomatic action and requested Jefferson's input. Adams wanted to send Jefferson to Paris to negotiate a truce with the French Government, but he acknowledged this plan wouldn't work because the president couldn't "send away the person destined to take his place" if he became ill or died suddenly.[48] In an age when Atlantic crossings took weeks, if not months, the vice president couldn't be that far from the seat of government.

Jefferson's history with France and personal prestige would have lent significant gravitas to the mission. If Jefferson was unavailable, Adams continued, Madison was the obvious next-best option. He asked Jefferson to "consult Mr. Madison for him," hoping that it might be more welcome coming from a close friend.[49] Jefferson replied that he thought Madison unlikely to accept the mission, but he would ask.

Jefferson was pleased with the tenor of the conversation. He concluded that Adams meant to "attend to self respect & national dignity with both" France and Great Britain, and that "perhaps the depredations of both on our commerce may be amicably arrested."[50]

After Adams departed, Jefferson packed up his belongings, left Madison's home, and took up rooms at the Francis Hotel. He could have stayed with Madison, but he recognized the value of the future president and vice president sleeping under one roof the night before the inauguration. It was a powerful way to demonstrate unity and bipartisan cooperation on the eve of a historic transition.

Jefferson's contemporaries appreciated the import of this gesture. Students celebrating the impending inauguration offered toasts to "Adams and Jefferson, or Checks and balances."[51] Alexander Hamilton ruefully noted that "the Lion & the Lamb are to lie down together. There is to be a united and vigorous administration." Or so they said. Hamilton wasn't so sure. "Skeptics like me quietly look forward to the event—willing to hope but not prepared to believe."[52]

Later that night, with Jefferson just down the hallway, Adams tossed and turned in anticipation of the events the following morning. February 8 had been an anxious day, but "Tomorrow will be a worse day," he wrote to Abigail. Once he had "take[n] the oaths," there would be no turning back.[53]

4

The "Sublimest Thing" Ever Exhibited in America

ON THE MORNING of March 4, Adams looked out the window as heavy rain pounded down and turned the streets to mud.[1] The president-elect had carefully planned the details of his transportation later that morning. He had purchased "a Pair of Young" and "clever" horses to pull the new "Simple but elegant" chariot. As president, Washington had used a luxurious cream-colored coach with gold trim, pulled by six matching horses, and was escorted to both inaugurations by an armed guard.[2] Some Republicans had questioned Washington's finery as that of aristocracy, but most citizens had accepted the splendor as appropriate to his status as president and father of the country. Adams knew he would not have the same latitude.

Adams also welcomed the opportunity provided by the inauguration to set aside some of the more aristocratic trappings of his predecessor. He turned down a military escort, which Washington had enjoyed on special occasions, and encouraged his family to adopt equally simple modes of travel. When John learned that Abigail had painted the Quincy coat of arms on their family carriage, he demanded that she paint over it immediately with "all the Arms totally obliterated." He explained, "It would be a folly to excite popular feelings and vulgar Insolence for nothing."[3]

Adams looked over his remarks and checked to be sure his outfit was prepared. He dressed in a new pearl gray suit he had ordered for the occasion. He eschewed black, as it was favored by his predecessor, but light gray still struck an appropriately somber tone.[4] He powdered his hair and placed the freshly brushed tricorne hat on his head. For the final touch, he strapped his ceremonial sword around his waist.[5]

Adams had first purchased the sword when he traveled to France as an American minister in 1778 because a ceremonial sword was required for presentation at Versailles, the court of the French kings. He donned the sword again for his official arrival at The Hague, the seat of government in the Netherlands, and the Court of St. James, King George III's residence in London, as dictated by custom. It was a smallsword, just under forty inches in length. Both the blade and the switch (the handle piece) were silver. A filigree pattern was carved into the blade, and the handle was covered with ornamental designs.[6] Washington had worn a ceremonial sword as president at all official gatherings; Adams knew of no other way for a gentleman to present himself at ceremonial occasions.

The sword embodied the challenge of the moment. Adams was attempting to craft an image that combined competing motivations: following Washington's example, but not replicating him too closely; cultivating respect for the presidency as an institution, while still embodying republican virtue. These details, from the sword to the carriage, were integral to that process. Adams could not control how the crowds mulling outside or the legislators gathering at Congress Hall would respond to the transfer of power, but he could make sure he surrounded himself with trappings of ceremony to instill the new institution with legitimacy. As Americans learned how to participate in democratic elections, lose gracefully, and observe inaugurations for the first time, Adams was crafting a tradition of peaceful transfer of power.

While Adams waited for his carriage to arrive, Thomas Jefferson carefully dressed in a long blue frockcoat and closed the door to his rooms. He walked the two blocks to Congress Hall, before climbing the stairs to the Senate chambers on the second floor. At 10 o'clock, the clerk announced the arrival of the vice president–elect.

Jefferson made his way down the central aisle of the room. Beneath his feet lay a large, ornate carpet decorated with an enormous eagle, holding thirteen arrows and an olive branch in its talons. Thirteen stars circled the head of the eagle, who held a scroll in its beak, which was inscribed with "E pluribus unum." Jefferson walked past the senators' desks and their large, crimson upholstered chairs, toward the small platform at the front of the room. William Bingham, a senator from Pennsylvania and the Senate president pro tempore, stood in front of the vice president's desk underneath the red damask canopy.[7]

Bingham then guided the vice president through the oath and Jefferson promised to "support and defend the Constitution of the United States against all enemies, foreign and domestic." Perhaps equally as important given the contentious election that found him sharing the executive branch with his opponent, he promised to "take this obligation freely, without any mental reservation or purpose of evasion; and that I will well and faithfully discharge the duties of the office."

After completing his role in the ceremony, Bingham climbed down from the dais and returned to his seat next to James Ross, his fellow senator from Pennsylvania. Jefferson, the new president of the Senate, took his seat at the desk under the canopy at front of the room. The clerk read the credentials of the eight new senators elected in the fall campaigns before Jefferson administered their oaths, completing his first official act as vice president. He then pulled out a few sheets of paper, cleared his throat, and delivered his brief speech.[8]

Jefferson tailored his remarks to avoid Adams's mistakes during his early years as vice president. Jefferson promised to take a hands-off approach to his role as the president of the Senate; there would be no excessive speechifying. As a nod to the growing partisan divide in Congress, he acknowledged that he would "concur with some" opinions and "differ from others," but he would enforce the chamber's rules with the "most rigorous and inflexible impartiality."

Speaking to the Federalist-dominated Senate, he expressed great confidence in Adams's ability to manage the responsibilities of the presidency. Indeed, he said Adams's "talents and integrity have been known and revered by me through a long course of years." The president's "eminent character" served as the "foundation of a cordial and uninterrupted friendship between us," Jefferson shared.[9]

Secretary of State Timothy Pickering sat in the back of the room, jotting down notes on Jefferson's short remarks. Jefferson praised Adams and appeared willing to work with the administration, but Pickering had no faith that the vice president would remain on the sidelines. Even worse, the secretary of state worried that Adams would be fooled by Jefferson's kind words and allow himself to be manipulated by the wily vice president. Pickering planned to share his concerns with Adams and appointed himself sentry against Republican conspiracies.[10]

Pickering's unease reflected the political system's lack of preparation and experience dealing with a president and vice president from two different parties. Pickering and many fellow citizens questioned whether the executive branch could withstand the internal stress as partisan tensions flared. There was a very real concern that Jefferson would form a shadow administration and tear the whole experiment apart.

After delivering his remarks, Jefferson ordered the special session of the Senate in recess and led the senators down the stairs to gather with their colleagues in the House chambers. The clerks had been busy arranging seating and the room was already full in anticipation of the day's events. The justices from the Supreme Court, the department secretaries, and visiting foreign ministers were seated in the reserved spaces toward the front of the room. Over 100 representatives were perched in their usual seats in three semicircular rows around the dais. On the sides of the room and behind the House seats, the senators lined up in additional chairs. Rows and rows of benches were crammed on the balcony to fill every inch of space. As the official hour drew close, leading citizens claimed every seat and bit of standing room.[11] One newspaper report observed that the ladies' colorful dresses and shawls added a "brilliancy to the scene."[12] From their perch on the balcony, leading ladies in Philadelphia and the wives of cabinet secretaries and foreign ministers observed the scene.

Noticeably absent were Abigail Adams, Martha Washington, Martha Jefferson Randolph, and Maria Jefferson Eppes, Jefferson's daughters. Jefferson's daughters were busy with their families in Virginia, but Martha's motivation for missing the event is more puzzling. She had not attended either of George's inaugurations, so maybe she hoped to avoid the spectacle or perhaps remained at home to avoid drawing attention to Abigail's absence.

While the attendees took their seats, Adams's carriage pulled up in front of the Francis Hotel to pick up the president-elect.[13] His servants, with the newly purchased matching livery, opened the front door. As Adams stepped through the doors, the clouds parted, and a few weak rays of sun shone on the gleaming carriage waiting outside.[14] It was an auspicious sign for the momentous day and could not have been better designed by Adams himself.

The carriage ride was short, only two blocks, which was just as well, because Adams was nauseous and dizzy with worry that he might not get through the ceremony without fainting.[15] As he traveled the short distance to Congress Hall, he missed Abigail desperately.[16] He could have used her thoughtful edits on his speech, her steady encouragement, or just a reassuring squeeze to his hand in the carriage.

A few minutes before noon, the carriage pulled to a stop on Chestnut Street. At the same time, Washington, dressed in his usual black velvet suit, walked down Sixth Street. Upon spotting the first president, the crowds gathered outside Congress Hall erupted into a spontaneous cheer. The roar moved inward and "a thunderous applause" shook the room as Washington walked into the House chambers.[17] "No sooner was his person seen than a burst of applause such as I had never before known, and which it would be as impossible for me to describe [was heard]," reflected Senator Theodore Sedgwick.[18]

The public cheers were more nuanced than they first appeared. No one expected Washington's attendance. Washington was leaving office and had no official role in the ceremony. There was no precedent of a former president's attendance at the inauguration. At the local and state level, outgoing executives were not typically present at the inauguration of their successors.[19] The crowd's cries revealed their surprise and appreciation for his participation in this momentous occasion. The most interesting aspect of the entire day "was the presence of the late President," wrote Sedgwick, describing the event to a friend. "He came unattended and on foot, with the modest appearance of a private citizen."[20]

A few minutes after Washington entered the House chambers, Adams followed and was met with similarly enthusiastic roars.[21] He strode down the center aisle of the room, climbed the raised dais, and took a seat behind the Speaker's desk. He nodded to acknowledge Jefferson, seated to his right, before turning to his left and recognizing the Speaker of the House, Jonathan Dayton, and the clerk, John F. Beckley. Finally, Adams greeted Washington and the justices of the Supreme Court, seated just in front of the dais.[22]

Observing the new federal officers from his spot at the front of the room, one of the justices described his pleasure at seeing Adams and Jefferson seated next to each other: "The thing looks well; it carries conciliation and healing with it, and may have a happy effect on parties."[23]

The applause and cheers tapered off and the room fell silent. Adams stood and pulled out his remarks from his coat pocket. He took a deep breath, willed his hands to remain steady, and began, "When it was first perceived . . . ," before launching into a brief history lesson to remind Americans why the Constitution and the government was unique and worthy of devotion.[24] Just ten years earlier, the new nation had stumbled under the weight of "universal languor, jealousies and rivalries" between the states, and "decline of navigation and commerce." The "discontents, animosities, combinations, partial conventions, and insurrection" provoked by this economic turmoil threatened "some great national calamity."

The president urged his fellow Americans to remember the conditions under which the nation had suffered without the federal government. Implicit in this reminder was a warning that the United States was still new, fragile, and susceptible to returning to those conditions.

The greatest threat to a prosperous future, Adams continued, was the threat to "the purity of our free, fair, virtuous, and independent elections." These threats could come from many sources, whether they be "through artifice," party corruption, or "foreign nations by flattery or menaces, by fraud or violence, by terror, intrigue, or venality." The American republic required a government chosen by its people for its people. Anything else would no longer be a republic, Adams proclaimed.[25] From the very beginning of his administration, Adams emphasized the importance of safe elections and the peaceful transfer of power to the democratic process.

The nation was under siege, Adams conceded, but there was reason for optimism. These threats had hovered over the new nation since its inception, but it had endured the first eight years largely thanks to Washington's leadership, "ardent patriotism and love of liberty." Those years had laid a shared foundation upon which Adams hoped to build. The norms and customs that were central to the republic took time to solidify. Every day, every year the nation endured would bolster its defenses against those who sought to tear it down.

Adams closed his tribute to his predecessor by acknowledging that Washington's presence was "a bulwark, against all open or secret enemies of his country's peace." Adams was far too savvy to think that once Washington went home, he would recede from the political scene. For better or worse, the first president would cast a long shadow.

Next, Adams recommended measures for Congress's consideration that he judged "necessary and expedient," as called for in the Constitution. His vision reflected his decades-long commitment to American industry, trade, and neutrality. At home, Congress should found "schools, colleges, universities, academies, and every institution for propagating knowledge." The economy had largely recovered from the Revolutionary War and trade was flourishing, but Americans still relied heavily on European manufacturers, while the merchant marine, the American ships that carried goods across the globe, depended on the goodwill of European navies to keep them safe. To be a truly independent nation, the United States needed its own industrial base and navy to protect its trade. Future growth and continued stability demanded government investment to help these industries flourish. Accordingly, Adams encouraged Congress to adopt measures "to improve agriculture, commerce, and manufacturers for necessity, convenience, and defense."

American prosperity shaped Adams's foreign policy agenda as well. He pledged his "inflexible determination to maintain peace and inviolable faith with all nations." American interests would be best served by maintaining "that system of neutrality and impartiality among the belligerent powers of Europe." Adams had no way of knowing what the next four years would bring, but his vision proved prophetic.

The pace and tenor of Adams's speech rose to a crescendo as he closed his inaugural address with an appeal to a higher power. He expressed his wish that the "Being who is supreme over all, the Patron of Order, the Fountain of Justice, and the Protector in all ages of the world of virtuous liberty, continue His blessing upon this nation and its Government and give it all possible success and duration consistent with the ends of His providence."[26] Not quite the modern-day "God Bless America," but it was close. He was met with a standing ovation and rapturous applause.

Having completed his speech without incident, Adams exhaled deeply. Amid the continuing roar, he pocketed his notes, stepped down from the dais, and stood in front of the table where the justices were seated for his last task. Unlike later inaugurations, Adams took the oath of office after his remarks, rather than before. Chief Justice Oliver Ellsworth stood and assumed his place next to the president-elect. He held out a Bible on which Adams placed his hand. Ellsworth administered the oath, which Adams "repeated with energy." When the new president lowered his hand, the attendees once again burst into deafening cheers.[27]

With the crowd still on its feet and cheering, the new president walked back down the aisle with Washington and Jefferson in his wake. It was the first time in nearly twenty years that Washington had walked behind another man as a measure of deference. As the front doors of Congress Hall opened, thousands upon thousands of people crammed should-to-shoulder along Sixth and Chestnut Streets, waiting to capture a glimpse of the first and second presidents.

American citizens had never witnessed a transition from one federal leader to another. The only transition they were familiar with was the spectacular failure of the French Revolution, and they had spent the last seven years reading lurid accounts of the atrocities. This crowd did not expect Adams's inauguration to devolve into a bloody, violent uprising, but they were canny enough to realize no one ever really expected a peaceful transition to fail. As the three men stepped outside, the throngs erupted in a roar, accompanied by the rounds of artillery fired to celebrate the occasion.

The new president turned toward the old and they nodded to each other before going their separate ways. Washington walked west on Chestnut Street toward the President's House, while Adams and Jefferson made their way east back toward the Francis Hotel. Large crowds escorted all three men back to their residences, while cannons continued to boom, and musicians played in the streets.[28]

Shortly after Adams returned to his rooms, the former president arrived. Washington had made no private calls while in office but received them regularly. By calling on Adams, he intentionally signified their reversal in status. A few hours earlier, when they were at Congress Hall, Adams was convinced that the twinkle in Washington's eye revealed his delight to be retiring. Washington's face was notoriously impenetrable, but Adams was fairly certain his predecessor was thinking "Ay! I am fairly out and you fairly in! see which of Us will be happiest." Later that afternoon, a private citizen once again, Washington could be more direct, and he heartily wished Adams a "happy, successful, and honorable" administration.[29]

The festivities continued later that evening. At 7 P.M. at College Hall, local luminaries offered "Readings and Recitations, Moral, Critical, and Entertaining," including "a poem, on the [former] President's Farewell Address, with a sketch of the character of his successor." The offerings continued with a two-part allegorical poem entitled "The Cave of Nature. Or, a picture of the virtues, vices, passions and attributes of the human mind."[30]

Other Philadelphia venues offered less intellectual pursuits. Several hundred local merchants pooled resources to host a feast at Oellers Hotel to honor Washington. The guests included "the heads of Departments, officers of the army, foreign ministers," and leading citizens of the city. While serenaded by musicians, attendees were treated to the "choicest" delicacies produced by nature, and "served up in the most elegant style." Jeremy Wadsworth, a former commissary general for the Continental Army, a successful businessman, and friend of Washington's, sent enough salmon to feed the nearly 400 guests.[31]

Although Adams had slept little the night before, he could not rest. He had survived the most "trying day," but the burdens of office weighed heavily. He left his bed in the early hours and lit the oil lamp on his desk. He described for Abigail the "solemn scene" and confessed that before the ceremony, he had feared that he would fail to meet the expectations of his fellow Americans. His concerns came to naught, he shared, as there was "Scarcely a dry Eye" in the chambers after he had delivered his address.

Adams mused on the historic nature of the moment. "The sight of the sun setting full-orbed, and another rising (though less splendid), was a novelty," he noted. Washington's attendance had surprised Adams. Both men understood that Washington's presence lent legitimacy to the proceedings and the new Adams administration. Washington remained a bastion against threats to the peaceful transfer of power and the republic.[32]

Their contemporaries offered equally euphoric praise for the ceremony and its participants. Senator Sedgwick called the event the "most august and sublime [he] had ever beheld."[33] Even longtime Republican critics offered praise. Senator Stevens T. Mason of Virginia concluded that the nation would survive the change in office, "for he never heard such a speech in public in his life."[34] The *Aurora*, the strident Republican paper and Washington's nemesis, applauded Adams's address, highlighting his efforts to confirm "himself the friend of France and of peace, the admirer of republicanism, the enemy of party."[35]

Americans knew that they were watching history being made in real time. Representative William Smith of South Carolina reflected that

> The change of the Executive here has been wrought with a facility and calm which has astonished even those of us who always augured well of the government and the general good sense of our citizens. The machine has worked without a creak. On the 4th of March John Adams was quietly sworn into office, George Washington attending as a private citizen. A few days after he went quietly home to Mt. Vernon; his successor as quietly took his place.[36]

One newspaper concluded its inauguration coverage by recognizing the power of the moment: "Thus ended a scene, the parallel of which was never before witnessed in any country- which forms a new era in our history, and in the history of Republican Freedom."[37]

5

A Scene of Ambition

THE NEXT MORNING, Secretary of the Treasury Oliver Wolcott Jr. paid his first official visit to the new president. They chatted briefly about the previous day's events before steering the conversation toward France and diplomacy. In the weeks leading up to the inauguration, rumors had swirled around Philadelphia that Charles Cotesworth Pinckney, the American minister to France, had been forcibly ejected from Paris. If the reports were true, Pinckney's removal was one small step short of a declaration of war by France against the United States under international law. From the American perspective, it was also a sharp and unprovoked escalation in Franco-American relations. Adams had received no official word yet and could take no decisive action until he received confirmation. But he worried about Pinckney's safety and wondered where the minister was currently located.

He asked Wolcott "what he thought of sending Mr. Madison to France, with or without others?" Perhaps he should reappoint Pinckney, Adams suggested, along with a few other respected figures to lend additional weight to the mission. Adams explored his various options out loud, revealing his commitment to resolving the tensions diplomatically.

Wolcott paused, caught off guard by the quick turn in the conversation. He asked if the president had determined to send another peace mission, should the rumors prove true.

Adams replied that he hadn't made up his mind, but he thought the idea "deserved consideration." Was the president "determined to send Mr. Madison?" Wolcott inquired? Again, Adams gave no firm commitment.[1]

Wolcott sputtered that "sending Mr. Madison will make dire work among the passions of our parties" in both Congress and the states. Having won the election, Wolcott argued, Federalists should set policy and enjoy the benefits of prestigious appointments.

Exasperated, Adams replied, "Are we forever to be overawed and directed by party passions?!" Cultivating bipartisan support for the new administration and its foreign policy was important, Adams explained, and a prominent Republican nomination would go a long way toward building goodwill, both at home and abroad.

Wolcott sat silently for a moment and thought about the president's response. He then said carefully, "Mr. President, we are willing to resign." Wolcott spoke for the entire cabinet, or at least Secretary of War James McHenry and Secretary of State Timothy Pickering.[2] Attorney General Charles Lee had a bit of an independent streak.

This threat was a huge blow to Adams's bipartisan vision. He thought they were having a friendly, perfectly civil, good-humored conversation. Adams had no intention of requesting resignations and he was shocked to hear that Wolcott was even thinking about such a severe step. Furthermore, Adams hadn't discussed this idea with any of the other secretaries, but clearly, they had been talking among themselves if Wolcott could confidently declare they would resign en masse.

Although Adams was stunned by the conversation, he wasn't willing to provoke a split in the Federalist Party this early into his term, especially after he had worked hard to provide continuity and consistency during the transition. For the time being, Adams backed away from his idea of appointing Madison and assured Wolcott that he wanted the cabinet secretaries to remain in office.

"From the Situation, where I now am, I see a Scene of Ambition, beyond all my former suspicions or Imaginations," he wrote to Abigail, reflecting that the presidency was already starting to look very different just twenty-four hours after the inauguration. Less than a day into his honeymoon period, Adams realized that the cabinet did not share his goals for bipartisan cooperation, nor would they afford Adams the same deference they had granted Washington. Adams would have to fight over every executive appointment, decision, and policy. Over the next several weeks, France offered additional evidence that it welcomed war and Vice President Jefferson flirted with treason. Adams's dreams of bipartisan comity were under assault from forces within the cabinet, the Republican Party, and from across the Atlantic.

The next night, George Washington hosted his final official dinner at the President's House. At the end of the evening, Adams and Jefferson walked back to the Francis Hotel together.[3] As they made their way down the street, avoiding potholes, puddles, and worse, Jefferson broached the subject of France. He had spoken to James Madison but had disappointing news to share. Madison was committed to his retirement and would turn down any appointment as an envoy to France. Or at least that was the excuse Jefferson provided. In truth, Madison wanted to distance himself from the Adams administration.

Adams turned to Jefferson, noticeably relieved. He confessed that there had been "opposition" to the proposal, but he had not wanted to insult Madison by withdrawing the offer. Adams didn't provide further details, but Jefferson speculated that the cabinet was behind the sudden change of heart. Flush with praise for Adams just a few days earlier, Jefferson now concluded that the president was controlled by "party views."

In his notes, Jefferson reflected that it was the last time they discussed policy.[4] For the next four years, Jefferson watched the administration from the outside. He never attended a cabinet meeting or offered advice, similar to how Adams had observed the Washington administration from a distance.

The chasm between the president and vice president was not preordained. Whatever Jefferson thought, Adams still desperately hoped to forge a bipartisan coalition. Jefferson and Madison immediately assumed the worst of the president and had more nefarious ideas. So too did the Essex Junto, the most radical wing of the Federalist Party, including Timothy Pickering and Oliver Wolcott Jr., ensconced in Adams's cabinet.

Over the next few weeks, information slowly trickled in from Europe as the winds shifted and ships battled weather across the Atlantic. From London, Rufus King, the American minister, sent a report confirming that Pinckney had left Paris. He couldn't say exactly when or why, or provide information on Pinckney's whereabouts, but it was clear that relations with France were on the warpath.

Adams wondered what happened in Paris as he prepared to convene his first cabinet meeting. Four outcomes seemed possible, he mused, from the best, in which "Mr Pinckney may be [received] in a fair and honourable Train of Negotiation," to the worst: "Mr Pinckney may be rejected, with Circumstances of Indignity Insult and Hostility."

Adams also jotted down some questions for the secretaries to consider. Should he convene Congress, and if so, what should he say in his speech? Which measures should he advocate? Was an embargo too extreme or should the army be further strengthened?[5]

FIGURE 5.1 Rufus King. Etching by Albert Rosenthal after a painting by John Trumbull. Library of Congress, Prints and Photographs Division, LC-DIG-ppmsca-31799.

Adams was weighing his options when the secretaries arrived at the Francis Hotel and gathered on the small sofas surrounding the fireplace. As the discussion unfolded, the secretaries quickly sorted themselves into two camps. On one side, Pickering and Wolcott opposed another peace commission. They believed another mission was beneath the nation's honor. If France wished to avoid hostilities, it would have to extend an olive branch and send envoys to the United States. So certain that war was inevitable, Pickering had drafted an anonymous pamphlet detailing the French outrages against American commerce and brought it to the meeting. Pickering explained that he planned to "hand it . . . to Mr. Fenno" for publication in the Federalist-leaning *Gazette of the United States*.[6] Adams recognized that the hostile tone of Pickering's pamphlet would only add fuel to the fire and forbade its publication. He had no interest in war, much to Pickering's chagrin.

On the other side, McHenry and Attorney General Charles Lee were more receptive to continuing diplomacy. They didn't have high expectations that another mission would secure peace, but they didn't think it would cause any further harm.

With the secretaries divided, Adams asked them to write written opinions considering two points. First, whether he should send another mission. Second, if he did appoint new ministers, how should he frame the scope and scale of the mission?

Washington had often requested written opinions when his cabinet was hopelessly divided.[7] Whether Adams learned of this practice from the department secretaries or he intuited that it would be helpful to have multiple perspectives, he intended to make a final decision after consulting advisors.

Adams then included an additional task for Pickering and Lee. Please examine the "practice of our Ancestors," he asked the men, "both in England and in the American Colonies before the Revolution" to determine how best to convene Congress. Should he issue a proclamation to summon Congress or did he need a legal writ from the Supreme Court? Adams reminded them that this "extraordinary occasion" had never happened "since the Establishment of this Government." There were "no precedents" from Washington "to Guide us." If he established this precedent, he wanted to be sure it "will hereafter require no Alterations."[8]

One week later, the cabinet gathered again, this time at the President's House. Adams had finally moved in a few days earlier and had set up his office in Washington's former study. The secretaries left no written record of their impressions of that first meeting, but it must have been startling to see someone other than Washington occupying that room.

Pickering laid a new dispatch on the table. The long-awaited reports from Paris had finally arrived and confirmed their worst fears. The French Directory had ordered Pinckney to leave the country. Pinckney had stubbornly remained in Paris until he received written orders, risking his personal safety to ensure he had a written record of the interactions.[9]

Even worse, Pinckney wrote that the French Directory had also issued a new decree, declaring the end of the "free ships, free goods" provision of the Franco-American Treaty of Commerce. Under a "free ships, free goods" agreement, belligerent nations couldn't seize the cargoes of vessels flying under the flag of neutral nations. The new French decree treated American ships transporting British goods as belligerent vessels. Additionally, unless American captains carried an exact list of crew members and passengers, they would all be treated as pirates.[10] The French had never insisted on that documentation before, and it was not consistent with American naval practices. In a panic, Rufus King wrote to Alexander Hamilton that the new measure would "render *all our Ships* liable to Capture . . . since no American Vessel has . . . the Document required."[11]

This new intelligence removed all remaining doubt that France was determined to provoke hostilities. With this evidence in hand, the cabinet easily settled on a consensus and advised Adams to convene an emergency session of Congress. Pickering dispatched Adams's proclamation, which instructed "the Senators and Representatives" to "meet and assemble in Congress" on "Monday the fifteenth day of May" to "consult and determine on such measures as in their wisdom shall be deemed meet for the safety and welfare of the said United States."[12]

Although the cabinet had settled the most pressing issue—what to do with Congress—Adams still had several unanswered questions. He pestered the secretaries for the written opinions he had requested to guide his planning for the upcoming congressional session. Adams did not know that many of the secretaries were intentionally delaying their responses until they received marching orders from Hamilton.

"I have this moment received the inclosed paper" from the president, McHenry wrote to Hamilton. He pleaded with the former secretary of the treasury "to give me your answer at length that I may avail myself of your experience knowledge and judgement." Similarly, Pickering begged Hamilton to continue to "communicate to me your ideas on public affairs, especially at the present interesting period."[13] Without the president's knowledge, many of the secretaries funneled secret cabinet information to Hamilton and requested his input on how they should respond to the president.

In late March, Hamilton wrote back to McHenry approving of the administration's decision to convene Congress. "'Tis well," he praised his mentee, before suggesting that the president should "send a Commission extraordinary to France." To Wolcott and Pickering, who had opposed diplomacy, Hamilton wrote that the cabinet must support a peace commission. "A suspicion begins to *dawn* among the friends of the Government that the *actual* administration" supported a war with France, Hamilton explained. It was "very important to obviate" this rumor and demonstrate that the secretaries endorsed peace, he counseled. The peace commission might not accomplish anything, but it would demonstrate that the administration had explored all diplomatic options before turning to force and would endear the cabinet to the American people, Hamilton advised.[14]

In other words, Hamilton viewed Adams as a figurehead to be managed or manipulated, while the real administration—the cabinet—did the work of governing the nation. Needless to say, Hamilton did not view the cabinet this way when Washington was president. This shift was not just personal, but rather reflected two different visions of executive power. The first featured a powerful president that controlled the entire executive branch, while the second envisioned an executive-by-committee like the modern British cabinet. These clashing interpretations of executive power would bedevil the Adams administration for the next several years.

News from Europe bolstered Hamilton's argument. The French army notched a series of victories against its enemies in Europe, and the Bank of England teetered dangerously close to insolvency. If the other European nations signed peace treaties with France and the Bank of England couldn't pay its expenses, Hamilton argued, Britain would have to abandon its war as well. That would leave the United States squaring off against the French army, the most powerful in the world, with no help.[15] Hamilton knew this prospect would chill Pickering and Wolcott's militaristic impulses.

Hamilton also waged a paper war in the Federalist ranks. He sent countless letters to other Federalist leaders, trying to persuade his friends and allies to back a peace commission in the coming congressional session. He borrowed rhetoric from his previous letters to the secretaries, arguing that he was "*anxious*" to avoid a "Rupture with a political monster."[16]

Whether it was the shifting winds in Europe or Hamilton's relentless correspondence, the secretaries gradually changed their minds about the wisdom of a peace commission. By the time congressmen began arriving in Philadelphia for the emergency session, Adams and his secretaries were mostly aligned, even if the president didn't know to whom he was indebted for this temporary unity.

On April 15, Adams sent another letter to the cabinet, asking each secretary to draft a memo including "in detail . . . Such particulars as the Secretary may think necessary or expedient to be inserted in the President's Speech at the opening of the ensuing Congress." The secretaries should also consider which "Articles" to include "in the Instructions of an Ambassador, Envoy ordinary or Extraordinary or Minister Plenipotentiary to be sent to France." Over the next few weeks, the secretaries drafted their memos for the president. Pickering, Wolcott, and especially McHenry lifted whole paragraphs from Hamilton's missives to include in their opinions.[17] Adams, however, remained ignorant of Hamilton's role in his presidency in the early days of his administration.

While the escalating conflict with France dominated Adams's attention, nagging details closer to home demanded his time. He had originally planned to move into the President's House on March 13, but after discovering its state of disrepair, he hired a few servants to clean the home from top to bottom, oversaw repairs, made a few necessary purchases, and instructed his servants to make the place habitable: "It proves to be a tedious Business to clear the Presidents house for me."[18]

Adams couldn't help feeling unmoored. He needed real feedback on his performance as president and the person he most trusted to tell him the truth was hundreds of miles away. Toward the end of April, he was wracked with a violent cold and cough and descended into full self-pity. He pouted that everyone else mourned the "the Loss of their beloved" Washington. "I never wanted your Advice & assistance more in my Life," he wrote to his wife, acknowledging that all his burdens would have been manageable had Abigail been by his side.[19]

Adams had originally planned to return to Quincy in the spring after his inauguration, then Abigail would join him when he returned to Philadelphia in the fall. But he quickly realized that the French crisis would keep him in town much longer than he anticipated and he simply could not do without her. Over the next several weeks, he wrote near daily letters pleading with her to abandon her responsibilities in Massachusetts and come to his side. "I pray you to come on immediately. I will not live in this State of Seperation." Pride be damned, he was willing to beg: "You, I must and will have."[20]

When Abigail reminded him that she had to care for their estate and their family, he replied that she "ought to think a little of the President as well as the Husband. His Cares! His Anxieties! his Health! . . . his Comfort." He knew he sounded ridiculous, however, and closed his letter, "dont laugh."[21]

In early May, Abigail relented and left Massachusetts to travel to Philadelphia. They might have been married for nearly thirty-three years, but John simply couldn't wait another moment to see her. He rode out in his carriage and met her north of the city, where they enjoyed a picnic and walked along the banks of the Delaware River. After their private afternoon, they returned to Philadelphia, arriving just as the sun was setting.[22]

Abigail immediately took charge of the house, staff, and domestic matters. She hired more servants, a combination of white, free Black, and enslaved workers from local owners.[23] She purchased additional housewares, planned menus, ordered food, and oversaw preparations for multiple events per week—and did so under the strictest economy to stretch their limited budget. To manage her workload, she rose every morning before 5 A.M., spent a few hours praying, reading the Bible, and writing letters home to manage their farm. She enjoyed breakfast with her husband before spending the next two to three hours with the servants. She issued instructions, made lists, and sent orders to local shops. At 11 A.M., she dressed to receive company, paid visits of her own, went for social walks, or drove out in the carriage.

In the afternoons and evenings, Abigail anchored the social events at the President's House. She was a warm, engaging hostess and a lively conversationalist, skills she employed to make guests feel at ease and to obtain valuable insider information about the political networks in Philadelphia. Not only did she fill a vital social function as part of eighteenth-century norms, but she also removed burdens from the president's plate and doted on him when he was ill.[24]

On Abigail's first Monday in town, she received "32 Ladies and near as many Gentlemen." The next night, she hosted all of the foreign ministers and their wives, "our own Secretaries & Ladies. . . . [A]dd to them, the whole Levee to day of senate & house strangers." In one day alone, she endured "near one Hundred" visitors who "askd permission to visit me, so that from half past 12 till near 4 I was rising up & sitting down."[25] In addition to the daily visits and Tuesday levees, she organized weekly state dinners on Thursday afternoons for about forty guests. Each dinner's guest list was carefully constructed to maximize political advantage. Abigail calculated that she will "have got through the whole of Congress, with their apendages" by the end of June.[26]

Grateful for Abigail's able management, John gladly relinquished charge of the house to her and devoted every spare moment to crafting his upcoming address to Congress. As he went through draft after draft, trying to strike the right balance, the political tempest simmering under the surface was about to explode.

On May 2, a translated letter to Philip Mazzei, a wine dealer and viticulturist living in Italy, was published in the New York *Minerva.* For months, rumors about the original version has churned through political conversations. Once copies of the New York paper filtered into Philadelphia, they collided with swirling political intrigues and reignited partisan battles.

The letter criticized the Washington administration, which wasn't all that unusual. But it included one line that caught readers' attention. "I should give you a fever," the author wrote, "if I should name the apostates who have embraced these heresies; men who were Solomons in council, and Sampsons in combat, but whose hair has been cut off by the whore England."[27]

Solomon was known for his wisdom and Samson for his feats of strength in battle, so readers immediately grasped that this allegory could refer to only one person—George Washington. Americans also instinctively recognized that shorn hair referred to Samson's humiliation and enslavement by the Philistines, described in the Book of Judges in the Bible. To suggest that the British had similarly emasculated Washington was a breath-taking insult.

The letter would have been galling even if the author had remained anonymous. The *Minerva* attributed the letter to Jefferson, the vice president and Washington's first secretary of state. The paper challenged him to refute it—he did not.[28]

Over the next few weeks, newspapers across the country scrambled to reprint the scandalous letter. In Philadelphia, where congressmen arrived for the upcoming session, residents exchanged whispers and watched to see what might happen next. Abigail noted, "The writer has never denied it, tho publickly calld upon to do it; You may be sure it has not escaped censure, and will never be forgotten."[29]

Hushed conversations and pointed glances reached a fever pitch when he returned to the city to resume his chair as president of the Senate. Jefferson made no public comment and refused to recognize the letter, but his authorship was widely accepted.

The letter solidified party lines and exacerbated misgivings between the two sides. Federalists, who had already been suspicious of Jefferson's motivations in the administration, viewed the letter as further evidence of the vice president's disloyalty. Thereafter, they viewed everything Jefferson did or said in the worst possible light. Jefferson also grew increasingly distrustful. He began to censor his own writing and urged friends and family to keep his letters private. The Federalists had demonstrated they would use anything and everything against him.

John Adams resented the letter's timing. The controversy kept the first president in the center of the public mind, which was exactly what Adams was trying to avoid. It doomed his efforts to chart a moderate course, which became increasingly impossible as Federalists attacked the vice president and Republicans responded in kind. Adams also felt his own niggling doubts. He knew better than to put any criticism of Washington in writing. Adams wondered, if Jefferson was willing to write such things about Washington—the father of the country—what might Jefferson write about him?

At that same moment, Adams returned to Congress Hall. Two months earlier, the chamber had been filled with spectators and cheers. This time, the senators and representatives sat solemnly in silence, waiting to hear the president's news. Adams confirmed the reports that the French Directory had ordered Pinckney "to quit the territories of the French Republic" and exclaimed that "they will not receive nor acknowledge another Minister Plenipotentiary from the United States" until their complaints "have been redressed."[30]

Despite this insult, Adams remained "desirous of preserving peace and friendship with all Nations," he told the assembly. He was convinced that "neither the honour nor interest of the United States forbid the repetition of" another peace commission. Accordingly, he planned to send another diplomatic mission to negotiate a new treaty "compatible with the rights, engagements & honour of our Country."[31]

However, in the meantime, he also recommended that Congress pass "defensive measures." Commerce must be defended from French depredations, coastal defenses must be bolstered in the event of "sudden & predatory incursions," and funds raised to pay for these improvements.[32] Adams explained that defensive improvements would both strengthen the nation's hand in negotiations and prepare the country if diplomacy failed.

Adams was met with polite applause and returned home in his carriage. This time, there were no jubilant crowds escorting him, no bands playing music, and no artillery firing booming cannons.

Federalists controlled both houses of Congress and applauded the president's speech. Using their twenty-two to nine majority in the Senate, they crafted a reply offering the Senate's full-throated support for the president's robust defense of the country.[33] Henry Van Schaack, an Arch Federalist from Massachusetts, offered similarly rapturous praise. "The speech of the President has relieved my mind of an infinite load of anxiety. It is in truth the very thing itself—In my opinion nothing from the federal chair since the government has existed, is in any ways equal to it."[34]

Republicans in the House interpreted the president's speech very differently. They condemned the "hot-headed Executive" for delivering a bellicose message that would only inflame relations with France.[35] The *Aurora*, which had previously lauded Adams's mild inaugural address, decried "the temper" which the president "shewed in his speech." Benjamin Franklin Bache, the editor, concluded that the cabinet secretaries, "Timothy and oliver," had warped the president's mind.[36]

The House was more closely divided, with a slimmer fifty-six to forty-nine Federalist majority. The fractures in the House spilled onto the floor and the representatives spent the next several weeks debating how to respond. Federalists in the House wanted to replicate the Senate's reply to the president, which heaped praise on Adams. Republicans knew better than to "openly countanance the conduct of France," but they hoped to gently "court and coax" the French back to friendly relations.[37] After weeks of debating the language, the entire House, all 100 representatives, visited the President's House to deliver their response.[38] It was perfectly tepid in its support for the administration.

No one was more disappointed in the president's speech than Jefferson. As president of the Senate, he was required to sign all official replies to the president. It irritated him to place his signature at the bottom of the Senate's "high toned" address which lavished praise on Adams. He concluded that the cabinet had "fixed" on war and convinced Adams to follow their lead."[39] Had Jefferson bothered to speak to Adams, he would have realized that they agreed on more than they disagreed. Instead, Jefferson increasingly turned away from the administration and toward his fellow Republicans.

While the House was embattled, the Adamses hosted a dinner for the secretaries and the senators.[40] The conversation naturally turned to politics and the possibility of another peace commission. Republicans in attendance urged Adams to appoint one of their own to ensure the inclusion of a pro-French voice on the commission, without knowing he had already approached Jefferson and Madison. The Federalists preferred the commission to be stacked with staunch allies. Adams did not reveal his intentions to his guests.

A few days later, the cabinet returned to discuss the commission in more detail. Pinckney's future was the first item on the agenda. He was waiting at The Hague for further instructions and could be easily ordered back to Paris. The secretaries agreed there were several reasons to send Pinckney back to France. He hailed from the powerful Pinckney family in South Carolina, which served as a bedrock of Federalist support across the South and would be instrumental to future Federalist campaigns. The Pinckneys were also notoriously touchy about family honor and clamored for retribution for the insult directed at their kin. Perhaps most important, independent and sovereign nations selected their own diplomatic representatives. They all agreed that France should not be given a veto over whom the administration selected for its diplomatic corps—Pinckney must be included on principle.

And yet, they also conceded Pinckney might be eager for revenge. He needed to be balanced by more level heads. Adams listed other potential candidates, including names suggested at dinner the night before: "James Maddison, John Marshall, Ludwell Lee, Thomas Lee, Bushrod Washington, William Vans Murray."[41] Wolcott and Pickering favored strong Federalists like

Rufus King or George Cabot. Attorney General Lee and McHenry suggested the president's son, John Quincy Adams.

Adams immediately dismissed these recommendations as impractical. He couldn't risk tainting the mission with claims of nepotism if he appointed his son, and King was the current minister to Great Britain. Since France and Britain were at war, sending King to Paris would be insulting to the French Directory and counterproductive. Instead, Adams suggested a moderate voice, like John Marshall. Adams already knew through Lee's intervention that Marshall would accept the appointment. Although Marshall had no diplomatic experience, he came from a crucial southern state, was a brilliant lawyer, and was almost universally regarded as reasonable and charismatic. As a war veteran and unimpeachable Federalist, Marshall would also be acceptable to the Federalists in Congress. The secretaries offered no objection.[42]

Adams also proposed a non-partisan representative: Elbridge Gerry. Gerry wasn't exactly a Republican, but he definitely wasn't a Federalist. This time the secretaries howled in opposition. Surprised by the "inveterate prejudice,"

FIGURE 5.2 John Marshall by John Wesley Jarvis, 1825. White House Collection/White House Historical Association.

Adams insisted Gerry was an "impartial man." The secretaries refused to budge and remained unanimous in their resistance.

Faced with the cabinet's determined opposition, Adams suggested Francis Dana instead. Dana was a moderate like Marshall, but compared to Gerry, the secretaries thought he was a reliable Federalist choice. Having secured the cabinet's support, Adams submitted to the Senate the nominations of Dana, Marshall, and Pinckney—all Federalists—as special envoys to France.[43]

Convinced that the administration was now hell-bent on war with France, Jefferson took matters into his own hands. Shortly after Adams's address, he visited Philippe de Létombe at his home at the corner of 12th and Chestnut Streets. Over the next week, Jefferson visited Létombe's house three more times.

These were not social visits. Jefferson shared his concerns that the president was "vain, suspicious, and stubborn, of an excessive self-regard, taking counsel with nobody." It was a dire situation, but Jefferson counseled that Adams's "presidency will only last five years [*sic*]; he is only President by three votes." The American people would certainly make a better decision next time and Jefferson was certain "the system of the United States will change with him."

Jefferson encouraged the French Directory to delay as long possible. They should accept the new envoy, but "drag out the negotiations at length." Perhaps France should consider an invasion of England to negotiate from a more powerful position, Jefferson suggested. Létombe demurred and insisted he knew little about the Directory's military plans.

When Jefferson returned a few days later, he again urged a French military incursion. In Létombe's dispatches back to Paris, he noted wryly, "Jefferson never ceases to repeat that the thing is practicable." Undeterred, Jefferson insisted that the current administration "will be of short duration." He would be in office before long and "all will return to order." For the moment, "It is for France, great, generous, at the summit of her glory, to pretend to take no notice, to be patient, to precipitate nothing."[44]

Jefferson's interference came remarkably close to treason. The United States had not declared war on France—yet—but vessels from both nations were engaging in open hostilities on the high seas. As vice president, Jefferson actively undermined the administration's foreign policy and encouraged its enemy to forestall peace.

Jefferson then turned to domestic politics. He regularly wrote to his Virginian allies, but now began building a network farther north. Writing a conciliatory letter to Aaron Burr, Jefferson smoothed any hurt feelings that might be lingering from the election loss. He reminded Burr of "my esteem for you" and confided that he was "much pleased to see a dawn of change in the spirit" of New York. He encouraged Burr to send "some general view of our situation and prospects since you left us."

After the Mazzei letter scandal, Jefferson refused to articulate his political plans in writing. However, he hinted to Burr that if they could organize in the North and reach the people, "who are unquestionably republican," then maybe there "might still hope for salvation."[45] Burr wrote back almost immediately, thanking Jefferson for the letter. A savvy politician himself, he knew the importance of discretion. Instead of replying in detail, he planned to travel from New York to meet "in person. Let me hope to meet you in Philadelphia on Sunday."[46]

When Burr arrived, Jefferson offered an assessment of the political scene and relayed his discussions with the French minister. They also sketched out plans to build out the Republican Party infrastructure. Burr would take the lead in New York, and Jefferson would gather James Monroe and James Madison at Monticello that summer to maximize their Virginia leverage. They would cultivate written networks, build up local organizations, and subsidize Republican editors. Not only was the vice president sabotaging Adams's foreign policy, but he was also actively colluding to undermine the administration at home while still in office.

Adams did not know about Jefferson's meetings with Létombe or his scheming with Burr. But he knew his vice president was writing letters. On June 23, Uriah Forrest, an old Adams friend and loyal Federalist, forwarded a letter containing "disgraceful insinuations, barefaced assertions and dangerous principles" apparently uttered by Jefferson against the administration. Adams thanked his friend for the news and acknowledged it was "a serious thing."[47] Adams might not have been willing or able to put into words his hurt and betrayal, but he shared the letter with his wife. Abigail did not hold back her disgust for Jefferson in a letter to John Quincy. She was loath to give up their friendship, she wrote, and "it is with much reluctance that I am obliged to look upon him as a man whose mind is warped by prejudice and so blinded by ignorance as to be unfit for the office he holds." Jefferson might be "wise and scientific as a philosopher," she conceded, but "as a politician he is a child and duple of party!"[48]

6

A Dishonorable Infidelity

IN MID-JUNE, ADAMS learned that Francis Dana had declined the appointment as minister to France, citing poor health and an intense aversion to sea travel after many missions abroad. Adams knew Dana well and perhaps expected the rejection all along. With this opening on the commission, Adams seized the opportunity to nominate Elbridge Gerry in Dana's place, just as he had wanted to do from the beginning. Adams was finally gaining traction on his foreign policy priority of peace with France, but he would face two unexpected obstacles in the coming months. First, over the summer, a series of scandals would rock the political world and exacerbate the existing partisan divide, making compromise nearly impossible. Second, Secretary of State Timothy Pickering waged a covert campaign to undermine Adams's control over the executive branch.

While Adams remained unaware of Pickering's intrigues in the summer of 1797, he had learned his lesson about diplomatic nominations. This time, Adams did not consult with his cabinet before sending Gerry's name to the Senate for consideration. Instead, he wrote a note to Gerry, revealing his plan. "I have this moment written a Message to the Senate nominating you to be an Envoy Extraordinary to the French Republic," Adams said. "Knowing as I did Mr Dana's aversion to the Sea . . . I was always apprehensive he would decline."[1]

As with almost all decisions, Adams had discussed the matter with Abigail, who was less enthusiastic about the appointment. She cared for Gerry as a friend but expressed doubts that he was suited for diplomatic work. She encouraged her husband to provide firm instructions so that Gerry wouldn't "obstruct the negotiation" by being "too rigid [in] opinion upon trivial matters."[2] Adams acknowledged that Gerry was a diplomatic novice and had "an unaccommodating disposition" and "obstinacy that will risk great things to secure small ones."[3]

The cabinet's resistance went much further than Abigail's concerns. After learning about the president's nomination, McHenry told Adams, "If sire, it was a desirable thing to distract the mission, a fitter person could not perhaps be found. It is ten to one against his agreeing with his colleagues."

Adams loved Gerry and respected his determined apolitical approach to public service. Ultimately, Adams put his faith in Gerry's unfailing principles and decided it was more important to have a loyal friend among the envoys whom he could trust.

When Adams ignored the cabinet's critiques, Pickering took matters into his own hands. Convinced that the president needed to be saved from his own "eccentricities," Pickering met secretly with his Massachusetts friends in the Senate and convinced them to vote against Gerry's nomination.[4] He shared that the president had made the appointment without the cabinet's "approbation" and had no trouble convincing his Federalist allies to vote against Gerry. Senator Theodore Sedgwick promised Pickering that he would "withhold [his] consent," as he "could not reconcile to myself to approve an appointment so highly improper."[5]

Pickering's efforts fell short—Gerry was confirmed 21 aye votes to 6 nays. All negative votes came from the president's own party.[6] Later that evening, Pickering called on the president to share the vote tally. Adams regretted that "his conduct was disapproved by his friends." Pickering responded that perhaps the president ought to "have consulted his council, & respected the opinion of his friends in the Senate, & in the U.S. none of which had any confidence in Gerry." He explained that "the former administration" had followed this policy, as "there was no other way in which the Executive could expect support."[7]

Adams "appeared astonished" that his predecessor had made his nominations in this manner. He had every right to be surprised because Pickering was lying. Washington had regularly made decisions independently of his secretaries and allies in Congress. Pickering had resented Washington's actions, just as he did Adams's, but he didn't dare go behind Washington's back and work with Federalists senators to vote against the president's candidate.[8]

Adams may have suspected a coordinated effort to undermine Gerry's nomination, but he did not know about Pickering's meetings with the senators, nor did he know that Pickering had made the first official break with his administration. While Pickering's objections to Gerry had merit, his subterfuge was a shocking breach of the president's trust and undermined the chain of command in the executive branch.

It was a defining moment for the cabinet, even if Adams did not yet grasp the full ramifications. Either way, he would not be deterred. He wrote grimly that he "would not be the slave" to his cabinet. He was determined to preserve presidential independence over executive branch policies and appointments.[9]

As Adams worked to assemble his peace commission and facilitate the departure of the envoys, a series of scandals rocked the seat of government.

James Monroe, the disgraced minister to France, was sailing toward Philadelphia and eager to cause trouble. In May 1794, President George Washington had nominated Monroe as the new minister to France, tasking him with smoothing relations between the countries.[10] Few ministers could have successfully altered the behavior of the revolutionary French government, but Monroe was particularly ill-suited to speak on behalf of American interests at that moment. Monroe hated the British and despised the Jay Treaty, which John Jay had negotiated in 1794 to resolve lingering tensions from the Revolutionary War. Monroe believed that the treaty had betrayed the "principles contained" in the Franco-American alliance by granting Britain equal standing with France. As a result, when the French government started seizing American ships and sailors in response to the treaty, Monroe had an increasingly difficult time defending Washington's policy of neutrality and demanding restitution for those losses.[11]

On August 22, 1796, President Washington ordered Monroe's recall and issued a stern rebuke to the wayward minister. The summons took weeks to cross the Atlantic before reaching a thoroughly unrepentant Monroe. He took his time closing up his home, savoring the last delights of Paris, and bidding inappropriately affectionate farewells to French counterparts before finally sailing for the United States.[12]

Describing Monroe's final days in France, John Quincy wrote that the French Directory refused to meet with his replacement and then hosted a dinner in Monroe's honor. At the event, the departing minister delivered a fiery speech that made clear he would return to the United States with "the same unqualified devotion to the french will."[13]

This behavior was far beyond the bounds of normal diplomatic conduct. "At the moment when a national indignity" had been inflicted on the nation, John Quincy wrote incredulously, Monroe refused to defend his country. Instead, he "condescends to flatter" France by declaring "that the principles of their Revolution and of ours were the same," either ignoring or excusing the violence and anarchy of the French Revolution.[14]

Monroe found redemption amid the partisan squabbling in Philadelphia. On the evening of July 1, Jefferson and his "knot of Jacobins," a derogatory term Federalists used for Republicans, hosted a dinner at Oeller's Hotel to toast Monroe's return. The attendees toasted Jefferson as the "Man of the people," rather than the current president.[15]

Federalists observed the dinner with horror and disgust. "Some of the violents were there," Abigail wrote, referring to the more radical Republicans. More important, "*the vice President*" showed his face at an obviously Republican opposition event while still serving in the Adams administration.[16]

The event demonstrated the stark divide between Federalists and Republicans over foreign policy. Congress was in session to address the recent French provocations and insults, but there was no public unity in the face of a foreign threat. Instead, a group of avowed Republicans were feting the recalled American minister who appeared to favor France over the United States. Republicans excused any behavior if the accused was a member of their party. As long as partisan identity trumped national loyalty, Adams would have to navigate his foreign policy without unified public support.

Bolstered by the encouragement he received from his fellow Republicans, Monroe went on the offensive. On July 6, he wrote to Secretary of State Pickering demanding an official explanation for his recall. Pickering refused to reveal privileged conversations with the former president since Washington was no longer in office.[17]

When Monroe insisted that he had a "right" to receive some sort of explanation, Pickering invited Monroe to his office to hear the "considerations which induced" the secretaries to advise Washington to remove Monroe.[18]

Outraged, Monroe published their entire exchange of letters and wrote a 500-page defense of his time as minister to France, criticizing the Washington administration and attempting to rehabilitate his career. He enlisted Jefferson and Madison's assistance in this herculean effort, and they helped produce the lengthy volume for publication just five months later.

Pickering alerted Washington that a forthcoming publication by Monroe, *A View of the Conduct of the Executive in the Foreign Affairs of the United States Connected with the Mission to the French Republic during the Years 1794, 5 & 6*, would be published later that summer.[19] He sent no such warning to the current President of the United States, even though the scandal would harden party lines and keep the Washington administration at the center of political debates.

Upon reading the volume, Abigail sarcastically described the book as shining "so Bright upon all good Democrats, that all Mistery is dispelld, and the Executive alone is found Guilty." Of course, Washington's only crime, according to Abigail, was of "loveing [his] own Country so well as whilst desireing and wishing to do justice to all, to be unwilling to subjugate it self to any one."[20]

While Abigail gloated that "the Jacobins do not even want to read Munroe," Jefferson disagreed. He wrote to Madison that "Monroe's book is considered as masterly by all those who are not opposed in principle, and it is deemed unanswerable."[21] Partisan loyalties even shaped how Americans read books.

Another publication soon added further fuel to the partisan fire. On June 26, James Callender published the first of several pamphlets alleging that Alexander Hamilton had abused his position as secretary of the treasury and speculated with public funds.[22] When these rumors first surfaced in Republican circles in early 1793, Hamilton had met with three Republican members of Congress: Senator James Monroe, Representative Frederick Muhlenburgh from Pennsylvania, and Representative Abraham Venable of Virginia. Wolcott also attended the meeting as a witness.

At the meeting, Hamilton confessed that he had engaged in an extramarital affair with Maria Reynolds and paid hush money to her husband, James Reynolds. The missing funds were all from his personal account and he provided documentation. The Republicans present accepted that Hamilton was guilty of bad judgment and infidelity, but not fraud.[23]

Four years later, when Callender published the allegations, he included details known only to the five people present at the meeting. Neither Hamilton nor Wolcott spoke to Callender, so that left one of the three Republicans—and Hamilton was certain Monroe was to blame. Wolcott agreed. "I am astonished at the villany of Munroe," he wrote, shocked that the Virginian had "utterly betrayed his promise" to keep the information private in the most "base, false, & malignant" manner.[24]

Hamilton dashed off a letter accusing Monroe of supplying the information in the publication. He demanded Monroe publish "a declaration" clarifying Hamilton was innocent of the charges and reminded Monroe that these statements were made "in the presence of Mr Wolcott by yourself and the two other Gentlemen." If Monroe was a man of honor, he would comply with this request. If not, Hamilton hinted he would be willing to take further steps to obtain satisfaction, a nod to the dueling code.[25]

By this point, Monroe had traveled from Philadelphia to New York and was staying with friends for a few days before returning south. He brushed off Hamilton's griping with little thought.

Hamilton then demanded an interview in person and suggested that they both bring friends to serve as witnesses or seconds "at what may pass."[26] At 10 A.M. on the morning of July 11, Hamilton arrived at 46 Wall Street, where Monroe was staying at the home of Thomas Knox. Hamilton brought John Barker Church and Monroe invited David Gelston as his witness.[27]

Monroe insisted he knew nothing of the publication until he had arrived back from Europe and, as far as he knew, the packet of papers detailing Hamilton's misdeeds "remained sealed with his friend in Virginia."

Leaping to his feet, Hamilton declared to Monroe:

"your representation is totally false!"

"Do you say I represented falsely? You are a Scoundrel!" Monroe exclaimed, who rose to his feet as well.

"I will meet you like a Gentleman," Hamilton hotly replied.

Monroe snapped, "I am ready; get your pistols."

"It will not be settled any other way," Hamilton agreed.

At this point, Church and Gelston jumped between the two men and urged caution. Gelston finally convinced Hamilton to interview Monroe, Veneable, and Muhlenberg in Philadelphia and obtain information from all witnesses present at the original 1793 meeting.

When Hamilton grudgingly accepted this proposal, Church suggested that "any warmth or unguarded expressions that had happened during the interview should be buried and considered as tho' it never had happened." Both men reluctantly agreed.[28]

Several weeks later, after additional meetings in Philadelphia and further correspondence, Hamilton remained unsatisfied. Exasperated, Monroe said, "If these do not yield you satisfaction I can give no other, unless called on in a way which . . . I wish to avoid, but which I am ever ready to meet."[29]

Hamilton replied that if Monroe's letter was "intended as an advance towards" a duel, though he didn't say the fateful word, "it is incumbent upon me not to decline it."[30]

Monroe quickly responded that it was never "my intention to give or even provoke" a challenge that would lead to a duel. But he also added that he would "stand on the defensive & receive one in case you thought fit to give it." If Hamilton intended his reply to be a challenge, Monroe requested he "say so."[31]

Hamilton was willing to defend his honor, but he wasn't willing to provoke the duel. At least not with Monroe's disavowal in writing. He responded tersely that "any further step on my part . . . would be improper."[32]

After this exchange, Hamilton ultimately decided he would not gain the appropriate retribution from private correspondence. He drafted an essay explaining his behavior in full, revealing that his "real crime is a loose connection" with Reynold's wife.[33] John Fenno published the final pamphlet, which was voraciously devoured by readers in Philadelphia before they mailed copies to friends and colleagues across the country.

Republicans gleefully reported the humbling of their longtime nemesis. John Dawson, a Republican in the House of Representatives said to Madison "that Mr. H. is given up wher'ever he has been, as an immoral man; and that the ease with which he acknowledges himself an adulterer inspires doubts that he was guilty of the other charge also."[34]

Adams left no written record of his observations in 1797, but he and Abigail certainly discussed the subject. She wrote to their son Thomas that the "confessions have not . . . cleard up the publick transactions, which stood fair and unshaken, by the disclosure of a private Amour. alass—alass—how weak is Humane Nature."[35] Ten years later, John blamed Hamilton's manic behavior on "a superabundance of secretions which he could not find Whores enough to draw off."[36] He may not have written anything in 1797, but he was convinced Hamilton's personal failures reflected pervasive moral rot. The scandal confirmed for Adams that Hamilton was not to be trusted.

While Hamilton and Monroe battled to salvage their reputations with dueling publications, the Adamses opened the doors of the President's House for a July 4 reception. At 12 P.M., "the Governor of this Commonwealth, officers of the general and state governments, members of both houses of Congress, the society of the Cincinnati, Officers of the militia in their uniforms, the Foreign Ministers and many private citizens waited on the President of the United States" to participate in the festivities.[37] So many citizens attended that the house could not hold the guests and Abigail had to place "long tables in the Yard" to serve the 200 pounds of cake and the two quarter casks of wine spiked with rum. Local militias and musicians formed a parade to entertain the guests and marched for four full hours.[38]

After the July 4 celebration, Adams returned his attention to the peace mission to France. There were instructions to write and envoys to meet before he could leave Philadelphia for the summer.

Adams instructed Pickering to draft the official instructions, but he also took care to offer his own guidance and wisdom based on diplomatic experience, which Pickering, the cabinet, and the envoys lacked. Shortly before departing for France, Marshall joined Adams at the President's House for a private dinner. They discussed the potential outcomes for negotiations, the non-negotiables, and what concessions the envoys could offer to appease the French directory.

Marshall was eager to hear Adams's recollections of France, ask questions about what he should expect, and consult on how to approach the deliberations. Adams shared his conviction that European powers had little respect for or interest in the United States and instead viewed the nation as a pawn in their centuries-old conflicts. He also revealed his difficulties negotiating with the French while he had been stationed in Paris. Adams found the French infuriating, utterly lacking in directness, obsessed with pleasure, and duplicitous. Marshall listened carefully and concluded that Adams was "a sensible plain candid good tempered man."[39]

On July 20, Marshall departed for Europe. He sailed for Holland to connect with Charles Cotesworth Pinckney, before they traveled together to Paris.[40]

Later that week, Adams received a note from Gerry, announcing that he planned to set sail as soon as he received his official instructions. He also asked for Adams's personal "opinion, as far as it can be communicated with propriety, on all matters left to the discretion of, or that have a near relation to the embassy." Gerry offered his assessment—it would be "necessary for the envoys" to set aside their differences "on important points," even if that meant that the "minority" would have to yield to the majority. The French already suspected that Americans were "a divided people," he continued, and disunity would "encourage an opposition to their measures."[41] Did the president agree?

Adams was relieved to read Gerry's astute assessment of the diplomatic situation. Many Federalists had voiced concerns that Gerry's "unaccommodating disposition" might risk interrupting the "happy and perfect harmony among all our Ministers abroad." He was delighted that Gerry was already on guard against disunity and assured him that no accusations could "Sap the foundation of the Confidence" he retained for his friend.

Nonetheless, Adams included one last warning, urging Gerry to remember that "It is of great Importance, that harmony Should be preserved among all our Ministers abroad."[42] Tellingly, Adams had not stressed this point so firmly with the other two ministers, revealing he did not have the same concerns about Marshall and Pinckney.

The next day, Pickering arrived at the President's House with a draft of official instructions.[43] Adams made a few tweaks and then approved the final product. Gerry received the instructions on July 23 and set sail on *The Union* a few days later.

The official instructions tucked safely in Gerry's trunk were remarkably circumspect and moderate. They encouraged the envoys to avoid getting bogged down debating French and American resentments over existing treaties. Instead, they should "terminate our differences," without specifically addressing "the merits of our respective complaints and pretensions," and draft a new treaty based on "mutual satisfaction and good understanding."[44]

The instructions authorized the envoys to make generous concessions, but in return the envoys were tasked with clarifying the existing agreements and terminating the mutual defense clause of the Treaty of 1778. As part of his decades-long campaign for neutrality, Adams sought to eliminate all treaty obligations that would require U.S. participation in European wars unless required for American national security. The envoys should also try to obtain compensation for the American commerce seized by the French navy, but the terms could be flexible and were not required for a new treaty.

Adams and Pickering gave the envoys incredible leeway to negotiate; the instructions imposed only three non-negotiable conditions. First, they could make no "engagement inconsistent with the obligations of any prior treaty." In other words, the envoys could make no arrangement with France that would abrogate the Jay Treaty. Second, they could offer no restrictions on American trade that were guaranteed under the law of nations. Third, they could not offer loans to France during its current war, knowing that the funds would be immediately deployed to fight the British.

With Congress in recess, the envoys on their way to France, and all remaining business tended to, Adams quickly left the "Bake House" in Philadelphia. On Monday, July 24, Abigail and John began the journey to Quincy and arrived at their beloved farm on Friday, August 4. Their thoughts lingered on events in Philadelphia, however.[45] "We know not what a day will bring forth— from every side we are in Danger. we are in Perils by Land, and we are in Perils by sea; and in Perils from false Breathern," Abigail concluded.[46]

7

Expect Nothing but the Most Unqualified Injustice

THE NEXT DAY, John Adams received a letter from Benjamin Lincoln, his old friend and Revolutionary War veteran. "A committee from a number of Citizens" planned to visit the president on Monday, August 7, "at half past ten oClock," Lincoln announced. He hoped that Adams would "be at Quincy" at that time "and in a situation to receive them."

Two days later, a committee of six men, including Lincoln, arrived at Adams's doorstep. They were shown into the front parlor just to the left of the entry hall, which Abigail had ordered freshly whitewashed to brighten the room. They welcomed the president home and proclaimed, "as Citizens of Massachusetts, we feel a peculiar pride & pleasure in your being placed at the head of the Union, when we recollect, that we have the honour to recognize you, as one of our number." They requested "the honour of [the president's] Company" at "a public Dinner" they had arranged to demonstrate their esteem.[1]

After months of reading attacks in Benjamin Franklin Bache's *Aurora* and receiving letters warning of Thomas Jefferson's nefarious dealings, Adams could barely contain his emotions at this vocal display of support. He spent that afternoon writing a response, spilling out all his frustrations and fears about the state of the nation, the "Jacobins," partisan politics, loyalty, and France. Adams routinely vented his feelings on paper, but wisely didn't make them public. In this case, he had the good sense to pen another draft in a more moderate tone. The second pass was less vitriolic but was still not fit for public consumption. He set that draft aside as well and started again.

The third version thanked the committee for their "kind Congratulations" and "accepted with Pleasure" their "polite Invitation." He shared their worry that "the profligate Spirit of falshood and malignity . . . are Serious Evils" that threaten the "Union of the states, their Constitutions of Government and the moral Character of the Nation." But he took heart that "the Citizens of Boston" condemned these "nefarious designs" and he was confident their actions would defeat the "Ennemies of Republican Governments."[2] Satisfied his third attempt had struck the appropriate tone, Adams sent the letter to the committee.

The following week, the festivities began with a parade of Boston cavalry marching "in front of the PRESIDENT's house in *Quincy*." After music performances and "an elegant collation which had been prepared," the crowds and troops "escorted the PRESIDENT and a numerous Cavalcade of the First Citizens of *Quincy*" to the governor's mansion on the corner of Washington and Cliff Streets, before processing to the State House. At precisely 3 P.M., the group marched two blocks around the corner to Faneuil Hall, where 300 attendees enjoyed a dinner. "The Hall was elegantly decorated, and particularly ornamented with two fine portraits of the PRESIDENT of the *United States*, and his predecessor, with apt and suitable encomiums on their respective merits." Even when crowds celebrated Adams, he could not escape Washington. After the dinner, Adams enjoyed a performance of "Macbeth" at the Haymarket Theatre, before returning home to Quincy.[3]

The celebration was the only time Adams left home between his arrival on August 4 and his departure on October 3, but it was a welcome distraction. Otherwise, all Adams could do was wait for news from France and he was not the most patient person.

Abigail spent her first weeks in Massachusetts checking on their various properties, stopping in on their neighbors, and visiting her family. Even afternoons spent at home were rarely quiet. Abigail regularly counted "a Family of 20" sitting around the dining table. She liked nothing more than gathering her children, grandchildren, and nephews under her roof.[4]

While Abigail renewed their ties with loved ones, the president spent his mornings monitoring the harvest, walking in his woods, and overseeing maintenance to walls and fences. In the afternoon, he tended to his papers and the dispatches delivered daily from Philadelphia. Most of the letters were workaday, if not downright annoying. Letters arrived from all over the country, from friends, family, and strangers, suggesting potential candidates for vacant positions and analyzing their respective merits. Adams spent countless hours that first summer fielding requests for financial support,

FIGURE 7.1 Peacefield: "View of the seat of John Adams, late President of the United States, in the town of Quincy." From the Eliza S. Quincy Memoir in the Quincy family papers, vol. 45, after page 52. Eliza S. Quincy, 1822. Massachusetts Historical Society.

rejecting supplications, and discussing candidates for appointments in the federal government.

These were not the letters Adams hoped to receive. He was desperate to hear how events were unfolding across the globe.

John Quincy Adams was running out of books to read. At the end of June, he had sailed from Rotterdam on the *Alexander & Alexander*, a ship under Prussian flags that carried around twelve passengers. They had made it only eighteen miles before a fierce headwind forced the vessel to make anchor.[5] As of July 7, he had spent eight days holed up in a small lodging house in Maassluis, Netherlands, waiting for the winds to change and speed his departure back to London.

That afternoon, he received a visit from Charles Lucas Pinckney Horry. Horry was visiting his uncle, Charles Cotesworth Pinckney, who was sheltering in The Hague after his exile from Paris. Horry delivered letters from "Genl: Pinckney and Mr: Murray." After they dined together, John

Quincy returned to his room to read the new correspondence. He discovered that the letters contained "some very unpleasant intelligence, personally concerning myself."[6] He had received news of his father's plans for him, and he was not pleased.

In May 1796, then President George Washington had nominated John Quincy Adams as the next minister to Portugal.[7] He had remained in the Netherlands, managing both portfolios until a replacement could be assigned to The Hague. The Hague was a regular stopping point for ministers abroad as ships sailing from North America followed the winds and the tides, often drifting into the North Sea before making port in the Netherlands. Captains and crews disembarked in port to resupply their ships and repair any damage sustained during Atlantic crossings, passengers recovered from seasickness, and diplomats sought out their colleagues to exchange news and letters. The Hague's value as a travel hub facilitated John Quincy's conversations with diplomats from around the globe and enabled him to oversee relations for both Portugal and the Netherlands.

On February 27, 1797, just five days before John Adams took office as the next president, Washington had appointed William Vans Murray as the next minister to the Netherlands. With his successor confirmed, John Quincy arranged to move to Lisbon. He spent weeks purchasing and packing books, shipped his clothes and household goods, and secured a companion for his future life. In May 1797, he proposed to "his best friend," Louisa Catherine Johnson, and they set a date to marry before sailing to Lisbon.

While his eldest son planned his voyage, the new president had other ideas. Everywhere he looked he saw signs of treachery, duplicity, and partisan machinations. Jefferson was writing defamatory letters about the administration, the cabinet resisted his diplomatic agenda, Federalists and Republicans were feuding in the papers, and France seemed determined to instigate a war with the United States. Adams needed all the allies he could find.

Over the past several years, he had come to rely on his son's reports from Europe. These reports were delivered directly to him rather than filtered through the newspapers or Timothy Pickering's partisan lens. They were the best intelligence available, and he depended on them when making foreign policy calculations.

The diligent son strove to meet his father's expectations. Every two weeks, and sometimes more frequently, John Quincy provided voluminous updates. In each missive, he carefully scratched out thousands of words, full of rumors, updates, observations, and advice about the state of diplomacy in Europe.

FIGURE 7.2 William Vans Murray by Mather Brown, 1787. Courtesy National Gallery of Art, Andrew W. Mellon Collection.

On May 20, 1797, Adams sent a letter to the Senate, nominating his son as the next minister to Prussia. A post in Berlin would give him a much better seat to observe and report back on political developments, military fortunes, and continental intrigues. Adams knew that Portugal was a fading power, but Berlin would provide a front-row seat to the squabbles between France, Prussia, Russia, and the Habsburgs in Austria-Hungary. His son was too good a diplomat and too valuable a resource to waste in Lisbon.

In early June, Adams wrote to his son, explaining his rationale for the choice: "You have wisely taken all Europe for your theatre, and I hope will continue to do as you have done." He urged John Quincy to "send us all the information you can collect." But he was also explicit about where that information should go: "I wish you to continue your practice of writing freely to me, and cautiously to the office of State."[8]

Abigail also wrote to John Quincy, knowing that he was already worried about accusations of nepotism and how another appointment might be perceived, but she hoped "the reason which opperated in affecting this Change will be obvious" to him. Nonetheless, she reminded him that his position in Berlin would be "more usefull to your Country at the present time, than you could be in Lisbon."[9] As a mother, she never shied away from reminding her children of their duty to the nation and she was confident he would meet her lofty expectations. John Quincy reluctantly "turned away from the Lisbon course," but he grumbled about it.[10]

In one of the most strident letters that he sent to his father, he huffed that "this appointment was . . . totally contrary to every expectation and every wish I had formed." The position was so unappealing that he had serious "hesitation with respect to accepting it." He had already leased housing in Lisbon and sent crates and crates of books, which would have to be retrieved at great expense. Then, there was an "embarrassing" circumstance that he did not know a single "human being" in Berlin. John Quincy wasn't just whining; serving as an effective diplomat required connections to smooth introductions, facilitate relationships, and foster negotiations.

John Quincy reminded his father that he had "explicitly declared" his resolution to never "hold any public office under your nomination," and he "indulged the hope, that my adherence to it would never be put to so severe a trial, as I have experienced." He continued, "the degraded and humiliating aspect in which it places me personally" would cause Adams's opponents to paint him as a "creature of favour, the "parent de Ministre."

John Quincy was right to worry. Not long after the Senate confirmed his nomination, Bache printed a report in the *Aurora* full of "Lies, falshoods calumny and bitterness." Bache asserted that John Quincy, a mere "twenty-three-year-old" received a "sallery of ten thousand dollers pr year." There were two problems with this report, Abigail reminded her sister. First, "these salleries are all setled by Law." A resident minister received "4 thousand 500 Dollors pr year," while a "Minister plenipotentiary Nine thousand." Second, John Quincy was thirty years old. Bache lied about his age to undermine his experience and credentials.[11]

For all his protestations, John Quincy almost never said no to his father, and he never said no to the President of the United States. He spent the next few months waiting for instructions, preparing to travel to Berlin, and enjoying life with his new bride. On October 19, they set sail and arrived in Berlin three weeks later. They were "questioned at the gates by a dapper lieutenant," who did not know "who the United States of America were" until one of his fellow soldiers explained to him. Only then were John Quincy and Louisa Catherine permitted to enter the city, find lodgings, and begin their duties.[12]

Over the next several months, as scandals and crises erupted in Philadelphia, Adams would be enormously grateful that his son was positioned to provide valuable intelligence directly from Europe.

On October 3, John and Abigail set off for their journey south. "Address all your future Letters to the Care of Charles Adams Counsellor at Law New York, unless you can be sure they may be delivered to me on the road, which is not probable," Adams instructed Pickering.[13] They planned to visit their daughter Nabby in East Chester until they received the latest intelligence on the pandemic in Philadelphia. Charles, their son, who lived in the city, would deliver the president's daily correspondence.

As they left Quincy, they "were escorted out of Town by a Troop of light Horse, and the citizens in carriages and on Horse back as far as Weathersfield."

FIGURE 7.3 Abigail "Nabby" Adams Smith. Miniature portrait on porcelain tile by unidentified artist. Collection of the Massachusetts Historical Society.

The entourage then proceeded to New Haven, enjoying the crisp weather and fall foliage along the way. "Six Miles from the Town," a troop of "near a Hundred Light Horse in a Red uniform very well mounted, Gentlemen in carriages and on Horse back" greeted the first family. The gathered troops escorted the Adamses "to our Lodgings, fired three rounds made their compliments and left us," Abigail reported to her sister. Perhaps equally as touching was the simple commitment demonstrated by a lone "Horseman in uniform." When the Adamses arrived at their inn for the evening, they learned that the soldier "had been waiting two days there, and had orders to stay untill we arrived."[14]

New York society determined to outshine their fellow citizens in Boston and fete the president. Five days before the Adamses arrived, "a light Horseman had been sent out to" East Chester, which was "20 miles from the city." They waited patiently, before escorting the first lady and president into town for a "a splendid dinner" with over "300 subscribers."[15]

Over the next several days, local towns between New York and Philadelphia kept up the busy schedule of festivities, before the Adamses finally arrived at the President's House on November 10.[16] They were met with the first scrap of news from Paris in many long months.[17] The *Commercial Advertiser* in New York announced: "Another Revolution in France."[18]

As reports filtered in from Europe, Adams and the cabinet gradually pieced together a picture of the political developments in Paris. Facing growing domestic opposition, the moderate faction in the French Directory had organized a coup. The foreign minister Charles Maurice de Talleyrand-Périgord partnered with the army and the moderate faction in the Directory to sideline the more royalist elements. They also ordered the arrest of at least fifty members in the Council of Five Hundred and Council of the Ancients.[19]

Adams's network of informants began to fill in the details. From The Hague, Murray reported that Paul-François-Jean-Nicolas, vicomte de Barras and powerful member of the French Directory, had ordered, "Thirty Three of the Journalists . . . imprisoned & their presses broken *without Trial* as was the case with the members who were seized & condemned for Banishment.[20] Murray also warned that if the current ruling faction in the Directory retained power, the American envoys would have little hope of success.[21]

John Quincy offered equally grave warnings that Adams should "expect nothing but the most unqualified injustice, under the Machiavellian mockery with which they have so long duped the world" while the current Directory reigned in France.

The intelligence left Adams with more questions than answers and he pondered what to say to Congress. He was constitutionally obligated to provide updates to Congress but found it nearly impossible to fulfill that duty without more information himself. As each day ticked by without further news, Adams's frustration about the slowness of communication escalated. Adams pleaded with the cabinet to provide subjects on which he could include in his upcoming address.[22]

Once the secretaries sent back their responses, Adams compiled his speech, pulling a bit from each letter and adding his own insight, history lessons, and flair. He shared the ominous reports from France but had little tangible information about the status of the peace commission, which was the information everyone wanted. Instead, he did his best to provide a more comprehensive global update.

Spain had failed to fulfill its obligations under the "execution of our Treaty with his Catholic Majesty," which both nations had signed in 1795. The treaty had clarified the boundary between the United States and Spain in the Florida and Louisiana territories and granted American merchants access to trade on the Mississippi River. Regretfully, Adams reported, "Spanish Garrisons were Still continued within our Country" and inspired "Foreign Agents" to insinuate "themselves among the Indian Tribes" to "incite hostilities against the United States." This language Adams pulled directly from Secretary of War James McHenry's memorandum.

In better news, Adams was happy to report that the British government had already fulfilled their side of the negotiations under the Jay Treaty by paying "The Sums awarded by the Commissioners" to United States citizens for "Losses and damages Sustained by reason of irregular and illegal captures or condemnation of their Vessells or Property." In return, the commissioners were hard at work examining "the Claims of British Subjects for Debts contracted before the Peace, and Still remaining due to them from Citizens of the United States." Adams also pulled several sections verbatim from Secretary of State Pickering's bulletin but omitted much of Pickering's editorializing.

Adams acknowledged their shared frustration at the slow pace of news and diplomacy but urged Congress to make the most of the forced downtime. He could not make specific recommendations pertaining to France yet, but he reminded Congress that he had recommended "precautionary measures" the previous spring. Since then, nothing had transpired in the last several months to reduce the need for defensive preparations. Yet Congress remained unwilling to act. If anything, Adams scolded, the "increasing depredations" upon American shipping "Strengthen the reasons for its Adoption."

The president reminded Congress that "The Commerce of the United States, is essential, if not to their Existence, at least to their Comfort, their growth, prosperity and Happiness." It must be protected at all costs and individual citizens should not be expected to bear the burden of defending "national honour."

Similarly, Adams urged Congress to make a plan for raising the funds that would be needed to bolster the nation's defenses. He warned against ongoing borrowing, arguing that the "Consequences arising from the continual Accumulation of public Debts in other Countries" were too fearsome to risk. All attendees knew crushing national debts had provoked the violence of the French Revolution. As members of Congress devoured reports of current events and waited impatiently to learn the fate of the American envoys in Paris, they did not miss the president's subtle but unmistakable warning.[23]

In the absence of concrete news from Europe, newspapers filled the vacuum by printing every rumor that crossed the editors' desks.[24] On January 4, the *Gazette of the United States* reported that "the American Hotel at Havre was . . . surrounded by guards." From the same source, the *Gazette* reported, "we learn that our commissioners are rejected by the French government." Four days later, it informed readers that Pinckney was preparing to leave Paris. The following week, the *Gazette* indicated that the commissioners weren't leaving France voluntarily but instead had been "ordered to quit Paris."[25]

Philadelphia vibrated with tension and anticipation as residents waited for further dispatches. If these reports were true and the envoys had been forced to leave France under threat of violence, war seemed inevitable. Jefferson kept Madison apprised of the situation: "Either the Envoys have not written to the government, or their communications are hushed up." Jefferson suspected Adams was keeping information secret because so many other ships had arrived "from Bordeaux & Havre," two ports where ships regularly docked before sailing for the United States. If those ships arrived safely, so too should letters from the American envoys.[26]

A few weeks later, when they still hadn't heard any news, Jefferson and his colleagues were convinced that Adams had intentionally sabotaged the negotiations. Monroe concluded that the administration had adopted a strategy "wh. will be best calculated to promote a rupture with France & overthrow our own govt."[27] Madison vented to Jefferson that the president was "without a single pretension to the character of Soldier, a perfect Quixotte as a Statesman," meaning Adams was full of grand ideals and ambitions but lacked the skills or hard-nosed realism to achieve them.[28]

On January 17, 1798, four and a half months after the envoys landed in Europe and two months since Adams had returned to Philadelphia, a letter from the envoys finally arrived. Those months had been filled with much speculation, wondering, and worry.

Three months earlier, on October 21, John Marshall had written William Vans Murray a hasty note: "We are not & I believe shall not be received. . . . I am persuaded that however unsuccessful our mission may be, our conduct can never be disapproved by our country. I am preparing for orders, which I daily expect, to leave France." On October 29, Murray mailed the dispatch to the secretary of state, along with his own cover letter. He had tried to send Marshall's letter earlier, Murray explained, but the ship's departure had been delayed by eastern winds. Finally, on October 29, the winds had shifted enough to carry the vessel from The Hague, out of the North Sea, and across the Atlantic.[29] The letter took an additional eleven weeks to reach Philadelphia.

Pickering immediately carried the package to the President's House. Adams read the letter with a sinking feeling. As of October 21, Marshall had planned to leave France, but the president had no idea what had transpired since then or where the envoys were located at present. Adams dashed off a letter to his cabinet asking for guidance on what he should do with the commissioners, Congress, and future diplomatic steps.[30] He had to decide whether to recall the commissioners or send them elsewhere, when to inform Congress of these developments and how much to tell them, what measures he should recommend in response to the French insult, and how much support to seek from Great Britain in the event of war.

Once Adams sent this missive to his secretaries, he waited for answers from the cabinet, for information from France, and for the events hurtling toward Philadelphia. Answers to these questions would shape the future of his presidency and the nation.

8

Not a Sixpence!

THE NEXT MORNING Timothy Pickering visited David Claypoole to share the contents of the dispatches. The following day, the *American Daily Advertiser* published a note:

> We are informed the Secretary of State yesterday received a letter from Mr. Murray . . . which informs, that the French government would not recognize the American Commission, and that they daily expected they would be obliged to quit the Republic. Mr. Marshall's letter is dated October the 21st.[1]

Pickering leaked the dispatch, without Adams's knowledge, to cultivate outrage among the American people and soften their resistance to war.[2] He hated France, sought a cozier alliance with Britain, and was eager to build up an army to pursue these goals. While the president had repeatedly called for defensive measures, he was not warmongering, so the secretary of state took matters into his own hands.

The publication radicalized the Republican Party. Republicans in Congress were certain that Federalists were negotiating with France in bad faith, while Federalists saw Republican outrage as proof that the party prioritized France over the United States. While ships carrying news sailed from Europe, partisans readied their battle plans, and the president was left to wait for what came next. In the eighteenth century, foreign policy was the president's primary responsibility. He had few domestic obligations, and Congress dominated the legislative agenda. And yet, there was almost nothing he could do to shape the historic developments taking place in Europe that would define his presidential legacy or the nation's future.

On September 1, 1797, John Marshall had landed in Amsterdam. A few days later, he met with Charles Cotesworth Pinckney in Rotterdam, where they spent several days closeted in Pinckney's rooms sharing intelligence while they waited for Elbridge Gerry to join them. Marshall brought letters and information from Philadelphia, and Pinckney described the state of diplomacy in Paris. Pinckney happily reported to Pickering that he and Marshall "agree perfectly in sentiment."[3]

Their mission was a challenging one. The envoys were tasked with defending the honor, independence, and sovereignty of the United States. When the United States declared independence in 1776, they believed they were creating a new nation but also a new type of nation. As part of their independence, Americans explicitly rejected the old-world norms of monarchy, aristocracy, corruption, and cronyism. The American envoys, therefore, were in Paris to assert their right to be an independent nation in the manner of their choosing at a time when few European empires were inclined to offer respect for those ideas. The clash between old-world and new-world sovereignty would define the envoys' experience in France over the next several months.

Two weeks later, they worried their delay might insult the French Directory. Before departing for Paris, they left letters for Gerry in The Hague, in Rotterdam, and in Amsterdam, unsure of where his ship would dock.[4] They arrived in Paris on September 27, alerted the French government of their presence, and requested permission to postpone their "official Notification of [their] arrival" until Gerry could join them.

Gerry arrived at The Hague after nearly two months at sea, missing his colleagues by just a few days. He took a brief respite from his travels to recover from a long, uncomfortable sea voyage beset by illness and fever, before straggling into Paris late on the evening of October 4, 1797. With the commission assembled, all three envoys delivered their official notification to the French foreign minister, Charles-Maurice de Talleyrand-Périgord.

Talleyrand was no stranger to the envoys. In 1792, he had fled Paris to avoid imprisonment and near certain execution during the Reign of Terror. He initially settled in London, before seeking refuge in Philadelphia, where he quickly joined the French refugee community and enjoyed the French restaurants, bookstores, salons, newspapers, and civic societies.[5]

Over the next few years, Talleyrand walked the same streets as Washington, Jefferson, Hamilton, and Adams. He dined with elite families, exchanged letters with Benjamin Rush, toasted with Hamilton, visited Aaron Burr's home in New York, and met Gerry in Boston.[6] A few months before Talleyrand sailed back to France, Marshall traveled to Philadelphia to argue a case before the Supreme Court. There is no record of whether Marshall and Talleyrand crossed paths, but they certainly knew of each other.

Since Talleyrand's return to France, he received reports from Alexandre d'Hauterive, the French consul in New York, and other French representatives in the United States.[7] They all insisted that Adams didn't seek war with France. When the American envoys announced themselves in Paris, Talleyrand had high hopes for fruitful negotiations. But he also believed the United States was weak, divided, and fearful of French aggression. Plus, he needed money. The peace commission offered an opportunity to pursue multiple goals simultaneously.

Initially, French hopes seemed well founded. On the afternoon of October 8, 1797, the envoys arrived at Talleyrand's office. His chief secretary, Pierre Paganel, informed the envoys that Talleyrand had unexpectedly been called to visit the Directory. Although a "little surprized" at the delay, they pledged to return two hours later.[8]

At 3:00 P.M., they returned, and waited again, this time while Talleyrand finished a conversation with the Portuguese minister. After about ten minutes, Talleyrand greeted them in French and accepted their "Letters of credence." His "personal demeanor" was "polite and easy." He then regretfully informed them, still speaking in French, that he was unable to offer official recognition. He explained that the Directory had ordered him to write a report on the state of Franco-American relations. Once that report was submitted, he would offer guidance about next steps.[9]

This delay was an unexpected setback, and after a moment, the envoys asked if they needed cards of hospitality in the meantime. The cards didn't offer official recognition, but they would at least guarantee their safety against deportation by the French police. Talleyrand agreed that would be a wise step. The envoys returned to their chambers and the following day, a messenger delivered cards that were drafted "in a Style suitable to our official Character."[10]

After their first meeting, the envoys awaited further instructions from their lodgings at 1131 La Rue Fontane Grenelle in the Saint Germain neighborhood—just a few blocks from Talleyrand's home.[11] Gerry's apartment on the ground floor off the courtyard entrance included a reception room, a drawing room which Gerry used as his study, and a bedroom. On the left side of the courtyard, Marshall occupied a similar suite of rooms. Both apartments were "furnished with sattin furniture & glasses, neat, but the furniture not very fresh."

Through the courtyard, a "lofty stone stair case" led to the second floor, where the Pinckneys enjoyed slightly more spacious accommodations, reflecting Mary Pinckney's presence. Mary had accompanied Charles when he planned to serve a longer tenure as American minister to France. She remained with him when they fled to The Hague and stayed by his side when he returned to Paris. Polly Marshall and Ann Gerry were both pregnant and expected their husbands' mission would be of short duration, so they stayed home. The Pinckneys had an antechamber, as well as "a dining room, a small room where [their daughter] Eliza play[ed] on the piano, a drawing room very Elegantly furnished, a handsome bed Chamber," where General and Mrs. Pinckney slept. The second-floor apartment also included "a light closet or Small room" which Pinckney had "fitted up for a study" for his private use.

While Mary Pinckney lamented the sparse furnishings in the "eating room," she happily reported to her cousin that the house was in a quiet part of the city, and they rarely heard street noise.[12] Gerry, however, complained to his wife that his apartments were badly furnished, "not even having a carpet." The chimney smoked and a stable was situated under ground, producing "constant noise, as of persons breaking through the wall." The constant racket "disturbed [his] rest" and he kept "a pair of pistols under [his] pillow" for safety.[13]

On Sunday, October 14, the envoys received the first indication that their negotiations might go awry. Major James Mountflorence visited the envoys at Talleyrand's direction. Mountflorence was an agent for an American mercantile firm and worked for the American consulate in Paris. Talleyrand selected Mountflorence, and all the subsequent agents, because he would appear trustworthy to the American envoys. Upon his arrival, Mountflorence reported that the Directory had taken offense at President Adams's speech to Congress in May and required the envoys to provide an official explanation for the more bellicose passages.[14] In fact, the Directory was inclined to postpone official recognition of the peace commission until they had received an explanation for the "harmful" remarks.[15]

Three days later, Pinckney received another unexpected visitor secretly dispatched by Talleyrand. Nicholas Hubbard worked for the House of Van Stophorst and Hubbard in Amsterdam, which served as the US government's European bank and regularly collected and held letters for Americans traveling across Europe. During the Pinckneys' time in the Netherlands, they had taken long rides, enjoyed meals, and attended the debates of the Dutch convention with Nicholas and Jeanne-Marie Van Den Velden Hubbard.[16] Hubbard was well-chosen to exploit Pinckney's trust.

Hubbard asked Pinckney to meet with Jean Conrad Hottinguer, another secret Talleyrand agent. Hottinguer was a man of honor, Hubbard assured Pinckney. Their shared history caused Pinckney to agree to the meeting, as Talleyrand had intended.

Later that evening, Hottinguer arrived and joined Pinckney's dinner party. After conversing with the rest of the guests, Hottinguer whispered to Pinckney that he had a private message to share from Talleyrand. Pinckney ushered him into his private study, where Hottinguer revealed his plan to appease the Directory and facilitate future negotiations. If the envoys could offer an official loan to the French government, as well as a private sum for the Directory and its ministers, then they would be officially recognized.

Pinckney asked for specifics. Which passages of the president's speech had offended the Directory? What size loan would be required? And how much would the Directory require for its bribe?

Hottinguer replied that he wasn't sure about the specifics of the offensive language, nor the "quantum of the loan," but the "douceur for the pocket" should be about "fifty thousand pounds sterling."[17]

Flabbergasted, Pinckney said that France had treated him and his colleagues with "great slight and disrespect," but they still "earnestly wished for peace and reconciliation." He could not possibly consider any terms, let alone these substantial demands, "before he had communicated them to his colleagues."[18]

As soon as Hottinguer left, Pinckney relayed his conversation to Marshall and Gerry.[19] The next night, Hottinguer returned to the envoys' residence at La Rue Fontane Grenelle and delivered a summary of Talleyrand's demands in writing to all three envoys. He agreed to meet Gerry for breakfast on October 21, 1797 to answer any follow-up questions the envoys might have after reviewing his letter.

The next morning, however, Hottinguer returned and said he hadn't actually heard the requests directly from Talleyrand. Instead, they had been passed along by Pierre Bellamy, a Swiss citizen, banker, and "confidential friend" of Talleyrand.[20] Going forward, Talleyrand preferred to communicate with the envoys through Bellamy and Hottinguer.

Caught off guard by the constantly evolving players and demands, as Talleyrand intended, the envoys committed a diplomatic misstep. By consenting to receive Hottinguer and Bellamy, the envoys had inadvertently agreed to open negotiations with unofficial representatives. The envoys debased themselves and their mission by meeting with agents who did not possess official negotiating powers or recognition from the French Directory.

Anyone less was beneath their official station. Additionally, any product of their negotiations could be more easily discounted because their French counterparts were not officially sanctioned by the Directory. Adams had warned Marshall about this exact sort of trickery. It was a rookie mistake.

At 7 P.M., the two French agents arrived in Marshall's suite.[21] After Bellamy recounted his travels in the United States and his "favorable impressions . . . which were made by the kindness and civilities he had personally received in America," he repeated the same demands: the envoys must provide an explanation of the president's speech, a loan for the French government, and bribes for the Directory and ministers.[22] Bellamy closed his remarks by returning to the subject of the bribe. "Gentlemen," he said, "il faut de l'argent—il faut beaucoup d'argent." *You must pay money—you must pay a great deal of money.*

The next day, the envoys discussed the terms in private and wrote a formal response. They reaffirmed their commitment to peace and stressed that they possessed expansive authority to negotiate a new treaty. However, the envoys wrote, a loan was beyond the "limits of our instructions." They proposed that one of the "American Ministers will . . . embark for America" to obtain updated instructions on a potential loan if, and only if, the Directory "will suspend all further captures on American vessels."[23]

Upon receiving the written response, Bellamy looked visibly disappointed that the envoys did not discuss the bribes. The sum "was exact [*sic*] as much as was paid to the antient kings," he rued. Bellamy was not wrong. The Old World had long operated on a system of bribes and gifts. French officials regularly offered and accepted such bribes, including paying 24,000 livres to Silas Deane in exchange for facilitating a large arms and ammunition purchase in 1776. Baron David Alphonse Sandoz Rollin, the envoy of the king of Prussia to France, wrote that "it has become the custom under the Directory that every large transaction should be preceded by a *douceur*." Most nations simply complied.[24]

Bellamy's reference to the ancient kings was the exact wrong thing to say to the three American envoys who were very proud of the role they had played in the American Revolution to free themselves from the shackles of monarchy. They replied, haughtily, that "America had demonstrated to the world, and especially to France, a much greater respect for her present government than for her former monarchy."

The envoys recognized they were at a turning point and agreed to document all their conversations with Talleyrand's agents thus far. Marshall wrote the first draft, pulling from his detailed diary. He substituted "X" for

Hottinguer's name and "Y" for Bellamy's name to keep their identities a secret, as he had promised. They were thereafter known as Agent X and Agent Y in the United States.[25]

Marshall shared his draft with Pinckney and Gerry, who made a few slight revisions before adding their signatures. Marshall's secretary made several copies, which they all signed, before mailing them back to Philadelphia.

Talleyrand commenced the next stage of negotiations through Lucien Hauteval, a wealthy West Indian sugar planter who had fled the violent revolution in Saint-Domingue for Boston in 1792. When Hauteval arrived at Rue Fontane Grenelle, he delivered a new message from Talleyrand, who expected Gerry to attend private events, where they could discuss, unofficially, the goals of their commission.[26] Hauteval explained, that in French custom, Talleyrand would expect such social calls from Gerry, as they had been previously introduced in the United States.

Gerry should have immediately rejected this request per Adams's instructions about maintaining unity among the commissioners. Instead, he agreed to schedule an individual interview with Hauteval and Talleyrand.[27]

In the meantime, Hottinguer and Bellamy reappeared. At 12 P.M. on October 27, they arrived full of bravado, bragging about the advantageous settlement the French armies had recently signed with Austria. The "change in the state of things" warranted "an expectation" of a shift in their negotiations with the Americans. The envoys expressed their regrets but repeated that their instructions remained unaltered.[28]

"Gentlemen," Hottinguer explained, "you do not speak to the point; it is money; it is expected that you will offer money."

"We have spoken to that point very explicitly," the envoys replied.

"No you have not: what is your answer?" Hottinguer demanded.

Infuriated, Pinckney burst out, "No, no, not a sixpence!"[29]

Whatever came next, the envoys had drawn a firm line in the sand. They would not pay any bribes, not even a sixpence.

Six days later, on October 28, Hauteval arrived to escort Gerry to the French minister's house for their scheduled meeting. As the envoys had planned, Gerry reminded Talleyrand that they didn't have the authority to offer a new loan but would be willing to send one of their trio back to the United States for further guidance, if they could continue to negotiate the other issues.

Talleyrand retorted that further instructions were meaningless if the envoys wouldn't first settle the matter of the bribe and explain the president's speech. Perhaps he should speak with each of the envoys individually,

Talleyrand suggested, probing for a weak spot in the commission.[30] Gerry returned to the residence and relayed the contents of the conversation to Marshall and Pinckney, who wrote a response to Talleyrand that "they had nothing to add to this conference."[31]

Over the next several days, Talleyrand's agents bombarded the envoys with visits and demands designed to chip away at their resistance. Hottinguer boasted that France was on the brink of destroying England and the Directory might not permit the envoys to remain in Paris unless they offered a private sum to secure their safety. Bellamy threatened to exacerbate internal tensions in the United States and turn the American people against the Federalist administration.[32] Two days later, Hottinguer and Bellamy returned and announced that Talleyrand was preparing to demand the recall of the envoys.[33]

After this flurry of activity, the envoys again recorded all their interactions with Talleyrand, Hottinguer (X), Bellamy (Y), and Hauteval, whom they dubbed "Z." On November 8, they sent thirty-six pages in code describing their efforts since their first dispatch, which they had mailed on October 22.

At this point, Talleyrand abandoned his efforts to work with the commission and focused solely on Gerry. The envoys held firm on refusing a bribe, but they fractured on all other issues going forward. Gerry believed that the best strategy to avoid war was to prolong talks as long as possible. Although Gerry had promised Adams that he would remain neutral, his decades-old Anglophobia lingered. He feared a war with France would lead to an alliance with Great Britain, which was his greatest fear. He shared with William Vans Murray, the American minister at The Hague, his concerns that "total failure [of the negotiations] would bring war" and "disgrace republicanism."[34]

Marshall and Pinckney disagreed. They doubted France would provoke a war when its navy and armies were preoccupied battling Britain and her allies. They also resented Gerry's outright Anglophobia, indecision, and willingness to deal with French agents behind their backs. Pinckney wrote to his brother, Thomas Pinckney, that Gerry was "habitually suspicious, and hesitates so much, that it is very unpleasant to do business with him."[35]

Gerry had failed to uphold his promise to the president that he would prioritize unity with his fellow commissioners above all else. With no immediate method of communication, Adams would not learn of this betrayal for many months and could offer no feedback or recourse. He could only hope that Gerry inflicted limited damage and the other envoys held the line.

This widening rift was reflected in their living situation. At the end of November, Marshall and Gerry left their shared residence. Gerry was convinced his life was in danger at the house, although curiously the other envoys hadn't voiced similar concerns. Marshall likely joined Gerry to keep an eye on the wayward envoy, and enjoyed the more plush accommodations provided by Madame de Villete, an attractive widow in her thirties. Villete also proved to be a useful hostess. She helped Gerry improve his French, accompanied Marshall to the theater, and organized parties and dinners for her lodgers.[36]

As the envoys struggled to gain Talleyrand's attention and remain cordial with one another, they dispatched reports through the complex network weaving across Europe to Rufus King in London and to William Vans Murray at The Hague.

Whenever possible, King and Murray forwarded this correspondence to Pickering and Adams for their review. This complex communication web was vital to ensure that letters escaped the clutches of the British and French navies. British and French vessels captured American ships to seize materials, money, and men that could be used in their war against each other, and letters between Americans in the United States and Europe were often a casualty of the conflict.

To avoid seizure, American representatives abroad sent copies of each official dispatch through three different routes. They mailed one letter with American merchants docked in French ports. The second letter usually went to King in London, who would forward the package on to the administration. Finally, they sent the third copy through Lisbon, which took the longest time to reach Philadelphia but was the safest option.

On January 6, 1798, King wrote to Pickering that he had just learned that the November ship destined "for New York has been captured and carried to France—this I very much regret as she had important Dispatches for you from our Envoys at Paris and likewise from me." King hoped that "the Duplicates or Triplicates which went by other but less favorable conveyances may arrive."[37]

When this letter finally arrived in Philadelphia, Adams and Pickering understood why they had received no word from the envoys. The letters had been seized, leaving the president, his cabinet, Congress, and their fellow Americans in the dark.

Meanwhile, the envoys continued in a holding pattern. Gerry hosted several social gatherings for Talleyrand and the French agents but excluded Marshall and Pinckney, actively participating in the sidelining of his colleagues. He sometimes shared the details of these meetings, but often did not.

By mid-January, the envoys were at a breaking point. Marshall drafted a lengthy letter to Talleyrand. The first portion gave a detailed "justification of the conduct of the American government" and the second portion offered a statement of "the claims of the United States upon France." As he finished each section, he shared it with his fellow envoys. Pinckney offered a few small edits, but readily applied his signature.

Gerry spent most of January considering the letter and devising reasons to delay its delivery, even as Marshall "repeatedly pressed [him] on the subject." Finally, Gerry gave his approval. The clerks spent nine days translating the dispatches into French for Talleyrand and made copies in English, which Marshall handed to Major Rutledge, a friend and colleague, for hand delivery to Philadelphia.[38] Pinckney also sent King a copy of the report, confiding in his fellow minister:. "It is probable that our stay here will be very short."[39]

Marshall then drafted a second letter demanding their passports to return home. The envoys agreed if they did not hear from Talleyrand within ten days, they would send the second letter.[40] Pinckney immediately signed the letter; Gerry vacillated.

A few days later, Talleyrand once again summoned Gerry. After the meeting, Gerry said that "he was not at liberty to impart to Genl. Pinckney or [Marshall]" the contents of his conversation with Talleyrand.[41] It was a stunning breach of diplomatic protocol, his official instructions, and his promises to the president.

In his journal, Marshall brooded, "This communication necessarily gives birth to some very serious reflections." He knew exactly what game Talleyrand was playing and feared it was working.[42]

Over the next week, Gerry continued to meet privately with Talleyrand and his agents. He repeated to Marshall and Pinckney that he was not at liberty to share the contents of the conversations, but that he believed the French might soon offer new proposals. Marshall and Pinckney remained firm that they "had given our ultimate decision upon [the subject of money] more than once."

Gerry protested that they were rejecting proposals without knowing the details, seemingly ignoring the fact that he was responsible for keeping them uninformed.

Marshall replied that "it was true I knew nothing of the particular propositions, but I thought I knew something of the general objects of the [French] government." Marshall noted in his diary that "Mr. Gerry was a little warm and the conversation was rather unpleasant."

After weeks of waiting, Talleyrand announced he would not respond to their official report, dashing all remaining hope for productive conversations. Marshall pushed Gerry to sign the letter requesting their passports. Gerry made several alterations, and promised to sign the letter once they returned from their trip to the countryside. Rather inexplicably, in the middle of these negotiations, Marshall and Gerry departed for a weekend trip with Madame Villete to her country house.[43] Perhaps Marshall hoped the trip would soften Gerry's resistance. Neither mentioned the trip or its purpose in their letters, but Marshall's fawning praise of Madame Villete in his letters to his wife, Polly, led her to believe he was engaging in an extramarital affair. She took to bed and refused to get up for weeks.

After their return, Marshall and Gerry invited Pinckney to a meeting. Once all assembled, Gerry revealed "that a secretary of M^r^. Talleyrand had called on him that morning." The agent suggested the envoys should promise to grant a loan to France, which would be payable after the French war with Great Britain concluded. Gerry was convinced this solution would avoid "the ill consequences of a war with France."[44]

Marshall and Pinckney protested, in disbelief at his naivete. They "had no power to make such a loan" by the terms of their instructions, they insisted. More important, even if they did offer a loan, they could not "prevent France from raising money upon it, and thus render it, in effect, an aid during the present war"—which would explicitly contradict President Adams's instructions.

The meeting ended badly. Pinckney reported to his brother that "we separated without convincing each other and agreed to meet the next evening." The envoys did meet again the next day, "but that meeting did not bring M^r^. Gerry over to our opinion, nor did it convince us that we were wrong."

At a fundamental impasse, the envoys "agreed to ask a joint interview of M^r^. Talleyrand, to see if any measures could be suggested which would form a basis of a reconciliation on terms in which we all coincided." On the morning of March 2, the envoys were shown in for a meeting with Talleyrand.

Two days later, on the one-year anniversary of Adams's inauguration, the envoys' October 22 dispatch finally arrived in Philadelphia.[45] It taken four and a half months to reach the president, an unusually long time even by eighteenth-century standards. Despite the late hour, Pickering immediately delivered the package to the President's House.[46] While it would take several days to decipher the coded messages, the meaning was clear.

The next morning, Adams sent a message to Congress, "The first dispatches from our Envoys Extraordinary, since their arrival at Paris, were received at the secretary of state's office at a late hour the last evening." Most of the documents were in code, he explained, except the last letter, "which is dated the 8th of January 1798." The contents of this letter were so important that they should be "immediately made known to Congress, and to the Public," Adams proclaimed. He enclosed the letter from the envoys, which read: "We can only repeat that there exists no hope of our being officially received by this Government, or that the objects of our mission will be in any way accomplished."[47]

9

Poured in from All Quarters

IN THE EARLY morning hours of March 17, Abigail Adams sat in her sunroom on the third floor of the President's House and wrote to John Quincy in Berlin. Affairs had progressed rapidly in the last few days, she wrote. "Not a single line came to Hand from [the envoys] untill the last of Feb'^{ry}," then suddenly, "dispatches poured in from all quarters." Practically overnight, they had received the envoys' updates "from october to Jan'^{ry} 9th." Remarkably, Abigail explained, "they arrived at Boston, Baltimore, N York, and Philadelphia in the course of the same week!" Letters from Rufus King also arrived on March 14, 17, and 20. All provided essential, if troubling, intelligence.[1]

By March 13, a small army of clerks had decoded the dispatches. For the first time, the president read all the details of the French demands from Talleyrand and his agents. He was disgusted by their obsession with bribes, he was heartened that the envoys had defended his speech to Congress, and he followed the convoluted debates over a potential loan. He saw with finality that the envoys had not been received by the French Directory and concluded that there was little hope remaining for a diplomatic solution. Perhaps most distressingly, Adams followed the escalating tensions among the envoys.

Adams shared the dispatches with his cabinet and asked how he should proceed. Should he "present immediately to Congress the whole of the communications from our minister in France?" And should he "recommend, in his message, an immediate declaration of war?"[2]

Attorney General Charles Lee offered the first and most temperate response. "I am respectfully of opinion that [the dispatches] ought not to be communicated to Congress at this *moment*," he wrote. If the dispatches were published and those publications made their way to France before the envoys departed Paris, their mission could be "entirely frustrated" or worse.

Lee's concern for the envoys' safety shaped his advice on a declaration of war. For the time being, the president should "recommend some defensive measures." Then, "whenever we shall hear of our envoys having left France," the president "may recommend a formal declaration of war" assuming the envoys' last efforts at negotiations failed.[3]

The same day, McHenry responded. He was less concerned with the envoys' safety and advised "a full disclosure therefore to Congress" of the dispatches. However, he counseled the president keep the French agents' identities secret, as the envoys had promised. Like Lee, McHenry suggested that the president recommend a "qualified hostility" with a "vigorous *defensive plan*," rather than an outright declaration of war.[4]

After Lee and McHenry sent their letters, Pickering and Wolcott arrived at the President's House. Wolcott mostly agreed that immediate war was impractical, and he seconded the concerns about the envoys' safety. There was little reason to trust the Directory to respect their integrity as American ministers, and therefore guarantee their safety, if it wouldn't recognize them for negotiations.

Pickering insisted on a prompt declaration of war to defend national honor.[5] While he was sensitive to the envoys' safety, he argued that Congress and "the people at large should know the conduct of the French Government towards our Envoys, and the abominable corruption of that Government; together with their enormous demands for *money*."[6]

The French demands "are so monstrous as to shock every reasonable man, when he shall know them," he continued. The dispatches would "convince all [our] countrymen that it was not *possible* to adjust our differences with the present government of France."[7] Pickering's motivations were political, but he made a good point. The nation would not support a more militaristic approach unless it believed all peaceful options had been exhausted.

Adams also wanted revenge for the humiliation endured by the envoys. But his decades of diplomatic experience served him well at this moment. He drafted his most bellicose message for Congress demanding war, then set it aside.[8] Instead, he formulated a plan to lay bare French misdeeds, while also protecting the safety of the American ministers. It was a far more politically savvy approach than either his friends or enemies admitted.

Adams consulted with trusted allies and advisors outside the cabinet as well. Abigail was the first to know of the dispatches' arrival and the contents of the messages.[9] To her sister, she revealed that she and John had spoken about publicizing the dispatches. "It is a very painfull thing to him that he cannot communicate to the public dispatches in which they are so much interested," Abigail shared. "But we have not any assurance that the Envoys have left Paris," she said, emphasizing that they were analyzing the situation together as a team. They determined that "our foreign ministers can never be safe, or they will cease to be useful to us abroad, if their communications are all to be communicated."[10]

Outside of the cabinet, Theodore Sedgwick was one of the most frequent guests at the President's House. Sedgwick and Adams had known each other since they were young lawyers in Massachusetts. They served together in the Continental Congress, regularly socialized during George Washington's administration, and shared many similar passions, including serving as founding members of the American Academy of Arts and Sciences. In the spring of 1798, Sedgwick was one of Adams's closest confidants.

Just a few days after receiving the first dispatches, Adams told Sedgwick that they were still deciphering the coded messages, but he didn't think he would be able to make any "further communication" about the contents to Congress. "The ministers had expressed . . . so much indignation as to the gross insults inflicted on themselves & their country," Adams explained, that he feared "the publication would expose them to assassination."[11]

On March 17, Adams met with Sedgwick again and described the contents of newly decoded intelligence. Adams also relayed that he had "determined not to communicate the full dispatches," at the moment. Sedgwick agreed "the publication would have exposed" the envoys to imprisonment or assault. But "if those communications are withheld," he worried, "the opposition will make a mischievous use of it." Sedgwick warned Adams that the Republicans will "say that the President dare not expose his conduct" because it would reveal he negotiated with France in bad faith.[12]

"Orders will be given immediately to withdraw [the envoys] from France," Adams explained to Sedgwick, reassuring his friend. After the envoys were safely on their way, "then will be told a tale at which every ear will tingle," Adams confided, revealing his conspiratorial plan. Sedgwick later wrote his friend and neighbor Henry Van Schaack: "Unless I am mistaken [the story] will give a most fateful blow to the Jacobins." [13]

While Adams developed his strategy, Pickering and McHenry sent Hamilton a summary of the dispatches (which were still top secret) and asked for his input. The Federalist mastermind happily weighed in, offering advice on proposed defensive measures in the president's address, which replicated almost exactly what Adams already planned to do.[14] They only diverged in one key area. Hamilton proposed "the increase of our army to 20 000 men and the establishment of a provisional army of 30 000 more."[15] Adams never mentioned an army.[16] McHenry and Pickering incorporated this advice into their conversations with the president. They never obtained the president's permission to share secret intelligence or request Hamilton's advice, nor did they reveal the source behind their recommendations.

Two days later, Adams visited Congress and announced that "the Dispatches, from the Envoys Extraordinary of the United States to the French Republic . . . have been examined and maturely considered." After decoding all the information, Adams concluded the peace mission could not be "accomplished on terms compatible, with the Safety, the honour, or the essential interests of the Nation."

Adams insisted this failure could not be attributed to the envoys or the administration. "I can discern nothing, which could have insured, or contributed to Success, that has been omitted on my part." Unless circumstances materially changed, Adams continued, no further diplomatic options remained to protect and preserve "our national Sovereignty." He urged Congress to adopt the recommendations for national defense that he had made the previous spring with "promptitude, decision and unanimity."

"In all your Proceedings," he reminded them, "it will be important, to manifest a Zeal, Vigour and concert in defence of the National Rights, proportioned to the danger, with which they are threatened."[17]

The Republican outcry was ferocious. For months, Jefferson and Madison had speculated that the administration was intentionally suppressing intelligence. With growing frustration, they pledged that "the public will have a right to expect also from our Ex. & the Negociators, the fullest communication of every circumstance that may attend the experiment if it should miscarry."[18]

Now that Adams announced he would withhold the contents of the dispatches, they launched into action.[19] On March 20, Senator Joseph Anderson, a Republican from Tennessee, proposed a motion calling on the president to "lay before the Senate the instructions given to the American Commissioners at Paris; and, also, all communications he hath received from them relative to the object of their mission."[20] Sedgwick suspected Jefferson was the true author of the motion.[21]

While Congress spent the next several days debating the dispatches, Benjamin Franklin Bache picked up the cause in the pages of his newspaper. He argued Adams and Pickering were "afraid" to hand over the instructions and the dispatches because the materials would reveal their duplicity. When

Bache's challenge went unanswered, he accused the president of "making war" without the constitutionally-required declaration from Congress.[22]

The Republican response was almost exactly as Adams anticipated.

Shortly after Adams delivered his address to Congress, he reviewed a set of new instructions for the envoys drafted by Pickering. "The President presumes that you have long since quitted Paris and the French dominions." In the most recent dispatch, they had promised to "make one more direct attempt . . . to draw the French Government to an open negotiation." If that attempt succeeded and the envoys negotiated a treaty, "then you are to remain and expedite the completion of the treaty." However, Adams instructed, "if you shall have discovered a clear design to procrastinate, you are to break off the negotiation, demand your passports and return." To be very clear, "in no event is a treaty to be purchased with money, by loan or otherwise," Adams declared.[23]

After making a few edits, Adams instructed Pickering to find the fastest vessel available. Pickering handed the private letters to Clement Humphreys, a Federalist ally, and booked him passage aboard the brig *Sophia.* The president ordered the captain, Henry Geddes, to sail immediately for France, deliver the message to the envoys, and convey them to safety.[24]

By this point, Adams fully expected to share the dispatches with the American people. Once he made the contents public, he knew the details would be published in newspapers and carried to France. Adams gave Humphreys a few weeks' head start to reach the envoys before the news made its way to the Directory in France.

While Republicans in Congress thrashed over Adams's secrecy, he shared the full contents of the dispatches with Sedgwick. Over the next week, Pickering, Sedgwick, and their allies in Congress worked behind the scenes to relay the contents of the dispatches to their fellow Federalists and to convince them to vote for Senator Anderson's motion.[25] "We wish much for the papers," one Federalist wrote to Harrison Gray Otis. "The Jacobins want them. And in the name of God let them be gratified; it is not the first time they have wished for the means of their destruction."[26]

Sedgwick was busy from dawn to dusk building support for their plan. On March 27, he was "called out of bed, in the morning by the Secretary of war," then pulled to a Senate committee meeting. He remained in committee until 11, when he "was summoned to the Senate where I labored till three o'clock." Sedgwick then "waited on the President" and remained at the President's House until dinner. After dinner, he spent an hour with "some members of the house, the speaker included." Sedgwick then walked to the Treasury Department, before returning to the President's House to report on the outcome of all these conversations.[27] And that was just one day.

Three days later, John Allen, a Connecticut Federalist in the House, stood from his desk and requested recognition by the Speaker. When granted permission, Allen affirmed that he was "satisfied with the information" they had received from the president, but he "believed there were many gentlemen in the House who wished for more." Allen accused these representatives of acting in bad faith. They weren't motivated by an effort to protect the nation, he alleged, but instead were hoping to show "the conduct of the Executive [had] been improper." Allen "wished the people to be undeceived," so he proposed the following resolution:

> *Resolved*, That the President of the United States be requested to communicate to this House the despatches from the Envoys Extraordinary of the United States to the French Republic, mentioned in his Message of the 19th instant.[28]

Sedgwick never revealed if Allen was one of the House members present at his gathering on March 27. It is certainly possible. They were close to many of the same people, and New England Federalists tended to join the same social circles, frequently seeking each other upon their arrival in Philadelphia.[29] Either Allen was present, or Dayton passed along news about the dispatches, and the Federalists concocted this plan to introduce a parallel resolution in the House.

After a few days of deliberation, the House passed the motion with broad bipartisan support. Many Federalists agreed to support the proposal, Sedgwick confessed to Peter Van Schaacke, because they were "confident the request will be complied with, and I am sure a disclosure will show that the conduct of our government has been fair and honorable and that of France, vile & detestable."[30] They could happily take this position because they already knew the contents of the dispatches and they knew Adams was ready and willing to comply.

With record-breaking speed, Adams delivered the instructions and the full dispatches to Congress the following morning. He had been prepared to do so for weeks. He asked that they consider the documents "in confidence, until the members of Congress are fully possessed of their contents, and shall have had opportunity to deliberate on the consequences of their publication, after which time, I submit them to your wisdom."[31]

The House cleared reporters and observers from its galleys before both chambers locked their doors and posted guards at the entrance. For the next three days, all present members of Congress pored over the hundreds of pages of communications.

A growing sense of horror spread among the members, mingled with self-righteous satisfaction among the Federalists that their distrust of the French had been well founded, and a sinking realization among the Republicans that their worst fears had come to pass. The president and his envoys had earnestly sought peace and, in return, had been subject to abuse, threats, and humiliating demands.

Republicans in both chambers immediately tried to distance themselves from France. The Jacobins "now promise" that "they really preferred their own country to France. And they declare that they believe the President a wise & honest man!" Sedgwick gloated.

The Federalists seized the opportunity to humiliate their rivals and put forth a motion to publish the dispatches and instructions.[32] Eager to prove their patriotism, many of the more moderate Republicans agreed. The motion passed, despite warnings from Jefferson that the disclosure would rebound against them.

Over the next few days, Philadelphia printers produced 1,200 copies of the dispatches and official instructions. They delivered the giant stacks to Congress, where each congressman received several copies for his personal use or for distribution to his constituents. Federalist Robert Troup said the complete transparency was without precedent "and a novel and extraordinary act in diplomatic concerns."[33]

Within days, the public reaction had united in its disgust for France and approval of Adams. "It would be difficult for you . . . to conceive the change which has taken place in this city," Abigail wrote to John Quincy. Of course, not everyone condemned the French, Abigail continued, "the center of foreign influence, and Jacobinism," by which she meant Jefferson, "*remain unchanged*." But most important, the "real Americans who have been deceived, and betray'd by falshood, and deception . . . are uniting & united."[34]

After the initial shock wore off, some of the more radical Republicans attempted to regroup. They suggested that the fault lay with Talleyrand and his crew of corrupt henchman. There was no evidence, Republicans claimed, that the Directory had known or authorized their extortion efforts, and thus there was no reason to go to war. "It is pretty evident that mr A's speech" from May 1797 was "the only obstacle to negociation," Jefferson explained.

France required "humiliating disavowals of that [speech] . . . as a preliminary," which was a price Jefferson was willing to pay. Once this concession was offered and "this obstacle removed," he continued, "they seem not to object to an arrangement of all differences and even to settle & acknolege themselves debtors for spoliations."[35] Jefferson assumed the Directory would not make similar demands for bribes or loans. Once again, Jefferson was countermanding the president's foreign policy, while serving as vice president in the administration.

The *Aurora* amplified these arguments and accused Federalists of trying to manufacture a crisis, but these protests fell on unsympathetic ears.[36] Within just a few weeks the *Aurora* had lost thousands of subscribers and was teetering on the brink of bankruptcy. Jefferson noticed a similar seismic shift in Congress. "The worst effect of these papers has been in the H. of Repr.," he wrote to his son-in-law; "they have carried over all the waverers to the other side. we now expect to lose every question which shall be proposed."[37]

While Jefferson sulked in the Senate, President Adams relished the praise. For nearly the first time in his entire adult life, he felt the full support and adoration of the American people.

In Paris, relations between the envoys had gone from bad to worse. Pinckney and Marshall remained convinced that their instructions forbade them from offering any sort of loan to France. Gerry insisted that they could offer a loan payable at the end of the conflict and argued that the "people of the United States would certainly approve the measure" if it "would prevent a war." Marshall wrote in his diary, "We parted, neither having made any sort of impression on the other."[38]

Marshall concluded there were three options available since they could come to no agreement. First, Gerry could remain in Paris and negotiate alone, which Marshall thought would be most improper. Second, he and Gerry could return home for more instructions. Finally, Gerry could return by himself for instructions. Marshall believed Gerry had to go, as he had met privately with Talleyrand and "had communications" from the French government, which the other two envoys "did not possess."[39] Even after several more days of debate, they came to no resolution.

On the morning of March 6, as Marshall dressed for the envoys' next meeting with Talleyrand, Gerry walked into his room. "If General Pinckney and [you] were willing," Gerry suggested, he would propose "a clause declaring that the complaints of the two governments had been founded in mistake."

Marshall was thunderstruck. "I could not say the complaints of our government were founded in mistake," he replied. "I should tell an absolute lye, if I should say that our complaints were founded in mistake!"

Gerry shouted back, "I wish to God that [you] would propose *something* which was accommodating!" You propose nothing and "objected to every thing!"

Perhaps they should not discuss the matter further, Marshall replied. This type of talk "was calculated to wound but not to do good."

Determined to fight, Gerry demanded of Marshall, what have you proposed that "was accommodating?! I have heard nothing from you yet."

Marshall lost his temper. "I [am] not accustomed to such language, and did not permit myself to use it, with respect to [you] or [your] opinions," he snapped. "I do not believe any part of [your] conduct" was designed to "unite the people of America, but the contrary."[40]

The conversation ended abruptly as their carriage arrived to take them to their meeting, where Talleyrand confirmed that France would use the promise of a loan from the United States for collateral for other loans, which they would deploy immediately in the war against Britain. This admission effectively ended any debate between the envoys and solidified Marshall and Pinckney's refusal.

There was nothing to gain from further meetings, so the envoys agreed to send one last official letter summarizing their mission, the complaints of the United States government, and their efforts to achieve a diplomatic resolution.[41]

Then Marshall set about trying to create a public relations win for their commission by ensuring that Talleyrand shouldered the blame for the breakdown in diplomacy. If the Americans made the first move to leave, both Talleyrand and Republicans at home would blame them for the collapse of the negotiations. Instead, Marshall and Pinckney refused to ask for their passports and forced Talleyrand to order them away. In this battle of wills, they had a wily foe as Talleyrand was equally as determined to make their life so miserable that they would voluntarily depart Paris.[42]

Two weeks later, one of Talleyrand's agents arrived and suggested Marshall and Pinckney request their passports. Marshall replied that "the act must be entirely [Talleyrand's]."[43]

When Marshall shared the conversation with his colleagues later that day, Gerry swore he would "sooner be thrown in the Seine than consent to stay" by himself, which was the appropriate diplomatic response. France could not dictate to other sovereign nations, including the United States, which minister they would accept.[44] "I was perfectly silent," Marshall wrote in his diary, suspecting this promise would not last.

On the morning of March 23, 1798, Mr. Dutrimond, Talleyrand's secretary, arrived with a message: if Marshall and Pinckney did not submit a request for their passports, Talleyrand would order all three envoys to leave France immediately.[45]

As Marshall expected, Gerry acquiesced, yet again. He said he would stay "to prevent a war."

Marshall gave him silent treatment.

One week later, Dutrimond returned, expecting Marshall and Pinckney to request their passports. Marshall said he was "ready to receive our passports, but we could not demand them." Dutrimond threatened, "If [you wish] to be ordered away . . . the order would soon be received." If negotiations were no longer possible, "the order could not come too soon," Marshall retorted.[46]

A few days later, Gerry finally finished his edits to the envoys' official letter to Talleyrand. When he delivered the revised document to his fellow commissioners, Pinckney remarked that Gerry's "conduct [was] calculated to embarrass our government, and to increase instead of diminishing the danger of war between the two nations." Pinckney was certain their fellow Americans would condemn Gerry after learning of his conduct.

Gerry retorted that Pinckney and Marshall "were embittered" against him and had not been candid in their communications with him.

"It is false, sir!" Pinckney insisted. They had shared everything with Gerry, but he had "not used the same candour!"

Gerry demanded to know what evidence they had for that claim.

Pinckney then detailed the many and repeated conversations between Gerry, Talleyrand, and his agents, which were supposed to be "jointly entrusted to us, and which [you] concealed from us!"

Gerry pleaded that he "had given his word not to reveal the purport of those conversations!" as though this excuse would be an acceptable explanation for his behavior.

"[You] ought never to have given such a promise!" Pinckney asserted.[47]

After an hour of further "unpleasant conversation," the envoys terminated their meeting. Gerry said, regretfully, that he had always felt a "strong attachment" for General Pinckney and that respect alone "had prevailed on him to accept the mission." With that sad final note, the envoys sent their missive to Talleyrand on April 3—the same day President Adams delivered their first set of dispatches to Congress.

Pinckney wrote to his brother that "Mister Gerry has agreed with Mister Talleyrand to remain here." Pinckney expected that he and "General Marshall" will be "ordered to depart" shortly. "I have remonstrated with mister Gerry on the ill consequences which will result from his remaining, and on the impropriety of his having carried on a negociation with Talleyrand under injunctions not to reveal it to his colleagues," Pinckney then vented his frustrations. "I never met with a man so destitute of candour, and full of deceit as Mister Gerry."[48]

At the same time, Gerry described the situation in a letter to his wife, which revealed his warped view of the negotiations. He insisted that he had "united with" his colleagues "in every measure which has been adopted: but their conduct to me has not been of that frank & friendly description which I expected."[49]

On April 13, Talleyrand finally capitulated and ordered Marshall and Pinckney to leave the country. He enclosed passports and letters of safe conduct, and gave Pinckney permission to reside temporarily in the countryside while his daughter recuperated from a lengthy illness.[50]

On April 23, Marshall sailed for the United States.[51] At the same time, Pinckney left Paris and slowly made his way to the south of France. He remained in Lyon for a few months while his daughter recovered her strength. While in Lyon, he received word that an American messenger had arrived in France. By May 21, Pinckney had received the new instructions from the president and sent Humphreys on his way to Paris to deliver the same message to Gerry.[52]

On August 7, Pinckney and his family finally left France. The next day, Gerry followed, empty-handed.[53]

Back in Philadelphia, Adams pored over the envoys' dispatches and jotted down his thoughts. He admired John Marshall's determined resistance in the face of Talleyrand's browbeating but criticized some of the envoys' decisions. The "Tittle Tattle" offered by agents X, Y, and Z, Adams wrote, ought to have been ignored "till the Envoys were received by the Directory and some one vested with full Powers to treat." They should have replied, "we will not say one Word in answer to any Proposition till We are recd and meet a Minister on Equal ground," Adams scribbled in the margins.[54]

Adams resigned himself to wait for the envoys' return to the United States to learn how their time in Paris had concluded. In the meantime, he prepared for the worst. The XYZ Affair, as the failed mission to France became known, would set the stakes for the remainder of Adams's presidency.

10

Massacre the Inhabitants

PRESIDENT JOHN ADAMS issued a proclamation setting aside May 9, 1798, for "Solemn Humiliation, Fasting and Prayer."[1] Drawing on a New England tradition of fast and repentance to protect against famine and disease, Adams encouraged all citizens to spend the day praying for "the safety and prosperity" of the nation in the looming crisis with France. As the sun rose over the banks of the Delaware River on the intended fast-day morning, Philadelphia was quiet. It would not remain so for long. Before the sun set, the warnings of political violence would prove prescient, provoking aggressive and punitive legislation designed to target citizenship, immigration, and free speech.

The poorest residents could ill afford to neglect their daily duties. Shopkeepers opened their doors and swept their hearths, housemaids emptied chamber pots into privies and back allies, clerks scurried to deliver their first batch of letters, stable hands mucked stalls and fed animals, destitute children picked through the trash for scraps they could use or resell, and sailors unloaded goods from ships at the docks.

A few hours later, the streets began to fill, as residents made their way to their various churches and religious institutions to hear sermons and give thanks. After the conclusion of the services, many men and women lingered to chat with friends and neighbors. Though spring was in full bloom, the crowds were adorned in somber tones for the day. Fripperies and adornments were frowned upon for fast days, with one key exception—the cockade.

Many attendees had selected the "American" cockade, a black fabric rosette with a white button at the center, pinned to men's hats and ladies' dresses. Others boldly chose the red, white, and blue tricolor cockade, which signified an allegiance to France and the Republican Party.

The tricolor cockade had been all the rage in the early 1790s when the French Revolution appeared to be the sister movement to the American

Revolution. Most Americans proudly displayed their tricolor cockade on every outfit, but as the French Revolution devolved into anarchy and indiscriminate violence during the Reign of Terror, many Americans' enthusiasm waned.[2]

In the rush of patriotism after the publication of the XYZ dispatches, citizens adopted the black and white cockade to demonstrate their loyalty to the United States and signify their distrust of France. For many, the tricolor cockade became a symbol of disloyalty and betrayal. While churchgoers mingled, they kept a watchful eye on the sartorial choices around them. As the crowds increased, hats with black cockades appeared to be congregating on one side of the city center, while a mass of tricolor cockades assembled at the other.[3]

Around 1 P.M., Adams, who had returned to the President's House after attending a service, heard a noise that sounded like a soft hum. As it grew louder, Adams started to detect marching and voices. He looked out the window from his second-story office and saw thousands of people gathering on Market Street, just a few feet from his front door. They were wearing tricolor cockades.

Adams quickly sent a servant to the Department of War offices two blocks away to obtain guns and ammunition.[4] While they waited for weapons, the servants closed the shutters, barricaded the doors and windows, and gathered buckets of water, in the event the mob turned to arson.

Returning down a maze of back alleys and lanes, the servant led a few War Department clerks, their arms full of heavy chests of weapons, to the President's House. They slipped through the back door and handed out muskets and shot to every man in the house, including the president. They took positions at the doors or windows and prepared to defend the house and their lives.[5]

Adams could hear the jeers and insults hurled from the mob and spotted a distinct change in the tenor. Peeking through the draperies, he noticed a mass of men with black cockades arriving from the opposite direction. They announced that they had come to protect the president and demanded the "Jacobin" rogues disperse at once.[6]

The tricolor mob responded with laugher, abuse, and threats, refusing to leave. The Federalists took a step forward, reached out, tore off the tricolor cockades from their opponents' hats and coats, threw them to the ground, and stomped them into the mud.[7] Their honor impugned, the Republicans ripped the black cockades from the gathered Federalists and ground them into the dirt as well.

Just as the mob, which Adams estimated was 10,000 strong, threatened to burst into a full-scale brawl, the militia and the light horse cavalry arrived. Better armed, and on horseback, the troops quickly dispersed the mob and restored order in front of the President's House. The inhabitants exhaled a sigh of relief but didn't dare let down their guard or venture outdoors for the rest of the day.[8]

The young men in the mob slipped down the countless alleys and lanes that made up the labyrinth of the city and hid in the dwellings and stables behind the stately houses. But they didn't go home. Some threatened the offices of newspapers, others brawled in small street skirmishes, and most consumed too much alcohol.

The following morning, Thomas Jefferson, ardent Francophile, leader of the Republican Party, and secret supporter of the tricolor cockade, wrote that the city was "so filled with confusion from about 6. to 10. oclock last night that it was dangerous going out."[9]

The next morning, May 10, most Federalists woke expecting to see the city in flames and thousands of people murdered in their beds. Instead, the buildings were intact, few residents were injured, and all was quiet, though tense. Philadelphians had every reason to expect violence and every reason to be relieved that it had not come to pass. Passions had been swirling for months, both in the papers and in the streets.

In the pages of the *Aurora*, Benjamin Franklin Bache had encouraged citizens to reject Adams's fast day, which Bache deemed a bid for absolute power. The only way to defy this tyranny, Bache argued, was to assemble and denounce it.[10]

The violence had begun in the halls of Congress a few months earlier when Representative Roger Griswold insulted Matthew Lyon's honor. In response, Lyon spat in Griswold's face. When Congress failed to banish Lyon, Griswold attacked him with a cane. The squabble ended in a full brawl on the floor of the House chambers, complete with wrestling and a duel with makeshift weapons.[11]

Taking cues from their political leaders, groups of volatile young men stormed the streets of the city, terrorizing editors and partisans. Bache's house and the *Aurora* press were attacked multiple times. The structures, and his wife and children hiding inside, were saved by neighbors who worked to prevent the spread of fire.[12]

Bache was also personally assaulted several times, including once by the son of his rival editor, John Fenno. Bache had bumped into John Ward Fenno on the street and called him a "dirty tool of a dirty faction." Fenno landed repeated punches to Bache's head, while Bache attempted to defend himself with his wooden cane.[13]

The Aurora hinted at a coordinated effort ahead of the May 9 mob, while more explicit warnings were printed in local newspapers and sent directly to the President's House. One letter, from "An Unfortunate Misled Man," cautioned, "it is the fix'd resolve of a very numerous party of Frenchmen (in conjunction with a few other *unsuspected Characters*) to set fire to several different parts of this City on the night of that day (in May next) which is set apart by you as a day of Solemn fasting & prayer." The conspirators plan to "Massacre man, Woman & Child, save those who are friendly to their interests," the anonymous letter writer alerted the president.[14]

"A Friend to America & Truth" penned a similar message to Adams, predicting that "all good men will shudder at" this plot. "Do not sleep in fearless security," the anonymous friend advised, "the hour of danger is near at hand. . . . Have an eye to the Frenchmen. Look to that grandest of all grand Villains—That traitor to his country—that infernal Scoundrel Jefferson—he has too much hand in the Conspiracy."[15]

Abigial also observed dark tidings of violence to come. Two weeks before the fast day, Abigail was visited by two young women. One had recently passed down the back alley behind the President's House and found a letter at "the Edge of a gutter." Abigail read the anonymous letter, which warned "that the French peeple who were in this city had formed a conspiracy, with some unsuspected Americans, on the Evening of the day appointed for the fast to set fire to the City in various parts, and to Massacre the inhabitants." Meanwhile, the *Gazette* had recently reported that several attempts had been made to set fire to the city of Charleston. A few days later, Abigail discovered that Representative Harrison Gray Otis had received a similar letter in Congress. The preponderance of evidence made it difficult to dismiss.[16]

The president was inclined to ignore the letters as attempts to rile up the people, but Abigail wrote to her sister, "I really have been allarmd for his Personal safety tho I have never before exprest it."[17] The president had no personal security, and anyone could walk up to the President's House. Political violence had repeatedly marked the streets of Philadelphia in recent months, and she had no reason to expect it to stop or spare her husband.

Out of an abundance of caution, Governor Thomas Mifflin dispatched armed patrols every night in May, ordered the militia at high alert, and placed guards at the local magazines and arms depots.[18] These preparations had proven necessary on the fast day, when roving mobs clashed in front of the President's House and militia enforcement prevented further violence. But many Federalists concluded these measures were insufficient to protect the republic over the long term.

The problem, many Americans concluded, is that there were too many immigrants coming to the United States, and they were the wrong sort of immigrant. In just one decade, 80,000 people emigrated from Great Britain, 60,000 from Ireland, and 20,000 from France and French Saint Domingue (now Haiti).[19] Most of the British and Irish immigrants were poor, in search of a better life for their families, and fleeing various rebellions. Most French immigrants, both white and Black, escaped the violence of the French and Haitian Revolutions. With few exceptions, they voted en masse for Republicans.

Both parties demonstrated xenophobia, but for very different reasons. Many of the French refugees came from wealthy, aristocratic families and brought enslaved servants when they fled. Republicans suspected the French refugees were still secret monarchists and were eager to restore their former social hierarchy. They also worried that the influx of enslaved refugees from Saint-Domingue would spark similar slave rebellions in the southern states.

On the other side, Federalists suspected that the Irish, who had recently attempted a failed uprising against the British Empire, would remain in league with conspirators at home. Not only would they funnel funds, ammunition, and information to Ireland to undermine the British, but they also would attempt an overthrow of the federal government on American soil.[20] Federalists saw a similar threat in the French emigre community. Although many had fled the French Revolution, Federalists feared they harbored equally radical tendencies. Once in the United States, they would join forces with the Francophile Republicans and conspire to destroy the union.

They weren't totally wrong. Many Irish immigrants had participated in the rebellion against the British, remained sympathetic to the cause, and retained connections to the network. They set up United Irishmen clubs, with the goal of supporting collaborators back home. They also founded and published newspapers that criticized the Federalists for their British sympathies and assumed an active role in local politics.[21]

For example, William Duane, a newspaper editor in Philadelphia, founded the United Irish Society to "promote the creation of Republican government in Ireland." He also organized and subsidized the "Greens," an armed militia company devoted to the Republican Party and comprised entirely of Irish immigrants.[22] Federalists feared that if the French army invaded American soil, the Greens might be called out to support their efforts.

Federalists also collected ample evidence of French schemes. The former French Minister, Pierre Adet, had engaged in prolonged and public interference in the 1796 presidential election. He had conspired with Republicans in New England, produced materials for their private use, and published addresses to the American people in Philadelphia newspapers.[23]

More recently, the envoys' dispatches from France shared warnings from one of the unnamed XYZ agents about the existence of a secret French party in America that was biding its time until it received commands from the French Directory.[24] After receiving the signal, it would revolt against the administration and partner with the invading French forces to seize control of the nation. The dispatches, including this threat, were shared with Congress and published for the nation to read.

Just a few weeks after the fast day riots, Bache published a letter from Charles-Maurice de Talleyrand, the French foreign minister.[25] Pickering had received the letter the day before, but his clerks were still hard at work decoding and translating the contents. The president hadn't read it.

Bache never revealed his source, but Pickering was convinced "it was transmitted to him, as I am very well informed, by Talleyrand himself, for the purpose of publishing it."[26] Regardless of his source, Bache clearly was well connected and could not be dismissed as a harmless rabble rouser.

Finally, Pickering was certain that he had obtained evidence that the French Directory had bribed members of Congress. In several secret sessions with Roger Gerard van Polanen, the Batavian minister to the United States, Pickering learned that Adet and the French consul general, Joseph Philippe Létombe, had paid up to $80,000 to several senators and representatives for inside information about congressional debates.[27] Pickering believed the bribes were just the beginning. What other plots were afoot?

President Adams reviewed all this evidence, combined with the publication of the XYZ dispatche, and the imminent return of the envoys, and concluded that war was on the horizon, from forces both foreign and domestic. Most Americans agreed.

When the XYZ dispatches reached the American public, Jefferson wrote to Madison, warning that "the impressions first made by those communications continue strong & prejudicial here. . . . [T]hey have also carried over to the war-party most of the waverers in the H. of R." He feared the crush of public opinion would lead to "great & dangerous follies."

On April 17, 1798, the first of these follies emerged from the House Select Committee to Consider Means for the Protection and Defense of the

Country. Representative Joshua Coit from Connecticut proposed a bill to suspend naturalization indefinitely.[28] During the House debates, Coit's colleague, Samuel Sitgreaves, bluntly admitted that the purpose of the bill was to "prevent them from ever becoming citizens" and to permanently reduce the number of Republican voters.

This extreme ban didn't sit well with moderate Federalists and horrified Republicans. Forming a temporary coalition, they forced revisions to the existing 1795 naturalization bill by extending the naturalization period from five years to fourteen years.[29] They included a provision that allowed current residents to apply for citizenship. The final bill also established a complicated process that required immigrants to register upon arrival and then proclaim their intention to naturalize years in advance. Failure to comply would delay citizenship and thus further prevent Republican voting.

Both parties had supported the naturalization bill in 1795. However, three years later, it was clear the legislation targeted one political base. On June 13, this legislation passed with the thinnest of majorities in the House, 41–40, along party lines.[30]

Jefferson confided in Madison that "one of the war-party, in a fit of unguarded passion declared some time ago they would pass a citizen bill, an alien bill, & a sedition bill." By mid-June the citizenship bill passed; Jefferson braced himself for what might come next.[31]

Fearing the extreme measures that might come out of the Federalist-dominated Senate, Republicans in the House proposed an Alien Enemy Act to preempt more radical legislation. The Republican bill would empower the president, in the event of war, to "apprehend, restrain, secure and remove" citizens of an enemy nation residing in the United States. The legislation exempted naturalized citizens and upheld the trial process by authorizing courts to convene hearings and impose sentences.[32]

While Federalists supported the Alien Enemies Act, it didn't go far enough to address the troublemakers they saw around every corner. A committee of Federalists in the Senate tabled the Enemies Act and proposed a much more radical Alien Friends Act. Their proposal allowed the president to "deport all such aliens as he shall judge dangerous to the *peace* and *safety* of the United States" and imposed harsh punishments on anyone that interfered.[33]

The Senate toned down some of the more punitive passages and passed the bill on June 8 on a party-line vote, 16 to 7. The bill then went to the House, where Albert Gallatin, a Swiss immigrant who had settled in western Pennsylvania, led the battle against the bill.

Gallatin attacked the constitutionality of the bill rather than the obviously xenophobic motivations or punitive provisions contained in the text. The Constitution had given the states the power to regulate aliens, Gallatin argued. Even if Congress decided to pass legislation, the current bill completely obliterated the right to trial by jury and left aliens "subject to the arbitrary control of one man only."[34]

Gallatin's best arguments were overpowered by the public fury provoked by the publication of the dispatches from France. Even hesitant Federalists were persuaded that more severe measures were required. The House moderated the text, but passed the bill, again along strict party lines, 46 votes to 40. James Madison called the final version "a monster."[35]

Federalists then realized they hadn't passed a war measure and returned their attention to the Alien Enemies Act, which languished in committee until early July. It was the only bill crafted by Republicans and adopted with bipartisan support. A version of this bill remains in effect today.[36]

Months earlier, as the Alien and Naturalization bills were introduced, Jefferson had lamented to Madison, "There is now only wanting, to accomplish the whole declaration beforementioned, a sedition bill which we shall certainly soon see proposed. The object of that is the suppression of the whig presses. Bache's has been particularly named."[37]

On July 4, while the president and the first lady celebrated the nation's birthday, the Senate passed a sedition law restricting freedom of speech. The bill had two purported goals: defend the government from insurrections and protect the nation from lies designed to provoke political violence.

The first section made it a crime to "unlawfully combine or conspire" to "oppose" a government measure, impede "the operation of any law," or "intimidate or prevent" an official from fulfilling his duties.

The second section made it a crime to "write, print, or publish" any seditious libel (in writing) or utter seditious speech. It defined sedition as speech or writing intended to "defame" the government, Congress, or the president, or to "bring them into contempt or disrepute," to "excite against them the hatred" of the America people, "to stir up sedition," to encourage others to oppose "a law or presidential act," to "resist, oppose, or defeat" any law or act, or to "aid, encourage or abet any hostile designs of any foreign nation."[38]

The legislation allowed truth as a defense, but most observers predicted that it would make little difference in court. Federalists had stacked the federal judiciary and appointed marshals who would pick juries hostile to Republicans. Perhaps more important, critics noted it was impossible to prove the veracity of a political opinion. The nature of an opinion is that it is personal and open to interpretation.

The Sedition Act effectively made campaign speech, political rallies, or partisan opinions illegal, which reveal the third, unspoken goal of the legislation—to crush the Republican Party.

Federalists saw 1798 as a turning point in a great battle between "good and evil on a scale almost without precedent since biblical times."[39] They were under attack, besieged from all sides by foreign forces in league with domestic collaborators, and they didn't trust the American people to come to their defense.

They started the year with genuine concerns about national security and offered compelling arguments about the trustworthiness of certain actors in cahoots with the French. They nurtured understandable dislike of Republican newspaper editors who spewed lies and perhaps libel. And they were operating under a legal framework that didn't protect against violent or violence-provoking speech.[40]

Federalists became so convinced of the existential nature of the threat and the righteousness of their cause, however, that they persuaded themselves that any and all measures were acceptable, and even required, to secure a victory against France and their domestic partners in the Republican Party. Even banning free speech.

As the Sedition Act made its way through Congress, Jefferson stopped writing about anything political—even to Madison. He couldn't risk postal workers intercepting his letters and using them as evidence of sedition. Senator Henry Tazewell noted the dark atmosphere when he wrote to Madison and promised to send "an account of whatever may occur that can be interesting . . . if I am not Guilotined."[41]

The final Sedition Bill, passed on July 10, protected Congress, the federal government, and the president. It did not mention the vice president. It would expire on March 3, 1801—the day before the next inauguration.[42]

President Adams had not asked for any of this legislation. He had not lobbied for it, nor had he instructed his cabinet to do so. And yet, when presented with these four bills, he signed them. He did not say why, but he wrote to Benjamin Chadbourn, a judge in Maine, "The Fate of our Republick is at hand."[43] Most republics fail when "the Virtues are gone," he theorized. "A free and equal Constitution of Government has rarely existed among Men," and requires constant vigilance to protect, Adams argued. They must watch for attempts by "the Minority [to cultivate] foreign Influence for support, and for assistance. To overthrow and take Vengeance on the Majority." These ruminations suggest that Adams saw the nation on the brink of destruction and was willing to accept radical measures to save it.

Adams had long feared that the republic would be short-lived, and he refused to oversee its collapse. Protective measures against internal threats seemed like a sound idea, especially because Abigail ardently supported them. In the spring of 1798, Abigail wrote to her sister that if the government did not suppress the radical Republican presses, "we shall come to a civil war."[44] The week before Congress passed the Sedition Act, she impatiently pushed for the legislation: "I wish our Legislature would set the example & make a sedition act, to hold in order the base Newspaper calumniators," she wrote. Once Congress passed the bill, she delighted in the defenses written by Pickering and other Federalists.[45]

Adams never revealed whether Abigail's advice was the deciding factor, but it often was. The choice would prove to be one of his worst errors of judgment and failures of morality in his lengthy public service career.

After signing the legislation, he largely turned his attention to other matters. The bills required him to approve all deportations, but he did not participate in the day-to-day pursuit of potential candidates or supervision of the presses for seditious material. He left those unsavory tasks to his secretary of state.

Pickering wasted no time. On July 7, 1798, he wrote to Richard Harrison, the US attorney for the New York District.[46] A newspaper in New York, the *Time Piece*, had printed a "most false inflammatory charge," Pickering claimed. The enclosed article alleged "that the executive in Communicating to Congress the letter from Mr. Gerry to the President, made additions & alterations in it to promote certain men in this country."

"I require you to examine the papers enclosed, as well as generally those of a similar seditious tendency," Pickering continued. "It appears that the Editor of the Time Piece is an Irishman & Alien, named John D. Burke." If Burke is "an Alien, no man is a fitter object for the operation of the Alien Act." Therefore, Pickering ordered, you will "ascertain this fact" and send me the proper evidence.

"If on the other hand he be a citizen," Pickering schemed, and "you should be of opinion, that the speech attributed to him is proved, & constitutes an offense against the law, you will institute a prosecution against him" under the Sedition Act. Pickering demanded a prosecution, but left it up to Harrison to decide which charges to bring.

"P.S.," Pickering wrote, "Altho Burke should prove to be an Alien, it may be expedient to publish him for his libels, before he is sent away: if the suffering of him to remain here until a Court competent to try the libels shall sit, will not be a greater evil than the libels unpunished."[47] It would be the first of many cases Pickering personally managed while he had free rein over sedition prosecutions.

While Congress debated potential legislation and Pickering pursued his political enemies, Adams's letters took a positive turn. He received hundreds of petitions and addresses from citizens across the country applauding his actions, condemning French treachery, and pledging their support in the event of war.[48] Over the next twelve months, he received over 300 petitions from civic organizations, state legislatures, college students, and social societies around the nation. Each address represented hundreds, if not thousands, of participants who voted to approve the text. The affection contained in the addresses cut across class, ethnicity, religion, and creed. All sixteen states sent their regards to the president, and no region was disproportionately represented. Western territories were as eager to proclaim their loyalty to the nation and affirm the unity of the American people as the Eastern seaboard. Even the *Aurora* was forced to admit that "the many addresses from different parts of the union" appeared to be a triumph for the Federalists and Adams in particular.[49]

The Boston region contributed over twenty addresses, but the one from the Massachusetts legislature was particularly gratifying for Adams:

> As a native citizen of this Commonwealth . . . we feel for you those sentiments of attachment and veneration, which the recollection of your long, distinguished, & successful services are calculated to excite.[50]

This tidal wave of support and popularity meant more to Adams than it would have almost anyone else. He had long toiled in Washington's shadow, often bitter that his hard work and sacrifice didn't merit the same adoration as military exploits. Thus, when the American people showered him with praise in 1798, he responded to every single letter, petition, and address. He knew many of his responses would be passed among family and neighbors, forwarded to friends, read aloud, or published. He took care with every word. No two responses were the same, and each received its own special treatment.[51]

Abigail did her best to support his efforts but confided in her sister the responses "have kept him at his pen three Hours in a day, upon an average for 5 or 6 weeks past." Despite these long hours, the president still had "more than 30 at this moment unanswerd." Abigail fretted, "he is really worn down. I never saw him so thin. Yet his Spirits are good, and his fortitude unshaken."[52]

The arrival of John Marshall increased Adams's determination. On June 18, word came that Marshall would enter Philadelphia the next morning. An official delegation, headed by "Sec^{y} of State & Mr Bingham in the latter Coach" and escorted by "three Companys of Light horse," marched six miles outside the city to meet him. A "Thousand spectators" in carriages, on horseback, and on foot followed the delegation, braving the hot and muggy weather to greet the incoming hero. On their parade back into town, all the "Bells in the City" rang to announce the procession's arrival. Marshall was "paraded through the streets" so the gathered crowds could catch a glimpse of the envoy before he was escorted to his lodgings at the City Tavern.[53]

Marshall's first order of business was to visit the President's House. The president and first lady offered an enthusiastic welcome; they were eager to hear every scrap of news from the last six months. Marshall did not disappoint. He had much to convey and an important letter to deliver.

The French had stumbled into the Quasi-War with the Americans, Marshall argued. Talleyrand and "the directory have been deceived with respect to the People of this Country," he explained. The Directory had assumed that the American people were much more divided, and they did not expect the United States to offer such unified resistance to French insults. Ultimately, Talleyrand and the Directory had no intention of restricting "our Rights and Liberties." Instead, they were motivated purely "from Interest. as they want our trade."

However, Marshall offered an important qualification to this good news. The French military victories had made the Directory "imperious haughty, and vindictive," Marshall observed. "They hold us in too much contempt to retreat from a single demand which they have made, or recede a single step."[54] Firm resistance to their bullying was the only possible option, Marshall counseled.

He then handed the president a letter from Elbridge Gerry. In it, Gerry explained that he had fully "expected my passport with my collegues" and had intended to leave France, but he was "informed the directory will not consent to my leaving" and his departure would "bring on an immediate rupture."

Gerry genuinely believed that his presence in France prevented the outbreak of war, but he knew enough to refuse to negotiate a treaty by himself.

Talleyrand wanted to "resume our reciprocal communications" and discuss the subject of a loan, Gerry explained. He assured Adams that he had objected to the loan and refused to enter negotiations until he received additional instructions from the president.

"I accepted of this mission, my dear Sir," Gerry continued, "to support your administration, & have brot myself into a predicament, from which you must assist me to extricate myself: by appointing some others to supply the places of myself & collegues, if a further progress in this business should be found practicable."[55]

The president thanked Marshall for bringing him the letter and praised his handling of the entire situation; he had served his nation well. Neither Marshall nor Adams left any written record of their conversation or indicated whether they met again for private consultations. But a warm working relationship had been established.

Over the next several days, nearly every leading figure in Philadelphia called on Marshall. On Saturday evening, one hundred twenty guests, including all Federalist members of Congress, dined at Oeller's Hotel to demonstrate their "affection, approbation and respect."[56] The sixteen rounds of toasts and endless speeches praised Marshall's "patriotic firmness with which he sustained the dignity of his country, during his important mission."[57]

On June 25, 1798, almost a year after he left, Marshall set out for his home in Virginia.[58]

Bolstered by Marshall's intelligence, Adams sent an update to Congress. "I think it my duty," Adams continued, "to communicate to you, a Letter received by him, from Mr. Gerry, the only one of the three, who has not received" his passport and departed from Paris. This correspondence, as well as the ongoing communications between Talleyrand and Gerry, "will shew the situation in which he remains, his intentions, and prospects—." By this time, Adams assumed, "he has received fresh Instructions (a copy of which accompanies this Message) to Consent to no Loans, and therefore the Negotiation, may be considered at an End." The president closed his message by promising to "never send another Minister to France without assurances, that he will be received, respected, and honored, as the representatives of a great, free, powerful and Independent Nation."[59]

Adams then instructed the secretary of state to write a very different type of letter.

"Sir, by the instructions dated the 23rd of March," Pickering wrote to Gerry, "You will have seen that it was expected that all of you would have left France long before those instructions could arrive." Surely, these instructions "reached you during the last month," as "six sets were transmitted, one by a dispatch boat" directly to France.

The French Directory had treated Gerry and the nation "with contempt." He should have turned his back on the French rather than permit himself to be separated from his fellow envoys, who were "men of such respectable talents, maintained honor and pure patriotism." The president and the country had entrusted all three envoys, but the French Directory had trampled on the "authority and dignity" of our government by "designat[ing] the Envoy with whom they would condescend to negotiate." Pickering concluded, "I am directed by the President to transmit to you this letter, and to inform you that you are to consider it as a positive letter of recall."[60] There was no further encouragement and no praise offered to soften the blow.

II

Decisive Measures

ON THE EVENING of June 22, 1798, John Adams finished his supper and climbed the steps of the main staircase to the second floor of the President's House. After a long day of meetings and hosting events, he was eager for sleep. But he had one more letter to write that couldn't wait for the morning. He dipped his quill into a pot of ink and carefully wrote,

> "Dear Sir,
>
> I have this morning received with great Pleasure, the Letter you did me the Honor to write me, on the Seventeenth of this month . . ."[1]

It was the first letter Adams had penned to his predecessor since taking office fifteen months earlier. Washington had written to invite the Adamses to stay at Mount Vernon if they planned to visit the new District of Columbia, which Congress had created a few years earlier to serve as the seat of government starting in 1800. Adams thanked the Washingtons for the invitation, before moving to much more serious business. If war with France broke out, the United States would need an army. Adams had never served in the military but would automatically become the commander-in-chief under the terms of the Constitution. He needed Washington's help and support but also risked ceding too much authority over the executive branch and the army. This battle to control the powers of the presidency would pit Adams against Washington, and the president against the cabinet. The outcome would have ramifications that reverberate into the twenty-first century.

Over the last few months, Congress had steadily marched toward war readiness. It had passed legislation to finally create a naval department, bulk up the nation's coastal defenses, and expand the new fleet.[2] As a proud New Englander, which served as the regional base for most sailing activity, Adams had long believed that a navy and a strong merchant marine were central to American economic success and national security. Both Washington and Adams had repeatedly recommended that Congress create a department of the navy, rather than leaving the activities to private citizens.

Initially, Adams nominated George Cabot as secretary of the navy. Cabot was an old friend and a Massachusetts native, but health concerns forced him to decline the position. Adams then turned to Benjamin Stoddert, a solid Federalist and merchant from Maryland.[3] Adams had known Stoddert since their time together on the Continental Board of War during the Revolution and he liked that Stoddert lived in Georgetown. Stoddert would be well-equipped to advise on the placement and construction of naval dockyards when the seat of government moved to Washington, DC, in just a few years. Stoddert's success as a merchant was also compelling because he regularly managed vessels as part of his business.

Perhaps most important, Stoddert wasn't Washington's appointee or loyal to Hamilton. He was his own man. By June 18, Stoddert had accepted the position, traveled to Philadelphia, and immediately began establishing the department. He commenced his official correspondence that very afternoon, before taking the oath of office as the first secretary of the navy the following morning.[4]

At the same time, Congress passed legislation empowering the president to call into service troops in the event of a declaration of war or an "actual invasion" of the United States. Initially, this Provisional Army was not to exceed 10,000 troops, but Congress quickly began discussing adding supplemental regiments to augment the forces. Congress also authorized the president to commission officers for the state militias and the Provisional Army.[5] Adams never requested an army, but the initial Provisional Army was far smaller than the 50,000-man force McHenry had suggested (at Hamilton's insistence).[6] The army would be summoned only in the event of an invasion, so Adams concluded it was relatively harmless, for the time being.

He was much more worried, however, about the public response to the direct tax which Congress passed to pay for the increased military expenses. The tax was levied on "dwelling-houses, lands and slaves." Enslaved individuals were taxed at 50 cents per person, and houses and land were assessed in

FIGURE 11.1 Benjamin Stoddert, Secretary of the Navy, May 1, 1798–March, 31, 1801. Portrait by E.F. Andrews. Courtesy of the Navy Art Collection, Washington, DC, US Naval History and Heritage Command Photograph.

proportion to the value of the buildings. It was the first direct tax passed in the United States and was progressive in its application.[7]

Adams sensed the pressure to prepare for war was building, both from Federalists in Congress and in the president's cabinet. Taking proactive steps, he wrote to Washington, "I have no qualifications for the martial part of it, which is like [*sic*] to be the most essential." One of the questions that vexed him was "whether to call out all the old Generals, or to appoint a young sett." Adams hoped Washington would be willing to provide feedback and advice. But most important, Adams wrote, "We must have your Name, if you, in any case will permit Us to Use it. There will be more efficacy in it, than in many an Army."[8] He wrote this letter to Washington without the cabinet's knowledge.

Adams understood the powerful symbolic value of Washington's affiliation with any political project. He admitted as much to Washington: "If the Constitution and your Convenience would admit of my Changing Places with you, or of my taking my old station as your Lieutenant civil, I should have no doubts of the Ultimate Prosperity and Glory of the Country."[9]

As the month ended, Congress continued its rumblings about a potential war declaration and the state of military preparedness. On the night of July 1, the Federalist senators gathered at William Bingham's mansion on Third Street, in the second-floor salon. Perched on ornate stuffed sofas, they strategized their approach for the final days of the congressional session.[10] The day before, Peleg Sprague, their Federalist colleague, introduced a measure in the House to allow US ships to capture all French vessels, regardless of whether they were armed. Thus far, American vessels had largely restrained themselves to self-defense, engaging French forces only when attacked. This proposal would have changed the nature of the Quasi-War, the current state of half conflict between France and the United States, to an offensive one.

Senator Bingham urged caution. If Congress passed this bill, the next step would be a full declaration of war. Uriah Tracy, one of the most militant voices, countered that the Federalists should embrace conflict. He suggested that Congress could pass the declaration on July 4.

Bingham disagreed. He supported "decisive measures" to defend the nation and had heartily backed the creation of the naval department. But a declaration without the president first calling for it seemed to go too far, he argued. The other moderates concurred. At the moment, the nation occupied the moral high ground as the victim of French aggression. A declaration might undermine public support, both at home and abroad.

Sedgwick, in his capacity as the unofficial Federalist whip in the Senate, "counted noses." Earlier in the spring, the Federalists had devised a new procedure to vote on proposals privately in their caucus at the Binghams' mansion before introducing anything publicly. If a majority supported a measure, they would all vote for it in the Senate as a show of unity. If a majority opposed the measure, they would not bring it to the floor.

On the night of July 1, Sedgwick employed this approach. He polled his members and concluded that a war declaration would fall short by five votes. Several members expressed reluctance, but Sedgwick suspected Bingham was the real impediment to a war declaration and the rest would follow his lead. Sedgwick shared these concerns with Pickering, who concluded that Bingham was no longer a dependable ally.[11]

Similar measures were underway in the House. There John Allen introduced a measure to declare war on July 4, forcing another caucus, this time on the House side. Joshua Coit of Connecticut and Samuel Sewall of

Massachusetts teamed up to defeat this measure without a roll call on the floor. The House also voted down Sprague's measure, 32 votes to 41.[12]

Coit's resistance earned him the ire of the pro-war forces in the Essex Junto. Stephen Higginson wrote Wolcott, "It is impossible for the government to get along whilst its friends are so divided and the opposition so firm and united. In times like the present," Higginson howled, "when dangers, novel in their kind and terrible in their aspect, press us on every side," he found it infuriating "to hear men talk of their independence, their candour, their love of conciliation, and their aversion to party like Mr. Coit." Sensing his colleagues' anger, Coit updated his will that evening. He wrote "July 4, 1798," on the previously undated document that he had drafted the preceding January—just in case.[13]

The fractures emerging in the Federalist Party revealed the increasing partisan pressure. Moderation was no longer allowed and party operatives reserved their most virulent rhetoric for colleagues who appeared to have gone soft or refused to toe the party line.

Federalist allies kept the president apprised of the pro-war developments in these gatherings. In Adams's next meeting with Pickering, he casually broached the subject of command: "Whom shall we appoint Commander in Chief?" he asked his secretary of state.

Pickering replied without hesitation, "Colonel Hamilton."

"Oh no," Adams replied, "it is not his turn by a great deal." There were many other generals with much more experience and higher rank, he explained. "I would sooner appoint Gates, or Lincoln, or Morgan," he said, referring to generals who had earned their high rank in the Revolution.

"Morgan is an excellent soldier," Pickering conceded, but he has "a broken constitution," and he "is utterly incapable of taking the field. As for Gates, he is now an old woman: and Lincoln is always asleep."[14]

Adams noted the vitriol in these criticisms and elected to say nothing. Their meeting ended without any further discussion of commanding generals. But that very same day, Adams wrote to the Senate: "I nominate George Washington of Mount Vernon to be Lieutenant General and Commander in Chief of all the Armies raised or to be raised in the United States."[15]

Federalists in Congress were stunned. This letter was the first they had heard of the nomination, and they had been caucusing nightly. They quickly scribbled notes and handed them to their clerks, who delivered them to Pickering and McHenry. The secretaries were equally flabbergasted. Pickering swore to his allies in Congress, "The president had never intimated to Mr Wolcott or me his intention" of naming Washington as commander-in-chief.[16]

Adams may not have discussed the move with his cabinet, but he did mull it over with Abigail. "Some were exerting every power and faculty for Col H——n," she wrote to her cousin, revealing the machinations behind the scenes. To counter these pressures, she explained, "the President decided without communication, and sent in the nomination of the old General."[17] Both Abigail and John concluded that Washington's appointment "stifled the Envy and Ambition, the thirst of power and command which was rising in a mass throughout the United States." Hamilton and his supporters, who "expected to have filled this place dare not publickly avow this disappointment," she gloated.[18]

Shortly after Adams sent the nomination to the Senate, he received Washington's response to his original letter. Washington pledged "as far as it is in my power to support your Administration, and to render it easy, happy & honorable, you may command me without reserve."[19] Adams had submitted the nomination before Washington had written this letter, but he was now reasonably confident that the general would not reject the position.

Buoyed by Washington's letter, Adams summoned McHenry to his office. He needed the secretary of war to travel to Mount Vernon and deliver Washington's commission in person. Adams sent McHenry as a sign of respect, but he also knew that Washington might have questions about the timing of the nomination. Adams asked McHenry to address Washington's concerns and convince him to accept the position.

After securing Washington's cooperation, Adams instructed McHenry to obtain the general's advice. "I wish to have his opinion of the man most suitable for Inspector General, and Adjutant General, and Quartermaster General." Washington's "opinion on all subjects must have great weight," Adams conceded.[20]

Adams repeated in his written instructions that "His Advice in the formation of a List of officers would be extreamly desirable to me. The Names of Lincoln Morgan, Knox, Hamilton, Gates Pinckney, Lee, Carrington Hand, Muhlenbourg, Dayton Burr, Brooks Cobb, Smith, as well as the present Commander in Chief may be mentioned to him, and any others that occur to you." Adams carefully worded his instructions. The president wanted advice but would have the final say in all matters.[21]

After meeting with the president, McHenry called on Hamilton, who had just arrived in Philadelphia. They spent several hours planning McHenry's trip to Virginia. Hamilton advised McHenry how best to approach Washington, what to say, and how to say it. Hamilton also handed over a sealed letter for

Washington and asked McHenry to hand-deliver it.[22] McHenry had a similar conversation with Pickering at the state department and promised to deliver a private letter to Washington from the secretary of state as well.[23]

In the early morning hours of July 9, McHenry departed from Philadelphia. In his bag, he carried three letters to Washington, from Adams, Pickering, and Hamilton. Hamilton and Pickering knew about the other letters. Adams did not.[24]

Two days later, a carriage carried McHenry down the long, circular driveway leading to Mount Vernon. Two enslaved men greeted McHenry at the guest house, took his luggage, and offered him a basin of water and a cloth to wash off the grime from the road.[25]

After freshening up, McHenry was escorted into the mansion, where he found the Washington family enjoying music and madeira after their supper. Although dinner had long been over, Martha Washington offered a few refreshments. Before heading to bed, McHenry handed the three letters to Washington.

The next morning, McHenry rose early, familiar with Washington's habits from their days in the Continental Army and the cabinet. He wasn't surprised to find Washington in his private study before sunrise, composing a list of potential names for the officer corps.

FIGURE 11.2 George Washington's Private Study, Mount Vernon. Courtesy of Mount Vernon Ladies' Association.

McHenry and Washington spent the next two and a half days in the former president's study.[26] Occasionally they left the room to dine with other visitors at Mount Vernon or to ride across Washington's plantation. But mostly they debated the merits of various candidates.[27]

They focused on three names: Charles Cotesworth Pinckney, Henry Knox, and Alexander Hamilton. Their ranking carried strategic implications. Because Washington planned to remain at Mount Vernon unless France invaded, the inspector general, or the second ranked officer, would exercise full operational control.

The problem, Washington acknowledged, was how much weight to give their military ranks from the end of their previous service. At the end of the Revolutionary War, Pinckney and Knox outranked everyone except Washington. Knox, a brilliant and innovative general of artillery, had been Washington's favorite officer. Hamilton had toiled as an aide-de-camp in Washington's household before finally securing a line command of his own. He had proven his value, but he still ranked far below the other two.

Events since then complicated matters significantly. Knox had served loyally as secretary of war for the Confederation Congress and then in Washington's administration. Toward the end of his tenure, however, he had lost Washington's trust during a domestic rebellion in western Pennsylvania. Knox rushed home to Maine to save his estate before it fell into bankruptcy and put his affairs in order relatively quickly, but then inexplicably dawdled.[28] Rather than returning to Washington as he had promised, he spent six weeks enjoying his land and his family.

Back in Philadelphia, Washington worried that something terrible had befallen his old, trusted friend. On October 1, 1794, Washington left Philadelphia and marched westward to meet up with state militias. He wrote to Knox with great sadness, "It would have given me pleasure to have had you with me & advantages might have resulted from it on my present tour, if your return, in time, would have allowed it."[29]

Washington accepted Knox's apology and when the secretary of war retired a few months later, they parted on good terms. But Washington never forgot that in a moment of crisis, Knox had put his personal needs above the duties of his office. Despite his utmost "love & esteem" for Knox, Washington no longer trusted him with the highest command.[30]

McHenry knew this history and preyed on it. He reminded Washington that Hamilton had only climbed in his estimation since the end of the Revolution. He had played an integral role securing the passage of the

Constitution, crafted a financial system that restored the national credit and economy, and demonstrated an unparalleled capacity for work.

Washington agreed that Hamilton's "services ought to be secured at *almost* any price."[31] But Charles Cotesworth Pinckney also deserved real consideration. During the Revolution, Pinckney served as a commander of the 1st South Carolina Regiment and led with distinction in the Battle of Brandywine and Battle of Germantown. After the war, Pinckney was promoted to a major general for his ongoing service in the South Carolina militia, making him one of the highest-ranking officers. Further, he gained additional prominence for his role in the XYZ Affair and his honorable diplomatic service on behalf of the nation. His loyalty was beyond question, and he was widely admired.

Pinckney's "connections [we]re numerous, powerful and more influential than any other in the three Southern States," which was an important asset in his favor.[32] Washington continued, "*If* the French should be so *mad* as openly, and formidably, to Invade these United States . . . their operations will commence in the Southern quarter" because this region was the weakest and most vulnerable to attack.[33] Pinckney's support in the South would be essential. If Pinckney refused to serve over a disagreement about rank, "disgust would follow, & its influence would spread" to the South.

McHenry suggested Pinckney might be willing to serve under Hamilton as they were close friends dating back to their time in the army. Perhaps the letters from Hamilton and Pickering offered some guidance, McHenry suggested, knowing full well what the other men advised.[34]

Hamilton elected to make no rank recommendations knowing his name was part of the conversation. Instead, he stressed the president's deficiencies and left the rest to his allies in the cabinet. "The President has no *relative* ideas & his prepossessions on military subjects in reference to such a point are of the wrong sort," Hamilton wrote. "It is easy for us to have a good army but the selection requires care," he warned.[35]

Pickering happily filled in the gaps. He wrote of his "extreme anxiety that our *army* should be organized in the most efficient manner." The president was disinclined "to place Colo. Hamilton in what we think is his proper station," Pickering relayed. But Hamilton "ought not to be, the Second to any other military commander in the U. States," other than Washington.[36] Hamilton could be abrasive, Pickering admitted, but "even Colo. Hamilton's political enemies, I believe, would repose more confidence in him than in any military character that can be placed in competition with him."[37] No one else had the capacity to do the job well.

After reading these letters, Washington conceded to McHenry that Hamilton would probably be his first choice. Additionally, "impediments to the return of General Pinckney, and causes unforeseen" might make it impossible for him to accept a position immediately. McHenry agreed that Pinckney's location was currently unknown, encouraging this train of thought.[38]

The next morning, Washington carefully wrote out his advice to the president and replied to a few important letters. Later that day, McHenry began his return to Philadelphia, carrying three letters from Washington.

To the president, Washington had written to officially accept the nomination. He knew how hard Adams had worked to avoid war, which was why he was willing to lend his support. "No one can more cordially approve of the wise and prudent measures of your Administration," Washington commended.

There was one caveat, however. "I shall not be called into the field until the Army is in a situation to require my presence, or it becomes indispensible by the urgency of circumstances." He hastened to explain, "I do not mean to withhold any assistance to arrange and organise the Army, which you may think I can afford." But he wanted to stay home as long as possible.[39] The letter did not mention his subordinate officers or any requirements about his staff, which would prove to be a critical silence in the following months.

Washington's letter to Knox was his most challenging. "I have placed you among those characters on whom I wish to lean, for support." There would be three major generals in the new army: "Colo. Hamilton, Genl Chas Cotesworth Pinckney and yourself," ranked in that order. Knowing that this ranking would cause great pain for his old friend, Washington was reluctant to take responsibility for this decision and instead hid behind "the public estimation," which preferred Hamilton. Washington then rushed to explain why Pinckney had to come second, reiterating his concerns about a French attack in the South and the Pinckney family connections.[40] Despite this hurtful news, Washington hoped "the difficulty will not be insurmountable, in your decision."[41]

Washington offered more positive updates to Hamilton. He listed the officers and their relative rank, then asked for Hamilton's advice. It is "my wish to put you first," Washington said, but he wasn't sure whether Pinckney "will consider a Junr. Officer?" My "fear of loosing him, is not a little embarrassing," Washington confessed.[42]

Ultimately, "it rests with the President" to make these appointments, Washington concluded—a position that was consistent with his previous approach to military and civilian authority.[43] In 1775, he had accepted a commission as the "Commander-in-Chief" of the Continental Army and spent the next eight years assiduously submitting to civilian oversight. He never challenged Congress's right to supervise the army and welcomed committees to observe conditions at winter quarters. He quickly responded to summons every time Congress demanded a report, either in writing or in person, even when it tested his resolve.[44]

The Confederation Congress also tempted Washington to abandon his commitment to republicanism on more than one occasion. At several moments, Congress gave Washington near unilateral authority to respond to the crisis. Washington employed that new power to seize food and supplies for his soldiers, but then he immediately handed back the special grant of force.[45] More famously, he returned his commission after the end of the war, and resumed life as a private citizen, breaking centuries of global precedent of military dictatorship.

As president, Washington had remained vigilant against any hint of blending civilian and military authority. In the fall of 1789, as Washington traveled to Boston, he refused to observe a series of military maneuvers by a local militia. He said could only "pass along the line" as a civilian leader of a country at peace.[46]

When rebels protesting a whiskey excise tax turned violent in 1794, Washington called up the militia from Pennsylvania, Maryland, Virginia, and New Jersey. He rode on horseback to meet them and conducted a thorough review.[47] All evidence suggests he remained in civilian dress. This sartorial choice declared a visible distinction between himself and the other military leaders. A few days later, the militias marched westward under the command of Alexander Hamilton and Henry Lee, while Washington rode back to Philadelphia. Perhaps he knew the optics would be poor if the president charged and arrested his own citizens. The message was clear: Washington was not a military commander.

Finally, Washington had willingly retired after two terms. He could have stayed in office for the remainder of his life—a king in all but name. Both Republicans and Federalists urged him to seek a third term, but he refused.

When Washington wrote to Hamilton that the president's authority remained absolute over the military, therefore, he was defending a position consistent with the actions and statements that defined his career over the last three decades. Just a few weeks later, Washington changed his mind.

On the morning of July 17, John and Abigail were eating breakfast in the family dining room when the secretary of war arrived. Abigail offered McHenry a seat at the table, but he declined, as he was still dusty from the trip. He had gone straight to the President's House to deliver the good news—Washington had accepted the appointment.

McHenry handed over the letter from Washington and pulled out a piece of paper with the list of officers and their recommended rankings. Adams quickly scanned the document, then handed it to Abigail. They both said they were pleased with the list.[48]

That afternoon, McHenry and the president drew up the appropriate paperwork for the nominations. As McHenry prepared to deliver the forms to the Senate, Pickering walked into the president's study and announced that "the Senate has just adjourned for the day" and the nominations would have to wait for the next morning. He then asked to look at the appointments, while he was there. Adams handed him the list.

Pickering was delighted to see Hamilton's name at the top, but asked if it was wise to appoint William Smith, the president's son-in-law, as the adjutant general. Adams's opponents might accuse him of nepotism, especially given that John Quincy Adams already had a position in the diplomatic corps. Adams waved away these concerns. The appointment was based solely on merit. Besides, Washington had listed him among the generals, not the president.

The next day, McHenry and Pickering returned to retrieve the documents and reiterated their concerns about Smith. This time, Pickering alleged that Smith's real estate speculation failures had tarnished his reputation beyond repair. Adams dismissed these claims and said, if financial failures were grounds to disqualify a candidate, then half the list and much of Congress would be ineligible.

Adams admitted he was also having second thoughts. Knox and Pinckney should surely be ranked higher than Hamilton since their years of service and seniority should count for something.

Panicked, both McHenry and Pickering pointed to Washington's letter and his list. They reminded the president that he had asked for Washington's input on the order of officers and this order is what Washington requested. Although he grumbled about it, Adams agreed to submit the list as written, but he left open the possibility that officers could appeal to Washington or a board of officers if they objected to their rank.[49]

McHenry and Pickering left for Congress Hall, determined to ensure the officer corps reflected the Essex Junto's preferences. Pickering walked upstairs to the Senate chambers and asked the clerk to summon several senators from their deliberations. In a small side room, he shared his concerns about Smith and urged them to vote against the nomination. "I spoke to so many, and with so little reserve," Pickering later confessed to John Jay, "that I thought it not improbable that my interference would eventually be known to the President." Pickering "chose to hazard [the president's] displeasure" because he believed Smith completely unworthy and unfit "to fill that important place." He said as much to the senators.[50]

Several of the senators were sympathetic to Pickering's anxieties, but they didn't want to embarrass the president. They agreed to try to convince Adams to withdraw the nomination instead.[51] That evening, Uriah Tracy, Benjamin Goodhue, and James Hillhouse, all members of the Essex Junto, called on the president and pleaded with him to remove Smith from consideration or perhaps make him a lower-ranking officer. The position of adjutant general was tasked with managing the army's correspondence and writing out all the general orders. That responsibility was far too important to entrust to someone who "had been a speculator and was a Bankrupt."

Adams challenged the senators "to look at the list" of officers. I think, you "would find many upon it who had been equally speculators and some whose circumstances were not more Eligible," he noted.

The senators changed tack. Smith was rumored to have played a role in the 1798 gubernatorial election in New York on behalf of the Republican candidate Robert R. Livingston. It was one thing for Smith's finances to be questionable, but his political loyalties must be beyond reproach.

Adams scoffed at these claims. He was persuaded there "could be no solid foundation" for the charges that Smith was a Republican, for "Gen^{ll} Washington had assignd to him that department." If the Senate "chose to negative him they had a right so to do, but he would not withdraw the nomination," Adams stated with finality.[52]

Sensing the president's obstinacy, the senators regretfully took their leave. The next day, the Senate voted on the nominations. The Senate rejected Smith's appointment. Every other officer was approved.[53]

Before the sun rose on July 25, the Adamses rode out of Philadelphia in their carriage. They told no one outside their household that they were leaving. The president purposely left the officer commissions unsigned.[54]

12

The "Majic" of His Name

THE TRIP NORTH to Quincy was the most unpleasant Adams could remember. He and Abigail had spent a week on the road, baking under the oppressive July sun. The dark walls of the carriage boiled the air, forcing them to rest every few hours at a local tavern. At each stop, Abigail removed her clothing and lay down to avoid fainting, while the horses, at risk of heatstroke, recovered in the shade. At night, they found every bed full at their usual stops. They laid pitiful mattresses, "not longer than one of [Abigail's] Bolsters on the floor," and tried to get comfortable.[1]

When they returned to the road, John was glum. The army weighed heavily on his mind and illustrated all the most perplexing challenges of his presidency. He had not wanted the army in the first place. He was keenly aware that Americans feared standing armies and those fears had been part of the cultural inheritance for generations of Americans. Many of the first white colonists in North America remembered the English Civil War, when two massive armies marched across England from 1642 to 1651, leaving death and destruction in their wake. Tales of fearsome armies were passed down to children around the family hearth and then brought to life a century later. In the 1750s, British regulars arrived on North American shores for the first time to seize French colonial holdings in Canada and protect British settlements from attack. But they also required housing, food, and supplies.[2] Like other soldiers, they came with a risk of violence, assault, and intimidation. After the British victory in the Seven Years' War, the regulars were left behind to guard the empire's expanded territory. The burgeoning costs of empire required new taxes and customs, which provoked colonial resistance and ultimately led to the American Revolution.[3] Fifteen years after the Revolution ended, when Congress created the Provisional Army, most Americans had lived through the British regulars, the much-detested taxes, and the war that had followed.

Now, the "Provisional Army" seemed poised to sabotage Adams's entire administration. Article II of the Constitution designates the president as commander-in-chief of the nation's forces and empowers him with the authority to give orders and appoint officers. Washington had enjoyed this authority completely. The Provisional Army forced Adams to discover if the same unqualified authority would be extended to him. Adams suspected that his command would be seriously undermined if Hamilton was installed as inspector general. On the other hand, Adams trusted his orders would be implemented if he installed Henry Knox in the upper echelons of the officer corps. Adams felt confident that Knox would keep him apprised of the army's development, but it was unclear if he would accept an appointment below both Hamilton and Pinckney.

The Senate had also rejected the nomination of his son-in-law, William Smith, as adjutant general. It was a personal embarrassment to be sure, but a strategic setback as well. Smith could have served as Adams's inside source of information for all army happenings, which was one of the main reasons he had been so unpopular with McHenry and Pickering.

Finally, the army also brought into stark relief the troublesome problem for Adams of serving as president while George Washington was alive. The Constitution was new and its meaning still under development. Politics were intensely personal. Any action Washington took, anything he refused to do, anything he said or didn't say, carried constitutional weight because of who he was and the position he occupied in the nation's imagination. He held all the leverage and there was nothing Adams could do about it.

How powerful was the president? Did he control the executive branch, or did he simply oversee cabinet secretaries who dominated their own fiefdoms? Did the Constitution place the army under his jurisdiction or was it managed by the top-ranked officers? The battle over the army's command structure compelled Adams to answer these questions and forced him to defend presidential authority.

All these concerns about the army's organization were temporarily banished from Adams's mind shortly after they arrived in Quincy in early August. The stress of the trip triggered an attack of Abigail's rheumatism, compounded with "Billious dierea" and "intermitting fever." She may have suffered from diabetes and the symptoms "baffeld the skill of [her] Physicians."[4]

For the next three months, Abigail left her room only a handful of times. The fever "depress[ed] her spirits" and deprived her of sleep, sometimes for days at a time. Weak from the ordeal, Abigail couldn't even write to her children. At the most perilous moments, John did not leave her side. "Her Destiny is Still very precarious, and mine in consequence of it," he confessed.[5]

As the president prayed desperately for his wife's survival, McHenry struggled in Philadelphia with his own "bilious fever." He was bombarded by letters and demands for action from all sides while on his sickbed.

McHenry was easygoing, honest, and loyal to his friends. He had served honorably as an officer in the Continental Army and had been Washington's choice for secretary of war in 1795, but the president quickly grew disenchanted with his abilities. McHenry was a good man, but he lacked the capacity to manage the demands of an executive department, and pretty much everyone knew it. Washington constantly urged McHenry, "In all important matters, to deliberate maturely, but to execute promptly & vigorously. And not to put things off until the morrow which can be done, and require to be done, to day."[6]

A few years later, McHenry was still the secretary of war, and Washington and Hamilton were still bemoaning his management of the department.[7] What had been a busy department during peacetime had exploded with details, decisions, and paperwork to build and outfit the Provisional Army, as well as the existing forces, and prepare for the impending war. As secretary, McHenry was responsible for the appointment of the entire officer corps, the logistics of recruitment, the organization of units, the design of uniforms, the development of supply lines, the construction of armories and factories to provide supplies, the purchasing of goods—among other duties. The limitations of eighteenth-century communication made his job harder. Letters took a few days to reach Washington at Mt. Vernon and Hamilton in New York, a week to reach the president in Quincy, and longer to reach Charles Cotesworth Pinckney in South Carolina. Then he had to wait for their responses.

All the cabinet secretaries observed McHenry struggling. Wolcott conceded to Hamilton that "Mr. McH's good sense, industry & virtues, are of no avail, without a certain address & skill in business which he has not & cannot acquire."[8] Defending himself, McHenry reminded Washington and Hamilton that they had imposed impossible conditions by demanding the right to review and approve any proposed course of action before he implemented a decision. While McHenry wasn't legally required to obtain their permission for every detail, it was a habit born from decades of subservience. Every decision was postponed by weeks until McHenry received Washington and Hamilton's letters containing their endorsement.[9]

Despite McHenry's valid point, Hamilton and Washington remained at their homes and kept up constant castigations of McHenry for his subpar execution. "I observe you plunged in a vast mass of details," Hamilton empathized.[10] Nonetheless, he urged McHenry to send Washington "frequent communications."[11] As commander-in-chief of the Continental Army, Washington had kept an eagle eye over every single detail of army organization and movement at headquarters. He continued to demand the same level of detail without being physically present—a nearly impossible request.[12]

At his wit's end, McHenry wrote to the president pleading for help, copying Hamilton's wording exactly. "I find myself plunged, in a vast mass of details," he lamented. He could offer "a general, but vigilant superintendence," but he couldn't manage all the new tasks while remaining responsible for "the permanent duties of the Department."

After making what he hoped was a compelling case, McHenry pleaded, "I hope Sir, after considering, this summary view, of a part of my business, that you will give me leave to call effectually to my aid, the Inspector General, and likewise General Knox; and to charge them with the management of particular branches of the service."[13]

At the same time, McHenry wrote to General Knox announcing that the President of the United States had appointed him "major General," and the Senate had confirmed the appointment.[14] "It may be proper to mention," McHenry added, "that the nominations to the Senate for General officers" were submitted "on the same day, and in the order, in which they appear in the annexed list."[15] Below this paragraph, McHenry wrote Washington's name, followed by the other generals. Henry Knox was third.

Knox had long expected an appointment and believed "our Country, is about to enter into a Contest in which its existence as an independent nation" would be tested. He replied to McHenry that he was "anxiously desirous, of endeavouring to serve my Country and its Government," but needed one clarification. Is the order of names "intended to establish, the priority of rank?" He reminded McHenry that under previous military rules, appointments "made *in the same grade and on the same day*, are to be governed by the former relative rank."

Knox referred to the system established by Congress during the Revolution, in which a series of factors determined an officer's rank, including length of service, previous experience, merit promotions, and geographic location. The states had jealously monitored the wartime promotions to ensure no one region had enjoyed a preponderance of high-ranking officers. Knox expected that his rank, as well as those of the other officers, would carry over from the previous conflict. In 1783, Knox had retired as the second highest-ranking officer behind Washington. Even if Hamilton received a massive promotion from lieutenant colonel to general in the interim, Knox should still rank first.[16]

These squabbles over rank reflected a deep commitment to honor culture. A man's reputation determined everything—every economic, educational, romantic, or employment opportunity. Accordingly, men defended their reputation with utmost vigilance. For military men, their ranks were irrevocably interwoven with their honor. A potential demotion would have been a huge insult to Knox. He hoped that the details could be sorted out to avoid "sensations of public degradation."[17]

After Knox mailed his reply to the secretary of war, he spent the next several days pacing around his house in Boston, anxiously awaiting the president's return to Massachusetts. As soon as he received word that Adams had settled back in Quincy, he rode south to meet with him.[18]

The president was relieved to see a friendly face as he struggled with Abigail's illness. After sharing family updates, Knox mentioned the purpose of his visit. "The names placed before mine, on the list are those of Generals Hamilton and Pinckney!" he protested.[19]

Adams confided his concerns to Knox, starting with his distrust of Hamilton's dangerous ambition. He much preferred to rank Knox first and believed he had the authority as president to make appointments. Adams had acceded to Washington's wishes under McHenry and Pickering's pressure because of his own military inexperience. Now that he had spoken to Knox, however, he felt empowered to assert his preferences.

For weeks, the president had mulled over the troublesome officer appointments, beginning to develop a strategy of delay and obfuscation. His conversation with Knox only strengthened his resolve to resist Hamilton's influence in the army.

Shortly after Knox's visit, Adams received McHenry's letter begging for help, which offered the perfect opportunity to reassert his control over the officer corps. Adams began by acknowledging McHenry's difficulties and the "importance" of the decisions on his plate. The secretary of war should feel free to "inform General Washington, that I consider him in the Public Service from the Date of his Appointment and intitled to all the Emoluments of it." Hopefully, Washington could be of some help to the beleaguered secretary of war.

However, Adams continued, he had changed his mind, and the ranks were unsettled.[20] New England would be insulted if Knox, a native son, was listed below Hamilton. "In my Opinion," he wrote to McHenry, "as the matter now Stands, General Knox is legally intitled to rank next to General Washington, and no other Arrangement will give Satisfaction." If Washington consented to Knox serving as his number two, Adams authorized McHenry to call the generals into immediate service. However, if McHenry chose "Any other Plan," he would bring upon himself "long delay and much confusion. You may depend upon it," Adams threatened.[21]

McHenry received the president's reply on August 22. Panicking, he rushed to Pickering's department of state offices with all the correspondence between Washington, Hamilton, Knox, and the president from the past several months. Pickering notified Hamilton and advised him to reach out to Washington immediately to ensure the old general held firm. They needed to be sure Washington didn't acquiesce to Adams's demands.

From Philadelphia, Pickering and McHenry would work on the president.[22] They spent the afternoon poring over the pages and pages of letters, looking for some wiggle room. McHenry recounted his visit to Mount Vernon. Based on his recollection, McHenry was convinced "that Genl. W. made [Hamilton's] appointment the *sine qua non* of his accepting the chief command."[23]

Reviewing the correspondence, they saw that Adams had written that the change in rank depended on Washington's "opinion and consent." Here was their opening, Pickering suggested. Washington must insist on Hamilton's rank and force Adams to back down. They needed to turn Washington against Adams and box the president into a corner.

First, McHenry replied to the president, protesting the change. He reminded Adams that the order of the generals had originated "exclusively from General Washington." Furthermore, Washington had insisted that he retain "the right to name the General officers & general staff" as one of the conditions of his acceptance of command.[24] After McHenry finished his letter to Adams, he began another to Washington.[25]

Pickering drafted a few messages of his own. He wrote to Washington complaining that Adams's personal animosity toward Hamilton had warped his mind. He criticized Knox as unpatriotic for threatening to withhold his service if he did not receive the top rank. Pickering also assured Washington that "Colo. Hamilton's" absence would be "*an irreparable loss,*" whereas Knox would not be missed according to every "man of information."[26]

Then Pickering wrote to Hamilton again. When the fight over ranks had started at the beginning of the summer, Hamilton had been willing to serve under Knox. Pickering insisted that Hamilton must not reveal this flexibility to Washington, or it would threaten their whole plan. Hamilton agreed.[27] After their first round of subterfuge, they sat back and waited for the president to respond.

While their letters made their way to Quincy, the secretaries were forced to quickly pack their belongings, as well as crates of department papers, and flee the city. Yellow fever had arrived. Yellow fever is a mosquito-transmitted virus that attacks the liver. In the eighteenth century, it was highly contagious and there was no cure. McHenry, Wolcott, Stoddert, and Pickering found lodging and temporary office space in Trenton. Most wealthy residents in Philadelphia escaped to their other homes, rented space in the country, or joined the department secretaries in nearby towns. "Our city is in the deepest mourning!" one New York City resident cried. "Our number of deaths to the 1st of this month exceed 1400."

Philadelphia was in "a much more deplorable state." The fever baffled "all medical skill" and many of the leading physicians fled, leaving the sick and poor to die without care. The city, which boasted over 50,000 inhabitants before the fever, had dwindled to only 7,000. "All private business is at an end, and nothing but distress, deep distress, prevails in that quarter," one observer concluded somberly.[28]

One afternoon when Adams briefly stepped away from Abigail's sickbed, he read about the horrific scenes in cities up and down the Atlantic coast. His heart ached for those who lost their loved ones or couldn't afford care when they needed it most. He wrote to Wolcott and asked the secretary of the treasury to draw $500 against his salary to help ease "the distress of the poor." He asked Wolcott to make the donation anonymously and "to let nobody know but yourself, from whom it comes."[29]

Adams then dragged his attention back to the officer ranks and wrote a reply to McHenry's letter. He reminded McHenry that Washington had acknowledged in his correspondence that "these points must ultimately depend upon the President." Adams had requested Washington's input, but "the power & authority is in the President. I am willing to exert this authority at this moment and to be responsible" for the consequences. Therefore, he concluded, it was his duty to "determine it exactly as I should now—Knox, Pinckney & Hamilton."

Adams closed by revealing that he was aware of the chicanery taking place behind his back. "There has been too much intrigue in this business both with

General Washington & me" and he had no intention of becoming "the dupe of it."[30]

After weeks of waiting, Pickering and McHenry finally received this much-anticipated response from the president. "I shall follow the order you prescribe," McHenry wrote to Adams, discomfited. But he insisted that he had "never even contemplated" any intrigues. Perhaps he protested a bit too much. McHenry babbled on, offering to "immediately retire," if Adams suspected him of such trickery.[31]

An exasperated Adams read this letter. No, he did not want McHenry to resign, the president assured his secretary of war. If Adams had sought that outcome, he would have asked for it. However, Adams continued, "I have Suspected . . . that extraordinary pains were taken" to persuade him that all Federalists demanded Hamilton as commander-in-chief. Once McHenry was convinced, he then expressed "this opinion to General Washington more forcibly" than he should have, coloring Washington's approach to the officer ranks. Adams was sure that Hamilton and Pickering had planned the conspiracy and connived to use McHenry as a pawn. Adams's hunch for how the scheme developed and who was behind it were shockingly accurate.[32]

Nonetheless, Adams concluded, the whole episode was behind them. He reassured McHenry, "I have no hard Thoughts concerning your Conduct in this Business." As far as the president was concerned, the matter was finished, and the delay had only postponed the army's development, which he preferred anyway.[33]

Back in Trenton, Pickering dispatched a flurry of letters enlisting allies in New England. He wrote to George Cabot, begging the Massachusetts Federalists to contact the president in support of Hamilton.[34] Pickering hoped Cabot's words would carry weight, given that he had been Adams's first choice for secretary of the navy a few months earlier.

Within days, Cabot happily joined the fray and sent a letter to Adams, intending "to prevent *a possible embarrassment* to the administration of our government." He urged Adams to ignore Knox's concerns about ranks and claims about Revolutionary-era military rules. Instead, Cabot argued, the appointments should be made based on aptitude. "On the comparative merits & talents of Hamilton and Knox I am well persuaded" that "the most enlightend men through New England" all prefer Hamilton. Cabot refused to apologize for any perceived interference, sure that Adams would understand his motives and forgive the impertinence.[35]

While Pickering's Essex Junto allies attempted to persuade the president to reinstate the order of appointment in Hamilton's favor, he urged McHenry to write to Washington at Mount Vernon, this time with more urgency. "The President is determined to place Hamilton last and Knox first," McHenry alerted Washington. "I know not how it will be received by Hamilton, and can only hope, that he will not refuse to serve."[36]

McHenry had good reason to be worried. While Hamilton had previously expressed willingness to serve under Knox, he had since changed his mind. The promise of military command and glory was too appealing and almost within his grasp: "My mind is unalterably made up. I shall certainly not hold the commission on the plan proposed."[37]

A few days later, McHenry wrote to Washington yet again. This time he enclosed copies of his private correspondence with the president and Knox, neither of whom knew that McHenry was sharing their confidential letters with Hamilton, Pickering, and Washington.[38]

After weeks of back and forth, Washington finally threw down the gauntlet. He informed McHenry that he would assert his right to appoint his own officers in the order he wished, or he would refuse his commission as Commander of the Armies.[39] It was one of the worst choices made by Washington in his long and storied public career. He was so thoughtful about the presidents that would come after him and the precedents he established in the abstract, but when it came time to support the real person who followed him, he fell short. Washington had spent decades fiercely protecting civilian command over the military and bolstering the power of the executive. In one stroke, he actively undermined the presidency, belittled executive authority over the military, and undercut Adams.

For their part, McHenry and Pickering were delighted to finally have their ultimatum in hand. That same day, they met to draft a joint address to the president. They tasked Wolcott with writing the letter, as he had "been absent in Connecticut from a day or two after Washington's nomination, until the Senate had adjourned." Adams could not suspect him of "*intermeddling* in the primary arrangements."[40]

On September 17, Wolcott posted his lengthy letter to Adams detailing all the reasons that prior rankings shouldn't apply. He assured the president that Hamilton's appointment would be popular with New Englanders and not perceived as an insult to Knox. Finally, Wolcott argued that Washington had agreed to serve with the understanding "his opinion on all subjects would have great weight." To go back on that pledge would be inappropriate.[41] A few days later, McHenry followed this warning with his own letter containing Washington's threat.[42]

In Quincy, the president read this pile of letters with growing outrage. Washington had said nothing about officer nominations being a condition of his acceptance of the position of commander-in-chief. He had only asked that he be allowed to stay home until a war began; Adams had happily obliged him.

Now, McHenry, Wolcott, and Pickering claimed that Washington had made additional demands, causing Adams to wonder if they intentionally withheld that information. He was certain that he never would have agreed to hand over all nominations. The Constitution gave the president complete authority over the armed forces, and Adams resented any attempt to limit that power.

Furious, Adams wrote out a response to Wolcott. He then set it aside and went for a walk around his property. Upon his return, he wrote "do not send" in the corner of the draft. Like he had so many times before, Adams used quill and paper to vent his frustrations, then wisely thought better of sending the emotional letter.[43] He never responded to Wolcott.

Adams knew he had a short fuse and a tendency to respond rashly. When provoked, Adams was at his worst—petty, jealous, and vain. But when given the opportunity to process his thoughts, he could be a master politician. This deft handling of the letters is even more remarkable given that Adams didn't have Abigail's support. She had survived the worst of her illness but was still weak and struggled to sleep. He didn't want to burden her or cause further upset with these troubles. They may have discussed the army briefly but did not pore over every detail together as usual.

The letters from Hamilton's supporters were even more insulting. Adams and Cabot had been friends since they had drafted the Massachusetts constitution together in 1780, and now Cabot had the audacity to lecture the president. Cabot and the others would not have dared hurl the same insult at Washington. Adams wrote "not to be answered" on the top of Cabot's letter.[44]

On September 30, Adams received the letter from McHenry, including Washington's threat, and finally comprehended the full scope of the plot. He also realized that he had been outmaneuvered. He could fight the cabinet and win, but he could not risk Washington resigning his commission. If Adams wanted to unite the nation, he would have to swallow the humiliation and surrender to Washington's demands.

That evening, he signed all three commissions and included a terse note:

> "Inclosed are the Commissions for the three Generals Signed and all dated on the Same Day. I am sir / your most obedient &c"[45]

He refused to write the words "Hamilton is ranked first," but the intent was clear.

Eight days later, he received a letter from Washington, which stated that he had "*accepted* and *retained* the Commission" on the grounds that he would have the authority to name his own officers. Washington pointedly asked whether the president's decision "to reverse the order of the three Major Generals is final." He did not explicitly threaten to resign, but the meaning was obvious.[46]

The letter was an attack on presidential prerogative that Washington would never have permitted while he was in office. He broke his own precedent, established dangerous new expectations for future presidents, and personally threatened his successor's ability to lead.

As president, Washington had determined the command of American forces, first appointing General Arthur St. Clair as commander of the army, and then replacing him with General Anthony Wayne once Clair proved incompetent.[47] He also determined the composition of the subordinate officer ranks. Now, Washington was arguing that he, as the highest-ranking general should manage the army, even though he was no longer elected or directly responsible to the American people. Washington could probably be trusted with that enormous authority, but it created a dangerous precedent for future generals who might be tempted to exploit the power for more devious purposes.

Washington understood his unparalleled stature. Henrietta Liston, the wife of the British minister, correctly observed that "such was the majic of his name that his opinion was a sanction equal to law."[48] He had used that power and influence with great effect to help foster legitimacy for the first peaceful transfer of power and the Adams administration. Now his resignation could fatally cripple Adams's presidency. He was either actively undermining Adams or recklessly naïve.[49]

Adams sensed the nature of the danger posed by Washington. He had resolved to deal with the army as a threat and refused to accept any diminution of presidential authority. He penned a friendly reply to his predecessor, determined to maintain Washington's goodwill. He replied, "I presume, that before this Day you have received Information, from the Secretary at War, that I some time ago signed the three Commissions and dated them on the same day."

But he saw the situation clearly and made sure Washington knew it. Adams reminded Washington of the enormous power he had formerly enjoyed over the army and hinted that Washington was depriving his successor of the same control: "There is no doubt to be made, that by the present Constitution of the United States, the President has Authority to determine the Rank of Officers.[50]

13

The Tocsin of Insurrection

WHILE ADAMS GRAPPLED with his secretaries over generals and ranks in the army, Thomas Jefferson was home with no constitutional responsibilities. Congress was out of session, there were no tie-breaking votes to cast, and he had a lot of free time to fill. Initially, Jefferson was content to wait out the Alien and Sedition Acts with the rest of the Adams administration, confident voters would punish Federalists in the upcoming elections and entrust Republicans with power. When one of his friends predicted that "the southern states must lose their capital and commerce—and that America is destined to war" because of the standing armies and oppressive taxation, Jefferson encouraged "a little patience and we shall see the reign of witches pass over, their spells dissolve." The people will recover "their true sight," he reassured fellow Republicans, and "restore their government to it's true principles." In the meantime, he recognized, the people were "suffering deeply in spirit, and incurring the horrors of a war, & long oppressions of enormous public debt," but disunion would be much worse. "Better keep together as we are," he counseled.[1]

Over the summer, however, two developments forced Jefferson to adopt increasingly militant responses to the administration's legislative agenda. On July 9, the House of Representatives passed a bill adding twelve regiments, or 50,000 soldiers, to the existing United States Army. This force was separate from the Provisional Army, which would only be summoned in the event of war.[2] The bill remained stuck in committee in the Senate, but it lingered on the horizon menacingly.[3]

Then, over the summer, district attorneys brought a series of indictments against leading Republicans in the first wave of sedition prosecutions. On June 26, Pennsylvania officials arrested Benjamin Franklin Bache, editor of the infamous Republican newspaper, the *Aurora*, at the request of Secretary of State Timothy Pickering. Bache was charged with seditious libel of government officials.[4] Bache argued his case in the pages of the *Aurora*, refusing to flee the yellow fever outbreak in Philadelphia. His case was never resolved because he died on September 10, 1798, one of thousands of victims of the latest outbreak of the pandemic. But it presaged many of the prosecutions to come.[5]

In October 1798, Representative Matthew Lyon of Vermont was indicted for sedition for publishing letters and campaign speeches critical of the president and the Senate. His trial on October 8 was a farce, even by eighteenth-century standards. Justice William Paterson presided and refused to permit the jury to consider the law and facts. Instead, he instructed them on how to convict Lyon, who was sentenced to four months in jail and a hefty fine of $1,000.[6]

Virginians saw the high-profile sedition prosecutions, increased taxes, and the threat of a standing army as evidence of a systemic, coordinated plot. On their own, each Federalist policy was tolerable, but taken together, they posed a diabolical threat to civil liberties. At any moment, the army might march south, enforce the draconian laws, and harass Republican candidates. In small towns from Vermont to Georgia, citizens submitted petitions protesting the recent tax. They often nailed a copy of the petition to posts and doors of nearby taverns. When those calls for reform went unanswered, angry citizens hoisted "liberty poles" in their town squares. At the base, they frequently placed an American cockade—the black rosette associated with the Federalist Party—and doused it with tar and feathers. These practices intentionally borrowed from Revolutionary Era resistance. Colonists had hoisted liberty poles to protest British imperial rule and patriots had frequently applied tar and feathers to tax collectors to dissuade other officials from enforcing the laws. Two decades later, citizens raised liberty poles to invoke the memory of the Revolution and to protest the new taxes.[7]

Jefferson himself concluded that if congressmen and leading newspaper editors were at risk, he might be next. He devised a plan to combat the threat posed by the Alien and Sedition Acts, starting with a series of resolutions that called for collective action by the states.

What type of collective action, however, was a complicated question. Jefferson believed the Alien and Sedition Acts unconstitutional, but they were passed through the duly approved constitutional process. In the 1770s, colonists had protested British taxation policy, complaining they had no voice in the legislative process. The same rationale could not be used in 1798, when Congress had passed the Alien and Sedition Acts over the objection of the Virginia delegation.

Instead, Jefferson struggled to define a new method to reject unconstitutional legislation with no precedent or model to follow. His drafting process reveals the convoluted development of his thinking. He drafted six resolutions on one piece of paper. Perhaps the next day, he returned and penned two more on another sheet. Little scraps of paper contained scribbles that would become one more resolution. He scratched out various words and phrases, inserted new thoughts, and sometimes went back and crossed them out again.[8]

Sometime in late September, Jefferson compiled these edits and wrote out all nine resolutions, cleanly, on one piece of paper. He mailed them to Wilson Cary Nicholas, who was a friend, a distant cousin, and his representative in the Virginia House of Delegates. He instructed Nicholas to share the resolutions with a receptive member of the North Carolina legislature as soon as possible. Either Jefferson worried the resolutions would be attributed to him if published in Virginia, or more likely, there was already another plan in the works for his home state.[9]

Nicholas received the draft in early October. Whether the contents of the letter and the resolutions were a previously discussed plan or a surprise to him remains a mystery. Whatever his immediate reaction, Nicholas supported the endeavor, as did his house guest.

Nicholas received the letter while he was hosting John Breckinridge.[10] Breckinridge was born and bred in Virginia, studied at William and Mary with Nicholas, and served alongside him in the Virginia House of Delegates.[11] In 1793, Breckinridge moved to Kentucky and won election to the state legislature four years later. He had spent the previous few weeks at the hot springs for his health and was visiting Nicholas on his trip home.[12] Nicholas immediately recognized the opportunity—an influential member of the Kentucky House of Representatives was sitting in his parlor at the exact moment that he was searching for a sympathetic ally.

After obtaining the most "Solemn assurances" of complete secrecy, Nicholas shared the resolutions with Breckinridge and asked if Kentucky would serve as a friendly venue for the resolutions. If so, would Breckinridge shepherd them through the adoption process? Breckinridge was enthusiastic and eager to contribute, but he wondered aloud if he should visit Jefferson to obtain his permission before designating Kentucky as the appropriate theater for action.

After mulling over this suggestion, Nicholas counseled against a visit. He would write to Jefferson to explain the situation and vouch for Breckinridge's trustworthiness. In the meantime, they agreed Breckinridge should avoid

Monticello to be sure that the resolutions were not attributed to the vice president.

On October 5, Jefferson received Nicholas's letter.[13] He immediately replied and expressed his approval for the happy turn of events. "I understand you intend soon to go as far as mr Madison's," he continued. "You know of course I have no secrets for him. I wish him therefore to be consulted as to these resolutions."[14] Jefferson's part was finished for the moment.

Ten days later, James Madison arrived at Monticello to confer about next steps. He had stopped at Nicholas's home on the way to Monticello, and the congressman had apprised him of the new arrangement. Perhaps Madison and Jefferson agreed at this meeting that the younger partner would draft resolutions for submission in Virginia, or maybe they had established that plan when visiting together in July.[15] Either way, Jefferson hired a trusted messenger to safely carry a copy of the resolutions to Madison for his review while he drafted the Virginia version.[16]

Meanwhile, Breckinridge got to work as soon as he arrived home in Kentucky. He made a few substantive changes to Jefferson's draft to tone down the fieriest passages with the most radical implications to increase the likelihood the proposal would pass.

In the eighth resolution, Jefferson had called for a committee of correspondence to communicate between the states. Breckinridge immediately noted the parallels between Jefferson's proposed committee and the committees of correspondence that had spearheaded the resistance in the years prior to the Revolutionary War—parallels he was eager to avoid. Instead, Breckinridge inserted a new clause calling for the resolutions to be transmitted to the state's representatives and senators in Congress, and for the governor to communicate the resolutions to the legislatures of the other states.[17]

Breckinridge also tempered Jefferson's language on the states' power to respond to national legislation. Jefferson had insisted that each state had the "natural right" to nullify legislation and to thwart enforcement of the offensive acts, in this case the Alien and Sedition Acts. Breckinridge was unwilling to go that far. His updated version declared that the acts were "unauthoritative, void, and of no force," but the word nullification was stricken.

On November 7, Breckinridge entered the chambers of the Kentucky House and gave notice to the clerk that he planned to make a motion the following day. The next morning, he moved that the House go into the Committee on the Whole to consider his resolutions.

After brief debate, the resolutions were laid on the clerk's table. Over the next two days, they were read aloud twice. On November 10, the House passed the resolutions with only three dissenting votes. Three dates later, the Kentucky Senate passed the resolutions unanimously. The governor, James Garrard, promptly expressed his approval and distributed the resolutions to the other states.[18] Breckinridge had fulfilled his pledge: the Kentucky legislature passed the resolutions before the Virginia legislature commenced its next session.[19]

While Jefferson's resolutions made their way through the Kentucky legislature, Madison crafted his own version. Madison was the first to credit Jefferson with genius, but he was also the first to recognize his friend's tendency for the dramatic. Madison hated the Alien and Sedition Acts just as much as the next Republican, but he urged a more cautious approach.

The Virginia Resolutions opened with a firm pledge to the Union. Rather than challenging the legitimacy of congressional action, Madison insisted that citizens protest "every infraction" of constitutional principles. He condemned the Alien and Sedition Acts as unconstitutional but offered no explicit recourse. The resolutions expressed a wish that the states, including Virginia, would take "the necessary and proper measures" to combat the bills. He did not specify what those measures should be; the people should decide.[20]

After Madison completed his draft, he handed it to Wilson Cary Nicholas, who would be traveling to Richmond for the upcoming legislative session. Before Nicholas left his home in Albemarle County, he called on the vice president to pay his respects. He also shared Madison's draft.[21]

A few days later, Jefferson wrote to Nicholas, requesting one key edit. "The more I have reflected on the phrase in the paper you shewed me," Jefferson shared, "the more strongly I think it should be altered." Instead of inviting the states to cooperate in the annulment of the legislation, the resolutions should "declare, that the said acts are, and were ab initio—null, void and of no force, or effect.'" Jefferson concluded, "I should like it better."[22] Eager to please, Nicholas complied with Jefferson's suggestion. He added the phrase "null, void, and of no force" without consulting Madison.

On December 3, the Virginia General Assembly opened its new session. One week later, John Taylor of Caroline, another distant cousin, introduced the resolutions drafted by Madison but significantly altered to reflect Jefferson's wishes. A copy of the resolutions made its way to Philadelphia, where the Republican *Aurora* published them on December 22 with Jefferson's critical words: null, void, and of no force.[23]

The Federalist reaction was swift. As the Virginia Assembly debated the resolutions, Theodore Sedgwick wrote to Rufus King in London that the resolutions would "doubtless pass both houses, and [were] little short of a declaration of war."[24]

The Federalists could not be certain who had authored the resolutions, but they had their suspicions. By December 13, Jefferson still had not arrived in Philadelphia for the new session of Congress and his absence attracted notice. William Hindman, a Federalist representative from Maryland, theorized that Jefferson, "the Fountain of Mischief in this Country," remained at Monticello to attend "the Legislature in Virginia, to aid Taylor, Giles & Junto in plotting some diabolical Plan against the Federal Government."[25]

Across the Atlantic, John Quincy Adams read the resolutions with disgust and frightening clarity. He wrote to William Vans Murray that the resolutions are "certainly meant as the tocsin of insurrection." Unlike some of his more histrionic colleagues, John Quincy doubted Virginia would withdraw from the Union in the near future. "Things appear to me very far from being ripe for the serious struggle," he reassured Murray. They might be spared for the moment, he prophesized, but that struggle "must, indeed, some day happen between the Ancient Dominion and the Union."[26]

A flurry of letters flew between Federalists closer to home. Samuel Henshaw relayed to Sedgwick that his neighbors in Massachusetts viewed the resolutions as nothing short of "withdrawing themselves from the Union."[27] Hamilton was more direct. He demanded of Sedgwick, "What, my Dear Sir, are you going to do with Virginia?"[28] The threat posed by the resolutions and the potential responses from Congress set the stage for one of the most dramatic legislatives sessions yet.

In every official document Madison crafted, he was specific and measured in his rhetoric. From his home at Montpelier, he immediately noticed Jefferson's inserted clause in the Virginia resolution and was not surprised that the additional language drew the hottest reaction in the House discussions. Madison had eliminated nullification rhetoric for good reason, knowing it would be an unnecessary distraction.[29] He left no record of his reaction to Jefferson's edits, but almost certainly objected both to the new language and to Jefferson's interference without talking to him first.

For two weeks, the Virginia House was roiled by contentious debates.[30] Republicans held the majority, but a vocal, determined Federalist minority put up a fight. Quietly, on the morning of December 21, 1798, Taylor removed the most offensive language and returned the proposal to Madison's original vision. Perhaps Madison insisted that Taylor make the change. If he did, they spoke in person or the letter did not survive. Madison certainly retained the influence in the Virginia legislature to engineer such an amendment and his instincts were sound.[31] The revised proposal simply declared the Alien and Sedition Acts unconstitutional rather than null and void.[32]

The final version, featuring Madison's more temperate language, passed the Virginia House on December 21, by a vote of 100 to 63, and the Virginia Senate on December 24, by a vote of 14 to 3.[33] Although the final resolution did not include the word "nullification," the publication of the earlier version inflicted real damage on the political atmosphere and the future of the nation. The resolutions introduced the principle into the political lexicon and Jefferson and Madison would be remembered as the authors of this divisive concept. John Quincy was correct that these ideas would eventually be deployed to fuel an insurrection.[34]

14

All Evidences That They Are Sincere

ON THE MORNING of October 1, the *Sophia* dropped anchor just off Nantasket, Massachusetts. The rocky peninsula was a welcome site for the passengers, who had just survived the Atlantic crossing in hurricane season.[1] A small rowboat, carrying sailors and a few fabric sacks, rode the waves toward the beach. The sailors purchased a few provisions and deposited letters at the local post office before returning to the ship. One letter was marked urgent. The front read:

John Adams, Esq.
President of the United States
Quincy, Massachusetts

The letter was from Elbridge Gerry, who had finally arrived home from France. Gerry's arrival marked the start of a new chapter in Adams's presidency. He developed a strategy to undermine the Essex Junto, sideline the army, and regain control over his foreign policy and the executive branch more broadly. He would need all the tools at his disposal—the navy, his intelligence network, and his unparalleled stubbornness.

The Massachusetts Arch Federalists learned of Gerry's impending arrival and fretted about how his presence might influence the president. Stephen Higginson wrote to Oliver Wolcott Jr., "I hope the President will forbid him any residence in our country, and that Gerry will be pushed into the shade with a strong arm, immediately on his arrival."[2]

Timothy Pickering agreed and wrote to the president, warning him to be suspicious of Gerry's promises. "Mr. G. might come home charged with some soothing," Pickering suggested, "but insidious propositions from the French Government" could not be trusted.[3]

Eager to ensure that Gerry would not find a warm welcome, the New England Federalists schemed about how to alienate him from the public sphere. George Cabot updated Wolcott on these plans: "I have just been canvassing this subject with Mr. Higginson and Mr. Sewall at Boston," he wrote. "We concluded to urge [Harrison Gray] Otis to make a visit to Quincy for the purpose of communicating freely to the President what passes abroad on the subject."

"Sewall offers to accompany Otis if required; but his known dislike of Gerry makes it best that he should not be a principal," Cabot explained. The Boston community was a small one and many of the Essex Junto had a long, contentious history with Gerry. Adams might suspect Sewall's motives, Cabot continued, and "you recollect enough of what passed at your own table to perceive that *I* am disqualified to speak of Mr. G to the President," he confessed.[4]

With all the other Federalists disqualified, Otis visited the president at his home, where he was greeted as an old friend. The president had met Otis when he was a child, as the Adamses were close with his aunt and uncle—James Otis and Mercy Otis Warren. They had served together at the Massachusetts state constitutional convention and spent time together in Philadelphia during Washington's administration when Otis served as a representative in the House.

On this occasion, however, Otis came not as a friend, but as an Arch Federalist. He urged Adams to avoid Gerry, despite their long relationship. The appearance of welcoming Gerry with open arms would undermine the president's strong stance against France. Adams should also ignore any excuses the disgraced diplomat might offer in his defense, Otis urged.

Adams listened politely to Otis's pleas but made it clear that the Federalists had no right to dictate whom he welcomed to his own house.[5]

After learning of the president's chilly response, a despondent Cabot suggested to Wolcott that the president should be cut out of official government business if a cabinet secretary wasn't present to serve as his keeper. "If at any time he is absent for the benefit of relaxation, let it be adhered to that he does no business and gives no opinions," Cabot proposed. "If some system like this is not established there will be no order nor consistency in our affairs," he warned.[6] It was an extraordinary suggestion that would have deprived Adams of all executive branch authority and rendered the president a mere figurehead.

Three days after Gerry's arrival in Boston, he mounted his horse and rode south from East Boston to Quincy to pay his respects to the president. After taking tea with Abigail in her upstairs chamber, the two men went into the president's private office located in the garden.[7] The room still carried a lingering scent of paint and wallpaper glue from the construction completed over the summer.[8] Freshly painted bookshelves flanked the room and held John's vast collection of books, organized under Abigail's careful supervision.[9]

Gerry insisted to Adams that he had "united with" his colleagues "in every measure which has been adopted" but they had been set against him from the beginning. Furthermore, Marshall and Pinckney were outwardly hostile to the French from the start and Talleyrand had made clear he resented the "conduct & disposition of my colleagues towards France."[10]

Adams reminded Gerry that he had issued explicit instructions to work closely with the other envoys and warned against the very split that had occurred. He scolded Gerry for allowing himself to be used by Talleyrand to drive a wedge through the commission.

Stung by this criticism, he protested that Gerry had only stayed to prevent war. "The directory would not consent to my leaving France," he insisted. Talleyrand warned that his departure would "bring on an immediate rupture!"[11]

And where is that rupture? Adams asked. Surely, Gerry could now see that remaining only undermined the unity of the American diplomatic mission.

Gerry admitted that he had failed to follow the president's instructions, but he maintained his lengthy stay in Paris had value. Over the summer, he had seen firsthand that neither Talleyrand nor France sought war. To be sure, Talleyrand was terribly corrupt and tried to exploit the envoys to line his pockets. But France was completely surprised by the absolute refusal of the Americans to participate in a little quid pro quo before official negotiations, and equally shocked by the firm and relatively united American response to the XYZ affair.[12]

Gerry explained that his relationship with Talleyrand had shifted dramatically after news reached France of the publication of the XYZ dispatches and the subsequent measures adopted by Congress to expand the American navy. Talleyrand became much more solicitous of Gerry, begged him to stay, and offered to abandon all the objectionable prerequisites to negotiations. Gerry assured the president that he had repeatedly reminded Talleyrand that he did not have the power to treat with France alone. His reluctance infuriated Talleyrand, and the French minister soon concluded Gerry was just as intractable as Marshall.

Gerry suggested further negotiations might still work. Shortly before he left France, Talleyrand had received a report from Victor Du Pont, who had been appointed the new consul general in Philadelphia. Du Pont did not stay long, as Adams had refused to provide the appropriate diplomatic credentials in retaliation for the recent treatment of the American envoys. Before Du Pont sailed back to France, however, he had time for a few important meetings.[13] First, he debriefed with Philippe de Létombe, Du Pont's predecessor, who suggested that the Directory did not know the extent of the French privateer depredations on American shipping in the West Indies. He urged Du Pont to brief the Directory on all the details.

Du Pont then visited with Vice President Thomas Jefferson, who demanded an explanation for the Directory's outrageous behavior. Their actions were driving the Republican Party to extinction and bringing war closer every day, Jefferson alleged. If France wished to avoid conflict and preserve its allies in the Republican Party, the Directory needed to take drastic steps to heal the breach. Jefferson suggested they recall all commissions to French privateers and reverse the decrees that had fostered the indiscriminate pillaging. Then the Directory should promise to recognize an American minister and offer to negotiate with the appointed envoy in Paris, Spain, or the Netherlands, whichever location made the Adams administration most comfortable.[14]

On July 3, Du Pont landed in Bordeaux. He made his way to Paris, where he delivered his report to Talleyrand, which blamed France for the conflict. "It appears that the Directory does not yet know," Du Pont informed Talleyrand, that the conduct of the French privateers "have been beyond limit and also contrary to the principles of justice as well as sane policy." The "acts of violence, of brigandage, of piracy committed by French cruisers" were too much for any nation to overlook. Additionally, the privateers "have nearly always been excited or protected" by French officials contrary to their professional duty to uphold international law.[15]

On July 31, the Directory followed Jefferson's instructions, revoking the offensive decrees and recalling all the commissioners and judges suspected of impropriety. Gerry never read Du Pont's report, but he witnessed Talleyrand's grave concern, and he saw the immediate response from the Directory. He relayed these observations and the subsequent developments to Adams.

These reports explained French behavior. Adams had long believed that France had nothing to gain from war. It needed American merchants to provide their Caribbean colonies with food and supplies; war would disrupt that essential supply pipeline, and conflict would only push the United States into the arms of the British, France's longtime enemy. Gerry's intelligence confirmed Adams's foreign policy instincts and bolstered his intention to follow them.[16]

Over the next few weeks, Adams received several important letters from his most trusted sources in Europe. Over the summer, William Vans Murray received several visits from a Mr. Louis André Pichon, who had previously worked in the Bureau of Foreign Affairs in Paris. Pichon was stationed as the "French secretary of legation here," Murray explained.[17]

Initially, Murray "had expected that they would probably attempt to use me as a vehicle of overtures to be made to the Government, for the purpose of distracting and dividing and of reviving that hope which has so much been our disease."[18] The public mind was made up against France, Murray had proclaimed definitively to Pichon. "We were now armed and arming," and this legislation "had pass'd without debate or opposition."

Yet, as the summer wore on, Murray began to change his mind, he wrote to Adams. Pichon regularly "admits . . . an American war would be highly unpopular in France."[19] Then in August, "the enclosed paper was given to me," Murray continued. He enclosed a "*written* answer" from Talleyrand, expressing his willingness to engage in negotiations—one of the prerequisites Adams had required in his last speech to Congress. This guarantee was not sufficient, Murray knew, but he thought the president should be aware of it.[20]

Critically, Murray sent much of this information separately from his official dispatches to the State Department. Adams, therefore, had the opportunity to read the intelligence before it was filtered by Pickering.

While Murray sent the president regular updates, he also updated John Quincy Adams in Berlin. Their relatively close posts facilitated frequent communication and they exchanged letters every few days. Murray trusted John Quincy's judgment , and he knew the president held his son in similarly high esteem.

Accordingly, over the summer, Murray sent detailed descriptions of his regular meetings with Pichon. On August 10, Pichon shared "the *arrêté*," which was the Directory's order to recall the privateers and restrict their actions in compliance with international law.[21] A few days later, Pichon confessed he had been sent to The Hague to offer "all evidences that they are sincere, and that things will be brought to a friendly conclusion, if we will but enter upon negotiation." At the end of August, Pichon revealed "that a great change had taken place in the mind of his government on American affairs." They concluded that "they had been deceived by men who meddled on both sides of the water." Murray acknowledged that many of these sentiments were likely offered as "the sweetest flattery to my ears" but he believed that Pichon acted in good faith.[22]

Armed with this intelligence and his own gathered from Berlin, John Quincy wrote a standard diplomatic dispatch to Pickering. He wrote frequent dispatches and numbered them for clarity. In this one, numbered 137, John Quincy urged the administration to consider another round of diplomacy if the Directory publicly promised to treat an American envoy with appropriate respect.

John Quincy also wrote a private letter to his father. "The present situation of the affairs of France," combined with "the spirit which she at length finds roused in the United States, have produced a great and important change in her conduct towards us." After Gerry departed Paris, John Quincy had noticed that France had "redoubled [its] pretences of moderation and peacable dispositions."[23]

Pickering received the official dispatches at the Department of State offices. He did not forward the official dispatch, nor did he ever mention dispatch 137 in his letters to the president. Pickering carefully preserved many of John Quincy's reports as part of the State Department archives; they remain at the National Archives today. Number 137 is missing. It is possible the dispatch was lost or destroyed by accident sometime before 1900 when scholars first flagged its disappearance. It is also possible Pickering destroyed Number 137 because he did not want the president to receive the information contained in the pages.[24] Unbeknownst to Pickering, however, the president received private letters from Murray and John Quincy with the same diplomatic updates.

All this evidence swirled around Adams's mind as he prepared for the upcoming session of Congress. He wrote to each secretary, asking him to provide an update on the state of his department and requested input on two questions of note:

First, should he recommend that Congress declare war against France? Second, should he send another peace commission? In Adams's previous "message to both houses of congress," he had promised never to send envoys to France until he received assurances they would be recognized. While Adams had no intention of backing down from this pledge, he could offer "to nominate a minister to the French republick, who may be ready to embark for France, as soon as [we] receive from the directory, satisfactory assurances."[25] This question revealed that Adams expected it was only a matter of time before he received those explicit assurances.

This letter reached the secretary of state just as Alexander Hamilton, Charles Cotesworth Pinckney, and George Washington rode into Philadelphia.

Just as President Adams began to seriously consider another round of diplomacy to end hostilities between France and the United States, Washington departed for Philadelphia to attend a war council. After months of desperate pleading, McHenry would finally have in-person assistance from Washington and the other senior generals to sort through the countless details required to organize and staff the new army.

On November 10, Washington arrived in the city and took up lodgings at Mrs. Rosannah White's boarding house.[26] That night, he drafted a list of fourteen questions to guide their discussions, including the likelihood of an invasion by France. The list of questions also included: where "is most likely to be first attacked," how to prevent France from possessing "the Floridas & Louisiana," how to improve American engineers, how to organize and recruit regiments, and how much artillery should be assigned to each regiment.[27] No detail was too small, as Washington's final question concerned the cockades pinned to soldiers' hats. One option he considered was "a small Eagle (of Pewter, tin, & in some instances silver) fixed by way of [a] Button in the center of a rose cockade."[28]

First thing Monday morning, Hamilton and Pinckney joined Washington in the parlor he had rented from Mrs. White.[29] For five hours they toiled over letters of application, recommendations, officer lists, regiment structure, and defense plans. Tobias Lear, Washington's longtime personal secretary, took notes, gathered materials, sharpened quills, and made copies of important documents. At 3 P.M., they broke to attend their various dinner engagements, before returning at 7 P.M. to finish the day's discussions.

For the next three weeks, they cloistered themselves in the parlor every day except Sunday. Toward the end of the extended war council, Washington grew frustrated with their pace and was eager to return home to Mount Vernon. On December 9, he insisted "a few moments for dinner *only* might interrupt our daily labour, having dispensed with the Sabbath on this occasion."[30]

McHenry and Pickering kept close tabs on the army's developments. Shortly after Washington's arrival, McHenry encouraged him to "confer with the Secretary of State, on the subject of our foreign relations, as well as the Secretary of the Treasury on the extent and reliance which may be placed on our resources and finances, to assist you to mature your opinion upon" army matters. "I need not add," McHenry wrote after consulting his cabinet colleagues, "that the Secretary of State and Secretary of the Treasury, will chearfully give you every information which you may think it necessary to request."[31]

The cabinet also arranged ample opportunity for collusion. Hamilton stayed at Wolcott's house for the duration of his visit and offered daily updates over family meals. Washington joined them for dinner on November 16, dined with McHenry a few days later in the middle of a snowstorm, and spent his dinner break on November 24 at Pickering's home.[32] In between, he dined with leading families and state officials in Philadelphia, often accompanied by Hamilton, Pinckney, and the secretaries.

Pickering never replied to the president, but he shared the contents of the letter with the cabinet and the generals without Adams's knowledge. Over dinner, they discussed Adams's recent questions about a new peace commission. They plotted to block Adams's foreign policy through cabinet coordination and army planning. Pickering and his allies reasoned that if the army was well developed, it would be harder to set the military aside in favor of negotiation. They hurried to complete the initial army planning to close off Adams's avenues for diplomacy.

Pickering collaborated with Wolcott and McHenry to coordinate their recommendations to the president and uniformly discouraged diplomacy. They all wrote responses encouraging Adams to maintain his firm stand against France, continue ongoing defensive preparations, and resist further national humiliation. The language varied slightly, but the sentiments were in lockstep.[33]

Stoddert remained detached from the cabal in the cabinet. He played no role in the military planning at Washington's lodgings, which was notable given the navy's presumed role in a future war, and he wrote his own recommendations independent of the other secretaries. "I never had a doubt," he wrote the president, "that a Navy, being our only means of carrying the War into the Country of an Enemy, or keeping it from our own, was the proper defence for this Country." He counseled against further expansion of the army, arguing that "the existing Laws . . . authorize the procurement of a sufficient quantity of arms & warlike stores."[34] Adams couldn't agree more.

As Pickering, Wolcott, and McHenry funneled information to Washington, Hamilton, and Pinckney, Adams prepared to return to Philadelphia. On November 3, he went to Cambridge to conclude an "indispensible piece of business." His carriage rattled down Brattle Street and pulled to a stop in front of Elbridge Gerry's large yellow house.[35]

Adams visited Gerry to ask for a personal favor—he needed Gerry to hold his tongue during the coming congressional season. The president knew the Federalists were spoiling for a fight with Gerry, no one more so than Pickering. Earlier that summer, Pickering had been apoplectic with rage when he learned that Gerry had ignored the instructions to return home. "What a contemptable animal!" he had screeched to his allies.[36] Pickering had been a bit more circumspect with the president, but he had already published letters in the *Boston Gazette* condemning Gerry's actions in France and he was pressing to release all of Gerry's documents to Congress.[37]

After reading Pickering's criticism, Gerry had complained to the president about the publication. He included a list of Pickering's errors and provided documentation that refuted the claims. "I am persuaded, that your Excellency will be convinced of the errors pointed out, & will be disposed, in the most publick & prompt manner, to do me justice: & because I presume, that Mr Pickering will readily promote the same measure."[38]

Adams understood all too well the pain of newspaper criticism and was eager to assure his friend that he believed him. But responding in print to Pickering's publications would do Gerry no good right now, Adams advised, as his conduct was "very unpopular on several Points."[39] A newspaper pamphlet war would only undermine national unity and further damage Gerry's reputation.

Adams knew the next several months would determine who controlled foreign policy. He fully expected a forthcoming battle with the members of the Essex Junto in his cabinet. A political fight in the newspapers between Pickering, Gerry, and their allies would entrench partisan divisions, force the president to take sides, and make diplomacy nearly impossible.[40] Adams pleaded for time to pursue diplomacy and regain control over his presidency. Gerry reluctantly agreed.

On the morning of November 12, Adams climbed into his carriage with a heavy heart. For the first time, he planned to face an entire season in Philadelphia without Abigail's counsel, company, and friendship. Her health was slowly improving, but he worried the trip would be dangerous. The hospitality demands of the President's House and the prevalence of disease in Philadelphia posed too great a risk to her health.

On his way out of town, he visited Governor Increase Sumner, who shared good news to buoy the president's spirits. For weeks, rumors of a British naval victory over the French had circulated in the papers, but that morning, *Russell's Gazette*[41] finally proclaimed,

> BUONAPARTE HAS BEEN DEFEATED BY THE ARABS;—
> AND HIS FLEET CAPTURED BY ADMIRAL NELSON.

The governor "told Us the News of last night," he shared with Abigail in a letter he wrote at his first stop. The British victory had dramatic implications for American foreign policy. Another enemy was the last thing France needed at this moment. The French Directory would be weakened both domestically and internationally by its defeat and would be desperate to avoid opening an additional front in the war. Adams immediately understood this development strengthened his hand and improved the chances of diplomacy.

On November 23, Adams's carriage made its way through the snowy streets of Philadelphia and arrived at the President's House. "Generals Washington, Hamilton & Pinckney are at Philadelphia, not waiting for me, I hope," he wrote to Abigail, revealing his unease about the coming months.[42] But he doggedly met with the cabinet secretaries and received their memorandums for his upcoming speech to Congress. Adams gave special attention to Benjamin Stoddert, as they had had little time to talk in person before the president left town in July. They spoke at length about the president's upcoming address to Congress, whether Adams should request a declaration of war, and the best way to protect the nation.[43] Adams also hosted Washington for a dinner at the President's House, which must have been a highly uncomfortable evening.[44]

Undeterred, Adams continued to gather as much additional information as possible from all sources. He received letters from American citizens in France and an unexpected visit from Dr. George Logan, who had conducted an unsanctioned diplomatic visit to France over the summer.[45] Adams offered tea and listened as Logan described his meetings with Talleyrand. He took Logan's word with a generous heaping of salt, but the circumstantial evidence was mounting.[46] John Adams wasn't the only one to notice.

A few days later, Noah Webster, published an open letter in the New York *Minerva*.[47] Under the pseudonym, "True American," Webster wrote in favor of the growing navy because it "affords the protection so essentially necessary to a commercial nation." Every "real friend to the American government" must be delighted "to observe how fast we are progressing towards raising a force which will rescue our flag from the insults to which it has been to[o] long exposed."[48]

Webster's readers immediately grasped the implications of his letter. "Noah Webster, I perceive, says we must have a fleet," Fisher Ames wrote to Pickering. "*Therefore*," he must mean, "we do *not* want an army," Ames concluded.[49] Webster argued in favor of robust diplomacy, backed by a powerful navy, and against warmaking with an army. His words carried unusual weight because of his high standing in the Federalist Party as an influential newspaper editor and author. Neither Webster's letter nor Logan's visit provided decisive intelligence that diplomacy was possible, but they did add to the pile of evidence the president was accumulating.

Public statements like Webster's also suggested that a growing number of Americans agreed with Adams's view of diplomacy.[50] They supported a strong navy to provide leverage in negotiations with France and to protect American commerce but were increasingly less interested in the army. Adams planned to exploit this wedge to undermine the Essex Junto's grip on his cabinet and his foreign policy.[51]

Adams turned his attention to his upcoming annual address to Congress. He analyzed the memos from the secretaries, scrutinized the language, and scratched out his own draft. For several nights, he wrote and rewrote sections until he had the rhetoric just right. Congress Hall would be packed, and the message would be printed and distributed to readers across the world who would scour the text for clues on the status of diplomacy.

On December 8, just before noon, the senators filed into the House chamber in Congress Hall. As the clock chimes indicated the top of the hour, Generals Washington, Hamilton, and Pinckney walked down the aisle and took their reserved seats to the right of the Speaker's dais. Next came the British and Portuguese ministers, and the British and Danish consuls, with their secretaries.

A few minutes later, the clerk announced the arrival of the President of the United States. Adams entered the chamber, followed by Pickering, Wolcott, Lee, McHenry, and Stoddert. The secretaries took their assigned seats, just next to the generals.[52] Adams sat in the Speaker's chair. One newspaper reported that the chamber had never been "more crowded with Spectators. Among whom were many ladies of the first respectability."[53] After a moment, Adams stood, cleared his throat, and began.[54]

As Adams delivered his speech, the secretaries recognized their contributions. Stoddert heard the president detail the naval improvements completed since the last session and the benefits to American trade and commerce from a strengthened navy.[55] McHenry recognized the president's argument that "vigorous preparations for War" were the best preventative against future attacks on American sovereignty.[56] Pickering noted that Adams reiterated his demand that France "make reparation for the Injuries heretofore inflicted on our Commerce and to do Justice in the future."[57] And Wolcott's careful assessment of France's outreach had made it into the speech. Wolcott had advised the president that France "appears to be unwilling to *open rupture* yet there exist no symptoms of a desire for *real peace*."[58]

Adams declared, "The French government appears . . . averse to a rupture with this country." And yet, the most objectionable laws authorizing French attacks on American commerce continue "in force." So far, "nothing is discoverable in the conduct of France, which ought to change or relax our measures of defence." This statement closely adhered to Wolcott's recommendation.

But the secretaries also recognized the one significant change inserted by the president. Pickering and Wolcott had both admitted the wisdom of receiving a French minister, provided the Directory offered assurances that they would negotiate in good faith. Pickering had insisted it was "impossible for the United States to originate a third mission to the French Republic without humiliation and dishonor."[59]

Instead, the president reaffirmed he had never "abandon[ed] the desire of Peace." He remained willing to send a new envoy to France, if the Directory took "the requisite steps" and offered the "determinate assurances" that another envoy would be received as a representative of a strong, powerful, and independent nation.[60]

This minor shift in language sent ripples through the audience present at Congress Hall, which gave "the most profound attention" to the president's words.[61] John Dawson, a Virginia representative sitting in the House chambers, wrote to James Madison the following day, describing the far-reaching implications of Adams's rhetorical evolution: "By the enclosed speech you will find that the tone of the president is much changed, and that we may still hope for peace."[62]

15

Solely the President's Act

JOHN ADAMS OPENED the door to negotiations with France in his address to Congress, then spent the next few months compiling additional intelligence to support such bold action. On the home front, the Arch Federalists' plans for the army and the unpopular tax burden required to support it pushed Adams toward diplomacy. Meanwhile, trusted international sources sent Adams reports that France welcomed another peace commission. To take this decisive step, the president would have to consolidate his hold over foreign policy.

Alexander Hamilton had other ideas about foreign policy and fully intended to pursue them. A few days after the president's address, he wrote to Representative Harrison Gray Otis, suggesting that Congress pass new legislation to expand the armed forces.[1] The Provisional Army, authorized in the initial surge of militant spirit after the release of the XYZ dispatches, had never been called to serve and was set to expire during the upcoming congressional session. Hamilton suggested that Congress should reauthorize the Provisional Army and augment the traditional forces under the president's authority.[2] Instead of 10,000 men, Congress should authorize a 50,000-man army.

While Adams increasingly believed a French invasion unlikely, the Arch Federalists fantasized about other uses for the army. Senator Theodore Sedgwick was particularly pleased about a provision that allowed the president to deploy volunteer companies to suppress domestic disorder or execute the laws. At the prospect of using the military on American citizens, he gleefully reported, "No Act of Congress has ever struck the Jacobins with more horror."[3]

Hamilton was thinking much more ambitiously. As early as 1790, he had noted that Spanish ownership of the Mississippi River and the port of

New Orleans was problematic for American merchants and farmers, who demanded access to the river to transport their goods. The Treaty of San Lorenzo, signed in 1795, had temporarily solved the problem by providing Americans access to the crucial waterway. But Spanish officials dragged their feet and resented the threat of American expansion into western territories.

Hamilton concluded that the United States should just own Florida, New Orleans, and the Mississippi River so that no foreign power could threaten the nation's access to the river in the future. In the summer of 1798, a plan emerged to exploit the latest war between France and Great Britain. Francisco de Miranda, a Venezuelan revolutionary, sought Hamilton's help freeing his people from the shackles of Spanish imperial rule. Miranda had served in the Spanish army and had visited the United States several times in the 1780s, before spending much of the following decade in France. He now endeavored to bring the principles of the American and French revolutions to South America.[4]

From his refuge in London, Miranda had approached William Pitt, the British prime minister, to inquire whether the British navy would be willing to participate in a joint effort with the United States army to liberate South America. Pitt demonstrated enough interest that Miranda felt empowered to approach Rufus King, the American minister in London. King welcomed the idea and encouraged Miranda to write to Hamilton, as the working head of the American army. This outreach was a huge breach in protocol. Hamilton was not the president or the secretary of war, nor was he empowered to dictate military policy.[5] Miranda peppered Hamilton with letters and even went so far as to write John Adams directly, ensuring that the president knew of the behind-the-scenes machinations long before his advisors broached the subject with him.

A few weeks later, King reported to Pickering that the British cabinet was content to leave South America untouched if Spain resisted French encroachment. However, if Spain succumbed to French control, Britain would intercede to prevent the resources of the Spanish colonies from falling into French hands.

"If England engages in this plan," King explained to Pickering, "she will propose to the United States to cooperate in its execution." Miranda planned to remain in London "until events shall decide the conduct of England." In the meantime, King suggested, Pickering should discuss this plan with the president and gauge his interest.[6]

Before consulting with Adams, Pickering enthusiastically sought out Robert Liston, the British minister in Philadelphia, and pledged his support for "such a concert" between the two nations. Almost as an afterthought, he mentioned that he had to move cautiously because "he has received no instructions on the subject from the President of the United States."[7]

Pickering sent the president several letters detailing the proposed plan. He also forwarded the dispatches from King and passed on reports he had requested from McHenry on naval vessels and British convoys, all to speed along the proposed alliance. Adams did not reply.[8] His silence was not dereliction of duty; he read every scrap of mail that crossed his desk. Instead, he used silence as a powerful tool to forestall plans he opposed, knowing that no treaty or major policy could move forward without his involvement. It was a forceful, but subtle method of upholding his constitutional supremacy over diplomacy.

Bolstered by Pickering's encouragement, Liston left for Quincy to present the case for joint Anglo-American action to Adams in person. The president was familiar with the details but listened attentively to Liston's proposal. Adams had noted a suspicious similarity among the plans put forth by Pickering, Liston, and Hamilton, but said nothing for the moment about the concerted effort.

"The people of this country are at present employed in deliberating" the question of an alliance, Adams demurred, "and it would perhaps not be wise to disturb their meditations" at this moment. "No doubt all will come out right by and by," the president assured Liston, committing to nothing, but equally rejecting nothing.[9]

Hamilton proved much easier to convince. By August 1798, his earlier doubts about Miranda had vanished and he wrote the aspiring revolutionary inquiring about a potential rank in the combined forces. With dreams of military glory in his grasp, he also wrote to King in London, lamenting the lack of a direct rupture with France and pondering how else they might move this project forward.[10]

"Our game will be to attack wherever we can," Hamilton wrote to co-conspirators. France and Spain, as allies, should be treated as one entity to plunder. "Tempting objects will be within our grasp," he wrote to James Gunn, knowing that the Federalist senator and former general from Georgia would share his goal of seizing Florida and Louisiana.[11]

Hamilton also put his allies in the House on notice. France had long been rumored to be planning to seize "possession of the Floridas and Louisiana," he reminded Otis.[12] At every moment this attack was possible, and the executive should be "cloathed with power to meet and defeat so dangerous an enterprise." The two countries were not at war yet, Hamilton acknowledged, but it would be better for the United States to terminate the "state of semi-hostility" with France than to remain in limbo. American forces would then seize the Floridas and Louisiana to prevent them from "falling into the hands of an Active foreign power." Hamilton concluded, "I have been long in the habit of considering the acquisition of those countries as essential to the permanency of the Union."[13]

Hamilton's plan was doomed from the start. The American people would rebel against a standing army marching south on a conquering mission. They did not like new taxes or a standing army any more than they had two decades earlier, as Adams well knew. He warned Sedgwick and the other Arch Federalists, ardent supporters of the army, "If you must have an army I will give it to you, but remember it will make the government more unpopular than all their other acts."[14]

Adams had the evidence to make these claims. On his trips home to Quincy and back again to Philadelphia, he had witnessed signs of widespread dissatisfaction with the army and the financial measures required to fund it. The liberty poles were so thick in eastern Pennsylvania and Massachusetts that Federalists formed associations with the specific goal in mind of destroying "the sedition poles."[15] The president grasped the symbolism.

Adams felt the sting of tax collection himself. He owned a decent sized farm in Massachusetts that provided for the basic needs of his family, but he was not a wealthy man and extra expenses required some juggling. Over the winter, Abigail described the potential obstacles of tax collection. The legislature surely did not comprehend the challenge of executing the house tax, she wrote. The officials have "to measure every House Barn out House count every square of Glass, collect every piece of Land, and its bounds—and then apprize the whole." The entire process "is a Labour indeed!"[16]

Armed with reports from his wife and the scenes he had witnessed with his own eyes, Adams fretted over the ballooning federal budget. In 1796, Congress authorized a budget of $5.8 million, which was mostly allocated to reducing debts from the Revolution, replenishing military stores, and paying government salaries.[17] Just four years later, Congress allocated $11.9 million for the army and navy alone. Hamilton's plan for a 50,000-man army would be so expensive that it would spark a rebellion in all sixteen states, Adams concluded.[18]

Adams had many reasonable objections to the army, but his dislike was also personal. He resented Hamilton's appointment as the inspector general and he begrudged his cabinet for interfering in the ranking of the generals. Years later, Adams still complained that the cabinet "biassed General Washington's mind . . . and induced him to place Hamilton on the List of Major Generals, before Generals Knox and Pinckney."

Adams might not have known the full scope of Hamilton's machinations, but he intuited enough. He realized that their visions for foreign policy were diverging rapidly, a development that threatened to undermine the presidency. Hamilton was scheming to make himself, as the inspector general of the army, the primary moving force behind foreign policy. This plot would sideline Adams and undermine the president's constitutional authority over both the army and foreign affairs. Adams was determined to thwart Hamilton's bid for power, no matter the cost.

Washington had empowered Hamilton to run the army, however, and afforded significant protection to his wily subordinate. Adams could not condemn Hamilton outright without risking another showdown with Washington. So, he said everything right about the army, at least in public. In his address to Congress, he urged continuing military preparedness as the best way to secure a diplomatic solution. He appointed officers to the army, decried the inefficiencies in the war department, and urged soldiers to enlist.

In private, however, the president welcomed every opportunity to delay, obfuscate, and erect obstacles to army organization. As McHenry attempted to fill the ranks in both the Provisional Army and the expanded US Army, Adams insisted that McHenry submit a list of proposed names. Once Adams mailed back his approval, then McHenry could fill out the commissions and send them back to Quincy for the president's signature. It was intentionally clunky and inefficient. When McHenry complained to the president about the pace of appointments, Adams made his distaste for the army clear, snapping, what would "induce men of common sense to inlist for five dollars a month, who could have fifteen when they pleased by sea or for common work at land?"[19]

Adams also prioritized anything navy-related over the army. He signed blank commission documents to streamline Secretary Stoddert's navy recruitment while refusing the same process for McHenry.[20] He regularly took several days to reply to McHenry's letters, if at all, whereas he replied to Stoddert instantly and urged haste.[21]

While delaying at every turn, Adams laid the groundwork for a policy shift.[22] In his annual address, he had pledged complete transparency about ongoing diplomatic developments and planned to fulfill that promise. He instructed Pickering to prepare a copy of the recently received envoys' communications from France to lay before Congress.

By January 8, Congress was getting anxious. Where were the dispatches? Why hadn't the president delivered them? Hoping to force the issue, Representative Albert Gallatin put forth a resolution calling for all documents produced by the envoys. That afternoon, Adams sent a note to the Department of State offices, again requesting the documents. Pickering demurred, insisting that he needed another day to finish his report on Gerry's correspondence.

The next day, Adams sent another note. Pickering again refused to comply with the request.

Abigail complained that Pickering's delay tactics would hurt the president. "The world knows that the President is not accustomed to be thus dilatory. yet the blame will fall upon him, by those who know not the cause," she complained to her nephew.[23]

Finally, after weeks of delays, Adams dispatched his chief clerk to command Pickering to hand over the documents immediately.[24] No report was required, Adams asserted, nor had he ever asked Pickering to write one. Pickering finally handed over Gerry's letters to the president, only after succeeding in delaying the release of the information and nearly completing his report.

Adams delivered the letters to Congress straight away. Over the previous summer, Gerry had written extensively about the change in France's disposition to the United States. The Arch Federalists read with horror that Talleyrand had been desperate to resume negotiations before Gerry left Paris. Republicans were thrilled.

That evening, Pickering visited the president to deliver the report. Adams read the document, crossing out entire sections that vilified Gerry or questioned his integrity. These sections were essential, Pickering insisted. They demonstrate that "Mr Gerry's conduct" was "wrong in principle, and in many particulars very reprehensible!"

Unmoved, Adams continued editing.

As Adams slashed through another page, Pickering protested that one paragraph was particularly important. It contextualizes "Mr Gerry's strange opinion of the sincerity of Talleyrand in his talks of negociation." Gerry's assertion could not stand, Pickering pleaded.[25]

Perhaps loyalty motivated Adams to omit this section. Or perhaps he recognized that Pickering had lost all objectivity and was determined to destroy Gerry. Or maybe Adams concluded that Congress did not need to read the secretary of state's observations about the documents. Abigail certainly thought Pickering was out of line. After reading his report, she asked, "Was it a part of the secretarys buisness, thus to teach the National Legislature what to think, and how to think upon matters of fact?"[26] The president had the constitutional duty to share his ideas with Congress. Article II, Section 3 requires the president to give "Congress Information of the State of the Union, and recommend to their Consideration such Measures as he shall judge necessary and expedient."[27] The Constitution grants the secretary of state no such rights or privileges. Adams's forceful edits reminded Pickering of the constitutional hierarchy in the executive branch.

On January 21, Adams delivered the revised report to Congress. Pickering immediately sent versions of the original to Washington, Sedgwick, Cabot, and his other Essex Junto friends. Cabot forwarded a copy of the report to King in London and hinted at more nefarious activities behind the scenes: "I dare not commit to writing my ideas on the subject but you wou'd be charmed with Pickering if you knew the great part he sustains."[28] What Pickering was doing behind the scenes isn't completely clear, but it definitely wasn't following the president's orders or serving him well.

As Adams tangled with his secretary of state, he grew increasingly impatient for a particularly important arrival which offered both personal and political implications. Several months earlier, Thomas Boylston Adams, the third and youngest of the Adams sons, left Berlin for home. He carried with him a bundle of priceless letters that he carefully transported across the European continent and Atlantic Ocean.

The previous September, when Louis-André Pichon, the chargé d'affaires of France at The Hague, had first produced a letter from Talleyrand expressing his commitment to diplomacy, Murray made three copies. He sent one to Secretary of State Pickering, one copy directly to the president, and one to John Quincy. After reading the letter, John Quincy wrote a memorandum offering a comprehensive view of the international scene. He argued neutrality was "an object of such inestimable value, and involves so deeply the welfare not of the present age only but of all posterity," that all honorable methods of avoiding war should be considered.[29] In Berlin, he heard reports that France feared cooperation between the United States and Great Britain. The time was ripe for diplomacy, he told his father. John Quincy also enclosed a copy of the letter from Pichon, in case the other copies had not arrived, before sealing the package and handing it to Thomas for safekeeping.[30]

John Quincy also wrote a lengthy letter to their mother. They all knew John would read the correspondence, but by addressing it to Abigail, John Quincy could write more freely. He assured his parents, "I had neither a thought nor a paper, upon any subject, public or private, which I could not communicate to [Thomas], with the most unlimited confidence."[31]

While in Berlin, John Quincy kept a letter book that contained a copy of every letter he wrote, both diplomatic and private. The letter book was copied in Thomas's hand.[32] He had read every scrap of correspondence produced by John Quincy for four years and had also accompanied his brother on most outings. He could provide firsthand insight on almost every conversation, negotiation, and situation in Europe. John Quincy was telling his parents to listen to Thomas.

Back in the United States, John and Abigail knew Thomas was en route, but that was the extent of their information. The ship that carried him remained a mystery, as was its port destination. The arrival date would depend on the wind, the weather, and the presence of enemy vessels. In early January, Abigail confided to her husband, "I think hourly of Thomas this dreadfull cold Weather. pray Heaven that he may return in safety to his affectionate Mother."

A few days later, John replied, "We must wait with Patience for the ship." He could not help but playfully continue, "Ought he to visit Father or Mother first?—I believe he must come here before he goes to Quincy.—But I shall leave it to him, to decide."[33]

Finally, on January 13, John received good news. He immediately relayed to Abigail that he had received "from the Post Office, a Letter from our dear Thomas dated the 12 informing me of his Arrival at New York."[34] Two days later, Adams, dressed in his best suit with a ceremonial sword hung at his waist, greeted levee guests who filed into the state dining room of the President's House. As the conversation concluded, a servant scurried into the room and whispered in the president's ear: "Sir, Mr Adams is up Stairs."[35]

The president immediately excused himself and bounded up the stairs, where he found his son standing in the family parlor. With tears streaming down his face, John embraced Thomas, and said "I thank, my God, my son that you have returned again to your native country."[36] William Smith Shaw, the president's secretary and Thomas's cousin, was in the room and wrote to Abigail that night, "I would not wish to live, if I could have seen such a scene and not have been moved."[37]

After four years apart, father and son had much to discuss. They spent most of the next several days discussing politics—both at home and abroad. John was delighted that Thomas's "Mind is well stored with Ideas and his Conversation entertaining."[38]

The president spent days poring over the letters hand-delivered by Thomas and probing his recollections. Adams added all this information, which no one else possessed, to his case for diplomacy. Thomas's arrival could not have been better timed.

The next day, Adams instructed Pickering to collaborate with the other members of the cabinet to prepare a draft treaty. Pickering ignored the request and left the note unanswered.[39]

Pickering might have responded differently had he known about the next letter Adams received. On February 1, Washington wrote to the president, vowing to help Adams "bring on Negotiation upon open, fair and honorable ground." Peace "is the ardent desire of all the friends of this rising Empire," Washington solemnly concluded.[40] Adams recognized the letter's significance immediately. He would have Washington's support if he decided to take this momentous step, or at the very least, avoid public condemnation.[41]

Adams would need every bit of support in the face of the Arch Federalists' war mongering. On the evening of February 6, Theodore Sedgwick called on the president. Over the last year, Sedgwick had drifted away from Adams and toward Hamilton and Pickering. Now, he welcomed war with France as an opportunity to bolster a standing army and crush Republicans. He was horrified by Adams's ongoing commitment to diplomacy and willingness to compromise.

Sedgwick called on Adams to share draft legislation for the upcoming session, including the Senate's bill to reorganize the army based on Hamilton's recommendations.[42] Adams noted that one of its provisions would create a new rank in the army, "General," and bestow it on Washington. Adams asked what additional responsibilities came with this rank. Nothing, Sedgwick replied, other than to make clear that the rank holder had no rivals.

Adams turned to Sedgwick, incredulously, and asked, "Are you going to appoint him general over the Presidents?" He continued, sputtering with rage, "I have not been so blind but I have seen a combined effort, among those who call themselves friends of the government to annihilate the essential powers given by the president." Sedgwick insisted that no one was trying to destroy the president's power, but Adams silenced any further conversation: "This sir my understanding has perceived and my heart felt," he said to his former friend and ally.[43] While Sedgwick and Adams interacted over the next two years as part of their duties, this visit marked the end of their productive relationship.

The next day, Sedgwick wrote a letter to Hamilton, "in the most perfect confidence," and described the conversation. He concluded, "This shews that we are afflicted with an evil for which certainly no compleat remedy can be applied."[44] No longer did the Essex Junto simply disagree with the president; now, he was evil.

Adams was equally despondent after their meeting. He was less concerned with Washington's rank than with who might inherit the exalted position when he was gone. Adams confessed to Gerry that he suspected a contingent of the Federalists were angling "to give Hamilton the command of it & thus to proclaim a Regal Government, [Col] Hamilton at the Head of it."[45] If Congress bestowed this rank on Washington, Adams couldn't veto it without causing a fatal uproar, but it only further motivated him to protect his authority over diplomacy and sideline the army. In early February, Federalists in Congress introduced the bill. After several weeks of debate, Congress passed the measure, authorizing the president to organize 30,000 troops in the event of war with France.[46]

The drumbeat of intelligence continued. On February 15, new dispatches arrived for Adams from William Vans Murray at The Hague. "I am sensible that I run some hazard in thus communicating to you Sir such things," Murray explained. "But I thought that you would on the whole wish to know all that I could collect." He could not risk Pickering filtering the details, so he took "the liberty of privately communicating" this intelligence.[47]

A French military postmaster had hand-delivered a sealed diplomatic parcel from Pichon, who had recently returned to Paris to meet with Charles Maurice de Talleyrand. Pichon relayed to Talleyrand that the United States needed concrete proof of French goodwill. On September 28, 1798, Talleyrand wrote his most straightforward letter to date, and Pichon forwarded it to The Hague. Murray was honored to share it with the president.[48] Four months later, the much-anticipated letter finally arrived in Philadelphia: "Whatever plenipotentiary the Government of the United States might send to France" would be "received with the respect due to the representative of a free, independent, and powerful nation," Talleyrand pledged.[49]

Equally as important, Murray relayed that the Directory had rescinded its decree of October 29, 1798. No longer would any American serving aboard a British ship be treated (and hanged) as a pirate. It was the essential precondition to future negotiations Adams had required in his December 1798 address. Adams had diligently worked for this outcome for the past seven months and he was determined to act decisively.[50]

That evening, the president carefully drafted a note to the Senate. He slept on its contents, then ordered his clerk to deliver the letter to the Senate chambers on the morning of February 18.

Joseph Philippe Létombe, the French consul stationed in Philadelphia, was sitting in the House chambers that morning, listening to the debates. He wrote to Talleyrand describing what he saw: "The debate at this moment was very brisk." The Federalists and Republicans were "highly animated. They were discussing a bill giving the president eventual authority to increase the army."

One of the members entered the chambers and shouted that there was "no more reason to work for this bill, since the President had just nominated a minister to the French Republic!"

Létombe reported, "The majority acted as if struck by a thunderbolt. The orator Otis, the friend and confidant of Adams, showed embarrassment, grew pale." Unsure of what to do next, many of the members rushed upstairs to the Senate chambers to corroborate the report. The Federalist senators confirmed that the nomination "had evidently been kept secret from the Feds of both houses."[51] They gestured to the table at the front of the room, where the president's letter lay:

> I transmit to you a document which seems to be . . . a compliance with a condition mentioned at the conclusion of my message to congress of the twenty first of June last. Always disposed and ready to embrace every plausible appearance of probability of preserving or restoring tranquility I nominate William Vans Murray. . . to be minister plenipotentiary of the United States to the French Republic."

Létombe concluded, "The House adjourned, and is still adjourned."[52]

16

Struck by a Thunderbolt

THE MORNING AFTER submitting the nomination, John Adams sat down at the desk in his private study on the second floor of the President's House in Philadelphia. He had a very important letter to write and wanted to be the first to share the news. "Dear Sir," he wrote to George Washington. "I Yesterday determined to nominate Mr. Murray to be Minister Plenipotentiary to the French Republic." Adams explained that he took this step based on "the Strength of a Letter from Talleyrand himself," which promised that "any Minister Plenitentiary from the United States shall be received" according the conditions he had required in "my Message to Congress of the 21 of June last."

There was always a possibility of some chicanery with the French, Adams acknowledged, so he had also issued instructions that "Murray is not to remove from his station at the Hague untill he shall have received formal assurances that he shall be received and treated in Character." Adams also confessed his worry that partisan politics might throw a wrench in the gears of diplomacy. "In Elective Governments, Peace or War are alike embraced by Parties when they think they can employ either for Electioneering Purposes," Adams mused. Maybe he hoped Washington would work behind the scenes to rally support for Murray's nomination, but he didn't ask outright.

Adams closed by thanking Washington for his previous letter. Adams quoted Washington's own words to demonstrate how much it meant to him. Adams agreed whole-heartedly that "Tranquility upon just and honourable terms is undoubtedly the Ardent desire of the Friends of this Country."[1]

Adams wasn't the only one writing frantically to Washington. Enraged, Pickering wailed that "we were all thunderstruck when we heard" of the nomination. "It is solely the President's act" and "Confidence in the President is lost," he grumbled. "The honor of the country is prostrated in the dust," Pickering concluded.[2]

Pickering shouldn't have been that surprised. The president had shown great interest in William Vans Murray's dispatches from The Hague, had indicated a willingness to listen to Gerry's report on the conditions in Paris, and had ordered Pickering to draft a blueprint treaty and instructions for a new peace commission. Pickering also knew Adams distrusted the army. Whether he had forgotten these indicators or had just chosen to ignore them, Pickering did not say.

Theodore Sedgwick expressed similar surprise and horror. "This measure, important & mischievous as it is, was the result of presidential wisdom without the knowledge of, or any intimation to, any one of the administration," Sedgwick complained to Hamilton. "In the dilemma to which we are reduced," he whined, they could either approve or reject the nomination. Both were evil.[3]

Adams confirmed to Abigail that the Federalists had been "kept in the dark," but he hoped when he shared all the intelligence he had compiled, the nomination "will be approved." He also shared with amusement, "Oh how they lament Mrs Adams's Absence!— she is a good Counseller! If she had been here Murray would never have been named nor his Mission instituted!"[4] He was not insulted that his peers thought Abigail controlled him. Rather, he cackled at the idea that she opposed diplomacy or that they somehow knew her views better than he did.

Abigail wrote back, equally tickled. Thomas had recently visited Boston, where he heard several Federalists say, "*we heartily wish* THE OLD WOMAN *had been with the President to prevent it*," she reported to her husband. "This was pretty sausy!" Abigail continued, "but the old woman can tell them they are mistaken, for she considers the measure as a master stroke of policy."[5]

Abigail was privy to the president's extensive intelligence-collecting efforts. She knew that Talleyrand had revealed his growing commitment to diplomacy over the past several months and believed the appointment "shows that the disposition of the [United States] Government" was equally committed to peace. "Upon them rests in the Eyes of all the World" and the responsibility to pursue peace. Yes indeed, she concluded, "I call it a master stroke of policy."[6]

Casting around for a solution, the Federalists in the Senate elected to refer the nomination to "a committee consisting of Sedgwick, Stockton, Read, Bingham and Ross"—all Federalists. Pickering explained to Washington, "They will study to find some remedy—or rather alleviation—for the mischief is incapable of a remedy."[7]

The committee discussed their options. They could accept the nomination—which none of them wanted to do. Or they could reject the nominee, but that posed thorny constitutional questions. If they rejected Murray on the grounds that he was unfit for the position, how would they explain their previous votes to confirm him as the American minister to The Hague?

Similarly, if they rejected the appointment outright, they knew they would be treading "upon the most important and useful prerogative of the executive." George Washington had insisted that the president alone had the right to determine where to send American ministers. The Senate could reject a candidate, but not the position, without improperly inserting itself into the diplomatic process.

Federalists were eager to uphold this principle, at least while they controlled the presidency. Rejecting the nomination would "open a door for concerning cabal and intrigue in the Senate," under future, potentially Republican presidents. After much deliberation, they agreed to send the president a letter asking permission to call on him to discuss the appointment.

John Rutherfurd, a Federalist from New Jersey who had recently retired from the Senate, counseled Sedgwick to approach the meeting with caution. Rejecting the nomination "will create fatal divisions and parties amongst the Federalists, and they may perhaps throw the Old Man [Adams] into the arms of his enemies." He urged Sedgwick to try to make the best of the situation. Perhaps they could try "to tie Murray down by instructions, which will prevent any risqué from the appointment."

Rutherfurd reminded his former colleagues that the president, our friend, "has an honest heart and the best intentions in the world, but he has high passions, is tenacious of authority and is precipitate, and if a breach takes place between him and the federal party in the Senate, I dread the consequences."[8]

Sedgwick did not heed Rutherfurd's sage advice.

On February 23, the committee arrived at the President's House.[9] The senators explained to Adams that they were worried about Murray's credentials to handle negotiations of such magnitude—or at least that's what they elected to say out loud at first. Perhaps the president could nominate two additional envoys, just as he had last time, they suggested. The senators mentioned John Quincy Adams and Rufus King, both of whom had extensive diplomatic experience and were already in Europe.[10]

Adams saw through the ploy. He accused them of trying to scuttle his diplomatic efforts before they had even begun. As he had said nearly two years earlier when Federalists first suggested King and John Quincy, "the nomination of either Mr King or Mr Adams would probably defeat the whole measure," Adams retorted. Since Republicans already accused him of nepotism when he appointed his son to Berlin, he reminded the senators, they would never confirm John Quincy for this new position. Furthermore, King's nomination would be a grave insult to France and the presence of the minister to Great Britain would doom the negotiations, as the senators well knew.[11]

Losing his temper, Sedgwick informed the president "that the measure is condemned—that it is considered as dishonourable and disastrous—by all his real friends and the friends of his country; and this without a single exception!"[12]

This outburst was much more honest than their supposed concerns about Murray's abilities, but it was the exact wrong thing to say to Adams to change his mind. Adams welcomed unpopularity if it was the result of a moral and just choice.

The party seemed "determined to rule him," Adams retorted, "but he would disappoint them." If they really wanted to meddle with foreign policy, the senators could reject Murray, he continued, but that choice would be "upon your own responsibility."

They were at a stalemate. The senators left, frustrated in their aims. Once his temper cooled, Adams wrote to Abigail. "I am not very angry now, nor much vexed or fretted"—at least not anymore. He vowed, "I will not take Revenge," even though he was sorely tempted.[13]

Both sides waited for two days to see if the other would flinch first.

On February 24, 1799, the senators gathered at 10 A.M. at Bingham's home for a caucus. They debated the nomination for five hours but found themselves divided and uncertain. They agreed to recess for dinner and to return at 7 P.M. Not until 11 P.M. did they finally reach a consensus—they would vote to reject the nomination.

The following morning, Sedgwick was sitting in the Senate chambers putting the final touches on a report explaining their rationale when a note from the president arrived. Adams asked him to refrain from voting on the nomination until they received his new message.[14]

Shortly thereafter, a new missive from the president was delivered to the Senate, nominating Patrick Henry and Chief Justice Oliver Ellsworth to join Murray as envoys extraordinary. Murray would still be the lead negotiator, but he would be buoyed by two reliable Federalists. Adams also promised to keep the envoys home until he had received word directly from Talleyrand that these specific nominees would be received properly.[15]

The senators agreed that this outcome was the best that could be achieved for the moment and confirmed the three-man peace commission on February 27.[16]

The nomination hadn't worked exactly as Adams had hoped, and there was still a possibility it could all fall apart as he waited for further assurances from France. In the meantime, he received welcome letters a bit closer to home.

Henry Knox wrote that he viewed the nomination as "one of the most dignified, decisive, and beneficial ever adopted by the cheif magistrate of any nation." Adams had put himself "above all prejudice" and pursued "the happiness of the nation as the primary object of his administration." As a result, he "nobly hazard[ed] his reputation until the mist of ignorance or party will subside." Knox urged the president to exercise patience. Most Americans trusted in "Your knowledge and virtue," he assured Adams, and they knew "those qualities are fully adequate to the important existing crisis." Despite the party rancor, the American people "will adhere and cling to you, in preference to all others."[17]

A few days later, Attorney General Charles Lee passed along a private letter from John Marshall. "I should not have sent [it] to you," Lee wrote, given that the letter was marked confidential. But Lee thought the president should know that his efforts enjoyed the "approbation of so good a judge as Mr. Marshall." Lee was happy to report that "it is with no small pleasure I find his opinion correspondent with my own."[18]

For all that Pickering and Sedgwick bayed about the entire Federalist Party opposing Adams's efforts, they discounted support for the nomination in Virginia, Massachusetts, and the president's own cabinet.[19]

Adams was immensely gratified by this support, especially as his former allies appeared to be deserting him in droves. One consolation, he wrote Lee, is that "the nomination of Murray has . . .shown to every observing & thinking man, the real strength or weakness of the constitution." The battle over the Murray nomination was a stark reminder of the constitutional powers of the executive. The president is entrusted with the authority to make nominations and treaties with the aid of subordinates of his choosing; the cabinet secretaries have no legally recognized role in that process. Adams demonstrated his intentional commitment to ensuring that the power dynamic remained unchanged.

The nomination has also "produced a display of the real spirit of the parties in this country, & the objects they have in view. To me, it has laid open characters," Adams confessed to Lee. He could clearly see the outlines of a war party in the Federalist ranks and resolved to do something about it. "If combinations of senators, generals & heads of department shall be formed such as I cannot resist and measures are demanded of me that I cannot adopt, my remedy is plain and certain." He would resign and leave the Arch Federalists to duke it out with Jefferson, he confided ominously to Lee. "I will try my own strength at resistance first however," Adams concluded.[20] The congressional session had only just begun.

17

The Spirit in the City Is Very High

THE TENSIONS THAT had roiled the nation for the last year were bubbling to the surface in Congress. On February 25, 1799, Representative Andrew Gregg from Pennsylvania presented two petitions from his constituents. 270 citizens from Cumberland County and 314 from Mifflin County had written to Congress requesting the repeal of the Alien and Sedition Acts. Representative Albert Gallatin followed with another petition from Chester County with 692 signatures. Representative Edward Livingston delivered a petition with 2,500 signatures from New York. Representative Joseph Hiester shared "one of the same kind" with 1,400 names. Representative James Bayard put forth a petition from the "inhabitants of Newcastle County, State of Delaware, signed by between 700 and 800 persons."[1]

A few weeks earlier, Alexander Hamilton had encouraged Theodore Sedgwick and their allies in Congress to take seriously the Virginia and Kentucky resolutions and the accompanying protests. To be sure, Hamilton disagreed with the Virginians' objections, but he argued that Federalists in Congress could seize the upper hand by treating their fellow citizens' concerns with at least the appearance of care.

In true Hamiltonian fashion, he offered a lengthy letter full of suggestions for how to proceed. First, the "proceedings of Virginia and Kentucke" should be "referred to a special Committee." Next, that committee should issue a report "exhibiting with great luminousness and particularity" the constitutional authority behind the Alien and Sedition Acts.

The report should also display the full evidence of the "regular conspiracy to overturn the government. . . . No pains or expence should be spared to disseminate this Report," Hamilton insisted. "A little pamphlet containing it should find its way into every house in Virginia."

The committee should also examine any potential modifications to the laws which would offer better "precautions against abuse and for the security of Citizens." These types of concessions, Hamilton assured Sedgwick, "have a good rather than a bad effect."[2]

The Federalists organized a caucus to deliberate on the petitions presented by their Republican colleagues. They considered Hamilton's wise counsel but dismissed it. Instead, they agreed to ignore the arguments put forth by their opponents and make no retort themselves.

The result was "a scandalous scene," Thomas Jefferson reported to James Madison. The House convened into the Committee of the Whole and "Gallatin took up the Alien" acts, while Wilson Nicholas, a Republican from Virginia, tackled "the Sedition laws." His arguments were initially met with "common silence." The Federalists then entered "into loud conversations, laugh, cough &c." The din was so overpowering that if anyone wanted to be heard, they "must have had the lungs" of an auctioneer, Jefferson lamented.

Undeterred, Livingston attempted to speak on behalf of his constituents. "But after a few sentences the Speaker called him to order & told him what he was saying was not to the question. It was impossible to proceed," Jefferson said with dismay.[3] After several hours of squabbling, the Speaker put forth a resolution "That it is inexpedient to repeal the act passed the last session." The House approved this resolution 52 votes to 48, along party lines.[4]

The results of the 1798 elections had offered Federalists a false sense of security. Most of the state elections for Congress took place in the immediate aftermath of the publication of the XYZ dispatches. Republicans left Congress in droves rather than address French perfidy, or they switched their allegiance, while voters rewarded Federalists for their strong stance on France. Voters weren't initially put off by the Alien and Sedition Acts, especially in the summer elections that were held before prosecutions had begun in earnest. The biggest swing came from the South, a former Republican stronghold. The North Carolina congressional delegation switched from nine Republicans and one Federalist to seven Federalists and three Republicans. Virginia Federalists remained in the minority, but they picked up considerable seats in both the state and national legislatures.[5]

However, as citizens began to see the implications of the Alien and Sedition Acts through local prosecutions of average citizens, the tide began to turn against the Federalist Party. The initial Sedition prosecutions focused on prominent Republican newspaper editors in New York and Philadelphia. Federal officials then turned their attention to average citizens like Benjamin Fairbanks, David Brown, and Lespenard Colie, who were charged with raising a liberty pole, reading an essay to a crowd that criticized the federal government, and shouting "Damn the President," respectively. The prosecution of paltry crimes instilled fear in their neighbors.[6]

Citizens increasingly grew distrustful of the Federalist Party as they saw the growing reach of the Sedition Act, experienced the effects of the new dwelling tax, and viewed the growing army with alarm. The Federalists would soon have to confront the public sentiment against the Sedition Act and their entire legislative agenda. As resistance to Federalist measures grew, citizens' petitions and protests offered Federalists an opportunity to lower the partisan temperature and notch an easy political win. Their failure to do so reflected the increasing partisan divide and extremism festering in the Federalist Party.

By January 1799, tax officials made their way through Bucks and Northampton counties in Pennsylvania, assessing the local dwellings. On receiving their bills, citizens were outraged and submitted petitions to their local representatives, asking for redress. They raised liberty poles to protest the tax and demonstrate their seriousness.

The residents of these communities were no radicals. Most were Federalists, served in local government positions, and were veterans of both the Continental Army during the Revolution and Washington's army to suppress the Whiskey Rebellion in 1794. They didn't burn effigies, pull down homes, or tar and feather federal officials.[7]

But when Samuel Clark, a tax collector, arrived at Lower Milford, Pennsylvania, on February 6, John Fries (pronounced Frees), a decorated war veteran deeply loyal to Washington, warned Clark to turn back. If Clark continued, he would "be confined in an old stable . . . and fed on rotten corn." Others threatened to "tie him to the Liberty Pole" in Milford Square. Clark lived nearby and had no interest in sparking violence with his neighbors, so he returned home empty-handed.[8]

Over the next few weeks, the citizens of Lower Milford and most of the surrounding towns successfully blocked assessments of their homes through coordinated but peaceful action. Fries and his fellow leaders formed an association of fifty local citizens who signed a pact with the word "LIBERTY" trumpeted across the top of the paper. As a group, they refused to turn over "valuation or measurement of the houses" until they could be sure the tax was "really authorized by law." While organizing the resistance, Fries also worked hard to prevent violence. He regularly asked after the health of the tax assessors and apologized for any verbal abuse they suffered.[9]

Despite the care taken by both citizens and collectors to avoid escalation, Judge Richard Peters ordered United States Marshal William Nichols to arrest a dozen men from Lehigh Township for threatening a local collector.[10] They would be transported to Peters's district, over fifty miles away, and their cases tried in an entirely different community. Rumors swirled that the prisoners would be sent to Philadelphia, which played on the fears of Northampton locals that their friends and family members would never receive a fair trial from a jury of their peers. This right had been a point of contention in the Revolution between colonists and British authorities. US officials recognized its legal importance, by enshrining the right in the Judiciary Act of 1789.

Meanwhile, tax officials James Chapman, John Roderock, and Everhard Foulke resolved to make another attempt to complete their assessments. On March 6, they made their way through Northampton County, initially meeting little resistance. But by the afternoon, protestors from Quakertown had gathered at Robert's Tavern, waiting to seize the collectors.

At dusk, Roderock and Foulke traveled down the main road. Initially, Fries tried to convince them to cease their efforts, arguing that the tax bill wasn't settled law. The community had sent petitions addressing both the Alien and Sedition Acts and the tax law, and they believed both bills would soon be repealed. Fries and the protestors insisted the laws shouldn't be enforced while under review. These comments reveal two key aspects of the protest. First, the protestors viewed both bills as part of a larger Federalist agenda to suppress their rights.[11] The Sedition Acts could not be separated from the taxes in the minds of citizens. Second, Fries was confident that their petitions would move officials in Congress to repeal the contested legislation, and thus the taxes should not be collected. This interpretation was naïve, if not ignorant of the workings of the legal system. No judge had stayed the collection, nor had Congress announced its intention to revisit the bill. Accordingly, citizens were still legally obligated to pay their taxes and comply with the law.

Fries's pleas failed to move the collectors, and they announced their intention to proceed. The crowd seized Foulke, but Roderock managed to escape by fleeing on horseback into the forest. The crowd escorted Foulke into the tavern, which was filled with inebriated, raucous locals eager to take out their frustrations on the unarmed collector. Fries managed to secure the collector's release, much to the consternation of his men, and Foulke rode away, shaken by the experience, but unharmed.

That night, Fries gathered with the other leaders, and they decided to travel to Bethlehem to rescue their imprisoned neighbors. The following morning, Fries donned his regimentals and pinned a black feather to his hat, just like he had worn in the Continental Army, to proclaim his loyalty to Washington.[12] He and a small contingent of twenty men set out for Northampton.

At about 2 P.M., they met up with other militia groups, creating a combined force of about 140 men. Before crossing the bridge into Bethlehem, Fries stopped to pay the toll for the entire group, as a demonstration of their commitment to order and the rule of law.[13]

Arriving at the tavern that operated as a makeshift prison, Fries politely greeted Marshal Nichols. Fries asked to post bail for the prisoners and remove them peacefully. He insisted he had no objection to a trial if it was held locally so the prisoners could be judged fairly. Nichols refused. He had orders to remove the prisoners and he intended to follow them.

Over the next several hours, Fries walked up and down the stairs between Nichols and his troops, attempting to negotiate a compromise. He made sure to disarm himself each time he reentered the building, eager to avoid any appearance of armed intimidation. Yet, by late afternoon, the militia men grew increasingly restless, no doubt egged on by the libations liberally poured by the tavern keeper. Around four o'clock, one particularly inebriated old man, Henry Huber, attempted unsuccessfully to rush the stairs, before a deputy shoved him to the bottom. To appease his men, Fries finally allowed an armed delegation to join him inside the tavern, but pleaded with his comrades not to fire unless fired upon first. Fries assured Nichols that he did not intend violence, but he wasn't sure how long he could restrain the crowd. By sundown, the threat of violence was palpable, and Nichols relented. He released the prisoners but refused to accept bail. Instead, he reported the prisoners as stolen. The militia dispersed without destruction or assault, and the prisoners returned home. They cheered the peaceful result and celebrated the parallels to the Revolution.[14]

Back in Philadelphia, Adams was in no mood to deal with an insurrection. "I have been so overwhelmed with Business at the Close of the session of Congress and Since, that I have not been able to write you for several Days," he wrote to Abigail. He wanted nothing more than to sit by the fire at night and talk to her in person about events of the day. He would have to settle for writing her a letter instead.[15]

On March 9, he summoned his cabinet for a meeting at 6 P.M. He instructed the secretary of state "to bring with him a Copy of the Instructions to our late Envoys to France."[16] Still smoldering over the nomination and the fact that it had been kept from him, Pickering arrived determined to do everything in his power to sabotage the mission. He proposed three conditions upon which the negotiations must take place.

First, France must indemnify American citizens for the losses caused by the seizure of ships and goods. Second, American vessels were not bound to have a *rôle d'equipage*, or a detailed crew log, as mandated by the October 1798 French decree. Third, the United States would not help France defend her colonial holdings, including those in the Caribbean, which it had previously promised to do in the Treaty of 1778.

Much to Pickering's surprise, Adams and the rest of the cabinet readily agreed to these conditions. Adams instructed Pickering to draw up more detailed instructions to send to the envoys as soon as Talleyrand sent the required reassurances. The president repeated his pledge that Murray would stay at The Hague and the other envoys would stay on American soil until Talleyrand's letter had arrived, but he wanted the instructions ready.

Pickering was delighted that "the evil of the nomination may thus be counteracted." He was convinced that France would never accept these terms. Even if France proved accommodating, the unpredictable and slow speed of communications across the Atlantic Ocean would cause an indeterminable delay—enough time for circumstances to change and war to begin. It would also give Pickering time to brainstorm other ways to scuttle Adams's foreign policy.[17]

As the cabinet meeting concluded, Captain William Nichols, marshal for the District of Pennsylvania, arrived with an urgent report to deliver to the president. Nichols was shown to the drawing room upstairs, where he briefed the president and Secretary of War McHenry. He insisted that "a daring combination of and treasonable opposition to the laws of the United States" had occurred, and he was certain that federal laws could not be enforced "without military force." He failed to mention that no violence had taken place.[18]

The next morning, McHenry returned to the President's House to plan their response. Adams drafted a proclamation, which decried the "combinations to defeat the execution of the law." Responding solely to Nichols's reports, Adams warned that the resistance might amount to "overt acts of levying war against the United States." He commanded all insurgents "on or before Monday next, being the eighteenth day of this present month, to disperse and retire peaceably to their respective abodes." The proclamation also announced

Adams's intention to "call forth military force to suppress such combinations, and to cause the laws to be duly executed" based on the "solemn conviction that the essential interests of the United States demand it."[19] Adams handed the proclamation to McHenry and asked him to distribute it to the appropriate state and local authorities, as well as the newspapers.

With the proclamation dispatched, the president considered how to suppress further resistance. The recent bill to create the Provisional Army also permitted the president to call up local volunteer militias in the event of a domestic rebellion. He ordered McHenry to summon the militia under this law.[20]

McHenry suggested they consider the regiments under the regular army instead, as it was already partially organized and could be summoned more quickly. Adams refused; he didn't want Alexander Hamilton or his army anywhere near the scene of battle. He was also wisely factoring in Americans' deep-rooted distrust of standing armies. Deploying regular troops to crush citizens had not worked well for kings in England, nor had it worked in the American colonies. Both Washington and Adams prudently sought to avoid this comparison. In 1794, Washington had summoned local militias to suppress the Whiskey Rebellion. Four and a half years later, Adams adhered to Washington's precedent. Siccing the New Army on citizens, paid for by the very taxes they were currently protesting, would be highly unpopular. Adams ordered McHenry to appoint William MacPherson as the commander of the temporary militia force.[21]

While McHenry was executing the president's orders, John Fenno Jr. printed a report in his Federalist newspaper, the *Gazette of the United States*, warning of a burgeoning rebellion in western Pennsylvania that threatened to quickly outpace the Whiskey Rebellion in both size and ferocity.[22] If these reports were true, the rebellion would quickly shut down the judicial system, prevent the enforcement of the rule of law, and render state and federal authorities impotent to suppress the insurrection.

By this point, Adams had obtained additional intelligence and offered a different assessment: "We have a silly Insurgence in Northampton County in this state, which will detain me, I suppose, some days," Adams wrote to Abigail. The problem was Pennsylvania, he concluded. "This state is not a moral Person, it has not Intelligence enough to make it accountable for its Actions." He wasn't particularly worried about the insurrection, but he noted that "The Spirit in the City is very high against them."[23]

The next morning, the president left for Quincy.[24] It would prove to be one of the worst and most inexplicable decisions of his presidency.

18

A Paltry Insurrection

ON MARCH 18, John Fries received a copy of the president's proclamation and gathered with his friends and neighbors in a local tavern to read it aloud. After a brief discussion, they agreed to "desist from opposing any public officer in the execution of his office and enjoined upon the citizens to use their influence to prevent any opposition, and to give due submission to the laws of the United States."[1] They kept their word. No further disruption or resistance emerged.

The rebellion was over, but the Federalist response was just beginning. Every step of the prosecution, from military enforcement to sentencing, reflected the increasing partisanship of the Arch Federalists and exposed Adams's distance from it—both ideologically and physically.

In the coming weeks, General William MacPherson toured the countryside, organizing Federalist supporters and seeking guides. No one interfered with his travels or hurled insults in his direction.[2] A few levelheaded Federalists accurately assessed the threat. Oliver Wolcott Jr. wrote, "There is a paltry insurrection here, which I am inclined to think will be subdued without difficulty." Supreme Court Justice James Iredell agreed that the insurrection "can be easily suppressed."[3]

The rebellion could still "be nursed into something formidable," Wolcott warned, especially if one was inclined to see connections where they might or might not exist.[4] An editorial in the *Gazette of the United States*, the leading Federalist paper, argued that the insurrection, "commenced in deceit and wickedness," was connected to past outrages and rebellions, including "the hostilities of Genet," the French foreign minister who attempted to drag the United States into its war against Great Britain. Surely the next step would be a French-provoked "Rebellion of the Land of Slaves." If left unchecked, the French Directory would dismantle the Union, the *Gazette* argued.[5] Federalists saw this rebellion, not as a unique, contained resistance event spearheaded by fellow Federalists, but as the latest in a long line of Republican outrages. Even John Quincy Adams, not normally prone to histrionics, worried that there was a spirit in "part of our country" that "will never be suppressed but by force." Until then, he warned his mother, these insurrections "injure very much the estimation of our country with the rest of the world."[6]

For Federalists inclined to see the worst-case scenario, all the requisite conditions were present. The house tax had been the immediate source of outrage, but many of the rebels lumped the taxes in with the Alien and Sedition Laws in their protests. Because the rebels appeared to be resisting their entire agenda, Federalists concluded that these acts of resistance were part of a broader Republican plot, including the Kentucky and Virginia Resolutions.

Federalists' preexisting biases intensified these suspicions. They had long assumed that Republicans were cultivating radical support among immigrant communities. The creation of armed United Irishmen militias in cities like Philadelphia and New York City appeared to validate these concerns. Pickering concluded that the United Irish companies were "probably formed, to oppose the authority of the Government; and in case of war and invasion by the French, to join them."[7] Many of the rebels in Fries's ranks were German Americans who had resisted assimilation. They spoke German, lived in ethnic enclaves, and voted for officials who represented their cultural interests. The rebels' "otherness" exacerbated Federalists' fears that Republicans were once again partnering with immigrants to overthrow the government.[8] They saw a nefarious, widespread, well-organized insurrection because that was what they expected to see.[9]

Whether the Federalists believed their own rhetoric or it was merely useful is harder to determine. Genuine or feigned, the Federalists' response to the rebellion was well calculated to crush political rivals, demonstrate the power of federal authority, and flex the new army's muscles. Eager to make the most of the opportunity, Hamilton recommended to McHenry that it would be much better to use too much force than not enough.[10]

On March 20, at 3 P.M., Governor Thomas Mifflin wrote to the adjutant general of the Pennsylvania militia: "The secretary of War has this moment communicated to me the President's intention to employ a military force in suppressing the insurrection now existing in the counties of Northampton, Bucks and Montgomery," he ordered. "You will, therefore, immediately issue general orders for complying with the President's request," Mifflin instructed.[11]

As MacPherson planned to ride west with the militia, the secretaries kept Adams apprised of developments. Wolcott reported, "The discontents in Northampton are not increasing, and no resistance to the force ordered to march is expected."[12] Stoddert agreed. "There seems to be every probability, that the Insurrection in Northampton will be subdued without Bloodshed," he noted. "A number of the prisoners who were rescued out of the hands of the Marshal, have delivered themselves up, at Philadelphia," Stoddert continued. "I believe those who appeared in Arms at Bethlehem, will not resist the Marshal," who planned to ride out shortly accompanied "by about 200 horse."[13]

McHenry confirmed these reports. "All necessary arrangements have been made and are making to subdue the insurrection," he wrote. However, he did make a change in the plans without obtaining Adams's prior consent. In addition to MacPherson's volunteers, "I have issued orders to draw five companies of the regular army to the scene of insurrection," McHenry explained. He elected to employ the regular army (i.e., Hamilton's forces), rather than relying on the militia, because it would produce a favorable impression, "which is alone intended to give due efficacy to the laws."[14] Once organized, the army would also develop into a useful tool for enforcing the Federalists' domestic agenda, McHenry explained to the Essex Junto. Crushing this rebellion would give the army useful practice. He notably left this rationale out of his correspondence with the president. Adams had wanted to produce the exact opposite impression, but his concerns were ignored and there was nothing he could do to countermand the order, because he had left town while the crisis was ongoing.

The damage inflicted by McHenry's insubordination was mitigated by the army's utter failure to deliver. A few days later, McHenry reluctantly admitted that only sixty men turned out, an insufficient force to take on the rebels. With the army failing him, McHenry returned to Adams's original plan and called on the governors of Pennsylvania and New Jersey to summon their militias. The governors complied and McHenry gathered a combined force of about 600 men, complete with a company of artillerists.[15] The volunteers and militia would be tasked with arresting the rebels, while the regular forces guarded their flanks to prevent further disturbances.

On April 4, at 8 A.M., General MacPherson met his volunteer forces on Market Street in Philadelphia. They marched west until they reached the Schuylkill River, then turned north. For eighteen miles, they marched along Wissahickon Creek, before setting up camp on the border of Montgomery and Bucks counties. The following day, MacPherson's forces established headquarters at David Sellers's tavern and prepared to ride out the next morning to arrest John Fries.[16]

As three cavalry units approached town, Fries stood atop a cider barrel, calling out auction bids in both English and German. Earlier that day, Fries had been tipped off about his impending arrest and pledged to stand his ground and submit peacefully. He had expected to face only a few soldiers or officers, but his resolve broke when he observed hundreds of MacPherson's forces draw their weapons. The townspeople attending the auction fled across the town square and through the fields, and Fries escaped into the woods. Just before sunset, the forces came upon a small black dog who inadvertently led them to his owner, Fries, hiding in a briar patch. He was arrested and escorted back to Philadelphia under heavy guard.[17]

Over the next two weeks, the troops processed the arrests of 120 people, most of whom submitted themselves voluntarily. A few days later, the only casualty of the campaign occurred when one volunteer on watch duty heard a rustling noise. Convinced he had found the remains of the "rebel army," he fired his gun, killing a bull rummaging through the cavalry's hay.[18]

A few officers noted the ridiculousness of the exercise and wondered what they were doing in Pennsylvania. "This expedition was not only unnecessary, but violently absurd," one officer wrote. "A sergeant and six men might have performed all the service for which we have been assembled at so heavy an expence to the United States."[19]

McHenry offered a more triumphal take. He wrote again to the president, with "the honor" of enclosing "a copy of the last letter which I have received from Brigadier General MacPherson." The letter contained "a list of persons made prisoners or who had voluntarily surrendered to Justice."[20]

MacPherson and his troops staged a parade and review of more than 1,000 troops in the tiny Millers Town, which had less than 500 residents, just to make a point.[21] They returned to Philadelphia on April 20 and declared the rebellion suppressed.[22]

Just a few short days later, the defendants' trial began. Justice James Iredell presided over the proceedings of ten defendants, all charged with treason. Federalist prosecutors insisted the resistance was an insurrection, if not full civil war, designed to subvert the nation's laws and stymy the judicial system, rather than a relatively simple airing of economic grievances over taxation policy.[23] Philadelphia Republicans pooled resources to hire the Pennsylvania secretary of state, Alexander James Dallas, and Federalist William Lewis, two of the best trial attorneys in the area.[24]

Iredell opened the trial by embarking on a lengthy rant explaining his views of the case. "The grievance," Iredell explained, "is the land tax act." The government had concluded that "public exigencies rendered [the tax] unavoidable" and took extra care that "the great part of it must fall on rich people only." Despite the law's careful construction, the insurgents intended to "prevent by force of arms the execution of any act of the Congress of the United States altogether." This violent opposition "was a levying of war against the United States, and of course an act of treason," Iredell proclaimed.[25]

He delivered this weighty statement before a single piece of evidence was presented to the jury, leaving observers with a good sense of the outcome of the trial before it had begun. Pickering wrote to the president that he had consulted with the judges. He sent them detailed notes asserting that Fries and his fellow defendants should be convicted of treason.[26] They "were perfectly agreed as to the treasonable matter, and the *guilt* of the prisoner."[27] Even before the adaption of modern standards of the independent judiciary, this collusion was inappropriate.

From May 1 to May 9, the jury listened to the testimony of eighteen prosecution witnesses who swore that Fries ordered his men to fire, carried a "large horse pistol," and intended to obstruct federal law. The jury then heard from four defense witnesses who spoke to Fries's peaceful nature and his willing submission to authorities afterward. The defense acknowledged Fries's participation in the resistance, but they presented his efforts as restrained and within constitutionally protected protest activities.

After the evidence and statements were delivered, Iredell again addressed the jury. He defined treason as obstructing a federal law, which was a very restrictive interpretation, and prohibited the jury from considering a more expansive definition of this grave charge. He ordered them to consider why Fries rode to Bethlehem. If the jury found that Fries schemed to rescue the prisoners "by any kind of force," he asserted, then they "ought to declare him guilty of the charge laid in the indictment." Under those terms, the jury was left with little choice.[28] At 10 P.M. on May 9, the jury delivered a guilty verdict on the charge of high treason.[29]

Wolcott wrote to the president that Fries had conducted himself respectfully during the proceedings and "continued tranquil until the verdict of the jury was returned." Since then, Wolcott continued, "he has been much affected." Apparently, Wolcott explained, Fries "confidently expected to be acquitted" because his defense counsel had convinced him that his "offence did not amount to treason."[30]

Adams read descriptions of the trial proceedings with growing concern. As a lawyer, he knew that any treason conviction would establish precedent for subsequent cases, and the broad definition articulated by Iredell could prove dangerous. Adams worried all future misdeeds might be swept up in this definition of treason, creating a much more punitive system of justice. He wrote to his attorney general and divulged his concerns. "I am told that Mr Lewis is of opinion that Fries Crime amounts not to Treason," Adams said. "Can you give me a minute of his reasons?"[31]

At the same time, Adams asked Wolcott, trying to get a sense of Fries's character, "Is Fries a Native or a Foreigner? Is he a Man of Property and independent, or is he in Debt? What has been his previous Life, industrious or idle? sober or intemperate?" His questions reveal the president attempting to put Fries's one misdeed in the context of an entire life.[32]

Adams was obligated to consider these questions by his constitutional authority and the precedent established by Washington. Article II, Section 2 of the Constitution grants the president the sole "Power to grant Reprieves and Pardons for Offences." It is one of the most influential and unlimited powers entrusted to the president. In 1795, Washington invoked this authority when he issued a blanket proclamation of amnesty for all the rebels convicted of resistance in the Whiskey Rebellion. He had followed the proclamation with a full pardon for the two defendants, John Mitchell and Philip Vigol, convicted of treason and sentenced to death.[33]

Washington had justified the pardons in his annual address to Congress by explaining that it was his duty "to exercise with firmness and energy the Constitutional powers with which I am vested." He also owed a duty to the public good, which obligated him to "mingle in the operations of Government every degree of moderation and tenderness, which the national justice, dignity and safety may permit." Because "the misled have abandoned their errors, and pay the respect to our Constitution and Laws," Washington saw ample reason to be merciful.[34]

Finally, Adams sympathized with many of the rebels' protests. He distrusted the army, felt queasy over the dwelling tax, and expressed deep ambivalence about the Sedition Act. Adams did not articulate these concerns while considering a pardon, but they almost certainly weighed on his mind.[35]

As Adams pondered these factors, he received a reply from Charles Lee. Lee hadn't attended the trial, so he could not provide a detailed explanation for "Mr. Lewis's reasons for the opinion that the crime of Fries was not treason," but he was able to secure and forward "a short note" on the subject from William Rawle, the US district attorney. Both Rawle and Lee rejected Mr. Lewis's argument and upheld the court's judgment of treason.[36]

Perhaps Wolcott and Lee mentioned the president's concerns to Pickering because he wrote to Adams that Fries's "conviction is of the highest importance." Pickering had polled "the real friends to the order & tranquillity of the country," meaning the Arch Federalists, and they all agreed "that an example or examples of conviction and punishment of such high-handed offenders were essential." Firmness would "ensure future obedience to the laws, or the exertions of our best citizens to suppress future insurrections," he persisted. "The idea of taking the life of a man" was painful, Pickering allowed, but there were larger concerns at stake. A conspiracy to "overturn the Government" survived.[37] This last sentence revealed Pickering's motivations for securing a conviction and an execution. For Pickering, McHenry, and their fellow Essex Junto allies, the trial was not about the rule of law but rather an opportunity to defend their partisan legislation and crush political enemies.

The justice system soon postponed Adams's deliberations. Before Fries could be sentenced, his counsel entered a motion requesting a new trial. Dallas alleged that one of the jurors had been overheard before the trial declaring that Fries "ought to be hung." Reluctantly, Iredell granted the motion and set a new trial date in the fall.[38]

For the moment, Adams was spared the pardon decision. But "the issue of this investigation has opened a train of very serious contemplations to me," he confessed to Pickering. It "will require the closest attention of my best understanding, & will prove a severe trial to my heart," Adams wrote, foreshadowing that this debate was far from over.[39] Over the next several months, the retrial, a potential pardon, and the fate of the army would highlight the growing distance between the president and some of his cabinet secretaries.

19

The Air of an Abdication

THE GULF BETWEEN the president and the Arch Federalists was palpable. While the cabinet managed the federal response to the insurrection, many Federalists questioned the president's absence. Adams's "stay from the seat of Government, which is likely to continue till next November or December, is a source of much disgust" one Federalist wrote to Rufus King. "It embarrasses the public business and has the air of an abdication."[1]

Timothy Pickering sent a similar letter to George Washington, announcing that the president planned to remain in Quincy for eight months, despite the "great Executive business arising out of the late Session, and with an Insurrection!"[2] The problem was not Adams's summer visit per se. Washington had regularly left the seat of government for visits home with no objection from his cabinet. In fact, his trips home in 1792, 1794, 1795, and 1796 had amounted to over three months away from Philadelphia. Until the summer of 1799, Adams had been away roughly the same number of days as Washington. But there were two important differences for the cabinet and the American public. Adams took one long trip, whereas Washington was able to make several, shorter visits home to Mount Vernon due to the closer proximity. And Washington was never absent during a crisis because he could rush back quickly from Virginia.[3] Adams's absence sent a poor message to the American people and undermined his efforts to assert control over the executive branch and foreign policy.

Pickering was outraged at the president's seemingly cavalier attitude toward his responsibilities, but he also secretly relished the opportunity provided by the lack of oversight. Over the next several months, with Adams absent, he pursued his own goals, whether or not they aligned with the president's agenda. When they clashed over issues, Pickering directly challenged the president's authority over foreign policy.

A few weeks after Adams left Philadelphia, British General Thomas Maitland sailed into port aboard a British sloop of war. His mission was to open Saint-Domingue to Anglo-American trade.[4]

In August 1791, enslaved workers on sugar plantations on the northern plains of Saint-Domingue had rebelled against the tyranny of their owners and oppressors. Inspired by the revolutionary rhetoric from Paris, the rebellion spread to nearby towns and quickly devoured most of the island. In 1793, faced with an ongoing war against Britain and an insurgency in the Caribbean, the French Republic agreed to abolish slavery in all its colonies, hoping to restore peace and to keep the rebellious forces from falling into the hands of European enemies.[5]

This plan was put to the test when the first British forces landed in Saint-Domingue, eager to seize the colony during the chaos. Over the next twelve months, up to 12,000 English troops died of disease.[6] General Maitland landed in Saint-Domingue a few years later, part of the second wave of British troops charged with capturing the French colony. His forces met the same fate. He sailed back to London to convince the British ministry to seek a peaceful solution.

Upon his return, Maitland met with the newly installed leader of independent Saint-Domingue, Toussaint Louverture. Born into slavery on a sugar plantation, Louverture took an early leadership role in the revolution. By 1798, he controlled most of the island and was poised to negotiate with the upper hand.

In August, Maitland and Louverture signed a secret treaty that guaranteed British troops a peaceful retreat. In return, Britain would make no further attack on Saint-Domingue, and Louverture would try to contain the revolution from spreading to the nearby British colony of Jamaica.

Although Louverture had dispatched the British threat, his people needed food to survive, and his forces desperately required supplies to counter future French attacks. Prior to the revolution, Saint-Domingue had relied on American merchants to buy its goods and deliver critical supplies in return. But that trade had slowed to a trickle over the past year in response to French naval seizures and President Adams's subsequent embargo on all French ports. Louverture needed to tempt American ships back into the ports at Saint-Domingue to reignite the critical trade.[7]

At the same time, Maitland arrived in Philadelphia with a proposal for Anglo-American cooperation to open trade in Saint-Domingue and stem the tide of further revolution in the Caribbean. The British foreign minister, Lord Grenville, hoped "to act in concert with the United States" and granted

Robert Liston "full powers" to solidify "arrangements which may be mutually advantageous."[8]

On April 5 at noon, Maitland and Liston arrived at the Department of State offices. Pickering expressed interest in the economic potential of a mutual arrangement but asked to see their proposed terms in writing. Liston and Maitland agreed to create a draft of the agreement and pledged to return the next day.

That evening, Pickering sat down at his desk and penned a letter to the president, describing the conversations thus far.[9] One week later, Adams received the letter and wrote back immediately that he was "anxious to receive the Result of the Conference with Mr. Liston, Gen. Maitland & Colo. Grant."[10]

Pickering relished the relative independence to conduct diplomacy according to his own values. He had long sought a closer relationship between the United States and Britain, and Adams's absence offered an opportunity to seize it.[11] Over the next several days, Maitland and Liston regularly walked along Arch Street, from Liston's home to Pickering's Department of State offices, and back again.[12]

On the afternoon of Saturday, April 20, they concluded the preliminary negotiations. "We have given the subject the best examination in our power, and we believed the interests of the U. States would be better secured and promoted than by any separate and independent arrangements of the United States," Pickering wrote to Adams that evening. He enclosed the draft of the articles and acknowledged that he had already offered the government's tentative approval. "But I have informed Mr. Liston & General Maitland," that their draft agreement was "subject to your decision, to approve or reject them. This is perfectly understood by them," Pickering assured Adams.[13]

On the morning of April 23, Maitland sailed for Saint-Domingue to carry the news to Touissant Louverture.[14] It was a remarkable moment. For the first time, a white American administration recognized a Black-led government and offered assistance.

A few days later, the president received Pickering's dispatches and read the results with delight. "I am very glad that you did not detain Gen Maitland till you could hear from me," Adams wrote to his secretary of state. "Upon the whole I think the negotiation has been conducted with caution & prudence & the result has my fullest approbation."[15] In this instance, Pickering's initiative had served the president well.

Over the next several weeks, Pickering drafted a proclamation declaring Saint-Domingue open to American trade and mailed it to the president for his consideration. If the anticipated response from Saint-Domingue provided "the proper basis for a proclamation," he wanted to be prepared. Every moment counted, Pickering urged, as "the impatience of the merchants, and the great interest of the country in the St. Domingo trade rendering it desirable to prevent every delay which can by any means be avoided."[16] Pickering had tremendous ability to work quickly and with initiative when it suited him. When he elected to procrastinate, as he did later that summer, it was an intentional choice.

On June 15, Adams signed the proclamation and returned it to the secretary of state so that "it may be completed and published at a proper season without loss of time."[17] The final pieces fell into place over the next two weeks. On June 21, Pickering received a diplomatic packet from Maitland announcing the ports of Cape Francois and Port au Prince would be opened to American ships on August 1. The secretaries met that evening, and again the next day, to discuss how best to spread the news and publish the president's proclamation.[18]

Pickering informed the president that the cabinet had decided on a publication schedule. The challenge was how to publicize the news in such a way that merchants across the country would have equal time to prepare for their voyage, set sail, and take advantage of the economic opportunity. Because news took days, if not weeks, to transmit to the farthest reaches of the nation, the most distant states would be notified first. On Friday, June 28, they would send copies of the proclamation to "Maine, Georgia, South and North Carolina, and the Ports on James River." The day after, copies would go to the remaining districts in Virginia, "New Hampshire, Massachusetts and Rhode Island." They would inform Connecticut on Monday. "New York, New Jersey, Delaware, and Maryland would be mailed copies on Tuesday. And on Wednesday, July 3, copies would be delivered in Pennsylvania.[19]

Pickering explained that this plan was the fairest one they could devise. "If there had been more time," he clarified, "we should have made greater differences in the periods of transmitting the proclamation" so that each state would have the same amount of time to prepare. "As it is," Pickering continued, "the merchants in general will have only about twenty five days to fit their vessels for sea, and to make their voyages to Saint-Domingue, to arrive on the first of August."[20] On June 27, Pickering mailed the president the final version of the proclamation, which officially "renewed a commercial intercourse" with Saint-Domingue.[21]

In the president's absence, Pickering kept a vigilant eye out for real and perceived attacks on the Federalist agenda. An item in the *Aurora* quickly captured Pickering's attention. On June 24, William Duane published an article claiming that the British had paid $800,000 in bribes to government officials. Duane claimed to have evidence written in the president's own hand.[22]

Duane was born in upstate New York in 1760 to Irish parents but spent most of his childhood in Ireland and Great Britain. As a young adult, he worked for newspapers in Ireland, London, and India before he was arrested for sedition. The harsh treatment radicalized Duane and turned him into a political agitator. Duane's political activities forced him to flee London and he arrived in Philadelphia on July 4, 1796. Nearly destitute, Duane found refuge and employment at the home of Benjamin Franklin Bache. Just before Bache died of yellow fever in the summer of 1798, he named Duane as his successor as editor of the *Aurora*.[23]

Bache's *Aurora* had long been a thorn in the side of the Federalists, and Duane readily picked up the mantle. In just a few months, he established himself as the most prominent Republican editor by waging relentless attacks on the Federalist Party and turning his office into a hub of political activity. He organized the Irish community into a powerful political force, coordinated protests, and authored petitions against the Alien and Sedition Acts.[24]

Just a few months before Duane captured Pickering's attention, he was brutally assaulted by a group of cavalry soldiers for criticizing the army. Thirty soldiers, recently returned from arresting rebels in Northampton, marched into Duane's *Aurora* offices. They dragged him from behind his desk into the streets, took turns punching him until he could no longer stand, and whipped him until they were satisfied. Undaunted, Duane published an article the following day describing the beating in gruesome detail, under the title "MORE OF GOOD ORDER AND REGULAR GOVERNMENT!"[25]

In a lather, Pickering wailed to Adams, "There is in the Aurora of this city, an uninterrupted stream of slander on the American Government." It was not the first time, but Pickering was determined that it would be the last. "I shall give the paper to Mr. Rawle," the local US attorney. "If he thinks it libellous," Pickering stressed, he would instruct "him to prosecute the Editor."[26]

A few days later, Adams replied, somewhat nonplussed. "Is there any Thing evil in the Regions of Actuality or Possibility, that the Aurora has not suggested of me?" he asked. Nonetheless, he agreed that the July 24 article is "imbued with rather more impudence than is common to that Paper." Adams had not sought the prosecution himself, but he approved Pickering's plan. "If

Mr. Rawle does not think this paper Libellous he is not fit for his office," he continued, "and if he does not prosecute it, he will not do his Duty."[27]

Before receiving the president's reply, Pickering wrote again, informing Adams that "a prosecution against Duane, editor of the Aurora, has been instituted." Not content with the one charge, Pickering encouraged prosecutorial vigilance. "I have desired Mr. Rawle to examine his news-paper and to institute new prosecutions as often as [Duane] offends." Almost as an afterthought, Pickering included, "This I hope will meet with your approbation."[28]

Pickering was convinced Duane wasn't just an annoyance, but a much more serious threat that required active squashing. "Wm. Duane pretends that he is an American Citizen," Pickering wrote snidely, but he "seemed bent on stirring "up sedition & work[ing] other mischief."[29] Within a week of Pickering's first letter to Rawle, the US attorney had arrested Duane for seditious libel "concerning the administration" under the Sedition Act.[30] Rawle demanded that Duane post an abnormally high bond, $2,000, to guarantee his appearance at the next court session a few months later. Duane replied that "neither persecution nor any other peril would make him swerve from the cause of republicanism."[31]

After spending the summer pursuing his own diplomatic goals with Britain and rustling up sedition prosecutions, Pickering turned his attention to the president's peace mission, which he was determined to thwart for good. In May, Adams had finalized the three commissioners who would travel to France. Patrick Henry had regretfully declined the appointment due to poor health, but William Davie agreed to serve with Chief Justice Oliver Ellsworth and William Vans Murray. Davie was a solid Federalist but less radical than some of the other potential candidates. As the governor of North Carolina, he also provided important geographic balance to the commission.[32]

At this point, or at any point in the previous months, Pickering could have drafted the detailed instructions for the envoys that Adams had requested at their last cabinet meeting on March 11. Instead, he intentionally stalled and hoped the French would prove incalcitrant.

When Pickering finally received updates from Europe, the contents of the letters only further enraged him. Earlier that spring, William Vans Murray had received a bundle of newspapers that announced his appointment. "I am profoundly grateful for and justly proud of this mark of [the president's] confidence!" Murray beamed in his letter to Pickering.[33] As soon as Murray received the official instructions, he wrote to Talleyrand announcing his new position and asking for direct assurances that he and his fellow envoys would be received with all appropriate respect, as the president had requested.[34] Less than two weeks later, Murray received a response from Talleyrand, promising he would be delighted to receive the commissioners. Murray quickly bundled up a copy of his letter and Talleyrand's answer and mailed them to Pickering in Philadelphia.[35]

The first of Murray's dispatches arrived in Philadelphia on July 8. Furious at the president's unwavering dedication to the peace mission, Pickering vented his wrath on the unsuspecting foreign minister. "Every man whom you knew and respected, every real patriot, every man who had steadily and faithfully supported his and his predecessor's administration was thunderstruck," Pickering condescendingly explained to Murray. The nomination was "done without any consultation with any member of the government . . . because he knew we should all be opposed to the measure!" Pickering sputtered.[36] He mailed this reply to The Hague and then sat on Murray's letters for several weeks.

At the end of July, Pickering finally wrote to the president, announcing that he had just received dispatches from Murray, which included a letter from Talleyrand.[37] He advised that Talleyrand's assurances were insufficient to proceed with negotiations. "The answer, I observe," Pickering noted, "does not exactly conform to the terms used in the instructions to Mr. Murray, & which he repeated in his letter of May 5th to the Minister." Furthermore, Pickering argued, Talleyrand continued to insult the president, while pretending to make "amicable professions!" Pickering huffily observed, "it was certainly not necessary for him to insinuate that the President of the United States was wasting many months of precious time."[38]

Adams took this letter from his touchy secretary of state with a grain of salt. After extensive diplomatic service, he knew better than to allow small aggravations to upend progress.[39] "It is far below the Dignity of the President of the United States, to take any notice of Talleyrand's impertinent Regrets," he wrote back to Pickering. "As long as I am in office," Adams pledged, France would find "a pacific & friendly disposition" in the United States. "In this Spirit I shall pursue the negotiation and I expect the Cooperation of the heads of Departments," Adams commanded in no uncertain terms.

With the preliminary conditions satisfied, Adams continued, "I pray you to lose no time in conveying to Governor Davie his Commission," as well as any other letters or paperwork the envoys might need to "make immediate Preparations for embarking." "I wish to delay nothing," he wrote to Pickering.

Adams closed by repeating his orders for Pickering to prepare official instructions "as promptly as possible." It shouldn't take long, the president continued, as "all the Points of the Negotiation were so minutely considered, and approved by me, and all the heads of departments before I left Philadelphia." He instructed Pickering to share them with the heads of the departments and send them immediately to Quincy. "My Opinions and determinations on these subjects are so well made up," Adams concluded, "that not many hours will be necessary for me to give you my ultimate sentiments concerning the Matter or form of the Instructions to be given to the Envoys."[40]

Pickering received Adams's very clear orders. He rejected them.

Instead, he spent the next several weeks trying to convince Chief Justice Oliver Ellsworth to refuse to serve on the mission.[41] Pickering wrote to George Cabot, asking him to write Ellsworth and "propose his attempting to dissuade the President" from sending the peace commission. "I also will write him," Pickering promised.[42] He sent similar sentiments to Stephen Higginson and Theodore Sedgwick. These efforts were so conspicuous that Liston noted them in his dispatches back to London.[43]

Adams's allies witnessed these developments with increasing discomfort. Uriah Forrest was a Revolutionary War veteran, former Federalist congressman, a loyal Adams supporter, and the close friend and neighbor of Secretary of the Navy Benjamin Stoddert. Forrest watched events unfold that summer and perhaps received behind-the-scenes information from Stoddert about cabinet deception. Alarmed, Forrest wrote to the president with a dire warning.

Forrest was motivated to write, he explained, by a deep conviction that the "happiness of this Country depends on the confidence the people have in the Government; and I feel that Yourself must be the Rallying point of confidence." That was not possible, Forrest explained, when Adams was "so much away from the Seat of Government."

Taking a more aggressive tone, Forrest reminded Adams that "The People Elected You to administer the Government—They did not Elect your officers—Nor do they . . . think them equal to Govern, without your Presence and control." He warned, there will always be men "not satisfied with their proper share of Power." Without the president around to keep a careful eye, these men will "increase in their own consequence and claims, until they fancy themselves exclusively entitled" to complete authority. He did not name names, but he challenged Adams to consider if the administration was "free from such Characters."[44]

Adams replied with thanks, but insisted he could manage the affairs of government in Quincy as well "as I could do at Philadelphia." He explained that the "Secretaries of State, Treasury, War, Navy & the Attorney General, transmit me daily by the post all the business of consequence." No decisions are made "without my advice & direction," he continued. "The post goes very rapidly, and I answer by the return of it, so that nothing suffers or is lost," Adams assured Forrest.[45]

The president missed the alarm contained in Forrest's letter, or he ignored it.

20

An Apple of Discord to the Federalists

THEODORE SEDGWICK'S LARGE brick mansion with white trim, columns, and black shutters dominated Main Street in Stockbridge, Massachusetts, and dwarfed its neighbors. Sedgwick had built the house in 1785 as a tribute to English gentry sophistication. Fourteen years later, the house offered little comfort as he sat in his private study, ruminating over his correspondence. He received regular updates from Timothy Pickering and James McHenry in Philadelphia, Alexander Hamilton in New York, and George Cabot, Stephen Higginson, and other members of the Essex Junto around Boston. The news was grim. "The delay in raising the army," he explained to Rufus King in London, "has been shameful & almost unpardonable." He was not "positive" whether the delay "is attributable" to the secretary of war alone, "or ought to be shared between him" and the president. But Sedgwick suspected the president had something to do with it. Those suspicions would only grow sharper in the coming months as Adams pursued his diplomatic agenda, intentionally undermined the growth of the army, and marched toward a confrontation with the Essex Junto.

"What makes this conduct the more unaccountable," Sedgwick fussed, was the comparison between the stagnation of the army and the success of the navy.[1] Sedgwick was right about the navy's extraordinary achievements in just one year. The prior summer, American merchant marine seizures by the French navy had reached an all-time high. In response, insurance rates skyrocketed to nearly 33 percent of the value of the ship and its cargo. Just months after the navy's creation in June 1798, the rates hovered between 15 and 20 percent. By the end of the year, they had dropped to 10 percent. In the first year of the navy's existence, the insurance savings totaled $8.5 million—three times the cost to build the navy.[2]

The navy also notched highly symbolic victories against pesky French privateers. The recent victory of the *Constellation*, a US naval vessel captained by Thomas Truxton, gave Americans particular pleasure. The *Constellation* destroyed *l'Insurgente*, the fastest French privateer, which had captured many American vessels. Newspapers across the country trumpeted Truxton's lopsided victory and cities and communities threw celebrations in honor of the naval commander. Revenge was sweet, but the naval victories also ushered in a new era of American participation on the world stage. They revitalized confidence and restored national honor after a series of naval and diplomatic humiliations.[3] The navy also encouraged merchants to expand their networks, confident that their ships and wares would be protected. Finally, the navy provided a powerful backstop to Adams's diplomatic efforts.

Eager to maximize the opportunity, Adams and Stoddert engineered the next phase of their naval strategy. As the summer faded, Stoddert reported to Adams that new frigates, recently constructed under the war readiness measures, were nearing completion and almost ready to set sail. With Adams's approval, Stoddert ordered one to patrol the waters around Saint-Domingue, the second to monitor the Guinea coast in Africa, and a third to hunt French privateers outside the ports of Guadaloupe.[4]

Around the same time, McHenry wrote to the president about the army. He downplayed the naval success and bombastically proclaimed that the nation needed three things to maintain its "proper grade among the powers of the earth." First, an army. Second, "a system calculated to keep its wants regularly supplied." Third, "genius in the general who commands it." McHenry continued, "If we can combine these three, with a navy," he said, almost as an afterthought, "we shall have nothing to fear from without or within."[5]

One week later, the president brought McHenry down to earth. "It is an excellent Principle for every Man in public Life, to magnify his office and make it honourable," he conceded. "I admire the Dexterity with which you dignify yours," Adams wrote somewhat condescendingly. But surely Secretary of the Navy Stoddert would "have felt the Importance of his office enough to have stated a Navy as the first and most indispensable" thing for the nation.. Do not make him prioritize between the two secretaries, Adams warned McHenry. "I shall be at no Loss. My answer would be ready."[6] The navy had proven its value to both diplomacy and the American economy, whereas the army appeared to be an endless pit for resources, manpower, and attention, while contributing little value back to the nation. Adams openly played favorites.

As the summer progressed and France issued no further threats, most Americans astutely assumed the chances of war were fading. Officers returned their commissions and soldiers deserted in droves. McHenry and Hamilton watched their carefully constructed regiments dwindle and spent hours poring over the reports of court martial proceedings for deserted infantry.[7] Adams secretly welcomed the army's deterioration and did nothing to stop it.

Sedgwick had guessed correctly: the president was partly to blame for the army's lackluster progress—and it had been intentional.

Events in Paris soon outpaced both Adams and Pickering's plans for the peace commission. On June 18, or 30 Prairial in the French calendar, several of the French directors were forced from office, the third time in two years that French constitutional practices had crumbled in the face of political pressure. Jacobin clubs, which had gained notoriety during the height of the Revolution, returned and held sessions in the former Tuileries Palace. Newspapers called for revolutionary dictatorship, and Napoleon Bonaparte racked up victories across Europe, the Middle East, and Africa. At the end of the summer, he set sail for France.[8]

Pickering was absolutely delighted; here was the excuse he needed to delay the mission. The men who had provided assurances to the president were no longer in power and the French army was on the brink of surrendering to the British and her allies. A newly victorious Britain might inflict vengeance on the United States for signing a treaty with France. Or at least that's what Pickering argued.[9]

He canvassed the other secretaries. Wolcott and McHenry echoed Pickering's sentiments and expressed enthusiasm for delaying the mission.[10] Charles Lee and Stoddert weren't so sure. And the secretary of the navy didn't particularly like the direction of the conversation.

On August 17, Stoddert wrote to the president, after "talking on this subject with some of the heads of Departments." He thought the president should know that some of the other secretaries expected that the mission should be delayed until the following spring.[11]

Pickering's attempt to delay the mission was aided by the annual arrival of yellow fever. On August 24, Stoddert wrote to the president to notify him that the secretaries were packing up their offices and relocating to Trenton, New Jersey.[12] Pickering borrowed some rooms in the New Jersey State House for the state department offices. The State House perched on the bluff above the Delaware River, and river breezes flowed through open windows.[13] A few blocks away, Stoddert rented a house for his family and offices. The nine-room row house was clean except for "a number of small ants," but smaller than Rebecca Stoddert, Benjamin's wife, preferred. They didn't bring any furniture with them when they fled the fever, and she found it challenging to entertain guests properly. But Trenton offered one bright spot; she could purchase excellent fat chickens, which she could not find in Philadelphia, despite her best efforts.[14]

A few days after settling in, Stoddert reported to Adams that "the Officers are now all at this place, & not badly accomodated." Adams had ignored the first subtle invitation, but Stoddert persisted, requesting that the president join the secretaries in Trenton "before our Ministers depart for France." Without naming names, Stoddert hinted that the other secretaries were discussing the "recent events in Europe" and the possibility "these events might be of a nature to require the suspension for a time of the mission." Stoddert urged the president to take into account "both Public considerations," like the nation's security, and "those which relate more immediately to yourself," like Adams's reelection chances. His presence was needed.[15]

On September 10, after weeks of intentional procrastination, Pickering finally invited the other secretaries to the temporary department of state offices to discuss the envoys' instructions. Pickering and McHenry insisted the mission should be suspended, or at least delayed until the president received assurances from the new Directory that the envoys would be received. They also weren't particularly subtle about their hatred for the mission and their preference for war. Stoddert alone spoke in favor of the mission, or at least supporting the president's preferred foreign policy. The secretary of the navy knew Charles Lee agreed with him, but the attorney general was back in Virginia and could only offer written support.

After intense deliberation, the secretaries finally agreed on the remaining details. Pickering dashed off a quick cover letter to the president, promising to include more specifics the following day. He sealed the package and handed it to the clerk just before the post rider departed Trenton for Boston.[16] The next day, Pickering wrote another, lengthier letter. He suggested that the president might wish to send a copy of the instructions to Chief Justice Oliver Ellsworth and "invite his observations upon them: as it is important that he should be satisfied."

Next, Pickering described the "very portentous scene" in Paris, which had expelled many of the ministers from the Directory. The "instability and uncertainty in the government" of France "have suggested to the Heads of

Departments some doubts of the expediency of an immediate departure of the envoys," Pickering explained.

Given these developments, Pickering continued, he thought it his duty to suggest "the question of a temporary suspension of the mission to that country." If the terrors of the French Revolution were to return, a permanent suspension of the mission "seems to the Heads of Departments to merit serious consideration."[17] Pickering used a clever turn of phrase to make it appear that all the secretaries opposed the mission. But he wasn't accurately describing the secretaries' conversations to the president. The "Heads of Departments" didn't agree unanimously, as the secretary of the navy made clear two days later.

At his wits' end, Stoddert abandoned all subtlety. "I have been apprehensive that artful designing men might make such use of your absence from the seat of Government," he disclosed to the president. Especially at this moment, when their deliberations were "so important to restore Peace with one country & to preserve it with another."[18]

Adams sat in his library in Quincy and watched these letters pour in from Trenton. He kept his cards close to his chest as he replied.

Adams's letters to Pickering were especially gracious, given the secretary's implicit insults. Pickering's suggestion that Ellsworth be given editorial control over the envoys' instructions was not standard practice. Washington had given Jay wide latitude to negotiate a treaty with Britain in 1794, but he didn't usually give his envoys veto power over their instructions.[19] Nor had Adams previously given editorial control to his envoys, which Pickering well knew. However, Pickering also knew that Ellsworth was wavering on the mission. If Ellsworth had reservations about the instructions, he might be able to further delay his departure.

Adams refused to accept Pickering's premise and turned the conversation on its head. "I am glad you have sent a copy to the Chief Justice," he wrote to Pickering. "I had several long conversations with him last winter on the whole subject. He appears to me to agree most perfectly in sentiment with me upon every point of our policy," Adams continued.

Adams then offered a very different interpretation of the developments in France. The new, more radical government shouldn't automatically doom negotiations, Adams argued. The French government during "the reign of terror" was "the most disposed to accomodate with us" of all the various regimes, he reminded Pickering. More important, the American response to French depredations had been so strong that any government would know better than to expect "complaisance" from us. While the situation was in flux, it would be prudent to have envoys on site to represent American interests and to take advantage of the shifting winds.[20] Adams closed by expressing his "great anxiety upon this whole subject," but noticeably did not give a concrete answer either way about the envoys' departure.[21]

A few days later, the president received a letter from the chief justice. Ellsworth said that "many seem to expect" that "the present convulsion in France, and the symptoms of a greater change at hand" would induce the president to "postpone for a short time, the mission to that country." If those expectations were correct, Ellsworth wrote, "I wish for the earliest notice of it."[22]

Adams did not miss the reference to "many seem to expect." At this point, he had not indicated to his secretaries how he planned to manage the mission's departure. And yet, someone had told Ellsworth there would be a delay.

Again, Adams tactfully made no mention of the behind-the-scenes deception clearly taking place. He wrote back immediately, "the Convulsions in France . . . will certainly induce me to postpone" the envoys' departure, but only for a few weeks at most. "If your Departure for Europe should be postponed to the 20th of October or even the first of November," the passage across the Atlantic will be as safe "as at any other season of the year," he assured Ellsworth. "This is all I can say at present," he concluded.[23]

The Essex Junto was just getting started, however. After Pickering and Ellsworth wrote to the president, Cabot visited Peacefield at the urging of "Great Men out of the Govt. as well as some that are in." Cabot confided in King about this multi-step campaign: "Infinite pains have been taken to prevent" the diplomatic mission, which he called an "indiscreet & impolitic step."

Upon his arrival, Cabot was "treated with great kindness & hospitality," but every time he tried to broach the subject that "bore affinity to those which I wished to touch," he found himself stymied. Abigail changed the subject, John refused to discuss foreign policy or said his mind was made up. When Cabot pressed the subject, the president conveniently found himself called out of the room. It was almost as if they colluded to ensure "every heart was locked & every tongue was silenced," Cabot groused to King.[24]

Adams made no mention of these intrigues in his letters to Ellsworth or Pickering. He never let on just how much he knew or, at least, how much he suspected. But the schemes were clearly at such an advanced stage that he could no longer stay in Quincy. That same night, he wrote to Pickering announcing that "sometime between the 10th & fifteenth of October, I shall join you at Trenton." He also decided to suspend until that time "the ultimate determination concerning the instructions."[25] Adams let the secretary of state believe that he had won.

Pickering replied, in his most supercilious manner, that he "consulted [his] colleagues; and they concur with me in opinion that it will be an eligible step" for Adams to join them in Trenton, as if the president needed their permission. "If, however," Pickering continued, they received more news from Europe which supported suspending the mission, then "the trouble of your journey may be saved."[26] Pickering suggested Adams could just stay home and leave the governing to them.

Earlier in the summer, Uriah Forrest had warned that some governing men "increase in their own consequence and claims, until they fancy themselves exclusively entitled" to complete authority.[27] He had been right; Pickering had been left to his own devices for too long.

If Adams had any remaining hesitation about going to Trenton, this letter from Pickering banished the thought from his mind. It may have also solidified his intention to push ahead with the mission, regardless of the circumstances in Europe. At the very least, it confirmed to Adams that Pickering was not to be trusted and decisive steps were required to reassert presidential authority over the executive branch and foreign policy.

On September 30, Adams set out under the cover of darkness. He had warned Stoddert that he would not be in Quincy to receive letters past September 29. He also told Gerry about his plans but asked his old friend to keep them a secret from the Essex Junto. Abigail did not reveal his departure date to anyone else.[28]

While Adams quickly made his way to Trenton, Ellsworth forwarded the letter he received from the president to the secretary of state. Delighted, Pickering gloated to his allies, "the most ⟨satisfactory⟩ communication I have it in my power now to make, is the probability that the mission to France will at least be suspended."[29] Cabot passed along the news to King: "It is this day announced to me as a public report that the Mission is suspended. I hope & believe it is so, but how much happier shou'd I have been if it had never been projected!"[30]

A few days later, the president arrived in Trenton.

On the night of October 10, Adams collapsed into "a bed of down, the finest Thing in the World." He had picked up one of his "great Colds" in his travels and his personal troubles weighed heavily on him.[31]

As usual, Adams stopped along the route to visit with his daughter Nabby in East Chester, and then made his way to New York City to visit Charles, his second son. What he found in New York horrified him and would be the cause of endless pain for both John and Abigail. Charles was fully in the throes of his alcohol addiction, had fled his home, and left his wife, Sally, and their children destitute.[32]

When Adams arrived in New York City, "Sally opened her Mind to me for the first time. I pitied her, I grieved, I mourned," he wrote to Abigail. He was able to find their son but could do nothing to help him. Charles was "a Madman possessed of the Devil."

Abigail was usually the tougher disciplinarian, but in this case, she found herself empathizing with Charles's plight. Abigail herself consumed little alcohol but had witnessed enough family members ravaged by the disease to suspect some hereditary connection.[33] She blamed herself since it appeared to travel through her bloodline. By the late eighteenth century, some doctors were beginning to explore the hereditary and physical aspects of addiction. Dr. Benjamin Rush, one of the Adamses' closest friends, was among these forward thinkers.[34] But mostly, society still treated addiction as a weakness or personal failing. John possessed nearly indominable will, so he could not understand Charles's addiction. The emotional pain caused by his son's decline was too painful for Adams to bear while serving as president, and he risked descending into his own darkness, to which he was prone. He closed his mind to his son: "I renounce him," John said with finality.[35]

John turned to his presidential duties once he reached Trenton. The bedroom and small drawing room he rented from "two old maids Miss Barnes" weren't fancy or spacious, but they were clean, "handsomely furnished," and comfortable.[36] Over the next several days, Adams and the secretaries met individually and as a group in his sitting room on Warren Street.[37] Adams also met with Chief Justice Ellsworth and Governor William Davie, who had both traveled to Trenton at the president's request.[38] But Ellsworth and Davie weren't the only temporary residents in Trenton.

Alexander Hamilton was in town for a series of meetings with McHenry, and Robert Liston, the British minister, who was staying nearby as well.[39] Perhaps they were in Trenton to flee the yellow fever epidemic, but Adams was already in a suspicious frame of mind and doubted it was a coincidence.[40]

On the afternoon of October 15, Adams gathered the secretaries for a cabinet meeting after dinner. They talked through the details of the instructions and debated when the envoys should leave. Pickering, McHenry, and Wolcott expressed concern over the safety of the envoys if they sailed during the fall. Here, they were showing their diplomatic inexperience. "I have been obliged to sail for Europe in the middle of winter" on two separate occasions, Adams insisted, and it was perfectly safe.[41]

Pickering, McHenry, and Wolcott then turned their attention to the circumstances in Paris. Surely, they should wait to determine whether Louis XVIII would be restored to the throne and more favorable circumstances might be established. Adams scoffed at this notion. The king would not be restored anytime soon. When the meeting finally ended at 11 P.M., the president gave no indication that he had changed his mind about the mission—one way or the other.

At some point, before or after the cabinet meeting, Adams had an unexpected visitor. Perhaps Hamilton called on the president to discuss the army, or perhaps he thought he could be more persuasive than Pickering or McHenry; he left no record revealing his intentions. Adams greeted Hamilton with cool indifference, and there was nothing that infuriated Hamilton more than being ignored. He launched into a "diatribe on politics" and offered his extensive, and unsolicited, advice.[42]

Adams was furious. This forty-something lieutenant colonel had ridden George Washington's coattails to fame and power. He had never served in a diplomatic capacity and had never visited the great courts in Europe. He had never even negotiated a treaty. And yet he unabashedly lectured the president, who had spent years toiling abroad in service to his nation. The crux of Hamilton's argument centered on his conviction that the all-powerful British would soon restore the French king to the throne. The king would offer better negotiation terms and would punish those who had treated with the revolutionary government.[43]

"I should as soon expect," Adams snapped, "that the Sun Moon & stars will fall from their orbits" before Louis XVIII would be back on the throne. And the idea that he would be restored before Christmas, as Hamilton claimed, was preposterous. If Hamilton knew anything about diplomacy, Adams insisted, he would know that European governments care only about themselves. France will be equally as disposed to "accommodate our differences" under a royal or directorial government, because it benefited her bottom line. The envoys would be perfectly positioned "to wait for new commissions" as needed, regardless of the conditions of the French government.

With most of his rage spent, Adams muttered, "Never, in my life did I hear a man talk more like a fool."[44]

Hamilton left no record of the clash. Adams wrote to Abigail that he expected the envoys to sail soon. He would share all the details of this interaction with her when they were reunited, but for now, there was no role "for impertinent Paragraphs fabricated by busy bodies who are forever meddling with Things they understand not."[45]

The morning after the cabinet meeting, Adams drafted a quick note to Pickering and instructed his clerk to deliver it before breakfast. "I request you to order fair copies of the instructions to be delivered to Judge Elsworth & Govenor Davie, with another for Mr. Murray without loss of time." The president also ordered the envoys to "take their passage for France" by November 1.[46]

Adams followed that letter with another to Stoddert, instructing the secretary of the navy to "transmit immediate orders" to a local captain to prepare his frigate to carry the envoys to France by the "first of November or sooner if consistent with their convenience."[47]

Adams left no clear record about why he decided to send the mission immediately after dithering for weeks, but three possible motives explain his behavior. First, he always intended to send a peace commission but got distracted over the summer and didn't realize the extent of the cabinet subterfuge until Stoddert's warnings jarred him awake. Second, he believed in the concept of a mission but was in no rush as the delay allowed him to strengthen American naval superiority in the Caribbean, which was both a long-prized goal and would enhance his negotiating hand in Paris.[48] Third, Adams hoped that by keeping his distance, he could slow-play the army and delay the inevitable confrontation between him and the Arch Federalists, including those in his administration.

The truth is probably some combination of all three possibilities. Adams wanted to be home with Abigail, and he put his personal needs above the duties of the office in the spring of 1799. He likely downplayed the threat posed by Pickering and Wolcott. They had never directly disobeyed an order, thus far, so perhaps he retained limited trust in their abilities to follow strict instructions. This trust was initially rewarded by Pickering's excellent diplomacy with Saint-Domingue. As a result, Adams may have assumed they would not actively harm his administration. Once he received word from Stoddert that matters were far worse than the president realized, Adams moved quickly to end their subterfuge, reassert his authority, and enforce his foreign policy.

Additionally, Adams did effectively undermine the army from Quincy. His refusal to fully participate made McHenry's job nearly impossible. At the same time, Adams zealously supported the navy and appeared to move with more alacrity and firmness to dispatch the envoys once he received word that the new squadron was ready to sail. At the very least, the squadron's readiness contributed to Adams's enthusiasm for diplomacy. The summer of 1799 displayed Adams's selfishness, naivete, political savvy, diplomatic expertise, and keen sense of the ambitions of those around him. They cannot be separated.

On November 3, 1799, Governor Davie and Justice Ellsworth set sail from Newport, Rhode Island on the *United States*, captained by Commodore Barry.[49] Three months later, they finally arrived in Paris.

Distraught, Cabot wrote to King, "Our envoys have sailed. Sic vult sic jubet Preses." *So he wills, so the President commands.*[50] Cabot concluded that the president had shut his ears and his heart to his true friends.[51] Adams had long been jealous of Hamilton, Cabot alleged, and he now indulged that animosity toward Pickering, Wolcott, and "*very many of their friends* who are suspected of having too much influence in the Community." Fisher Ames agreed with this sentiment and observed that "Federal men already begin to divide" over the mission.[52]

In a private letter to Washington, McHenry confirmed the accuracy of these observations. "The President believes, and with reason," McHenry confessed, "that three of the heads of departments have viewed the mission as impolitic and unwise." Adams was particularly displeased with "Mr Pickering and Mr Wolcott, thinking they have encouraged opposition to it." McHenry acknowledged the president was annoyed with him too, although not to the same extent as Pickering and Wolcott, and "not at all with Mr Stoddert and the attorney General, who appear to enjoy his confidence."

This fracture had sparked rumors of cabinet dismissals. "I believe," McHenry explained, "the Attorney General and Secretary of the Navy" advised the president to dismiss at least one secretary. "There are however," McHenry noted vaguely, "powerful personal reasons, especially at this juncture, which forbid it." He didn't need to further expound on these insinuations. Washington fully understood that a presidential election was looming. If Adams hoped to win reelection, he couldn't further fracture his party.

"But in my view of the subject," McHenry mused, "the evil does not lay in a change of Secretaries," but rather, "in the mission, which as far as my information extends, [has] become an apple of discord to the federalists."[53] Without realizing it, McHenry had just identified the fundamental misunderstanding between Adams and the Arch Federalists. The Arch Federalists believed the president had shattered their party when he nominated a new peace mission. They were wrong. It had fractured six months earlier, when they forced Adams to accept Hamilton as inspector general and turned the New Army into a political project. McHenry and the Arch Federalists were only now realizing, however, that the president was determined to defeat them.

21

The Late President of the United States, Is No More!

BY THE END of October, the threat of yellow fever had mostly subsided, and the residents of Philadelphia slowly trickled back into the city. Pickering and Wolcott moved at the first opportunity, perhaps looking to put some distance between themselves and the president.[1] James McHenry, Charles Lee, and Benjamin Stoddert followed a few days later, once the secretary of the navy had ensured that the envoys had set sail.

Adams remained in Trenton until the second week of November, when he could be certain Philadelphia was safe. Only then did he encourage Abigail to meet him. She had left Quincy on October 10, stopping to visit with family for several weeks.[2] In early November, she resumed her travels, met John in Trenton, and they made their way back to the President's House. They would not spend another winter apart.

Upon their return to the city, Abigail remarked on the changed political atmosphere in a letter to her sister. "Some of the federalists have been so deluded" as to oppose the "Mission to France." She suspected the instigator was one "Man in the cabinet, whose Manners are forbidding, whose temper is sour and whose resentments are implacable." The problem, Abigail continued, is this secretary "would like to dictate every Measure," but the president insisted on acting independently. She never wrote Pickering's name, but the meaning was clear.[3]

The secretaries noted the altered atmosphere as well. Wolcott wrote that the president "has more than once observed in my hearing that divisions in the executive Departments, will cause the people to be divided." He insisted, disingenuously, that he supported "the importance of harmony in the public Councils, and have been concerned in no factious projects to defeat them."[4]

Wolcott's protestations aside, the Adamses returned to a city carved into conflicting factions with two unexpected political forces that would shape the coming congressional term: the arrival of a new face and the surprise departure of an old one.

In September 1798, John Marshall had visited Mount Vernon at George Washington's request. For the next three days, Washington waged a pressure campaign to convince Marshall to run for Congress in the upcoming election. Washington was concerned about the growing power of the Republican Party in their home state and believed Marshall would make a compelling candidate.

Despite the strength of Washington's arguments, Marshall refused. Congressional politics weren't appealing, and he needed the money his law firm provided. On the morning of September 6, Marshall rose before dawn, planning to leave before the family awoke to avoid having to say "no" to Washington once more. As Marshall tiptoed down the stairs, he saw Washington standing in the middle of the hall—outfitted in full military uniform, complete with a dress sword. Marshall found he simply could not refuse his old commander-in-chief. He caved and agreed to submit himself as a candidate.[5]

The campaign between Marshall and John Clopton, his opponent, was one of the most fiercely contested battles in the election cycle. Republicans hammered Marshall with the hated Alien and Sedition Acts, but Marshall deftly undercut these critiques by expressing his opposition to the legislation. He said nothing about their constitutionality, but instead argued they were ineffective and pointless. In return, Marshall and his supporters attacked Clopton for the Virginia Resolutions, which threatened to tear apart the Union.[6]

The election came down to the wire, and Patrick Henry's warm endorsement may have proven to be the decisive factor. On April 25, residents from Hanover, Henrico, New Kent, and James City counties traveled to the courthouse green to cast their votes. Each white man who met the property qualifications walked up to the justices' bench, where Marshall stood to one side and Clopton on the other. The voter verbally indicated his preference and received a mug of whiskey from his selected candidate.[7] The event soon became rowdy, as some citizens elected to sample the beverage options first to determine which libation they preferred before casting their vote. When the ballots were counted, Marshall won by 108 votes.[8]

In late November 1799, John and Polly Marshall traveled together to Philadelphia. Polly was six months along in her eighth pregnancy and refused to be separated from her husband.[9] They took up temporary lodging at a boarding house. She had never fully mentally recovered from the childbirth she endured while John was in Paris and generally avoided social gatherings. They rented accommodations in a boarding house, where there was less pressure to host teas or dinner for the elite social circle in Philadelphia.

On December 3, Marshall was seated in the crowd when the president arrived at Congress Hall to deliver his annual address and officially open the session of Congress. The Federalist majority in this session was larger than in recent years, but the numbers belied the party's internal divisions. Southern Federalists applauded Adams's diplomacy and were wary of the growing unpopularity of the army, while Northern Federalists seethed over Adams's "betrayal." The House appointed a five-person committee, headed by Marshall, to draft its response to the president's address.[10]

Marshall was generally well liked by everyone in Congress and showed a real knack for making friends on both sides of the aisle. He had expressed public support for Adams's peace mission but also retained unimpeachable patriot credentials. He had suffered through the brutal winter at Valley Forge with Washington and the Continental Army, served in the Virginia House of Delegates, and played a pivotal role securing the ratification of the Constitution in the Virginia Ratification Convention. More recently, Marshall had won national acclaim for his stalwart defense of the nation's honor in the face of Charles Maurice de Talleyrand's insults. No one could accuse him of being soft on France or afraid of war.[11]

On December 10, Marshall led a contingent of the House members to the President's House, where he delivered the tepid address. Adams responded with equally lukewarm language.[12]

Marshall's deft handling of the situation drew praise from all quarters. "Considering the state of the House," Wolcott wrote to Fisher Ames, "it was necessary and proper that the answer to the speech should be prepared by Mr. Marshall." There was no one else who could "unite all opinions, at least of the federalists," Wolcott explained.[13]

A few days later, Marshall was sitting at his desk on the floor of the House chambers when a clerk rushed in to hand him a message. After Marshall opened the envelope, all color drained from his face. He swallowed hard, before standing up and interrupting the proceedings.

"Information has just been received," Marshall said with an anguished voice, "that our illustrious fellow-citizen, the Commander in Chief of the American Army, and the late President of the United States, is no more!"[14]

While John Marshall received news of George Washington's death in the House, a clerk delivered a letter to the president from Tobias Lear, Washington's longtime private secretary. "It is with inexpressible grief that I have to announce to you the Death of the Great and the Good General Washington," Lear wrote. "He died last evening between ten and eleven O'clock, after a short illness of about twenty hours."[15]

The president said all the right things. To the army, he wrote that he shared "the grief which every heart must feel for so heavy and afflicting a public loss." Adams directed full funeral honors at all military stations to "express his high sense of the vast debt of gratitude which is due to the virtues talents and ever memorable services" of the "beloved Chief General George Washington."[16]

The next morning, the House resumed its session and John Marshall delivered brief remarks. He put forth motions recommending the House call on the president "in condolence of this national calamity" and don mourning wear for the remainder of the session. Marshall also suggested a joint committee be created to determine the appropriate mourning procedures that would be "expressive of the profound sorrow with which Congress is penetrated on the loss of a citizen, first in war, first in peace, and first in the hearts of his countrymen."[17] This description of Washington—first in war, first in peace, and first in the hearts of his countrymen—would echo through the generations.

At 1 P.M. that afternoon, the House committee called on the president at his official residence.[18] Again, Adams offered the appropriate sentiments in his reply. He recognized the pain of "the death of the most illustrious and beloved personage which this country ever produced" and closed by sympathizing "with you, with the nation, and with good men through the world in this irreparable loss sustained by us all."[19]

The following Monday, Marshall stood on the House floor and delivered a report from the joint committee. In honor of Washington's extraordinary service, the committee recommended "that a marble monument be erected by the United States, in the Capitol, in the city of Washington." More immediately, Congress would host a mock "funeral procession from Congress Hall to the German Lutheran Church," since Washington was already buried at Mount Vernon, "in honor of the memory of General George Washington, on Thursday the 26th." Finally, the committee recommended that Americans "wear [black] crape on left arm, as mourning for thirty days."[20]

On the morning of the funeral, Representative Harrison Gray Otis sat at his desk on the House floor and wrote a letter to his wife, Sally, setting the scene. "Before my eyes and in front of the Speaker's chair lies a coffin covered with a black pall, bearing a military hat & sword," he described. "The chair itself & tables shrouded with black. In the background is Washington's portrait." In one hour, "we shall march attended by the military in grand procession to the German Lutheran Church" he wrote, with matching "black crape" on our arms and "white scarfs" around our necks.

At the appointed time, the congressmen gathered to march down Fourth Street. The processional took longer than expected because the streets were clogged with thousands of residents eager to pay their respects.[21] Major General Henry Lee delivered the oration to the president, first lady, cabinet secretaries, their wives, foreign emissaries, and the leading figures in town.[22] "It was a handsome performance," Abigail told her sister.[23] Notably, New York Assemblyman Aaron Burr and Vice President Thomas Jefferson—leading figures in the Republican Party—were absent.[24]

After the official congressional ceremony concluded, opportunities for mourning continued across the country. At her drawing room on Friday evening, Abigail noted the ladies present showcased their grief by "ornamenting their white dresses [with] 2 yds of Black Mode, in length, of the narrow kind pleated upon one Shoulder, crossed the Back in the form of a Military Sash tied at the side, crossed the Petticoat & hung to the bottom of it." Others wore "black Epaulets of Black silk trimmed with fringe upon each shoulder, black Ribbon in points, upon the Gown & coat." The ladies' "caps were crape with black plumes or black flowers," while they donned "black Gloves" and carried black fans. The gentlemen were "all in Black."[25]

Towns, organizations, and civic groups in all sixteen states staged mock funerals, complete with empty caskets, processionals, eulogies, and mourning wear, to provide citizens outside of Philadelphia the opportunity to grieve publicly.[26]

Not content with the funeral in Philadelphia and the haphazard ceremonies across the country, Congress resolved that "the people of the United States" should "assemble on the 22d day of February next" to publicly "testify their grief for the death of Gen. George Washington, by suitable eulogies, orations and discourses; or by public prayers."[27] The mourning process would take months, by design.

By February, Abigail and John's grief was wearing a little thin. "On Saturday the 22d I went to hear Major Jackson deliver his oration," Abigail wrote to her sister. "It was a very handsome one, and much better delivered than I had any Idea he could perform." But she was growing tired. The last "two Months have chiefly been appropriated to funeral honours to the Memory of Gen'll Washington," she continued. "I know not that in any modern Time's, either

Kings or Princess have received equal honors," she wryly observed.[28] Perhaps she feared that the ceremonies weren't befitting a republic. Or perhaps she felt that some of the eulogies, bordering on ridiculous, were counterproductive. "Simple Truth is his best his greatest Eulogy," she wrote to her sister. That "alone can render his Fame immortal."[29]

The president was slightly more circumspect. "An eminent character and example of public virtue has now been sufficiently celebrated. I hope we shall now let him enjoy his heaven in tranquility and no longer disturb his ghost with fulsome adulation."[30] He was ready to move on, and there was much to do.

What Adams actually thought is harder to decipher. Surely, Abigail knew, but he intentionally left no written record of his emotions during those pivotal days. He knew the nation needed to mourn. Perhaps he genuinely felt sorrow at the passing of the first chief. Certainly, Adams respected Washington's lengthy service and unprecedented contributions to the nation.

Adams was also acutely aware of the implications of his predecessor's death. Washington had retained an unparalleled stature until the end. Only one president was in office at a time, but as long as Washington lived, there were always two presidents in the American imagination. His precedents still carried weight, but not with the same emotional power as when he was alive. He could no longer speak out or challenge Adams's authority.

Equally as important, Washington's name and symbolic importance was no longer an asset to be exploited by the Arch Federalists. Hamilton grasped this change in status immediately. "Perhaps no man in this community has equal cause with myself to deplore the loss," Hamilton wrote to Tobias Lear. "I have been much indebted to the kindness of the General, and he was an Aegis very essential to me," he acknowledged honestly.[31]

And yet, new concerns emerged. Washington had been present as a central, unifying, stabilizing force for as long as most Americans could remember. Henrietta Liston, the wife of British minister Robert Liston, cried, "He stood the barrier betwixt the Northernmost and Southernmost States." Without him, she noted, the states might fall apart. "He died at a moment when his life was as critically necessary to his Country as at any preceding one," she mourned.[32] How would the country respond to the gaping hole in public civic life left by his death? Who would hold together the American people in the face of diverging goals and interests? His absence was profoundly unmooring.

Free from Washington's shadow, Adams was standing on unstable political ground. But for the first time, he could carve his own path without a presence menacing from Mount Vernon.

22

Their Gag in My Mouth

AS THE EIGHTEENTH century ended, Theodore Sedgwick reflected on the state of the nation and found it wanting. Washington's death had provided a brief moment of unity, but once the temporary distraction offered by grief and mourning rituals faded, Federalists found little to hold together their members. With the Arch Federalists' split with the president now out in the open, they moved to consolidate their power, close ranks, and punish those who expressed disagreement. They used all means at their disposal to enforce unanimity and reserved their fiercest enmity and vitriol for moderates in their own party who refused to fall in line.

Timothy Pickering didn't despair like Sedgwick; he was consumed with bitterness. Raging, he returned to Philadelphia in disbelief that the president dictated foreign policy without him. Unable to scream at the president, he poured forth his wrath on William Vans Murray. Murray had sent another round of dispatches from The Hague, including a copy of his letter to Talleyrand discussing the new peace mission. Pickering regretted "the style of your letter to Talleyrand," he wrote to Murray. The mission is "viewed by every member in the administration, and by all the ablest and best supporters of the government throughout the Union, as the most unfortunate and the most humiliating event to the United States," Pickering snarled, ignoring the members of the cabinet, moderate Federalists in Congress, and huge numbers of Americans who supported diplomacy. He viewed the French as an enemy and thus objected to Murray's friendly tone when corresponding with Talleyrand. "This is not the necessary diplomatic style," Pickering haughtily informed Murray. The joy Murray expressed at the "prospect of reconciliation" was "injurious and degrading" to the nation's honor.[1]

A few days later, Pickering resumed his diatribe. "In the bitterness of my indignation, chagrin and distress on the appointment of new envoys to the execrable government of France, I have vented my feelings in some private letters to you," Pickering continued. Other men shared the same opinion, he wrote, including those "whom I am sure you remember with respect, esteem, and affection," such as "General Hamilton, Mr. Cabot and Mr. Ames." Pickering revealed that he had shown Murray's letter to McHenry and Wolcott, who both agreed that the letter "exceeded the bounds of prudence and propriety." The president himself remarked of Murray, "that young man will ruin me," upon reading the letter. "Perhaps this single remark would have supplied the place of all other comments," the secretary of state concluded.[2]

Pickering's words were designed to inflict maximum pain. He shared the diplomatic correspondence with the other secretaries to intentionally humiliate Murray. And Pickering knew how much Murray respected and adored the president. It was cruel.

Pickering also listed his grievances against the president, and he was lucky the correspondence wasn't intercepted. The country would have been humiliated if the secretary of state had been caught castigating the president in a letter to the American minister at The Hague. Pickering was so blinded by rage over the mission that he no longer approached his official duties with the professionalism and clarity expected of a secretary of state.

When Murray received the letters, he was shocked. He didn't mind guidance or constructive criticism—he was a young and relatively inexperienced diplomat who still had much to learn. But these letters were not designed to improve his tradecraft or benefit the nation's foreign policy. Trying to make sense of the situation, he made copies and sent them to John Quincy Adams in Berlin. "I feel deeply hurt," Murray confessed.[3]

John Quincy sympathized with Murray's plight. "I had understood that the Colonel disapproved altogether of the new mission to France," he wrote to Murray. But Pickering showed little sense or judgment, John Quincy acknowledged. "He has even intimated in a letter to me, that he thought there was a kind of *infatuation* in the mere idea of treating" with the French. The letter showed the depth of Pickering's fanaticism—he believed John Quincy would side with him over the president.

"It is therefore possible," John Quincy continued, "that his letter censuring the expressions of your letter to Talleyrand was not anything more than his own sentiments." Pickering's objections read like "the cavils of a captious, or at least of an angry mind," he assured Murray.[4]

More important, John Quincy dismissed Pickering's comments about the president's criticisms. He knew his father well and knew his foreign policy even better, and "I cannot believe that he partook of the Colonel's dissatisfaction concerning the manner of address in your letter to Talleyrand. Your style in that case probably displeased only those who disproved of the mission itself."[5]

Boosted by his friend's kind words, Murray replied to Pickering. He defended himself and objected to Pickering's tone. "I cannot help regretting sincerely the loss of your friendship; the terms, the harsh and ungenerous terms, on which you have withdrawn it."[6]

Pickering's campaign for vengeance did not end with Murray. He colluded with his allies to block any praise for the president in official documents and newspapers. Fisher Ames reported back to Pickering that he had obtained an early copy of Massachusetts governor Moses Gill's Thanksgiving message and convinced him to remove the section which thanked God for the peace commission and prayed for its success.[7] The final version did not mention the mission at all. It was an extraordinarily petty act to ensure that the president received no support.

Pickering then rededicated himself to enforcing the Sedition Act with as much venom and vigor as possible. Earlier that summer, US Attorney William Rawle had arrested William Duane on sedition charges for alleging that the Adams administration had accepted bribes from the British government. Duane was released on bail until the October federal court session commenced.

In the meantime, Pickering scoured the pages of the *Aurora* for any additional transgressions that could be prosecuted. On October 15, the court opened the session and Duane arrived with his lawyer, Alexander James Dallas, the Pennsylvania secretary of state who also served as defense counsel for John Fries. Rawle introduced a second sedition charge, this time for Duane's allegations that the British paid bribes to influence American policy in Saint-Domingue.[8]

Dallas announced that he intended to present the "truth" defense against the sedition charges. His client had in his possession a letter written by then vice president John Adams that they intended to present as evidence. Newly appointed Associate Justice Bushrod Washington, who was presiding over the case, expressed uncertainty that the letter was genuine. Duane offered to immediately stand trial and hand over his documents, including the authenticated letter. Duane's gambit rendered the justice and district attorney mute "with astonishment."

While the court reeled and Rawle scrambled for a solution, Dallas asked for a postponement of the trial. He planned to call Tench Coxe, Timothy Pickering, and James Monroe to the stand as witnesses, but they were still out of town due to the yellow fever outbreak.

With Rawle's agreement, the court postponed the trial until June 11, 1800, when the court would be back in Philadelphia, and again ordered an enormous bail for Duane—$3,000 this time.[9] Once again Pickering's quest for revenge was thwarted, or at least delayed.

The Sedition Act was proving harder to enforce than expected and the "army everywhere to the southward is very unpopular, and is growing, daily, more so," Sedgwick wrote to Rufus King.[10] Sensing the mood of the country, John Nicholas, a Republican congressman from Virginia, introduced a resolution on January 1, 1800, to repeal authorization of twelve regiments of regulars. The proposal also called for the disbanding of the dragoons and the decommissioning of all new officers.[11] Nicholas's bill consumed the House's attention for the next week, with debate dragging into "a later hour every afternoon," until the representatives, tired, hungry, and irritable, left for the night to escape "the polluted atmosphere of the Hall."[12]

On one side, the Republicans pointed to the budget to justify killing off the army. The proposed budget for the 1800 fiscal year detailed $14 million in expenditures, of which $9 million would be quickly consumed by the army and navy alone. However, the revenue was only projected to be $9 million, leaving a gap to be covered with expensive loans. Why take on prohibitively expensive loans, they asked, when it was clear that France had no intention of invading?[13] Republicans left their most pressing concerns unstated. They were pretty sure Federalists would use armed force to intimidate voters or suppress civil resistance if they seemed on the brink of losing control of the federal government in the upcoming election.

On the other side, Harrison Gray Otis, the Federalist chairman of the committee on defense, argued that the army offered much more than just defense in the event of a potential French invasion. "The army is evidence of our spirit rather than of our strength, a pledge of our union and further exertions," he declared on the House floor.[14] Federalists believed that a strong national defense would boost the chances of successful diplomacy. French officials would offer better terms if they believed the United States was willing to defend itself against aggression. But Federalists also left their private fears unsaid. The threat of war and the Federalists' strong response to national insult made their party more popular. Without a potential war, and the patronage positions supplied by the army, their political base might collapse.

On January 7, as the debate raged, Marshall stood and suggested that "a middle ground might be taken." Perhaps they could modify the law, "so as to diminish the estimated expense, without dismissing the troops already in actual service."[15] Marshall knew personally that Charles Maurice de Talleyrand could be unpredictable. He would not undermine the army until he received positive news from the envoys, but he grew increasingly confident that a larger army was unnecessary.[16]

Marshall's proposal had no immediate effect on the members, and the debate continued for several more days. But behind the scenes, he went to work piecing together a coalition for this compromise position and revealed his extraordinary political talents.[17] He counted among his friends Albert Gallatin and John Randolph, both radical Republicans, and Sedgwick and Robert Goodloe Harper, members of the Essex Junto. Marshall went from boarding house to boarding house, shaking hands, sharing meals, and offering toasts with congressmen from both parties and from all states.[18] He left no documentation of his behind-the-scenes activities, but others alluded to these efforts. "I have been much in company with General Marshall since we arrived in this city," Sedgwick wrote to King. He "possess great powers & has much dexterity in the application of them. . . . In short, we can do nothing without him."[19]

Marshall obtained support from the Arch Federalists, including Sedgwick, who desperately wanted to maintain the army at full strength, but recognized that a reduced army was better than none. Marshall also secured the approval of more conservative Republicans, like Samuel Smith from Baltimore, who had been one of first Republicans to sponsor the New Army bill in 1798.[20] Late in the afternoon of January 10, the House finally cast its vote on the Nicholas resolution. It was defeated 60 votes to 39, with a handful of Republicans casting their votes with the Federalists.[21]

A few days later, Harrison Gray Otis introduced a new resolution, authored by Marshall, which would retain the 4,000 troops already activated but suspend further enlistments to save money.[22] From Jefferson's perch in the Senate, he wrote to Madison, "you will see by the papers that a motion to disband the army has failed, by a majority of 60. to 39. . . . Another motion will be tried to-day, to stop recruiting: but I see no reason to expect it to succeed."[23] He underestimated Marshall's abilities to count the votes.

Over the next ten days, the House debated Otis's resolution. Some members proposed amendments designed to kill the legislation, but they were defeated. The House read the amended law the requisite three times before passing it on January 24. One month later, the Senate caved and agreed to the bill as well.[24]

John Adams made no mention of the legislation in his correspondence, but he was paying attention. He continued to host dinners and attend Abigail's drawing rooms at the President's House. Marshall was certainly a guest at some of these events and the president likely thanked him for his support of the peace commission. Whether they spoke about the details of Marshall's plan or what might come next is impossible to know. They both intentionally left no record. But it is clear Adams enthusiastically approved of any attempt to weaken the army's political influence and Marshall knew he had the president's support.

While the House was debating the army's future, the Senate was roiled by the first major threat to the sanctity of the vote, the presidential election, and the peaceful transfer of power in the nation's short history.

On January 23, 1800, Senator James Ross introduced a resolution to create a thirteen-member committee to investigate "irregular elections." The committee would be comprised of six members selected by the House, six members chosen by the Senate, and the chief justice. Because Federalists controlled both houses of Congress and entirely dominated the Supreme Court, the committee would be an arm of the Federalist Party.[25]

The committee would be empowered to determine what qualified as an irregularity and thus when to seize jurisdiction over the election. The members would meet in private, have the authority to summon witnesses and examine correspondence, and determine which electoral votes to count and which to discard. Based on those determinations, they would then declare the winner of the presidential election in a report delivered on March 1, 1801—three days before the inauguration. The proposal provided no mechanism to appeal the committee's decision.[26]

Presiding over the Senate while Ross introduced this proposal, Jefferson saw the measure for the ploy it was. The Federalists were trying to create a committee, Jefferson wrote to James Monroe, which would "decide who is elected President. Their decision to be without appeal & Congress to have no power to dissolve them."[27]

Charles Pinckney, a Republican senator from South Carolina and the cousin of Charles Cotesworth Pinckney, reminded his colleagues that "By the Constitution, Electors of a President are to be chosen in the manner directed by the State Legislatures—that is all that is said."[28] Here Pinckney drew an important distinction. He agreed that the language in the Constitution could be vague or incomplete at times. But on the right of elections, it was quite clear. Not a "single word in the Constitution" could be construed to give "Congress, or any branch or party of our Federal Government, a right to make or alter the State Legislatures' directions on this subject." Even the "most tortured construction" failed.[29]

While the Senate debated the proposal, three Republican senators slipped a copy of the bill to William Duane, editor of the *Aurora*. On February 19, he published the text of the bill in full.[30]

The outrage was instantaneous. Most Americans objected to the blatant attempt to undermine their right to elect the president, at least indirectly through their states. In the pages of the *Aurora*, Duane described the bill as a measure "calculated to influence and affect the approaching presidential election." In no uncertain terms, the Federalists were attempting "to frustrate in a particular manner, the wishes and interests of the people."[31]

Inside the Senate, the Federalists howled that Duane's publication was an unsanctioned breach of the Senate's closed-door policy.[32] Senator Uriah Tracy, a rabid member of the Essex Junto, led the charge to prosecute Duane. Tracy claimed it was a crime for an unsanctioned newspaper to publish a bill while still under Senate consideration. The First Amendment did not give the press the right to publish "untruths respecting the official conduct of that body."

Continuing his heated diatribe, Tracy reminded his colleagues that Article I, Section 6 of the Constitution declared that congressmen "shall not be questioned in any other Place" for "any Speech or Debate in either House."[33] This clause was initially designed to shield congressmen from arrest or prosecution for speech made during congressional debates, but Tracy took the privilege one step further. They had all agreed that the Senate has "the right of protecting ourselves within these walls, from attacks made on us in our presence." If they had that right within the Senate chambers, then surely "we are not to be slandered or questioned elsewhere."[34] In other words, Tracy argued that senators could not be held accountable for their words anywhere. After making this absurd logical leap, Tracy concluded that Duane must be punished, and the Senate must do it.[35]

The Federalists crammed through a new "standing committee of privileges" to adjudicate the issue. The five-man committee would investigate the origins of the leak, determine whether the publication was a breach of Senate privileges, and decide the appropriate retribution.[36]

In early March, the committee introduced charges of "seditious utterances" against Duane and called for an immediate vote. Republicans protested the irregular proceedings. How could they vote on charges when they had heard no evidence, no defense had been offered, and Duane wasn't even present? They suggested he should be prosecuted under the Sedition Act instead.

Republicans despised the Sedition Act, but at least that case would be heard in a proper court, with evidence, defense counsel, and a jury. Federalists rejected these pleas and rammed through a vote, 20 votes to 8, declaring Duane's behavior defamatory and malicious.[37]

The Senate then introduced a new, special form of proceedings. They ordered Duane to appear on March 24. On the appointed day, Jefferson, in his capacity as president of the Senate, would read the charges. Duane would have the opportunity to defend his conduct or offer evidence "in excuse or extenuation" at the end of the day. If no exculpatory evidence was presented, Duane would be held by the Sergeant-at-Arms until the Senate determined his sentence.[38]

Duane couldn't be certain, but he suspected that this new procedure was designed to embarrass Jefferson by forcing him to read the charges and sign the arrest warrant. He colluded with the ever-present Alexander James Dallas and Thomas Cooper, a prominent Republican lawyer, to extricate himself from the situation. For the next several days, Duane kept up his relentless attacks on the Federalists in the pages of the *Aurora*, until he received the official summons on March 21.[39]

Duane requested the right to be aided by defense counsel, which the Senate granted, but with severe restrictions. Defense counsel could only aid Duane in "denial of facts" or when offering evidence "in excuse or extenuation."[40]

As planned, Duane sent official engagement letters to Dallas and Cooper, asking them to appear with him on March 26 at noon. They both replied and refused to serve under such limited conditions. "I will not degrade myself by submitting to appear before the Senate with *their gag in my mouth*," Cooper wrote. The intended audience was not the Senate—Duane printed these responses in the *Aurora* for maximum effect with his readers.[41]

The next day, the senators waited in anticipation. At the appointed hour, bells clanged in the many churches across Philadelphia. All eyes gradually drifted to the door, but it remained closed. When it was clear Duane would not appear, the sergeant-at-arms issued an arrest warrant, which required all persons to "aid and assist" the sergeant in seizing Duane.[42]

"You will have seen their warrant to commit Duane," Jefferson wrote to Monroe. "They have not yet taken him," he gloated.[43] Jefferson knew Duane had no intention of being found, for Cooper had written to detail their extensive plan prior to the commencement of the Senate hearing. The vice president took no direct role in hiding the fugitive, but he certainly could have identified who was involved and chose to remain silent.

While federal officials and the forces they hired combed the city searching for Duane, he continued to publish the *Aurora* on a regular schedule and insisted he spent most of his time at home.[44]

Meanwhile, the federal court commenced its session postponed from the previous fall and ordered Duane to appear to answer the previous charges of sedition regarding the allegation of British bribes. By this point, the original indictment for sedition had expired and US Attorney William Rawle had to reissue the indictment. And yet, when the court opened, Rawle declined to bring forth a new charge.

Duane crowed in the pages of the *Aurora* that Rawle had withdrawn the charge "by order of the President." More likely, at some point during the last few months, Duane had showed the certified letter to Rawle, who declined to prosecute the charge to avoid entering the letter as evidence in the case or calling the president and other government officials as witnesses, which would have been highly embarrassing for the administration.[45]

Rawle refused to let Duane win, however, so he brought forth another indictment on charges of sedition for defaming the president and alleging the acceptance of British bribes. The marshal wrote on the back of the arrest warrant, "Duane is not to be found." Duane hadn't gone underground to avoid this specific sedition charge, but it was fortuitous timing.[46]

Meanwhile, on March 31, the House finally picked up the "disputed elections" bill, which Duane had first published on February 19. The House called for a preliminary vote and the bill failed—with Marshall leading the opposition. Marshall believed the bill unconstitutional and confided to his brother that the bill would "be very warmly contested."[47] Marshall regularly visited the President's House over the next several months. No record remains of the conversations between the two men, but the president certainly knew of Marshall's plan to oppose the legislation.

Over the next two weeks, the House debated the bill, but mostly off the floor. Representatives gathered in groups in the hallways, in the cloakroom, and in their boarding houses to hash out the details. Eager to salvage the bill, Arch Federalists proposed a postponement until December, when the election results would be clear. If Republicans were winning, then Federalists could reintroduce the committee to investigate "irregularities," and overturn the results. If Federalists were winning, they would not need the committee. Again, Marshall led the opposition and the proposal failed.

By mid-April, Marshall had proposed so many amendments to the bill that Theodore Sedgwick, the new Speaker of the House, referred the bill to committee. Frustrated with the entire thing, Sedgwick instructed Marshall to draft a new version. Toward the end of the month, Marshall unveiled his clean copy for House consideration. The new bill gave the committee the power to announce the votes, but no authority to accept or reject electors from the states, and therefore no authority to determine the outcome of the election. Marshall had entirely defanged the proposed legislation.

On May 2, the House passed the "John Marshall amendment."[48] The Senate rejected the amendments but declined to send the bill to a joint committee between the chambers for resolution.[49] Congress adjourned on May 14 with no agreement between the two chambers on the bill, and it officially expired.[50]

The efforts to condemn Duane in the Senate chambers also collapsed. With the session ending and Duane still on the loose, the senators gave up. On the final day of the session, the Senate passed a resolution requesting the president "commence and carry on a prosecution against William Duane" under the Sedition Act for "certain false, defamatory, scandalous, and malicious publications."[51]

When Congress commenced a new session in the fall, no one reintroduced the election measure. Congress had defeated the first real threat to the sanctity of democratic elections and upheld the will of the people as described in the Constitution—but just barely.

23

Hocus-Pocus Maneuvers

THE COMING ELECTION was on the minds of many Americans, and not just because the Senate was attempting to intervene in the certification process. As citizens went to the polls to elect their legislatures, the results would shape the presidential election in the fall. At the state level, both parties meddled with their selection practices to seize the upper hand. In Philadelphia, partisans convened their respective caucuses to select presidential candidates. The election season had officially commenced.

In the spring of 1800, Aaron Burr was out for revenge. He had lost his reelection bid to the New York Assembly the prior year and was determined to seize control of the Assembly for the Republicans in the upcoming election. Such a victory would boost his own position within the growing Republican Party and would have important implications for the presidential election in the fall.

The Constitution empowers each state to select its electors however it sees fit. In 1800, New York law dictated that the state legislature would make the selection. The party that won control over the legislature in the coming election would win the right to pick Federalist or Republican electors, thus determining if the state voted for the Federalist or Republican candidates in the upcoming presidential election. Because of New York's size and bounty of Electoral College votes, it would be a hotly contested swing state, and everyone knew it.[1]

Burr focused on the thirteen districts in New York City, which had previously been bastions of Federalist support. He wooed the commercial elite, worked with a series of local newspapers, and created teams of campaign staffers to go door-to-door to turn out the vote—the first political machine.[2]

Burr also assembled a lineup of well-known names to run for office, including George Clinton, the longtime former governor of the state, and

Horatio Gates, a Revolutionary War hero. Burr intuited that name recognition might win over undecided voters, but he kept the names a secret until after the Federalist ticket was set. Unaware of Burr's strategy, the Federalists in New York City, led by Alexander Hamilton, put forth "two grocers, a ship chandler, a baker, a potter, a bookseller, a mason, and a shoemaker." The party had battled allegations of elitism for years and hoped their slate of "common men" would counter that criticism. This ticket was more representative of the American population but struggled to compete with the roster of Republican luminaries.[3]

On April 29, voters went to the polls for the first of three days of balloting, where they found candidates and supporters from both sides addressing citizens and debating each other. Burr himself spent at least ten hours each day checking on polling places across the city.[4]

By midnight on the evening of May 1, the results in New York were clearly an overwhelming triumph for Burr and the Republicans over Hamilton and the Federalists. Burr's forces had won all thirteen districts in the city and captured enough votes in the Assembly to determine the electors in the upcoming presidential election.[5]

As word of the New York results reached Philadelphia, Republicans cheered the news. "REPUBLICANISM TRIUMPHANT," crowed one correspondent to Representative Albert Gallatin. "We find with particular satisfaction that Hamilton no longer rules that opulent and happily situated city," a newspaper editorialist jeered.[6] Both the Adamses similarly placed the blame at Hamilton's feet. "The conduct of the little General has done more injury to that cause than he has ever done service to this country," Abigail complained to her sister. "The fact is," she continued, "the Antifederal party carried the [presidential] election." Hamilton "will draw upon his own head a total annihilation of all his own schemes, for Jefferson will in spite of all his efforts be President."[7]

While Republicans celebrated their victory in New York, the president received dire warnings about the upcoming election in other parts of the Union. One anonymous supporter wrote of a "cabal . . . whose object is to have Mr Ellsworth elected President." Many of the leading Federalists in Congress, including Sedgwick, Harper, Dayton, and Hillhouse, "have embarked with great zeal in the project." Even more important, Hamilton, Pickering, and Wolcott were playing leading roles in this plot, warned the writer. "The picture I have drawn, Sir, is an alarming one but it is full of truth."[8]

A few weeks later, another concerned supporter wrote that "General Hamilton and Mr. Wolcot are organizing their plan of supporting Mr

Ellsworth, & the military & revenue officers under the direction of their respective chiefs are to be arrayed against you." In Congress, Senator Jonathan Dayton from New Jersey, "talks openly of opposing your election" and pledges that the New Jersey electors will support Ellsworth. In Massachusetts, Sedgwick had the support of local political leaders to vote for Ellsworth, while James McHenry partnered with Representative William Craik, Senator Robert Goodloe Harper, and former Senator Charles Carroll to campaign for Ellsworth in Maryland. "I pray to god you may be able to frustrate their diabolical projects!" this supporter pleaded.[9]

Adams was always reluctant to take anonymous letters at face value, but these struck close to home. He already suspected that the Essex Junto was lining up in opposition, and Hamilton had campaigned against him in a presidential election once before. After their confrontation in October, Adams had no doubt that he would try again.

Rumors of election machinations spread so far and wide that they reached Rufus King in London. He wrote to Federalist allies in New York, hoping they would deny these reports. "I don't believe that the wise men of the East will do so indiscreet a thing as to offer MR. E., or any other in lieu of Mr. A.," he pleaded. "The consequence will be defeat," he continued, so "I conclude that Mr. A. will be supported by his former friends."[10]

On May 3, the Federalists in Philadelphia gathered for a caucus at William Bingham's house, their unofficial meeting spot. The Essex Junto, including Sedgwick, Pickering, and Harper, argued desperately for another candidate. They proposed either Chief Justice Oliver Ellsworth or Charles Cotesworth Pinckney as well respected and dependably Federalist candidates.

Moderate Federalists, like Harrison Gray Otis and John Marshall, insisted the party remain loyal to Adams. Even if Federalists didn't like the president personally, changing candidates at this point was a dramatic and unprecedented step that would weaken the party and aid Jefferson and the Republicans, they argued.

From New York, Hamilton wrote to the Federalist caucus urging them "to support Adams & Pinckney, equally, as the only thing that can possibly save us from the *fangs* of Jefferson." He reminded them that he had been desirous of pursing this policy "at the last Election," but it was "now recommended by motives of additional urgency."[11]

Hamilton was proposing a departure from previous elections. In 1800, the Constitution called for electors to cast ballots for two candidates. The person who received the "great Number of Votes shall be President," and the person with the second "greatest Number of Votes of the Electors shall be the

Vice President."[12] Electors cast both of their votes on the same ballot; there was not a separate category for the vice presidency. In 1796, both Federalists and Republicans had nominated two candidates, but there was a clear understanding about which individual was intended for the presidency and vice presidency. Accordingly, in 1796, most Federalists had supported Adams and Thomas Pinckney as the president and vice-presidential candidates, respectively. Now, Hamilton was suggesting Federalists support both Adams and Charles Cotesworth Pinckney as equal candidates, without making a distinction about which position they were intended to fill.

"Pray attend to this & [let] me speedily hear from you that it is done," Hamilton ordered.[13]

After a lengthy debate, the Federalists finally settled on an unhappy compromise. "Mr. Adams & General Charles C. Pinckney are proposed." If all went according to plan, Pickering reported to King, New England would vote unanimously for "both candidates," while "South Carolina and part of North Carolina vote for General Pinckney." If this plan worked, "the *federal election* of President will perhaps not be in jeopardy," Pickering confided.[14]

Sedgwick confirmed that "we have had a meeting of the whole federal party," and we "have agreed that we will support" both "Mr. Adams and General Pinckney." Using the same rhetoric employed by Hamilton a few days earlier, Sedgwick confirmed that the Federalists could escape the "fangs of Jefferson," but only if they "faithfully execute" this plan.[15]

After the meeting, news of the Federalists' decision percolated through Philadelphia. "Last Saturday evening the Federal members of Congress had a large meeting," Representative Albert Gallatin wrote to his wife, Hannah. They "agreed that there was no chance of carrying Mr. Adams," but acknowledged that if they removed him from the ticket they would lose "the votes in New England." Showing a keen grasp of the Federalist electoral strategy, Gallatin explained that they selected a candidate from South Carolina "ostensibly as Vice-President, but really as President," to receive the same votes as Adams, plus "the votes of his own State." Gallatin and the Federalists understood that South Carolina leaned Republican but might be persuaded to split its votes between Jefferson and their hometown candidate. For that purpose, Gallatin concluded, "they have selected General Charles Cotesworth Pinckney."[16]

John Adams saw the agreement for exactly what it was—a plan to try to sneak Pinckney past him into the presidency. The plan was deeply insulting; the Federalists would have never attempted such a maneuver with Washington. Thomas Jefferson also saw the subterfuge clearly. The Federalists "held a caucus on Saturday night," he wrote to his son-in-law. They "have determined on some hocus-pocus maneuvers by running Genl. Charles C. Pinckney with mr Adams."[17]

A few days later, forty-three Republicans from both houses of Congress gathered for their own caucus.[18] With no dissent, they unanimously selected Thomas Jefferson as their presidential candidate. They also agreed to put forth Aaron Burr as the vice-presidential candidate. Following established electoral practice, Republicans selected a northern candidate to provide geographic balance to the ticket. A few weeks earlier, New York had proven to be a Republican stronghold, largely thanks to Burr's efforts in the state election. George Clinton, the former governor, declined to be considered, due to age and poor health, making Burr the easy choice.[19]

The attendees swore each other to secrecy, and the bond mostly held. No word of the meeting leaked to the press and only a few sentences survive describing the meeting, written by Gallatin to his wife, Hannah.

Although Jefferson was in Philadelphia, he did not attend the conference and swore that "nothing ever passed between" Burr and himself about the Republican ticket. "It is our mutual duty to leave those arrangements to others, and to acquiesce in their assignment," Jefferson insisted. He supported Burr's selection, however, as he "has certainly greatly merited of his country, and the Republicans in particular, to whose efforts his have given a chance of success."[20] Four days later, Jefferson left Philadelphia to spend the summer at Monticello.[21]

Farther north, Hamilton was constitutionally incapable of leaving the fate of the election to someone else. On May 7, 1800, he wrote to Governor John Jay and urged him to act while the Federalists still controlled both chambers of the state legislature. The recently elected assemblymen (including many more Republicans) wouldn't be seated until the coming fall. While the legislature was still controlled by a Federalist majority, Hamilton suggested that Jay put forth a bill that would change how the state selected its electors. If the state employed a different method, such as a committee appointed by the governor or a committee pulled from both chambers, the electors could be reliably Federalist. In other words, Jay could put New York safely in the Federalist column in the presidential election. "I am aware that there are weighty objections to the measure," Hamilton admitted, but it "will not do to be overscrupulous." In "times like these," Hamilton pleaded, "scruples of delicacy and propriety . . . ought to yield to the extraordinary nature of the crisis."[22]

Hamilton's proposal came remarkably close to a coup. Voters had cast their ballots for legislature candidates with the understanding that Federalist assemblymen would pick Federalist electors and Republican assemblymen would pick Republican electors. The overwhelming Republican victory demonstrated the voters' expectations that the state would select Republican electors and therefore, Republican candidates for president and vice president. Hamilton's plan would have deprived New York citizens of their votes.

On the back of this letter, Jay wrote that it proposed "a measure for party purposes which I think it would not become me to adopt."[23] Jay was a staunch Federalist, but he put the Constitution and the nation above party. He demonstrated a basic level of civic virtue required to uphold democratic norms and institutions. His example would be important in the coming months. Hamilton's proposal was not the first, nor the last challenge to the sanctity of the vote before the inauguration on March 4, 1801, and the Constitution would require many acts of civic virtue to survive.

24

A Change in the Administration

THE RESULTS OF the New York election and the Federalist caucus changed everything for the president. Adams insisted that "Age, Infirmities, family Misfortunes have conspired, with the Unreasonable Conduct of Jacobins and insolent Fœderalists, to make me too indifferent to whatever can happen."[1] But he protested a bit too much. He still desperately sought the validation of reelection. Now it seemed nearly impossible.

Since his inauguration, he had battled with Pickering and McHenry for control over foreign policy. Over the past year, he grew to doubt their loyalty but retained their services in the cabinet to avoid splitting the party. Maybe he worried about the nation's future with a fractured Federalist Party or perhaps he knew that a divided party would harm his election chances. Either way, he now had the Federalist Party nomination in hand, at least nominally.

However, the manner of the nomination was embarrassing and infuriating. The Federalist deal was an insult to the president's authority and an affront to Adams's decades of public service. "The President's mind is in a state which renders it difficult to determine what prudence and duty require from those about him," Wolcott confided to Fisher Ames. "He consider[s] Col. Pickering, Mr. McHenry and myself as his enemies; his resentments against General Hamilton are excessive."[2]

Freed from concerns about the Federalist Party nomination, Adams was determined to manage the remainder of his presidency unencumbered. He concluded that it was time to introduce a change to the administration. His actions would further inflame passions within the Federalist Party, define the limits of cabinet authority, defend presidential power, and establish precedents that still govern the cabinet today.

On the night of May 5, two days after the caucus, Adams summoned the secretary of war to the President's House. On arrival, McHenry was shown to the drawing room.[3] Usually, Adams met with his secretaries in his study. But this was no run-of-the-mill conversation. Initially, Adams chatted about vacancies and potential nominees in the war department—a conversation that could have easily waited until morning. He then paused, before mentioning the recent election in New York. "Hamilton has been opposing me in New York!" Adams insisted. McHenry protested that he had heard nothing of the sort and insisted that Hamilton would not campaign against the president. Adams knew McHenry's denials were almost certainly a lie and told him so. "You are subservient" to Hamilton, Adams retorted.[4]

If Adams had been writing McHenry a letter, he would have set it aside and drafted something more temperate like he usually did when discussing a contentious topic. But once he started this rant, he had trouble stopping. He accused McHenry of biasing "General Washington's mind" against him and for excessively praising Hamilton in his congressional reports. "Hamilton is an intriguant—the greatest intriguant in the World—a man devoid of every moral principle—a Bastard, and as much a foreigner as Gallatin," Adams snapped.

Then Adams got personal. "Wolcott is a very good Secretary of the Treasury, but what do any of you know of the diplomatic interests of Europe? You are all mere children, who can give no assistance in such matters." He criticized every element of McHenry's management of the war department, from the recruiting to the design and cloth of the uniforms.

McHenry expected Adams's rants about elections and Hamilton. He had heard them before. But he could not ignore the president disparaging his reputation and his honor. "I shall certainly resign," McHenry declared.

Perhaps the president began to regret unleashing all his frustrations on McHenry. He replied that he had always "considered you as a man of Understanding and of the strictest Integrity," and he had "no Reasons to be dissatisfied" with "your general Behaviour towards me," the president reassured McHenry.

Nonetheless, McHenry repeated his intention to resign, promised to send in his official notice the next day, and left late in the evening.[5]

The next morning, McHenry submitted his official resignation and asked that he be allowed to remain in office for the rest of the month to put his affairs in order. Adams agreed.[6] Neither man left any immediate documentation of the encounter. At the end of the month, McHenry wrote a lengthy description of their conversation and sent a copy to all his closest allies in the Essex Junto. He also sent a copy to the president. Adams did not reply. How the president would describe the interaction, or the veracity of McHenry's recollections remains a mystery.[7]

Adams had considered a change in the cabinet for months, if not years, but he never indicated why he started with McHenry. Perhaps he hoped that McHenry, when confronted, would confess the extent of cabinet duplicity or maybe McHenry was the most incompetent and thus, his removal was expected. Adams believed McHenry was disloyal, but the secretary of war was not an evil mastermind. Once this first step was taken, Adams determined to remove all the malicious forces from his administration.[8]

A few days later, an unexpected conversation strengthened Adams's resolve. On May 9, Benjamin Goodhue, one of the senators from Massachusetts and a central member of the Essex Junto, called on the president to say goodbye before he headed home. Adams accused Goodhue of conspiring with a "damned faction" to wound him personally, obstruct his foreign policy, and cram "Hamilton down [his] throat."[9]

Goodhue denied these charges, but Adams had proof. He had seen letters exchanged by members of the Essex Junto "filled with expressions of hatred" and "calculated to injure him in the view of the public." Goodhue described the conversation as "a perfect rage of passion that I could not have expected from the supreme executive." He absolved himself of all involvement and insisted he was entirely innocent. Goodhue's intransigence and inability to take responsibly for his actions galled Adams. The conversation spurred him to cut the Essex Junto rot from its source in the cabinet.

The next day, Saturday, May 10, he wrote a letter to Pickering. "As I perceive a necessity of introducing a change in the Administration of the office of State, I think it proper to make this communication of it to the present Secretary of State that he may have an opportunity of resigning, if he chooses." Furthermore, Adams continued, "I should wish the day on which his resignation is to take place to be named by himself." He asked for Pickering's answer "on or before Monday Morning" so he would have time to submit "the Nomination of a Successor" before the end of the legislative session.[10] The president's intent was clear, but he was permitting Pickering to choose how he left office.

The letter wasn't a surprise. Relations between the two men had been downright hostile since the fall, and rumors of cabinet turnover had filtered among the political elite for months. If anything, Pickering was surprised that Adams had waited this long. But he did not reply that day, nor the next.

Monday morning, Pickering sent a letter to the president. He acknowledged Adams had offered him the "opportunity of resigning, if he chooses." However, "several matters of importance in the office, in which my agency will be useful, will require my diligent attention until about the close of the present quarter." Pickering pled financial difficulties, explaining that he had planned to remain "in office until the fourth of March next"—another ten unbearable months—so that he might save enough to "enable me to subsist my family a few months longer." In conclusion, Pickering wrote, "after deliberately reflecting on the overture you have been pleased to make to me, I do not feel it to be my duty to resign."[11]

The letter was breathtakingly haughty and a direct challenge to the president's authority. Adams had offered Pickering the gentleman's way out. Resignation by cabinet secretaries was common and honorable. Pickering declined, convinced that the president would not take the bold step of firing him.

The president read Pickering's reply and dashed off another letter. This one left no room for argument: "Diverse Causes and considerations essential to the Administration of the Government, in my Judgment requiring a Change in the Department of State you are hereby discharged from any further Service as Secretary of State."[12]

That afternoon, Adams sent a message to the Senate: "I nominate the honorable John Marshall Esqr. of Virginia to be Secretary of State in the place of the Honorable Timothy Pickering Esqr. removed."[13] It was the first the Arch Federalists had heard of Pickering's removal, and they were furious.

The next day they assembled at Senator Jacob Read's house on the corner of Fourth and Cyprus Streets to strategize.[14] Dubbed the "Pickeroors" or the "Pickeronians" by the *Aurora*, this group was comprised of members of the Essex Junto and the Arch Federalists, including Pickering, Gouverneur Morris, James McHenry, Benjamin Goodhue, Uriah Tracy, and Theodore Sedgwick. Over the next two days, they explored the possibility of a new election caucus or supporting a different presidential candidate.[15]

While this caucus was gathering at Senator Read's house, another group, the "Adamites," met two blocks away, at Senator William Bingham's mansion.[16] Members of the Adamites included John Marshall, Senators Henry Latimer, Samuel Dexter, Dwight Foster, John Howard, John Laurance, William Wells, and Ray Greene—the more moderate wing of the Federalist Party. They all supported Adams, or at least opposed changing candidates this close to the election.

While the Pickeroors and the Adamites battled over which candidate to support, a serious question of constitutional power undergirded their disagreement. What was the nature of the relationship between the president and the cabinet secretaries? What did the president owe to the secretaries and what did they owe him? Did the president have the unilateral right to remove them for any reason?

The Constitution was maddeningly vague on this subject. Article II mentions the executive departments and authorizes the president to nominate "Officers of the United States," with the "Advice and Consent of the Senate." The president is also empowered to request written opinions from the department secretaries on "any Subject relating to the Duties of their respective Offices." Those are the only mentions of the departments in the original Constitution.[17]

In the summer of 1789, the First Federal Congress set about creating the executive departments and established the departments of war, state, and treasury, as well as the attorney general. The formation of the departments turned out to be easier than determining how the secretaries could be removed from office. Some congressmen believed the president should have unilateral authority to remove the secretaries, while others argued the president needed Senate consent. Another faction argued that secretaries could only be removed for impeachable offenses, while a fourth group argued it was up to Congress to decide.[18]

The final compromise side-stepped the issue. The bills included language that tasked the chief clerk of each department with taking custody of the official records when the secretary was removed by the president. The bill made no explicit mention of how the secretary would be removed or the president's power in this situation.[19] The bill was purposely ambiguous to secure passage. As a result, most officials assumed the president had some authority in this area, but it was still poorly defined and very much untested.

Many congressmen probably expected that Washington would figure it out, like he did so many aspects of the presidency. On this one issue, however, Washington's administration provided little guidance. His stature had been so unparalleled that the department secretaries never questioned his authority. Even Thomas Jefferson, who had regularly disagreed with Washington's decisions while serving as secretary of state, had complied with the president's directives.[20] Furthermore, the turnover in his cabinet had been voluntarily. Jefferson, Hamilton, and Henry Knox all retired when they chose, and Edmund Randolph resigned when he realized he had lost Washington's confidence. The first president had never even requested a resignation.[21]

Adams's relationship with his secretaries revealed how much cabinet precedent had yet to be established. As their working relationship began to fray, McHenry wrote to Washington and suggested that the president ought "to conciliate his ministers." If Adams would listen to the secretaries and follow their advice, he could "restore mutual confidence and harmony of action," McHenry argued.[22] It was the president's duty to compromise, McHenry suggested, not the secretaries'.

Pickering didn't necessarily expect the president to cave to his secretaries, but he also didn't believe the secretaries were obliged to obey the president. "I do not subscribe" to the idea that the department secretaries owe "*implicit obedience*" or resignation, he wrote to McHenry. "On the contrary, I should think it is their duty to prevent, as far as practicable, the mischievous measures of a wrong-headed president."[23] To be clear, Pickering did not think Adams was violating the Constitution. He just did not like Adams's policies. Pickering envisioned a parliamentary-style administration, in which the president would share power with the unelected cabinet, similar the one that has emerged in modern Britain.

In Berlin, John Quincy Adams learned about the cabinet shakeup and came to a very different conclusion. "I must place that confidence in the discretion of the President, which the Constitution has placed there," he wrote to his brother. The Constitution, he continued, has made the secretaries' "removal entirely dependent upon him." The secretaries were supposed to be "assistants & promoters of the system," but if they instead became "enemies & opponents," they cannot "be retained."[24]

John Adams agreed and articulated a similar vision shortly after his inauguration. The president's power to remove secretaries "I hold to be a Sacred Part of the Constitution without which the Government could not exist," Adams declared. "If Executive officers, hold their offices independent of the head," he continued, they can intrigue to oppose "the Execution of the Laws." If the president doesn't control his secretaries, he concluded, "the Executive Authority would be a Nose of Wax."[25]

These warring visions came to a head on May 12, when Adams fired Pickering and nominated Marshall as the next secretary of state. The Senate did not object to Pickering's removal or insist on his reinstatement. Instead, the next day it quietly confirmed John Marshall as the new secretary of state and Samuel Dexter as the new secretary of war.[26] While many Arch Federalists seethed, they trusted Marshall to manage the state department. They worried that Adams's next choice might be far more objectionable.

The Senate's quiet acceptance of Pickering's firing ended the speculation around the president's constitutional power to remove cabinet secretaries. Adams had removed Pickering unilaterally without Senate participation, ensuring that future presidents could do so as well.[27] The Senate's tacit approval also effectively endorsed Adams's vision of the relationship between the secretaries and the president.

At the peak of cabinet activity during Washington's administration, he had met with the cabinet up to five times per week. But in Washington's final years in office, he had convened only a handful of cabinet meetings. As a result, he had established the precedent that the secretaries have no institutional right to participate in the decision-making process. They can offer their advice and support but can't demand to be in the room where decisions are made. Because of Washington's unparalleled stature, that precedent was theoretical and untested. Adams made it a tangible governing power. After Adams, all department secretaries understood they served at the president's pleasure.

Fully liberated, the president issued all the orders Pickering and McHenry had vociferously opposed.

A few days earlier, Marshall had put forth a proposal in the House that granted the president authority to demobilize the army once he was confident the peace commission would produce results. The House agreed to the proposal and referred it to a committee to ensure it was attached to the existing army legislation.[28] Marshall almost certainly had Adams's blessing. Two days after dismissing Pickering, Adams signed the bill discharging the soldiers in the newly created regiments.[29]

Outraged at the president's treatment of Pickering but unwilling or unable to do anything about it, the Arch Federalists in the House decided on a petty retort. They voted to remove the president's authority to discharge so that they could exercise the power themselves. They passed a resolution ordering that the army be demobilized on or before June 15, 1800.[30] The outcome was the same, but the swipe at the president gave them some solace.

Adams created the cabinet he wanted and commenced the disintegration of the army, then turned to clemency. He spent the next few days pondering forgiveness, vengeance, justice, and the value of human life. He had been ruminating on the Fries Rebellion for over a year. In late April, Fries's retrial had concluded. "The trial of Fries for Treason has been, this last week before the Court," Abigail reported to her sister. "He is found Guilty this is his second trial, in both of which he has received the same verdict."[31]

Months earlier, Adams had asked his department secretaries for their opinions on a potential pardon for Fries, assuming the second trial produced the same result as the first. "I have the honor to inclose the opinions of the attorney general and heads of departments," Pickering had written. They all agreed "that no pardon should now be granted, nor any answer given."[32]

Unconvinced, the president returned to the conversation once he had removed the most poisonous elements from his cabinet. First, he asked the attorney general if he had the authority to issue a pardon in this case. Charles Lee replied, "The Attorney General of the United States most respectfully reports to the President his opinion that the President may reprieve for offences against the United States in all cases except in cases of impeachment."[33]

Convinced he had legal authority, Adams then asked Wolcott and Stoddert whether it was the right thing to do. "Is it clear beyond all reasonable doubt that the Crime of which they Stand convicted, amounts to a Levying of War against the United States, or in other Words to Treason?" the president asked. Adams was a bit of a hothead and was prone to saying things he regretted in the heat of the moment, as his exchange with McHenry just a few weeks earlier had shown. Wasn't there a danger in "establishing such a Construction of Treason," which could be "applied to every Sudden, ignorant, inconsiderate heat, among a Part of the People," he asked? Wouldn't it be more effective for "the Advantage of Government and the public Peace," Adams wondered, to reward Fries's "professions of deep Repentance and promises of obedience" with a pardon? He had already served a lengthy term in prison and leniency might be more persuasive than vengeance.[34]

Wolcott and Stoddert both replied that their minds were unchanged since the previous fall. They believed an example had to be made of Fries, or other potential rebels would interpret Adams's leniency as an invitation to cause trouble.

Adams thanked the secretaries for their input. However, "as I differ in opinion, I must take on myself alone the responsibility of one more appeal to the humane and generous natures of the American People."

"I pray you therefore to prepare, for my Signature this morning a Pardon for each of the Criminals John Fries, Frederick Hainey and John Gettman," Adams wrote to Charles Lee. He also requested that the attorney general prepare a proclamation for a "General Pardon of all Treasons and Conspiracies" committed in Pennsylvania "in opposition to the Law laying Taxes on Houses."[35] That afternoon, Adams issued a public announcement granting "a full, free, and absolute pardon, to all and every person or persons concerned in the said insurrection" and specific pardons to those defendants sentenced to death."[36]

The convicted rebels, Fries, Hainey, and Gettman, received word of the president's decision just twenty-four hours before their scheduled executions. News of the presidents' pardons spread across Philadelphia and up and down the coast. Most locals learned about them on the morning of the scheduled hangings.

Nearly everyone was shocked. Pickering, Gouverneur Morris, and other Arch Federalists were convinced that the pardons demonstrated a diabolical "coalition" between Adams and Jefferson to jointly capture the upcoming election.[37] Others offered a happier reaction. On her trip back to Quincy, Abigail stopped in New York and reported that the pardon was very unexpected. The Republicans, according to Aaron Burr, had "Supposed that Fries would have been made an example of," Abigail wrote.[38]

Abigail didn't seem all that surprised, nor did John Quincy. The pardons were "sanctioned by the example of the former President" and "conformable to the true principles of policy, which should prevail in a popular Government," he wrote. Unlike monarchies or authoritarian governments, republics depended on the goodwill of the people. Accordingly, they were obligated to show "greater lenity than in any other formal polity."[39] John Quincy understood that it was not sufficient to establish precedents and exercise executive authority. Presidents must cultivate trust among American citizens so that they will uphold democratic institutions.

25

The Seat of Government

IN MID-MAY, JOHN MARSHALL was at home in Richmond attending his neglected law practice. He was sitting in his study on the first floor of the large brick house on the northwest corner of 9th and Marshall Streets, just across from City Hall, when he received news that the President of the United States had nominated him as secretary of state.[1] A few weeks earlier, while he was still in Philadelphia, Adams had offered him the position of secretary of war. Marshall had declined this position, thinking it beneath his talents and eager to return to his law practice and its profits.

A few weeks later, however, Marshall's prospects in Richmond looked far gloomier. His time in Congress had scared away many legal clients, and the Republicans in Virginia had been hard at work preparing for the coming campaign. The secretary of state was the most respected cabinet position and would offer him an escape from the "political man" label.[2] In the last week of May, Marshall accepted the position. He packed up his belongings once more and traveled to Washington City (now Washington, DC) on June 5, sharing a coach with Supreme Court justice Samuel Chase.[3]

Marshall arrived in Alexandria on June 7 and took up lodgings at the Washington City Hotel just across the street from the Capitol building under construction. He was joined by Samuel Dexter, the new secretary of war.[4] Dexter was a Federalist, born in Boston and educated at Harvard University. For the previous several years, he had served in the House of Representatives and the Senate, where he generally supported Adams's more moderate agenda.

After settling into the hotel, the secretaries waited for the president's arrival.[5] As Adams traveled south from Philadelphia to Washington at the end of May, he delivered a series of speeches, toasts, and addresses to citizens gathered to greet him.[6] On June 1, during his Fredericksburg, Maryland, stop, Adams received word that Marshall had accepted the nomination. He

FIGURE 25.1 *A view of the Capitol of Washington before it was burnt down by the British.* William Russell Birch, ca. 1800. Library of Congress Prints and Photographs Division, LC-DIG-ppmsca-22593.

finally had a cabinet of his own. The secretaries would prove their value over the coming months as Adams did his best to ignore the campaigning around him and waited impatiently for news from France. For the first time, most of Adams's administration pursued the same goals and worked to make his policy a reality. Whether this coordinated effort would produce a diplomatic win in time to influence the election remained unclear.

Adams arrived in Alexandria on June 9 and spent the first evening in town dining with Charles Lee. Describing the evening for Abigail, he wrote, "I am particularly pleased with Alexandria. Mr Lee lives very elegantly neatly and agreably there among his sisters and friends" and on a beautiful piece of land covered in "Clover and Timothy. I scarcely know a more eligible situation."[7]

The next morning, Adams rode the twelve miles from Alexandria to Mount Vernon to pay his respects to Martha Washington. Continuing the narrative of his trip, he shared with Abigail, "Mrs Washington and her whole

Family very kindly enquired after your health and all your Children and Louisa; and send many friendly Greetings."[8] After spending the day with the Washingtons, Adams returned to Alexandria. A "troop of cavalry" met him on King Street, where he offered remarks to the gathered citizens before the militia escorted him to dinner with local dignitaries at Gadsby's Tavern on the corner of Cameron and Royal Streets.[9]

In mid-June, Adams finally crossed the Potomac River into the new federal district. He addressed a gathering of local citizens, proclaiming: "May the future councils of this august temple be forever governed by truth and liberty, friendship, virtue and faith, which . . . can never fail to insure the union safety, prosperity and glory of America."[10] He then traveled to the Washington City Hotel, where he took up temporary lodgings with Marshall and the other secretaries until the Executive Mansion (now the White House) was completed later that fall. Until then, white and black laborers, both free and enslaved, toiled around the clock cutting stone, making brick, applying plaster, and painting.[11]

Upon first arriving in the city, the navy, state, war, and treasury departments all crammed into the recently completed Treasury Building, right next to the east side of the Executive Mansion. Although the building was large, it was not big enough to accommodate the growing number of clerks and ever-expanding boxes of files of all four departments. In early June, the navy department took up residence at 2107 Pennsylvania Avenue, in a large brick townhouse. A few months later, the State Department moved in next door, facilitating easy communication between the secretaries. Dexter, Marshall, and Stoddert established standing meetings at the navy department offices every Tuesday and Friday mornings. Lee occasionally traveled from Alexandria to join them, and they invited Wolcott to attend after he moved to Washington City at the end of the month.[12]

Adams left the department organization to his secretaries but welcomed the opportunity to sort through his foreign policy with Marshall, the continued disbanding of the army with Dexter, and the ongoing success of the naval department with Stoddert. The most pressing topic of conversation was the prospect of diplomatic success in Paris. Adams reasoned that the envoys could have signed a new agreement with France as early as April 1 if everything had unfolded smoothly. Newspapers regularly printed that "dispatches from [the envoys] are momently expected."[13] And yet, they still had no news.

FIGURE 25.2 “Six Buildings” on the north side of the 2100 block of Pennsylvania Avenue NW, 1905. Junior League photograph collection, DC History Center.

Adams could not track the progress of his envoys, but their initial travels and reception would have provided hope for a quick, peaceful resolution. The *United States* made nearly record time, crossing the Atlantic in just twenty-four days. Chief Justice Oliver Ellsworth and Governor William Davie rested in Lisbon for a few weeks, gathering intelligence on the ever-fluctuating French government, before departing for Paris on December 21. They battled storms in the Bay of Biscay of the coast of France for twenty-six days, before giving up, retreating, and landing in Corunna, Spain. They notified Charles Maurice de Talleyrand of their arrival and their intention to travel to Paris by land.[14] While the two envoys trekked up the Iberian Peninsula and into France, Talleyrand notified William Vans Murray that his colleagues were in Europe. The French minister sent a French passport a few days later, and Murray sailed from Rotterdam on an adventure he “NEVER anticipated when in America, and on one so greatly important!”[15]

Murray arrived with his family on March 1 and reserved a temporary suite of rooms at “the Hotel de l’Empire—a splendid and dear hotel, (formerly Labord’s the bankers, guillotined),” he wrote to John Quincy Adams. The next day, Ellsworth and Davie arrived in Paris and secured lodgings at Maison des Oiseaux on the Rue de Sevres, a large, stone house that had been used as a prison during the revolution.[16]

With the commission assembled, the envoys could finally begin their work and were hopeful they could meet the president's April 1 goal. On March 2, 1800, Talleyrand greeted them with the expected cordiality. A few days later, the envoys were presented to Napoleon Bonaparte in the Hall of Ambassadors at the Tuileries Palace. "The Premier Consul received us with a courtly frankness," Murray told John Quincy, and asked after each envoy "by name." He spoke "of the death of General Washington, of whom he spoke in praise, and then passed on" to the next guests.[17] Ellsworth was reportedly so dazzled by Napoleon that he declared "that no other man ever had given him so vivid an impression of mental power."[18] Having spent several years in Europe, Murray was less easily impressed.

The next day, Talleyrand shared the names of the commissioners selected by Napoleon to represent France in the negotiations. Joseph Bonaparte, Napoleon's brother, was the president of the commission, and he was joined by Pierre-Louis Roederer and Charles-Pierre Claret Fleurieu.[19]

The American envoys immediately responded to Talleyrand and sent a letter opening communications with their French counterparts, but their timeline was quickly derailed.[20] Illness in the French commission delay their first meeting until April 2, at the Maison des Oiseaux.

At the first meeting, the commissions were able to establish terms for their negotiations. None of the French commissioners were fluent in English, and only Murray possessed passable French. They agreed to conduct their negotiations in writing, which would further slow their pace, but was the only way to avoid miscommunication.[21]

After years of contentious cabinet interactions, the cordial and harmonious meetings were a welcome change, even if Adams was facing another summer impatiently waiting for letters to arrive.

In the evenings, Adams continued his social tour. On the night of June 13, he went to Georgetown, where the president thanked the crowd gathered for "the approbation, you have the goodness to express, is both a reward and an encouragement.[22] He attended "an entertainment" at "Mr. McLaughlin's Tavern," where toasts were drunk to "John Adams—the early, the uniform, the steady and unshaken friend of his country." The hosts offered further remarks on "the utmost harmony and conviviality" at the event, "which was given, to the Chief Magistrate of the Nation, as a testimony of respect for his office, gratitude for his numerous and important services and veneration for his eminent talents and virtues."[23]

Reflecting on this stage of his journey, John wrote to Abigail, "An Abundance of Company and many tokens of respect have attended my Journey, and my Visit here is well [received]."[24] The reception was noteworthy because this trip was not just a sightseeing adventure. Adams was not outright campaigning, which was still considered inappropriate, but he was marshalling support for his foreign policy, and by extension, his reelection bid.

He continued these efforts on his return trip north. On June 18, he arrived in Baltimore, where he "was escorted into town by captains Holingsworth's and Bray's troop of horse." The next day "the honorable Mayor and Corporation waited on him about two o'clock," to deliver their own remarks.[25] "While they deplored the loss of General Washington, it afforded [them] consolation to find that America had other sons, in whom she may safely confide the management of her affairs," they shared.

One observer noted that these remarks were "rather unkind" and the mayor "ought to have confined the compliment to Mr. Adams alone." After years of battling Washington's shadow, however, Adams knew how to manage the backhanded compliment. "Our country, I trust," he pithily retorted, "will always abound, as it ever has abounded with Characters in whom she may safely confide the management of her affairs." Under their steady stewardship, the nation will "avoid all the Calamities which can be avoided by good plain human Understandings and sound Integrity of heart." These factors, he proclaimed, were much more important to the country's success than "refinement of Genius or Taste."[26] Adams subtly reminded the audience that the nation didn't need heroes like Washington, just a basic level of civic virtue. The same observer wryly concluded, "Let the mayor and city council wash down this answer."[27]

Adams stopped briefly in Philadelphia on his way north to pick up any remaining mail and permanently close the President's House on High Street. He finally arrived home on the evening of July 3, 1800, in time to celebrate the nation's birthday on July 4 in Quincy.[28]

By the end of July, Adams's inability to shape events across the globe was driving him to distraction and he searched for something, anything he could do. At the end of July, he finally received the first dispatches from the envoys, sent from Paris to Marshall in Washington City, and then on to Quincy. The envoys conveyed their frustrations at the slow pace of negotiations and the seemingly impassible conflict over whether to first tackle a new treaty or damages sustained.

Adams gloomily concluded in his letter to Marshall that the dispatches were insufficient to form a conclusion about the future of the commission, but "there are reasons to conjecture" that the French government was deploying "all the resources of their diplomatic Skill to protract the negotiation." He began to suspect that "the French Government is flattered with full Assurances of a change at the next Election," and expected Jefferson would be "more favourable to their Views."

The president supposed that the envoys might need additional instructions if they found themselves at an impasse. "I shall propose to your consideration and that of the heads of departments," Adams wrote Marshall, "the propriety of writing to our Envoys by the Way of Holland and England or Hambourg, or any other more expeditious and certain conveyance."

Two points deserve additional attention, Adams proposed. First, they should "repeat and confirm" their instructions to discontinue the previous Franco-American treaties. Second, Adams refused to discontinue "our Naval protection of our Commerce" or reopen "our Commerce" until France acted in a way "to justify or excuse Us in the Smallest Relaxation." Adams therefore concluded, the "Envoys may be instructed to be as explicit, as decency and delicacy will admit in rejecting all propositions" that opened commerce between the two nations before a new treaty is signed.[29]

Before Marshall could draft these instructions, new dispatches from the envoys arrived, revealing that the commissioners had quickly found themselves at an impasse, despite their best intensions.[30] President Adams's instructions required the envoys to negotiate reparations for damages inflicted on American commerce before discussing any new or revised treaty. The French commissioners insisted that any claims would have to be addressed under the previous Franco-American treaties, which Adams had abrogated in the spring of 1798. The French insisted, therefore, a new treaty would have to be negotiated first before claims could be settled. The commissioners went back and forth but were faced with a fundamentally intractable chicken or egg situation.

As the negotiations ground to a halt, the American envoys grew frustrated with each other.[31] Murray lamented that Ellsworth was "ignorant of the world & its manners," and "thought little about anything but the Logic of the points—as if Logic had much to do with events in Europe," Murray griped. Ellsworth was a good man and an "excellent & austere Judge," but his talents and personality were ill-suited to diplomacy, Murray concluded.[32]

The envoys kept their shared goal in mind, however, unlike the previous American commission that had fractured under French pressure. Murray confided in John Quincy that "Mr. E[llsworth] was supposed in the United States to be originally against the mission," but he should "be assured that he is heart and soul occupy'd to make it succeed. So is D[avie]. So am I."[33]

By mid-August, the envoys had been in Paris for several months with nothing to show for their efforts. The envoys wrote to Marshall of their decision that negotiations "must be abandoned, or our instructions deviated from." If the envoys altered their instructions, "the deviation will be no greater than a change of circumstances may be presumed to justify," they wrote, referring to France's recent military victories.[34]

Eager to try something new, the envoys submitted a new proposal to their French counterparts, suggesting that the old treaties be reestablished with a few modifications and that both nations pay indemnities to citizens of the other. Finally, both nations would be given a grace period to buy out the other nation from certain trade and defense obligations. The French ministers countered with a proposal that completely reestablished the old treaties and created commissioners to adjudicate claims. However, no reparations would be paid if the treaties were not reestablished in full.

The Americans could not accept a complete restoration of the treaties because they would invalidate the Jay Treaty and impose military obligations on the United States to come to the aid of France—the two requirements Adams had explicitly prohibited. The president would never sign this agreement.

On the French side, Joseph Bonaparte declared in his first fit of temper that he would rather resign than accept a modified treaty, while also providing indemnities to American citizens.[35]

Back in Washington City, Marshall received the first round of dispatches from the envoys in late August and read them with disappointment. He forwarded them to the president, advising, "We ought not to be surprizd if we see our envoys in the course of the next month without a treaty. This produces a critical state of things which ought to be contemplated in time."[36]

Adams replied, sharing his agreement with Marshall's interpretation. He also expected that the envoys might be sent home with "Professions and

Protestations of Love, to serve as a substitute for a Treaty." He didn't have to tell Marshall these protestations would be useless.

If the envoys returned home empty handed, Adams wondered if he should recommend "to Congress an immediate and general Declaration of War, against the French Republic." For years, the nation had suffered under a warlike state with "restrictions and Limitations," Adams reasoned. "If War in any degree is to be continued, it is a serious question whether it will not be better to take off all the Restrictions and Limitations," he asked Marshall.[37]

Marshall understood the gravity of the situation, but he urged the president to proceed warily. "It is certainly wise to contemplate the event of our envoys returning without a treaty," he acknowledged, "but it will very much depend on the inteligence & assurances they may bring." They should not advocate any policy without that intelligence, he argued.

"I am greatly disposd to think that the present government is much inclind to correct, at least in part, the follies of the past," he shared, remaining optimistic that a positive resolution was possible. Since the XYZ Affair, the French Directory had adopted "considerable retrograde steps" to make amends, and he expected "the same course will be continued." If he was right, "there will be security—at least a reasonable prospect of it—for the future—& there will exist no cause of war, but to obtain compensation for past injuries." Past injuries would not be "a sufficient motive" for war, Marshall concluded.[38]

Back in Paris, the American envoys adopted a similar view. On September 13, they proposed a radically different approach to the negotiations. They suggested that because neither side could agree to a plan "respecting the former treaties and indemnities," both sides could agree to "further treat on those subjects" in the future. Until then, "the said treaties would have no operation." This proposal provided a blank slate for a temporary agreement.

On September 19, both teams of envoys gathered at Roederer's home.[39] With the impasse cleared, the commissioners quickly crafted a new agreement that was much more robust than the terms they had debated over the previous months. Ironically, by not considering the previous treaties, they were able to agree on new terms that covered many of the details in the treaty of 1778 and convention of 1788.[40]

In the closing days of September, the commissioners sparred over the official language of the document and debated what to call the agreement, as "convention," "treaty," and "provisional treaty" all carried various weight and legal meanings. They finally settled on a "provisional treaty" that would be copied in both English and French, with the understanding that the French version was the original. Bonaparte then took the document to his brother for review, before returning to the Americans the next day with two additional requests.[41]

Napoleon preferred the agreement be called a convention, signed in the name of "the First Consul of the French Republic and the President of the United States," rather than the previously agreed upon "governments of the nations." In return, Joseph Bonaparte offered to sign both the French and English versions at the same time, declaring them both originals. With these terms agreed, the American envoys traveled to Bonaparte's estate, where they signed the convention that evening of October 3, 1800.[42]

The ministers sent official dispatches to the secretary of state acknowledging they did not obtain everything they had hoped. But they believed the treaty was better than nothing. Walking away empty handed would have "left the United States involved in a contest," without any allies, and with little prospect of peace "with honor."[43] Murray also wrote John Quincy, just as he had every step of the way for the last three years. "We have the honor to inform you that a provisional treaty was yesterday signed between France and the United States." If ratified, the treaty would reestablish "the relations of amity between the two nations," he proudly declared.[44]

On the night of October 3, after the envoys signed the treaty, Joseph Bonaparte threw an elaborate party to celebrate the agreement. Describing the festivities for John Quincy, Murray wrote that the three French consuls offered toasts, followed by a "splendid dinner" for at least 150 people, including "the ministers of state, members of the senate, tribunat, council, secretary of state, generals, all the family of the Bonaparte, and the foreign corps." The room was decorated in a pastoral theme, covered by "temporary berceaux of foliage, and wreaths, and flowers, full of emblems, transparencies, busts, and lustres, etc." After the dinner, "the most celebrated performers of Paris" put on a concert featuring the works of "Banti, Garnt, Kuntgre and Frederick," followed by a cannon fire display and coffee in the brightly illuminated gardens.

The entertainment continued, Murray relayed, with "fire works in the gardens; after, a comedy in one wing of the building ended by songs in honour of the treaty, or reconciliation." The evening ended "round 3 o'clock in the night," and Bonaparte graciously offered the envoys a place to sleep. "It was a very pleasing noble compliment to our government and country!" Murray concluded.[45]

Now, the news needed to reach the United States as soon as possible.

At home in Quincy, Adams received Marshall's letter urging patience. He acknowledged that the advice was prescient and well-reasoned. Nothing would have been gained from preemptively declaring war and impulsive action threatened to undermine the steady steps toward peace Adams had so carefully cultivated. Marshall's loyal service demonstrated the value of a secretary of state who pursued and supported his president's foreign policy.

Adams had gambled his popularity, the leadership of his party, and his reelection campaign on the peace commission. As Federalist and Republican leaders ramped up their electioneering, Adams remained silent and resigned himself to wait for news from Paris that had the potential to fundamentally alter his political career, the coming election, the nation, and the world.

26

Death or Liberty

ON AUGUST 1, 1800, the citizens of Chester County, Pennsylvania, hosted a July 4 festival that had been postponed until after the completion of the harvest. The celebrations began with the firing of guns and cannons. At noon, the "Republican Females of Chester county" presented the militia with a new flag. Mrs. Cloyd then delivered remarks thanking the militia for their duty combating the "infectious poison of aristocracy beginning to spread her baneful influence in our peaceful and simple abodes." After the remarks, a parade of Republican militia, volunteers, clergy, and ladies of the committee marched to a park, where the Declaration of Independence was read, and music played. "Two hundred ladies and gentlemen" enjoyed a "sumptuous" meal with sixteen toasts to cap off the day's events.[1]

The Chester County Republican festival served as a microcosm of the broader Republican campaign. At the local level, elites hosted balls, galas, parades, and barbeques to fire up support for their preferred candidate.[2] In Lancaster, Pennsylvania, Republicans delivered one toast for each of the sixteen states. Their celebrated topics included Jefferson and the peace commission. The attendees then consumed half a ton of beef and pork. In a working-class neighborhood in Philadelphia, artisans toasted the vice president as "the choice of the people". They also attended parades complete with floats that conveyed obvious political messages, such as "Liberty Under Siege," and street shows that culminated in the burning of John Adams in effigy.[3] The partisan forces that had roiled the country for the past three years burst forth in both Republican and Federalist electioneering.

These events were advertised ahead of time and then covered by an ever-growing number of Republican newspapers. Starting in the summer of 1798, a wave of Republican newspapers cropped up to protest the Alien and Sedition Acts. The editors were mostly laborers and artisans, but their efforts were supplemented by rich donors who helped cover costs before advertising developed into a profitable industry.[4] The newspapers were so effective that Federalists complained that Republicans had founded a partisan printing press in every town in the country. Federalists were exaggerating but only slightly. In 1795, Republican papers comprised 14 percent of the nation's newspapers. By 1800, they accounted for 40 percent of the papers and were growing.[5] Party elites also supported the spread of political news by writing public letters, which they distributed to friends and family members with the understanding that they would be passed along to acquaintances, shown to supporters, and even printed in sympathetic newspapers. The campaign of 1800 depended on the combination and coordination of newspapers, correspondence networks, social festivities, and private visits.

From the spring until the last day of voting on December 3, the Republican Party established a model for party organization, discipline, and unity. To promote their arguments and scurrilous claims, Republicans in Virginia built up committees of correspondence in counties across the state, as well as with Republicans in other states.[6] The committees exchanged copies of newspapers, pamphlets, and letters, as well as coordinated election tactics across state lines.

Republican elites in Virginia set the tone for the campaign. They resurrected accusations that Adams aimed to create a monarchy in the United States and planned to name John Quincy as his heir. As evidence of Adams's interest in monarchy, Republicans alleged that he had dispatched Charles Cotesworthy Pinckney to obtain four "pretty Girls two of them for my Use and two for his own." Adams dismissed the rumors with humor, long accustomed to the drivel printed in the papers: "If this is true Gen. Pinckney has kept them all four to himself and cheated me out of my two."[7]

A letter printed in the *Aurora* proved much more damning. In 1792, Adams had written to Tench Coxe, then a Federalist, sharing his distrust of the Pinckneys. The Pinckney family had waged a "long Intrigue" to obtain a diplomatic posting in London, Adams wrote, and he suspected "British Influence" in the recent appointment of Thomas Pinckney. "Were I in Any Executive Department I should take the Liberty to keep a vigilant Eye upon them," he concluded.[8]

After Coxe switched his allegiance to the Republican Party, he shared this letter with William Duane, who promptly published it in the *Aurora* on August 28, 1800. Duane reminded readers this letter had been written while Washington was president and Adams vice president. As such, the letter proved the existence of British influence in the federal government, Duane argued, and implicated both Thomas and Charles Cotesworth Pinckney in these schemes.[9] The allegations carried additional weight, given that both Pinckneys had lived in England for nearly twenty years and been educated at British institutions. Republicans were already targeting Federalist sympathies for Britain; this letter appeared to confirm their fears.

Coxe's letter was embarrassing for both Adams and the Pinckneys, but it played little role in the overall Republican campaign strategy. Republicans ultimately concluded that Adams was too independent to marshal the Federalists behind him, and thus, less menacing. Republicans also dismissed Charles Cotesworth Pinckney as a threat because he tended toward moderation, like most of the Federalists from South Carolina.

The real danger, Republicans asserted, came from Arch Federalists in the north. As a result, most of the campaign focused on the Federalist Party agenda, espoused by Alexander Hamilton and the Essex Junto.[10] The Republican press submitted the Alien and Sedition Acts, the New Army, and the hated taxes as evidence that the Federalists had betrayed the Constitution and attempted to crush their liberties. If Federalists remained in power, Republicans argued, they would enrich an aristocracy, backed by a tyrannical president and standing army.

The latest chapter of the Duane sedition trials offered further proof of this plot. In October 1800, a grand jury approved the indictment requested by the Senate five months earlier. The indictment alleged that Duane libeled the Senate by describing it "as actuated by factious and improper Views and Motives, as governed by Intrigue and the Influence of private, secret meetings, as unfit to be trusted." Duane secured a delay of the trial because most of the witnesses were in Washington City, while the case was tried in Philadelphia.[11] The case would resume the following May, unless Jefferson won the presidential election and dismissed the charges.[12]

At the end of the century, Americans still expected their politicians to avoid campaigning, at least publicly, but the line was growing fuzzy. By 1800, Jefferson was so convinced the Federalist Party posed a mortal threat to the nation that he could not remain on the sidelines. He wrote several letters articulating his principles and his vision for the nation. To Gideon Granger, a rare Connecticut Republican, Jefferson affirmed he was a stalwart friend "to the freedom of religion, freedom of the press, trial by jury & to economical government, opposed to standing armies, paper systems, war, & all connection other than of commerce with any foreign nation."[13] The heart of the contest between the two parties was over "the great question which divides our citizens," Jefferson explained. Should the "preponderance of power" be lodged "with the monarchical or the republican branch of our government?" He shared this letter with John Vanmetre, a Republican deputy in Berkeley County, Virginia.[14] Unlike previous years when Jefferson instructed his subordinates to keep his correspondence private, these letters were intended for a broader audience.

Jefferson also demonstrated significant enthusiasm for the presidency, whereas he had previously appeared to shun political office and claimed to abhor politicking. "It has been the greatest of all human consolations to me to be considered by the republican portion of my fellow citizens, as the safe depository of their rights."[15] He even considered making a campaign stop in Richmond on his return from Philadelphia to Charlottesville. "Nothing should be spared to eradicate" the city's displays of "federalism & Marshalism," he wrote to Governor James Monroe.[16]

Monroe waved him off, concerned that his presence would provoke Marshall into campaigning for Adams. "Nothing of the kind is necessary here," Monroe replied, because it could have a detrimental effect on the elections in "the other states," he deftly advised Jefferson.[17]

Once Jefferson had returned to Monticello, he eagerly gathered any evidence he could find about the state of the race in the important swing states. Before the creation of polling, Jefferson and his contemporaries relied on letters and newspaper descriptions to gauge the mood of the people. This method was imperfect, however, and Jefferson confessed to an ally in South Carolina that "the state of the public mind in N. Carolina appears mysterious to us." He peppered friends and colleagues with questions, begging them to send any intelligence they acquired. "What will be the effect" in the South of the joint nomination of the Federalists, he asked. Will Pinckney's "personal interest, or local politics derange the votes in that quarter?"[18]

As Jefferson struggled to get a handle on the race, events seventy miles east threatened to upend the election.

In the spring of 1800, an enslaved blacksmith named Gabriel made his way across Henrico County to Richmond and back again to Thomas Prosser's plantation. Along the way, he stopped at other farms and plantations, offering his services. Most of his wages went to his enslaver, Prosser, but he kept a small percentage. He also made important connections among the enslaved community.

At some point in the spring, Gabriel met with his brother, Solomon, and a few other enslaved men at "Prosser's black smith's shop in the woods" to plan an armed rebellion. The first goal would be to kill Prosser, Gabriel's playmate as a child, and Absalom Johnson, a white neighbor who had played a central role in Gabriel's branding and imprisonment the previous year.[19]

The men would then march on Richmond, armed with "cutlasses, knives, pikes, and muskets," and rally supporters along the way.[20] Gabriel planned to lead the conquering forces, carrying a homemade flag that declared "Death or Liberty."[21] He intentionally inverted Patrick Henry's famous phrase to emphasize the stakes of their revolt, the consequences for whites who did not step aside, and the obvious limitations of the promises of the American Revolution.[22]

Once they reached Richmond, the rebels would split into three units to seize the guns held at Capitol Square and kidnap Governor James Monroe. He would not be executed immediately, unlike many other whites, because they expected he might be persuaded to support their demands given his vocal support for French liberty.[23]

By August 25, everything was in place. Gabriel and Solomon distributed the swords they had been making since the previous fall and marshaled their forces. They estimated their "associates to the number of 5-600," spread across Richmond and ten surrounding counties.[24]

When the appointed day arrived, winds thrashed the rivers, streams, and bays into a swirling, foamy morass. Roads from the far-flung plantations into Richmond, Petersburg, and Norfolk flooded with flash rains, and lightning lit up the sky. From his jail cell in Richmond, newspaper editor James Callender wrote to Jefferson that it was the most "terrible thunder storm, accompanied with an enormous rain, that I ever witnessed in this State."[25]

The historic storm rendered the waterways dangerous and the roads impassable, stranding the enslaved population on the outlying plantations. Gabriel planned to reconvene his forces a few days later, but before he could spread the word, a few participants reconsidered the consequences of their involvement.

Late that evening, an enslaved man named Pharoah approached his enslaver, Mosby Sheppard, and revealed the plot.[26] Mosby Sheppard then passed the news to William Mosby, who was on the list of intended targets. Mosby rushed to warn William Austin, the local militia captain.[27] Around the same time, another enslaved man in Petersburg confessed the plot to his enslaver, Benjamin Harrison, who alerted the authorities.

The next day around noon, Governor James Monroe was briefed on the thwarted revolt. In the previous weeks, he had received warnings about an uprising but had dismissed them as unserious rumors. With this intelligence, he acted to crush any remaining threat. He ordered the "publick arms" removed from government buildings and sent to the local penitentiary for safekeeping. He then called up the Fourth and Nineteenth Regiments from the state militia.[28] While the militia traveled to the capital, armed patrols combed the back roads outside Richmond and arrested any Black men they could find.

Not until the trials began, however, did the Virginia authorities fully grasp the extent of the plot. Richmond and Henrico County were the heart of the rebellion, but there were parallel plans in Norfolk, Petersburg, and across the state. The authorities struck quickly and with little mercy. "Will, Mike, Nat, and Issac" were the first conspirators executed at the gallows on 15th and Broad Streets in Richmond.[29] By mid-September, the executions were so numerous that "Ladies of Richmond who lived not far distant" from gallows asked authorities to move the execution site "because the exhibition was offensive" to their sensibilities.[30]

As the militia arrested more suspects every hour over the next several weeks, Gabriel evaded capture.[31] Each day he remained free, his rebellion became more scandalous and more menacing in the imagination of white residents in Richmond. Evidence that emerged during the trials only fueled their worst fears. Several defendants mentioned the participation of white men and at least two French citizens., Charles Quersey and Alexander Beddenhurst, who offered to show the rebels how to fight and "furnish" them with guns and "all things needful."[32]

Federalists cackled with delight. "The sound of French Liberty and Equality in the ears of these Blacks led them to this desperate measure," wrote one Federalist press. "Behold America the French doctrine of Insurrection!"[33] They had long warned that Republican sympathies for revolutionary France belied a closer, more nefarious plot. Many Federalists were convinced that Republicans conspired with the French to agitate the Whiskey Rebellion in western Pennsylvania in 1794 and Fries's Rebellion in Northampton County, Pennsylvania in 1799.[34] Now, those efforts were coming home to roost, proving correct the Federalist argument that anarchy, once unleashed, could not be confined.[35] Robert Troup, a New York Arch Federalist and Hamilton's college roommate, wrote to Rufus King, gloating "in Virginia they are beginning to feel the happy effects of liberty and equality."[36]

Republican presses did their best to tamp down any rising panic. In the *Aurora*, William Duane wrote, "the insurrection we are told, was organized upon the French plan." On the contrary, he assured readers, the insurrection was clearly the work of the British, "for only Albion could be so perfidious." The reports of two Frenchmen, was a "Federalist good joke."[37]

While Republican newspapers attempted to dismiss or downplay any French connection, the evidence was significant enough to provoke serious action from Monroe. The court officials gathered all evidence of French involvement uncovered during the trials and delivered it to the governor's residence, rather than filing it with the rest of the court records. Monroe then destroyed the evidence to ensure it did not leak further and damage Republican chances in the coming elections.[38]

On September 23, Gabriel was finally captured in Norfolk and sent to Richmond in chains. That same day, Maryland voters went to the polls to elect representatives in their state legislature. Whether the rebellion would influence voters was unclear. Like Virginia, Maryland's economy was built on slave plantations, dotted by small cities with both enslaved and free black populations. Federalists had long held power in the state and were eager to make the most of the French connection to the rebellion, but they were also deeply divided as a party. The Arch Federalist wing of the state was loyal to their neighbor, James McHenry, and expressed reluctance to support Adams in the coming election, while the moderate wing insisted the party back its candidates.[39]

With Gabriel in irons, Monroe was convinced the imminent threat had passed and reduced the "Guard of Militia." He then wrote to Jefferson, as he so often did when faced with tricky questions. "It is unquestionably the most serious and formidable conspiracy we have ever known of the kind," Monroe confessed. Thus far, he continued, "10. have been condemned & executed, and there are at least twenty perhaps 40. more to be tried, of whose guilt no doubt is entertained." But "when to arrest the hand of the Executioner is a question of great importance," he mused. "I shall be happy to have yr. opinion on these points," he concluded.[40]

A few days later, Jefferson wrote a thoughtful reply, revealing the many considerations at play. "Where to stay the hand of the executioner is an important question," he wrote, borrowing Monroe's phrase. "Those who have escaped from the immediate danger," understandably want to "extend the executions." Yet, "there is a strong sentiment that there has been hanging enough."

"The other states & the world at large will for ever condemn us if we indulge a principle of revenge, or go one step beyond absolute necessity."[41] He wasn't concerned about the enslaved population, he explained, but rather how states like Pennsylvania might view their harsh form of justice. Home to a large Quaker population and vibrant free black community, Pennsylvania had long led the anti-slavery agitation. It was also a critical state in the coming election. Monroe needed to demonstrate that Republicans could be trusted to keep the peace, but not alienate the antislavery votes in key swing states.[42]

Jefferson's guidance confirmed Monroe's instincts, and on October 2, he issued pardons for Abraham and Solomon, two of earliest participants.[43] The other convicted individuals were sold further south, enabling their enslavers to secure compensation under Virginia law, but removing the threat from the neighborhood.[44] This clemency did not extend to the original instigators. After Gabriel was sentenced to death, he asked to be hung on the same morning as the remaining men. On October 10, Gabriel, George Smith, and Sam Byrd were executed just outside the city limits of Richmond. They were the last executions stemming from this rebellion. But their plan had consequences that outlived them.[45]

The affected communities remained forever altered, long after the justice system, such as it was, had completed its work. For months, white patrols stalked the streets and outlying plantations searching for lingering evidence of rebellion. For the enslaved population, conditions for the survivors worsened, distrust fueled cruelty at the hands of enslavers, and many mourned the loss of loved ones. The fledging anti-slavery movement in Virginia was quickly extinguished by the threat of widespread violence, but not for future generations of enslaved people. Gabriel was not the last enslaved man in Virginia to dream of revenge and freedom.[46]

The president largely stayed above the fray. He did not comment on the rebellion, nor did Abigail—a notable omission for the chatty political observer. Adams did not contact Governor Monroe to offer support or federal assistance. He viewed it as a state matter. But John Quincy did not hold his tongue. "If the negro keepers will have French democracy," he wrote of the Republicans and the violence and anarchy of the French Revolution, "I say let them have it."[47]

27

The Unqualified Conviction of His Unfitness for the Station

ON JUNE 27, Richard Stockton wrote to Oliver Wolcott about the state of the campaign in New Jersey. Stockton came from a founding family, had represented the state in the United States Senate, and would be one of the states' prized electors in the coming election. In his letter, he bemoaned the split in the Federalist Party but urged Wolcott and the other Federalists to hold their tongues against the president. The New Jersey electors preferred Charles Cotesworth Pinckney to John Adams, but "they will act, at all events, in conformity with the plan proposed in Philadelphia." Stockton then articulated the motivating principle for the Federalists in the coming election: "Mr. A. with all his weaknesses, surrounded by his present council, and more or less influenced by all, or at least by some of its members," was not "a worse man than J[efferson] with Gallatin, Burr, etc."[1]

The challenge for the Federalist Party would be keeping this goal front and center in the coming months, especially as news from the envoys in Paris still had not arrived. The party initially focused its efforts on attacking Thomas Jefferson, but as the summer wore on, internal divisions became increasingly impossible to ignore. By fall, the open hostility between the Essex Junto and Adams and his supporters dominated political discourse, with critical ramifications for the coming election, the future of the Federalist Party, and the nation.[2]

While the Republicans resuscitated old claims of monarchism to hurl at Adams, the Federalists recycled old material as well. They reprinted the Mazzei letter in newspapers, reminding readers that Jefferson was consumed with "hatred of WASHINGTON." Now that Washington was no longer on the political scene, he had undergone an apotheosis. Criticism of the father of the country was sacrilege and tarnished Jefferson as disloyal.[3]

Jefferson was not just disloyal to Washington, the Federalists argued, but he was also more attached to France than to his own nation. They alleged he had fomented a "French party in America," which attempted to import the violent leveling witnessed during the French Revolution and more recently in Virginia during Gabriel's thwarted rebellion. "If the Jeffersonians wish more republicans, what must it result in?" one writer asked his readers. "Not in the freedom of equal laws, which is true republicanism, but in the licentiousness of anarchy," Federalists answered. He was the "greatest villain in existence."[4]

Federalists anchored their claims about Jefferson on his questionable religiosity. Jefferson believed in the freedom of religious expression and rejected any state role in religion. Personally, he sometimes identified as a Christian, but also found deist ideas compelling, which suggested that religious truth came from human reason, rather than divine revelation. Deists rejected the Bible as the word of God and scripture as religious doctrine.[5] Jefferson crafted his own Bible for his private use that focused on the works and teachings of Jesus Christ but removed the miracles and spiritual elements.

The United States in 1800 was a deeply religious society and Jefferson understood that these ideas and practices would have been disqualifying for higher office and perhaps polite company, so he kept them secret. And yet enough of Jefferson's writings hinted at distrust for organized religion to give Federalists material for their accusations.

The *Gazette of the United States*, the leading Federalist paper in the nation, published nearly the same article every day in September and October. "THE GRAND QUESTION STATED" was splashed across the top of the page. The article challenged their readers to consider "the only question to be asked by every American." Shall they swear "allegiance to GOD—AND A RELIGIOUS PRESIDENT; or impiously declare for JEFFERSON—AND NO GOD!!!"[6]

The religious stakes of the nation were also personal. Federalists alleged that if Jefferson won, he planned to raid their homes and seize their Bibles. They urged readers to bury their religious texts to protect them from the radicals.

Jefferson rued that "the floodgates of calumny have been opened against me."[7] He wrote to Madison that the Federalist papers "of Massachusets & Connecticut continue to be filled with the old stories of deism, atheism, antifederalism &c." When pressed by a supporter to take action, however, Jefferson acknowledged that he could have "filled the courts of the United

States with actions for these slanders," but he was convinced anything he said would be misinterpreted and just exacerbate the tensions.[8]

From Quincy, Adams watched Federalists criticize Jefferson's most private religious moments and seethed with indignation. What do Jefferson's private religious habits have to do with the American public? Adams demanded of his fellow Federalists. Fisher Ames reported to Rufus King that the president even defended Jefferson as "a good patriot, citizen and father."[9] But Adams said nothing publicly to defend Jefferson, which he later conceded was a moral failing, and left himself open to counterattacks.

Republicans did not let the opportunity pass. They reached out to members of smaller denominations, like Quakers, Baptists, and Methodists, and reminded them of Jefferson's support for religious liberty. They pointed to provisions in the Massachusetts state constitution, which Adams had drafted in 1780, that deferred to established churches, and contrasted them with Jefferson's defense of religious toleration in Virginia.[10]

Republicans also noted the rank hypocrisy of the Federalist claims on morality. "Mr. Jefferson stands preeminent for his political, social, moral, and religious virtues. He is in fact what his enemies *pretend to be*," they wrote. "But what shall we say of a faction who has at its head a confessed and professed adulterer," they asked, referring to Hamilton's publication in 1798 confessing to an extramarital affair.[11] Notably, Jefferson's relationship with Sally Hemings was not yet widespread knowledge, so it could not be deployed by Federalists to counter these accusations.

Republican allegations against Hamilton gained traction as he once again inserted himself into politics and assumed an increasingly prominent role in the campaign. In June, as Adams traveled south to visit the new capital, Hamilton set out from New York for a tour of New England under the guise of bidding farewell to the disbanding troops. In practice, he planned to urge Federalist allies to vote equally for both Adams and Pinckney.[12]

The façade fooled no one, least of all Abigail Adams. "It was Soon understood that the Gen'll did not come to disband troops," she wrote to her son Thomas in Philadelphia. Instead, "his visit was merely an Electioneering business." He traipsed across Connecticut, Massachusetts, and Rhode Island, "to feel the pulse of the N England states, and to impress those upon whom he could have any influence to Vote for Pinckney." In Oxford, Massachusetts, he delivered a "formal speech" to the gathered troops in his capacity as the "Head of the Army," in which he declared that Adams could not win reelection.[13]

It was an outrageous breach of military ethics. Hamilton was traveling as an army official paid by the federal government, yet he was campaigning against the commander-in-chief. He flagrantly insulted the structure of command and violently flouted the unspoken divide between civilian and military affairs. Eighteenth-century America did not yet have the strong tradition of apolitical generals, but Hamilton's behavior crossed whatever line did exist.

Hamilton was met with a mixed reaction that characterized the chasm in the Federalist Party. The Essex Junto applauded his presence. Robert Troup crowed to Rufus King, "Hamilton lately returned from a tour through the Eastern States, where he was very attentively and affectionately received."[14]

On the night of June 19, the Essex Junto threw an elaborate feast at Boston's Concert Hall. The *Gazette* claimed that "the company was the most respectable ever assembled in this town, on a similar occasion." The guests were served "every dainty the season affords, and every luxury which could be procured," and "at no public feast ever prevailed greater harmony, good humor, and public spirit."[15] Troup offered a similarly bombastic report to King that it was "the most honorary dinner ever known in Boston."[16]

The moderate Federalists saw Hamilton's tour clearly. He sought "to create Divisions and Heart burnings against the President merely because he knows that he cannot Sway him, or carry such measures as he wishes untill he can be instrumental of getting in a President to his mind," Abigail snarked. Through "his intrigues he will lose many more votes for Pinckney than he will obtain," she accurately prophesized.[17]

Abigail proved to be a more skillful pundit on New England politics than the Essex Junto. Many moderate Federalists and New Englanders were queasy at Hamilton's display of politicking, unlike his Essex Junto allies. Some Boston Federalists, like J. Hale, were loyal to the president and announced, "I am decidedly for the re-election of Mr. Adams." Others objected to Hamilton's strident, bombastic approach, and observed that "he did not appear to be the great general which his talents designate him."[18]

After Hamilton's celebratory dinner in Boston, he began his return journey to New York. Along the way, he encountered further Federalist opposition when he stopped in Rhode Island to visit Governor Arthur Fenner. Fenner scolded Hamilton: "I see what You are after. You mean to bring in Gen'll Pinckney!" He raged that he would "not engage in any such jockying trick." Hamilton protested that Adams could not be trusted to pursue Federalist policies, like supporting the army and pursuing war with France. The lack of news from the envoys suggested that Adams had debased himself and the nation for nothing, Hamilton argued. His pleas fell on unsympathetic ears. Fenner professed that his admiration for Adams had only increased after the president sent envoys to secure peace with France and disbanded the unnecessary and expensive army—an intentional swipe at Hamilton, who was the figurehead of the army and its supporters.[19] Perhaps most important, Fenner continued, he would "sooner give My Vote for Mr Jefferson," than elect someone he did not know or trust—and he knew John Adams.[20]

Fenner was not alone. "A real or affected alarm is attempted to be spread," Fisher Ames, another member of the Essex Junto, wrote to King in despair. "The Massachusetts feelings are to be called up to defend their own State born patriot." Hamilton's visit had the opposite outcome than the one he intended.[21]

While Hamilton was stirring up trouble in Boston, Adams engaged in election activities of his own in his backyard. Shortly after returning to Quincy, Adams attended a parallel banquet at Faneuil Hall. As the guest of honor, he delivered a toast to the revolutionary "Patriots, Hancock & [Samuel] Adams."[22] Adams chose his words carefully. He called upon the memory of two hometown heroes to assume the mantle of revolutionary virtues. His toast reminded Americans that he had worked closely with both Hancock and his cousin to declare independence and then make it a reality.

In his public remarks, Adams also went on the offensive against his Arch Federalist nemeses. He alluded to a "British faction" in the nation that was working to prevent peace with France and to secure a more permanent alliance with Britain. The label, "British faction," was originally devised by the Republicans to reignite American prejudices lingering from the Revolution. Everyone knew he was referring to the Essex Junto, even though he didn't call them out by name.

"It is getting to be the fashion here again to call the federalists the British faction," Ames rued. "Nothing can be more false," he insisted. It is true the Arch Federalists respected "the laws and Courts and Government of Britain and detest the arbitrary tyrants of France," but they would never countenance "any kind of competition in point of respect & affection with our own" nation.[23]

Sedgwick sent nearly identical complaints to King, sputtering that Adams denounced the men "in whom he confided at the beginning of the administration, as an oligarchick faction, and what is still more odious, as a British faction, who are combined to drive him from office!"[24]

For all their complaints, Hamilton's allies reluctantly admitted Adams's campaigning was effective. "There is no doubt that our Legislature was strongly disposed to chose Electors to vote for Adams & P.," Ames wrote of the Massachusetts legislature. But ever since "a certain Great Man," meaning Adams, returned from Washington City, the legislature clamored that he is to be "sacrificed and tricked out of his place. The Essex Junto is cursed and lampooned." Ames concluded all electoral hopes were likely lost: "Jefferson will have a majority and be chosen."[25]

Adams's supporters launched their own attacks on the Essex Junto. "Our Friend Webster has lately been on to the Eastward, has visited Quincy & has returned," a fellow Arch Federalist wrote to Wolcott. Along his travels, Webster affirmed that he harbored similar suspicions about Hamilton and the Essex Junto. "The President has done perfectly right," Webster declared to his Massachusetts hosts. The loss of Webster's support for Arch Federalist policies was keenly felt by Hamilton and his allies.[26]

Webster's words carried so much weight that Wolcott felt compelled to write to the editor and demand an explanation. A report had reached him, Wolcott informed Webster, that "you have lately declared that a British Party exists in this Country & that you possess documents which if published, would hurt the reputation of sundry persons high in office." These reports "do much mischief by inciting unfounded suspicions against honest men," Wolcott admonished. He demanded a justification of "the grounds of your opinion."[27]

Webster was unrepentant. "Until these Gentlemen change their conduct" toward the president, Webster maintained, "I hold myself bound to use the little influence I have to oppose their policy." The Essex Junto had conspired to "divide the federal interest irreconcilably," weaken the government, and "strengthen opposition." He considered it his duty to support the president's "policy in all essential points," as they have been "more consistent with the true interests of this Country," and the precedents established "by his predecessor, than the policy of his opposers."[28] Webster was right—Adams was following the foreign policy prescriptions Washington had articulated in his Farewell Address.[29] Adams's foreign policy was Washington's foreign policy, not because he was blindly following his successor, but because they both genuinely believed neutrality was in the best interest of the nation.

Reluctantly, Wolcott concluded that an Adams victory would be just as "dangerous [as] the election of Mr. Jefferson may prove to the community." Adams's temperament was "revolutionary, violent, and vindictive," Wolcott wrote. "His passions and selfishness would continually gain strength" and he would corrupt "the fountains of virtue and honour" and "destroy the principles" upon which the government was founded.[30]

Wolcott wrote this letter while serving as Adams's secretary of the treasury but said none of it to the president's face, nor did he resign in protest. His criticism exposed the toxic, irreversible conflict in the Federalist Party. Wolcott and Adams agreed on most things, including how to manage the banking system, opposition to taxes, avoiding war with Great Britain, and the need for the best men to lead the nation. But Wolcott had allowed their personal differences to blind him to their similarities.

Hamilton shared Wolcott's dismay but passive resignation was not in his vocabulary. The president's insinuations against him and the ongoing dismantling of the army were too much to bear. He wrote to the president about the rumors that Adams had repeatedly, "on different occasions, asserted the existence of a British Faction in this Country," and had "named me, at other times plainly alluded to me, as one of this description of persons." He demanded to know whether these allegations were true, and "if correct what are the grounds upon which you have founded the suggestion."[31]

Adams ignored the letter.

When the president refused to respond, Hamilton started collecting information that could be used to prove the president's "unfitness" for office. He had already obtained extensive documentation from James McHenry, who had sent records of his time as secretary of war shortly after leaving office. Now, Hamilton sought incriminating evidence from other members of the cabinet. He contacted Pickering and Wolcott, asking for intelligence against the president and "facts which denote unfitness in Mr. Adams." "You must be exact & much in detail," he instructed.[32] They both enthusiastically agreed. "I will readily furnish the Statement you desire from a firm conviction, that the affairs of this Govt. will not only be ruined, but that the disgrace will attach to the federal party, if they permit the reelection of Mr. Adams," Wolcott replied.[33] In Pickering's response, he lamented that he had not had time to make copies of important documents before he was removed from office as secretary of state, but he forwarded whatever he could find.[34]

With Pickering and McHenry's information in hand, Hamilton started exploring how best to undermine the president. "I have serious thoughts of giving to the public my opinion respecting Mr. Adams with my reasons in a letter to a friend with my signature," he explained to Wolcott. "This seems to me the most authentic way of conveying the information & best suited to the plain dealing of my character."[35]

Wolcott reasoned it was "perfectly proper & a duty, to make known those defects & errors which disqualify Mr. Adams," but he continued with a note of caution. "The situation in which we are both placed is delicate & somewhat perplexing." He recommended Hamilton "ought to publish nothing with your signature *at present*."[36]

Hamilton ignored Wolcott's advice, finished a draft, made several copies, and mailed them to Troup, Cabot, Ames, and other Essex Junto allies for review. They all urged him to reconsider. Cabot agreed with every word, he told Hamilton, but readers would read the letter as a personal attack on the president. The publication would only confirm Adams's claims that Hamilton was "dangerous."[37] Knowing Hamilton as well as he did, Cabot worried his warnings might not be heard. So, he wrote to Wolcott, hoping that the secretary might have more influence with his former colleague. Hamilton must not publish a declaration with his name, or in any way that could be traced to him, Cabot insisted. He could make "a strong appeal to the sense and principles of the real Federalists," but it would have to be "*accompanied with suitable acknowledgments that [Adams] is to be supported as one of the candidates, notwithstanding [his] defects.*"[38]

Hamilton received these responses a few days later, but he had made up his mind and would not be deterred.

"I have drafted a letter which it is my wish to send to influential individuals in the New England States. I hope from it two advantages the promoting of Mr. Pinckney's election and the vindication of ourselves," Hamilton wrote to Wolcott. "Decorum may not permit going into the news papers," but he insisted that he could still address the letter "to so many respectable men of influence as may give its contents general circulation." Anonymous publications would not carry enough weight, so his name would have to be attached.[39] In a display of stunning naivete or dangerous ignorance, Hamilton somehow believed he could send his letter to large numbers of influential men, and they would not leak it to the newspapers.

"What say you to the measure?" Hamilton asked. "Some of the most delicate of the facts stated, I hold from the three Ministers, yourself particularly," Hamilton conceded, and he would not "take the step without your consent."[40]

Wolcott replied, "The style & temper is excellent," but he reminded Hamilton that all the advice from Massachusetts was "opposed to any publication with your signature." Reluctantly, however, he acknowledged that "anonymous publications do no good."[41]

The same day, Troup wrote to King, "Hamilton has thoughts of publishing the grounds of his opposition to Mr. Adams; and from circumstances I expect daily to see him in the newspapers on this subject."[42] As one of Hamilton's closest friends and neighbors in New York, Troup would know.

Hamilton then wrote once more to the president, protesting "a base wicked and cruel calumny" committed against him, and condemning Adams's silence. He mailed the letter on October 1, 1800.[43]

The president did not respond.

Hamilton could not tolerate this insult to his honor. In mid-October, he sent his pamphlet to the printer to make copies for select distribution.[44] Perhaps Hamilton genuinely believed he could keep the pamphlet contained in select elite circles. Or perhaps he believed that he could convince enough electors to withhold their votes and produce an Electoral College tie. In that case, perhaps he wrote to persuade members of the House of Representatives to select Pinckney.[45] It was not the first grave political miscalculation Hamilton had made, but it was certainly among his worst.

The final version, one long, bitter, anguished diatribe, ran fifty-four pages.[46] On October 24, the *American Citizen* in New York posted a notice alerting readers that they had printed "A letter from ALEXANDER HAMILTON, concerning the public CONDUCT and CHARACTER of JOHN ADAMS, Esq. PRESIDENT OF THE UNITED STATES." Interested readers could purchase a copy at 136 Pearl Street, the newspaper announced.[47]

The next day, Duane began publishing the pamphlet in installments in the *Aurora*, the first headline announcing "ALEXANDER HAMILTON. AGAIN!"[48] Some reports suggest that Aaron Burr obtained a copy and swiftly delivered it to the *Aurora*. Other evidence indicates that John Beckley, the editor responsible for leaking Hamilton's Maria Reynolds pamphlet, was behind this leak as well.[49] Either way, the publishing world in New York City and Philadelphia was a small one.

Hamilton was arguing a case in front of the New York state court in Albany when a messenger ran into the court room. He whispered in Hamilton's ear, relaying the news that the *Aurora* had just printed a portion of his pamphlet. Hamilton fell silent, but quickly recovered and professed his relief that his honest sentiments were finally public. He was the only one.

Troup was in Albany as well when the publication was released and found "the general impression at Albany among our friends was that it would be injurious and they lamented the publication of it." After traveling home to New York City, Troup reported to King "a much stronger disapprobation of it expressed every where." Every single man "in the whole circle of our friends" condemns it, he concluded glumly.[50]

As newspapers made their way north containing Hamilton's harsh words, Massachusetts readers offered even more sharp condemnation. "Your friends are dismay'd by your letter," Cabot wrote to Hamilton at the end of November. "Even those who approved the Sentiments thought the avowal of them imprudent & the publication of them untimely." Everyone agreed "that the execution is masterly, but I am *bound* to tell you that you are accused by respectable men of Egotism, & some very worthy & sensible men say you have exhibited the same *vanity* in your book which you charge as a dangerous quality & great weakness in Mr. Adams."[51]

Readers in the South expressed equal shock. "We are all thunderstruck here by Genl. Hamilton's pamphlet," Bushrod Washington, George's nephew and a Supreme Court justice, wrote to Oliver Wolcott. "If it was intended to promote the election of Genl Pinckney, it is seriously believed by his best friends here that it will produce quite a contrary effect."[52]

Hamilton's shockwaves then rippled across the Atlantic. William Vans Murray had recently returned to The Hague when he received news of "a pamphlet against the President!" He wrote to John Quincy in solidarity, expressing his horror. "I have always respected [Hamilton as] among the most illustrious men of our nation," but there was nothing rational, ingenious, or persuasive in the pamphlet, Murray assured his friend.[53]

Other Federalists were compelled to make a more forceful defense of the president. Webster marshaled the pro-Adams voices when he printed an open letter to Hamilton: "You accuse the President of *vanity*," but surely this pamphlet was nothing if not an exercise in vanity, he snarked. Hamilton alleged "the President is *unmanageable*," which Webster agreed that was "in a degree true." Hamilton and his "supporters can not manage him," Webster acquiesced, "but this will not pass in this country as a crime" because Americans valued independent thinkers. Finally, Hamilton suggested Adams is "unstable." But Webster demanded, "did he waver during the Revolutionary War?"[54]

John Jay was not willing to publish an open letter in a newspaper while governor of New York, but he felt compelled to do something. On November 5, John Jay sent a note to the state assembly responding to their measures for port security. He included a passage at the end that endorsed "the patriotic zeal and important services of the President, to which I have been a witness." He was persuaded "that nothing will be wanting on his part to promote and expedite every proper measure for the defence and security" of "the United States in general, as well as to this State in particular."

On its surface, the passage was relatively innocuous, but it was cleverly crafted. Jay did not attach this passage to his annual address to the state legislature because the assembly always wrote a response. This type of letter from the governor required no reply from the assembly, thus offering the Republicans no opportunity to criticize the president. Coming less than two weeks after Hamilton's publication, Jay's statement was a clear vote of support for the embattled president and the administration's foreign policy. He forwarded a copy of the note to the president. He didn't mention Hamilton's pamphlet, but he didn't have to—the meaning was clear.

In mid-October, the president departed from Quincy for his journey to Washington, DC. Along the way, he stopped in New York to see his daughter and spent the night in Philadelphia, before arriving in Washington City on November 1. That evening he slept in the Executive Mansion for the first time.

Adams left no record revealing when he first learned of Hamilton's publication, but he probably received a copy during a brief stop in Philadelphia. He said nothing about his emotions while reading the pamphlet. Certainly, he viewed the publication as confirmation that Hamilton was dangerous, unpredictable, and hell-bent on seizing power for himself. As Adams scanned the fifty-four pages, he started drafting a point-by-point refutation. He jotted a note mentioning Hamilton's use of "a long Conversation between the President and secretary of War." He then asked, rhetorically, "How did Mr.

FIGURE 27.1 The White House, November 1800, by Tom Freeman, 2000. White House Historical Association.

Hamilton hear of any private Conversation between the President and one of his Ministers"?[55] The material leaked from confidential conversations with his cabinet secretaries was a monstrous betrayal. He had fired Pickering and asked for McHenry's resignation, but he expected their interactions would remain private.

Adams made no mention about the information Wolcott supplied to Hamilton, nor did he ever indicate that he knew of his secretary of the treasury's involvement.[56] But when Wolcott offered his resignation a few days after the president arrived in Washington City, Adams accepted it without comment or hesitation.

On November 2, he wrote to Abigail, "I Shall Say nothing of public affairs," but he was very grateful she agreed to come to Washington for the winter. "It is fit and proper that you and I should retire together and not one before the other," he rued, acknowledging that he almost certainly would not win reelection.[57] She had been his partner every step of the way and he wanted her by his side if this was the end.

Abigail left their home a few weeks later. From Philadelphia she replied, "I met upon my journey . . . the polite Letter of the Gen'lls." She dismissed the pamphlet, writing that "it is as Wise and judicious as the former Precious confessions" Hamilton had published about his own extramarital conduct. She reassured her husband that it would "produce upon the public mind an effect exactly the reverse of what was intended."[58]

Neither Abigail nor John Adams responded publicly to the pamphlet. To her sister, she wrote, "I shall not say any thing to You upon political subjects, no not upon the little Gen'll," whom she called a little "cock sparrow." But she would have plenty to say when they saw each other in person. In the meantime, she could only "laugh at the folly, and pitty the Weakness Vanity and ambitious views" depicted in "his fables."[59]

Adams's refutation came to a full ninety pages. He wisely set it aside, just as he regularly set aside his most virulent writings.[60] He offered no public rebuttal for nearly a decade, but he did write one poignant letter to an old friend.[61]

At the end of November, Adams received Jay's note and the enclosed copy of the governor's letter to the state assembly. "The assurance of the continuance of your friendship was unnecessary for me, because I have never had a doubt of it," Adams replied. Always honest and blunt to a fault, Adams addressed the elephant in the room. "Among the very few Truths in a late Pamphlet," he wrote, "there is one that I shall ever acknowledge with pleasure." The "principal Merit of the negotiation for Peace" at the end of the Revolution "was M^{r}. Jays." This was not mere flattery. Seventeen years earlier, when they worked together to negotiate the treaty in Paris, Adams had written the very same thing in his diary.[62]

"I often say that when my Confidence in Mr Jay shall cease, I must give up the Cause of Confidence and renounce it with all Men," Adams closed warmly. After so many betrayals, the president treasured those friends he still trusted.[63] In the coming weeks, as voters went to the polls, Adams would discover which friends remained loyal, how much damage Hamilton had wreaked on the Federalist cause, and the outcome of the presidential election.

28

Storms of a New Character

ON OCTOBER 31, voters began traveling to their local court houses, taverns, and city squares to cast their ballots in the presidential election. They would continue to do so for the next thirty-four days.[1] The process was much more complicated than twenty-first century presidential elections and gave ample room for political maneuvering and intrigue.

Article II, Section I of the Constitution grants each state the right to determine how their electors will be chosen. In the twenty-first century, most states have an automatic "winner take all" system, meaning the candidate who receives a bare majority of the vote, wins all the state's Electoral College votes. A few states have carved exceptions into their laws, giving certain districts a single Electoral College vote.[2]

In the Early Republic, this process was constantly evolving. In the 1796 presidential election, eight states empowered their legislature to pick the electors, six states held special elections for the electors, and two states divided their electors between legislature selections and special elections.[3] By 1800, many of the states had passed new laws that reflected the increasing partisan ferocity of elections. Eleven states granted their legislatures the right to name electors, while only five remained committed to special elections.[4] Just a few months earlier, both Federalists and Republicans had viciously campaigned to win seats in the New York state legislature and control the state's vote in the coming presidential election. In the remaining ten states whose legislatures determined the electors, therefore, elections for the state legislatures took on extra significance.

As a result, the presidential election was actually a series of elections, first at the state level to control legislatures, then in states with direct elections for electors, and finally at the electoral college level. And all these elections occurred in an overlapping, interwoven patchwork of events from mid-summer to December 3, when the Constitution mandated that all states submit their electoral college votes. There was no one election day or a few weeks of early voting, but rather months of voting, guesswork about the results, and uncertainty about when the result would be determined.

Republican leadership in Virginia crafted their party's national strategy, beginning with guaranteeing a victory in their home state. Madison and Jefferson were determined that Virginia's electoral votes would go for both Jefferson and Burr, rather than splitting between candidates from two parties like they had in 1796. They adopted a three-part plan to achieve this goal.

First, Republicans altered the state election process to cultivate the best possible conditions for success. Republican allies in the state legislature passed a bill changing the method of elector selection from district elections to state-wide elections. Instead of the twenty-one districts independently voting for their one elector, citizens voted for a general ticket with the top twenty-one candidates qualifying as electors. This system prevented local pockets of Federalists, like those who lived near Mount Vernon or John Marshall's home in Richmond, from picking off votes.[5]

Next, Republicans crafted a sophisticated statewide campaign. They named a slate of electors on the "Republican Ticket," filled with big names, including James Madison, George Wythe, General Joseph Jones, and Edmund Pendleton.[6]

Republicans then tapped the county committee system, founded earlier in the year, to turn out all eligible citizens (which was mostly property-owning white men), and ensure voter cohesion. In 1800, Virginia required each voter to hand write the names of his preferred candidates on a ballot, sign it, and deposit the paper into a ballot box. However, the state did not require the handwriting of the names and the signature to match. Over the summer, the Republican committees borrowed from the strategy implemented by John Beckley in Pennsylvania four years earlier. They hand-wrote thousands of ballots with their candidates' names and distributed them across the state.

Republicans understood that it might be difficult for voters to remember the names of twenty-one candidates, especially if they did not know them personally. They also knew that some eligible voters did not know how to write and would struggle to fill out a ballot. On election day, voters simply had to sign their name and deposit their ballot.[7]

Federalists in the state watched this process in horror and did their best to muddy the waters. They ran on the "American Republican Ticket," hoping to confuse voters, but lacked the statewide infrastructure to match Republican efforts.[8] As the Republican committees distributed ballots across the state, most observers assumed they would sweep the election in the fall.[9]

Leadership on both sides relied on word-of-mouth reporting, newspapers, and letter networks. Although Federalists and Republicans used different sources, by September they had reach similar conclusions: Republicans would win all the votes in New York, Georgia, Virginia, Kentucky, and Tennessee. New York was already decided, Virginia appeared to be a blow out, and the other southern states were notoriously hostile to Federalists.[10] They also guessed that Federalists would carry Delaware, New Jersey, and all the New England states (Massachusetts, Vermont, New Hampshire, and Connecticut). Rhode Island would probably be divided. If this speculation was accurate, Federalists entered the fall with roughly forty-eight votes to forty-four Republican votes. Whichever side reached seventy votes would win.[11]

These calculations focused public attention on Pennsylvania, Maryland, and both Carolinas, which carried forty-five votes in the Electoral College.[12] All four states held back-to-back elections in the coming weeks. None had received news from the envoys in Paris.

Maryland was up first, and the stakes of the general assembly elections were front of mind for all voters. Maryland had a tradition of permitting the voters to directly choose their electors, but Federalists knew that direct election would likely split the vote between Adams and Jefferson. In response, Federalist candidates for the assembly promised, if they were elected, to change the law and give the legislature the power to select the electors.[13] For years, Republicans had warned that Federalists wanted to seize power from the people and now Maryland Federalists had said the quiet part of their strategy out loud.

The "Electioneering warfare," from August to October, was carried on with "much warmth & some acrimony," Thomas Boylston Adams reported to his father from Philadelphia, where he was building his law practice.[14] In "Anapolis—Elk Ridge, & elsewhere," candidates took their campaigning directly to the people. They "assemble with their partizans—they mount the Rostrum, made out of an empty barrel or hogshead . . . praise & recommend themselves at the expence of their adversary's character & pretentions," he described for family at home in Massachusetts.[15]

While delivering fiery speeches, candidates referenced national issues and tied themselves to Jefferson or Adams. Republicans pointed to the Federalist electoral strategy as a power grab befitting a monarchy, which echoed the criticisms they made of Adams and the Arch Federalists at the national level.[16] On October 6, Maryland voters overwhelmingly cast ballots for

Republican candidates. Federalists maintained a majority in the state senate, but Republicans seized the majority in the lower house. As a result of the divided legislature, Maryland continued to select its electors through direct elections.[17]

Maryland Federalists consoled themselves that their position on electors had prompted the loss and would not affect the direct elections for electors a few weeks later. But "the astonishing increase of Republicans" in the legislature convinced many partisans that the upcoming elections would produce more Republican electoral votes than they had anticipated that summer.[18] "I congratulate you most sincerely on the Change in Maryland," one politician from South Carolina wrote to Jefferson, revealing how carefully observers from outside the state monitored news of the state's election.[19] How far that change would carry, however, no one could say. Both sides would have to wait until November for the next round of balloting to determine how Maryland would affect the election.

A few days later, attention shifted to Pennsylvania and South Carolina, which both held their legislative elections on October 14. The Pennsylvania election would reflect national political issues. Pennsylvania voters had a front row seat to national politics because the state had hosted the federal government for the last ten years, produced the Fries's Rebellion, and served as the jurisdiction where many Sedition cases were tried.

For the past year, Federalists in the Pennsylvania state senate and Republicans in the state assembly had battled over how the state would choose its electors. The Federalist Senate preferred for the legislature to have the power, while the Republican Assembly demanded local elections. Prognosticators anticipated that the upcoming election would not alter the breakdown in the state legislature. Federalists would probably retain control of the state senate, while Republicans would keep the assembly. The gridlock over how to pick electors would not budge and as a result, "Pennsylvania will probably have no vote in the College of Elector's," Thomas Boylston Adams predicted for his father.[20] Without Pennsylvania votes, neither candidate was likely to reach the seventy-vote threshold needed to win.

The Pennsylvania election unfolded as expected. Republicans won ten of the thirteen available congressional seats at the national level. Locally, they did even better. They picked up fifty-five of seventy-eight available seats in the assembly, and six of the seven state senate races. Republicans swept all the races in western towns, like Pittsburgh, and found overwhelming support in the east, where many counties had previously voted Federalist. The *Herald of Liberty* gloated, "The Republicans will carry every candidate from the Coroner to the Congressman. Never was there such a change known!"[21] The lopsided victory was a thorough repudiation of the Federalist tax program, the heavy-handed approach to Fries's Rebellion, and the Sedition Act.[22]

Despite the Republican success, Federalists still controlled the state senate and refused to approve any electoral vote plan that did not give them at least partial control over the state's electors. Federalists in the Pennsylvania Senate were willing to completely ignore the will of the people to protect their hold on power. As the calendar ticked toward December 3, the deadline for submitting electors, no one could be sure whether Pennsylvania would cast votes in the Electoral College.[23]

Two weeks later, Virginia and North Carolina held their statewide elections for electors.[24] From Monticello, Jefferson rued that the election "is the only thing of which anything is said here."[25] Virginia voted unanimously for the Republicans, leaving one Federalist to gripe "Virginia is sold and past salvation." North Carolina split between the two parties, with eight Republican votes and four Federalists votes.[26] Neither state altered electoral college expectations.

Meanwhile, in Maryland, Federalists and Republicans resumed their electioneering. At any public gathering, whether it be a "horse race—a cock fight—or a Methodist quarterly meeting" candidates presented their case and solicited support.[27]

The internal dynamics were messy, however, and rarely as neat as Federalists versus Republicans. Consumed with bitterness, James McHenry told other Federalists to "make little or no exertions for the federal candidate." He still believed in "the good old cause," but was convinced that "our labour would be lost" because of the "utter unfitness of one of the federal candidates to fill the office of the President."[28]

Other Federalists remained devoutly loyal to Adams, including Supreme Court Justice Samuel Chase and Secretary of the Navy Benjamin Stoddert, and they cultivated support among potential electors. Moderate Republicans backed their efforts and opposed the Arch Federalist schemes to sneak Pinckney into the presidency. If need be, their votes and support were an insurance plan for Adams. Samuel Smith was one such moderate Republican. Smith came from a leading family in Baltimore, made his fortune as a merchant, earned acclaim as an officer during the Revolutionary War, and currently served as one of Maryland's senators in Congress. His friendly ties with other merchants, like Stoddert, and officers, like Hamilton and Pinckney, would prove essential in the coming months.[29]

On November 10, Maryland voters went to the polls to cast their ballots. Federalists bounced back from the previous election defeat, but not to their full strength from years prior. The voters selected five Republican electors and five Federalist electors.[30] The results notched up both the vote totals, Adams with fifty-four votes and Jefferson with fifty-seven, but gave no further insight into the outcome of the race. Public attention shifted back to Pennsylvania once more.

Desperate to ensure that Pennsylvania's votes counted, Governor Thomas McKean convened a special session of the legislature on November 8. There wasn't enough time to call a new election, so he instructed both houses to come up with a compromise to allocate the votes. Republicans proposed a bill that authorized the legislators to select the electors. Each member would receive one vote; a majority would win.

Federalists rejected this proposal out of hand. Republicans possessed a two to one majority of members of the assembly, plus a minority in the senate. Their numerical superiority would overpower any Federalist votes. Federalists in the state senate countered with an alternative that granted the assembly the right to choose eight electors and the senate seven electors. They knew the assembly would pick Republican electors and the senate would pick Federalist electors but were willing to concede one vote.[31]

This proposal would not secure a victory for either Jefferson or Adams, but the Federalists had nothing to lose. If the legislature refused to adopt a plan and Pennsylvania did not register electoral college votes, South Carolina would decide the election. Either Federalists would secure some Electoral College votes, or they would deprive both parties of votes. They refused to compromise, and Pennsylvania remained undecided.[32]

On November 19, Rhode Island voted unanimously for the Federalists. Adams was now one vote ahead of Jefferson, fifty-eight to fifty-seven, at least according to the best unofficial tally. As many observers had expected from the beginning, the election came down to Pennsylvania and South Carolina.[33] Both states had fourteen days left to cast their Electoral College votes, or they wouldn't count.

From Washington City, Marshall wrote to Charles Cotesworth Pinckney that "the Senate of Pennsylvania will maintain their ground" and insist the state split its electoral votes. If the two houses agreed upon a compromise, then the race would be tied. "It is now reduced to an absolute certainty," Marshall warned, that Jefferson would win if he "gets any votes in South Carolina."[34]

Over the next several days, Federalists rejected every single proposal from the Republicans in the state assembly. The *Philadelphia Repository* reported resignedly, "The Legislature of Pennsylvania, it is thought, will not be likely to agree in choosing electors for President and Vice President of the United States."[35] Finally, two days before the deadline, Republicans blinked.

On December 1, both houses nominated eight candidates, as the Federalists had suggested. The next day, the state senators and assemblymen gathered in one joint session. They cast votes, selecting the top fifteen as electors—eight Republicans and seven Federalists. The Republican electors cast votes for Jefferson and Burr, and the Federalist electors voted for Adams and Pinckney.[36] On the morning of December 2, Jefferson and Adams were now tied at sixty-five votes each. "On your legislature I believe depends absolutely the election," Marshall confirmed for Pinckney upon hearing the news.[37]

The South Carolina legislature selected its electors, but the law mandated a unique process. The state's eight electors had to be chosen by a majority vote of all legislators. Neither party could force its candidates on the other, and the atmosphere was ripe for secret negotiations. The state cast its ballots on October 14, but the legislature did not convene until late November to choose its electors. Because of the distance and limited means of communication, neither South Carolina nor Pennsylvania knew what was going on in the other state.[38]

The political atmosphere in South Carolina was equally unusual. There were 161 seats in the legislature, but ten members were absent. Republicans controlled eighty-five votes to sixty-six Federalist votes. Both parties were institutionally weak and moderate, however, and they had avoided the partisan wave that wracked northern states. At least fifteen Republican votes were willing to cross the aisle depending on the issue.[39] Government was a small world in the eighteenth century, and politicians often knew each other or were related. Nowhere was that truer than in South Carolina. The Federalist Party was dominated by Charles Cotesworth Pinckney, the Federalist candidate, and his brother, Governor Thomas Pinckney. The Republican Party was led by their cousin, Charles "Blackguard Charlie" Pinckney.[40]

Charles wrote to Jefferson, acknowledging that he had become the face of the Republican Party in South Carolina, as the Federalists "single me out, as the object; my situation is difficult & delicate, but I push Straight on."[41] To Madison, he was more forthcoming about the personal toll. "I am charged with being the *sole cause* of all the Opposition in South Carolina," he wrote. "M*y two Kinsmen* have of course divided & will be separated from me in future."[42]

Into this sprawling morass of personal ties and weak party affiliations, Alexander Hamilton added his pamphlet condemning the president. The

City Gazette of Charleston challenged Charles Cotesworth Pinckney, questioning whether he would "stand for the presidency on such terms? Or does he patiently bear the dishonor of being brought forward" by Hamilton, a man so driven by "private ambition?" Goading Pinckney, the paper wondered if he would "bear such an insult on his affection to his country?"[43] Monroe noted that he was "inclined to believe, from what I have heard of the work, it will do" the whole Federalist Party "more harm than good."[44] John Barnes, a Republican ally from Maryland, was more direct. The pamphlet produced "the very *contrary purpose* intended by the Author—in respect—to Mr C.C. P."[45]

Unlike other states where party affiliation trumped other considerations, some electors were willing to split their votes between parties, one for Jefferson and one for Charles Cotesworth Pinckney. In the last week of November, a committee of both Republican and Federalist delegates proposed a new ticket with Pinckney and Jefferson as the candidates. Several of the delegates approached Pinckney, seeking his support. He refused "any inducement to be associated with Mr. Jefferson, at the expence of Mr. Adams."[46]

Charles Cotesworth had pledged to support the Federalist ticket equally per the agreement at the caucus in Philadelphia in May. Once Hamilton's letter was made public, he refused to seek votes independent of the president as a matter of personal honor, even if it meant losing the election.[47] Like many eighteenth-century men, especially southerners, nothing was more important than his personal honor. "I am sorry to inform you that the anti-federalists will have a *small* majority in our legislature," Pinckney wrote to Marshall. "As it rests on South Carolina, the election is settled."[48]

With Charles Cotesworth refusing to participate, the delegates retreated to their party platforms. Just after noon on December 2, the legislature put forward two slates of electors—one Republican and one Federalist. The next day, they cast their ballots. The Federalist delegates voted for Adams and Pinckney, and the Republicans cast their votes unanimously for Jefferson and Burr. The Republican slate won.[49]

On December 12, Jefferson received a report from Republican printer Peter Freneau, who was covering the South Carolina elections for his paper. On December 2, Freneau had written, "The Vote tomorrow I understand will be Thomas Jefferson 8. Aaron Burr 7. Geo Clinton 1."[50] Freneau believed that one elector would switch his vote to avoid a tie between Jefferson and Burr in the Electoral College. He was wrong.

A few days later, Jefferson received final tallies and realized with horror that he and Burr had tied.[51] For nearly a decade, Madison and Jefferson had worked closely to form a political party, establish a party infrastructure, and organize campaigns to seize power from the Federalists. Yet somehow, they had failed to arrange for one elector to drop his vote for Burr.

Earlier in the fall, while Adams and Hamilton had waged dueling campaigns in Massachusetts, Burr had conducted his own swing through New England to cultivate support among Republican electors. During his travels, Burr had sent reports to Madison and Jefferson, proclaiming enormous enthusiasm for Republicans in the north. Once the electoral results were reported, Madison and Jefferson realized that Burr had overstated Republican support in the north. Perhaps Burr was simply overly optimistic. Or maybe he intentionally exaggerated the strength of Republican sentiment so that southern voters would feel safe to vote for Burr and Jefferson together.[52]

At the same time, Virginia Republicans found themselves under increasing pressure from their northern allies. In 1796, many southern electors had dropped Burr votes to give Jefferson the edge. Four years later, northern Republicans demanded assurances that all southern electors would vote equally for Burr and Jefferson. In October, David Gelston, a Republican operative in New York, wrote to Madison of his "extreme anxiety" about the coming election. Northern Republicans feared that southern electors might drop Burr from their ballot, delivering the second-place spot, and thus the vice presidency, to Adams or Pinckney. "*Can we, may we* rely on the integrity of the southern States?" Gelston asked Madison. He requested assurance of "the integrity of Virginia & the southern States." In return, he also promised that electors in New York "shall be faithful & honest."[53]

Madison wrote back immediately, guaranteeing Gelston that the southern electors would uphold their end of the bargain. He was true to his word. "It seems important that all proper measures should emanate from Richmond for guarding against a division of the Republican votes," Madison wrote to Governor Monroe.[54] Perhaps Madison felt that he could not break that promise and arrange for one southern elector to drop a Burr vote, but surely someone else could be responsible.

Jefferson rarely got his hands messy with the political dirty work required by elections, so he likely presumed that someone else had made the necessary arrangements. And Monroe almost certainly wouldn't take decisive action without implicit direction or approval from Madison or Jefferson. They took for granted that someone else had arranged the single vote drop.

By the time they realized their mistake, it was too late.[55] The results "produced great dismay & gloom on the republican gentlemen" in Washington City, Jefferson wrote to Madison. The tie prompted "equal exultation in the federalists, who openly declare they will prevent an election," he confided darkly. In the coming weeks, the country would grapple with its first electoral tie. The forthcoming constitutional crisis produced "storms of a new character," including mass protests, threats of political violence, and plots to overturn the election results. The nation's survival was in the balance.[56]

29

Nothing but a Forest and Woods Along the Way

IN EARLY NOVEMBER, Abigail left Quincy, stopping for a day or two in Philadelphia and Baltimore, before making her way to Washington City. "You find nothing but a Forest & woods on the Way," Abigail wrote of her journey to her sister. They did not see a single village "for 16 and 18 miles," and the wilderness was only occasionally dotted by "a thatchd cottage without a single pane of glass."

By mid-morning, Abigail realized they had taken a wrong turn and "were wandering more than two hours in the woods in different paths, holding down & breaking bows of trees which we could not pass." Just as she was beginning to despair, they came upon a "black fellow with a horse and cart," who showed them back to the road and offered directions.[1]

The next morning, her carriage rattled down Pennsylvania Avenue, avoiding the tree stumps and corn stalks local citizens had stubbornly planted in defiance of the city commissioners.[2] She was immediately struck by the "beautifull situation" with a view of the Potomac River in front of the Executive Mansion. She could also see the potential for the city, remarking, "the country arround is romantic but a wild—a wilderness at present."[3]

She offered similarly mixed observations of the Executive Mansion. "The house is upon a grand and superb scale," but still very much under construction, she wrote to her daughter. The surrounding area was littered with construction equipment and muddy pits. Without fences or walls, the grounds were open to the public and visible to travelers passing by on Pennsylvania Avenue. Inside, the East Room, the largest public space on the first floor, was still under construction, and most fireplaces had to burn day and night to dry the paint and keep the damp at bay.

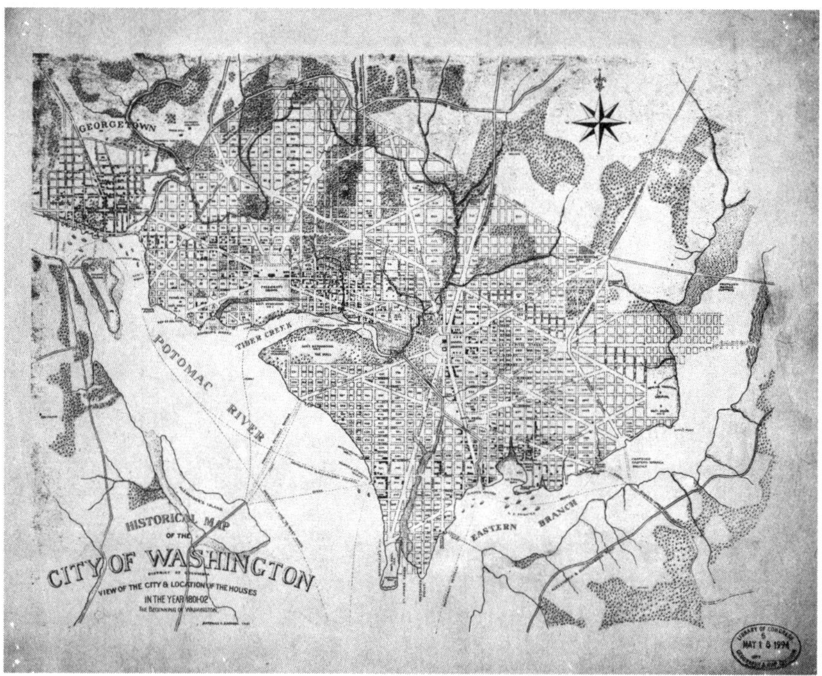

FIGURE 29.1 Map of Washington, DC by A. C. Harmon. *Historical map of the city of Washington, District of Columbia: view of the city & location of the houses in the year - 1801–02: the beginning of Washington*. Library of Congress Geography and Map Division, Washington, DC.

Once finished, the house would require an enormous labor force to maintain. Abigail anticipated future presidents would need at least "thirty servants to attend and keep the apartments in proper order, and perform the ordinary business of the house and stables." The Adamses could only afford to employ a small staff, so "lighting the apartments, from the kitchen to parlours and chambers, is a tax indeed." Communication was also a challenge, Abigail rued, as "bells are wholly wanting, not one single one being hung through the whole house." Most large houses, including the Adams's Peacefield in Quincy, the President's House in Philadelphia, and Mount Vernon, relied upon a system of bells to communicate between residents, guests, and hired or enslaved laborers. "This is so great an inconvenience, that I know not what to do, or how to do," she fretted.

Abigail and John largely contained themselves to a few rooms on the second floor that were relatively comfortable. She scattered lavender sprigs across the building to mask the scent of fresh paint, and she hung ropes across the East Room to hang drying laundry. When leaks sprang in the new roof, which they did frequently, she instructed servants "to Sit tubs to catch the water."[4] And she was constantly on the hunt for more firewood. They were "surrounded with forests," but she could not find wood because "people cannot be found to cut and cart it!" she exclaimed with exasperation.[5]

These troubles were nothing compared to the onslaught of news that arrived in the next few weeks. In early December, a letter arrived from New York. Charles, their second son, had died.[6] "I came to this city with a heavey Heart; in daily expectation of his Death, which took place on the first of December," she wrote to John Quincy.[7] "He was beloved, in spight of his errors," and Abigail would mourn his passing for the rest of her days.[8]

Adams had tried to block Charles from his mind with little success. He wrote that Charles had been "the delight of my Eyes and a darling of my heart." Charles's death was "the greatest Grief of my heart and the deepest affliction of my Life."[9]

Just a few days later, a clerk delivered a packet of letters and papers, including the news that the South Carolina electors had voted for Republicans. "The consequence to us personally is that we retire frm public life: for myself and family I have few regrets," she assured her son Thomas.[10]

That same day, another mail delivery arrived in Washington City that could have changed the outcome. Reports of a new Franco-American treaty had swirled around town for a few weeks. Not until early December, however, did the president finally receive a copy of the Treaty of Mortefontaine and the full dispatches from his envoys in Paris.[11] His foreign policy had triumphed. The treaty validated Adams's judgment, his risk-taking, and his willingness to fracture the Federalist Party for the long-term good of the nation.[12]

As the Adamses struggled under the weight of grief and the certain knowledge that their stay in the Executive Mansion would be short, the final piece of news arrived. The papers announced that "Mr. Jefferson & Mr. Burr have an equal number of votes" and "the house of representatives must chuse between" the two Republicans. "It is extremely uncertain on whom the choice will fall," Secretary of State John Marshall wrote to Charles Cotesworth Pinckney. "Having myself no voice in the election," he pledged to play no role and swore he would "not intermeddle with it." However, Marshall was already hearing rumors and witnessing "the anxiety of parties."[13] And with good reason. The next three months would pose an unprecedented threat to the Constitution, the sanctity of elections, and the peaceful transfer of power—fundamental cornerstones of the American republic. If the threats succeeded, the republic would fail.

After receiving word of their victory, Burr initially deferred to Jefferson, just as Republicans expected him to do. "My personal friends are perfectly informed of my Wishes on the subject and can never think of diverting a single Vote from you," he assured Jefferson. "On the Contrary, they will be found among your Most Zealous adherents."[14] Jefferson described Burr's conduct as purely honorable in letters to colleagues, and yet, he noted that Burr had not promised to refuse the presidency should it be offered to him. Jefferson was right to be suspicious.

Over the next several weeks, Republicans stridently insisted that Jefferson was the people's choice and the intended president, which began to grate on Burr. They had no objection to voting for him as vice president; why should they now expect he would reject the presidency? He had nursed a chip on his shoulder since the 1796 election, when he believed southern Republicans had betrayed him by splitting their votes. Now he saw their influence behind the campaign to pressure him to step aside.[15]

By the end of the month, Burr hedged his bets. Samuel Smith, a Republican representative from Maryland, visited Burr to encourage him to withdraw. Burr refused to commit one way or another. Smith reported back to Jefferson, Madison, and other Republicans that Burr could no longer be trusted.[16]

By January, Jefferson no longer described Burr as honorable in his correspondence. On February 1, he wrote Burr directly, "It was to be expected that the enemy would endeavor to sow tares between us, that they might divide us and our friends. every consideration satisfies me you will be on your guard against this, as I assure you I am strongly."[17] Burr wrote back, assuring Jefferson he had discounted all "slander and intrigue." But notably, he remained silent on the election results.[18]

The Federalists, disgruntled from the election, had several reasons to prefer Burr and encourage his ambitions. "I think Burr is preferred to Jefferson in Boston and as I am told in [Connecticut]," Fisher Ames wrote to Theodore Sedgwick. "He is more likely to preserve the Union, the first of political cares," Ames continued. He reasoned that Burr would be willing to "entrust [Federalists] with power," since he would need their votes to win the election. Furthermore, Burr had not expressed opposition to the entire Federal program, nor was he hostile to New England. "I am not in favor of the election of Jefferson," Sedgwick agreed with Ames. Jefferson absolutely "has the will to do mischief." Even if Burr was similarly inclined, Sedgwick argued, he did not have "the same <u>means</u>" to accomplish nefarious ends. Sedgwick concluded Burr could be made to see reason.

Jefferson, on the other hand, had little reason to compromise with Federalists. He retained the loyalty of Republicans and would throw all current Federalist officeholders out of their positions.[19] He had expressed hostility to the army and navy, deplored the national bank, and showed untoward friendliness toward France. "Should we be able to prevent the election of Jefferson on the first ballot," Sedgwick speculated, "we shall be able to exclude him altogether."[20] As Speaker of the House of Representatives, Sedgwick planned to use the powers of his position to pursue this outcome.

Sedgwick had one obstacle in his path he did not foresee. Alexander Hamilton hated Thomas Jefferson, but he feared Burr. He knew that Jefferson was steadfast in his beliefs—beliefs which Hamilton adamantly opposed. But he would rather see a president with convictions than one with none. Hamilton declared that Burr was without principle and, therefore, far more dangerous.[21]

"Our friend Hamilton," Robert Troup wrote to Rufus King, "is exerting all his might against Burr." If Federalists continued to "play so dangerous a game as to support Burr," Hamilton threated to "withdraw from the party and from all public concerns," Troup relayed.[22]

Hamilton's efforts were persuasive. Marshall replied that he had initially been "disposd to view with less apprehension any other character" besides Jefferson. Marshall knew Jefferson well, and he had a long list of flaws he attributed to his cousin. "His foreign prejudices" made him unfit "for the chief magistracy of a nation," Marshall wrote to Hamilton. He feared Jefferson would weaken "the office of President" to "increase his personal power," and he would "sap the fundamental principles of the government." Worst of all, "the Morals of the Author of the letter to Mazzei," that is, Jefferson's morals, "cannot be pure."

However, after reading Hamilton's letter, Marshall agreed that Burr might present "still greater danger than even from Mr. Jefferson . . . Such a man as you describe is more to be feard & may do more immediate if not greater mischief." Marshall reaffirmed that he could not bring himself "to aid Mr. Jefferson," but he would take no action to help Burr.[23]

While Hamilton continued to pepper his allies in Congress, Federalists began discussing other options offered by the Constitution.[24] Article II, Section 1 of the Constitution pronounced that if "no Person have a majority" in the presidential election, "the Votes shall be taken by States, the Representation from each State having one Vote."[25] Accordingly, each state delegation in the House of Representatives had to agree on their candidate. Eight state delegations voted for Jefferson: Georgia, Kentucky, New York,

New Jersey, North Carolina, Pennsylvania, Tennessee, and Virginia—all controlled by Republicans. Six state delegations voted for Burr: Connecticut, Delaware, Massachusetts, New Hampshire, Rhode Island, and South Carolina—all controlled by Federalists. Two state delegations, Vermont and Maryland, were evenly divided between Republicans and Federalists.

A loophole embedded in Article I of the Constitution, which established the commencement and closing dates of each session of Congress, further complicated the process. The states had voted, and Republicans had secured a majority in the House, picked up seats in the Senate, and won the presidency and vice presidency. But the new congressmen would not take their seats until the following November. As a result, Federalists still controlled a numerical majority in both houses of Congress and retained considerable power to affect the outcome of the presidential election, even though Republicans controlled a majority of state delegations. It was a strange system and contemporaries noted as much.[26]

Albert Gallatin, observing the Federalist machinations from the House, noted three distinct Federalist strategies. First, the Federalists would try to pick off states to vote for Burr, convinced that they could control him as president. Second, they would force a delay until March 4 when John Adams's term expired, and then call upon the Presidential Succession Act of 1792 to convene a new election. Third, using the same delay tactics, they would pass legislation appointing an interim president, who would campaign as the incumbent in a new election.[27]

Jefferson offered the same conclusions in his reporting to Madison. "The Feds appear determined to prevent" the "certification of the results," he wrote. They planned "to pass a bill giving the government to Mr. Jay, appointed Chief justice, or to Marshall as Secy. of state."[28] Gallatin agreed that Marshall was the most likely candidate under Federalist schemes.

Republicans offered several responses to Federalist machinations. The Federalists could not outright elect Burr if Republican states held firm, and Gallatin, Madison, and Jefferson pledged to do so. If Federalists moved on to more extreme plans, Gallatin had responses prepared for those scenarios. He argued that Republicans should accept a new election, as they would likely win again. If the Federalists used their remaining authority in state legislatures to suppress the popular vote, Republicans could thwart their attempts when Congress convened in the fall. By then, Republicans would be seated with a majority in Congress. They could reject the results if produced through Federalist voter suppression, which would send the election to the House. Since Republicans would control more states in the House starting in the fall of 1801, they could elect Jefferson as the people's choice. There was always the possibility, Gallatin acknowledged, that they might lose. If the Federalists won fair and square, then Republicans would have to accept their defeat. Gallatin did not like the idea, but he was willing to accept that his side would not always win in a democracy.

If Federalists appointed an interim president, the most drastic option, there was little Republicans could do. They did not have a majority, so they could not completely stifle proceedings, but they could boycott the proceedings in protest. Gallatin hoped the dramatic statement would spark widespread protests across the country, forcing Federalists to retreat.

Madison wondered if the possibility of defeat in a new election was too great. Instead, perhaps the new Congress should be summoned "by a joint proclamation or recommendation of the two characters" that received "a majority of votes for President," meaning Jefferson and Burr. Madison reasoned that under normal circumstances, the newly inaugurated president would convene the legislature. Either Burr or Jefferson would be president, so "the prerogative of convening the Legislature must reside in one or other of them," he argued. If they both agree, then "the intentions of the people would undoubtedly be pursued." Madison acknowledged that this plan was not "strictly regular" in "reference to the Constn." However, he concluded that "the irregularity" would be more in keeping with constitutional intent than "the other remedies proposed," which were "substantial violations of the will of the people, of the scope of the Constitution, and of the public order & interest."[29]

Madison and Gallatin's competing plans exposed the constitutional crisis of the moment. When constitutional text is vague or the Constitution is faced with an unprecedented situation, there are two approaches. First, follow the will of the people under the rationale that the Constitution was drafted to "promote the general Welfare" of the country, even if it risks violating the text of the document.[30] Second, adhere closely to the strict construction of the text, even if it risks rejecting the will of the people.

Gallatin rejected Madison's plan as taking dangerous liberties with the Constitution. While catering to the will of the people was appealing, Gallatin argued, it risked tearing down the very institutions they were trying to protect. Once they started improvising with constitutional mandates, it would be difficult to stop or prevent the Federalists from adopting the same strategy in the future. It could provoke the "dissolution of Union," or permanently undermine the Constitution, he argued. Assuming power by means not "strictly warranted" by the Constitution posed a real threat to "our republican institutions."[31]

These ideas were swirling as congressmen arrived in the new capital city for the upcoming session.[32] Residents, congressmen, and executive branch officials all noted the flaws in the Constitution and grappled with how best to address the silences and vagaries in real time. They knew the coming session of Congress would be unprecedented. They were responsible for resolving the looming crisis with no model to follow.

All eyes were locked on February 11, when the House of Representatives would certify the election results, but the president's job was unfinished. He had victories to secure for the future, a transition to plan, and precedents to set. No president had ever left office after losing—a first Adams intended to handle with care.

On December 16, he wrote to the Senate and sent "for their consideration and decision," the Treaty of Mortefontaine between "the United States of America and the French Republic."[33] The treaty was not perfect, and the envoys had not secured everything they hoped, but all treaties required compromise and were almost always better than war. Adams argued that the treaty "leaves us at full Liberty to Place England and France on a footing of Equality in their relations with Us, which I think is the precise point" of our foreign policy, he wrote to his son. The treaty represented the pinnacle of Adams's lengthy diplomatic foreign policy career and validated his diplomatic instincts.[34]

The envoys agreed. Oliver Ellsworth, the most Arch Federalist of the envoys, wrote to several of his allies, urging them to support ratification. "My best efforts & those of my colleagues, have not obtained all that justice required," he acknowledged. "Enough is however done," he argued, "to extricate the United States from a contest which it might be as difficult to relinquish with honor." Ellsworth had witnessed Napoleon's spectacular successes across Europe, and he knew France would make an imposing enemy. Given these shifting tides in Europe, Ellsworth hoped the Federalists would agree that "it was better to do this than to have done nothing."[35]

Ellsworth had too much faith in his fellow Federalists, who were still hopelessly divided over foreign policy. The Arch Federalists mourned the demise of the army and their dreams of military glory. They wanted to punish Adams for his perceived weakness toward France. From Massachusetts, Pickering wrote to Wolcott in disgust, "The Treaty with France, as you Suppose, has excited my utter astonishment. Davie and Murray always appeared to me fond of the mission; & and I supposed that they had made the treaty: but when informed that our friend, our highly respected restable friend Mr. E[llsworth] was most urgent for its adoption, my regret equaled my astonishment."[36] The Federalists in the Senate followed Pickering's lead and rejected the treaty at the end of January. All negative votes were cast by Federalists.[37]

Abigail described the Senate's response accurately. "The party had rather the whole convention should be negatived and every thing put again at the mercy of France" just because the president initiated the mission, she explained to her son. They "pretend that they are fearfull of Mr Jeffersons prediliction in favour of France" but were willing to let him make a much more lenient treaty if it meant depriving the president of a political victory.[38] The Federalists in Congress chose political vendetta and personal retribution over the good of the nation.

Undeterred, Adams resubmitted the treaty, urging the Senate to reconsider. Meanwhile, Marshall met with Federalist senators to remind them of the stakes. They would have fewer votes in the next Congress and no control over the executive branch. Did they really want to trust Jefferson to protect American commerce, he asked his fellow Federalists? Marshall's argument received unexpected support from the most ardent voice for war. Abruptly changing his mind, Hamilton wrote to Senator Gouverneur Morris that the treaty, in "its present form," should be ratified, if only to prevent the "Jacobin Administration" from doing far worse.[39] Looking to the future, Hamilton argued that it would benefit the Federalists to argue, "The Federal Administration steered the vessel through all the storms raised by the contentions of Europe into a peaceable and safe port."[40]

Marshall and Hamilton's lobbying efforts paid off and the Senate ratified the treaty on February 3, twenty-two votes to nine. The ten Republicans present voted to ratify, along with twelve Federalists. All nine nay votes were obstinate, unrepentant Arch Federalists.[41] Many years later, Adams recognized the treaty as his greatest accomplishment and hoped his tombstone would plainly declare: "Here lies John Adams who took upon himself the Responsability of the Peace with France in the Year 1800."[42]

With the treaty resolved, Adams had only one more foreign policy task. He wrote to Marshall, asking him to prepare official letters "recalling Mr John Quincy Adams as Minister Plenipotentiary" from Prussia. He asked for copies of the recall "to go by the Way of Hamburgh, another by Holland, a third by France, a fourth through Mr King in England, and a fifth if you please by the Way of Bremen or stettin or any other Channel most likely to convey it soon." He wanted the news to reach his son as quickly as possible.

"Justice would require" that John Quincy should be sent to "France or England if he should be continued in Europe," the president remarked. John Quincy was among the most experienced and successful diplomats in the nation. He had earned the right to serve in the most prestigious positions in the diplomatic corps. But Adams believed it was his "duty to call [his son] home," rather than leave his fate in Jefferson or Burr's hands.[43] The letter was marked with a sense of deep sadness. Adams accepted that his political career had ended, but he regretted that his political fortunes limited John Quincy's prospects.

There was one bright spot that temporarily cheered the president. When word of the treaty arrived from France, so too did a note for Adams from Ellsworth resigning his position as Chief Justice due to poor health. Adams immediately appointed his old friend, John Jay, to this post as a mark of respect and admiration. "I had no permission from you to take this Step," Adams admitted, "but it appeared to me that Providence had thrown in my Way an Opportunity" of demonstrating Jay's value to the public. Perhaps more important, the appointment would furnish "my Country with the best Security, its Inhabitants afforded, against the increasing dissolution of Morals."[44]

Jay replied that the "nomination so strongly manifests your Esteem, that it affords me particular Satisfaction." But he had to regretfully decline the position. He had left the bench because he was convinced that the judicial "System [was] so defective" that it would never "obtain the Energy weight and Dignity" which were required for it to "support to the national Governmt."[45]

Jay's appointment caught most Arch Federalists by surprise. "When the office of Ch. Justice became vacant, it was the wish of all the federal men," Sedgwick wrote, "that J[ustice William] Paterson should be appointed." If Paterson was not nominated, Sedgwick continued, then they hoped, "that Gen.l Pinckney who had conducted with the most honourable disinterestedness, should be rewarded." Instead, Sedgwick sputtered, the president nominated Jay "without even consulting his ministers or any" Federalists, when "every man of common sense [knew] he could not accept."[46]

Sedgwick expected Paterson's elevation because he was the most senior justice on the bench and an avowed Arch Federalist. They suspected that he was excluded because he had "given an honest opinion that Mr. Adams and General Pinckney ought to be equally supported at the late election."[47] It's certainly possible that the president avoided promoting Paterson after the political insult. However, Marshall's comments at the time indicate that the president was listening to his advisors, and they had suggested other nominees.[48]

Marshall opposed Paterson's nomination for two reasons, he explained in a letter to Charles Cotesworth Pinckney. First, Paterson was old and in poor health. If Jefferson or Burr were going to be president, Marshall wanted a Federalist to serve as Chief Justice for as long as possible. Second, Paterson had played a prominent role in many of the Sedition Act trials, often imposing hefty bails and punitive sentences on defendants. As a vocal opponent of the Alien and Sedition Acts, Marshall disapproved of the harsh punishments.[49]

Adams never disclosed why he refused to promote Paterson to chief justice. However, Marshall's appointment as secretary of state six months earlier hints at one explanation. Shortly after Marshall publicly condemned the Alien and Sedition Acts, Adams brought him into the cabinet. Either Adams agreed with Marshall's critique of the legislation or the criticism wasn't so offensive that it disqualified Marshall as a close colleague and advisor. Furthermore, once Marshall was installed as secretary of state, he served as the president's closest confidant, aside from Abigail. Adams and Marshall were both moderates, opposed to the Arch Federalists' extreme measures, and suspicious of the Essex Junto. They rarely disagreed; Paterson's nomination was no exception.[50]

Perhaps more important, Adams reflected on the long-term importance of the bench and was determined to appoint a justice who could serve a lengthy tenure. "The office of Chief justice" is too important to entrust to an older man, he wrote to a friend in January 1801. Besides, he continued, he had already selected "a gentleman in the full vigor of middle age—in the full habits of business and whose reading in the science is fresh in his head." He was referring to John Marshall, though the secretary of state did not know it yet. Marshall was not just a convenient candidate, Adams reasoned, but the right one.[51]

The appointment surprised Marshall. He fully expected to return home to Richmond and resume his practice as a private attorney.[52] He took two full weeks to mull over the offer before accepting. The position would require at least partial residence in Washington City, circuit riding, and life in the political arena. And yet, it offered an opportunity to shape American jurisprudence. He finally accepted the nomination and Adams immediately sent his name to the Senate on January 20.[53]

The Arch Federalists howled in outrage. "General Marshall is brought forward although it is known that his appointment is disagreeable to the federal party & must be offensive to every gentleman on the bench," Sedgwick wailed.[54] As Speaker of the House, Sedgwick could do little about the nomination. But his ally, Senator Jonathan Dayton of New Jersey, hatched a plan with the other Arch Federalists to thwart yet another of the president's nominees. Dayton wrote to Justice Paterson, divulging that the Senate had temporarily postponed Marshall's appointment. They planned to visit Adams to determine whether he "could be induced under any circumstances whatever to nominate you." If the president acquiesced, they planned "to prevail on Mr. Marshall" to decline "the highest for a lower seat upon the Bench," Dayton explained to Paterson. If Marshall refused to cooperate, the Federalists would reject the nomination.[55]

In late January, Dayton and a handful of like-minded senators called on the president to lobby him to withdraw the nomination. The senators found the president as stubborn and immovable as ever. "The President alone was inflexible and declared that he would never nominate you," Dayton relayed to Paterson.

After Adams called their bluff, the senators concluded that rejecting Marshall "would have been . . . painful indeed to the Federalists on account of their esteem for that gentleman and their respect for his talents," Dayton confessed.[56] "Under these circumstances, we thought it advisable to confirm Mr. Marshall, lest another not so well qualified and more disgusting to the Bench should be substituted," Dayton concluded.[57] On January 27, 1801, the Senate confirmed Marshall as the next Chief Justice of the United States.

Adams had asserted his will over the Arch Federalists once more. He ensured that Marshall, not the Essex Junto, would define American jurisprudence and establish legal precedents still cited today. Marshall's appointment was one of Adams's longest lasting contributions to the nation.

The Senate then turned its attention to the judiciary branch more broadly and the circumstances that had caused Jay to reject the appointment in the first place. When Jay spoke of the system's defects, he was referring to the justices' obligation to ride circuit. In the 1790s, there were no federal circuit courts. Instead, Supreme Court justices traveled across the nation, convening court sessions to hear federal cases. These "circuits" were onerous, dangerous, and highly uncomfortable. The conditions of the roads and public lodging were poor, and justices spent months away from their families.[58]

Justices began advocating substantive reform as early as 1790, less than a year after the First Federal Congress passed the Judiciary Act of 1789, which created the federal judicial system. They urged Congress to create another level of courts in between the local districts and the Supreme Court. These districts would offer fairer and quicker justice. They would be in session most of the year to immediately address complaints and handle the burgeoning load of federal cases. They would also eliminate the need for justices to ride circuit, enticing qualified candidates to accept the position. The first three attorneys general supported these proposals.[59]

George Washington had also urged Congress to adopt judicial reform in many of his addresses to Congress (today's State of the Union), and Adams picked up the cause once he was in office. Every year, he encouraged Congress to tackle judicial legislation, but with little success. On March 11, 1800, Federalists in the House had put forth a bill radically reforming the judiciary, but it made little progress.[60]

On December 3, 1800, Adams again appealed to Congress to consider judiciary legislation.[61] A month later, with a Republican victory looming, Federalists in Congress finally discovered urgency. Over the next several weeks, the House and Senate debated the levels of courts, the number of judges, and when the legislation should go into effect. The final bill passed on February 13, 1801. It created the circuit court system, staffed by sixteen judges, and reduced the Supreme Court to five seats, effective after the next vacancy.[62]

The bill was a good one, based on real and serious challenges plaguing the judicial system. It offered substantive and effective solutions to the existing problems and adhered to the recommendations made by justices, attorneys general, and presidents. It was also remarkably close to the reforms adopted in the early twentieth century, which finally abolished riding circuit.[63] The bill genuinely improved the judicial system and made it more responsive to the needs of the American people.

The bill was also politically motivated. Congress had not yet resolved the tie between Jefferson and Burr, but the next president would almost certainly be a Republican. The proposed bill would stack the judicial system with Federalists eager to stymy the Republican agenda and limit Republican influence on the Supreme Court. Old and sickly, Justice William Cushing was likely to retire or die soon. Upon his departure from the bench, President Jefferson or Burr would be deprived of the opportunity to replace him.

Republicans decried the move as "One of the most expensive and extravagant, the most insidious and unnecessary schemes that has been conceived by the Federal party." The *Aurora* alleged the bill was totally unnecessary to handle the federal case load and it was instead designed to provide "sinecure places and pensions for thoroughgoing Federal partisans."[64] Jefferson concurred. "I dread this above all the measures meditated," he wrote to Madison, warning that the "effect will be very mischievous" because it will be "difficult to undo what is done."[65]

While Congress debated the bill, Adams began collecting names and recommendations for potential nominees. He submitted most of his nominations in the days immediately following the passage of the bill, but the Senate was slow to consider the positions and did not approve the final nominees until early March. No judges were submitted at midnight before the inauguration.[66] And yet, Jefferson complained about Adams's "midnight judges" for decades after his presidency, referring to the judges Adams appointed before leaving office.

To be sure, Adams welcomed the opportunity to expand Federalist control over the judiciary and diminish Republican influence in the legal system. But his motives were not entirely political. Adams was also following precedent. George Washington had nominated candidates for vacant positions until the day before he left office with little comment or objection from the American people.[67] Adams and Washington were both Federalists, but Adams had his own ideas about potential candidates and would have happily filled those positions once he was in office. Now that he was preparing to leave the presidency, he followed Washington's example in the absence of any other model to follow.

As soon as Jefferson arrived in Washington City for the new congressional term, he wrote to Madison. "I propose . . . to aim at a candid understanding with mr. A. I do not expect that either his feelings, or his views of interest will oppose it."[68]

By this point, Jefferson and Adams agreed on little. Their supporters had spent the past four years trashing each other in print, battling over votes, and occasionally coming to blows in the streets. Both believed the other was a threat to the future of the nation. And yet, over the next several months the president and vice president upheld the Constitution, even if just barely. Jefferson flirted with political violence and came perilously close to upending democratic institutions. But he redeemed himself in the end. Both Jefferson and Adams put aside petty grievances and worked together, honoring their commitment to basic civic virtue. It was not comfortable, but they did it.

Over the next several weeks, Adams and Jefferson met several times, including at least two private dinners at the Executive Mansion. In early January, Abigail confided in her son that "Mr Jefferson dines with us, and in a card of replie to the Presidents invitation, he begs him to be assured of his *Homage* and *high consideration.*"[69] Abigail, John, and Jefferson dined in the family quarters on the second floor.[70] Perhaps they reminisced about their time traveling together in Europe or chatted about their families. But they also spoke about the election and the looming balloting in the House of Representatives.

In one of their conversations, Jefferson alerted Adams that the Federalists would try to force him to nominate a temporary president or "devolve on him the government during an interregnum." Republicans would use force to resist these measures, Jefferson warned, and he urged the president to take steps to prevent "such an act."[71]

Adams was shocked. He knew his old friend was a revolutionary at heart and had downplayed the violence in the French Revolution. But for Jefferson to resort to armed resistance so casually demonstrated a worryinging lack of commitment to the constitutional process. Adams could only hope that Jefferson was exaggerating for rhetorical effect.

Adams replied that the American people clearly intended for Jefferson to be president. Both John and Abigail desired that outcome. Adams encouraged Jefferson to offer Federalists reassurance that they had nothing to fear. If Jefferson promised to keep the navy, honor the national debt, and retain some lower-ranking Federalists in office, then the presidency would be his. Adams's recommendations were sensible. He was not asking Jefferson to betray his principles but rather reach out to voters in the House, like any other politician. Adams himself had made countless compromises as president to preserve harmony or garner support for his agenda.[72]

Jefferson retorted that he would make no deal.[73] Many years later, when discussing the conversation, Jefferson accused Adams of supporting the Federalist schemes to appoint a temporary president or assume the powers himself.

But, shortly after the dinner, Abigail wrote to their daughter, describing John's plans. If the House could not resolve the tie between Jefferson and Burr, she wrote, "the President will immediately refuse being considered as a candidate," and would reject any other participation in the schemes. "The spirit of party has arisen to such a height, that it cannot be appeased by the wisest and best measures," she regretted. At best, the president hoped he might be able to arrest "the progress" of the mind-boggling partisanship.[74]

In other words, Adams planned to do exactly what Jefferson wanted but refused to say so to his former friend's face. Perhaps Adams was so shocked by Jefferson's threats of violence that he wasn't willing to offer solace at that moment. Or maybe he was feeling a little salty about having just lost the election. Adams had already told Jefferson that he was the rightful winner of the election. What more did Jefferson want from him? Adams did have a powerful stubborn streak and he refused to be backed into a corner. Whatever his reasons, Adams did not say exactly what Jefferson wanted to hear.

Adams's true response was more accurately revealed in Abigail's correspondence with their daughter, Nabby. Abigail wrote shortly after the conversations with Jefferson, while her recollections were fresh. Jefferson's accusations, however, were written fifteen years later, in the shade of retirement, when he was compiling thirty years of grievances and political defenses for publication in his *Anas*. The *Anas* was designed to rebut John Marshall's *Life of George Washington*. The accounts were penned with political motives in mind.[75]

Over the next several weeks, Adams fulfilled the pledge contained in Abigail's letter. He demonstrated his commitment to the Constitution both through concerted action and through intentional inaction. Restraint is much harder to quantify and less exciting to celebrate, but it is an essential quality during a constitutional crisis.

Adams started by undercutting Federalist schemes. "It has been the practice of this Government to Summon the Senate of the United States to meet on the fourth of March after a new Election of a President and Vice President," he wrote to Marshall. The uncertain electoral situation rendered "it probable that it will be at least as necessary this year as it ever has been at any former period." Accordingly, he requested the secretary of state to "prepare Summons's for all the Senators, who are to serve after the third of March next, to meet at the Capitol in the Chamber of the Senate in Congress on the fourth day of March 1801." He concluded, "There is no time to be lost."[76]

Many Republicans interpreted this letter as Adams's complicity with Federalist machinations.[77] Once a new Senate was convened, they would be expected to swear in a president and vice president. If the election was still unresolved, the senators could select a president pro tempore to supervise the Senate in the vice president's absence. Under the Presidential Succession Act, the president pro tempore also became the temporary president until a more permanent candidate was selected.[78] Republicans feared Adams would appoint Marshall or himself as the president pro tempore.

Instead, this letter reveals Adams's efforts to erode the Federalist majority in the Senate because he did not trust the extreme members of his own party to uphold their oaths to the Constitution. Federalists enjoyed a twenty-one to eleven seat majority in the Senate at the end of the Sixth Congress, which concluded on March 3. Under the terms of Article I of the Constitution, the Senate term did not automatically expire. Senators served six-year terms and therefore could continue their session indefinitely until the Seventh Congress began. By convening the Seventh Congress, Adams ensured that the new

Republican senators were sworn in, and the Federalist majority decreased from eighteen seats to fourteen. Federalists still controlled the Senate, but the narrower majority impaired their ability to impose radical measures.

He also trusted that a president pro tempore would not be required. A president pro tempore was only elected in the absence of the vice president. As long as Jefferson remained in his seat as vice president, no pro tem could be elected in the Sixth Congress. Adams knew Jefferson wasn't going anywhere. Furthermore, he fully expected Jefferson to win once the House balloting commenced. In late December, before meeting with the vice president, he predicted, "I presume mr. Jefferson will finally be agreed upon; *neither party can tolerate Burr*."[79]

Worst case scenario, if another election was required, Adams refused to participate and he had complete confidence that "Mr. Jefferson would be chosen."[80] In the meantime, he pledged not to meddle in the constitutional process and to permit the election to play out in Congress.[81]

When faced with uncertainty, Adams adhered to the strict text of the Constitution. He trusted that the process would produce an outcome that was consistent with the will of the people. More important, as a student of history, Adams knew republics were fragile. He refused to meddle with the Constitution, fearing that any interference would lead to its demise.[82]

30

The Prey of Anarchy and Faction

THE SMALL CITY of Washington bustled with activity. Lodging houses, shops, and services sprang up around two central hubs: the Executive Mansion and the in-progress Capitol. Albert Gallatin, a representative from Pennsylvania, described the scene around the Capitol for his wife, Hannah. There were "seven or eight boarding-houses, one tailor, one shoemaker, one printer, a washing woman, a grocery shop, a pamphlets and stationery shop, a small dry-goods shop, and an oyster house."[1]

As the February 11 certification date ticked closer, visitors flocked to Capitol Hill and crammed into the limited boarding houses, eager to play their part witnessing history. We have "hardly any other society than ourselves," Gallatin complained to Hannah. "A few, indeed, drink, and some gamble, but the majority drink naught but politics, and by not mixing with men of different or moderate sentiments, they inflame one another."[2]

In early February, rumors spread across the country of a Federalist plot to pass legislation and appoint a new president. From neighboring states, citizens traveled to Washington City to register their protest. One observer reported to a Baltimore paper, "vast numbers have crowded hither from all parts of the Union. . . . [T]he hotels and lodging houses have been so much crowded that in the house where I lodge fifty have slept on the floors, with no other covering than their great coats—no other underlay than their blanket."

In the days just before Congress certified the election results, the new arrivals began milling about in front of the Capitol, where Congress was in session. The crowd was determined to ensure that either Burr or Jefferson became president rather than a Federalist plant. "If any man should be thus appointed President by law and accept the office, he would instantaneously be put to death," the crowd shouted. In between votes on other legislation, some of the Republican congressmen slipped out the side doors of the building and joined the crowd. Gallatin decried their participation in the "excitement out-of-doors" as dangerous and likely to instigate violence.[3]

Philippe de Létombe, the French minister to the United States wrote to Paris describing the mob that descended on the Capitol as 100,000 strong.[4] Washington City was not equipped to contain 100,000 people, but whatever the size, the protest was large enough to make a significant impression on the congressmen and residents present in the city.

Rumors of other plots gave credence to the mob's threats. Gallatin heard reports that "fifteen hundred" men "determined to repair to Washington the 4th of March for the purpose of putting to death" anyone that the Federalists appointed as "the usurping pretended President." Gallatin still believed these rumors to be accurate nearly fifty years later when he wrote about the election to a friend.[5]

Around the same time, word arrived at the capital from Pennsylvania and Virginia, warning that Governors Thomas McKean and James Monroe prepared their militias to march on Washington.[6] Republicans intended for these militias to prevent "civil war and the shedding of a single drop of blood."[7] The Republican governors stood ready to defend the election results, the will of the people, and the Constitution—as they saw it—if Federalists tried to pass legislation and appoint a new president.

In the summer of 1800, McKean and Monroe had made a pact, pledging their combined efforts to protect "those liberties we acquired by our revolution" and promote "the sacred cause of our country."[8] McKean secured weapons for 20,000 men and compiled brass pieces, before sending out orders to his militia officers ordering them to obey Jefferson "as President and Mr. Burr as Vice President." As the balloting neared, they both maintained constant contact with agents in the city through express riders between Richmond, Philadelphia, and Washington.[9]

Neither Jefferson nor Adams commented on these plans, but the vice president certainly knew of them. Gallatin had communicated "all the facts to Governor McKean" and suggested he ready "a body of militia, who might, if necessary, be in Washington on the 3d of March."[10] Both Gallatin and Jefferson stayed at the same hotel and spoke nightly. Then, on January 27, Monroe wrote to Jefferson that he would convene the assembly "without delay" if the Federalists attempted "any plan of usurpation." He did not put more details in writing, and Jefferson dared "not trust more through the post."[11] But they understood one another.

Federalist papers in the city reported on these preparations with outrage, suggesting "the constitutional rights" of Congress were "soon to become the prey of anarchy and faction."[12]

Sedgwick wrote to his neighbor Daniel Dewey that "the Jacobins say you must chose a President or the Government comes to an end—and they say you must vote for Jefferson because they will not vote for Burr—the consequence therefore is unless you will give up your opinions to them, that they will tear the Government in pieces."[13] Sedgwick had a point. In a republic, one side loses in elections. They don't get to threaten violence to force their desired outcome.

While tensions were already on a knife's edge, the offices of the war and treasury departments went up in smoke. In the early morning hours of January 20, flames licked up the walls of the first floor of the Treasury Department. Residents rushed out into the snow and passed buckets of water to extinguish the fire. Others used the Treasury Department's engine to pump water from a local well. One man threw the "public accounts of the Revenue" out the windows to save them from destruction.[14] Adams ran from the Executive Mansion and joined his neighbors to combat the blaze and prevent its spread. The combined effort saved the building's roof and prevented the fire from leaping to neighboring buildings.[15]

Fires were regular occurrences in the eighteenth-century, but this blaze seemed no accident after the War Department had burned to the ground two months earlier.[16] Federalists accused the Republican mob of starting the fires, while Republicans accused Federalists of deliberating setting the fire to obscure evidence of corruption and wrongdoing. One witness breathlessly reported to the *Aurora* that they saw Oliver Wolcott "removing trunks of materials from the Treasury Department!"[17] There was no evidence either fire was intentional, but the fear of arson elevated the already tense mood in the city.

As tempers flared, a snowstorm reached Washington City on the night of February 10. By the next morning, a thick blanket of snow covered the entire city. The flakes continued to fall fast and heavy, quieting the protests and discouraging the mob from leaving their homes and hotels.[18]

At the other end of Pennsylvania Avenue, Adams remained cozy in the Executive Mansion. He had no official role in the House proceedings, he could not cast a vote, and his presence would be a distraction. Furthermore, the unprecedented nature of the transition forced Adams to establish precedent for this type of constitutional crisis. There were no laws or statutes that offered guidance. The president's role was undefined, and his options were limited. He couldn't call up the army without Congress, and he worried it would have been exploited by the Arch Federalists for partisan aims. There was no national guard. The governors controlled the state militias, except in rare cases of domestic rebellions, like Fries's Rebellion in 1799. But now, the threat of rebellion came from Congress and the states themselves. Adams concluded that silence and restraint was the most prudent and constitutionally appropriate course of action. The best he could do was refuse to cooperate or give succor to Federalist plans and trust the House to elect the right candidate.

On February 11, the day of the certification, congressmen bundled up against the cold and trudged through the deep snow to the Capitol. In Philadelphia, they had gathered in the House chamber because it was the larger of the two. This time, they all piled into the Senate chambers because the House chambers remained unfinished. At 12 P.M., Vice President Thomas Jefferson sliced open the first envelope and began to read off the electoral returns. Everyone anticipated that the results would be a tie, but it was finally confirmed as Jefferson read off the electoral return tallies: Thomas Jefferson, seventy-three votes; Aaron Burr, seventy-three votes; John Adams, sixty-five votes; Charles Cotesworth Pinckney, sixty-four votes; John Jay, one vote from a particularly ornery elector.[19]

Jefferson, in his capacity as president of the Senate, declared that the tie remanded the outcome to "the House of Representatives to determine the choice." The representatives left the Senate chambers, walked down the wooden corridor, and found seats in their temporary chambers. They congregated by state delegation, rather than by party. Each state would receive one vote in the balloting process, so the delegates had to first vote in their state delegation, before each state could cast its vote.[20]

Before any voting could occur, Federalists pushed through an agreement that the House would remain in session until a president was selected. Federalists retained the majority of seats, but Republicans controlled the majority of state delegations. Federalists could not force their desired outcome, but they could compel the House to remain in session, increasing the pressure on Republicans to defect and support Burr. The Federalists reasoned that the longer the session continued, the harder it would be for Republicans to stand firm behind Jefferson because the pressure to compromise would build.[21]

The first ballot began at 1 P.M. As expected, eight state delegations voted for Jefferson: Georgia, Kentucky, New York, New Jersey, North Carolina, Pennsylvania, Tennessee, and Virginia—all controlled by Republicans. Six state delegations voted for Burr: Connecticut, Delaware, Massachusetts,

New Hampshire, Rhode Island, and South Carolina—all controlled by Federalists. Two state delegations, Vermont and Maryland, were evenly divided between Republicans and Federalists and could not come to an agreement. They could cast no vote.[22] Nine votes were required for the next president to be elected.

The House immediately moved onto the second ballot. It deadlocked, eight states to six, just like the first ballot.

The third ballot produced the same outcome.

And the fourth.

Over the next nineteen hours, the House cast twenty-seven votes with no further resolution.

In between ballots, representatives curled up in chairs or lay down on their coats to catch a quick nap. Porters and clerks offered sandwiches, snacks, and beverages in the cloak room in the hall. One representative, Joseph Nicholson, had been ill for several days, but he was determined to cast his vote. If he missed a single ballot, the Federalist delegates from his home state of Maryland would swing the state to Burr. He insisted that friends carry him for two miles on a stretcher in the swirling snow from his lodgings to the Capitol. The Republican committee room was outfitted with a bed, where Nicholson shivered under blankets. Nicholson's wife carried his vote back and forth between the room and the floor of the House twenty-six times, in between nursing her husband and tending the fire.[23]

As the balloting proceeded and the session continued into the early hours of the morning of February 12, Federalists pushed for Republican defections. Representative James Bayard, a moderate Federalist from Delaware who was friendly with many mid-Atlantic Republicans, approached Samuel Smith (from Baltimore) to offer a compromise. If Smith, a moderate from Maryland, switched his vote, he would put his state in Burr's column. In return, Burr would appoint Smith as secretary of the navy. Bayard did not offer a specific position to Edward Livingston, a representative from New York, but they did discuss what it might take to flip the state from Jefferson to Burr. Both Smith and Bayard refused these offers, before reporting the content of the conversations to Jefferson.[24]

At 8 A.M., after the twenty-sixth ballot, the congressmen agreed to recess for four hours. Gallatin wrote to his wife that he promptly fell asleep on the floor. Others managed to make it to their beds in nearby lodging houses. Later that afternoon, the House cast two more ballots, both deadlocked at eight states to six. Reluctantly, the House agreed to recess until the next morning, when they would cast their twenty-ninth ballot on Friday, the thirteenth.

The twenty-ninth vote stalemated, just as the previous twenty-eight had done.

On Saturday, the House cast four more ballots with no change in the results. Frustrated, tired, and hungry, the House agreed to reconvene on Monday, February 16.

Over the weekend, the two parties met with their caucuses to resolve the impasse. Adams stayed away and played no role, just as he had pledged. Republicans remained unified behind Jefferson, but the vice president had lost patience.[25] "Four days of ballotting have produced not a single change of a vote," he complained to Monroe.

Determined to break the deadlock, Jefferson met with a handful of unnamed Federalists. He suggested that Republicans planned to convene "a convention to reorganize the government, & to amend it." His threats "shook" the Federalists" and "the very word Convention, gives them the horrors," he reported casually to Monroe.[26] Then, for the first time, Jefferson explicitly confirmed the plans in Virginia and Pennsylvania. He declared "openly & firmly" that "the middle states would arm" if Federalists attempted to thwart the election. Jefferson's threats removed any doubt about the rumors that had plagued the city for weeks. Americans had watched the French repeatedly overturn their constitution and devolve into anarchy and terror. Suddenly, Republican violence and the destruction of the Constitution seemed terrifyingly close to reality.

While Jefferson might have overstated the likelihood of a convention or military force to intimidate Federalists, he had embraced political violence as an acceptable political tactic. His behavior was unacceptable for a democratically elected leader and disgraced his oath to the Constitution.

Alarmed by Jefferson's warnings, the Federalists gathered and sought an honorable way to end the stalemate. Initially, they approached Jefferson directly. He refused to discuss "terms & promises," and proclaimed that he "would not receive the government on capitulation."[27] The Federalists were not asking for much. They asked Jefferson to "stipulate" to "no French love, nor British quarrel, nor war on Commerce, nor on the funded or other paper property." In other words, if he maintained neutrality with both France and Britain, protected the economy, and safeguarded private property, Federalists would "give him the preference," Sedgwick exclaimed with exasperation to Fisher Ames.[28]

Rebuffed by the vice president, Federalists tried a more circuitous route. Their allies in New York repeatedly approached Burr about making a deal to share power. Those in Congress urged him to travel to Washington City to meet in person. Burr promised to travel immediately to New York City, and on to Washington by "3d March at the utmost; sooner if the intelligence . . . shall be such as to require my earlier presence." But then he abruptly altered his plans and remained in New York. Burr never explained why he changed his mind.[29] William Cooper, a Federalist representative from New York, rued, "Had Burr done any thing for himself, he would long ere been President."[30]

Bayard again entered the scene, this time seeking a Jefferson victory under acceptable terms. At the Federalist Party caucus over the weekend, he had hinted that he might switch his vote to Jefferson. His comment was met with jeers of "Deserter!" from his fellow Federalists and deterred him from making a change. For the moment anyway.[31]

But after days more of balloting and no movement, Bayard resolved to end the logjam. He arranged another meeting with Samuel Smith and invited John Nicholas of Virginia, another close ally of Jefferson. Bayard articulated the Federalist demands: preserve the financial system and honor the national debt, maintain the navy, and keep Federalist officeholders below the level of cabinet secretary, if they were qualified.[32]

After their conversation, Smith returned to his lodgings at Conrad and McMunn's boarding house, where Jefferson, Gallatin, and most of the Republican leaders were staying. They had a private "tête à tête" between friends to discuss the Federalist requests. Jefferson indicated his willingness to cooperate in a roundabout fashion but made no firm commitment.[33]

Smith returned to the House after their chat, where he met Bayard and delivered the good news that Jefferson would uphold his end of the bargain. For his part, Jefferson wrote to Monroe that "it is confidently believed by most that tomorrow there is to be a coalition," suggesting he knew exactly what was happening.[34]

Later, Jefferson vehemently denied that he had made a deal to secure the election. Technically, he was probably correct. John Quincy later observed that Jefferson had "a memory so pandering to the will that in deceiving others he seems to have begun by deceiving himself."[35] Most likely, Jefferson indicated to Smith, with a wink and nod, that he would work with the Federalists, while never agreeing to precise demands and thus, maintaining his deniability.[36]

Pickering observed from Massachusetts, where he had retreated after his firing, that some Federalists had "*sold* their votes to Mr. Jefferson and *received their pay* in appointment to public offices." Burr would have been president if he had "been at the seat of government and made similar promises of appointments."[37]

On Monday morning, February 16, the House once again convened and tallied the thirty-fourth and thirty-fifth ballots. They were tied. That night, Federalists held a final caucus. Jefferson was gaining support, and no one was confident what the outcome might be if they pursued legislation to appoint a different president. They agreed to swing the necessary votes and end the process. Adams received updates as the House counted ballots but continued to practice restraint and trusted the will of the people would prevail.

The next morning, February 17, the Federalists from Vermont and Maryland "retired" from the House chamber. Their absence gave the Republicans from their states control of their delegation's vote. Vermont and Maryland cast votes for Jefferson. Bayard and the Federalists from South Carolina cast blank ballots, which removed two states from Burr's tally. The final result was ten states for Jefferson, four states for Burr, and two states with no vote. On the thirty-sixth ballot, Jefferson was finally elected the third President of the United States.[38] The next day, the Senate certified the results. They sent notice of the election to Adams and included the official certificates for state department records.[39]

On Abigail's trip home to Quincy, she received updates of the deadlocked ballots at each stop. While she rested in Philadelphia, the bells at Christ Church suddenly began to clang with wild abandon. Although she had supported Jefferson over Burr, she could not help ruing darkly that the religious establishments were celebrating the election of "an infidel."[40]

The bells were only the beginning of the celebration. The Federalist *Gazette of the United States* reported with perhaps a touch of sarcasm that the price of gin and whisky had risen 50 percent since 9 A.M. The paper complained, "Bells have been ringing, guns firing, dogs barking, cats mewling, children crying, and Jacobins getting drunk ever since the news of Mr. Jefferson's election arrived in this city."[41]

31

The New Order of Things Begins

PRESIDENT-ELECT THOMAS JEFFERSON had no time for celebrations. He had two weeks to conduct his entire transition, including hiring staff for the Executive Mansion, appointing a cabinet, and writing his inaugural address.[1] There was no formal transition process, no staff to ease the burden, and no written rules to guide his actions. Jefferson leaned heavily on the Adamses and the Federalist cabinet members to ensure the unprecedented transition was successful. A few days earlier, Jefferson had threatened political violence and the destruction of the Constitution. Now he sought to repair the damage. All participants in the transition put the Constitution and the survival of democratic institutions above their own personal political beliefs or egos. The transition of 1801, and all productive transitions that followed in the two centuries since, made for strange bedfellows.

Before Abigail left town, Jefferson had called at the Executive Mansion to say goodbye. While no votes had been cast in the House yet, both expected that he would eventually win. Accordingly, she showed him around the mansion and offered a few notes "respecting the house, and furniture." He thanked her for the advice and shared his plan "to retain all domesticks" that Abigail recommended, should he be elected. After securing the presidency, Jefferson returned to the list of servants Abigail suggested and hired three: Christopher, Jack, and the groom that worked in the stables.[2]

Jefferson then inquired if there was anything he could do to be of service to "to *mr Adams*," Abigail, or their family, in particular John Quincy. He asked Abigail if her son "liked his residence at Berlin." Jefferson made no offers, but he was clearly debating whether to keep the Adamses' son in his diplomatic post. Abigail replied "frankly, that I expected mr Adams would return to America."[3] This moment was an odd one. Jefferson and Abigail had been extremely close friends and while she never forgave him for his criticism of her husband, they both knew it was likely the last time they would see each other.

After the House finally elected a successor, Adams set the tone for a conciliatory and peaceful transition. In his final acts as president, he set an example for statesmanship and a model for his successors to follow. "This part of the Union is in a State of perfect Tranquility and I See nothing to obscure your prospect of a quiet and prosperous Administration, which I heartily wish you," he wrote to Jefferson.[4]

Adams also offered information and aide to the president-elect whenever possible. "In order to save you the trouble and Expence of purchasing Horses and Carriages," he wrote just a few days after the election was decided, "I shall leave in the stables of the United States seven Horses and two Carriages with Harness the Property of the United States. These may not be suitable for you: but they will certainly save you a considerable Expence" and they belong to "the Presidents Household."[5]

One week later, Adams sent John Briesler, his longtime steward, to visit Jefferson. Briesler had served as a manager at the President's House in Philadelphia and the Executive Mansion in Washington City (today's Chief Usher). Adams instructed him to offer assistance and answer any questions from the president-elect.[6]

Following the president's example, each secretary wrote to Jefferson and extended their service and support. Stoddert penned a heartfelt message, acknowledging that he was "not among the number of those who desired your elevation to the important station you are about to fill," but that he would "sincerely pray that your administration may realize the most sanguine expectations which have been formed of it." In his capacity as a private citizen going forward, Stoddert would "zealously support the Just measures of the Government."[7]

The secretaries also passed along, at the "direction of the President," any information that Jefferson would need once he assumed office. "I have the honor to enclose, for your information," Stoddert wrote, "a letter addressed to me" from the Chamber of Commerce in Philadelphia, complaining of recent captures of American vessels by British privateers in the West Indies. Stoddert readied an American naval vessel in Norfolk, Virginia, but did not issue any orders without Jefferson's knowledge and permission.[8]

This thoughtful interaction reveals how carefully and responsibly Adams and his cabinet managed policy decisions in the final days of the administration. There were no statutes requiring cooperation or mandating intelligence sharing. Instead, Adams and the secretaries demonstrated their commitment to facilitating Jefferson's smooth entrance into office.

Jefferson's response acknowledged these efforts. "The declarations of support to the administration of our government are such as were to be expected from your character and attachment to our constitution," he replied to Stoddert with his thanks.[9] He also asked Stoddert and Samuel Dexter (the former secretary of war and new secretary of treasury after Wolcott's resignation) to remain in office after his inauguration while he selected his own candidates. They agreed and served him respectably for several months until Jefferson's cabinet was complete.[10]

Two days before the inauguration, Jefferson wrote to his cousin, Chief Justice John Marshall. "I propose to take the oath or oaths of office as President of the US on Wednesday the 4th. inst. at 12. o'clock in the Senate chamber," he wrote. "May I hope the favor of your attendance to administer the oath?" he asked, reflecting his uncertainty about how the ceremony would proceed.

In the meantime, Jefferson asked Marshall if he would be saying "the oath prescribed in the constitution?" He acknowledged that he did not "know what has been done in this heretofore; but I presume the oaths administered to my predecessors are recorded in the Secretary of state's office." Jefferson's question hints at a bit of nerves and perhaps he wanted to practice before saying the oath in front of a large audience.

Finally, Jefferson confessed he had not yet hired a private secretary. After his inauguration, he would need a clerk to deliver messages to Congress, because it would be inappropriate for him to deliver the messages himself. He asked Marshall to send "the chief clerk of the department of state" to serve as "the bearer of a message or messages" to Congress. If possible, Jefferson continued, please send the clerk to meet him at "my lodgings" after the inauguration.[11]

Marshall loathed his cousin and spent most of his professional career obstructing Jefferson's agenda. But he put the duties of his position and the stakes of the moment above his personal feelings. Later that afternoon, Marshall graciously replied, "The chief clerk of this department will attend you at the time requested." He added, "I shall with much pleasure attend to administer the oath of Office on the 4th." After consulting the "records of the office of the department of state," Marshall concluded that the oath "prescribd in the constitution seems to me to be the only one which is to be administerd."[12]

With these final details sorted, Jefferson spent the remaining days before the inauguration holed up in his rooms at Conrad and McMunn's boardinghouse, editing and reediting his address. At one point, he scratched out so many lines that he pasted a square of fresh paper on top of one passage to start again. On the evening of March 3, he wrote out two copies of the address: one in shorthand for him to read the following day and the other for public consumption.[13]

On the morning of March 4, President John Adams boarded a stagecoach at 4 A.M. He planned to travel all the way to Baltimore in one day and needed an early start. At 12 P.M., he would no longer be president. Adams had ridden into the presidency in his private carriage but would be leaving as an average citizen. He asked his valet to book a seat on the public coach north to Massachusetts, a notable symbolic gesture to his new status. Upon climbing into the coach, he saw that Theodore Sedgwick, his onetime friend and enemy, was on the bench across from him. It would be an awkward and silent trip home.

Adams was in a dark place; he was mourning the death of his son Charles and the end of his presidency. He was certainly bitter about the loss and had no interest in attending the inauguration or celebrating Jefferson. There is no question that he wanted to flee Washington City as quickly as possible. But his actions were not necessarily those of a poor loser.

There was no precedent of a defeated president attending his successor's inauguration. Nor was there a history of defeated governors attending their successors' ceremonies at the state level. Adams had not received an invitation to the inauguration and had no idea how his attendance would be received. Over the previous weeks, Adams had demonstrated a commitment to forging a smooth transition. He had shown real statesmanship, not petulance—even when he was sorely tempted.

True, Adams had taken great comfort in Washington's attendance at his inauguration. But the first president's presence served as an endorsement of the Adams administration, and they had served together in the same party. In 1801, Adams worried that his appearance might be a distraction and undermine the healing process required at this inauguration. March 4 would be the first transfer of power between political parties and Adams would do nothing to risk the survival of the republic.[14]

Adams was a complex, nuanced man who could hold two separate thoughts in his head at once. He both wished to avoid celebrations honoring Jefferson's inauguration and operated with loftier motivations for removing himself from the scene. He reflected on the loss of Jefferson's friendship and the presidency, while also focusing on the long-term health of democratic institutions and the republic.

For his part, Jefferson does not appear to have expected, nor did he request, that Adams attend the ceremony. Some Republican newspapers noted Adams's early departure, but they did not condemn his absence so much as mocked him for losing. They gloated over his forced departure and toasted his return to private life. The *Massachusetts Spy* did write, "Sensible, moderate men of both parties would have been pleased had he tarried until after the installation of his successor. It certainly would have had good effect."[15] Later generations of Americans agreed and created an expectation that the defeated president would attend the inauguration of their successor. But that process did not begin until 1845 when John Tyler attended the inauguration of James K. Polk—the first defeated president to do so.[16]

A few hours after Adams left Washington City for the last time, a company of artillery lit their fuses and boomed their cannons to proclaim the start of the festivities. At 10 A.M., a company of Alexandria riflemen gathered outside Conrad and McMunn's to greet the new president.[17]

At precisely noon, Jefferson appeared, wearing a simple suit, and eschewing the ceremonial sword favored by Washington and Adams.[18] Dress swords were required at European court and smacked of aristocracy and false airs, at least to Republicans. Jefferson carefully selected his clothing and transportation to signify the dawn of a simple, republican administration.[19] A line of militia officers drew their swords and led the procession to the Capitol, followed by local citizens, congressmen, and the president-elect. When they arrived at the door of the Capitol, the officers opened ranks, flanked the steps, and saluted.[20]

As Jefferson walked through the door, the artillery discharged once again, this time to announce his arrival and prompt the 1,140 guests to rise to their feet. Jefferson took the ceremonial seat at the raised dais at the front of the room.[21] After a few moments, he stood again and read his remarks.

Jefferson pledged his fidelity to the Constitution and promised to uphold democratic institutions. He swore his commitment to the vital principles of the republic, including "the supremacy of the civil over the military authority," "the honest payment of our debts," and "freedom of religion; freedom of the press, and freedom of person under the protection of the habeas corpus, and trial by juries impartially selected."

Jefferson then acknowledged the unprecedented hostility of the election and the toll it had inflicted on the nation. "Let us, then, fellow-citizens, unite with one heart and one mind," he urged. The American people disagreed on how to best protect themselves and the nation, but "every difference of opinion is not a difference of principle," Jefferson insisted.[22] "We have called by different names brethren of the same principle." He paused, before proclaiming, "We are all Republicans, we are all Federalists."[23]

Seated next to the dais, Chief Justice Marshall heard every word. He interpreted Jefferson's words as a genuine effort to bridge the divide and perhaps, a subtle acknowledgment of his own role dragging the country to the constitutional brink. The speech was "well judgd & conciliatory," he wrote that afternoon. Marshall was never disposed to give Jefferson the benefit of the doubt, but on this occasion, he believed his cousin was well intentioned. The address gave "lie to the violent party declamation which has elected him," he continued.[24] At this moment, parties and political culture were shifting and evolving. Marshall hoped that the inauguration signaled the moderation of both parties and the birth of a new political era.

It was a remarkable and history-defining event. Most presidents since Jefferson have used their inaugural addresses to heal the wounds inflicted during a bruising campaign. They have adopted rhetoric designed to remind the American people of their shared values and similarities. Presidents embrace the opportunity offered by their inaugurations to unite the American people during the most tumultuous moments. Jefferson was the first. His address would be less extraordinary today because it would be expected. In 1801, it was revolutionary.

After completing his address, Jefferson walked to the clerk's desk. Chief Justice Marshall stood and administered the oath of office. The new president spoke so softly that few members in the audience could hear him, but it did not matter. Earlier that morning, he had delivered his remarks to Samuel Harrison Smith, the editor of the *National Intelligencer*. Smith had copies of the address ready for distribution as soon as Jefferson became the third President of the United States.[25]

For the third time that day, the artillery issued a barrage. After sixteen rounds, cannons at the base of the hill delivered their own sixteen-round response.[26] Later that afternoon, Marshall wrote to Charles Cotesworth Pinckney, "To day the new political year commences—The new order of things begins."[27]

Epilogue

MAY NONE BUT HONEST AND WISE MEN

A FEW WEEKS after the inauguration, Thomas Jefferson moved into the Executive Mansion. The transition process was complete, with no violence or bloodshed—though it had been a close call. The election of 1800 and the transition of 1801 set the tone for American politics for the next two centuries, for both good and ill.

This moment revealed the constitutional loopholes and darkest aspects of political life that have plagued Americans since the ratification of the Constitution. The campaign of 1800 exposed the perils of weak parties and intense partisanship. The Republican Party at the turn of the century was stronger and better organized than the Federalists and therefore able to assert a more uniform approach to the election and voting. It was also able to tolerate dissent without collapsing into intraparty turmoil. The Federalists, on the other hand, were divided and chaotic, and they attacked moderate voices that did not toe the party line. This internal discord produced intense partisanship that appealed to the party's radical base, while shunning the more moderate, inclusive approach that engaged centrist or independent voters.

Timothy Pickering, Theodore Sedgwick, Alexander Hamilton, and the Arch Federalists blamed John Adams's moderation for undermining the Federalist platform in the 1800 election, but the results suggest Adams's balanced agenda was a much better fit for the American people.[1] At the district level, Adams received more votes than many Federalist congressional candidates. He also outperformed the 1796 election results in many states, except New York.[2] Federalist infighting and extreme electoral tactics cost the party valuable votes in Maryland, New York, and South Carolina, not Adams's moderation and conciliatory foreign policy like the Essex Junto claimed. The phenomenon of a weak party structure, leading to party fratricide and strident partisanship, has emerged again and again over the last two centuries.

Thomas Jefferson and Aaron Burr carried nine states in the electoral college, amounting to seventy-three electoral votes. Of those nine states, six had sizable populations of enslaved men and women. Article I, Section 2 of the Constitution allocated representation in Congress based on population, which was to be determined by adding "the whole Number of free Persons" with "three fifths of all other Persons."[3]

Federalist audiences could not help but remark on the leverage this clause provided to the southern states in the Electoral College. "There are above 500,000 negro slaves in the *United States*, who have no more *voice* in the Election of President and Vice-President of the *United States*, than 500,000 New-England horses, hogs and oxen," an anonymous writer in Boston noted. "Yet those 500,000 slaves (at least their masters for them) chose 15 Electors of Presidents of the United States!—Whereas the owners of the 500,000 New-England horses, hogs, and oxen, have not a single vote more."[4]

Southern, and often slaveholding, politicians, like Jefferson, benefited from this constitutional advantage until the Civil War. Based on the total population in the South, rather than the voting population, southern politicians received more seats in the House of Representatives and southern states had outsized power in the Electoral College. From Washington to Abraham Lincoln, nine of the sixteen presidents were from the South, and ten enslaved individuals. In the Jim Crow Era, roughly 1880 to 1964, southern politicians received similar electoral boosts from the free Black population, while systematically depriving Black citizens of their right to vote. Without the three-fifths clause, Adams likely would have won reelection in 1800. His defeat was only the first in a long line of racially charged victories in the Electoral College.

The delegates at the Constitutional Convention deliberately designed the three-fifths loophole to ensure that southern states ratified the Constitution. But the Constitution unintentionally produced other perils in the electoral system that only emerged over time.

The Federalists' machinations during the extended transition in 1800 revealed the potential pitfalls of empowering the previous Congress to adjudicate contested or undecided elections. Right before the Civil War, during the lengthy transition in 1860–1861, most southern Democrats forfeited their seats in Congress and returned home to join their states in the Confederacy. Northern Democrats and Republicans were hamstrung without a quorum and impotent to face the crisis until the newly elected congressmen arrived in Washington, DC, later that spring.

Seventy years later, in 1932, while the country descended into an ever-worsening depression, the American people overwhelmingly elected Franklin D. Roosevelt and endorsed the Democratic Party's vision for change. Yet, for over four months, while the economy continued to crumble, the outgoing Congress, split between a Democratic House and a Republican Senate, refused to stem the tide of the worsening bank crisis, and President Herbert Hoover tried to sabotage Roosevelt's New Deal plans.

Two days before FDR's inauguration, Congress passed the 20th Amendment to improve the transition process. The amendment moved the start of future congressional sessions from March 4 to January 3, ensuring that each new class of congressmen took office much faster than the 1931–1932 transition. The amendment also ensured that the new session of Congress was in place to certify the results of the election. The 20th Amendment makes schemes like those of the Federalists in 1801 much more difficult in the future—though not impossible.

For all the shadows of the election of 1800, there were critical precedents that shaped the way future generations participated in the democratic election process. Despite the threats, none of the worst violence came to pass. No blood was shed, the transition was peaceful. Voters did not face intimidation at the ballot boxes. Partisans and foreign actors did not tamper with votes.

The transition had been a close call, however, and partisans were appropriately sobered by their near miss with violence and constitutional crisis. Americans conceded that meaningful political change must be achieved through ballots, not bullets. With a dash of luck and a generous helping of civic virtue, the final outcome of the election both adhered to the strict text of the Constitution and reflected the will of the people.

This peaceful transfer of power was not the result of a clearly articulated process in the Constitution or a specific statute. In 1800, very few details of the transition process had been written down or codified. While we might assume today that eighteenth-century Americans revered the Constitution and respected the sanctity of their elections as a central feature of the republic, they did not. Instead, this defining characteristic of American democracy emerged because the first two administrations established precedents that crystallized into norms and customs. These political practices were not guaranteed. They required repetition and practice over decades to become a cherished feature of the political system. The Constitution's quasi-sacred status emerged slowly over the centuries.

None of this would have been possible without John Adams. He refused to meddle in Congress, he rejected Federalist schemes, he steadfastly adhered to the text of the Constitution, and he walked away after losing with no fuss. These invaluable contributions ensured the survival of the presidency. And yet, the details of Adams's presidency and the important role he played establishing democratic norms are rarely remembered.

Thanks to the handiwork of his contemporaries, especially Alexander Hamilton and Thomas Jefferson, Adams became a bit player in this early American political drama. Hamilton, in particular, hated Adams, mostly because he could not control or influence his actions. Adams's blatant contempt for Hamilton's opinions did not help either. In the fall of 1800, Hamilton's relentless campaign to undermine Adams's reelection left its mark. His pamphlet, "Letter from Alexander Hamilton, Concerning the Public Conduct and Character of John Adams, Esq. President of the United States," did little to sway votes outside of South Carolina, but it shaped the historical narrative.

Since 1800, Adams has usually been described as unpredictable, jealous, unreliable, mad with power, and vindictive—the same language Hamilton used in his pamphlet.[5] There is no doubt Adams had a temper and was prone to outbursts. He resented that his service wasn't glorified like Washington's, and he distrusted Hamilton's influence among the Federalists. But he was relentlessly dependable. He was protective of executive power, but not often precious about his own. He demonstrated a capacity for forgiveness and was extraordinarily loyal to his friends and family. When he harbored suspicions about a political rival or foreign diplomat, he was almost always correct.

Adams also showed nearly unrivaled diplomatic instincts. The Treaty of Mortefontaine receives little credit in the history books, but it was a remarkable achievement. It saved the United States from a costly and dangerous war that the nation might not have survived. The treaty also laid the groundwork for one of the longest, continuous alliances in the world. The United States and France have been trusted allies since 1800. Adams pursued this treaty in the face of resistance from many of his closest advisors and his party. He showed real personal and political courage.

Adams's reputation and legacy might have withstood these efforts to besmirch them had Hamilton acted alone. Thomas Jefferson picked up where Hamilton left off and inflicted unparalleled and long-lasting damage on Adams's legacy and his place in the historical record. Jefferson kept detailed notes and records over the course of his long political career and used them to dismiss rivals, boost his and his allies' reputation, and shape the narrative of the nation's founding. In retirement, he compiled many of these notes in his *Anas* to provide a history of the Early Republic. Three years after his death, Thomas Mann Randolph, Jefferson's son-in-law, published the *Anas*.[6] Over the next several decades, Jefferson's heirs and supporters published more of his papers in some of the earliest editorial collections.

In all these records, John Adams appears small, focused on his personal grievances, and driven by party animus. Despite Jefferson's protest that he had no interest in politics or higher office, few figures in the Early Republic were more political in their daily lives. His writings are those of an operative, pursuing partisan aims and combating political enemies. When Jefferson described Adams as war-mongering or erratic, he was driven by partisan motivations and eager to downplay Adams's success with the Treaty of Mortefontaine. Ten or twenty years after the Adams administration, he supplemented the notes recorded in real time with memory-addled recollections. That does not mean he was always wrong, but it does require readers to recognize the bias and motivations behind these writings, and to weigh them accordingly when trying to determine what actually happened. As with most historical accounts, the truth is usually somewhere in the middle.

These nuances, however, rarely make it into the historical record. Instead, Jefferson's narrative that Adams spent "the last day of his political power, the last hours, & even beyond the midnight . . . employed in filling all offices, & especially permanent ones, with the bitterest federalists," took hold.[7] Jefferson's protégés, including his successors, James Madison and James Monroe, repeated his views again and again, ensuring that his version of events became the accepted account. Historians then propagated this version of the story for centuries.[8] As a result, Americans believed Adams to be vengeful, petty, egomaniacal, and untrustworthy.

The evolution of the political parties accelerated Adams's marginalization. The fracturing of the Federalist Party during Adams's presidency left him without supporters to champion his record. His most vocal supporters, like Noah Webster, Benjamin Stoddert, and Elbridge Gerry, were moderates, or even Republicans. As the Federalist Party became increasingly radical in the decades after Adams left office, most moderate voters were subsumed into the Republican Party or were labeled Republicans by later generations of historians. As a result, we remember Hamilton as the leader of the Federalists, while Jefferson led the Republicans, leaving Adams a man with no party in American memory.

During the War of 1812, after many Federalists vocally debated seceding from the nation, the party itself ceased to exist as a viable political operation. The Republican Party expanded its control during the Era of Good Feelings, before fracturing in the 1820s. The dominant wing reorganized as the "Democratic Party" under the leadership of Andrew Jackson, touting its roots in the Jeffersonian Republicans. The party has survived in one form or another since then, albeit with constantly shifting voting blocs, agendas, and principles, while the history of the Federalists—including Adams—has faded in public imagination.

Despite all these developments, biographies of Adams can fill plenty of library shelves, including excellent works by David McCullough, John Ferling, Joe Ellis, Page Smith, James Grant, and Ralph Brown. And yet, most books on Adams treated his presidency as the low point of his lengthy public service career and give it short shrift within their accounts of his life.

But all these works were written before the failed insurrection on January 6, 2021. The violent coup attempt was a shocking moment in American history, and it has changed the way historians approach the nation's institutions and its legacy. Most Americans took the peaceful transfer of power for granted before this moment.[9] They did not fully appreciate the fragility of that norm or how much civic participation is required to uphold it, until they saw it trampled beneath the feet of violent rioters desecrating the halls of the Capitol Building. This moment exposed Adams's presidency in a new light and forces us to understand the role he played in ensuring that this fundamental cornerstone of our democracy would endure.

Shortly after spending his first night in the Executive Mansion, Adams wrote to Abigail. "I pray Heaven to bestow the best of Blessings on this House and all that shall hereafter inhabit it. May none but honest and wise Men ever rule under this roof."[10] He did everything in his power to make that prayer a reality.

Acknowledgments

SHORTLY BEFORE ABIGAIL Adams died, as the story goes, she asked her husband, John, to burn their letters. This book would have been impossible if he had obeyed. I remain eternally grateful that the Adams family had such a keen sense of their place in history and worked so hard to preserve the historical record.

I always believed in this book, but I have an amazing team that backed this project from the beginning. My agent, Lisa Adams, took a chance on me when I knew I wanted to write something, but wasn't quite sure what or how. She helped me define this story and showed incredible patience with way too many drafts of the proposal and even more terrible proposed titles. I feel incredibly lucky that I can trust half-baked and hairbrained ideas with her and receive the benefit of her guidance. My editor, Susan Ferber, immediately understood my vision and offered so much constructive feedback to help me achieve it. I benefited from many rounds of feedback from readers, and I found my conversations with Susan essential to processing that feedback and making editing game plans. Finally, my publicist, Sarah Russo (and the Page One Media team), have been so encouraging every step along the way. They have lived with John Adams for several years and helped me plan to share him with the world. Thank you for protecting my time and running my life. You make everything better.

One of the challenges of writing history books is that you can't make stuff up (or at least you really shouldn't). Research fellowships and centers that support writers are so essential because they give you a place to find all the gems and funding to focus on your work. I had the great privilege of spending a year at the International Center for Jefferson Studies (ICJS), culminating in a manuscript workshop. Thank you to John Ragosta, Whitney Pippin,

Andrew Jackson O'Shaughnessy, Anna Berkes, and everyone at the library for welcoming me to write about John Adams at Jefferson's home. My year was so productive, and it was such a pleasure to spend time with you. I spent the next year at the Kluge Center at the Library of Congress. Few Americans realize the extraordinary treasure we have at the heart of our capital. The Library of Congress is mind-bogglingly huge and has everything you could ever hope to see. Plus, there is a team of amazing book fairies that deliver books to fellows' desks. Walking the stunning hallways, getting lost in the tunnels (many times), and speaking at special events was such an enormous privilege. Thank you to Kevin Butterfield, Travis Hensley, Michael Stratmoen, Sophia Zahner, and the entire Kluge team for all that you do to support scholarship.

Aside from libraries, edited collections are the most valuable resource to scholars. I cherish the work of the editing teams at the Adams, Washington, Madison, Hamilton, Jefferson, and Jay Papers projects. Sara Georgini deserves extra cheers for gamely receiving random texts with super specific Adams collections questions. No amount of recognition for their massive effort would be sufficient, but I hope my endnotes are a small testament to the incredible value of the work you produce.

I started working with two writing groups at the beginning of this project and I have become an evangelist. They provide an essential community as well as early and frequent feedback. Thank you to my Classified Writing Group (Ben Park, Rick Bell, Megan Kate Nelson, and Bob Elder) for pushing me to write with clarity, delivering harsh feedback in a way that makes me cry from laughter, and bringing so much creativity to my writing life. Thank you to my Early Government Working Group (Rachel Shelden, Jonathan Gienapp, Julian Davis Mortenson, Emily Sneff, and Liv Covart) for being so stinking smart about Early America and so relentlessly supportive. My arguments benefited greatly from your sharp insight, and I am always in awe of your work and your brains.

ICJS hosted a manuscript workshop for me when I had about 80 percent of the manuscript drafted and it was a most valuable, uplifting, meaningful professional experience. I remain flabbergasted that Christa Dierksheide, Eliga Gould, Frank Cogliano, Joanne Freeman, Gautham Rao, John Ragosta, Whitney Stewart, William Hitchcock, and Steve Sarson read my work in progress, sat in one room, and helped me make it better. Thank you for your time and thoughtfulness, it was such an incredible gift.

Thank you to Tessa Payer for your incredible initiative, organization, precision, and creativity. I hope you recognize your finds deeply woven into this book; I adore working with you. Caitlin Hopkins photographed the

Theodore Sedgwick Papers at the Massachusetts Historical Society, which quickly became one of my favorite sources. Thank you for tackling the project with such care. Evan Axelbank read the entire manuscript and offered much cheer and encouragement along the way. I really owe you, bud. The SHEAR Book Two workshop read my first chapter of this book when it was in its infancy and gave me hope that it could be a thing. Clay Jenkinson welcomed me as a regular guest on Listening to America and introduced me to his incredibly supportive podcast community. He has also relentlessly encouraged my work and career, and I treasure our friendship.

Amazing friends make life worth living, but amazing friends who understand your work and passion are priceless treasures. Whitney Nell Stewart is the most loyal, uplifting friend. Thank you for 100 percent seeing me, and being with me during the hardest, best, and most important times. At this point, I'm not sure I know how to write without texting Megan Kate Nelson about every step of the process. You have made me a better writer and a better version of myself. I can't wait for more books together, even if it is sometimes an insane thing to do.

I love my work and I do it a lot, but I am intensely fortunate to have a supportive family waiting for me when I step away from the words. I dedicated this book to my parents because they have believed in me, without hesitation, from day one. They supported my education and attended every theater performance, mock trial competition, singing recital, and sports game. I get to go to some pretty cool places for work these days, and it is such a privilege to be able to share those experiences with them. This career is sort of an odd one and I'm so appreciative to my siblings who cheer me on and support my goals, even when they probably think I'm nuts. Our family is a bit of a circus, but the best families are, and I'm thankful they all have my back always.

None of anything I do would be possible without Jake and Quincy. Quincy makes me laugh daily, offers a warm spot to land at the end of a hard day, keeps me company during early morning writing sprints, provides a daily structure, and a constant excuse to escape outside. My best writing advice is to have a dog, but John Quincy Dog Adams is really a once-in-a-lifetime friend.

Jake is the very best partner I could ever want. He puts tea and food in front of me when I'm on a deadline, answers the inanest grammar questions, challenges me to clarify the "so what," and is always there when I really need him. But most of the time, he gives me space to pursue my biggest dreams and prioritizes them like his own. He is my dearest friend.

Notes

ABBREVIATIONS

AFC — *The Adams Family Correspondence*, ed. L. H. Butterfield et al. Cambridge, MA: Harvard University Press, 1963–2022, 15 vols.

AOC — *Annals of Congress*, Library of Congress.

Aurora — *Aurora General Advertiser*

CRK — *The Life and Correspondence of Rufus King: Comprising His Letters, Private and Official, His Public Documents, and His Speeches*, ed. Charles R. King, New York: G. P. Putman's Sons, 894–1900, 6 vols.

JMO — *Papers of John Marshall Digital Edition*, ed. Charles Hobson. Charlottesville: University of Virginia Press, Rotunda, 2014.

Letters of WVM — *Letters of William Vans Murray to John Quincy Adams, 1797–1803*, ed. Worthington Chauncey Ford (Washington, 1914).

PAH — *The Papers of Alexander Hamilton*, ed. Harold C. Syrett, New York: Columbia University Press, 1961-1987, 27 vols.

PGW — *The Papers of George Washington*, Presidential Series, Dorothy Twohig et al, Charlottesville: University Press of Virginia, 1987–2020, 21 vols. Retirement Series, W.W. Abbot et al. Charlottesville: University of Virginia Press, 1998–1999, 4 vols.

PJM — *The Papers of James Madison*, Congressional Series, ed. William T. Hutchinson et al. Chicago: University of Chicago Press, 1962–1977, 10 vols. Charlottesville: University of Virginia Press, 1977–1991, 7 vols.

PTJ — *The Papers of Thomas Jefferson*, ed. Julian P. Boyd et al. Princeton, NJ: Princeton University Press, 1950–2021, 45 vols.

RES — The Papers of the Revolutionary Era Pinckney Statesmen. Charlottesville: University of Virginia Press, 2016.

Rotunda — Rotunda, Founders Early Access, Adams Papers

TPP — Timothy Pickering Papers, Massachusetts Historical Society

TSP — Theodore Sedgwick Papers, Sedgwick Family Papers, Massachusetts Historical Society

ABBREVIATIONS OF NAMES

AA	Abigail Adams
AG	Albert Gallatin
AH	Alexander Hamilton
BS	Benjamin Stoddert
CCP	Charles Cotesworth Pinckney
CL	Charles Lee
EG	Elbridge Gerry
GW	George Washington
JA	John Adams
JM	James Madison
JQA	John Quincy Adams
MSC	Mary Smith Cranch
OW	Oliver Wolcott Jr.
RK	Rufus King
TBA	Thomas Boylston Adams
TJ	Thomas Jefferson
TP	Timothy Pickering
TS	Theodore Sedgwick
WVM	William Vans Murray

INTRODUCTION

1. Apparently, the house was to be repainted and the carpets replaced before John Adams moved in. But those tasks were not completed. Who dropped the ball is unclear. JA to AA, 22 March 1797, *AFC*, 12: 44–45, n1.
2. Washington, George, Inventory of Goods in the President's House, February 1797. Washington Papers, Library of Congress.
3. JA to AA, 22 March 1797, *AFC*, 12: 44–45.
4. Alexander DeConde, *The Quasi-War* (New York: Charles Scribner's Sons, 1966), 9.
5. Francois Furstenberg, *When the United States Spoke French: Five Refugees Who Shaped a Nation* (New York: Penguin Books, 2014), 95–97.
6. JQA to TBA, 20 December 1800, AFC, 14: 361–68. Edward J. Larson, *A Magnificent Catastrophe: The Tumultuous Election of 1800, America's First Presidential Campaign* (New York: Free Press, 2007), 148.
7. US Census Data for 1790–1800, https://courses.lumenlearning.com/suny-ushistory2os2xmaster/chapter/united-states-population-chart/, accessed May 13, 2023. Slavery statistics, https://www.statista.com/statistics/1010169/black-and-slave-population-us-1790-1880/, accessed May 13, 2023.
8. JA to AA 31 January 1797, *AFC*, 11: 529–30.

9. Many thanks are due to Sarah Longwell, who helped me articulate civic virtue and my vision for the role it played during Adams's presidency. I remain eternally grateful for that conversation, which has shaped so much of my thinking since.
10. There were a few examples of congressional resistance in Washington's final years in office, but the deference Washington enjoyed has never been repeated.
11. Benjamin Franklin to Robert R. Livingston, 22[–26] July 1783, *Papers of Benjamin Franklin*, ed. Ellen R. Cohn (New Haven: Yale University Press, 2011), 40: 355–70.
12. David McCullough, *John Adams* (New York: Simon and Schuster, 2001). John Ferling, *John Adams: A Life* (Knoxville: University of Tennessee Press, 1992). Paige Smith, *John Adams* (New York: Doubleday, 1962). James Grant. *John Adams: Party of One* (New York: Farrar, Straus and Giroux, 2005). Gordon Wood, *Friends Divided: John Adams and Thomas Jefferson* (New York: Penguin, 2017). Stanley Elkins and Eric McKitrick, *Age of Federalism* (New York: Oxford University Press, 1994).

CHAPTER 1

1. TP to JA, 19 September 1796, *Rotunda*.
2. Quincy Tercentenary Committee, *Quincy Massachusetts Historical Guide and Ma.* (Quincy: Published by the Quincy Historical Society, 1925)..
3. GW to JM, 19 February 1792, *PGW*, Presidential Series, 9: 575.
4. Edward J. Larson, *The Return of George Washington: Uniting the States, 1783–1789* (New York: William Morrow, 2014), 85–97, 201–33.
5. Lindsay M. Chervinsky, *The Cabinet: George Washington and the Creation of an American Institution* (Cambridge, MA: Harvard University Press, 2020).
6. "John Adams's Address to Senate, 21 April 1789," *AFC*, 19: 417–19. John Avlon, *Washington's Farewell: The Founding Father's Warning to Future Generations* (New York: Simon and Schuster, 2017), 45–51.
7. "Madison's Conversations with Washington, 5–25 May 1792," *PGW*, Presidential Series 10:349–54. Avlon, *Washington's Farewell*, 46–49.
8. Ron Chernow. *Alexander Hamilton* (New York: Apollo, 2020), 505.
9. TJ to GW, 23 May 1792, *PGW*, Presidential Series, 10: 408–14.
10. AH to GW, 30 July–3 August 1792, *PGW*, Presidential Series, 10: 594–96. Avlon, *Washington's Farewell*, 45–51.
11. TJ to GW, 23 May 1792, *PGW*, Presidential Series, 10: 408–14. Avlon, *Washington's Farewell*, 45–51. Chernow, *Alexander Hamilton*, 505. Jay Cost, *James Madison: America's First Politician* (New York: Basic Books, 2021), 219.
12. Elkins and McKitrick, *Age of Federalism*.
13. JA to Benjamin Stoddert, 16 November 1811, *Rotunda*.
14. Robert Morris to AH, 10 February 1796, *PAH*, 20: 54. Hylton v. United States, 3 U.S. 171 (1796).

15. At every previous trip, Hamilton had stayed at a house on Market Street. In 1787, he stayed at Mrs. Dailey's boarding house at 3rd and Market. In 1796, Martha Archer ran a boarding house at 214 Market.
16. Oliver Wolcott Jr. to Alexander Hamilton, 15 January 1796; Robert Morris to AH, 10 February 1796; GW to AH, 13 February 1796, *PAH*, 20: 40–41, 54–55.
17. Griffith John McRee, *Life and Correspondence of James Iredell*, vol. 2 (New York: Appleton, 1857), 461–62.
18. Avlon, *Washington's Farewell*, 78–89.
19. AH to GW, 10 May 1796, *PGW*, Presidential Series, 20: 121–23. Chernow, *Alexander Hamilton*, 505–7.
20. GW to AH, 15 May 1796, *PGW*, 20: 143–45.
21. AH to GW, 10 May 1796, *PGW*, 20: 121–23.
22. AH to GW, 20 May 1796, *PGW*, 20: 166–70. AH to GW, 5 July 1796; 30 July 1796; 10 August 1796, *PGW*, 20: 380–81, 513–15, 572–73. Avlon, *Washington's Farewell*, 82. Chernow, *Alexander Hamilton*, 505–7.
23. New-York City Directory (New-York: Printed by John Buel, 1796), 82. Chernow, *Alexander Hamilton*, 505–7.
24. John Jay to Richard Peters, 29 March 1811 in Victory Hugo Paltsits, *Washington's Farewell Address* (New York: New York Public Library, 1935), 270–71. Avlon, *Washington's Farewell*, 81.
25. AH to GW, 20 May 1796, *PGW*, 20: 166–70. AH to GW, 5 July 1796; 30 July 1796; 10 August 1796, *PGW*, 20: 380–81, 513–15, 572–73. Avlon, *Washington's Farewell*, 82.
26. GW to JA, 10 May 1789, *PGW*, 2: 245–50.
27. Kathleen Bartoloni-Tuazon, *For Fear of an Elective King: George Washington and the Presidential Title Controversy of 1789* (Ithaca, NY: Cornell University Press, 2014).
28. GW to David Stuart, 26 July, 1789, *PGW*, 3: 321–27.
29. John Trumbull to JA, 6 February 1790, *Rotunda*.
30. JA to John Trumbull, 9 March 1790, *Rotunda*.
31. JA to AA, 13 February 1796, *AFC*, 11:174–75.
32. JA to AA, 26 January 1796, *AFC*, 11: 150–51.
33. Furstenberg, *When the United States Spoke French*, 11, 112.
34. JA to AA, 25 March 1796, AFC, 11, 228–30. John Ferling, *Adams vs. Jefferson: The Tumultuous Election of 1800* (New York: Oxford University Press, 2004), 84.
35. JA to AA, 25 March 1796, *AFC*, 11: 228–30.
36. Avlon, *Washington's Farewell*, 88–91.
37. Certification of David C. Claypoole, 22 February 1826 in Paltsits, *Washington's Farewell Address*, 290–92.
38. Avlon, *Washington's Farewell*, 88–91.

CHAPTER 2

1. Jeffrey L. Pasley, *The First Presidential Contest: 1796 and the Founding of American Democracy* (Lawrence: University Press of Kansas, 2013), 346.
2. JM to Monroe, 26 February 1796, Noble E. Cunningham Jr., *The Jeffersonian Republicans: The Formation of Party Organization, 1789–1801* (Chapel Hill: University of North Carolina Press, 1957), 89.
3. Moore Furman to Tench Coxe, 28 November 1796, Tench Coxe Papers, Historical Society of Pennsylvania, Philadelphia, PA. Joanne B. Freeman, "The Presidential Election of 1796," *John Adams and the Founding of the Republic*, ed. Richard Alan Ryerson (Boston: Northeastern University Press for the Massachusetts Historical Society, 2001), 147.
4. Pasley, *The First Presidential Contest*, 204.
5. Stephen G. Kurtz, *The Presidency of John Adams: The Collapse of Federalism, 1795–1800* (Philadelphia: University of Pennsylvania Press, 1957), 100–110. Chernow, *Alexander Hamilton*, 510–11.
6. R. Troup to R. King, 16 November 1796, *CRK*, 110. Susan Dunn, *Jefferson's Second Revolution: The Election Crisis of 1800 and the Triumph of Republicanism* (New York: Houghton Mifflin Harcourt, 2004), 80–83. Kurtz, *The Presidency of John Adams*, 100–110.
7. Manning J. Dauer, *The Adams Federalists* (Baltimore: Johns Hopkins University Press, 2019), 101–2. Chernow, *Alexander Hamilton*, 510–11.
8. Pasley, *The First Presidential Contest*, 204–7.
9. JM to Monroe, 26 February 1796, *PJM*, 16: 232–34.
10. Pasley, *The First Presidential Contest*, 187–95.
11. Robert G. Harper to AH, 4 November 1796, *PAH*, 20: 369–72. TJ to GW, 23 May 1792, *PTJ*, 23: 535–41.
12. John Beckley to William Irvine, 15 September 1796, Irvine Papers, XIII, Historical Society of Pennsylvania, Philadelphia, PA. Cunningham, *The Jeffersonian Republicans*, 89.
13. Freeman, "The Presidential Election of 1796," 146.
14. Pasley, *The First Presidential Contest*, 202–203. Cunningham, *The Jeffersonian Republicans*, 92.
15. TJ to Benjamin Austin Jr., 28 June 1803, *PTJ*, 40: 620–21n. *AFC*, 10: 306, Digital Edition https://www.masshist.org/publications/adams-papers/index.php/volume/AFC10/pageid/AFC10p306. *AFC*, v. 9, Digital Edition https://www.masshist.org/publications/adams-papers/index.php/view/ADMS-04-09-02-0219. Page Smith, *John Adams* (New York: Doubleday, 1962), II: 901.
16. Freeman, "The Presidential Election of 1796," 148.
17. Cunningham, *The Jeffersonian Republicans*, 106, Beckley to Madison, 15 October 1796)
18. Cunningham, *The Jeffersonian Republicans*, 104. Dunn, *Jefferson's Second Revolution*, 81.

19. Ital. in original. JM to Monroe, 29 September 1796, *PJM*, 16: 403–5.
20. Cunningham, *The Jeffersonian Republicans*, 97.
21. Smith, *John Adams*, II: 901.
22. Dumas Malone, *Jefferson and the Ordeal of Liberty* (Boston: Little, Brown, 1962), 285 (Adet to Minister of Foreign Relations, 9 June 1796, *Correspondence of French Ministers to the United States* (hereafter *C.F.M.*). p. 920).
23. Kurtz, *The Presidency of John Adams*, 114–33.
24. TP to Adet, 19 October 1796, *State Papers*, Foreign Relations, I: 636. *TPP*, "From Pickering, July–December 1796," 81.
25. "Authentic," *Aurora*, 31 October 1796, 3. "Authentic." *Aurora*, 5 November 1796, 2. Malone, *Jefferson and the Ordeal of Liberty*, 286–87. Dunn, *Jefferson's Second Revolution*, 82.
26. Gerard H. Clarfield, *Timothy Pickering and American Diplomacy* (Columbia: University of Missouri Press, 1969), 49–69. Malone, *Jefferson and the Ordeal of Liberty*, 249–51. Kurtz, *The Presidency of John Adams*, 114–33.
27. JM to TJ, 5 December 1796, *PTJ*, 29: 214–15. Malone, *Jefferson and the Ordeal of Liberty*, 288. Smith, *John Adams*, II: 899.
28. Emphasis in original. JM to James Monroe, 26 February 1796, *PJM*, 16: 232–34. Malone, *Jefferson and the Ordeal of Liberty*, 274.
29. JM to James Monroe, *PJM*, 16: 403–5.
30. JA to JQA, 11 November 1796, *AFC*, 11: 401–2. Dunn, *Jefferson's Second Revolution*, 81.
31. JA to AA, 12 December, 1796, *AFC*, 11: 443–45.
32. AA to JA, 28 January 1797, *AFC*, 11: 520–23.
33. JA to AA, 1 December 1796, *AFC*, 11: 427–28.
34. JA to AA, 1 December 1796, AFC, 11: 427–28
35. JA to AA, 1 December 1796, *AFC*, 11: 427–28.
36. Smith, *John Adams*, II: 903.
37. *Political Correspondence and Public Papers of Aaron Burr*, ed. Mary-Jo Kline, Joanne Wood Ryan, et al. (Princeton, NJ: Princeton University Press, 1982) I: 275, 278.
38. Merrill D. Peterson, *Thomas Jefferson and the New Nation: A Biography* (New York: Oxford University Press, 1975), 555.
39. JM to TJ, 5 December 1796; 10 December 1796, *PJM*, 16: 422–23, 424–25.
40. TJ to JM, 17 December 1796. Cunningham, *The Jeffersonian Republicans*, 107.
41. TJ to JM, 17 December 1796, *PJM*, 16: 431–32. Smith, *John Adams*, II: 909. Dunn, *Jefferson's Second Revolution*, 83–84.
42. JM to TJ, 10 December 1796, *PJM*, 16: 424–25.
43. JM to TJ, 5 December 1796, *PJM*, 16: 422–23.
44. JA to AA, 7 December 1796, *AFC*, 11: 438–39. Smith, *John Adams*, II: 905.
45. JA to AA, 18 December, 20 December 1796, *AFC*, 11: 446–48, 450–51.
46. JM to TJ, 19 December 1796, *PJM*, 16: 432–34.
47. JA to AA, 3 January 1797, *AFC*, 11: 481–82

48. TJ to JM, 17 December 1796, *PTJ*, 29: 223–24n. Dunn, *Jefferson's Second Revolution*, 84–85.
49. JA to AA, *AFC*, 11:462–63.
50. Electoral results, https://www.270towin.com/1796_Election. Smith, *John Adams*, II: 901–2.
51. JA to AA, 30 December 1796, *AFC*, 11: 467–68. Smith, *John Adams*, II: 908.
52. Smith, *John Adams*, II: 907.
53. AA to JA, 28 January 1797, *AFC*, 11: 520–23. Smith, *John Adams*, II: 908.
54. Smith, *John Adams*, II: 910.
55. JA to AA, 12 December 1796, *AFC*, 11: 443–45. Smith, *John Adams*, II: 901. McCullough, *John Adams*, 465. Charles Francis Adams, *The Works of John Adams* (Boston: Little, Brown, 1856), I: 495.
56. JA to AA, 11 January 1797, *AFC*, 11: 495–96.
57. JA to AA, 7 February 1797, AFC, 11: 542–43.
58. JA to AA, 7 December 1796, *AFC*, 11: 438–39.

CHAPTER 3

1. Ferling, *John Adams*, 331–32.
2. *AOC*, 4th Cong., 2d sess., 2095–98. AA to JA, 8 February 1797, *AFC*, 11: 545–46 n2.
3. "Declaration of Votes in Elections for P and VP, 8 February 1797," *Rotunda*. JA to AA, 9 February 1797, *AFC*, 11: 553–54.
4. JA to AA, 3 March 1797, *AFC*, 12: 7–8. JA to David Jackson, 8 February 1797, *Rotunda*.
5. Smith, *John Adams*, II: 915.
6. *AOC*, Senate, 4th Cong., 2nd session, 1550–51.
7. *AOC*, Senate, 4th Cong., 2nd session, 1551–52.
8. *AOC*, Senate, 4th Cong., 2nd session, 1555–56.
9. JA to United States Senate, 23 February 1797, *Rotunda*. Smith, *John Adams*, II: 914.
10. AA to Thomas Boylston Adams, 8 November 1796, *AFC*, 11: 394–98.
11. AA to JA, 23 December 1796, *AFC*, 458–59. Joseph J. Ellis, *The First Family: John and Abigail* (New York: Alfred A. Knopf, 2010), 175.
12. JA to AA, 3 January 1797, *AFC*, 11: 481–82. Smith, *John Adams*, II: 911.
13. JA to Gerry, 13 February 1797, *Rotunda*. Luke Mayville, *John Adams and the Fear of American Oligarchy* (Princeton, NJ: Princeton University Press, 2016), 150–51 R. B. Bernstein, *The Education of John Adams* (New York: Oxford University Press, 2020), 138–51. Jeanne E. Abrams, *A View from Abroad: The Story of John and Abigail Adams in Europe* (New York: New York University Press, 2021), 195–223.
14. Liston/Grenville, 13 February 1797, quoted in Bradford Perkins, *The First Rapprochement* (University of Pennsylvania Press, 1955), 58–59. Smith, *John Adams*, II: 911. x
15. JA to AA, 30 December 1796, *AFC*, 11: 467–68.

16. AA to Elizabeth Smith Shaw Peabody, 10 February 1797, *AFC*, 11: 554–56.
17. JQA to AA, 14 November 1796, *AFC*, 11:404–8. JA to AA, 20 February 1797, *AFC*, 11: 567–68.
18. GW to JA, 20 February 1797, *Rotunda*. JA to AA, 20 February 1797, *AFC*, 11: 567–68. Smith, *John Adams*, II: 917.
19. C. Bradley Thompson, *John Adams and the Spirit of Liberty* (Lawrence: University Press of Kansas, 1998), 131. Bernstein, *The Education of John Adams*, 138–51.
20. Mary Sarah Bilder, "The Soul of a Free Government: The Influence of John Adams's *A Defence* on the Constitutional Convention," *Journal of American Constitutional History*. 1 (2023), 1–40.
21. "Volume 1 of John Adams' A Defence of the Constitutions of Government of the United States of America: Editorial Note," *The Adams Papers*, Papers of John Adams, 18: 544–50. John Adams to Roger Sherman, 20 July 1789, *Rotunda*. Gilbert Chinard. *Honest John Adams* (Boston: Little, Brown, 1933), 234.
22. Bernstein, *The Education of John Adams*, 179–81.
23. Dauer, *The Adams Federalists*, 120–24.
24. Ralph Adams Brown, *The Presidency of John Adams* (Lawrence: University Press of Kansas, 1975), 27–30.
25. Kurtz, *The Presidency of John Adams*, 269–70.
26. Clarfield, *Timothy Pickering and the American Republic*, 181.
27. Bernstein, *The Education of John Adams*, 181.
28. JA to Benjamin Rush, 22 April 1812, *Rotunda*.
29. Kurtz, *The Presidency of John Adams*, 277.
30. George Washington kept a daily diary for the month of February 1797 and noted the high temperature in Philadelphia each day. Most days, the highs did not exceed the mid-30s, not including wind chill. "February 1797," *The Diaries of George Washington*, ed. Donald Jackson and Dorothy Twohig (Charlottesville: University Press of Virginia, 1979), 6: 232–36. JA to Benjamin Rush, 22 April 1812, *Rotunda*.
31. JA to Gerry, 13 February 1797, *Rotunda*. Dauer, *The Adams Federalists*, 120–24. Brown, *The Presidency of John Adams*, 27–30.
32. Octavius Pickering and Charles Upham, eds., *Life of Timothy Pickering* (Boston: Little, Brown, 1863), 3: 360.
33. GW to AH, 9 August 1798, *PAH*, 22:62–64. Chernow, *Alexander Hamilton*, 504.
34. AH to GW, 5 November 1796, *PAH*, 20: 374–75.
35. Kurtz, *The Presidency of John Adams*, 114–33.
36. JA to TP, March 1797, *Rotunda*.
37. JA to EG, 13 February 1797, *Rotunda*. Dauer, *The Adams Federalists*, 112–13.
38. TJ to John Langdon, 22 January 1797, *PTJ*, 29: 269–70. Malone, *Jefferson and the Ordeal of Liberty*, 294.
39. "I. To John Adams, 28 December 1796," *PTJ*, 29: 235–36. Smith, *John Adams*, II: 910. McCullough, *John Adams*, 466. Dunn, *Jefferson's Second Revolution*, 86. Kurtz, *The Presidency of John Adams*, 214–21.

40. Dunn, *Jefferson's Second Revolution*, 86–87. Dauer, *The Adams Federalists*, 112–13.
41. AA to JA, 15 January 1797, *AFC*, 11: 499–501. Ellis mistakenly suggests that Jefferson did send this letter to John Adams. He did not. Ellis, *First Family*, 175.
42. TJ to JM, 30 January 1797, *PJM*, 16: 479–80.
43. TJ to Martha Jefferson Randolph, 28 February 1797, *PTJ*, 29: 308–9.
44. "Philadelphia, March 3." *Claypoole's American Daily Advertiser* (Philadelphia, Pennsylvania), no. 5586, 3 March 1797, 3. Malone, *Jefferson and the Ordeal of Liberty*, 295.
45. 1796 directory: https://archive.org/details/philadelphiadire1796phil/page/n25/mode/2up?q=city+tavern; LOC picture: https://www.loc.gov/item/pa0921/.
46. JA to AA, 3 March 1797, *AFC*, 12: 7–8.
47. March 2, 1797, *The Complete Anas of Thomas Jefferson*, ed. Franklin B. Sawvel (New York: Round Table Press, 1903),184. Peterson, *Thomas Jefferson and the New Nation*, 560.
48. March 2, 1797, *Jefferson's Anas*, 184. Peterson, *Thomas Jefferson and the New Nation*, 561.
49. March 2, 1797, *Jefferson's Anas*, 184. Peterson, *Thomas Jefferson and the New Nation*, 561.
50. JM to TJ, 22 January 1797, *PJM*, 16: 473–74.
51. AA to JA, 18 March 1797, *AFC*, 12: 38–40.
52. AH to Rufus King, 15 February 1797, *PAH*, 20: 515–16. Freeman, "The Presidential Election of 1796," *John Adams and the Founding of the Republic*, 158.
53. JA to AA, 3 March 1797, *AFC*, 12: 7–8.

CHAPTER 4

1. Diary of Elizabeth Sandwith Drinker, March 1796, written by Elizabeth Sandwith Drinker, 1735–1807 (1796); edited by Elaine Forman Crane; in *The Diary of Elizabeth Drinker*, vol. 2 (Boston: Northeastern University Press, 1991), 17–25.
2. JA to AA, 14 January 1797; 24 February 1797, *AFC*, 11: 496–97, 575–76.
3. JA to AA, 2 February 1797, *AFC*, 11: 527; McCullough, *John Adams*, 468; Ferling, *John Adams*, 334.
4. Peterson, *Thomas Jefferson and the New Nation*, 562.
5. Chernow, *Alexander Hamilton*, 523. McCullough, *John Adams*, 468.
6. I have found no record of the sword's survival, but a brief description was featured in an inventory of his belongings at The Hague. "Household Inventories of the U.S. Legation at The Hague, 14 May 1782–24 June 1784," *PJA*, 13: 26–48. Adams was also painted wearing the sword in several portraits, including one by William Winstanley in 1798, Adams National Historical Park, and one by John Singleton Copley in 1783, Harvard University Portrait Collection.

7. "Furnishing Plan for the Second Floor of Congress Hall," Independence National Historic Part, National Park Service, https://irma.nps.gov/DataStore/DownloadFile/603653, accessed March 14, 2023. Kurtz, *The Presidency of John Adams*, 223. "United States," 17 March 1797, *Impartial Herald*, (Newburyport, MA), 2. "Vice-President's Speech." 15 March 1797, *Columbian Centinel*, (Boston, MA), 2.
8. *AOC*, Senate, 5th Congress, 1581. "United States," March 17, 1797, *Impartial Herald*, (Newburyport, MA), 2. "Vice-President's Speech." 15 March 1797, *Columbian Centinel*, (Boston), 2.
9. *AOC*, Senate, 5th Congress, 1581–1582. "United States," 17 March 1797, *Impartial Herald*, (Newburyport, MA), 2. "Vice-President's Speech." 15 March 1797, *Columbian Centinel*, (Boston), 2.
10. *TPP*, Misc. Journals, 1795–1797, 337A.
11. "Furnishing Plan for the First Floor of Congress Call, Independence National Historical Park, National Park Service, July 1959, https://irma.nps.gov/DataStore/DownloadFile/603740, accessed March 14, 2023.
12. "March 15, 1797," *Columbian Centinel*, (Philadelphia, PA).
13. Peterson, *Thomas Jefferson and the New Nation*, 562.
14. Diary of Elizabeth Sandwith Drinker, March 1796, 17–25.
15. JA to AA, 5 March 1797, *AFC*, 12: 9–11.
16. Adams wrote to Abigail regularly about how much he missed her, but for examples: JA to AA, 14 January 1797, *AFC*, 11: 496–97; 22 March 1797, *AFC*, 12: 44–45.
17. *Columbian Centinel*, Boston, MA, 15 March, 1797. *Connecticut Gazette and Medley*, (New Bedford, MA_, 24 March 1797.
18. Theodore Sedgwick to Rufus King, 12 March 1797, *CRK*, II: 158–59. Dunn, *Jefferson's Second Revolution*, 87.
19. There is little record of former or defeated governors attending the ceremonies of their successors. "Legislative Acts/Legal Proceedings," 6 June 1787, *Essex Journal*, Newburyport, MA. *Memoir of Increase Sumner*, ed. William Hyslop Sumner (S. G. Drake, January 1954), 20–21. "Lancaster, December 18," 20 December 1799, *Claypoole's American Daily Advertiser*, Philadelphia, PA, 3.
20. Theodore Sedgwick to Rufus King, 12 March 1797, *CRK*, 2: 158–59.
21. *Columbian Centinel*, 15 March 1797, 2.
22. Senate Journal, 4th Cong., Special Session, 4 March 1797, 107.
23. McCullough, *John Adams*, 474.
24. John Adams, *Inaugural Address*, 4 March 1797, https://avalon.law.yale.edu/18th_century/adams.asp. JA to AA, 5 March 1797, *AFC*, 12: 9–11.
25. John Adams, *Inaugural Address*, 4 March 1797, https://avalon.law.yale.edu/18th_century/adams.asp.
26. John Adams, *Inaugural Address*, 4 March 1797, https://avalon.law.yale.edu/18th_century/adams.asp. "United States," 17 March 1797, *Impartial Herald*, (Newburyport, MA), 2. "Vice-President's Speech," 15 March 1797, *Columbian Centinel*, (Boston, MA), 2.

27. *Columbian Centinel*, 15 March 1797; Peterson, *Thomas Jefferson and the New Nation*, 563.
28. *Columbian Centinel*, 15 March 1797, *Philadelphia Gazette* (Philadelphia, PA), March 1797.
29. JA to AA, 5 March 1797, *AFC*, 12: 9–11. Peterson, *Thomas Jefferson and the New Nation*, 563.
30. *Gazette of the United States, & Philadelphia daily advertiser.* (Philadelphia, PA), 3 March 1797. *Chronicling America: Historic American Newspapers*. Library of Congress, https://chroniclingamerica.loc.gov/lccn/sn83025881/1797-03-03/ed-1/seq-2/.
31. *Columbian Centinel*, 15 March 1797. GW to Jeremiah Wadsworth, 6 March 1797, *PGW*, Retirement Series, 1: 17.
32. JA to AA, 5 March 1797, *AFC*, 12: 9–11.
33. Theodore Sedgwick to Rufus King, 12 March 1797, *CRK*, II: 158–59.
34. Smith, *John Adams*, II: 920
35. Peterson, *Thomas Jefferson and the New Nation*, 563.
36. Kurtz, *The Presidency of John Adams*, 208, William Smith to Rufus King, 3 April 1797, *CRK*, 2: 167.
37. *Columbian Centinel*, 15 March 1797 (Boston, MA).

CHAPTER 5

1. John Adams, "Boston Patriot," Letter XIII, *Memoirs of the Administrations of Washington and John Adams, Edited from the Papers of Oliver Wolcott*, ed. George Gibbs (New York: W. Van Norden, 1846), I: 465–66.
2. Gibbs, *Memoirs of the Administrations of Washington and John Adams*, I: 465–66. Ferling, *John Adams*, 344–45. Dunn, *Jefferson's Second Revolution*, 89. Dauer, *The Adams Federalists*, 125–27. Clarfield, *Timothy Pickering and American Diplomacy*, 97.
3. Peterson, *Thomas Jefferson and the New Nation*, 561; Malone, *Thomas Jefferson and the Ordeal of Liberty*, 314.
4. Jefferson, *Anas*, , 184–85. Kurtz, *The Presidency of John Adams*, 229. Dunn, *Jefferson's Second Revolution*, 89–91. Dauer, *The Adams Federalists*, 125–27.
5. "Notes on Pinckney Case, 19 March 1797," *Rotunda*.
6. TP to AH, 30 March 1797, *PAH*, 20: f558–59. JA to Knox, 30 March 1797, JA to JQA, 31 March 1797, JA to Cranch, 25 March 1797, *Rotunda*. Clarfield, *Timothy Pickering and the American Republic*, 182. Clarfield, *Timothy Pickering and American Diplomacy*, 100–101.
7. Chervinsky, *The Cabinet*, 194.
8. John Adams to Timothy Pickering, 20 March 1797, *Rotunda*.
9. CCP to TP, 17 January 1797; 18 February 1797, *RES*.
10. Elkins and McKitrick, *Age of Federalism*, 552.

11. Rufus King to AH, 2 April 1797, *PAH*, 21: 8–12.
12. *AOC*, 5th Congress, 1st Session, 50.
13. TP to AH, 26 March 1797, *PAH*, 20: 548–50.
14. AH to TP, 29 March 1797; 11 May 1797, *PAH*, 21: 81–84. Dauer, *The Adams Federalists*, 127. Gilbert L. Lycan, *Alexander Hamilton and American Foreign Policy: A Design for Greatness* (Norman: University of Oklahoma Press, 1970), 305–9.
15. AH to Oliver Wolcott Jr., 5 April 1797, *PAH*, 21: 22–23.
16. AH to William Loughton Smith, 5 April 1797, *PAH*, 21: 20–21.
17. TP to JA, 1 May 1797; McHenry to JA, 29 April 1797; OW to JA, 21 April 1797, all in *Rotunda*. AH to OW, 5 April 1797; AH to McHenry, *PAH*, 21: 22–23, 72–75. Lycan, *Alexander Hamilton and American Foreign Policy*, 305–9.
18. JA to AA, 13 March 1797, *AFC*, 12: 23–24.
19. JA to AA, 22 March 1797, *AFC*, 12: 44–45.
20. JA to AA, 3 April 1797, *AFC*, 12: 59–60.
21. JA to AA, 24 April 1797, *AFC*, 12: 87–88.
22. AA to Mary Smith Cranch, 16 May 1797, *AFC*, 12: 116–18.
23. Lindsay M. Chervinsky, "The Households of President John Adams," *Slavery in the President's Neighborhood*, White House Historical Association, https://www.whitehousehistory.org/spn/timeline#the-households-of-president-john-adams, accessed May 19, 2023.
24. Brown, *The Presidency of John Adams*, 34.
25. AA to Mary Smith Cranch, 16 May 1797, *AFC*, 12: 116–18.
26. AA to MSC, 23 June 1797, *AFC*, 12: 171–73. Brown, *The Presidency of John Adams*, 34.
27. "Editorial Note: Jefferson's Letter to Philip Mazzei," *PTJ*, 29: 73–81.
28. "Editorial Note: Jefferson's Letter to Philip Mazzei," *PTJ*, 29: 73–81.
29. AA to JQA, June 15, 1797, *AFC*, 12: 162–65.
30. JA to United States Congress, 16 May 1797, *Rotunda*.
31. JA to United States Congress, 16 May 1797, *Rotunda*.
32. JA to United States Congress, 16 May 1797, *Rotunda*. Ferling, *John Adams*, 344–45.
33. United States Senate to John Adams, 18 May 1797, *Rotunda*.
34. Henry Van Schaack to Theodore Sedgwick, 28 May 1797, *TSP*, Box 4, Folder 20, MS. N-851.
35. Ferling, *John Adams*, 345.
36. Kurtz, *The Presidency of John Adams*, 232.
37. AA to Mary Smith Cranch, 24 May, 1797, *AFC*, 12: 124–27.
38. AA to Mary Smith Cranch, 3 June 1797, *AFC*, 12: 139–41.
39. TJ to JM, 18 May 1797, *PJM*, 17: 7–10.
40. AA to Mary Smith Cranch, 24 May 1797, *AFC*, 12: 124–27.
41. "Questions to Be Proposed Concerning Negotiators to be Sent to France, 27 May 1797 to 28 May 1797," *Rotunda*.

42. R. Kent Newmyer. *John Marshall and the Heroic Age of the Supreme Court* (Baton Rouge: Louisiana State University Press, 2007), 113.
43. *Memoirs of the Administrations of Washington and John Adams*, I:465–66. Ferling, *John Adams*, 344–45.
44. Frederick J. Turner, ed. "Correspondence of the French Ministers to the United States, 1791–1797," Annual Report of the American Historical Association for the Year 1903, vol. 2. Elkins and McKitrick, *Age of Federalism*, 566.
45. TJ to Aaron Burr, 17 June 1797, *PTJ*, 29: 437–40.
46. Aaron Burr to TJ, 21 June 1797, *PTJ*, 29: 447–48.
47. Uriah Forrest to JA, 23 June 1797, *Rotunda*. John Adams to Uriah Forrest, 28 June 1797, *Rotunda*.
48. AA to JQA, *AFC*, 12: 276–80. Peterson, *Thomas Jefferson and the New Nation*, 568–69.

CHAPTER 6

1. JA to Elbridge Gerry, 20 June 1797, *Rotunda*.
2. AA to JQA, 23 June 1797, *AFC*, 12: 169–71.
3. Elkins and McKitrick, *Age of Federalism*, 556–57. Grant, *John Adams: Party of One*, 386.
4. Clarfield, *Timothy Pickering and American Diplomacy*, 110.
5. Theodore Sedgwick to Rufus King, 24 June 1797, *TSP*, Box 3, Folder 23, MS. N-851.
6. *AOC*, Senate Executive Journal, Thursday June 22, 1797, 245–46.
7. Theodore Sedgwick to Ephraim Williams, 23 June 1797, *TSP*, Box 5, Folder 24, Ms. N-851.
8. Theodore Sedgwick to Ephraim Williams, 23 June 1797, *TSP*, Box 5, Folder 24, Ms. N-851.
9. "JA to Boston Patriot, 29 May 1809," *Rotunda*. Ferling, *John Adams*, 345.
10. GW to United States Senate, *PGW*, Presidential Series, 16: 143–44.
11. Elkins and McKitrick, *Age of Federalism*, 498–513, 550–51. Lycan, *Alexander Hamilton and American Foreign Policy*, 267–71. Tim McGrath, *James Monroe: A Life* (New York: Dutton, 2020), 157–64.
12. Elkins and McKitrick, *Age of Federalism*, 498–513, 550–51. Lycan, *Alexander Hamilton and American Foreign Policy*, 267–71. McGrath, *James Monroe*, 157–64.
13. JQA to JA, 14 January 1797, *Rotunda*.
14. JQA to JA, 14 January 1797, *Rotunda*.
15. William Smith to Ralph Izard, May 23, 1797. AA to TBA, 20 June 1797, *AFC*, 12: 207–8.
16. Rogers, Jr., George C. *Evolution of a Federalist: William Loughton Smith of Charleston* (Columbia, SC: University of South Carolina Press, 1962), 302. DeConde, *Quasi-War*, 33.

17. TP to James Monroe, 17 July 1797, *TSP*, 215A. DeConde, *Quasi-War*, 33.
18. TP to James Monroe, 25 July 1797, *TSP*, 218.
19. TP to GW, 25 July 1797, *PGW*, Retirement Series, 1: 273–74.
20. AA to TBA, 3 January 1798, *AFC*, 12: 343–36.
21. TJ to Madison, 3 January 1798, *PJM*, 17: 64–68.
22. OW to AH, 3 July 1797, *PAH*, 21: 144–45.
23. Pasley, *The First Presidential Contest*, 141–42. John Ferling, *Jefferson and Hamilton: The Rivalry That Forged a Nation* (New York: Bloomsbury Press, 2013), 291–96.
24. OW to AH, 7 July 1797, *PAH*, 21: 151.
25. AH to James Monroe, 5 July 1797, *PAH*, 21: 146–48.
26. AH to James Monroe, 10 July 1797, *PAH*, 21: 157. Joanne B. Freeman, *Affairs of Honor* (New Haven, CT: Yale University Press, 2001).
27. James Monroe to AH, 10 July 1797, *PAH*, 21: 157–58.
28. "David Gelston's Account of an Interview between Alexander Hamilton and James Monroe, 11 July 1797," *PAH*, 21: 159–62. Chernow, *Alexander Hamilton*, 533–45. Ferling. *Jefferson and Hamilton*, 291–96.
29. James Monroe to AH, 31 July 1797, *PAH*, 21: 192–93. Chernow, *Alexander Hamilton*, 533–45.
30. AH to James Monroe, 4 August 1797, *PAH*, 21: 200.
31. James Monroe to AH, 6 August 1797, *PAH*, 21: 204–5.
32. AH to James Monroe, 9 August 1797, *PAH*, 21: 208–9. Chernow, *Alexander Hamilton*, 533–45.
33. "Draft of the 'Reynolds Pamphlet,' 25 August 1797," *PAH*, 21: 215–38. Ferling. *Jefferson and Hamilton*, 291–96.
34. Madison to TJ, 27 October 1797, *PTJ*, 29: 565–66. John Barnes to TJ, 3 October 1797, *PTJ*, 29: 542–43. Chernow, *Alexander Hamilton*, 533–45.
35. AA to TBA, 3 January 1798, *AFC*, 12: 343–46.
36. JA to Benjamin Rush, 11 November 1806, *Rotunda*.
37. *Gazette of the United States*, Philadelphia, PA, 5 July 1797.
38. AA to MSC, 23 June 1797, *AFC*, 12: 171–73. AA to MSC, 6 July 1797, *AFC*, 12:190–93.
39. John Marshall to Mary Marshall, 3 July 1797, *JMO*.
40. Brown, *Presidency of John Adams*, 44; DeConde, *Quasi-War*, 35.
41. Elbridge Gerry to JA, 3 July 1797, *Rotunda*. Smith, *John Adams*, 934.
42. JA to Elbridge Gerry, 17 July 1797, *Rotunda*.
43. TP to JA, 18 July 1797, *Rotunda*.
44. Elkins and McKitrick, *Age of Federalism*, 562
45. AA to MSC, 21 July 1797; AA to MSC, 29 July 1797, *AFC*, 12: 211–12, 221–22.
46. AA to MSC, 6 July 1797, *AFC*, 12:190–93.

CHAPTER 7

1. "Benjamin Lincoln to John Adams, 5 August 1797," *Rotunda.*
2. "John Adams to Benjamin Lincoln, 7 August 1797," *Rotunda.*
3. "August 16, 1797," *Columbian Centinel,* (Boston, MA).
4. AA to Elizabeth Smith Shaw Peabody, 25 September 1797, *AFC,* 12: 245–46.
5. John Quincy Adams diary 24, 1 March 1795–31 December 1802, page 176 [electronic edition]; *The Diaries of John Quincy Adams: A Digital Collection* (Boston: Massachusetts Historical Society, 2004). https://www.masshist.org/publications/jqadiaries/index.php.
6. John Quincy Adams diary 24, 1 March 1795–31 December 1802, page 177 [electronic edition]. *The Diaries of John Quincy Adams: A Digital Collection.*
7. GW to US Senate, 31 March 1796, *PGW,* Presidential Series, 19: 643–44.
8. Brown, *Presidency of John Adams,* 28; JA to JQA, Adams Papers microfilm, reel 384, Massachusetts Historical Society, 2 June 1797.
9. AA to JQA, 15 June 1797, *AFC,* 12: 162–65.
10. John Quincy Adams diary 24, 1 March 1795–31 December 1802, page 179 [electronic edition]. *The Diaries of John Quincy Adams: A Digital Collection.*
11. AA to Mary Smith Cranch, 6 June 1797, *AFC,* 12: 142–44.
12. John Quincy Adams diary 24, 1 March 1795–31 December 1802, page 194 [electronic edition]. *The Diaries of John Quincy Adams: A Digital Collection.*
13. JA to TP, 2 October 1797, *Rotunda.*
14. AA to MSC, 13 October 1797, *AFC*: 12: 260–61. JA to TP, 20 October 1797, *Rotunda.*
15. AA to Cotton Tufts, 17 October 1797, *AFC,* 12: 263–67.
16. OW to JA, 6 October 1797. JA to OW, 7 November 1797. JA to OW, 7 November 1797, *Rotunda.* AA to William Smith, 21 November 1797, *AFC,* 12: 301–2.
17. JA to OW, 7 November 1797, *Rotunda.*
18. "Another Revolution in France or the Triumvirate Victorious," *Commercial Advertiser* (New York) I, no. 31, 6 November 1797: 2.
19. Clarfield, *Timothy Pickering and American Diplomacy,* 117. Jeremy Popkin, *A New World Begins: The History of the French Revolution* (New York: Basic Books, 2019), 487–89.
20. WVM to GW, 16 September 1797, *PGW,* Retirement Series, 1: 361–63.
21. Clarfield, *Timothy Pickering and American Diplomacy,* 115–17.
22. JA to McHenry, 10 October 1798; JA to OW, 12 October 1797; JA to CL, 15 October 1797; JA to TP, 20 October 1797, *Rotunda.*
23. OW to JA, 16 October 1797; McHenry to JA, 22 October 1797; CL to JA, 29 October 1797; TP to JA, 2 November 1797; JA to United States Congress, 22 November 1797, *Rotunda.*
24. WVM to TP, 10 October 1797, *Dutch-American Relations Online,* Despatches from United States Ministers to the Netherlands, 1797–1798.

25. "January 4, 1798," *Gazette of the United States & Philadelphia Daily Advertiser*, (Philadelphia, PA), 3. "January 8, 1798," *Gazette of the United States & Philadelphia Daily Advertiser*, (Philadelphia, PA), 3.
26. TJ to JM, 24 January 1798, *PJM*, 17: 71–73.
27. Monroe to TJ, 12 February 1798, *PTJ*, 30: 96–97.
28. JM to TJ, 18 or 19 February 1798, *PTJ*, 30: 116–18.
29. William Vans Murray to Timothy Pickering, 29 October 1797, Despatches from the United States Ministers to the Netherlands, 1797–1798, *Dutch-American Relations Online,* https://primarysources.brillonline.com/browse/dutch-american-diplomatic-relations-online-1784-1973.
30. JA to TP, 24 January 1798, *Rotunda*.

CHAPTER 8

1. "January 19, 1798," *Claypoole's American Daily Advertiser*, (Philadelphia, PA).
2. Clarfield, *Timothy Pickering and the American Republic*, 185.
3. CCP to TP, 1 September 1797; CCP to Rufus King, 11 September 1797; CCP to TP, [14] September 1797, *RES*.
4. CCP to McHenry, 19 September 1797, *RES*.
5. Furstenberg, *When the United States Spoke French*, 73–75, 97–117. Earl, "Talleyrand in Philadelphia," 282.
6. Earl, "Talleyrand in Philadelphia," 289. Furstenberg, *When the United States Spoke French*, 73–75, 97–117.
7. William Stinchcombe, "The Diplomacy of the WXYZ Affair," *William and Mary Quarterly* 34, no. 4 (October 1977): 593–97.
8. Marshall to Charles Lee, 12 October 1797, *The Papers of John Marshall*, 3: 246–47.
9. Elkins and McKitrick, *Age of Federalism*, 570–71.
10. CCP, Marshall, and EG to Timothy Pickering, 22 October 1797, *The Papers of John Marshall*, 3: 255–56.
11. Now Rue de Grenelle.
12. CCP to Harriott Pinckney Horry, 11 October 1797, MSP to MIM, 5 October 1797, *RES*.
13. EG to Mrs. Gerry, 25 November 1797, *Elbridge Gerry's Letterbook, Paris 1797–1798*, ed. Russell W. Knight (Salem, MA: Essex Institute, 1966), 22.
14. Envoys to TP, 22 October 1797, *The Papers of John Marshall*, 3: 256–66; CP notes on meeting with Talleyrand and conversations with James C. Mountflorence, 8–14 October 1797, *RES*.
15. Stinchcombe, "Diplomacy of the WXYZ Affairs," 596.
16. Mary Stead Pinckney to Margaret Izard Manigault, 23–28 May 1798, *RES*.
17. Envoys to TP, 22 October 1797, *Papers of John Marshall*, 3: 258–66.

18. Envoys to TP, 22 October 1797, *Papers of John Marshall*, 3: 258–66. Stinchcombe, "Diplomacy of the WXYZ Affairs," 598. William Stinchcombe, *The XYZ Affair* (Westport: Praeger, 1980), 50–58. DeConde, *The Quasi-War*, 45–57.
19. Envoys to TP, 22 October 1797, *Papers of John Marshall*, 3: 258. Stinchcombe, "Diplomacy of the WXYZ Affairs," 598. Stinchcombe, *The XYZ Affair*, 50–58. DeConde, *The Quasi-War*, 45–57.
20. Elkins and McKitrick, *Age of Federalism*, 571. DeConde, *The Quasi-War*, 45–57.
21. Elkins and McKitrick, *Age of Federalism*, 570–71. DeConde, *The Quasi-War*, 45–57. Envoys to Pickering, 22 October 1797, *Papers of John Marshall*, 3: 260.
22. Envoys to Pickering, 22 October 1797, *Papers of John Marshall*, 3: 260.
23. Envoys to Pickering, 22 October 1797, *Papers of John Marshall*, 3: 260. Stinchcombe, *The XYZ Affair*, 50–58. DeConde, *The Quasi-War*, 45–57.
24. Jean Edward Smith, *John Marshall: Definer of a Nation* (New York: Henry Holt, 1996), 203. J. F. Berard, *Talleyrand: A Biography* (New York: G. P. Putnam's Sons, 1974), 205.
25. Carol Berkin, *A Sovereign People: The Crises of the 1790s and the Birth of American Nationalism* (New York: Basic Books, 2017), 152–81.
26. Elkins and McKitrick, *Age of Federalism*, 573.
27. Envoys to TP, 8 November 1797, *Papers of John Marshall*, 3: 280–91.
28. Stinchcombe, "Diplomacy of the WXYZ Affairs," 600.
29. Envoys to TP, 8 November 1797, *Papers of John Marshall*, 3: 277–91.
30. Berkin, *A Sovereign People*, 152–81.
31. Envoys to TP, 8 November 1797, *Papers of John Marshall*, 3: 280–91.
32. Elkins and McKitrick, *Age of Federalism*, 573–75.
33. Envoys to TP, 8 November 1797, *Papers of John Marshall*, 3: 280–90. DeConde, *The Quasi-War*, 51.
34. WVM to JQA, 1 October 1797, Murray papers, Pierpont Morgan Library, Gerry to Murray, 28 December 1797, Gratz Collection, Historic Society of Pennsylvania, Philadelphia, Gerry to JA, 3 July 1797.
35. CCP to Thomas Pinckney, 22 December 1797, *TPP*, VIII, CCP to Rufus King, 14 December 1797, *RES*.
36. Stinchcombe, *The XYZ Affair*, 66–69.
37. Rufus King to TP, 6 January 1798, *TPP*.
38. Marshall, Paris Journal, *Papers of John Marshall*, 3: 190–94. Elkins and McKitrick, *Age of Federalism*, 575–76.
39. CCP to RK, 9 February 1798; CCP to WVM, 10 March 1798, *RES*.
40. American Envoys to Talleyrand, *Papers of John Marshall*, 3: 330–31, editorial note.
41. Berkin, *A Sovereign People*, 152–81.
42. Marshall, *Paris Journal*, *Papers of John Marshall*, 3: 195.
43. Mary Stead Pinckney to Margaret Izard Manigault, 14 March 1798, *RES*. Stinchcombe, *The XYZ Affair*, 108–10.
44. Stinchcombe, *The XYZ Affair*, 108–11.

45. Charles Cotesworth Pinckney, John Marshall, Elbridge Gerry to Timothy Pickering, 22 October 1797, *The Papers of John Marshall*, 3: 255, n2.
46. Ferling, *John Adams*, 352.
47. *AOC*, 5th Cong. 2nd Sess. 1201. John Adams to United States Congress, 5 March 1798, *Rotunda*. Dauer, *The Adams Federalists*, 141. Chernow, *Alexander Hamilton*, 550.

CHAPTER 9

1. Rufus King to TP, 6 January 1798, *TPP*. TS to Peter Van Schaack, 17 March 1798, *TSP*, Massachusetts Historical Society, Box 5, Folder 11.
2. JA to Heads of Department, 13 March 1798, *Rotunda*.
3. Italics in original. CL to JA, 14 March 1798, *Rotunda*. Ferling, *John Adams*, 352–53.
4. Italics in original. McHenry to JA, 14 March 1798, *Rotunda*.
5. DeConde, *The Quasi-War*, 67. Clarfield, *Timothy Pickering and American Diplomacy, 1795–1800*, 144–47.
6. TP to AH, 25 March 1798, *PAH*, 21: 370–77.
7. TP to AH, 25 March 1798, *PAH*, 21: 370–77.
8. DeConde, *The Quasi-War*, 67. Smith, *John Adams*, II: 955.
9. AA to Hannah Phillips Cushing, 9 March 1798, *AFC*, 12: 443–44.
10. AA to MSC, 20 March 1798, *AFC*, 12: 454–55. Smith, *John Adams*, II: 937.
11. TS to Henry Van Schaack, 12 March 1798, *TSP*, Box 4, Folder 23.
12. TS to Henry Van Schaack, 12 March 1798, *TSP*, Box 4, Folder 23.
13. TS to Henry Van Schaack, 17 March 1798, *TSP*, Box 4, Folder 24.
14. TP to AH, 25 March 1798, *PAH*, 21: 370–77.
15. AH to Jonathan Dayton, 15 March 1798, *PAH*, 27: 14–16.
16. Smith, *John Adams*, II: 952–54. Clarfield, *Timothy Pickering and American Diplomacy, 1795–1800*, 144–47.
17. John Adams to United States Congress, 19 March 1798, *Rotunda*. Elkins and McKitrick, *Age of Federalism*, 581–89. Smith, *John Adams*, II: 956–67.
18. JM to TJ, 21 January 1798, *PJM*, 17: 69–71. Malone, *Jefferson and the Ordeal of Liberty*, 363.
19. TJ to JM, 21 March 1798, *PJM*, 17: 99–100.
20. AH to TP, *PAH*, 21: 368–70, n1. *AOC*, VII, 525.
21. TS to Henry Van Schaack, 21 March 1798, *TSP*, Box 4, Folder 24.
22. James Tagg, *Benjamin Franklin Bache and the Philadelphia Aurora* (Philadelphia: University of Pennsylvania Press, 1991), 337. Smith, *John Adams*, II: 956–67.
23. TP to AH, 25 March 1798, *PAH*, 21: 378–79.
24. JQA to AA, 4 March 1798, *AFC*, 13: 10–14, n.3. "Notes on British Instructions and on Clement Humphreys, 13 April 1798," *PTJ*, 30: 271–72. Clement Humphreys to Charles Cotesworth Pinckney, 29 May 1798, *RES*. Elkins and McKitrick, *Age of Federalism*, 581–89.
25. TS to Henry Van Schaack, 21 March 1798, *TSP*, Box 4, Folder 24. Peterson, *Jefferson and the New Nation*, 590–97.

26. Jonathan Mason to Harrison Gray Otis in Samuel Eliot Morison, *Harrison Gray Otis, 1765–1848: The Urbane Federalist* (Boston: Houghton Mifflin, 1969), I: 112.
27. TS to Henry Van Schaack, 27 March 1798, *TSP*, Box 4, Folder 24.
28. *AOC*, House of Representatives, 5th Congress, 2nd Session, 1357–58.
29. Allen's family was close to the Dwight family, Sedgwick's in-laws, and Allen was well connected with Alexander Hamilton, one of Sedgwick's closest allies.
30. Underline in original. TS to Peter Van Schaack, 2 April 1798, *TSP*, Box 5, Folder 11. Elkins and McKitrick, *Age of Federalism*, 581–89.
31. JA to United States Congress, 3 April 1798, *Rotunda*.
32. Jonathan Mason Jr. to Otis, Boston, 30 March 1798, in Morison, *Harrison Gray Otis*, I: 93, cited in DeConde, *Quasi-War*, 71–73. Smith, *John Adams*, II: 956–67.
33. DeConde, *Quasi-War*, 73.
34. AA to JQA, 21 April 1798, *AFC*, 12: 516–19.
35. TJ to Peter Carr, 12 April 1798, *PTJ*, 30: 266–68. Ferling, *John Adams*, 354. Peterson, *Jefferson and the New Nation*, 590–97.
36. Tagg, *Benjamin Franklin Bache and the Philadelphia Aurora*, 341.
37. TJ to Thomas Mann Randolph, 19 April 1798, *PTJ*, 30: 282–84. Malone, *Jefferson and the Ordeal of Liberty*, 369–74. Smith, *John Adams*, II: 956–67. Chernow, *Alexander Hamilton*, 550–51.
38. John Marshall, "Paris Journal," *The Papers of John Marshall*, III: 219-20.
39. Marshall, "Paris Journal," 219–20. Berkin, *A Sovereign People*, 182.
40. Marshall, "Paris Journal," 222–24. The Marshall journal, his correspondence, and Pinckney's correspondence are the only sources on these conversations, so they must be taken with a grain of salt, as Marshall's reflections are obviously biased. However, when the envoys compiled their dispatches to report back to Pickering and Adams, they often copied whole passages from Marshall's diary and then all three signed off on the veracity of the details. Therefore, one can conclude that at least most of Marshall's entries in his Paris journal are pretty close to accurate.
41. Envoys to Talleyrand, 3 April 1798, *The Papers of John Marshall*, III: 428–59.
42. Berkin, *A Sovereign People*, 183–84.
43. Marshall, "Paris Journal," 229–30.
44. Marshall, "Paris Journal," 230–33. Berkin, *A Sovereign People*, 184–85.
45. Elkins and McKitrick, *Age of Federalism*, 574–79.
46. Marshall, "Paris Journal," 233–35. Berkin, *A Sovereign People*, 184–85. DeConde, *Quasi-War*, 57–59. Stinchcombe, *XYZ Affair*, 112–13.
47. Elkins and McKitrick, *Age of Federalism*, 574–79.
48. CCP to Thomas Pinckney, 4 April 1798, *RES.*
49. EG to Mrs. Gerry, 26 March 1798 in Russell W. Knight. *Elbridge Gerry's Letterbook Paris 1797-1798* (Salem, MA: Essex Institute, 1966), 34.
50. Talleyrand to Marshall, 13 April 1798. Marshall to Talleyrand, 13 April 1798. *The Papers of John Marshall*, III: 461–62. DeConde, *Quasi-War*, 54–59.
51. Marshall to CCP, 21 April 1798, *The Papers of John Marshall*, III: 463–64.
52. Clement Humphreys to Charles Cotesworth Pinckney, 29 May 1798, *RES.*

53. Berkin, *A Sovereign People*, 185
54. "Epitome, and Remarks on Actions of Ministers at Paris, [22 October 1797]," *Rotunda.*

CHAPTER 10

1. John Adams, "Proclamation Proclaiming a Fast-Day, 23 March 1798," *Rotunda.*
2. DeConde, *Quasi-War*, 83. Rachel Hope Cleves, *The Reign of Terror in America: Visions of Violence from Anti-Jacobinism to Antislavery* (Cambridge: Cambridge University Press, 2009), 58–82. Dunn, *Jefferson's Second Revolution*, 99.
3. JA to TJ, 30 June 1813, *PTJ*, Retirement Series, 6: 253–56. "Philadelphia," 10 May 1798; 11 May 1798, *Aurora*, 3. "Extract of a letter from a gentleman of reputation in Philadelphia dated May 11," 21 May 1798, *Aurora*, 2. John Miller, *Crisis in Freedom: The Alien and Sedition Acts* (New York: Atlantic Little, Brown, 1952), 62. DeConde, *Quasi-War*, 83–84.
4. https://archive.org/details/philadelphiadire1798phil/page/92/mode/2up.
5. JA to TJ, 30 June 1813, *PTJ*, Retirement Series, 6: 253–56. Miller, *Crisis in Freedom*, 62. DeConde, *Quasi-War*, 83–84. TJ to Thomas Mann Randolph, 9 May 1798, *PTJ*, 30: 341–42.
6. JA to TJ, 30 June 1813, *Rotunda.* Terri Diane Halperin, *The Alien and Sedition Acts of 1798: Testing the Constitution* (Baltimore: Johns Hopkins University Press, 2016), 2–5.
7. *The Pennsylvania Herald, and York General Advertiser*, 11 May 1798. TJ to Thomas Mann Randolph, 9 May 1798, *PTJ*, 30: 341–42. "Extract of a letter from a gentleman of reputation in Philadelphia dated May 11," 21 May 1798, *Aurora*, 2.
8. Adams probably exaggerated this number, at least slightly. Nonetheless, at least a few thousand men were in the streets. "Extract of a letter from a gentleman of reputation in Philadelphia dated May 11," 21 May 1798, *Aurora*, 2. DeConde, *Quasi-War*, 83–84. Miller, *Crisis in Freedom*, 62. TJ to Thomas Mann Randolph, 9 May 1798, *PTJ*, 30: 341–42.
9. TJ to JM, 10 May 1798, *PJM*, 10:128–30. "Extract of a letter from a gentleman of reputation in Philadelphia dated May 11," 21 May 1798, *Aurora*, 2. Halperin, *The Alien and Sedition Acts*, 2.
10. Miller, *Crisis in Freedom*, 62.
11. "Whereas: Stories from the People's House," January 19, 2018, Office of the Historian, U.S. House of Representatives, https://history.house.gov/Blog/2018/January/1-19-Lyon-Griswold/.. Joanne B. Freeman, *Affairs of Honor: National Politics in the New Republic* (New Haven, CT: Yale University Press, 2001), 173–75. Halperin, *Alien and Sedition Acts*, 82–84.
12. Jeffrey L. Pasley, *The Tyranny of Printers: Newspaper Politics in the Early American Republic* (Charlottesville: University of Virginia Press, 2002), 98.
13. Hoffer, *The Free Press Crisis of 1800*, 3. Tagg, *Benjamin Franklin Bache*, 350.

14. Italics in original. "An Unfortunate Man" to JA, 18 April 1798, Rotunda.
15. Smith, *Freedom's Fetters*, 26.
16. AA to MSC, 10 May 1798, *AFC*, 13: 23–26.
17. AA to MSC, 7 April 1798, *AFC*, 12: 489–91.
18. 11 May 1798, *The Pennsylvania Herald, and York General Advertiser.*
19. Halperin, *Alien and Sedition Acts*, 15, 35.
20. Smith, *Freedom's Fetters*, 23.
21. Halperin, *Alien and Sedition Acts*, 37. Elkins and McKitrick, *Age of Federalism*, 590–93. Bernstein, *The Education of John Adams*, 186–89.
22. "Newhampshire, Concord, November 23," 5 December 1799, *Green Mountain Patriot*, (Peacham, VT), 3. Halperin, *Alien and Sedition Acts*, 38. Elkins and McKitrick, *Age of Federalism*, 590–93. Bernstein, *The Education of John Adams*, 186–89.
23. Malone, *Jefferson and the Ordeal of Liberty*, 286–87.
24. Dispatch (30 October 1797), *American State Papers*, Foreign Policy, 2: 163–64. Smith, *Freedom's Fetters*, 14. Wendell Bird, *Criminal Dissent: Prosecution under the Alien and Sedition Acts of 1798* (Cambridge, MA: Harvard University Press, 2020), 23.
25. "Important State Paper," *Aurora*, no. 2310, 16 June 1798: [2].
26. TP to David Humphreys, 18 June 1798, *TPP*, History Vault.
27. Pickering notes, 14 May 1798, *TPP*, 303–303A.
28. *AOC*, 5th Cong., 2nd Sess., 1427.
29. Naturalization Act of 1795, ch. 20, § 1, 1 Stat. 414, 414 (repealed 1802).
30. Halperin, *Alien and Sedition Acts*, 53–54. Bird, *Criminal Dissents*, 32–37. Smith, *Freedom's Fetters*, 32–33.
31. TJ to JM, 26 April 1798, *PTJ*, 17: 120–22.
32. *AOC*, 5th Cong., 2nd Session, 1785. Smith, *Freedom's Fetters*, 35–49.
33. Bird, *Criminal Dissents*, 38–39.
34. Bird, *Criminal Dissents*, 39. Smith, *Freedom's Fetters*, 50–93. Halperin, *Alien and Sedition Acts*, 54–61.
35. Bird, *Criminal Dissents*, 40. Halperin, *Alien and Sedition Acts*, 56–57. AH to TP, 7 June 1798, *PAH*, 21: 494–95. TJ to Thomas Mann Randolph, 9 May 1798, PTJ, 30: 341. JM to TJ, 20 May 1798, *PJM*, 17:133–34. *Freedom's Fetters*, 50–93. Halperin, *Alien and Sedition Acts*, 54–61.
36. "Alien and Sedition Acts," *National Archives*, https://www.archives.gov/milestone-documents/alien-and-sedition-acts. Bird, *Criminal Dissents*, 38–39. Halperin, *Alien and Sedition Acts*, 56.
37. TJ to JM, 26 April 1798, *PTJ*, 17: 120–22. Dauer, *The Adams Federalists*, 161–67.
38. Text of legislation: https://www.archives.gov/milestone-documents/alien-and-sedition-acts; Bird, *Criminal Dissents*, 42–46. Smith, *Freedom's Fetters*, 112–50. Halperin, *Alien and Sedition Acts*, 62–65. *AOC*, 5th Cong., 2nd Sess., 2093–94.
39. Miller, *Crisis in Freedom*, 21. Dunn, *Jefferson's Second Revolution*, 101–8.

40. Speech that provoked violence wasn't carved out as a First Amendment exception until 1919, when the Supreme Court ruled, "The Free Speech Clause of the First Amendment does not shield advocacy urging conduct deemed unlawful under the Espionage Act." This case articulated the "clear and present danger" test for the first time. In 1969, the Court held in *Brandenburg v. Ohio* that speech "directed to inciting or producing imminent lawless action and is likely to incite or produce such action" is not protected under the First Amendment. "Schenck v. United States." *Oyez*, www.oyez.org/cases/1900–1940/249us47. Accessed September 9, 2022. Foundation for Individual Rights and Expression (FIRE). "BRANDENBURG v. OHIO." Oyez. https://www.thefire.org/first-amendment-library/decision/brandenburg-v-ohio/ (accessed September 9, 2022).
41. Henry Tazewell to JM, *PJM*, 17: 158–59. Smith, *John Adams*, II: 977–78.
42. *AOC*, 5th Cong., 2nd Sess., 2138–72.
43. JA to Benjamin Chadbourn, 11 June 1798. JA to James Wood, 10 June 1798, *Rotunda*.
44. AA to MSC, 10 May 1798, *AFC*, 13: 23–26.
45. Miller, *Crisis in Freedom*, 72. Dauer, *The Adams Federalists*, 159. Smith, *John Adams*, II: 977–78. Woody Holton, *Abigail Adams: A Life* (New York: Atria Books, 2010), 317.
46. "Office History," Southern District of New York, https://www.justice.gov/usao-sdny/office-history.
47. TP to Richard Harrison, 7 July 1798, *TPP*, 315.
48. Thomas M. Ray, " 'Not One Cent for Tribute': The Public Addresses and American Popular Reaction to the XYZ Affair, 1798–1799," *Journal of the Early Republic* 3, no. 4 (Winter 1983): 389–412.
49. *Aurora*, May 30, 11 June 1798, in . Ray, " 'Not One Cent for Tribute,' 389–412.
50. Samuel Phillips to JA, 7 June 1798, on behalf of Legislature of MA, *Rotunda*.
51. For one example, see JA to Students of Harvard College, July 1798, *Rotunda*.
52. AA to Elizabeth Smith Shaw Peabody, 22 June 1798, *AFC*, 13: 138–41,
53. TJ to JM, 21 June 1798, *PJM*, 17: 155–57. Henry Glen to John Jay, 22 June 1798, *The Selected Papers of John Jay*, 6: 653–54.
54. AA to Elizabeth Smith Shaw Peabody, 22 June 1798, *AFC*, 13: 138–41.
55. Gerry to JA, 16 April 1798, *Rotunda*.
56. Smith, *Freedom's Fetters*, 3–5.
57. Henry Glen to John Jay, 22 June 1798, *The Selected Papers of John Jay*, 6: 653–54. Smith, *Freedom's Fetters*, 3–5.
58. Marshall to TJ, 24 June 1798, *PTJ*, 30: 424.
59. JA to United States Congress, 21 June 1798, *Rotunda*.
60. TP to Gerry, 25 June 1798, *TPP*.

CHAPTER 11

1. JA to GW, 22 June 1798, *PGW,* Retirement Series, 2: 351–52. Elkins and McKitrick, *Age of Federalism*, 600.
2. Navy Department, 10 U.S.C. 5011, 5031. Kurtz, *The Presidency of John Adams*, 305.
3. JA to United States Senate, 18 May 1798, *Rotunda.*
4. Harriot Stoddert Turner, "Memoirs of Benjamin Stoddert, First Secretary of the United States Navy," *Records of the Columbia Historical Society* (Washington, DC, 1917), 20: 141–66
5. US Congress, *U.S. Statutes at Large*, 28 May 1798, 1: 558. William J. Murphy Jr., "John Adams: The Politics of the Additional Army, 1798–1800," *New England Quarterly* 52, no. 2 (June 1979): 237–38.
6. Stevens Thomson Mason to Thomas Jefferson, 6 July 1798, *PTJ*, 30: 443–45. Dunn, *Jefferson's Second Revolution*, 96–98.
7. *U.S. Statutes at Large*, 1:597–604. Kurtz, *The Presidency of John Adams*, 305.
8. JA to GW, 22 June 1798, *PGW*, Retirement Series, 2: 351–52.
9. JA to GW, 22 June 1798, *PGW*, Retirement Series, 2: 351–52.
10. Furstenberg, *When the United States Spoke French*, 170–75.
11. Alberts, *The Golden Voyage: The Life and Times of William Bingham*, 341. Kurtz, *The Presidency of John Adams*, 307–14.
12. DeConde, *Quasi-War*, 105.
13. Destler, *Joshua Coit, American Federalist*, 126–28.
14. TP to GW, 13 September 1798, *PGW*, Retirement Series, 2: 608–10.
15. JA to United States Senate, 2 July 1798, *Rotunda.*
16. TP to GW, 13 September 1798, *PGW*, Retirement Series, 2: 608–10.
17. AA to William Smith, 7 July 1798, *AFC*, 13: 176–79. Richard H. Kohn, *Eagle and Sword: The Federalists and the Creation of the Military Establishment in America, 1783–1802* (New York: Free Press, 1975), 231–37.
18. AA to [Cotton Tufts], 10 July 1798, Adams Papers, reel 390. Kohn, *Eagle and Sword*, 231.
19. GW to JA, 4 July 1798, *PGW*, Retirement Series, 2: 368–71.
20. Smith, *John Adams*, II: 973. Kurtz, *The Presidency of John Adams*, 325–27. Chernow, *Alexander Hamilton*, 555–59. Kohn, *Eagle and Sword*, 231–37.
21. Smith, *John Adams*, II: 973.
22. AH to GW, 8 July 1798, *PAH*, 21: 534–36.
23. TP to GW, 6 July 1798, *PGW*, Retirement Series, 2: 386–87.
24. Brown, *The Presidency of John Adams*, 65–66. Chernow, *Alexander Hamilton*, 555–59. Kohn, *Eagle and Sword*, 231–37.
25. "July—1798," *Diaries of George Washington*, 6: 303–11. Washington sent his carriage to Alexandria to pick up McHenry: GW to TP, 11 July 1798, *PGW*, Retirement Series, 2: 397–400.
26. Brown, *The Presidency of John Adams*, 65–66.

27. Brown, *The Presidency of John Adams*, 66–68.
28. HK to GW, 8 August 1794; GW to HK, 8 August 1794, *PGW*, Presidential Series, 16: 539–40.
29. GW to HK 9 October 1794, *PGW*, Presidential Series, 17: 43. Kurtz, *The Presidency of John Adams*, 325–27. Kohn, *Eagle and Sword*, 231–37.
30. GW to AH, 14 July 1798, *PAH*, 22: 17–21.
31. GW to TP, 11 July 1798, *PGW*, Retirement Series, 2: 397–400.
32. GW to TP, 11 July 1798, *PGW*, Retirement Series, 2: 397–400. James H. Broussard, *The Southern Federalists, 1800–1816* (Baton Rouge: Louisiana State University Press, 1999), 12–19.
33. GW to TP, 11 July 1798, *PGW*, Retirement Series, 2: 397–400. Chernow, *Alexander Hamilton*, 555–559.
34. Kohn, *Eagle and Sword*, 231–37.
35. AH to GW, 8 July 1798, *PAH*, 21: 534–36. Ralph, *The Presidency of John Adams*, 65–68.
36. Clarfield, *Timothy Pickering and American Diplomacy*, 170–71.
37. TP to GW, 6 July 1798, *PGW*, Retirement Series, 2: 386–87. Chernow, *Alexander Hamilton*, 555–59.
38. GW to TP, 11 July 1798, *PGW*, Retirement Series, 2: 397–400. Kohn, *Eagle and Sword*, 231–37.
39. GW to JA, 13 July 1798, *Rotunda*. Chernow, *Alexander Hamilton*, 555–59.
40. Elkins and McKitrick, *Age of Federalism*, 602.
41. GW to HK, 16 July 1798, *PGW*, Retirement Series, 2: 423–36. Kurtz, *The Presidency of John Adams*, 325–27. Ralph, *The Presidency of John Adams*, 65–68.
42. Chernow, *Alexander Hamilton*, 555–59. Kohn, *Eagle and Sword*, 231–37.
43. GW to AH, 14 July 1798, *PAH*, 22: 17–21. Elkins and McKitrick, *Age of Federalism*, 601. Brown, *The Presidency of John Adams*, 66–68.
44. GW to Benjamin Harrison Sr., 21 March 1781, *Rotunda*.
45. Worthington C. Ford, ed., *Journals of the Continental Congress, 1774–1789*. 6: 1027.
46. Chervinsky, *The Cabinet*, 147.
47. "September [1794]," *The Diaries of George Washington*, 6: 178–79.
48. McHenry to GW, 18 July 1798, *PGW*, Retirement Series, 2: 432–34. Kohn, *Eagle and Sword*, 231–37.
49. Kohn, *Eagle and Sword*, 232–35. Elkins and McKitrick, *Age of Federalism*, 601–3.
50. TP to JJ, 20 July 1798, *Selected Papers of John Jay*, 6: 666–68. Clarfield, *Timothy Pickering and American Diplomacy*, 172–74. Dauer, *Adams Federalists*, 213.
51. Kohn, *Eagle and Sword*, 233.
52. AA to William Smith, 23 July 1798, *AFC*, 13: 204–6, n1. Chernow, *Alexander Hamilton*, 560–61.
53. *AOC*, Senate, 5th Congress, 2nd Session, 623.
54. TP to JA, 25 July 1798, *Rotunda*. Kohn, *Eagle and Sword*, 235.

CHAPTER 12

1. AA to MSC, 29 July 1798, *AFC*, 13: 220–21.
2. Kohn, *Eagle and Sword*, 2–10. Elkins and McKitrick, *Age of Federalism*, 594–95. James Kirby Martin and Mark Edward Lender, *'A Respectable Army': The Military Origins of the Republic, 1763–1789* (West Sussex, UK: John Wiley and Sons, 2015), 19–27.
3. Kurtz, *The Presidency of John Adams*, 321–23.
4. AA to JQA, 15 November 1798, *AFC*, 13: 271–74.
5. JA to GW, 9 October 1798, *Rotunda*. Ferling, *Adams vs. Jefferson*, 117.
6. GW to McHenry, 13 July 1796, *PGW*, Presidential Series, 20: 428–30.
7. GW to AH, 9 August 1798, *PGW*, Retirement Series, 2: 500–502.
8. OW to AH, 9 August 1798, *PAH*, 22: 64–66.
9. AH to McHenry, 19 August 1798, *PAH*, 22: 81–83. Kohn, *Eagle and Sword*, 242.
10. AH to McHenry, 30 July 1798, *PAH*, 22: 41–43.
11. AH to McHenry, 25 August 1798, *PAH*, 22: 163. Kohn, *Eagle and Sword*, 235.
12. GW to McHenry, 10 August 1798, *PGW*, Retirement Series, 2: 508–11. GW to McHenry, 14 September 1798, *PGW*, Retirement Series, 2: 610–12.
13. McHenry to JA, 4 August 1798, *Rotunda*.
14. McHenry to AH, 25 July 1798, *PAH*, 22: 29–30. McHenry sent nearly identical letters to Knox and Pinckney. Enclosure: HK to McHenry, 5 August 1798, *PAH*, 22: 69–71, n3.
15. Enclosure: HK to McHenry, 5 August 1798, *PAH*, 22: 69–71.
16. Enclosure: HK to McHenry, 5 August 1798, *PAH*, 22: 69–71.
17. Enclosure: HK to McHenry, 5 August 1798, *PAH*, 22: 69–71.
18. Mark Puls, *Henry Knox: Visionary General of the American Revolution* (New York: St. Martin's Press, 2008), 236–37. Kurtz, *The Presidency of John Adams*, 325.
19. Enclosure: HK to McHenry, 5 August 1798, *PAH*, 22: 69–71.
20. AA to AAS, 19 July 1798, *AFC*, 13: 194–96.
21. JA to McHenry, 14 August 1798, *Rotunda*.
22. TP to AH, 21[–22] August 1798, *PAH*, 22: 147–52. Kohn, *Eagle and Sword*, 235–36.
23. TP to AH, 23 August 1798, *PAH*, 22: 159–61. Kurtz, *The Presidency of John Adams*, 325–27.
24. McHenry to JA, 20 August 1798, *Rotunda*.
25. McHenry to GW, 25 August 1798, *PGW*, 2: 559–62.
26. TP to GW, 1 September 1798, *PGW*, Retirement Series, 2: 573–77. Clarfield, *Timothy Pickering and American Diplomacy*, 177.
27. TP to AH, 21[–22] August 1798, *PAH*, 22: 147–52.
28. Robert Troup to Rufus King, 2 October 1798, *CRK*, II: 428–29. Dunn, *Jefferson's Second Revolution*, 95–96.
29. JA to OW, 13 September 1798, *Rotunda*.

30. JA to McHenry, 29 August 1798, *Rotunda*. John Lamberton Harper, *American Machiavelli: Alexander Hamilton and the Origins of U.S. Foreign Policy* (New York: Cambridge University Press, 2004), 219–23.
31. McHenry to JA, 6 September 1798, *Rotunda*.
32. Smith, *John Adams*, II: 981. Kurtz, *The Presidency of John Adams*, 325–27.
33. JA to McHenry, 13 September 1798, *Rotunda*.
34. Brown, *The Presidency of John Adams*, 68–69.
35. Italics in original. George Cabot to JA, 29 September 1798, *Rotunda*.
36. McHenry to GW, 7 September 1798, *PGW*, Retirement Series, 2: 589–90.
37. AH to McHenry, 8 September 1798, *PAH*, 22: 177. "Introductory Note: From George Washington, [14 July 1798]," *PAH*, 22: 4–17.
38. McHenry to GW, 10 September 1798, *PGW*, Retirement Series, 2: 600–601.
39. GW to McHenry, 16 September 1798, *PGW*, Retirement Series, 3: 4–6.
40. TP to GW, 18 September 1798, *PGW*, Retirement Series, 3: 11–13. Kurtz, *The Presidency of John Adams*, 326–27.
41. OW to JA, 17 September 1798, *Rotunda*.
42. McHenry to JA, 21 September 1798, *Rotunda*.
43. Elkins and McKitrick, 605. Brown, *The Presidency of John Adams*, 69.
44. Brown, *The Presidency of John Adams*, 68–69.
45. JA to McHenry, 30 September 1798, *Rotunda*. Harper, *American Machiavelli*, 219–23. Lycan, *Alexander Hamilton & American Foreign Policy*, 354. Kurtz, *The Presidency of John Adams*, 325–27.
46. GW to JA, 25 September 1798, *PGW*, Retirement Series, 3: 36–44.
47. GW to United States Senate, 4 March 1791, *PGW*, Presidential Series, 7: 510–11. GW to United States Senate, 9 April 1792, *PGW*, Presidential Series, 10: 236–40.
48. December 19, 1799, Bradford Perkins, "A Diplomat's Wife in Philadelphia: Letters of Henrietta Liston, 1796–1800," *William and Mary Quarterly* 11, no. 4 (October 1954): 628.
49. GW to JA, 25 September 1798, *PGW*, Retirement Series, 3: 36–44.
50. JA to GW, 9 October 1798, *Rotunda*. Harper, *American Machiavelli*, 219–23. Lycan, *Alexander Hamilton and American Foreign Policy*, 354. Brown, *The Presidency of John Adams*, 70.

CHAPTER 13

1. John Taylor to TJ, 13 May 1798, *PTJ*, 30: 347–48. TJ to John Taylor, 4 June 1798, *PTJ*, 30: 387–90. Chernow, *Alexander Hamilton*, 573–74.
2. *AOC*, 5th Congress, 2nd Sess., 2089. Murphy, "John Adams: The Politics of the Additional Army," 235–39.
3. *AOC*, 5th Congress, 2nd Sess., 2132. Dunn, *Jefferson's Second Revolution*, 111.
4. Bache's lawyers argued that he could not be charged with seditious libel under common law and the Sedition Act wouldn't pass for another week.

5. Bird, *Criminal Dissent*, 65–69. John Ragosta, *For the People, For the Country: Patrick Henry's Final Political Battle* (Charlottesville: University Press of Virginia, 2023), 109–16.
6. Bird, *Criminal Dissent*, 85–95.
7. Bradburn, *Citizenship Revolution*, 175–77. Shira Lurie, *The American Liberty Pole: Popular Politics and the Struggle for Democracy in the Early Republic* (Charlottesville: University Press of Virginia, 2023).
8. Jefferson, "I. Jefferson's Draft, [before 4 October 1798]," *PTJ*, 30: 536–43. Ferling, *Jefferson and Hamilton*, 303–5. "Editorial Note: The Kentucky Resolutions of 1798," *PTJ*, 30: 529–35.
9. Malone, *Ordeal of Liberty*, 400–401.
10. Adrienne Koch, *Jefferson and Madison: The Great Collaboration* (New York: Knopf, 1950), 187–888. Halperin, *The Alien and Sedition Acts*, 102–7. "Editorial Note: The Kentucky Resolutions of 1798," *PTJ*, 30: 529–35.
11. Lowell H. Harrison, "A Young John Breckinridge," *Virginia Magazine of History and Biography* 71, no. 1 (1963): 26.
12. Bradburn, Douglas. *The Citizenship Revolution: Politics and the Creation of the American Union, 1774-1804* (Charlottesville: University of Virginia Press, 2009), 175. Malone, *Ordeal of Liberty*, 401–2.
13. Wilson Cary Nicholas to Thomas Jefferson, 4 October 1798, *PTJ*, 30: 556–57.
14. TJ to Wilson Cary Nicholas, 5 October 1798, *PTJ*, 30: 557. "Editorial Note: The Kentucky Resolutions of 1798," *PTJ*, 30: 529–35.
15. While no records survive that reveal the depth of their partnership at this moment, I find it utterly incomprehensible that Jefferson didn't know Madison was drafting his own resolutions—the argument made by Noah Feldman (*Three Lives of James Madison*, 420).
16. TJ to JM, 26 October 1798, *PTJ*, 30: 567–68. Dunn, *Jefferson's Second Revolution*, 111. Cost, *James Madison*, 263–69. Halperin, *The Alien and Sedition Acts*, 102–7.
17. Jefferson, "II. Jefferson's Fair Copy, [before 4 October 1798]," "III. Resolutions Adopted by the Kentucky General Assembly, 10 November 1798," *PTJ*, 30: 543–56. Ragosta, *For the People, for the Country*, 121–24. Malone, *Ordeal of Liberty*, 401–5.
18. Bird, *Criminal Dissents*, 155. "III. Resolutions Adopted by the Kentucky General Assembly, 10 November 1798," *PTJ*, 30: 549–56.
19. Wilson Cary Nicholas to Thomas Jefferson, 4 October 1798, *PTJ*, 30: 556–57. "Editorial Note: The Kentucky Resolutions of 1798," *PTJ*, 30: 529–35.
20. "Virginia Resolutions, 21 December 1798," *PJM*, 17: 185–91. Cost, *James Madison*, 263–69.
21. "Virginia Resolutions, 21 December 1798," *PJM*, 17: 185–91. Halperin, *The Alien and Sedition Acts*, 102–7.
22. TJ to WCN, 29 November 1798, *PTJ*, 30: 590. Ragosta, *For the People, for the Country*, 124–29.

23. The "of Caroline" was often added to John Taylor's name as a nod to the county where he lived and worked to distinguish him from the many other John Taylors in Virginia. "Virginia Resolutions, 21 December 1798," *PJM*, 17: 185–91. Cost, *James Madison*, 263–69. Ragosta, *For the People, for the Country*, 124–29.
24. TS to RK, 20 January 1799, *TSP*, Folder 23.
25. William Hindman to Rufus King, 13 December 1798, *CRK*, II: 492. Ragosta, *For the People, for the Country*, 129–32.
26. JQA to WVM, 30 March 1799, *Writings of John Quincy Adams*, 2: 398–400.
27. Samuel Henshaw to TS, 26 January 1799, *TSP*, Folder 19.
28. AH to TS, 2 February 1799, *PAH*, 22: 452–454. Ragosta, *For the People, for the Country*, 129–32.
29. Malone *Ordeal of Liberty*, 401–7.
30. "New York, Dec. 17," December 31, 1798, *Rutland Herald*, (Rutland, VT). "Hartford, Dec. 17," December 31, 1798, *Rutland Herald*, (Rutland, VT).
31. "Virginia Resolutions, 21 December 1798, *PJM*, 17: 185–91.
32. Watkins, *Reclaiming the American Revolution*, 71. Halperin, *The Alien and Sedition Acts*, 102–7. Ragosta, *For the People, for the Country*, 124–29.
33. Bird, *Criminal Dissents*, 155.
34. JQA to WVM, 30 March 1799, *Writings of John Quincy Adams*, 2: 398.

CHAPTER 14

1. JA to TP, 3 October 1798, *Rotunda.*
2. Gibbs, *Memoirs of the Administrations of Washington and John Adams*, II: 107
3. TP to JA, 18 August 1798, *Rotunda.*
4. Gibbs, *Memoirs of the Administrations of Washington and John Adams*, II: 110.
5. Cabot to TP, 12 October 1798; Cabot to OW, 16 October 1798; Cabot to TP, 7 November 1798, Henry Cabot Lodge, ed., *Life and Letters of George Cabot* (Boston: Little, Brown, 1877), 172–80.
6. Gibbs, *Memoirs of the Administrations of Washington and John Adams*, II: 110–11. Smith, *John Adams*, II: 984.
7. Caroline Keinath, *Adams National Historical Park, Quincy, Massachusetts.* (Lawrenceburg, IN: Creative Company, 2008): 11.
8. Katharina Lacy, "Cultural Landscape Report- Adams National Historic Site, Quincy, Massachusetts." Olmsted Center for Landscape Preservation Cultural Landscape Publication No. 13 (1997), 41.
9. Laurel A. Racine, "Historic Furnishings Report: The Birthplaces of Presidents John Adams and John Quincy Adams," vol. I. National Park Service. April 2001, 267–68, https://irma.nps.gov/DataStore/DownloadFile/449277.The quote comes from Abigail Adams to Mary Cranch, 12 July 1798, quoted in *New Letters of Abigail Adams, 1788–1801*, ed. Stewart Mitchell (Westport, CT: Greenwood Press,

1973), 202. AA to MSC, 22 April 1798, *AFC*, 12: 519–23. AA to Cotton Tufts, 25 May 1798, *AFC*, 13: 49–52.

10. No record of the conversation exists. These arguments are ones that Gerry put forth repeatedly in writing to anyone who would listen, including the president, so they likely came up in his meeting with the president. EG to Mrs. Gerry, 26 March 1797, Gerry Letterbook, 36.
11. EG to JA, 16 April 1798, *Rotunda*.
12. Stinchcombe, *Diplomacy of the WXYZ Affair*, 613–15. Stinchcombe, *XYZ Affair*, 113–21. Harper, *American Machiavelli*, 225–26.
13. JM to TJ, 31 May 1798, *PJM*, 17: 138–140, n5.
14. Lycan, *Alexander Hamilton and American Foreign Policy*, 393.
15. Lyon, E. Wilson, "The Directory and the United States," *The American Historical* Review, 43: 3 (April 1938), 528–29. DeConde, *Quasi-War*, 148–51. Elkins and McKitrick, *Age of Federalism*, 648–49, 666–68.
16. Ferling, *Adams vs. Jefferson*, 118–24. Manuel Covo, *Entrepôt of Revolutions: Saint-Domingue Commercial Sovereignty, and the French American Alliance* (New York: Oxford University Press, 2022) 8–11.
17. Smith, *John Adams*, II: 995.
18. WVM to JA, 17 July 1798, *Rotunda*. Peter P. Hill, *William Vans Murray: Federalist Diplomat: The Shaping of Peace with France, 1797–1801* (Syracuse, NY: Syracuse University Press, 1971), 122–31.
19. WVM to JA, 3 August 1798, *Rotunda*. Elkins and McKitrick, *Age of Federalism*, 609, 615, 666–68. DeConde, *Quasi-War*, 147–48.
20. WVM to JA, 20 August 1798, *Rotunda*.
21. WVM to JQA, 10 August 1798, *Letters of WVM to John Quincy Adams, 1797–1803*, ed. Worthington Chauncey Ford (Washington, 1914), 453. Hill, *William Vans Murray*, 122–31.
22. WVM to JQA, 31 August 1798, *Letters of WVM*, 462–63. Elkins and McKitrick, *Age of Federalism*, 609, 615, 666–68. DeConde, *Quasi-War*, 147–48.
23. JQA to JA, 25 September 1798. *JQA Letters*, II: 367–68
24. Samuel Flagg Bemis, *John Quincy Adams and the Foundations of American Foreign Policy* (New York: A. A. Knopf, 1949), 100, n59.
25. JA to TP, 20 October 1798, *Rotunda*.
26. "November 1798," *The Diaries of George Washington*, 6: 321–26. *Philadelphia Public Directory*, ed. Cornelius William Stafford. William W. Woodward, 1799. https://archive.org/details/philadelphiadire1798phil/page/112/mode/2up?view=theater. McHenry to GW, 9 November 1798, *PGW*, Retirement Series, 3: 189–90
27. "Notes on an Interview with George Logan and Robert Blackwell, 13 November 1798," *PGW*, Retirement Series, 3: 200–202.

28. "Enclosure: Queries Propounded by the Commander in Chief, [10 November 1798]," *PAH*, 22: 244–46.
29. "Notes on an Interview with George Logan and Robert Blackwell, 13 November 1798," *PGW*, Retirement Series, 3: 200–202.
30. GW to Lawrence Lewis, 2 December 1798, *PGW*, Retirement Series, 3: 241–42. GW to Elizabeth Willing Power, 9 December 1798, *PGW*, Retirement Series, 3: 247–48.
31. McHenry to GW, *PAH*, 22: 239–44.
32. "November 1798," *The Diaries of George Washington*, 6: 321–26. *The Philadelphia Directory*, 1798, https://archive.org/details/philadelphiadire1798phil/page/112/mode/2up?view=theater. Kohn, *Eagle and Sword*, 243–45.
33. Brown, *The Presidency of John Adams*, 84. OW to JA, 26 November 1798; McHenry to JA, 25 November 1798; TP to JA, 27 November 1798, *Rotunda.*
34. BS to JA, 23 November 1798, *Rotunda.*
35. https://iiif.lib.harvard.edu/manifests/view/ids:2568922. National Register of Historic Places Inventory, "Elmwood," National Archives Catalog, https://catalog.archives.gov/id/63793751, accessed March 21, 2023.
36. TP to Goodhue, September 11, 1798, *TPP*, IX, 302. Clarfield, *Timothy Pickering and American Diplomacy,* 183.
37. EG to JA, 20 October 1798, *Rotunda.*
38. EG to JA, 20 October 1798, *Rotunda.*
39. JA to EG, 15 December 1798, *Rotunda.*
40. JA to Francis Dana, 7 November 1798, *Rotunda.*
41. *Boston Russell's Gazette*, 15, 18, 22 October 1798, 15 November 1798; JA to AA, [22] November 1798; Shaw to AA, 25 November, Adams Papers Digital Edition, https://www.masshist.org/publications/adams-papers/.
42. JA to AA, 16 November 1798, *AFC*: 276–77.
43. BS to JA, 25 November 1798, *Rotunda.*
44. "November 1798," *The Diaries of George Washington*, 6: 321–26.
45. Brown, *The Presidency of John Adams*, 85. Federalists condemned these efforts as traitorous and passed legislation, named the Logan Act, prohibiting private citizens from meddling in diplomacy going forward. It is still in effect. *Acts of the Fifth Congress*, https://govtrackus.s3.amazonaws.com/legislink/pdf/stat/1/STATUTE-1-Pg613.pdf. Richard Codman to Harrison Gray Otis, 26 August 1798 in *The Life and Letters of Harrison Gray Otis*, 1: 168–70.
46. Brown, *The Presidency of John Adams*, 86. WSS to AA, 18 December 1798, *AFC*, 13: 311–13.
47. Kurtz, *The Presidency of John Adams*, 324. Brown, *The Presidency of John Adams*, 85.
48. "Communication," *Commercial Advertiser*, November 21, 1798, 3.
49. Fisher Ames to Timothy Pickering, 22 November 1798, Gibbs, *Memoirs of the Administrations of Washington and John Adams*, II: 1297–18.
50. Clarfield, *Timothy Pickering and American Diplomacy*, 185–86.
51. DeConde, *Quasi-War*, 106
52. *Poughkeepsie Journal*, 18 December 1798. Harper, *American Machiavelli*, 229.

53. "Congressional," 24 December 1798, *The Farmer's Weekly Museum: Newhampshire and Vermont Journal*, (Walpole, NH), 2.
54. JA to United States Congress, 8 December 1798, *Rotunda.*
55. Stoddert to JA, 23 November 1798; Stoddert to JA, 25 November 1798, *Rotunda.*
56. McHenry to JA, 25 November 1798, *Rotunda.*
57. TP to JA, 27 November 1798, *Rotunda.*
58. OW to JA, 26 November 1798, *Rotunda.*
59. TP to JA, 27 November 1798, *Rotunda.* Chernow, *Alexander Hamilton*, 593.
60. JA to United States Congress, 8 December 1798, *Rotunda.*
61. "Congressional," 24 December 1798, *The Farmer's Weekly Museum: New Hampshire and Vermont Journal*, (Walpole, NH), 2.
62. John Dawson to JM, 9 December 1798, *PJM*, 18: 183. Chernow, *Alexander Hamilton*, 593.

CHAPTER 15

1. AH to Harrison Gray Otis, 27 December 1798, *PAH*, 22: 393–95.
2. Murphy, "John Adams: The Politics of the Additional Army," 235–37.
3. Kohn, *Eagle and Sword*, 252.
4. Francisco de Miranda to AH, 1 April 1797, *PAH*, 21: 1–3, n1. Chernow, *Alexander Hamilton*, 567–68. Harper, *American Machiavelli*, 210–26. Lycan, *Alexander Hamilton and American Foreign Policy*, 84–89.
5. Brown, *Presidency of John Adams*, 141–48. (LS [deciphered], RG 59, Dispatches from United States Ministers to Great Britain, 1791–1906. Vol. 7, 9 January–22 December 1798, National Archives, Washington, D.C.
6. Copy [deciphered], RG 59, Despatches from United States Ministers to Great Britain, 1791–1906. Vol. 7, January 9–December 22, 1798, National Archives, Washington, D.C. Francisco de Miranda, 7 February 1798, *PAH*, 21: 348–50. Dauer, *The Adams Federalists*, 178–84.
7. Clarfield, *Timothy Pickering and American Diplomacy*, 146–47. Lycan, *Alexander Hamilton and American Foreign Policy*, 384–95.
8. Dauer, *Adams Federalists*, 187. Harper, *American Machiavelli*, 210–26.
9. Liston to Grenville, 27 September 1798, Public Record Office (PRO), Foreign Office (FO) 5/11, 155- 61, Great Britain, cited in Dauer, *Adams Federalists*, 183.
10. Dauer, *Adams Federalists*, 188. Harper, *American Machiavelli*, 210–26. Lycan, *Alexander Hamilton and American Foreign Policy*, 384–95.
11. Lycan, *Alexander Hamilton and American Foreign Policy*, 377.
12. AH to Harrison Gray Otis, 26 January 1799, *PAH*, 22: 440–42.
13. AH to Harrison Gray Otis, 26 January 1799, *PAH*, 22: 440–42. Chernow, *Alexander Hamilton*, 567–68. Kohn, *Eagle and Sword*, 231–37. Harper, *American Machiavelli*, 210–26. Lycan, *Alexander Hamilton and American Foreign Policy*, 384–95.
14. TS to AH, 7 February 1799, *PAH*, 22: 469–72.

15. Douglas Bradburn, *Citizenship Revolution*, 176–77.
16. AA to JA, 23 December 1798, *AFC*, 13: 319–21.
17. Albert Gallatin, *A Sketch of the Finances of the United States* (New York: W. A. Davis, 1796), 49–56.
18. Adams wrote about the potential for rebellion in 1809 in his articles for the *Boston Patriot* but made similar sentiments to contemporaries in 1799. Kurtz, *The Presidency of John Adams*, 360. Kohn, *Eagle and Sword*, 252–55.
19. McHenry to GW, 31 March 1799, *PGW*, Retirement Series, 3: 453–58.
20. For example, see JA to BS, 20 May 1799, *Rotunda*.
21. JA to BS, 31 May 179, *Rotunda*.
22. JA to AA, 1 January 1799; 10 January 1799, *AFC*, 13: 337–38, 346–48.
23. AA to William Smith Shaw, 25 January 1799, *AFC*: 13: 375–77. Clarfield, *Timothy Pickering and American Diplomacy*, 180–86, 197–200.
24. "Memorandum by Elbridge Gerry of a Conversation with JA, 26 March 1799," *Rotunda*.
25. TP to GW, 2 February 1799, *PGW*, Retirement Series, 3: 355–56. Kurtz, *The Presidency of John Adams*, 342–53.
26. AA to JA, 14 February 1799, *AFC*: 13: 402–3.
27. United States Constitution, National Archives.
28. George Cabot to RK, 7 February 1799, *CRK*, III: 536.
29. Edel, Charles N. *Nation Builder: John Quincy Adams and the Grand Strategy of the Republic* (Cambridge, MA: Harvard University Press, 2014), 83.
30. Samuel Flagg Bemis, *John Quincy Adams and the Foundations of American Foreign Policy* (New York: Alfred A. Knopf, 1951), 100–103. James Traub, *John Quincy Adams: Militant Spirit* (New York: Basic Books, 2016), 102. Edel, *Nation Builder*, 87. Smith, *John Adams*, II: 996.
31. JQA to AA, 8 October 1798," *AFC*, 13: 250–55.
32. John Quincy Adams, *Letter-press* copies, 26 December 1795–30 May 1801, Reel 133, Adams Papers, MHS.
33. AA to JA, 6 January 1799; JA to AA, 10 January 1799, *AFC*, 13: 342–43, 346–48.
34. JA to AA, 13 January 1799, *AFC*, 13: 353–54.
35. JA to AA, 16 January 1799, *AFC*, 13: 363–64.
36. William Smith Shaw to AA, 15 January 1799, *AFC*, 13: 359–61.
37. William Smith Shaw to AA, 15 January 1799, *AFC*, 13: 359–61.
38. JA to AA, 16 January 1799, *AFC*, 13: 363–64.
39. JA to TP, 15 January 1799, *Rotunda*. Bemis, *John Quincy Adams and the Foundations of American Foreign Policy*, 101. Traub, *John Quincy Adams*, 102.
40. GW to JA, 1 February 1799, *PGW*, Retirement Series, 3: 350–51.
41. Brown, *The Presidency of John Adams*, 95. Kurtz, *Presidency of John Adams*, 347. Elkins and McKitrick, *Age of Federalism*, 617.
42. *AOC*, 5th Congress, 3d Session, 3045–46.

43. TS to AH, 7 February 1799, *PAH*, 22: 469–72. Elkins and McKitrick, *Age of Federalism*, 616–17.
44. TS to AH, 7 February 1799, *PAH*, 22: 469–72. Elkins and McKitrick, *Age of Federalism*, 616–17.
45. "Memorandum by Elbridge Gerry of a Conversation with JA, 26 March 1799," *Rotunda*.
46. *AOC*, 5th Congress, 3d Session, 3045–46.
47. WVM to JA, 7 October 1798, *Rotunda*. Kurtz, *The Presidency of John Adams*, 342–53.
48. DeConde, *The Quasi-War*, 158–59.
49. TJ to JM, 19 February 1799, *PTJ*, 17: 233–36. WVM to JA, 7 October 1798 *Rotunda*. Elkins and McKitrick, *Age of Federalism*, 616–17.
50. Brown, *The Presidency of John Adams*, 95. Elkins and McKitrick, *Age of Federalism*, 616–17.
51. TJ to JM, 19 February 1799, *PTJ*, 17: 233–36.
52. Morison, *Harrison Gray Otis*, I: 159. Smith, *John Adams*, II: 999–1001.

CHAPTER 16

1. JA to GW, 19 February 1799, *Rotunda*. Brown, *The Presidency of John Adams*, 97.
2. TP to GW, 21 February 1799, *PGW*, Retirement Series, 3: 389–91. Elkins and McKitrick, *Age of Federalism*, 618–19.
3. TS to AH, 19 February 1799, *PAH*, 22: 487–90. Smith, *John Adams*, II: 999–1001.
4. JA to AA, 25 February 1799, *AFC*, 13: 418–19.
5. TBA to JA, 1 March 1799, *AFC*, 13: 423–26.
6. AA to JA, 27 February 1799, *AFC*, 13: 421–23. Holton, *Abigail Adams*, 326–27.
7. TP to GW, 21 February 1799, *PGW*, Retirement Series, 3: 389–91. Elkins and McKitrick, *Age of Federalism*, 619. Lycan, *Alexander Hamilton and American Foreign Policy*, 396. DeConde, *Quasi-War*, 184–85.
8. John Rutherfurd to TS, 27 February 1799, *TSP*, Box 7, Folder 9.
9. AA to Catherine Nuth Johnson, 20 August 1800, *AFC*, 14: 380–84.
10. JA to AA, 22 February 1799, *AFC*, 415–16. Elkins and McKitrick, *Age of Federalism*, 619. Lycan, *Alexander Hamilton and American Foreign Policy*, 396. DeConde, *Quasi-War*, 184–85.
11. JA to AA, 22 February 1799, *AFC*, 415–16. Bemis, *John Quincy Adams and the Foundations of American Foreign Policy*, 102.
12. TP to GW, 21 February 1799, *PGW*, Retirement Series, 3: 389–91.
13. JA to AA, 22 February 1799, *AFC*, 415–16.
14. TS to Henry Van Schaack, 25 February 1799; TS to Henry Van Schaack, 26 February 1799, *TSP*, Box 5, Folder 1. Brown, *The Presidency of John Adams*, 100. DeConde, *Quasi-War*, 184–85.
15. JA to United States Senate, *Rotunda*. Elkins and McKitrick, *Age of Federalism*, 619.
16. Elkins and McKitrick, *Age of Federalism*, 619.

17. Henry Knox to JA, 5 March 1799, *Rotunda.*
18. CL to JA, 14 March 1799, *Rotunda.* DeConde, *Quasi-War*, 184–85. Smith, *John Marshall*, 252n, 255.
19. Bemis, *John Quincy Adams and the Foundations of American Foreign Policy*, 102.
20. JA to CL, 29 March 1799, *Rotunda.*

CHAPTER 17

1. *AOC*, 5th Cong. 3d Session, 2985.
2. AH to TS, 2 February 1799, *PAH*, 22: 452–54.
3. TJ to JM, 26 February 1799, *PJM*, 17: 243–45.
4. *AOC*, 5th Cong. 3d Session, 3001–15. Malone, *Jefferson and the Ordeal of Liberty*, 414.
5. John W. Kuehl, "Southern Reaction to the XYZ Affair: An Incident in the Emergence of American Nationalism," *Register of the Kentucky Historical Society* 70, no. 1 (January 1972): 29–30.
6. Bird, *Criminal Dissent*, 121–28.
7. Paul Douglas Newman, *Fries's Rebellion: The Enduring Struggle for the American Revolution* (Philadelphia: University of Pennsylvania Press, 2005), 97. Simon Newman, "The World Turned Upside Down: Revolutionary Politics, Fries' and Gabriel's Rebellions, and the Fears of the Federalists," *Pennsylvania History* 67, no. 1 (Winter 2000): 7.
8. Newman, *Fries's Rebellion*, 119. Newman, "The World Turned Upside Down: Revolutionary Politics, Fries' and Gabriel's Rebellions, and the Fears of the Federalists," 7.
9. Newman, *Fries's Rebellion*, 119–21. Elkins and McKitrick, *Age of Federalism*, 696–700.
10. Newman, *Fries's Rebellion*, 135. Paul Douglas Newman, "The Federalists' Cold War: The Fries Rebellion, National Security, and the State, 1787–1800," *Pennsylvania History* 67, no. 1 (Winter 2000), 89. "Another Insurrection," *Gazette of the United States, and Philadelphia Daily Advertiser* (Philadelphia, PA), 11 March 1799, 3.
11. Kurtz, *The Presidency of John Adams*, 358–59. Robert H. Churchill, "Popular Nullification, Fries' Rebellion, and the Waning of Radical Republicanism, 1798–1801," *Pennsylvania History* 67, no. 1 (Winter 2000): 111.
12. Newman, *Fries's Rebellion*, 133. "Another Insurrection," *Gazette of the United States, and Philadelphia Daily Advertiser*, Philadelphia, PA, 11 March 1799, 3.
13. Newman, *Fries's Rebellion*, 140. Chernow, *Alexander Hamilton*, 578–79.
14. "Columbian Intelligence. Pennsylvania. Philad, March 25." *Farmer's Museum or Lay Preacher's Gazette* (Walpole, NH), 8 April 1799, 3. Newman, *Fries's Rebellion*, 141. Elkins and McKitrick, *Age of Federalism*, 696–700. Newman, "The Federalists' Cold War: The Fries Rebellion, National Security, and the State, 1787–1800," 89.
15. JA to AA, 7 March 1799, *AFC*, 13: 433.

16. JA to TP, 9 March 1799, *Rotunda.*
17. Brown, *The Presidency of John Adams*, 101.
18. Newman, *Fries's Rebellion*, 143.
19. "Proclamation on Insurrection in Pennsylvania, 12 March 1799," *Rotunda.* Newman, *Fries Rebellion*, 145.
20. McHenry to AH, 13 March 1799, *PAH*, 22: 529–32. Elkins and McKitrick, *Age of Federalism*, 696–700.
21. Newman, *Fries's Rebellion*, 145. Kohn, *Eagle and Sword*, 251. Francis Wharton. *State Trials during the Administrations of Washington and Adams* (Philadelphia: Carey and Hart, 1849), 459.
22. *Gazette of the United States*, (Philadelphia, PA) 15, no. 2021, 11 March 1799, 3. Newman, *Fries's Rebellion*, 142. Elkins and McKitrick, *Age of Federalism*, 696–700.
23. JA to AA, 11 March 1799, *AFC*, 13: 435.
24. Brown, *The Presidency of John Adams*, 101.

CHAPTER 18

1. Newman, *Fries's Rebellion*, 144.
2. Memorandum from General MacPherson, 25 March 1799, MacPherson Manuscripts, Military Papers, Correspondence, March–April 1799, Historical Society of Pennsylvania. Newman, *Fries's Rebellion*, 149.
3. James Iredell to Hannah Iredell, 14 March 1799, *Documentary History of the Supreme Court*, ed. Maeva Marcus, 3:324 in Bird, *Criminal Dissent*, 187–88.
4. OW to Frederick Wolcott, 2 April 1799 in Gibbs, *Administrations of Washington and John Adams*, II: 230.
5. *Gazette of the United States*,(Philadelphia, PA) 15, no. 2059, 26 April 1799,3.
6. JA to AA, 7 May 1799, *AFC*, 13: 463–68. Newman, "The World Turned Upside Down: Revolutionary Politics, Fries' and Gabriel's Rebellions, and the Fears of the Federalists," 8–15.
7. TP to JA, 24 July 1799, *Rotunda*. Elkins and McKitrick, *Age of Federalism*, 696–700.
8. Newman, *Fries's Rebellion*, 153.
9. Newman, *Fries's Rebellion*, 153.
10. AH to McHenry, 18 March 1799, Harper, *American Machiavelli*, 235. OW to AH, 1 April 1799, *PAH*, 23: 1–3.
11. Wharton, *State Trials*, 459.
12. OW to JA, 25 March 1799, *Rotunda.*
13. BS to JA, 26 March 1799, *Rotunda*. Elkins and McKitrick, *Age of Federalism*, 696–700. Newman, "The Federalists' Cold War: The Fries Rebellion, National Security, and the State, 1787–1800," 91.
14. McHenry to JA, 16 March 1799, *Rotunda.*

15. McHenry to JA, 5 April 1799, *Rotunda.*
16. Newman, *Fries's Rebellion*, 155
17. "Extract of a letter from an officer . . ." *Aurora*, 8 April 1799, 3. Newman, *Fries's Rebellion*, 157–58. Jane Shaffer Elsmere, "The Trials of John Fries," *Pennsylvania Magazine of History of Biography* 103, no. 4 (October 1979): 435–36.
18. "Philadelphia, April 8," *Kentucky Gazette* (Lexington, KY), 2 May 1799, 3. Newman, *Fries's Rebellion*, 161. Elkins and McKitrick, *Age of Federalism*, 696–700.
19. Bird, *Criminal Dissents*, 189.
20. McHenry to JA, 11 April 1799, *Rotunda.*
21. Newman, *Fries's Rebellion*, 159.
22. Newman, *Fries's Rebellion*, 160. Elkins and McKitrick, *Age of Federalism*, 696–700.
23. Bird, *Criminal Dissents*, 189.
24. "The trial of the Insurgents . . ." *Wilkesbarre Gazette and Luzerne Advertiser* (Wilkes-Barre, PA), 7 May 1799, 2.
25. *State Trials*, 479–80. Newman, *Fries's Rebellion*, 207. Elkins and McKitrick, *Age of Federalism*, 696–700. Elsmere, "The Trials of John Fries," 437–45.
26. TP to JA, 10 May 1799, *Rotunda.*
27. Newman, *Fries's Rebellion*, 210.
28. *State Trials*, 597. Newman, *Fries's Rebellion*, 172.
29. TP to JA, 10 May 1799, *Rotunda.*
30. OW to JA, 25 May 1799, *Rotunda.* DeConde, *Quasi-War*, 198–99.
31. JA to CL, 17 May 1799, *Rotunda.*
32. JA to OW, 17 May 1799, *Rotunda.* Smith, *John Adams*, II: 1006–7. DeConde, *Quasi-War*, 198–99.
33. Edmund Randolph to GW, 21 July 1795, *PGW*, Presidential Series, 18: 392–94, n3. TP to GW, 2 November 1795, *PGW*, Presidential Series, 19: 113–14, n1.
34. GW to US Senate and House of Representatives, 8 December 1795, *PGW*, Presidential Series, 19: 221–27.
35. Kurtz, *The Presidency of John Adams*, 358–61.
36. CL to JA, 28 May 1799, *Rotunda.*
37. TP to JA, 10 May 1799, *Rotunda.*
38. Bird, *Criminal Dissents*, 213. CL to JA, 28 May 1799, *Rotunda.*
39. JA to TP, 17 May 1799, *Rotunda.* Smith, *John Adams*, II: 1006–7. DeConde, *Quasi-War*, 198–99.

CHAPTER 19

1. Troup to RK, 6 May 1799, *CRK*, III: 14. Chauncey Goodrich, April 1799 in Gibbs, *Administrations of Washington and John Adams*, II: 232–33
2. TP to RK, 12 March 1799, *CRK*, II: 557–58.

3. For examples of Washington's summer schedule, see GW to TJ, 4 July 1793, *PTJ*, 26: 436–37. "For August [1795]," *Diaries of George Washington*, 6: 208–9. GW to James Anderson, 18 August 1796, *PGW*, Presidential Series, 20: 590–92.
4. TP to JA, 4 April 1799, *Rotunda*.
5. Ronald Angelo Johnson, *Diplomacy in Black and White: John Adams, Toussaint Louverture, and Their Atlantic World Alliance* (Athens: University of Georgia Press, 2014), 14–16, 48–53.
6. Perry, James, *Arrogant Armies: Great Military Disasters and the Generals Behind Them* (Edison, NJ: Castle Books, 2005), 69.
7. Johnson, *Diplomacy in Black and White*, 42–45.
8. TP to JA, 5 April 1799, *Rotunda*. Johnson, *Diplomacy in Black and White*, 42–45.
9. TP to JA, 5 April 1799, *Rotunda*. Clarfield, *Timothy Pickering and American Diplomacy*, 148–49.
10. JA to TP, 14 April 1799, *Rotunda*.
11. DeConde, *Quasi-War*, 120.
12. *Philadelphia Public Directory*, ed., Cornelius William Stafford (William W. Woodward, 1799), 86.
13. TP to JA, 23 April 1799, *Rotunda*.
14. TP to JA, 23 April 1799, *Rotunda*.
15. JA to TP, 1 May 1799, *Rotunda*.
16. TP to JA, 7 June 1799, *Rotunda*.
17. JA to TP, 15 June 1799, *Rotunda*.
18. TP to JA, 22 June 1799. TP to JA, 24 June 1799, *Rotunda*.
19. TP to JA, 27 June 1799, *Rotunda*.
20. TP to JA, 27 June 1799, *Rotunda*.
21. "Proc. Open. Trade W/ Cert. Pts. of St. Domingo, 26 June 1799." TP to JA, 27 June 1799, *Rotunda*.
22. TBA to AA, 8 August 1799, *AFC*, 13: 533–36, n2. Dunn, *Jefferson's Second Revolution*, 113.
23. Pasley, *The Tyranny of Printers*, 94. Bird, *Criminal Dissents*, 227.
24. Pasley, *The Tyranny of Printers*, 176–91. Bird, *Criminal Dissents*, 229. Bradburn, *Citizenship Revolution*, 182.
25. Capitalization in original. "May 16, 1799," *Aurora* . Pasley, *The Tyranny of Printers*, 176–91. Bird, *Criminal Dissents*, 364.
26. TP to JA, 24 July 1799, *Rotunda*.
27. JA to TP, 1 August 1799, *Rotunda*.
28. TP to JA, 1 August 1799, *Rotunda*.
29. TP to JA, 24 July 1799, *Rotunda*.
30. Bird, *Criminal Dissents*, 231.
31. "William Duane . . ." *Gazette of the United States, and Philadelphia Daily Advertiser* (Philadelphia, PA), 3 August 3 1799, 3. Bird, *Criminal Dissents*, 232.

32. Patrick Henry to JA, 16 April 1799. JA to TP, 8 May 1799. TP to JA, 15 May 1799. TP to JA, 29 June 1799, *Rotunda.*
33. WVM to TP, 13 April 1799, *Letters of WVM*, 538.
34. WVM to JQA, 7 May 1799, *Letters of WVM*, 549.
35. WVM to Talleyrand, 18 May 1799, *Letters of WVM*, 553.
36. TP to WVM, 10 July 1799, *Letters of WVM*, 573–74.
37. TP to JA, 29 July 1799, *Rotunda.*
38. TP to JA, 31 July 1799, *Rotunda.*
39. Brown, *The Presidency of John Adams*, 104.
40. JA to TP, 6 August 1799, *Rotunda.*
41. Brown, *The Presidency of John Adams*, 107.
42. TP to Cabot, 13 September 1799, *Life and Letters of George Cabot*, 236–37.
43. Brown, *The Presidency of John Adams*, 108. Clarfield, *Timothy Pickering and American Diplomacy*, 208.
44. Uriah Forrest to JA, 28 April 1799, *Rotunda.*
45. JA to Uriah Forrest, 13 May 1799, *Rotunda.*

CHAPTER 20

1. TS to RK, 26 July 1799, *TSP*, Box 3, Folder 23.
2. DeConde, *Quasi-War*, 130. Elkins and McKitrick, *Age of Federalism*, 653.
3. DeConde, *Quasi-War*, 128–30. Elkins and McKitrick, *Age of Federalism*, 654.
4. BS to JA, 14 August 1799, *Rotunda*. Stephen Kurtz, "The French Mission of 1799–1800: Concluding Chapter in the Statecraft of John Adams," *Political Science Quarterly* 80, no. 4 (December 1965): 543–57.
5. McHenry to JA, 29 June 1799, *Rotunda.*
6. JA to McHenry, 7 July 1799, *Rotunda.*
7. For one example of an officer returning his commission, see Samuel Osburn to AH, 7 August 1799, *PAH*, Digital Edition, https://founders.archives.gov/documents/Hamilton/02-01-02-0807. Kurtz, *The Presidency of John Adams*, 334–35, 367–73.
8. Popkin, *A New World Begins*, 512–17.
9. Clarfield, *Timothy Pickering and American Diplomacy*, 206–7. DeConde, *Quasi-War*, 207.
10. McHenry to GW, 5 August 1799, *PGW*, Retirement Series, 4: 223–24.
11. BS to JA, 17 August 1799, *Rotunda.*
12. BS to JA, 24 August 1799, *Rotunda.*
13. "State House, Trenton, August–November 1797, 1798, 1799," Office of the Historian, Department of State, https://history.state.gov/departmenthistory/buildings/section18, accessed March 3, 2023.
14. Kate Mason Rowland, "Philadelphia a Century Ago," *Lippincott's Monthly Magazine*, December 1898, 804.
15. BS to JA, 29 August 1799, *Rotunda*. Smith, *John Adams*, II: 1012–13.

16. TP to JA, 10 September 1799, *Rotunda*.
17. TP to JA, 11 September 1799, *Rotunda*. Smith, *John Adams*, II: 1012–14.
18. BS to JA, 13 September 1799, *Rotunda*.
19. "The Jay Treaty: Appointment and Instructions: Editorial Note," *Selected Papers of John Jay*, 5: 609–21.
20. JA to TP, 19 September 1799, *Rotunda*.
21. Smith, *John Adams*, II: 1012–14.
22. Oliver Ellsworth to JA, 18 September 1799, *Rotunda*.
23. JA to Oliver Ellsworth, 22 September 1799, *Rotunda*.
24. Cabot to RK, 23 September 1799, *CRK*, III: 110–11. Kurtz, *The Presidency of John Adams*, 389.
25. JA to TP, 21 September 1799, *Rotunda*.
26. TP to JA, 24 September 1799, *Rotunda*.
27. Uriah Forrest to JA, 28 April 1799, *Rotunda*.
28. G. Cabot to RK, October 6, 1799. JA to BS, 21 September 1799, *Rotunda*. Brown, *Presidency of John Adams*, 109. Smith, *John Adams*, II: 1012–14.
29. TP to GW, 29 September 1799, *PGW*, Retirement Series, 4: 330.
30. George Cabot to Rufus King, 16 October 1799, *CRK*, III: 134–35.
31. Smith, *John Adams*, II: 1015. Chernow, *Alexander Hamilton*, 597–98.
32. "Charles Adams," Massachusetts Historical Society, https://www.masshist.org/adams/biographies#CA, accessed March 6, 2023.
33. AA to MSC, 31 October 1799, *AFC*, 14: 44–45.
34. Stephen Fried, *Rush: Revolution, Madness, and Benjamin Rush, the Visionary Doctor Who Became a Founding Father* (New York: Crown, 2018).
35. JA to AA, 12 October 1799, *AFC*, 14: 6. Holton, *Abigail Adams*, 327.
36. JA to AA, 12 October 1799; William Smith Shaw to AA, 12 October 1799, AFC, 14: 6–7. JA to AA, 30 October 1799, *AFC*, 14: 43, n1.
37. William J. Backes. *A History of Trenton, 1679–1929*. Trenton: Trenton Historical Society, 1929. T. Gordon, "Map of Trenton, 1800," J. F. and C. A. Watson, Lithrs. No. 62 Walnut Street Philadelphia.
38. JA to BS, 21 September 1799, *Rotunda*. JA to TP, 21 September 1799, *Rotunda*. TP to Ellsworth, 4 October 1799, *TPP*.
39. AH to James Wilkinson, 3 August 1799, *PAH*, 23: 303–5.
40. Smith, *John Adams*, II: 1015–17. Chernow, *Alexander Hamilton*, 597–98.
41. JA to TP, 21 September 1799, *Rotunda*.
42. Ferling, *John Adams*, 384–85.
43. Chernow, *Alexander Hamilton*, 597–98. Ferling, *Jefferson and Hamilton*, 310–11.
44. AA to MSC, 30 December 1799, *AFC*, 14: 92–95. Elkins and McKitrick, *Age of Federalism*, 640. Smith, *John Adams*, II: 1015–17. Chernow, *Alexander Hamilton*, 597–98. Ferling, *Jefferson and Hamilton*, 310–11.
45. JA to AA, 30 October 1799, *AFC*, 14: 43. The evidence surrounding this pivotal meeting is limited. Hamilton made only passing references to it in later documents,

and Adams's most complete description came a decade later. However, the description Abigail included in a letter to her sister on December 30, 1799 matches John's account many years later. Elkins and McKitrick, who usually can be relied to judge Adams harshly, determined that the account is fairly accurate, though readers won't be faulted for wanting to take Adams with a grain of salt. Elkins and McKitrick, *Age of Federalism*, 639–41.

46. JA to TP, 16 October 1799, *Rotunda*.
47. JA to BS, 16 October 1799, *Rotunda*.
48. This argument is made most persuasively by Stephen G. Kurtz, "The French Mission of 1799–800: Concluding Chapter in the Statecraft of John Adams," *Political Science Quarterly* 80, no. 4 (December 1965): 543–57.
49. "November 11, 1799," *Jenk's Portland Gazette*, Portland, ME, 3. Dauer, *Adams Federalists*, 240.
50. Cabot to RK, 9 November, 1799, *CRK*, III: 144.
51. Cabot to RK, 26 April 1799, *CRK*, III: 8–9.
52. Fisher Ames to TP, 19 October 1799,*Works of Fisher Ames*, ed. Seth Ames (Carmel, IN: Liberty Classics, 1983), II: 1317.
53. McHenry to GW, 10 November 1799, *PGW*, Retirement Series, 4: 397–402. Lycan, *Alexander Hamilton and American Foreign Policy*, 402.

CHAPTER 21

1. JA to AA, 30 October 1799, *AFC*, 14: 43.
2. AA to JA, 13 October 1799; AA to JA, 20 October 1799; JA to AA, 25 October 1799, *AFC*, 14: 8–9, 21–22, 38.
3. AA to MSC, 11 December 1790, *AFC*, 14: 73–75. Ferling, *John Adams*, 386. Smith, *John Adams*, II: 1017–19.
4. OW to either Henry Knox or Jedediah Morse, 2 January 1800. Oliver Wolcott Jr. Papers, Connecticut Historical Society.
5. Smith, *John Marshall*, 241. R. Kent Newmyer, *John Marshall and the Heroic Age of the Supreme Court* (Baton Rouge: Louisiana State University Press, 2007), 118.
6. "Richmond, May 7," 29 May 1799, *The North American*, Philadelphia, 2. Jean Edward Smith. *John Marshall: Definer of a Nation* (New York: Henry Holt, 1996), 245–47.
7. "Richmond, May 7," 29 May 1799, *The North American*, (Philadelphia, PA), 2. Editorial Note: Congressional Career, *JMO*.
8. "The Gazette," 30 April 1799, *The North American*, Philadelphia, 3. Editorial Note: Congressional Career, *JMO*. Smith, *John Marshall*, 248–50.
9. Smith, *John Marshall*, 252.
10. *AOC*, 6th Congress, 1st Session, 192–94.
11. Smith, *John Marshall*, 252–55.
12. *AOC*, 6th Congress, 1st Session, 198.

13. OW to Fisher Ames, 29 December 1799, Gibbs, *Memoirs of the Administrations of Washington and John Adams*, 313–14.
14. *AOC*, 6th Congress, 1st Session, 203. Smith, *John Marshall*, 255.
15. Tobias Lear to JA, 15 December 1799, *Rotunda*.
16. JA to United States Army, 18 December 1799, *Rotunda*.
17. *AOC*, 6th Congress, 1st Session, 203–4. Dunn, *Jefferson's Second Revolution*, 122–25
18. *AOC*, 6th Congress, 1st Session, 206.
19. JA to United States House of Representatives, 19 December 1799, *Rotunda*.
20. *AOC*, 6th Congress, 1st Session, 207–8.
21. Harrison Gray Otis to Sally Otis, 26 December 1799, in Samuel Eliot Morison, *Harrison Gray Otis, 1765–1848: The Urbane Federalist* (Boston: Houghton Mifflin, 1969), 141.
22. *AOC*, 6th Congress, 1st Session, 210.
23. AA to MSC, 7 January 1799, *AFC*, 14: 98–100.
24. Editorial Note on John Marshall's Congressional Career, *JMO*.
25. AA to MSC, 30 December 1799, *AFC*, 14: 92–95.
26. Mary Thompson, "In a Private Manner, without Parade or Funeral Oration: The Funeral George Washington wanted, But Didn't Get," *Mourning the Presidents: Loss and Legacy in American Culture*, ed. Lindsay M. Chervinsky and Matthew R. Costello (Charlottesville: University of Virginia Press, 2023), 11–32.
27. John Marshall, Resolution, 30 December 1799, *JMO*.
28. AA to MSC, 27 February 1800, *AFC*, 14: 158–61. Smith, *John Adams*, II: 1021.
29. AA to MSC, 28 January 1800, *AFC*, 14: 114–17.
30. JA to William Stephens Smith, 3 March 1800, Reel 120, Letterbook 32, Adams Papers, MHS, cited in Jonathan Horn. *Washington's End: The Final Years and Forgotten Struggle* (New York: Scribner, 2020), 206.
31. AH to Tobias Lear, 2 January 1800, *PAH*, 24: 155.
32. Liston, 19 December 1799 in Bradford Perkins, "A Diplomat's Wife in Philadelphia: Letters of Henrietta Liston, 1796–1800," *William and Mary Quarterly* 11, no. 4 (October 1954): 628.

CHAPTER 22

1. TP to *WVM*, 4 October 1799, *Letters of WVM*, 600–602.
2. TP to *WVM*, 25 October 1799, *Letters of WVM*, 610–12.
3. WVM to JQA, 29 November 1799, *Letters of WVM*, 622.
4. JQA to WVM, 15 December 1799, *Writings of JQA*, II: 444.
5. JQA to WVM, 6 January 1800, *Writings of JQA*, II: 446.
6. WVM to TP, 1 December 1799, *Letters of WVM*, 623.
7. Ames to TP, 19 October 1799, *Works of Fisher Ames*, I: 254. Dauer, *Adams Federalists*, 243.
8. Bird, *Criminal Dissents*, 233.
9. Smith, *Freedom's Fetters*, 285–86. *Aurora*, October 22, 1799.

10. TS to RK, 29 December 1799, *TSP*, Box 3, Folder 23. Elkins and McKitrick, *Age of Federalism*, 730.
11. *AOC*, 6th Congress, 1st Session, 227.
12. Harrison Gray Otis to Sally Otis, *Harrison Gray Otis*, I: 179.
13. *AOC*, 6th Congress, 1st Session, 247–48. Kohn, *Eagle and Sword*, 260.
14. Kohn, *Eagle and Sword*, 261.
15. *AOC*, 6th Congress, 1st Session, 252.
16. Marshall to Charles Dabney, 20 January 1800, *JMO*. Smith, *John Marshall*, 257.
17. Everyone except Thomas Jefferson. They hated each other.
18. Smith, *John Marshall*, 248.
19. TS to RK, 29 December 1799, *TSP*, Box 3, Folder 23.
20. Editorial Note: Congressional Career, *JMO*. US *House Journal*. 17980. 5th Cong., 2nd sess., 9 July.
21. *AOC*, 6th Congress, 1st Session, 369.
22. *AOC*, 6th Congress, 1st Session, 375–75.
23. TJ to Thomas Mann Randolph, 13 January 1800, *PTJ*, 31: 304–7.
24. *AOC*, 6th Congress, 1st Session, 375–425. Smith, *John Marshall*, 257. Kohn, *Eagle and Sword*, 261–63.
25. Malone, *Ordeal of Liberty*, 463.
26. Smith, *Freedom Fetters*, 288–89. Elkins and McKitrick, *Age of Federalism*, 730.
27. TJ to James Monroe, 16 February 1800, *PTJ*, 31: 381–82. James Roger Sharp, *The Deadlocked Election of 1800: Jefferson, Burr, and the Union in the Balance* (Lawrence: University Press of Kansas, 2010), 187–88. Bernard A. Weisberger, *America Afire: Jefferson, Adams, and the First Contested Election* (New York: HarperCollins, 2011), 235–36.
28. The Pinckneys had a confusing habit of recycling names even within the same generation.
29. *AOC*, Senate, 6th Congress, 1st Session, 128–29.
30. "Philadelphia," 19 February 1800, *Aurora*, 2.
31. "February 19, 1800," *Aurora*; "March 1800," *Aurora*, 2. Bird, *Criminal Dissents*, 236. Edward J. Larson, *A Magnificent Catastrophe: The Tumultuous Election of 1800, America's First Presidential Campaign* (New York: Free Press, 2007), 79–81. Dunn, *Jefferson's Second Revolution*, 171–72.
32. Katlyn Marie Carter. *Democracy in Darkness: Secrecy and Transparency in the Age of Revolutions* (New Haven: Yale University Press, 2023), 228–30.
33. United States Constitution, National Archives and Records Administration.
34. Smith, *Freedom's Fetters*, 289–91.
35. Smith, *Freedom's Fetters*, 289–91. Carter, *Democracy in Darkness*, 228–30.
36. 29 March 1800, *Aurora*, 2. *AOC*, Senate, 6th Congress, 1st Session, 63. Pasley, *Tyranny of the Printers*, 190.
37. Smith, *Freedom's Fetters*, 291–94. Sharp, *The Deadlocked Election of 1800*, 187–88. Weisberger, *America Afire*, 235–36. Dunn, *Jefferson's Second Revolution*, 172–73.

38. "Form of the Warrant issued by the Senate for the apprehension of William Duane," 29 March 1800, *The North American*, (Philadelphia, PA), 3.
39. Malone, *Ordeal of Liberty*, 466.
40. *AOC*, Senate, 6th Congress, 1st Session, 68–96, 116.
41. "To A. J. Dallas, Esq.," 27 March 1800, *Aurora*, 2. Thomas Cooper to William Duane, 25 March 1800, *American State Papers*, cited in Bird, *Criminal Dissents*, 237. *AOC*, Senate, 6th Congress, 1st Session, 121–22. Smith, *Freedom's Fetters*, 297. Larson, *A Magnificent Catastrophe*, 81–82. Dunn, *Jefferson's Second Revolution*, 172–73. Carter, *Democracy in Darkness*, 228–30.
42. "Form of the Warrant," 31 March 1800, *Aurora*, 3.
43. TJ to JM, 4 April 1800, *PJM*, 17: 378–79. Weisberger, *America Afire*, 235–36.
44. Smith, *Freedom's Fetters*, 298. Larson, *A Magnificent Catastrophe*, 81–82.
45. Smith, *Freedom's Fetters*, 287.
46. Bird, *Criminal Dissents*, 235.
47. Marshall to James Markham Marshall, 4 April 1800, *JMO*.
48. *AOC*, 6th Congress, 1st Session, 693. Smith, *John Marshall*, 264.
49. *AOC*, Senate, 6th Congress, 1st Session, 175–77. Dauer, *Adams Federalists*, 244.
50. *AOC*, 6th Congress, 1st Session, 720.
51. *AOC*, Senate, 6th Congress, 1st Session, 183. "Philadelphia, May 15," 21 May 1800, *Lancaster Intelligencer*, (Lancaster, PA), 3. "Raleigh," 27 May 1800, *Weekly Raleigh Register*, (Raleigh, NC), 3.

CHAPTER 23

1. "Extract of a letter, dated New York, March 31," April 3, 1800, *Aurora*, 2.
2. Harper, *American Machiavelli*, 253. Dunn, *Jefferson's Second Revolution*, 176–81. Bernard A. Weisberger, *America Afire: Jefferson, Adams, and the First Contested Election* (New York: HarperCollins, 2011), 94–95. Ferling, *Adams vs. Jefferson*, 130–31.
3. Sharp, James Roger. *The Deadlocked Election of 1800: Jefferson, Burr, and the Union in the Balance* (Lawrence: University Press of Kansas, 2010), 85–87. Harper, *American Machiavelli*, 253.
4. "Extract of a letter, dated New York, March 31," 3 April 1800, *Aurora*, 2.
Sharp, *The Deadlocked Election of 1800*, 86–87. Larson, *A Magnificent Catastrophe*, 99–101.
5. "Philadelphia," 6 May 1800, *Aurora*, 2. Sharp, *The Deadlocked Election of 1800*, 86–87. Larson, *A Magnificent Catastrophe*, 101. Dunn, *Jefferson's Second Revolution*, 176–81. Weisberger, *America Afire*, 94–95. Ferling, *Adams vs. Jefferson*, 130–31.
6. "Philadelphia," May 6, 1800, *Aurora*, 2.
7. AA to Abigail Adams Smith, 4 May 1800, *AFC*, 14: 224–27. "Philadelphia," May 6, 1800, *Aurora*, 2. Harper, *American Machiavelli*, 254.

8. Anonymous to JA, 11 March 1800, *Rotunda.*
9. Anonymous to JA, 19 March 1800, *Rotunda.*
10. RK to Troup, 8 May 1800, *CRK,* III: 235–36.
11. "Philadelphia," 3 April 1800, *Aurora*, 2. Ferling, *Jefferson and Hamilton*, 316–17. Harper, *American Machiavelli*, 253–54.
12. United States Constitution, Article II, Section 1.
13. AH to TS, 4 May 1800, *PAH*, 24: 444–53. Harper, *American Machiavelli*, 253.
14. TP to RK, 7 May 1800, *CRK*, III: 232
15. TS to RK, 11 May 1800, *CRK*, III: 238.
16. AG to Hannah Nicholson Gallatin, 6 May 1800, *The Life of Albert Gallatin*, ed. Henry Adams (Philadelphia: J.B. Lippincott & Co., 1879), 241. https://www.google.com/books/edition/The_Life_of_Albert_Gallatin/AbYEAAAAYAAJ?hl=en&gbpv=1&pg=PP7&printsec=frontcover.
17. TJ to Thomas Mann Randolph, 7 May 1800, *PTJ*, 31: 561–63.
18. *Political Correspondence and Public Papers of Aaron Burr*, ed. Mary-Jo Kline (Princeton, NJ: Princeton University Press, 1983), 1: 433–34. Albert Gallatin to Hannah Gallatin, 12 May 1800, *Life of Albert Gallatin*, 1: 247.
19. AG to Hannah Gallatin, 6 May 1800; Hannah Gallatin to Albert Gallatin, 7 May 1800, *Papers of Albert Gallatin*, Reel 4. Larson, *Magnificent Catastrophe*, 116–17.
20. TJ to Pierce Butler, 11 August 1800, *PTJ*, 32: 91. Larson, *Magnificent Catastrophe*, 118.
21. TJ to Thomas Mann Randolph, 14 May 1800, *PTJ*, 31: 581
22. AH to John Jay, 7 May 1800, *Selected Papers of John Jay*, 7: 80–82. Harper, *American Machiavelli*, 254.
23. AH to John Jay, 7 May 1800, *Selected Papers of John Jay*, 7: 80–82. Larson, *A Magnificent Catastrophe*, 108–9. Walter Stahr, *John Jay* (New York: Hambledon and London, 2005), 360–61.

CHAPTER 24

1. JA to John Trumbull, 10 September 1800, *Rotunda.*
2. OW to Fisher Ames, 29 December 1799, in Gibbs, *Administrations of Washington and Adams*, 313–14. Ferling, *Adams vs. Jefferson*, 132–34. Chernow, *Alexander Hamilton*, 611–15.
3. McHenry to JA, 31 May 1800, *Rotunda.*
4. Smith, *John Adams*, II: 1027–31. Chernow, *Alexander Hamilton*, 611–15.
5. AA to Abigail Adams Smith, 11 May 1800, *AFC*, 229–30, n2.
6. McHenry to John Adams, 31 May 1800, *Rotunda.* AA to AAS, 11 May 1800, *AFC*, 14: 229–30, n2.
7. Chernow, *Alexander Hamilton*, 611–15.
8. Ferling, *Adams vs. Jefferson*, 132–34. Smith, *John Adams*, II: 1027–31.

9. TP to Cabot, 16 June 1800, *Correspondence of George Cabot*, 275–77. Benjamin Goodhue to TP, 2 June 1800 *CRK*, III: 263–64.
10. JA to TP, 10 May 1800, *Rotunda*. Smith, *John Adams*, II: 1027–31. Chernow, *Alexander Hamilton*, 611–15.
11. TP to JA, 12 May 1800, *Rotunda*. Clarfield, *Timothy Pickering and American Diplomacy*, 213–14. Ferling, *Adams vs. Jefferson*, 132–34.
12. JA to TP, 12 May 1800, *Rotunda*. DeConde, *Quasi-War*, 271–72.
13. JA to United States Senate, 12 May 1800, *Rotunda*. Smith, *John Adams*, II: 1027–31.
14. *Philadelphia Public Directory*, 115.
15. "Friday, May 16, 1800"; "Monday, May 19, 1800," *Aurora*.
16. Robert Alberts, *The Golden Voyage: The Life and Times of William Bingham, 1752–1804* (Boston: Houghton-Mifflin, 1969), 391. Kurtz, *The Presidency of John Adams*, 395. Ferling, *Adams vs. Jefferson*, 132–34.
17. United States Constitution, Article II.
18. Jonathan Gienapp, "Removal and the Changing Debate over Executive Power at the Founding," 13. James Hart, *The American Presidency in Action, 1789: A Study in Constitutional History* (New York: Macmillan, 1948), 155. Michael McConnell. *The President Who Would Not Be King*, 164–65.
19. Gienapp, Jonathan, "Removal and the Changing Debate over Executive Power at the Founding," *American Journal of Legal History*, 63: 3 (September 2023), 229-250. Gienapp, *Second Creation*, 159–60.
20. Chervinsky, *The Cabinet*.
21. Chervinsky, *The Cabinet*, 293–297.
22. McHenry to GW, 10 November 1799, *PGW*, Retirement Series, 4: 397–402.
23. TP to McHenry, 13 February 1811, Bernard C. Steiner, ed., *The Life and Correspondence of James McHenry* (Cleveland: Burrows Brothers, 1907), 568.
24. JQA to TBA, 20 December 1800, *AFC*, 14: 361–68.
25. JA to Elbridge Gerry, 3 May 1797, *Rotunda*.
26. *U.S. Congress. Senate Exec. Journal.* 6th Cong., 1st sess., 13 May 1800, 354. Smith, *John Adams*, II: 1027–31.
27. With one exception. On March 27, 1867, Congress passed the Tenure of Office Act, prohibiting the president from removing cabinet secretaries without Senate approval. On 21 February 1868, President Andrew Johnson proceeded to dismiss Secretary of War Edwin Stanton. As a result, Johnson was impeached in the House of Representatives but acquitted in the Senate. The Tenure of Office act was rescinded in 1887. In 1926, the Supreme Court ruled in *Myers v. United States* that the president has the power to remove officials. United States Senate, https://www.senate.gov/about/powers-procedures/impeachment/impeachment-johnson.htm#:~:text=Johnson%20vetoed%20legislation%20that%20Congress,1868%2C%20to%20impeach%20the%20president, accessed June 23, 2023. "Myers v. United States." Oyez. Accessed November 27, 2023. https://www.oyez.org/cases/1900-1940/272us52.
28. *AOC*, 6th Cong., 1st sess., 704.

29. Harper, *American Machiavelli*, 252.
30. *AOC*, 6th Cong., 1st sess., 713–16. TJ to Thomas Mann Randolph, 14 May 1800, *PTJ*, 31: 581. Elkins and McKitrick, *Age of Federalism*, 731.
31. AA to JQA, 27 April 1800, *AFC*, 14: 218–20.
32. TP to JA, 9 September 1799, *Rotunda*.
33. CL to JA, 13 May 1800, *Rotunda*.
34. JA to BS, 20 May 1800, *Rotunda*. DeConde, *Quasi-War*, 198–99.
35. JA to CL, 21 May 1800, *Rotunda*.
36. JA to Pennsylvania Insurgents, 21 May 1800, *Rotunda*. Newman, *Fries's Rebellion*, 182–83.
37. TP to Benjamin Goodhue, 26 May 1800, TP to Samuel Gardener, 21 June 1800, TP to James Pickering, 7 June 1800, *TPP*, 13:526, 551, 542. "Tuesday 13 May[1800; Philadelphia]," Melanie Randolph Miller, ed., *The Diaries of Gouverneur Morris, New York, 1799–1816* (Charlottesville: University of Virginia Press, 2018), 91. Newman, *Fries's Rebellion*, 184.
38. AA to JA, 23 May 1800, *AFC*, 14: 252–54.
39. JQA to TBA, 20 December 1800, *AFC*, 14: 361–68.

CHAPTER 25

1. "Commission," 13 May 1800, *JMO*. United States Coast Survey, *Map of the city of Richmond, Virginia*. [Washington, DC: US Coast Survey, 1864] Map. https://www.loc.gov/item/2006626036/.
2. "Secretary of State: Editorial Note," *JMO*.
3. "Federal Account," 13 June 1800, *Aurora*, 3.
4. "Massachusetts," 18 June 1800, *Green Mount Patriot*, (Peacham, VT), 3.
5. *Aurora*, Philadelphia, 27 May 1800.
6. JA to Citizens of York, PA, 30 May 1800, *Rotunda*. JA to AA, 13 June 1800, *AFC*, 14: 283–84. Ferling, *Adams vs. Jefferson*, 138–39. Sharp, *The Deadlocked Election of 1800*, 102–3.
7. JA to AA, 13 June 1800, *AFC*, 14: 283–84. Smith, *John Adams*, II: 1036–37.
8. JA to AA, 13 June 1800, *AFC*, 14: 283–84.
9. "Alexandria, June 11, 1800," 27 June 1800, *Weekly Raleigh Register*, (Raleigh, NC), 3. *Aurora*, 16 June 1800; *Vermont Gazette*, 7 July 1800. *The Portland Gazette*, 23 June 1800. Kurtz, *The Presidency of John Adams*, 398–99. Ferling, *Adams vs. Jefferson*, 138–39.
10. JA to Citizens of Washington City, 5 June 1800, *Rotunda*.
11. The boardinghouse was located at the current site of the US Supreme Court building. Ferling, *Adams vs. Jefferson*, 138–39. Lina Mann, "Building the White House," *Slavery in the President's Neighborhood*, White House Historical Association, https://www.whitehousehistory.org/building-the-white-house.

12. Samuel Dexter to OW, 30 June 1800, Wolcott volume, 364. William Gardner Bell, *Secretaries of War and Secretaries of the Army* (Washington, DC: Center of Military History, United States Army, 2010), 10. "Buildings of the Department of State," Office of the Historian, United States State Department, 1977, https://history.state.gov/departmenthistory/buildings/section32.
13. "Communication," 10 June 1800, *Raleigh Minerva*, Raleigh, NC, 3.
14. Lyon, E Wilson, "The Franco-American Convention of 1800," *The Journal of Modern History*, 12: 3 (September 1940), 309.
15. WVM to JQA, 17 February 1800, *Letters of WVM*, 642–43.
16. Guy Périer de Féral, "La maison d'arrêt des Oiseaux, d'après les souvenirs de captivité du président de Dompierre d'Hornoy" *Mémoires de la Fédération des Sociétés historiques et archéologiques de l'Ile-de-France*, vol. 4, 1952 https://gallica.bnf.fr/ark:/12148/bpt6k3361501d; Olivier Blanc, *Last letters: prisons and prisoners of the French Revolution*, English translation by Alan Sheridan, 1987, 65–72. WVM to JQA, 7 March 1800, *Letters of WVM*, 644.
17. WVM to JQA, 7 March 1800, *Letters of WVM*, 644.
18. William Garrott Brown, *The Life of Oliver Ellsworth* (New York: Macmillan, 1905), 284.
19. "Journal of the Envoys' Mission," *Despatches from U.S. Minister to France, 1789–1906*, US National Archives, Record Group 59, Series: Despatches from Diplomatic Officers, 18 April 1800–2 August 1801, 83 [hereafter "Journal of the Envoys' Mission"]. Lyon, "The Franco-American Convention of 1800," 310–11.
20. "Journal of the Envoys' Mission," 84.
21. Lyon, "The Franco-American Convention of 1800," 311. DeConde, *Quasi-War*, 223–31.
22. JA to SC., Citizens of Georgetown, 31 May 1800, *Rotunda.*
23. *Raleigh Minerva*, 17 June 1800.
24. JA to AA, 13 June 1800, *AFC*, 14: 283–84.
25. *Poughkeepsie Journal*, 24 June 1800.
26. JA to James Calhoun, 16 June 1800, *Rotunda.*
27. *Aurora*, 21 June 1800.
28. AA to TBA, 12 July 1800, *AFC*, 14: 297–99.
29. JA to Marshall, 31 July 1800, *Rotunda.*
30. There is no record that Marshall started drafting these instructions. *Letters by secretaries of State, 1798–1801,* General Records of the Department of State, Record Group 59, National Archives, United States.
31. Hill, *William Vans Murray*, 170.
32. William Vans Murray Papers, April 24, 1801, Library of Congress, Manuscript Division.Alexander DeConde, "The Role of William Vans Murray in the Peace Negotiations between France and the United States, 1800," *Huntington Library Quarterly* 15, no. 2 (February 1952), 192. Hill, *William Vans Murray*, 170.
33. WVM to JQA, 20 August 1800, *Letters of WVM*, 651.

34. Lyon, "The Franco-American Convention of 1800," 310–11. Hill, *William Vans Murray*, 172–76. DeConde, *Quasi-War*, 253–58.
35. "Instructions to Oliver Ellsworth, William Richardson Davie, and William Vans Murray," 22 October 1799, *Despatches from U.S. Minister to France, 1789–1906*, US National Archives, Record Group 59, Series: Despatches from Diplomatic Officers, 18 April 1800–2 August 1801, 20–44. Lyon, "The Franco-American Convention of 1800," 323–24. Hill, *William Vans Murray*, 179–81. DeConde, *Quasi-War*, 244–51.
36. Marshall to JA, 25 August 1800, *Rotunda.*
37. JA to Marshall, 4 September 1800, *Rotunda.*
38. Marshall to JA, 17 September 1800, *Rotunda.* Kurtz, "The French Mission of 1799–1800: Concluding Chapter in the Statecraft of John Adams," *Political Science Quarterly,* 80, no. 4 (December 1965), 546.
39. Lyon, "The Franco-American Convention of 1800," 324.
40. Hill, *William Vans Murray*, 192–95. DeConde, *Quasi-War*, 253–58.
41. WVM to John Marshall, 1 October 1800, *Despatches from United States Ministers to the Netherlands*, 1798–1801.
42. Lyon, "The Franco-American Convention of 1800," 326. DeConde, *Quasi-War*, 253–58.
43. WVM to Marshall, 1 October Lyon, Despatches from United States Ministers to the Netherlands, 1798–1801.
    "The Franco-American Convention of 1800," 327.
44. WVM to JQA, 1 October 1800, *Letters of WVM*, 654.
45. WVM to JQA, 5 October 1800, *Letters of WVM*, 654. DeConde, *Quasi-War*, 253–58.

CHAPTER 26

1. "Chester County Republican Festival," 10 August 1800, *Aurora*, 2–3.
2. For a few precious decades after the Revolution, New Jersey offered the franchise to propertied women. It was rescinded in 1807, along with the right to vote for free men of color.
3. Ferling, *Adams vs. Jefferson*, 155.
4. Pasley, *The Tyranny of Printers*, 154–57.
5. Ferling, *Adams vs. Jefferson*, 144. Dunn, *Jefferson's Second Revolution*, 139–41.
6. Ferling, *Adams vs. Jefferson*, 118, 144.
7. JA to William Tudor, 13 December 1800, *Rotunda.* Larson, *Magnificent Catastrophe*, 209.
8. JA to Tench Coxe, May 1792, *Rotunda.*
9. *Aurora*, August 28, 1800, 2. Ferling, *Adams vs. Jefferson*, 158. Larson, *Magnificent Catastrophe*, 179.
10. Ferling, *Adams vs .Jefferson*, 146–53. Brown, *The Presidency of John Adams*, 187.

11. Bird, *Criminal Dissent*, 238–39. "Lancaster, October 28," October 28, 1801, *Lancaster Intelligencer*, (Lancaster, PA), 3. "Extract of a letter from a gentleman in Richmond, dated the 8th inst. to his friend in Norfolk," 11 May 1801, *The Recorder*, (Greenfield, MA), 3.
12. In May 1801, Jefferson instructed his attorney general to dismiss the case. The clerk incorrectly copied the documents, so the case was not finally dismissed until October 1801 when a grand jury dismissed the charges.
13. TJ to Gideon Granger, 13 August 1800, *PTJ*, 32: 95–97.
14. TJ to John Vanmetre, 4 September 1800, *PTJ*, 32: 126–27.
15. TJ to John Vanmetre, 4 September 1800, *PTJ*, 32: 126–27.
16. TJ to Monroe, 13 April 1800, *PTJ*, 31: 499–500.
17. Monroe to TJ, 8 April 1800; 23 April 1800, *PTJ*, 31: 489–90, 537–38.
18. TJ to Pierce Butler, 11 August 1800, *PTJ*, 32: 91.
19. Dunn, *Jefferson's Second Revolution*, 153–58.
20. Douglas Egerton, *Gabriel's Rebellion: The Virginia Slave Conspiracies of 1800 and 1802* (Chapel Hill: University of North Carolina Press, 1993), 50–51.
21. Larson, *Magnificent Catastrophe*, 191.
22. Newman, Simon P., "The World Turned Upside Down: Revolutionary Politics, Fries' and Gabriel's Rebellions, and the Fears of the Federalists," *Pennsylvania History* 67, no. 1 (Winter 2000), 8.
23. "United States," 31 October 1800, *The Recorder*, (Greenfield, MA), 2. Egerton, *Gabriel's Rebellion*, 50–51.
24. "Extract of a Letter from a Gentleman in Washington, dated the 19th inst.," 17 September 1800, *Lancaster Intelligencer*, (Lancaster, PA), 2. Egerton, *Gabriel's Rebellion*, 68.
25. James Thomson Callender to TJ, 13 September 1800, *PTJ*, 32:136–38. Larson, *Magnificent Catastrophe*, 192. Egerton, *Gabriel's Rebellion*, 69. Dunn, *Jefferson's Second Revolution*, 153–58. Sharp, *The Deadlocked Election of 1800*, 109–11.
26. Egerton, *Gabriel's Rebellion*, 70.
27. "United States," 31 October 1800, *The Recorder*, (Greenfield, MA), 2. Egerton, *Gabriel's Rebellion*, 71–72.
28. Egerton, *Gabriel's Rebellion*, 72–75.
29. Egerton, *Gabriel's Rebellion*, 77–85.
30. "Thursday September 25," 25 September 1800, *The Vergennes Gazette and Vermont and New-York Advertiser*, (Vergennes, VT), 3. Egerton, *Gabriel's Rebellion*, 92.
31. "By-the Governor of the Commonwealth of Virginia," 23 September 1800, *Poughkeepsie Journal*, (Poughkeepsie, NY), 2.
32. Douglas R. Egerton, "Gabriel's Conspiracy and the Election of 1800," *Journal of Southern History* 56, no. 2 (May 1990): 204–5. Dunn, *Jefferson's Second Revolution*, 153–58.
33. Larson, *Magnificent Catastrophe*, 195.
34. Shays' Rebellion, the Whiskey Rebellion, and Fries' Rebellion, respectively.

35. Michael L. Nicholls, "'Holy Insurrection': Spinning the News of Gabriel's Conspiracy," *Journal of Southern History* 78, no. 1 (February 2012): 39–40. Sharp, *The Deadlocked Election of 1800*, 109–11. Cleves, *The Reign of Terror*, 94.
36. Robert Troup to Rufus King, 1 October 1800, *CRK*, II: 315. Dunn, *Jefferson's Second Revolution*, 153–58.
37. 24 September 1800; 26 September 1800, *Aurora*. Egerton, *Gabriel's Rebellion*, 114.
38. "United States," 31 October 1800, *The Recorder*, Greenfield, Massachusetts, 2. Egerton, *Gabriel's Rebellion*, 103.
39. Egerton, *Gabriel's Rebellion*, 94.
40. Monroe to TJ, 15 September 1800, *PTJ*, 32: 144–45. Egerton, *Gabriel's Rebellion*, 89. Larson, *Magnificent Catastrophe*, 194. Dunn, *Jefferson's Second Revolution*, 153–58.
41. TJ to Monroe, 20 September 1800, *PTJ*, 32: 160–61.
42. TJ to Monroe, 20 September 1800, *PTJ*, 32: 160–61. Larson, *Magnificent Catastrophe*, 194. Sharp, *The Deadlocked Election of 1800*, 109–11.
43. Egerton, *Gabriel's Rebellion*, 94.
44. Egerton, *Gabriel's Rebellion*, 111. Dunn, *Jefferson's Second Revolution*, 153–58.
45. "United States," October 31, 1800, *The Recorder*, (Greenfield, MA), 2. Egerton, *Gabriel's Rebellion*, 110.
46. Nat Turner's Rebellion broke out in Southampton County, Virginia in August 1831 and was the deadliest revolt in US history. The rebels killed between fifty-five and sixty-five white people before the rebels were subdued.
47. JQA to WVM, 14 August 1798, *Writings of John Quincy Adams*, II: 349. This letter was written before Gabriel's Rebellion, but referred to other potential uprisings and was a regular sentiment.

CHAPTER 27

1. Richard Stockton to OW, 27 June 1800, Oliver Wolcott Jr. Papers, Connecticut Historical Society. Gibbs, *Memoirs of the Administrations of Washington and John Adams*, 375–76.
2. Harper, *American Machiavelli*, 256.
3. Ferling, *Adams vs. Jefferson*, 153. Dunn, *Jefferson's Second Revolution*, 1.47.
4. Christian Federalist, "Short Address," *Gazette of the United States* (Philadelphia, PA), 5. Ferling, *Adams vs. Jefferson*, 151–54. Larson, *Magnificent Catastrophe*, 180.
5. Darren Staloff, "Deism and the Founding of the United States," National Humanities Center, http://nationalhumanitiescenter.org/tserve/eighteen/ekeyinfo/deism.htm#:~:text=Deism%20or%20%E2%80%9Cthe%20religion%20of,reason%20rather%20than%20divine%20revelation.
6. *Gazette of the United States*, September 13, 1800, (Philadelphia, PA) 3. Larson, *Magnificent Catastrophe*, 173. Dunn, *Jefferson's Second Revolution*, 148.
7. TJ to Uriah McGregory, 13 August 1800, *PTJ*, 32: 98–99.

8. TJ to JM, 29 August 1800, *PJM*, 17: 406–7.
9. F. Ames to RK, September 24, 1800, *CRK*, III: 303–4
10. "Mr. Adams and Mr. Jefferson," October 1, 1800, *Lancaster Intelligencer*, (Lancaster, PA). Larson, *Magnificent Catastrophe*, 174.
11. Larson, *Magnificent Catastrophe*, 175.
12. Brown, *The Presidency of John Adams*, 181. Chernow, *Alexander Hamilton*, 616–17. Kurtz, *The Presidency of John Adams*, 402. Dauer, *The Adams Federalists*, 253. Sharp, *The Deadlocked Election of 1800*, 98–99.
13. AA to TBA, 12 July 1800, *AFC*, 14: 297–99. Dauer, *Adams Federalists*, 2253.
14. Troup to RK, *CRK*, 9 August 1800, 3: 290. Chernow, *Alexander Hamilton*, 616–17.
15. *Gazette of the United States*, 3 July 1800, Philadelphia, 3. Larson, *Magnificent Catastrophe*, 153.
16. Troup to RK, *Letters of Rufus King*, 9 August 1800, *CRK*, III: 290.
17. AA to TBA, 12 July 1800, *AFC*, 14: 297–99.
18. J. Hale to RK, 9 July 1800 (Boston), *CRK*, 3: 269–70. Kurtz, *The Presidency of John Adams*, 402. Dauer, *The Adams Federalists*, 253.
19. Larson, *Magnificent Catastrophe*, 154.
20. AA to TBA, 12 July 1800, *AFC*, 14: 297–99. Chernow, *Alexander Hamilton*, 616–17. Elkins and McKitrick, *Age of Federalism*, 734–35.
21. F. Ames to RK, 15 July 1800, *CRK*, III: 275
22. F. Ames to RK, 15 July 1800, *CRK*, III: 275. Dauer. *Adams Federalists*, 254.
23. F. Ames to RK, 15 July 1800, *CRK*, III: 275. Larson, *Magnificent Catastrophe*, 149.
24. TS to RK, 26 September 1800, *TSP*, Box 4, Folder 23, Letterbook to Rufus King.
25. F. Ames to RK, 19 August 1800, *CRK*, III: 295.
26. Timothy Phelps to OW, 15 July 1800, Oliver Wolcott Jr. Papers, Connecticut Historical Society. Larson, *Magnificent Catastrophe*, 149.
27. OW To Noah Webster, 4 September 1800. Oliver Wolcott Jr. Papers, Connecticut Historical Society.
28. Webster to OW, 14 September 1800, Oliver Wolcott Jr. Papers, Connecticut Historical Society. Smith, *John Adams*, II: 1045.
29. GW, "Farewell Address," 19 September 1796, *PGW*, Presidential Series, 20: 703–22.
30. OW to Fisher Ames, 10 August 1800, Gibbs, *Memoirs of the Administrations of Washington and John Adams*, 400.
31. AH to JA, 1 August 1800, *PAH*, 25: 51–52. Brown, *The Presidency of John Adams*, 182–84. Dunn, *Jefferson's Second Revolution*, 162–64.
32. AH to OW, 1 July 1800, *PAH*, 25: 4–5. DeConde, *Quasi-War*, 277. Sharp, *The Deadlocked Election of 1800*, 112–15. Chernow, *Alexander Hamilton*, 621.
33. OW to AH, 7 July 1800, *PAH*, 25: 15–17. Brown, *The Presidency of John Adams*, 182–84.
34. AH to TP, 14 May 1800; TP to AH, 15 May 1800, *PAH*, 24: 487, 490–91.

35. AH to OW, 3 August 1800, *PAH*, 25: 54–56. Larson, *Magnificent Catastrophe*, 215. Dunn, *Jefferson's Second Revolution*, 162–64. Sharp, *The Deadlocked Election of 1800*, 112–15. Chernow, *Alexander Hamilton*, 611–15.
36. OW to AH, 3 September 1800, *PAH*, 25: 104–11. Kohn, *Eagle and Sword*, 269–70. Smith, *John Adams*, II: 1045.
37. Kohn, *Eagle and Sword*, 269–70. Fisher Ames to Alexander Hamilton, 26 August 1800, *PAH*, 25: 86–88.
38. Cabot to OW, August 23, 1800, *Correspondence of George Cabot*, 288. Emphasis in the original.
39. Brown, *The Presidency of John Adams*, 182–84. Chernow, *Alexander Hamilton*, 623–24.
40. AH to OW, 26 September 1800, *PAH*, 25: 122–23. Larson, *Magnificent Catastrophe*, 216.
41. OW to AH, 1 October 1800, *PAH*, 25: 126–27.
42. Troup to RK, 1 October 1800, *CRK*, III: 315:
43. AH to JA, 1 October 1800, *PAH* 25: 125–26. Larson, *Magnificent Catastrophe*, 215. Brown, *The Presidency of John Adams*, 182–83.
44. Harper, *American Machiavelli*, 255.
45. John Ferling makes this argument in *Adams vs. Jefferson*, 143. I'm not persuaded, though it is the first plausible explanation for Hamilton's behavior that attributes some rationality to his actions.
46. Larson, *Magnificent Catastrophe*, 216.
47. *American Citizen*, 24 October 1800, (New York, New York), 2. Dunn, *Jefferson's Second Revolution*, 162–64. Sharp, *The Deadlocked Election of 1800*, 112–15. Chernow, *Alexander Hamilton*, 623–24.
48. *Aurora*, 25 October 1800, 2.
49. Chernow, *Alexander Hamilton*, 622.
50. Troup to RK, 9 November 1800, *CRK*, III: 330. Chernow, *Alexander Hamilton*, 623–26.
51. George Cabot to AH, 29 November 1800, *PAH*, 25: 247–50. Larson, *Magnificent Catastrophe*, 221. Dauer, *The Adams Federalists*, 255. Dunn, *Jefferson's Second Revolution*, 162–64. Brown, *The Presidency of John Adams*, 182–86.
52. Bushrod Washington to OW, 1 November 1800, Oliver Wolcott Jr. Papers, Connecticut Historical Society.
53. WVM to JQA, 30 December 1800; 20 January 1801, *Letters of WVM*, 670, 674–75.
54. November 6, 1800, *American Mercury*, 2. Larson, *Magnificent Catastrophe*, 221. Brown, *The Presidency of John Adams*, 185.
55. "Letter from Alexander Hamilton, Concerning the Public Conduct and Character of John Adams, Esq. President of the United States, [24 October 1800]," *PAH*, 25: 186–234, n163.
56. Lycan, *Alexander Hamilton and Foreign Policy*, 404.
57. JA to AA, 2 November 1800, *AFC*, 432–33.

58. AA to JA, 11 November 1800, *AFC*, 14: 437–38.
59. AA to MSC, 10 November 1800, *AFC*, 14: 434–35.
60. AA to MSC, 10 November 1800, *AFC*, 14: 434–35, n2.
61. In 1809, Adams published a series of "Boston Patriot" letters which addressed many of Hamilton's claims.
62. 30 November 1782, *Diary and Autobiography of John Adams*, ed. L. H. Butterfield, Leonard C. Faber, and Wendell D. Garrett, (Cambridge, Mass., 1961), 3: 85. Jeanne E. Abrams, *A View from Abroad: The Story of John and Abigail Adams in Europe* (New York: New York University Press, 2021), 83–84.
63. JA to TJ, 24 November 1800, *Selected Papers of John Jay*, 7:118–19. Larson, *Magnificent Catastrophe*, 220.

CHAPTER 28

1. Bruce A. Ackerman, *Failure of the Founding Fathers: Jefferson, Marshall, and the Rise of Presidential Democracy* (Cambridge, MA: Harvard University Press, 2005), 21
2. For example, in 2020 both Nebraska and Maine had separate districts with a single electoral vote.
3. Pasley, *The First Presidential Contest*, 346.
4. Larson, *Magnificent Catastrophe*, 201. Dunn, *Jefferson's Second Revolution*, 183.
5. "To the Citizens of Virginia," 24 October 1800, *Virginia Argus*, (Richmond VA), 4. Larson, *Magnificent Catastrophe*, 160.
6. "Republican Ticket," *The Times; and District of Columbia Daily Advertiser*, 26 July 1800, (Alexandria, VA), 2. "To the Citizens of Virginia," 24 October 1800, *Virginia Argus*, (Richmond VA), 4. Dunn, *Jefferson's Second Revolution*, 184–85. Sharp, *The Deadlocked Election of 1800*, 120.
7. Larson, *Magnificent Catastrophe*, 162. Sharp, *The Deadlocked Election of 1800*, 120.
8. Larson, *Magnificent Catastrophe*, 162.
9. "Introductory Note: To Theodore Sedgwick, [4 May 1800]," *PAH*, 24: 444–52.
10. CCP to AH, 17 July 1800, *PAH*, 25: 27–29.
11. Larson, *Magnificent Catastrophe*, 183.
12. Larson, *Magnificent Catastrophe*, 183.
13. Larson, *Magnificent Catastrophe*, 185. Dunn, *Jefferson's Second Revolution*, 183.
14. TBA to JA, 20 September 1800, *AFC*, 14: 400–401.
15. TBA to William Smith Shaw, 8 August 1800, *AFC*, 371–73.
16. "To the Citizens and Free Voters of the Fifth District," September 11, 1800, *Maryland Gazette*, (Annapolis, MD), 3. Robert Harper to Harrison Gray Otis, 28 August 1800, *Life and Letters of Harrison Gray Otis*, 1: 194. "Introductory Note: To Theodore Sedgwick, [4 May 1800]," *PAH*, 24: 444–52.
17. 4 September 800, *The Maryland Gazette*, (Annapolis, MD), 2. Larson, *Magnificent Catastrophe*, 186–88.
18. Charles Peale Polk to JM, 10 [October] 1800, *PJM*, 17: 423.

19. Charles Pinckney to TJ, 12 October 1800, *PTJ*, 32: 214–17.
20. TBA to JQA, 12 October 1800, *AFC*, 14: 417–20.
21. "Election Results," *Herald of Liberty*, 20 October 1800, Washington, Pennsylvania, 3.
22. "Lancaster, October 16," 16 October 1800, *Lancaster Intelligencer*, (Lancaster, PA), 3. Larson, *Magnificent Catastrophe*, 209. Brown, *The Presidency of John Adams*, 190–91.
23. "Elections in Pennsylvania," 29 October 1800, *Lancaster Intelligencer*, (Lancaster, PA), 3.
24. Larson, *Magnificent Catastrophe*, 201.
25. Larson, *Magnificent Catastrophe*, 230–31.
26. Dunn, *Jefferson's Second Revolution*, 185. Sharp, *The Deadlocked Election of 1800*, 120.
27. Sharp, *The Deadlocked Election of 1800*, 121.
28. McHenry to OW, 9 November 1800, Gibbs, *Memoirs of the Administrations of Washington and John Adams*, 2:445. Sharp, *The Deadlocked Election of 1800*, 121. Larson, *Magnificent Catastrophe*, 228.
29. Dunn, *Jefferson's Second Revolution*, 187.
30. Dunn, *Jefferson's Second Revolution*, 187.
31. "Extract of a letter from a gentleman at Lancaster, dated Tuesday evening, the 18th instant," 27 November 1800, *Maryland Gazette*, (Annapolis, MD), 2.
32. Larson, *Magnificent Catastrophe*, 233.
33. Sharp, *The Deadlocked Election of 1800*, 122.
34. Marshall to CCP, 20 November 1800, *JMO*.
35. "Philadelphia, November 22," *Philadelphia Repository, and Weekly Register*, 22 November 1800, 7.
36. "Extract of a letter from a gentleman at Lancaster, dated Tuesday evening, the 18th instant," 27 November 1800, *Maryland Gazette*, (Annapolis, MD), 2. Larson, *Magnificent Catastrophe*, 234. Ackerman, *Failure of the Founding Fathers*, 31. Dunn, *Jefferson's Second Revolution*, 188.
37. Marshall to CCP, 22 November 1800, *JMO*.
38. Larson, *Magnificent Catastrophe*, 235.
39. "South Carolina in the Presidential Election of 1800," *American Historical Review* 4, no. 1 (1898): 113.
40. Larson, *Magnificent Catastrophe*, 210. Dunn, *Jefferson's Second Revolution*, 188–89. Ferling, *Adams vs. Jefferson*, 158. Sharp, *The Deadlocked Election of 1800*, 124–25.
41. Charles Pinckney to TJ, 12 October 1800, *PTJ*, 32: 214–17.
42. Charles Pinckney to JM, 26 October 1800, *PTJ*, 17: 427–29.
43. "Federal Sedition and Anti-Democracy," *City Gazette*, 21 November 1800, (Charleston, SC), 2. *America's Historical Newspapers*.
44. Monroe to JM, 3 November 1800, *PJM*, 17: 430. James Thomson Callender to TJ, 17 November 1800, *PTJ*, 32: 254–55.
45. John Barnes to TJ, 20 November 1800, *PTJ*, 32: 255–56.

46. "Election Intelligence," 17 December 1800, *Lancaster Intelligencer*, (Lancaster, PA), 3. "South Carolina in the Presidential Election of 1800," *American Historical Review* 4, no. 1 (1898): 113.
47. Larson, *Magnificent Catastrophe*, 237.
48. CCP to Marshall, 29 November 1800, Appendix, *JMO*.
49. "Extract of a letter from a gentleman at Washington to his friend in this city, dated Dec. 13," 29 December 1800, *Portland Gazette*, (Portland, ME), 2. Ferling, *Adams vs. Jefferson*, 159–61. Sharp, *The Deadlocked Election of 1800*, 124–25.
50. Peter Freneau to TJ, 2 December 1800, *PTJ*, 32: 265–66. Dunn, *Jefferson's Second Revolution*, 183.
51. TJ to JM, 19 December 1800, *PJM*, 17: 444–46.
52. Larson, *A Magnificent Catastrophe*, 159.
53. David Gelston to JM, 8 October 1800, *PJM*, 17: 418–19.
54. JM to Monroe, 21 October 1800, *PJM*, 17: 426.
55. Larson, *A Magnificent Catastrophe*, 119, 239–43.
56. TJ to JM, 19 December 1800, *PJM*, 17: 444–46.

CHAPTER 29

1. Holton, *Abigail Adams*, 329.
2. Chernow, *Alexander Hamilton*, 635. Smith, *John Adams*, II: 1036–37.
3. AA to MSC, 21 November 1800, *AFC*, 14: 439–42. Brown, *The Presidency of John Adams*, 197.
4. AA to TBA, 15 January 1801, *AFC*, 14: 519–21.
5. AA to MSC, 21 November 1800; AA to AAS, 21 November 1800, *AFC*, 14: 439–45. Smith, *John Adams*, II: 1049.
6. Ferling, *Adams vs. Jefferson*, 163.
7. AA to JQA, 29 January 1801, *AFC*, 14: 547–51.
8. Holton, *Abigail Adams*, 329–31. Smith, *John Adams*, II: 1049.
9. JA to TJ, 24 March 1801, *PTJ*, 33: 426.
10. AA to TBA, 13 [December] 1800, *AFC*, 14: 479–81. Ferling, *Adams vs. Jefferson*, 160. Brown, *The Presidency of John Adams*, 189.
11. Smith, *John Marshall*, 277.
12. William R. Davie to Marshall, 4 October 1800; WVM to Marshall, 1 October 1800, *JMO*. Ferling, *Adams v. Jefferson*, 160. Brown, *The Presidency of John Adams*, 197. DeConde, *Quasi-War*, 283.
13. Marshall to CCP, 18 December 1800, *JMO*.
14. Aaron Burr to TJ, 23 December 1800, *PTJ*, 32: 342–43. Dunn, *Jefferson's Second Revolution*, 194–96.
15. Sharp, *The Deadlocked Election of 1800*, 133–35.
16. Larson, *Magnificent Catastrophe*, 246–47.
17. TJ to Burr, 1 February 1801, *PTJ*, 32: 528–29.

18. Burr to TJ, 12 February 1801, *PTJ*, 32: 577. Sharp, *The Deadlocked Election of 1800*, 133–36. Dunn, *Jefferson's Second Revolution*, 194–96.
19. Fisher Ames to TS, 7 January 1801, Box 7, Folder 15, *TSP*.
20. TS to Unknown, 24 January 1801, Box 3, Family Letters, *TSP.* Sharp, *The Deadlocked Election of 1800*, 136–39.
21. Harper, *American Machiavelli*, 261.
22. Troup to RK, 31 December 1800, *CRK*, III: 358–59. Sharp, *The Deadlocked Election of 1800*, 136–44. DeConde, *Quasi-War*, 287.
23. Marshall to AH, 1 January 1801, *PAH*, 25: 290–92. Dunn, *Jefferson's Second Revolution*, 197–204.
24. Troup to RK, 12 February 1801, *CRK*, III: 390–91. Sharp, *The Deadlocked Election of 1800*, 139–41.
25. United States Constitution, National Archives.
26. Ackerman, *Failure of the Founding Fathers*, 37.
27. Albert Gallatin, "Plan at the Time of Balloting for Jefferson and Burr. Communicated to Nicholas and Mr. Jefferson," *The Writings of Albert Gallatin*, ed. Henry Adams, I: 18–23. Ackerman, *Failure of the Founding Fathers*, 81–82. Sharp, *The Deadlocked Election of 1800*, 144–46.
28. TJ to JM, 26 December 1800, *PJM*, 17: 448.
29. JM to TJ, 10 January 1801, *PJM*, 17: 453–57.
30. United States Constitution of the United States, preamble.
31. Akerman, *The Failure of the Founding Fathers*, 42–45, 83–84.
32. "Washington City," 17 November 1800, *National Intelligencer and Washington Advertiser*, (Washington, DC), 2.
33. *AOC*, 6th Cong. 2nd Sess, 359. Smith, *John Adams*, 2: 1062–63.
34. JA to TBA, 27 January 1801, *AFC*, 546–47. Smith, *John Marshall*, 277.
35. TP to OW, 3 January 1801, Oliver Wolcott Jr. Papers, Connecticut Historical Society. Murray wrote a similar letter to John Marshall. Murray to Marshall, 1 October 1800, *JMO*.
36. TP to OW, 3 January 1801, Oliver Wolcott Jr. Papers, Connecticut Historical Society.
37. "Friday 23d Jany.," *Diaries of Gouverneur Morris*, 157. "Philadelphia," 23 December 1800, *Aurora*, 2. Smith, *John Marshall*, 277–79. Hill, *William Vans Murray Federalist Diplomat*, 201–3.
38. AA to TBA, 25 January 1801, *AFC*, 14: 539–43. "Remarks on the French Convention," 1 January 1801, *Alexandria Advertiser and Commercial Intelligencer*, (Alexandria, VA), 2. DeConde, *Quasi-War*, 288–93.
39. AH to Morris, 24 December 1800, *PAH*, 25: 271–73. Matthew Q. Dawson, *Partisanship and the Birth of America's Second Party, 1796–1800: "Stop the Wheels of Government"* (Westport, CT: Praeger, 2000), 178.
40. AH to Gouverneur Morris, 10 January 1801, *PAH*, 25: 305–8. Chernow, *Alexander Hamilton*, 630.

41. Senate Executive Journal, *AOC*, 371. "Alexandria Advertiser," 5 February 1801, *Alexandria Advertiser and Commercial Intelligencer*, (Alexandria, VA), 3. Smith, *John Marshall*, 278. Elkins and McKitrick, *Age of Federalism*, 687.
42. JA to James Lloyd, 28 January 1815, *Rotunda*. DeConde, *Quasi-War*, 288–93. Hill, *William Vans Murray Federalist Diplomat*, 201–3. Lycan, *Alexander Hamilton and American Foreign Policy*, 405–6.
43. JA to Marshall, 31 January 1800, *JMO*.
44. JA to JJ, 19 December 1800, *Rotunda*. *Alexandria Advertiser and Commercial Intelligencer*, 15 January 1801, 3. Smith, *John Marshall*, 279.
45. JJ to JA, 2 January 1801, *Rotunda*
46. TS spelled the justice's name Patterson, but to avoid confusion, I've corrected the spelling in the quotation. TS to Unknown, 24 January 1801, Box 3, Family Letters, *TSP*. Newmyer, *John Marshall and the Heroic Age of the Supreme Court*, 128–32.
47. TS to Unknown, 24 January 1801, Box 3, Family Letters, *TSP*. Charles Warren, *The Supreme Court in United States History* (New York: Cosimo Classics, 2011), 1: 175.
48. Marshall to CCP, 18 December 1800, *JMO*.
49. Marshall to CCP, 18 December 1800, *JMO*.
50. Newmeyer, *John Marshall and the Heroic Age of the Supreme Court*, 128–32.
51. JA to Elias Boudinot, 26 January 1801, *Rotunda*.
52. Marshall to CCP, 18 December 1800, *JMO*.
53. Newmeyer, *John Marshall and the Heroic Age of the Supreme Court*, 128–32.
54. TS to Unknown, 24 January 1801, Box 3, Folder 14, *TSP*.
55. Jonathan Dayton to William Paterson, 1 February 1801, in Warren, *The Supreme Court in United States History*, 1: 177–78. Newmyer, *John Marshall and the Heroic Age of the Supreme Court*, 128–32, 142.
56. Jonathan Dayton to William Paterson, 1 February 1801, in Warren, *The Supreme Court in United States History*, 1: 177–78. Newmyer, *John Marshall and the Heroic Age of the Supreme Court*, 128–32, 142.
57. Jonathan Dayton to William Paterson, 1 February 1801, in Warren, *The Supreme Court in United States History*, 1: 177–78. Newmyer, *John Marshall and the Heroic Age of the Supreme Court*, 128–32, 142.
58. Brown, *The Presidency of John Adams*, 199–200.
59. Warren, *The Supreme Court in United States History*, I: 186.
60. Warren, *The Supreme Court in United States History*, 185–86.
61. Brown, *The Presidency of John Adams*, 198.
62. Richard E. Ellis, *The Jeffersonian Crisis: Courts and Politics in the Young Republic* (New York: Oxford University Press, 1971), 15. Brown, *The Presidency of John Adams*, 199.
63. Warren, *The Supreme Court in United States History*, 185.
64. *Aurora*, 21 January 1801, Philadelphia. Warren, *The Supreme Court in United States History*, 187.
65. TJ to JM, 26 December 1800, *PJM*, 17: 448. TJ to Thomas Mann Randolph, 1 January 1801, *PTJ*, 32: 385–86.

66. JA to United States Senate, 18 February 1801. JA to United States Senate, 3 March 1801, *Rotunda*. Brown, *The Presidency of John Adams*, 198.
67. For one example, see GW to US Senate, 3 March 1797, *PGW*, 21: 792. Smith, *John Adams*, II: 1064–65.
68. TJ to JM, 19 December 1800, *PJM*, 17: 444–46.
69. AA to TBA, 3 January 1801, *AFC*, 14: 508–9. Emphasis in original.
70. Based on Abigail's notations they dined sometime the first week of January and again on January 22. AA to TBA, 3 January 1801, *AFC*, 14: 508–9. TJ to JA, 17 January 1801, *PTJ*, 32: 476. Brown, *The Presidency of John Adams*, 205. Jon Meacham, *Thomas Jefferson: The Art of Power* (New York: Random House, 2012), 340–41.
71. *Anas of Thomas Jefferson*, 240.
72. TJ to Thomas Mann Randolph, 23 January 1801, *PTJ*, 32: 499–500. Brown, *The Presidency of John Adams*, 202. Smith, *John Adams*, II: 1060–61.
73. *Anas of Thomas Jefferson*, 240.
74. AA to Abigail Adams Smith, 17 January 1801, *AFC*, 14: 530–32.
75. Meacham, *The Art of Power*, 335–36.
76. JA to JM, 28 January 1801, *JMO*.
77. Many historians have accepted this interpretation as well. See Ackerman, *Failure of the Founding Fathers*, 80–90. Dunn, *Jefferson's Second Revolution*, 206. Larson, *A Magnificent Catastrophe*, 259. Dumas Malone, *Jefferson the President: First Term, 1801–1805* (Boston: Little, Brown, 1970), 6–8.
78. "Presidential Succession," United States Senate, https://www.senate.gov/legislative/landmark-legislation/presidential-succession-1792.htm, accessed July 30, 2023.
79. JA to AA, 16 February 1801, *AFC*, 14: 569. Brown, *The Presidency of John Adams*, 201.
80. JA to EG, 7 February 1801, *Rotunda*.
81. Brown, *The Presidency of John Adams*, 202–4. Smith, *John Adams*, II: 1060–61.
82. AA to William Smith Shaw, 14 February 1801, *AFC*, 14: 565–66.

CHAPTER 30

1. Brown, *The Presidency of John Adams*, 197. Meacham, *The Art of Power*, 332.
2. AG to Hannah Gallatin, quoted in Ackerman, *Failure of the Founding Fathers*, 26. Brown, *The Presidency of John Adams*, 197.
3. AG to Muhlenberg, 8 May 1848, *The Life of Gallatin* , 248–49. Margaret Bayard Smith. *The First Forty Years of Washington Society*, ed. Gaillard Hunt (New York: Charles Scribner's Sons, 1906), 10-11. Ackerman, *Failure of the Founding Fathers*, 89.
4. Letombe to Directory, 24 February 1801, in Dan Sisson, *The American Revolution of 1800* (New York: Knopf, 1974), 463–68. Ackerman, *Failure of the Founding Fathers*, 89.

5. AG to Muhlenberg, 8 May 1848, *The Life of Gallatin*, 248–49.
6. Sharp, *The Deadlocked Election of 1800*, 131–32.
7. AG to Muhlenberg, 8 May 1848, *The Life of Gallatin*, 248–49.
8. Monroe to McKean, 12 July 1800, Thomas McKean Papers, Historical Society of Pennsylvania quoted in Sharp, *Deadlocked Election of 1800*, 154.
9. Thomas McKean to TJ, 21 March 1801, *PTJ*, 33: 391–93. Sharp, *Deadlocked Election of 1800*, 154–55. Dunn, *Jefferson's Second Revolution*, 209–10.
10. AG to Muhlenberg, 8 May 1848, *The Life of Gallatin*, ed. Henry Adams, 248–49.
11. Monroe to TJ, 27 January 1801; TJ to Thomas Mann Randolph, 29 January 1801, *PTJ*, 32: 511, 516–18.
12. "WASHINGTON FEDERALIST," *Washington Federalist*, 12 February 1801, (Georgetown, Washington, DC), 2. Ackerman, *Failure of Founding Fathers*, 3.
13. TS to Daniel Dewey, 8 February 1801, *TSP*, Box 7, Folder 16.
14. "Philadelphia," 25 January 1801, *Aurora*, 2.
15. "Fire," 22 January 1801, *Alexandria Advertiser and Commercial Intelligencer*, (Alexandria, VA), 3.
16. "Washington City, Nov. 10," 19 November 1800, *Lancaster Intelligencer*, (Lancaster, PA), 3.
17. Sharp, *The Deadlocked Election of 1800*, 130. Dunn, *Jefferson's Second Revolution*, 206–7.
18. Sharp, *The Deadlocked Election of 1800*, 149.
19. *AOC*, 6th Cong., 2nd Sess., 1024.
20. *AOC*, 6th Cong., 2nd Sess., 1024. Sharp, *Deadlocked Election of 1800*, 148–49.
21. Sharp, *Deadlocked Election of 1800*, 149, 151–63.
22. *AOC*, 6th Cong., 2nd Sess., 1025–26. Sharp, *Deadlocked Election of 1800*, 148–49.
23. Sharp, *Deadlocked Election of 1800*, 152. Dunn, *Jefferson's Second Revolution*, 207.
24. This promise was particularly ironic because Smith was Jefferson's first choice for naval secretary. Jefferson ultimately settled on Samuel's brother Robert when Samuel refused. Jefferson, "Notes on a Conversation with Edward Livingston," 12 February 1801, *PTJ*, 32: 583.
25. Sharp, *Deadlocked Election of 1800*, 152–53. Chernow, *Alexander Hamilton*, 636.
26. TJ to Monroe, 15 February 1801, *PTJ*, 32: 594. Dunn, *Jefferson's Second Revolution*, 207–9.
27. TJ to Monroe, 15 February 1801, *PTJ*, 32: 594. Sharp, *Deadlocked Election of 1800*, 161
28. Jefferson followed these requirements once in office. He was just being petulant. TS to Fisher Ames, 23 January 1801, *TSP*, Box 7, Folder 15. Sharp, *Deadlocked Election of 1800*, 149, 151–63.
29. "To the Editor of the Register, "February 10, 1801, *Weekly Raleigh Register*, (Raleigh, NC), 4. Chernow, *Alexander Hamilton*, 638. Dunn, *Jefferson's Second Revolution*, 201.

30. William Cooper to Thomas Morris, 13 February 1801, *Memoirs of Aaron* Burr, 2:113, cited in Larson, *Magnificent Catastrophe*, 266.
31. Chernow, *Alexander Hamilton*, 637–38. Sharp, *Deadlocked Election of 1800*, 158–59. Meacham, *The Art of Power*, 338. Dunn, *Jefferson's Second Revolution*, 210–13.
32. Sharp, *Deadlocked Election of 1800*, 161.
33. *Anas of Thomas Jefferson*, 240.
34. TJ to Monroe, 15 February 1801, *PTJ*, 32: 594.
35. Chernow, *Alexander Hamilton*, 637.
36. Especially because Jefferson did honor the debt and kept the navy, just as Federalists asked. He did remove some Federalists from office, but it was not the widespread purge Federalists feared.
37. Chernow, *Alexander Hamilton*, 638. Sharp, *Deadlocked Election of 1800*, 149, 151–63.
38. Dunn, *Jefferson's Second Revolution*, 210–13.
39. JA to Marshall, 19 February 1801, *JMO*.
40. Smith, *John Adams*, II: 1063.
41. Smith, *John Adams*, II 1062.

CHAPTER 31

1. Evidence suggests he did not begin drafting his inaugural address until after the vote was decided. "Editorial Note: First Inaugural Address," *PTJ*, 33: 134–38.
2. William Cranch to JA, 13 June 1801, *Rotunda*.
3. AA to TBA, 3 February 1801, *AFC*, 14: 554–56. Smith, *John Adams*, II: 1060–61. Meacham, *The Art of Power*, 340–41.
4. JA to TJ, 24 March 1801, *PTJ*, 33: 426. Brown, *The Presidency of John Adams*, 205.
5. AA to TJ, 20 February 1801, *PTJ*, 33: 23–24.
6. Brown, *The Presidency of John Adams*, 207.
7. BS to TJ, 18 February 1801, *PTJ*, 33: 18–19.
8. BS to TJ, 25 February 1801, *PTJ*, 33: 68.
9. TJ to BS, 21 February 1801, *PTJ*, 33: 35.
10. "Philadelphia, March 10," 19 March 1801, *The Maryland Gazette*, (Annapolis, MD), 2. "Peacham," 26 March 1801, *Green Mountain Patriot*, (Peacham, VT), 3.
11. TJ to Marshall, 2 March 1801, *JMO*.
12. Marshall to TJ, 2 March 1801, *JMO*.
13. "Editorial Note: First Inaugural Address," *PTJ*, 33: 134–38. Brown, *The Presidency of John Adams*, 198.
14. Larson, *Magnificent Catastrophe*, 271. Brown, *The Presidency of John Adams*, 206–8.
15. McCullough, *John Adams*, 564.
16. Sharp, *Deadlocked Election of 1800*, 165–66. Dunn, *Jefferson's Second Revolution*, 218–20.
17. "Editorial Note: First Inaugural Address," *PTJ*, 33: 134–38. Dunn, *Jefferson's Second Revolution*, 219. Ferling, *Adams vs. Jefferson*, 201–6. Smith, *John Adams*, II: 1065–66.

18. March 6, 1801, *Alexandria Times,* 6 March 1801, *National Intelligencer.* Lynne Cheney, *The Virginia Dynasty: Four Presidents and the Creation of the American Nation* (New York: Viking, 2020), 215. Ferling, *Jefferson and Hamilton*, 333.
19. G. S. Wilson, *Jefferson on Display: Attire, Etiquette, and the Art of Presentation* (Charlottesville: University of Virginia Press, 2018), 131–36.
20. "Editorial Note: First Inaugural Address," *PTJ*, 33: 134–38.
21. "Adams Leaves," *Windsor Federal Gazette*, (Windsor, VT), 24 March 1801, 2.
22. Dunn, *Jefferson's Second Revolution*, 220–25.
23. Jefferson, "III. First Inaugural Address, 4 March 1801," *PTJ*, 33: 148–52.
24. Marshall to CCP, 4 March 1801, *JMO*. Dunn, *Jefferson's Second Revolution*, 221–25. Ferling, *Adams vs. Jefferson*, 201–6. "Philadelphia," 18 March 1801, *Aurora*, 2.
25. "Editorial Note: First Inaugural Address," *PTJ*, 33: 134–38. Sharp, *Deadlocked Election of 1800*, 167. Larson, *Magnificent Catastrophe*, 272–74.
26. "Editorial Note: First Inaugural Address," *PTJ*, 33: 134–38. "President's Speech," 11 March 1801, *Lancaster Intelligencer*, (Lancaster, PA), 3. "Philadelphia," 17 March 1801, *Aurora*, 2.
27. Marshall to CCP, 4 March 1801, *JMO*. Dunn, *Jefferson's Second Revolution*, 221–25. Ferling, *Adams vs. Jefferson*, 201–6.

EPILOGUE

1. Lycan, *Alexander Hamilton and American Foreign Policy*, 408.
2. Brown, *The Presidency of John Adams*, 190–93.
3. United States Constitution, Article I, Section 2. Dunn, *Jefferson's Second Revolution*, 192–93.
4. "Boston," 24 December 1800, *Columbian Centinel*, (Boston, MA), 2. Ackerman, *Failure of the Founding Fathers*, 34.
5. "Letter from Alexander Hamilton, Concerning the Public Conduct and Character of John Adams, Esq. President of the United States, [24 October 1800]," *PAH*, 25: 186–234, n163.
6. "Editorial Note: The Anas," *PTJ*, 22: 33–38.
7. TJ to Benjamin Rush, 16 January 1811, *PTJ*, 3: 304–8.
8. Malone, *Jefferson the President: First Term*, 6–8. Dunn, *Jefferson's Second Revolution*, 220. Chernow, *Alexander Hamilton*, 638–50.
9. I count myself among the Americans who took a peaceful transfer of power for granted. Here I am drawing two distinctions. First, the nation has endured violent transfers of power at the state level, often in the South, to prevent Black voters from exercising their franchise and Black politicians from holding office. Second, while Abraham Lincoln's election provoked the southern states to secede, they did not prevent his assumption of office. Horrifying, yes, but not the same thing.
10. JA to AA, 2 November 1800, *AFC*, 432–33.

Bibliography

ARCHIVAL COLLECTIONS

Adams Papers microfilm, Massachusetts Historical Society, Boston, MA.

America's Historical Newspapers, Readex, https://www.readex.com/products/americas-historical-newspapers.

Despatches from U.S. Minister to France, 1789–1906, Record Group 59, Series: Despatches from Diplomatic Officers, National Archives, Washington, DC.

Despatches from U.S. Minister to the Netherlands, 1794-1906, Record Group 59, Despatches from Diplomatic Officers, National Archives, Washington, D.C. https://catalog.archives.gov/id/177380730

George Washington Papers, Manuscript Division, Library of Congress, Washington, DC.

Letters by secretaries of State, 1798–1801, General Records of the Department of State, Record Group 59, National Archives, Washington, DC.

Oliver Wolcott Jr. Papers, Connecticut Historical Society, Connecticut Digital Archive, http://hdl.handle.net/11134/40002:OWP001

Papers of Albert Gallatin, National Archives, Washington, DC. 46 reels.

Tench Coxe Papers, Historical Society of Pennsylvania, Philadelphia, PA.

Theodore Sedgwick Papers, Sedgwick Family Papers, Massachusetts Historical Society, Boston, MA.

Timothy Pickering Papers, Massachusetts Historical Society, Boston, MA.

American State Papers, Foreign Relations, Library of Congress, https://memory.loc.gov/ammem/amlaw/lwsplink.html#anchor1.

William Vans Murray Papers, Manuscript Division, Library of Congress, Washington, DC.

EDITED PRIMARY SOURCE COLLECTIONS

The Adams Papers, The Adams Family Correspondence, ed. L. H. Butterfield et al. Cambridge, MA: Harvard University Press, 1963–2022, 15 vols.

The Complete Anas of Thomas Jefferson, ed. Franklin B. Sawvel. New York: Round Table Press, 1903.

The Diary of Elizabeth Drinker, ed. Elaine Forman Crane. Boston, MA: Northeastern University Press, 1991, 3 vols.

The Diaries of George Washington, ed. Donald Jackson and Dorothy Twohig. Charlottesville: University of Virginia Press, 1976-1979, 6 vols.

The Diaries of Gouverneur Morris, New York, 1799-1816, ed. Melanie Randolph Miller. Charlottesville: University of Virginia Press, 2018.

Diary and Autobiography of John Adams, ed. L. H. Butterfield, Leonard C. Faber, and Wendell D. Garrett, 4 vols., Cambridge, Mass., 1961.

Journals of the Continental Congress, 1774–1789, ed. Worthington C. Ford. Washington: General Printing Office, 1904-1937, 34 vols.

Letters of William Vans Murray to John Quincy Adams, 1797–1803, ed. Worthington Chauncey Ford. Washington: American Historical Association, 1914.

The Life of Albert Gallatin, ed. Henry Adams. Philadelphia: J.B. Lippincott & Co., 1879. Public domain: https://www.google.com/books/edition/The_Life_of_Albert_Gallatin/AbYEAAAAYAAJ?hl=en&gbpv=1&pg=PP7&printsec=frontcover.

The Life and Correspondence of James McHenry, ed. Bernard C. Steiner. Cleveland: Burrows Brothers, 1907.

Life and Letters of George Cabot, ed. Henry Cabot Lodge. Boston: Little, Brown, 1877.

The Life and Letters of Harrison Gray Otis, Federalist, 1765-1848, ed. Samuel Eliot Morison. Boston: Houghton Mifflin, 1913, 2 vols.

New Letters of Abigail Adams, 1788–1801, ed. Stewart Mitchell. Westport, CT: Greenwood Press, 1973.

The Papers of Alexander Hamilton, ed. Harold C. Syrett, New York: Columbia University Press, 1961-1987, 27 vols.

Papers of Benjamin Franklin, ed. Leonard W. Labaree et al. New Haven: Yale University Press, 43 vols., 1959-present.

The Papers of George Washington, Presidential Series, Dorothy Twohig et al, Charlottesville: University Press of Virginia, 1987–2020, 21 vols. Retirement Series, W.W. Abbot et al. Charlottesville: University of Virginia Press, 1998–1999, 4 vols.

The Papers of James Madison, Congressional Series, ed. William T. Hutchinson et al. Chicago: University of Chicago Press, 1962–1977, 10 vols. Charlottesville: University of Virginia Press, 1977–1991, 7 vols.

The Papers of John Marshall, ed. Charles F. Hobson. Chapel Hill: Omohundro Institute of Early American History and Culture and the University of North Carolina Press, 12 vols., 2015.

The Papers of Thomas Jefferson, ed. Julian P. Boyd et al. Princeton, NJ: Princeton University Press, 1950–2021, 45 vols.

Political Correspondence and Public Papers of Aaron Burr, ed. Mary-Jo Kline, Joanne Wood Ryan, et al. Princeton, NJ: Princeton University Press, 1982, 2 vols.

The Selected Papers of John Jay, ed. Elizabeth M. Nuxoll. Charlottesville: University of Virginia Press, 2010-2021, 7 vols.

Smith, Margaret Bayard. *The First Forty Years of Washington Society*, ed. Gaillard Hunt. New York: Charles Scribner's Sons, 1906.

The Writings of Albert Gallatin, ed. Henry Adams. Philadelphia: J.B. Lippincott & Co., 1879, 3 vols., https://catalog.hathitrust.org/Record/000365280

Writings of John Quincy Adams, ed. Worthington Chauncey Ford. New York: The Macmillan Company, 1913, 7 vols.

Works of Fisher Ames, ed. Seth Ames. Carmel, IN: Liberty Classics, 1983.

SECONDARY SOURCES

Abrams, Jeanne E. *A View from Abroad: The Story of John and Abigail Adams in Europe*. New York: New York University Press, 2021.

Ackerman, Bruce A. *The Failure of the Founding Fathers: Jefferson, Marshall, and the Rise of Presidential Democracy*. Cambridge, MA: Belknap Press of Harvard University Press, 2005.

Alberts, Robert C. *The Golden Voyage: The Life and Times of William Bingham, 1752–1804*. Boston: Houghton-Mifflin, 1969.

Ames, Fisher, W. B. Allen, and Seth Ames. *Works of Fisher Ames*. Indianapolis: Liberty Classics, 1983.

Avlon, John. *Washington's Farewell: The Founding Father's Warning to Future Generations*. New York: Simon and Schuster, 2017.

Backes, William J. *A History of Trenton, 1679–1929*. Trenton: Trenton Historical Society, 1929.

Baldridge, Edwin R. "Talleyrand's Visit to Pennsylvania, 1794–1796," *Pennsylvania History: A Journal of Mid-Atlantic Studies* 36, no. 2 (1969): 145–60.

Bartoloni-Tuazon, Kathleen. *For Fear of an Elective King: George Washington and the Presidential Title Controversy of 1789*. Ithaca, NY: Cornell University Press, 2014.

Bell, William Gardner. *Secretaries of War and Secretaries of the Army*. Washington, DC: Center of Military History, United States Army, 2010.

Bemis, Samuel Flagg. *John Quincy Adams and the Foundations of American Foreign Policy*. New York: Alfred A. Knopf, 1951.

Bemis, Samuel Flagg. *John Quincy Adams and the Union*. New York: Alfred A. Knopf, 1956.

Berkin, Carol. *A Sovereign People: The Crises of the 1790s and the Birth of American Nationalism*. New York: Basic Books, 2017.

Bernard, Jack F. *Talleyrand: A Biography*. New York: Putnam, 1973.

Berns, Walter. "Freedom of the Press and the Alien and Sedition Laws: A Reappraisal." *Supreme Court Review* 1970 (1970): 109–59.

Bernstein, R. B. *The Education of John Adams*. New York: Oxford University Press, 2020.

Bilder, Mary Sarah. "The Soul of a Free Government: The Influence of John Adams's *A Defence* on the Constitutional Convention," 1 Journal of American Constitutional History, 1, 2023.

Bird, Wendell. *Criminal Dissent: Prosecutions under the Alien and Sedition Acts of 1798*. Cambridge, MA: Harvard University Press, 2020.

Bird, Wendell. "Liberties of Press and Speech: 'Evidence Does Not Exist to Contradict the . . . Blackstonian Sense' in Late 18th Century England?" *Oxford Journal of Legal Studies* 36, no. 1 (2016): 1–25.

Bird, Wendell. "Reassessing Responses to the Virginia and Kentucky Resolutions: New Evidence from the Tennessee and Georgia Resolutions and from Other States." *Journal of the Early Republic* 35, no. 4 (2015): 519–51.

Blanc, Olivier. *Last letters: prisons and prisoners of the French Revolution*, English translation by Alan Sheridan. Budapest: A. Deutsch, 1987.

Blumberg, Phillip I. *Repressive Jurisprudence in the Early American Republic: The First Amendment and the Legacy of English Law*. Cambridge: Cambridge University Press, 2010.

Bradburn, Douglas. *The Citizenship Revolution: Politics and the Creation of the American Union, 1774-1804*. Charlottesville: University of Virginia Press, 2009.

Broussard, James H. *The Southern Federalists, 1800–1816*. Baton Rouge: Louisiana State University Press, 1999.

Brown, William Garrott. *The Life of Oliver Ellsworth*. New York: Macmillan, 1905.

Brown, Ralph Adams. *The Presidency of John Adams*. Lawrence: University Press of Kansas, 1975.

Bushnell, Eleanore. *Crimes, Follies, and Misfortunes: The Federal Impeachment Trials*. Urbana: University of Illinois Press, 1992.

Carroll, Thomas F. "Freedom of Speech and of the Press in the Federalist Period; The Sedition Act." *Michigan Law Review* 18, no. 7 (1920): 615–51.

Carter, Katlyn Marie. *Democracy in Darkness: Secrecy and Transparency in the Age of Revolutions*. New Haven: Yale University Press, 2023.

Cheney, Lynne. *The Virginia Dynasty: Four Presidents and the Creation of the American Nation*. New York: Viking, 2020.

Chernow, Ron. *Alexander Hamilton*. New York: Apollo, 2020.

Chervinsky, Lindsay M. *The Cabinet: George Washington and the Creation of an American Institution*. Cambridge, MA: Belknap Press, 2020.

Chinard, Gilbert. *Honest John Adams*. New York: Little, Brown, 1964.

Churchill, Robert H. "Popular Nullification, Fries' Rebellion, and the Waning of Radical Republicanism, 1798–1801," *Pennsylvania History* 67, no. 1 (Winter 2000): 105–40.

Clarfield, Gerard H. *Timothy Pickering and American Diplomacy, 1795–1800*. Columbia: University of Missouri Press, 1969.

Clarfield, Gerard H. *Timothy Pickering and the American Republic*. Pittsburgh, PA: University of Pittsburgh Press, 1980.

Cleves, Rachel Hope. *The Reign of Terror in America: Visions of Violence from Anti-Jacobinism to Antislavery*. Cambridge: Cambridge University Press, 2009.

Coleman, Aaron N. *The American Revolution, State Sovereignty, and the American Constitutional Settlement, 1765–1800*. Lanham, MD: Lexington Books, 2017.

Cooper, William J. *The Lost Founding Father: John Quincy Adams and the Transformation of American Politics*. New York: Liveright, 2017.

Cost, Jay. *James Madison: America's First Politician*. New York: Basic Books, 2021.

Covo, Manuel. *Entrepôt of Revolutions: Saint-Domingue, Commercial Sovereignty, and the French-American Alliance*. New York: Oxford University Press, 2022.

Crane, Elaine Forman. "Political Dialogue and the Spring of Abigail's Discontent." *William and Mary Quarterly* 56, no. 4 (1999): 745–74.

Cunningham Jr., Noble E. *The Jeffersonian Republicans: The Formation of Party Organization, 1789–1801*. Chapel Hill: University of North Carolina Press, 1957.

Dauer, Manning J. *The Adams Federalists*. Baltimore, MD: Johns Hopkins University Press, 2019.

Dawson, Matthew Q. *Partisanship and the Birth of America's Second Party, 1796–1800: "Stop the Wheels of Government."* Westport, CT: Praeger, 2000.

DeConde, Alexander. *The Quasi-War: The Politics and Diplomacy of the Undeclared War with France, 1797–1801*. Scribner, 1966.

DeConde. "The Role of William Vans Murray in the Peace Negotiations between France and the United States, 1800." *Huntington Library Quarterly* 15, no. 2 (1952): 185–94.

de Féral, Guy Périer. "La maison d'arrêt des Oiseaux, d'après les souvenirs de captivité du président de Dompierre d'Hornoy" *Mémoires de la Fédération des Sociétés historiques et archéologiques de l'Ile-de-France*, vol. 4, 1952.

Destler, Chester McArthur. *Joshua Coit, American Federalist, 1758–1798*. Middletown, CT: Wesleyan University Press, 1962.

Diggins, John Patrick. *John Adams: The American Presidents Series: The 2nd President, 1797–1801*. Times Books, 2003.

Dunn, Susan. *Jefferson's Second Revolution: The Election Crisis of 1800 and the Triumph of Republicanism*. New York: Houghton Mifflin Harcourt, 2004.

Earl, John L. "Talleyrand in Philadelphia, 1794–1796." *Pennsylvania Magazine of History and Biography* 91, no. 3 (1967): 282–98.

Edel, Charles N. *Nation Builder: John Quincy Adams and the Grand Strategy of the Republic*. Cambridge, MA: Harvard University Press, 2014.

Egerton, Douglas R. *Gabriel's Rebellion: The Virginia Slave Conspiracies of 1800 and 1802*. Chapel Hill: University of North Carolina Press, 1993.

Elkins, Stanley, and Eric McKitrick. *The Age of Federalism*. New York: Oxford University Press, 1995.

Ellis, Joseph J. *First Family: Abigail and John*. New York: Alfred A. Knopf, 2010.

Ellis, Richard E. *The Jeffersonian Crisis: Courts and Politics in the Young Republic*. New York: Oxford University Press, 1971.

Elsmere, Jane Shaffer. "The Trials of John Fries." *Pennsylvania Magazine of History and Biography* 103, no. 4 (1979): 432–45.

Feldman, Noah. *The Three Lives of James Madison: Genius, Partisan, President*. New York: Random House, 2017.

Ferling, John. *Adams vs. Jefferson: The Tumultuous Election of 1800*. New York: Oxford University Press, 2004.

Ferling, John. *Jefferson and Hamilton: The Rivalry That Forged a Nation*. New York: Bloomsbury, 2013.

Ferling, John. *John Adams: A Life*. New York: Oxford University Press, 2010.

Ferling, John. "John Adams, Diplomat." *William and Mary Quarterly* 51, no. 2 (1994): 227–52.

Freeman, Douglas Southall, John Alexander Carroll, and Mary Wells Ashworth. *George Washington, a Biography*. New York, Scribner, 1948.

Freeman, Joanne B. *Affairs of Honor: National Politics in the New Republic*. New Haven, CT: Yale University Press, 2002.

Fried, Stephen. *Rush: Revolution, Madness, and Benjamin Rush, the Visionary Doctor Who Became a Founding Father*. New York: Crown, 2018.

Furstenberg, Francois. *When the United States Spoke French: Five Refugees Who Shaped a Nation*. New York: Penguin Books, 2014.

Gelles, Edith. *Abigail and John: Portrait of a Marriage*. New York: Harper Perennial, 2010.

Gibbs, George, and Oliver Wolcott. *Memoirs of the Administrations of Washington and John Adams: Edited from the Papers of Oliver Wolcott, Secretary of the Treasury*. New York: B. Franklin, 1971.

Gienapp, Jonathan. "Removal and the Changing Debate over Executive Power at the Founding," *American Journal of Legal History*, 63: no. 3 (September 2023), 229-250.

Gienapp, Jonathan. *The Second Creation: Fixing the American Constitution in the Founding Era*. Cambridge, MA: Harvard University Press, 2018.

Grant, James. *John Adams: Party of One*. New York: Farrar, Straus and Giroux, 2005.

Griffith, John McRee. *Life and Correspondence of James Iredell*. New York: Appleton, 1857, 2 vols. Gutzman, K. R. Constantine. "The Virginia and Kentucky Resolutions Reconsidered: 'An Appeal to the Real Laws of Our Country.'" *Journal of Southern History* 66, no. 3 (2000): 473–96.

Halperin, Terri Diane. *The Alien and Sedition Acts of 1798: Testing the Constitution*. Baltimore, MD: Johns Hopkins University Press, 2016.

Hamburger, Philip. "The Development of the Law of Seditious Libel and the Control of the Press." *Stanford Law Review* 37, no. 3 (1985): 661–765.

Harper, John Lamberton. *American Machiavelli: Alexander Hamilton and the Origins of U.S. Foreign Policy*. New York: Cambridge University Press, 2004.

Hart, James. *The American Presidency in Action, 1789: A Study in Constitutional History*. New York: Macmillan, 1948.

Hemphill, C. Dallett. *Philadelphia Stories: People and Their Places in Early America*. Edited by Rodney Hessinger and Daniel K. Richter. Philadelphia: University of Pennsylvania Press, 2021.

Hill, Peter P. *William Vans Murray, Federalist Diplomat: The Shaping of Peace with France, 1797–1801*. Syracuse, NY: Syracuse University Press, 1971.

Hobson, Charles F. *The Great Chief Justice: John Marshall and the Rule of Law.* Lawrence: University Press of Kansas, 1996.

Hoffer, Peter Charles. *The Free Press Crisis of 1800: Thomas Cooper's Trial for Seditious Libel.* Lawrence: University Press of Kansas, 2011.

Holder, Jean S. "The Sources of Presidential Power: John Adams and the Challenge to Executive Primacy." *Political Science Quarterly* 101, no. 4 (1986): 601–16.

Holton, Woody. *Abigail Adams: A Life.* New York: Atria Books, 2010.

Howe, John R. *The Changing Political Thought of John Adams.* Princeton, NJ: Princeton University Press, 1966.

Isenberg, Nancy, and Andrew Burstein. *The Problem of Democracy: The Presidents Adams Confront the Cult of Personality.* New York: Penguin Books, 2019.

James, J. A. "Louisiana as a Factor in American Diplomacy, 1795–1800." *Mississippi Valley Historical Review* 1, no. 1 (1914): 44–56.

John Adams' A Defence of the Constitutions of Government of the United States of America: Editorial Note," *The Adams Papers*, Papers of John Adams, 18: 544–50

Johnson, Ronald Angelo. *Diplomacy in Black and White: John Adams, Toussaint Louverture, and Their Atlantic World Alliance.* Athens: University of Georgia Press, 2014.

Journal of the American Revolution. "John Adams and the Molding of William Vans Murray, Peacemaker," November 14, 2017. https://allthingsliberty.com/2017/11/john-adams-molding-william-vans-murray-peacemaker/.

Kaplan, Fred. *John Quincy Adams: American Visionary.* New York: HarperCollins, 2014.

Knight, Russell W. *Elbridge Gerry's Letterbook Paris 1797–1798.* Salem, MA: Essex Institute, 1966.

Koch, Adrienne. *Jefferson and Madison: Tthe Great Collaboration.* New York: Knopf, 1950.

Koch, Adrienne. "Hamilton, Adams and the Pursuit of Power." *Review of Politics* 16, no. 1 (1954): 37–66.

Koch, Adrienne, and Harry Ammon. "The Virginia and Kentucky Resolutions: An Episode in Jefferson's and Madison's Defense of Civil Liberties." *William and Mary Quarterly* 5, no. 2 (1948): 145–76.

Kohn, Richard H. *Eagle and Sword: The Federalists and the Creation of the Military Establishment in America, 1783–1802.* New York: Free Press, 1975.

Kramer, Eugene F. "Some New Light on the XYZ Affair: Elbridge Gerry's Reasons for Opposing War with France." *New England Quarterly* 29, no. 4 (1956): 509–13.

Kuehl, John W. "Southern Reaction to the XYZ Affair: An Incident in the Emergence of American Nationalism." *Register of the Kentucky Historical Society* 70, no. 1 (1972): 21–49.

Kurtz, Stephen G. "The French Mission of 1799–1800: Concluding Chapter in the Statecraft of John Adams," *Political Science Quarterly,* 80, no. 4 (1965): 543-557.

Kurtz, Stephen G. "The Political Science of John Adams: A Guide to His Statecraft." *William and Mary Quarterly* 25, no. 4 (1968): 605–13.

Kurtz, Stephen G. *The Presidency of John Adams: The Collapse of Federalism, 1795–1800*. Philadelphia: University of Pennsylvania Press, 1957.

Lacy, Katharina. "Cultural Landscape Report- Adams National Historic Site, Quincy, Massachusetts." Olmsted Center for Landscape Preservation Cultural Landscape Publication No. 13, 1997.

Larson, Edward J. *A Magnificent Catastrophe: The Tumultuous Election of 1800, America's First Presidential Campaign*. New York: Free Press, 2007.

Lash, Kurt T., and Alicia Harrison. "Minority Report: John Marshall and the Defense of the Alien and Sedition Acts." *SSRN Electronic Journal*, 2006.

Leonard, Gerald, and Saul Cornell. *The Partisan Republic: Democracy, Exclusion, and the Fall of the Founders' Constitution, 1780s–1830s*. New York: Cambridge University Press, 2019.

Levinson, Sanford, ed. *Nullification and Secession in Modern Constitutional Thought*. Lawrence: University Press of Kansas, 2016.

Levy, Leonard W. "Liberty and the First Amendment: 1790–1800." *American Historical Review* 68, no. 1 (1962): 22–37.

Lurie, Shira. *The American Liberty Pole: Popular Politics and the Struggle for Democracy in the Early Republic.* Charlottesville: University of Virginia Press, 2023.

Lycan, Gilbert L. *Alexander Hamilton and American Foreign Policy: A Design for Greatness*. Norman: University of Oklahoma Press, 1970.

Lyon, E. Wilson. "The Directory and the United States," *The American Historical* Review, 43: 3, April 1938, 514-532.

Lyon, E Wilson, "The Franco-American Convention of 1800," *The Journal of Modern History*, 12: 3, September 1940, 305-333.

"Madison's Conversations with Washington, 5–25 May 1792," *PGW*, Presidential Series 10:349–54

Malone, Dumas. *Jefferson and the Ordeal of Liberty*, vol. 3. Boston: Back Bay Books, 1969.

Malone, Dumas. *Jefferson the President: First Term, 1801–1805*. Boston: Little, Brown and Company, 1970.

Mann, Lina. "Building the White House," *Slavery in the President's Neighborhood*, White House Historical Association, https://www.whitehousehistory.org/building-the-white-house.

Martin, Robert W. T. *Government by Dissent: Protest, Resistance, and Radical Democratic Thought in the Early American Republic*. New York: New York University Press, 2013.

Mayville, Luke. *John Adams and the Fear of American Oligarchy*. Princeton, NJ: Princeton University Press, 2016.

McCoy, Drew R. *The Last of the Fathers: James Madison and the Republican Legacy*. Cambridge: Cambridge University Press, 1989.

McCullough, David. *John Adams*. New York: Simon and Schuster, 2002.

McFadden, David W. "John Quincy Adams, American Commercial Diplomacy, and Russia, 1809–1825." *New England Quarterly* 66, no. 4 (1993): 613–29.

McGrath, Tim. *James Monroe: A Life.* New York: Dutton, 2020.

McRee, Griffith John. *Life and Correspondence of James Iredell,* vol. 2. New York: Appleton, 1857, 461–62.

Meacham, Jon. *Thomas Jefferson: The Art of Power.* New York: Random House, 2012.

Miller, John. *Crisis in Freedom: The Alien and Sedition Acts.* Atlantic Little Brown, 1952.

Morgan, William G. "The Origin and Development of the Congressional Nominating Caucus." *Proceedings of the American Philosophical Society* 113, no. 2 (1969): 184–96.

Morison, Samuel Eliot. *Harrison Gray Otis, 1765–1848: The Urbane Federalist.* Boston: Houghton Mifflin, 1969.

Murphy, William J. "John Adams: The Politics of the Additional Army, 1798–1800." *New England Quarterly* 52, no. 2 (1979): 234–49.

Nagel, Paul C. *John Quincy Adams: A Public Life, A Private Life.* New York: Knopf, 2012.

Newman, Paul Douglas. *Fries's Rebellion: The Enduring Struggle for the American Revolution.* Philadelphia: University of Pennsylvania Press, 2005.

Newman, Paul Douglas. "The Federalists' Cold War: The Fries Rebellion, National Security, and the State, 1787–1800," *Pennsylvania History* 67, no. 1 (Winter 2000): 63–104.

Newman, Simon P. *Parades and the Politics of the Street: Festive Culture in the Early American Republic.* Philadelphia: University of Pennsylvania Press, 1997.

Newman, Simon P. "The World Turned Upside Down: Revolutionary Politics, Fries' and Gabriel's Rebellions, and the Fears of the Federalists," *Pennsylvania History* 67, no. 1 (Winter 2000): 5-20.

Newmyer, R. Kent. *John Marshall and the Heroic Age of the Supreme Court.* Baton Rouge: Louisiana State University Press, 2007.

New-York City Directory. New-York: Printed by John Buel, 1796, 82.

Office of the Historian. "Buildings of the Department of State," United States State Department, 1977, https://history.state.gov/departmenthistory/buildings/section32.

Paige Smith. *John Adams* (Garden City, NY: Doubleday & Company, Inc., 1962), II: 901

Paltsits, Victor Hugo. *Washington's Farewell Address.* New York: New York Public Library, 1935.

Pasley, Jeffrey L. *The First Presidential Contest: 1796 and the Founding of American Democracy.* Lawrence: University Press of Kansas, 2016.

Pasley, Jeffrey L. *The Tyranny of Printers: Newspaper Politics in the Early American Republic.* Charlottesville: University of Virginia Press, 2002.

Paul, Joel Richard. *Without Precedent: Chief Justice John Marshall and His Times.* New York: Riverhead Books, 2018.

Pencak, William. "From 'Salt of the Earth' to 'Poison and Curse'? The Jay and Adams Families and the Construction of American Historical Memory." *Early American Studies: An Interdisciplinary Journal* 2, no. 1 (2004): 228–65.

Perkins, Bradford. "A Diplomat's Wife in Philadelphia: Letters of Henrietta Liston, 1796–1800." *William and Mary Quarterly* 11, no. 4 (1954): 592–632.

Perkins, Bradford. *The First Rapprochement: England and the United States, 1795–1805*. Berkeley: University of California Press, 1967.

Perl-Rosenthal, Nathan. "Private Letters and Public Diplomacy: The Adams Network and the Quasi-War, 1797–1798." *Journal of the Early Republic* 31, no. 2 (Summer 2011): 283–311.

Peterson, Merrill D. *Thomas Jefferson and the New Nation: A Biography*. New York: Oxford University Press, 1975.

Philadelphia Public Directory, ed. Cornelius William Stafford. William W. Woodward, 1799.

Pickering, Octavius, and Charles Wentworth Upham. *The Life of Timothy Pickering*. New York: Little, Brown, 1873.

Pickering, Timothy. *A Review of the Correspondence Between the Hon. John Adams, Late President of the United States, and the Late Wm. Cunningham, Esq., Beginning in 1803, and Ending in 1812*. Salem, MA, 1824. HardPress Publishing, 2014. hardpress.net.

Popkin, Jeremy. *A New World Begins: The History of the French Revolution*. New York: Basic Books, 2019.

Puls, Mark. *Henry Knox: Visionary General of the American Revolution*. New York: St. Martin's Press, 2008.

Quincy Tercentenary Committee, *Quincy Massachusetts Historical Guide and Ma.* Quincy: Published by the Quincy Historical Society, 1925.

Ragosta, John. *For the People, for the Country: Patrick Henry's Final Political Battle*. Charlottesville: University of Virginia Press, 2023.

Rakove, Jack. *James Madison and the Creation of the American Republic*. New York: Pearson, 2006.

Ray, Thomas M. "'Not One Cent for Tribute': The Public Addresses and American Popular Reaction to the XYZ Affair, 1798–1799." *Journal of the Early Republic* 3, no. 4 (1983): 389–412.

Robbins, Karen E. *James McHenry, Forgotten Federalist*. Athens: University of Georgia Press, 2016.

Rogers, Jr., George C. *Evolution of a Federalist: William Loughton Smith of Charleston*. Columbia, SC: University of South Carolina Press, 1962.

Rohrs, Richard C. "The Federalist Party and the Convention of 1800." *Diplomatic History* 12, no. 3 (1988): 237–60.

Ryerson, Richard Alan, ed. *John Adams and the Founding of the Republic*. Boston: Northeastern University Press for the Massachusetts Historical Society, 2001.

Schlesinger, Arthur Meier. *The Coming to Power: Critical Presidential Elections in American History*. New York: Chelsea House, 1972.

Sharp, James Roger. *The Deadlocked Election of 1800: Jefferson, Burr, and the Union in the Balance*. Lawrence: University Press of Kansas, 2010.

Shaw, Peter. *The Character of John Adams*. Chapel Hill: Omohundro Institute and University of North Carolina Press, 1976.

Smith, James Morton. *Freedom's Fetters: The Alien and Sedition Laws and American Civil Liberties*. Ithaca, NY: Cornell University Press, 1956.

Smith, Jean Edward. *John Marshall: Definer of a Nation*. New York: Henry Holt , 1996.

Smith, Jeffery Alan. *Printers and Press Freedom: The Ideology of Early American Journalism*. New York: Oxford University Press, 1987.

Smith, Page. *John Adams:* vol. 1: *1735–1784*. vol. 2: *1784–1826*. New York: Doubleday, 1962.

"South Carolina in the Presidential Election of 1800," *American Historical Review* 4, no. 1 (1898): 111-129.

Stahr, Walter. *John Jay*. New York: Hambledon and London, 2005.

Staloff, Darren. "Deism and the Founding of the United States," National Humanities Center, http://nationalhumanitiescenter.org/tserve/eighteen/ekeyinfo/deism.htm#:~:text=Deism%20or%20%E2%80%9Cthe%20religion%20of,reason%20rather%20than%20divine%20revelation.

Stinchcombe, William. "The Diplomacy of the WXYZ Affair." *William and Mary Quarterly* 34, no. 4 (1977): 590–617.

Stinchcombe, William. *The XYZ Affair.* Westport, CT: Praeger, 1980.

Tagg, James. *Benjamin Franklin Bache and the Philadelphia "Aurora."* Philadelphia: University of Pennsylvania Press, 1991.

Thompson, C. Bradley. *John Adams and the Spirit of Liberty*. Lawrence: University Press of Kansas, 1998.

Thompson, Robert R. "John Quincy Adams, Apostate: From 'Outrageous Federalist' to 'Republican Exile,' 1801–1809." *Journal of the Early Republic* 11, no. 2 (1991): 161–83.

Traub, James. *John Quincy Adams: Militant Spirit*. New York: Basic Books, 2016.

Turner, Harriot Stoddert. "Memoirs of Benjamin Stoddert, First Secretary of the United States Navy." *Records of the Columbia Historical Society* (Washington, DC) 20 (1917): 141–66.

Unger, Harlow Giles. *John Quincy Adams*. Boston: Da Capo Press, 2012.

Warren, Charles. *The Supreme Court in United States History*, vol. I. New York: Cosimo Classics, 2011.

Watkins, W. *Reclaiming the American Revolution: The Kentucky and Virginia Resolutions and Their Legacy*. New York: Palgrave Macmillan, 2004.

Watkins, William J. "The Kentucky and Virginia Resolutions: Guideposts of Limited Government." *Independent Review* 3, no. 3 (1999): 385–411.

Weisberger, Bernard A. *America Afire: Jefferson, Adams, and the First Contested Election*. New York: HarperCollins, 2011.

Wharton, Francis. *State Trials during the Administrations of Washington and Adams*. Philadelphia: Carey and Hart, 1849.

William J. Backes. *A History of Trenton, 1679–1929*. Trenton: Trenton Historical Society, 1929.

Wilson, G. S. *Jefferson on Display: Attire, Etiquette, and the Art of Presentation.* Charlottesville: University of Virginia Press, 2018.

Wood, Gordon. *Friends Divided: John Adams and Thomas Jefferson*. New York: Penguin, 2017.

Index

For the benefit of digital users, indexed terms that span two pages (e.g., 52–53) may, on occasion, appear on only one of those pages.

Adams, Abigial: 1, 61, 72, 86, 125, 133, 169–70, 187, 226, 227, 228–29, 328
as first lady: 70–71, 84, 110, 133, 147, 235–36, 304–6, 329–30
as political commentator: 9, 33–34, 37, 42–44, 78–79, 81–82, 84, 92, 111–12, 141, 147, 158, 176, 185, 192, 228–29, 231, 261, 280, 284, 312, 314, 318–19
at home: 21–23, 34, 54, 57, 61, 64, 86, 87, 88–89, 150, 176, 183, 194, 201, 225, 263–64
away from John: 21–23, 35–36, 37, 38, 40, 41, 51, 53, 70, 201, 231
correspondence with John Quincy Adams: 44, 77, 91–92, 110, 116, 186–87
health of: 150–51, 155, 176, 229
on Hamilton: 37, 84, 141, 283–84, 292
on Gerry: 78–79
on Jefferson: 72, 77, 81, 328, 329–30
on Republicans: 81–82
on Sedition Act: 131
Adams, Abigail "Nabby" Smith: 93, 226–27, 291, 304, 318–19
Adams, Charles: 93, 226–27, 306, 332
Adams, John:
allegations of British faction: 285–87
as Federalist candidate: 27–28, 33, 35–37
as president-elect: 38, 40, 41, 43, 45–46, 54, 57–58
as vice president: 3–4, 15, 20–23, 36, 41
at home: 87–88, 229
background of: 2–3, 8, 18, 55
charges of monarchism: 31, 274, 281–82
challenges as second president: 2, 7
commitment to neutrality: 3, 7–8, 43–44, 59–60, 73, 179, 189, 217, 272, 286–87, 306, 311, 312
commitment to peaceful transfer of power: 8, 330–33, 337–38
correspondence of: 88–89, 93, 132–33, 194, 228–29, 263–64, 292
courage of: 272, 338
criticism of: 9, 31, 33, 144, 154, 191, 211, 238–39, 261, 286–87, 335–36
defensive of executive power: 7, 258
diplomacy expertise of: 3, 7–8, 111, 171, 217, 224–25, 228, 254
distrust of cabinet: 155–56, 158, 176, 230, 253–56
drafting practice to control emotions: 88, 158
ideas on executive power: 45, 46
legacy of: 9, 338–40
management of army: 140, 147–48, 149–50, 152–60, 178, 184, 189, 221–22, 229–30, 241–42, 259
missing Abigail Adams: 53, 57, 70, 176–77, 201, 231

Adams, John (*cont.*)
on Fries's Rebellion: 201, 202–3, 209–10
on Hamilton: 37, 84, 183–84, 189, 228–29, 254, 291–93
on Sedition Act: 130–31
patriotism of: 9
political savvy of: 112–15, 250–51
relationship with Jefferson: 35, 49–50, 51, 52–53, 64–65, 317–20, 332–33
relationship with Knox: 153–54
relationship with Marshall: 85, 133–34
relationship with Washington: 20, 23, 47, 48–49, 136, 145, 158, 159–60, 177, 188, 191, 234, 236
role in contested election in 1800: 317–20, 323–24, 326, 328, 337–38
role in transition of 1801: 330–33, 337–38
sense of humor: 9
stubbornness of: 2, 194, 195–96
support for navy: 175, 177, 184, 221–22, 229–30
trips to and from Quincy: 23, 34, 86, 93–94, 149, 176–77, 226–27, 231, 262–63, 266–67, 291
view of Americans: 6
Adams, John Quincy: 33, 44, 74–75, 77, 80, 89–92, 110, 167, 172–73, 193, 261, 274, 280, 327, 329–30
and nepotism: 44, 45, 75, 91–92, 193–94
as asset to president: 90–91, 93, 94, 172–73, 186–87
as minister to Prussia: 92, 258, 312–13
correspondence with Murray: 166, 172, 186, 238–39, 265–66, 290
Adams, Louisa Catherine (Johnson): 92
Adams, Thomas Boylston: 186, 187–88, 192, 296, 297
address to Congress: 65, 68, 69, 71, 73, 95–96, 173, 177, 178–79, 180, 233
reactions to: 73–74, 179
Adet, Pierre: 31–32, 126–27
Alien Acts: 128–29, 166–67, 197, 198–99, 200, 205, 215, 232, 273–74, 275, 314
Allen, John: 115, 139–40
Ames, Fisher: 177–78, 230, 233, 237–38, 239, 253, 283, 285, 286, 288, 307, 326
Arch Federalists: 5, 7, 40, 51, 168, 180, 183, 185, 188, 195–96, 204, 210, 211, 229, 230, 236, 237, 241, 245, 256, 258, 259, 261, 275, 285, 296–97, 311–12, 313, 314–15, 323–24, 335–36
campaign in 1800: 249–51, 253, 281, 284–85, 288
Aurora Daily Advertiser: 24, 29, 33, 37–38, 62, 73, 87, 92, 117, 124, 125, 132, 161–62, 165, 215–16, 239, 243, 244–45, 256, 274–75, 278–79, 289, 316, 323

Bache, Benjamin Franklin: 29, 73, 87, 92, 113–14, 124–25, 127, 129, 161–62, 215
Bayard, James: 197, 325, 327, 328
Beckley, John: 30–31, 32, 58, 289, 295
Bellamy, Pierre: 102–4, 105
Bingham, William: 36, 55–56, 133, 139, 192, 194, 249, 256
bipartisanship: 53, 64, 65
Boston Massacre: 3, 8
Breckinridge, John: 163–65
Briesler, John: 34, 330
Buonaparte, Napoleon: 176, 182, 270–71, 311
Burr, Aaron: 5–6, 39–40, 41–42, 76–77, 235, 261, 289
as Republican candidate: 29–31, 34, 41–42, 251, 281, 295, 300, 301–3, 306, 310, 320, 321–22, 323, 324, 328, 336
role in 1800 campaign: 247–48, 302, 307–10, 316, 318, 324–25, 326–27
role in contested election: 307–10, 326–27
cabinet: 2, 46–49, 64, 65, 69, 79, 110, 138, 141, 217, 262–63
controlling Adams: 74
George Washington's cabinet: 13, 15–16, 17, 19–20, 24, 25, 28–29, 39, 46, 47–48, 67, 69, 79, 142, 259
meeting: 65, 66–67, 74, 202, 227–28, 266
responsibilities of: 230, 257–59
subterfuge: 218, 222–26, 227–28, 229, 248–49

tensions in: 64, 80, 155–56, 158, 176, 178, 183–84, 230, 231, 253–56

Cabot, George: 4–5, 37, 74–75, 137, 156, 158, 169, 186, 218, 220, 225, 226, 230, 237–38, 288, 290
Callender, James: 82, 277
calling customs: 52, 61
campaign (political): 27, 30–31, 33
ceremonial sword: 54–55, 333
Chase, Samuel: 298
civic virtue: 8, 252, 284
civil–military relations: 7, 145–46, 150, 157, 184, 203
Claypoole, David: 10, 23–24, 98
Clinton, George: 29, 30–31, 247–48, 251, 301
cockade: 54, 122–23, 124, 162, 174
Coit, Joshua: 127–28, 139–40
Congress Hall: 39, 55, 57–58, 60, 61, 72–73, 147–48, 178, 179, 233, 234
Conrad and McMunn's boarding house: 327, 331–32, 333
Constitutional Convention: 11, 13, 24, 45, 169, 336
Continental Army: 3, 4, 16–17, 24, 29–30, 61, 142, 145–46, 151, 152, 199, 201, 233
Continental Congress: 3, 8, 11, 13, 18, 20, 34, 49, 112
Coxe, Tench: 31, 32, 239, 274–75

Dallas, Alexander James: 207, 210, 239, 244
Dana, Francis: 76, 78
Davie, William: 216, 217, 227, 229, 230, 265–66, 311–12
Dayton, Jonathan: 58, 115, 141, 248–49, 314–15
Declaration of Independence: 13, 34, 273
decree: 67–68, 171, 189, 202
depredations on American shipping: 95, 170–71
Dexter, Samuel: 256, 258, 262, 264, 331
diplomatic dispatches: 67, 94, 97, 98, 103–4, 106, 108–9, 110, 111–14, 115–16, 119–21, 127, 184–85, 192, 217, 264, 268, 269
diplomatic instructions: 69, 84, 85–86, 114, 134–35, 188, 202, 216, 217–18, 223–24, 229, 268
drawing rooms: 21, 46–47, 71, 235, 241–42
Duane, William: 126, 215–16, 239–40, 243–45, 246, 274–75, 278–79, 289
Du Pont, Victor: 170–71
dwelling tax: 137–38, 183, 199–200, 205, 297–98
resistance to (*see* Fries's Rebellion)

Election of 1796: 26–28
certification of the vote: 39–40, 324
foreign interference in: 32, 59
uncertainty of results: 35–36, 38
results: 36–37, 39–40
Election of 1800: 281, 294–303
certification of election: 245–46, 328
contested election: 309, 321–22, 324–28
New York election: 247–48, 251–52, 294
response to Hamilton's pamphlet: 289–93, 300–1
results of: 336
Ross resolution on election irregularities: 242–43, 245–46
tie in: 301–3, 306, 307–9, 317–18, 321–22, 324–28
Electoral College: 26, 28, 39–40, 47, 247, 289, 296, 297, 301
state selection of electors: 26–27, 247–48, 296–98
Ellsworth, Oliver: 37, 60, 216, 218, 223, 224, 225, 226, 227, 230, 248–49, 265–66, 268–69, 311–12, 313
Essex Junto: 5, 65, 140, 147–48, 157, 168, 169, 176, 178, 186, 188–89, 206, 210, 220, 225, 226, 241, 243, 249, 254, 255, 256, 275, 281, 284–86, 288, 314, 315
Executive Mansion (White House): 264, 291, 304–6, 321, 323–24, 329, 330, 335
executive power: 6–7, 45, 64, 69, 79, 136, 146, 150, 155, 157, 158, 159–60, 169, 178, 184, 185–86, 193, 194, 195–96, 209, 217, 230, 256–59, 261, 316–17
to pardon: 209–10, 259–61

Farewell Address: 10, 12, 15, 17–19, 23–24, 30, 61
Federalist Party: 4–5, 281
  allegations of British faction: 285–87
  split in: 29, 41, 64, 140, 190, 193, 194, 195–96, 199, 211, 230, 231–32, 233, 237, 253, 284–91, 298, 335, 339
Fenno, John: 66, 84, 124–25
First Federal Congress: 5, 257, 315–16
Forrest, Uriah: 77, 218–19, 226
Francis Hotel: 1, 21, 52, 53, 57, 60–61, 64–65
French Directory: 67–68, 72–73, 75, 76, 94, 100, 101, 102–3, 110, 111, 116–17, 120–21, 133, 135, 189, 204–5, 270
  shift in policy: 170–72, 179, 189, 222, 223–24, 270
French Revolution: 4, 52, 60, 80, 96, 99, 122–23, 126, 212, 318
Fries, John: 199–201, 207, 239, 259–61
  trial of: 207–10
Fries Rebellion: 199–201, 259, 278, 297–98
  Federalist response to: 204–8

Gabriel's Rebellion: 276–80
Gallatin, Albert: 128–29, 185, 197, 198, 241, 248, 250, 251, 254, 281, 309–10, 321–22, 325, 327
Gazette of the United States: 24, 66, 96, 125, 203, 204–5, 282, 284, 328
Gerry, Elbridge: 31, 34, 47, 49, 78, 85, 226
  in France: 99–108, 117–21
  meeting with Adams: 170–71, 175–76
  objections to as minister: 75–76, 78–79
  return to US: 168–70, 173
  squabbling with Pickering: 134–35, 175–76
  split from other envoys: 104, 105–8, 117–21, 133–34, 170
Goodhue, Benjamin: 148, 255, 256
Great Britain: 4, 23, 43, 69, 97

The Hague: 3, 33, 55, 90, 94, 97, 99, 172, 186, 189, 190, 191, 192, 193, 202, 217, 237, 238, 290

Haiti (*see* Saint-Domingue)
Hamilton, Alexander: 4–5, 17, 67–68
  advising the cabinet: 68, 69
  and the army: 112–13, 137, 144, 154–55, 156–58, 173–75, 178, 183, 188–89, 205
  election intrigues: 28–30, 34, 35, 37, 49–51, 247–48, 249–52, 283–91, 308–9
  in Trenton: 227, 228–29
  in the cabinet: 13–14, 15
  on Adams: 144, 335–36, 338–39
  on Pickering: 48
  pamphlet on Adams: 287
  reaction to Kentucky and Virginia resolutions: 166, 197–98
  receiving secret information from the cabinet: 68, 112–13
  relationship with Washington: 17–19, 24, 47–48, 143–44, 236
  Reynold's pamphlet: 82–84, 283
  role in election of 1800: 247–48, 249–52, 283–91, 308–9
  supporting a peace mission: 68, 69, 312
  on territorial expansion: 180–81, 182–83
  view of presidency: 69
  war council: 173–75, 178
Harper, Robert Goodloe: 28–29, 241, 248–49
Hauteval, Lucien: 104, 105
Henry, Patrick: 194, 216, 232, 277
Higginson, Stephen: 37, 140, 168, 169, 218, 220
honor: 74, 111, 152
Hottinguer, Jean Conrad: 102–4, 105
Hubbard, Nicholas: 101–2

immigration: 4, 126, 127–28
inaugural address: 58–60, 331–32, 333–34
inauguration: 54, 55–60, 332–34
Iredell, James: 204, 207–8, 209, 210

Jacobin: 81, 82, 87, 112, 114, 116, 123, 180, 222, 253, 312
January 6, 2021: 8, 340
Jay, John: 18–19, 24, 34, 45–46, 47–48, 80, 147–48, 224, 251, 290–91, 292–93, 309, 313, 324

Jay Treaty: 80, 86, 95, 224, 269
Jefferson, Thomas: 5–6, 8, 13
accusations of atheism: 282–83
as author of Kentucky resolution: 163–64
as author of Mazzei letter: 72, 282
as president: 335
as president-elect: 329–34
as Republican candidate: 29–30, 31, 33, 34, 35, 36–37, 251, 302–3
as Republican leader: 17–18, 76–77, 81, 82, 161–67, 242, 244, 273, 295, 300
as vice president: 35, 36–37, 49, 51, 52–53, 55–57, 64–65, 235, 324
in the cabinet: 13–14, 15, 257
correspondence with Madison: 34–35, 36, 51, 52, 82, 96–97, 127, 128, 198, 241, 282–83, 309, 316, 317–19, 320
meeting with the French: 76, 171
on Adams: 74, 96–97, 113, 338–39
on Gabriel's Rebellion: 279–80
on Sedition Act: 130, 161, 162–63
on US Army: 161
public support of: 52
relationship with Adams (*see* Adams, relationship with Jefferson)
relationship with Madison: 29, 33, 35, 50–51, 53, 302–3
role in 1800 campaign: 275–76
role in contested election: 307–10, 322, 326–27
undermining Adams administration: 76, 77
Judiciary Act of 1801: 315–17
July 4: 84, 129, 139–40, 215, 267, 273

Kentucky and Virginia resolutions: 163–67, 197, 205, 232
King, Rufus: 4–5, 28, 65, 67–68, 74–75, 106, 181–82, 186, 193–94, 211, 220, 225, 226, 230, 240, 241, 249, 250, 278, 283, 284, 285, 288–89, 308, 312
Knox, Henry: 15, 16, 141, 143, 145, 147, 150, 152–55, 156–58, 183–84, 195, 257

Lear, Tobias: 23, 24, 174, 234, 236
Lee, Charles: 5, 47, 64, 66–67, 74–75, 110–11, 178, 195–96, 209–10, 222, 223, 231, 260, 263, 264
Létombe, André Joseph de: 43, 76, 77, 127, 170–71, 190, 322
levees: 21, 38, 46–47, 71
liberty pole: 162, 183, 198–99
Lincoln, Benjamin: 87, 140, 141, 336
Liston, Robert: 43, 159, 181–82, 212–13, 218, 227, 236
Livingston, Edward: 197, 198, 325
Louverture, Toussaint: 212, 213
Lyon, Matthew: 124

MacPherson, William: 203, 204, 206–7
Madison, James: 5–6, 11–13, 15, 17–18, 20, 63, 64–65, 74, 179
as author of Virginia resolution: 164–65, 166–67
as Republican leader: 27, 31, 32, 35, 36, 77, 113, 295
electioneering: 29, 31, 33, 34
correspondence with Jefferson (*see* Jefferson, correspondence with Madison)
on Hamilton: 84
relationship with Jefferson (*see* Jefferson, relationship with Madison)
role in election of 1800: 309–10
Maitland, Thomas: 212–14
Marshall, John: 133–34, 195
as congressman: 232–35, 245–46, 259
as envoy: 74–75, 84–85, 97, 99–108, 117–21
as secretary of state: 256, 258, 262–63, 264, 268, 269–70, 272, 312, 314
as chief justice: 314–15, 331, 334
opposition to Alien and Sedition Acts: 232
relationship with Adams (*see* Adams, relationship with Marshall)
role in election of 1800: 299, 300, 306, 308
Marshall, Polly: 101, 107–8, 232–33

Mazzei, Philip: 71–72, 77, 281–82, 308
McHenry, James: 16–17
as secretary of war in Adams administration: 64, 66–67, 111, 114–15, 230
in Washington's cabinet: 16–17, 46
intrigues with Hamilton: 69, 141–42, 144, 147–48, 154–55, 156–58, 174–75, 279, 287, 298
management of war department: 151–52, 153–54, 184, 221–22
on peace commission: 222, 223, 227–28
resignation of: 253–55
role in Fries's Rebellion: 202–3, 205, 206–7
support for army: 137, 174–75
unfitness for office: 48, 151–52
visit to Mount Vernon: 141–45
McKean, Thomas: 299, 322
Mifflin, Thomas: 51, 125–26, 205
Miranda, Francisco de: 181, 182
Monroe, James: 5–6, 27, 77, 96–97, 244
as governor of Virginia: 277, 278, 279–80, 302, 322
as minister to France: 80
as Republican: 81–82, 242, 276
role in Reynold's pamphlet: 82–83
Monticello: 33, 51, 77, 163–64, 166, 251, 276, 298
Morris, Gouverneur: 256, 261, 312
Mount Vernon: 10, 136, 141–45, 154, 174, 211, 232, 234, 236, 263–64, 295, 305
Murray, William Vans: 74–75, 90, 94, 97, 106, 171–73, 186, 189, 195–96, 216–17, 229, 237–39, 290
nomination of: 190, 191, 193–95
correspondence with John Quincy Adams (*see* Adams, John Quincy, correspondence with Murray)
in France: 265–66, 268–69, 270–71

navy department: 137, 175, 177–78, 184, 220–22
newspapers: 40, 114, 273–74, 296
Nicholas, Wilson Cary: 163–64, 165, 198
Nichols, William: 200, 201, 202–3
nullification: 165–67

Oellers Hotel: 61, 81, 134
Otis, Harrison Gray: 5, 114, 125, 169, 180, 182–83, 190, 234–35, 240, 241, 249

partisan tensions: 72, 98
Paterson, William: 313–15
peace mission to France: 52–53
concern for envoys' safety: 111–12, 114
of 1798: 63, 66–67, 73, 74–75, 80, 84, 97, 99–108, 110, 113, 134
of 1799: 173, 179, 180, 190, 193, 194–95, 216–18, 229, 264–66, 268–69, 270–71
peaceful transfer of power: 6–7, 8, 55, 61, 62, 245–46, 329–34, 337, 340
Pennsylvania, role in election: 31, 297–98, 299–300
Pichon, Louis André: 171–73, 186, 189
Pickering, Timothy: 4–5, 10
and Hamilton: 69, 140, 141–42, 144, 154–55, 156–58, 174–75, 287
as Arch Federalist: 111, 335–36
as secretary of state in Adams administration: 64, 65, 66, 67–68, 108, 210
correspondence with Vans Murray: 216–17, 237–39
fear of French influence: 127
firing of: 255–56, 259
in favor of war: 111
in Washington's cabinet: 16, 23, 32, 46, 47, 48
negotiating treaty with Saint-Domingue: 213–14
on Jefferson: 56, 327
on Gerry: 134–35, 168, 175–76, 185–86
on Great Britain: 182
on US Army: 174–75
opposition to peace mission: 66, 191, 237–39, 311–12
role in the Federalist Party, 46

role in Sedition prosecutions: 131–32, 161–62, 215–16
undermining Adams nominations: 78, 79–80, 147–48
undermining Adams foreign policy: 173, 188, 202, 211, 216–18, 222–26, 227–28, 229
view on executive power: 79, 255–56
Pinckney, Charles "Blackguard": 242–43, 300
Pinckney, Charles Cotesworth: 274–75, 306, 314, 334
as envoy: 63, 65, 67–68, 72–73, 74–76, 85, 89–90, 96, 99–108, 117–21
as Federalist candidate: 250–51, 281, 299, 300–2
as general: 144, 173–75, 178
Pinckney, Mary: 101
Pinckney, Thomas: 28–29, 30, 34, 35, 36–37, 40, 274–75, 300
political violence: 123, 124, 125–26, 318, 322–23, 326, 337
President's House: 1, 12, 23–24, 41, 60–61, 64–65, 67, 70–71, 84–85, 94, 97, 108, 110, 111, 112, 114–15, 123, 125–26, 133, 136, 147, 177, 191, 193, 202–3, 253–54, 267, 305, 330
presidential precedent: 7, 20, 67, 257, 259, 317, 332
Presidential Succession Act of 1792: 309, 319
presidential transition: 6–7, 40, 45, 49, 329–34
privateer: 170–71, 172, 221, 330

Quasi–War: 7–8, 124, 170–71, 240
Quincy: 21–23, 34, 42–43, 70, 86, 87, 88, 93–94, 150, 169–70, 182, 183, 184, 187, 203, 211, 218, 219, 224, 225, 226, 229–30, 231, 261, 267–68, 272, 283, 285, 286, 291, 304, 305, 328

Rawle, William: 209–10, 215–16, 239–40, 245
Reign of Terror (*see* French Revolution)
Republican Party: 5–6
campaign in 1796: 30–31
campaign in 1800: 274–76, 295
Revolutionary War: 3, 29–30, 59, 298
Ross, James: 56, 192, 242
Rush, Benjamin: 36, 45–46, 99–100, 227

Saint–Domingue: 4, 126, 212–14, 221, 229
Sedgwick, Theodore: 4–5, 41–42, 57–58, 62, 112, 113, 114–15, 139–40, 166, 180, 183, 186, 188–89, 192, 193, 194, 195, 197, 198, 218, 220, 222, 237, 240, 241, 245–46, 248–49, 250, 256, 285, 307–8, 313, 314–15, 323, 326, 332, 335–36
Sedition Act: 129–31, 166–67, 197, 198–99, 200, 205, 215, 232, 240, 243–44, 273–74, 275, 314
Pickering role in: 131–32, 161–62
prosecutions under: 161–62, 198–99, 215–16, 246, 275, 314
public response to: 197–12, 199, 200, 205, 209, 273–74, 297–98
Sewall, Samuel: 139–40, 169
Smith, Samuel: 241, 298, 307, 325, 327
Smith, William: 141, 147–48, 150
South Carolina: 28, 37, 74, 144, 297, 299–301, 306
state dinner: 21, 23, 46–47, 71
State of the Union (*see* address to Congress)
Stoddert, Benjamin: 5, 137, 155, 175, 177, 178, 184, 206, 218, 221, 222–23, 224, 226, 229, 230, 231, 260, 264, 298, 330–31, 339
Supreme Court: 17, 45–46, 57, 58, 99–100, 313–16

Talleyrand–Périgord, Charles Maurice de: 94, 99–100, 101–8, 117–20, 127, 134, 170–71, 172, 177, 185, 186, 189, 190, 191, 192, 195, 202, 216–17, 233, 237, 238–39, 240–41, 265, 266
Taylor, John (of Caroline): 165, 166–67
Tracy, Uriah: 41–42, 139, 148, 243, 256
treason: 208–9, 210, 259–61
Treaty of Mortefontaine: 7–8, 271, 306, 311–12, 338

Trenton: 155, 156, 224, 226–30
Troup, Robert: 28, 116, 278, 288–89, 308

United Irishmen: 126, 205
United States Army: 136, 149–50, 206, 220
  Provisional Army: 137, 150, 180, 184, 203
  ranks of officers: 141, 143–45, 147–48, 152–60, 183–84
  reduction of: 240–42, 259
United States Capitol: 321–22, 324–26, 328, 333–34, 340
United States Constitution: 5–6, 8, 26, 27, 28, 40, 41, 45, 55–56, 58, 59, 88, 129, 130–31, 136, 138–39, 143–44, 150, 158, 160, 185–86, 209, 233, 242–43, 246, 247, 249–50, 252, 257, 258–59, 275, 294–95, 308–9, 310–11, 317, 319–20, 322, 326, 329, 331, 333, 335, 336, 337–38
  3/5ths clause: 336
United States Senate: 21, 41, 56–57, 91, 117, 128, 129, 147, 150, 190, 193, 241, 242–46, 257, 258–59, 309, 311–12, 316, 319–20, 324, 328
  prosecution of Duane: 243–45, 246, 275

Van Schaack, Henry: 73, 112, 115
vice presidency: 49, 51

war between Great Britain and France: 69, 176–77
war, preparation for: 73, 96, 113, 137, 138
war, threat of: 7, 127
Washington, Bushrod: 74–75, 239, 290
Washington City (Washington, DC): 262, 264, 267–68, 269, 275, 286, 292, 299, 304, 306, 317, 321–28, 329–34
Washington, George:
  as commander-in-chief: 3, 11, 20, 145–46, 152, 232
  as general in Adams administration: 138–39, 140, 141, 145–46, 152, 154–56, 157–60, 173, 189
  as president: 8, 9, 17–19, 23–25, 38, 39, 42–43, 45, 47, 48–49, 52, 54, 55, 57–58, 80, 90, 146, 159, 203, 209, 211, 224, 257, 286–87, 316, 317, 333
  as unifier: 6–7, 59, 138–39, 236
  criticism of: 71–72
  death of: 233–36, 237, 266
  excluded Adams from administration: 20–21, 23, 24–25, 48–49
  legacy of: 1–2, 7, 42–43, 45, 59, 61
  relationship with Adams (*see* Adams, relationship with Washington)
  retirement of: 10–11, 12, 13–15, 17, 23, 27–28, 46, 62
  in retirement: 61, 136
  shadow of: 6–7, 30, 35, 46, 59, 72, 132, 150, 159–60, 236, 267
  war council: 173–75, 178
Washington, Martha: 21, 38, 57, 142, 263–64
Webster, Noah: 5, 177–78, 286–87, 290, 339
Wolcott Jr, Oliver: 16, 47
  as member of Essex Junto: 140
  as secretary of treasury in Adams administration: 63, 65, 264, 292, 323
  election intrigues of: 28–29, 35
  in favor of war: 111
  in Washington's cabinet: 46
  intrigues with Hamilton: 69, 154–55, 156–58, 174–75, 231–32, 287–88
  on Fries's Rebellion: 204–5, 208, 209, 210, 260
  opposition to peace mission: 66, 222, 223, 227–28, 311–12
  role in election of 1800: 281, 286–88
  role in Reynold's pamphlet: 82
Whiskey Rebellion: 5, 143, 146, 199, 203, 209, 278

xenophobia: 4, 126, 205
XYZ Affair: 99–108, 117–21, 270
  bribes: 102, 103, 104–5, 110, 111
  loans: 102, 103, 105, 107, 108, 110, 118
  passports: 107–8, 118–19, 120
  public response: 111, 113, 114, 116–17, 123, 127, 129, 170, 198
  split in commission: 104, 105–8

yellow fever: 155, 222–23, 227, 231